Stanley Cobb: A Builder of the Modern Neurosciences

Snapshot of Stanley Cobb in his office at the Massachusetts General Hospital, taken by the author in 1938

Stanley Cobb

A Builder of the Modern Neurosciences

BENJAMIN V. WHITE, M.D.

with the Assistance of
RICHARD J. WOLFE
EUGENE TAYLOR

1984

Published by The Francis A. Countway
Library of Medicine   Boston

Distributed by the University Press
of Virginia   Charlottesville

Copyright © 1984 by Benjamin V. White

Dedicated to the
Students and Colleagues of Stanley Cobb
And Especially To
Helen Cobb White and Hildegarde Cobb Forbes

Contents

List of Illustrations viii

Preface xi

Acknowledgments xiii

Chapter

1. Childhood 1
2. Education at Harvard 20
3. Baltimore and World War I 52
4. New Life in Boston 69
5. European Study 101
6. The Later Twenties 124
7. The Neurological Unit at Boston City Hospital 160
8. Epilepsy 179
9. Psychoanalysis 197
10. Psychiatry at the Massachusetts General Hospital (1934–1939) 219
11. Wartime Frustrations (1940–1946) 241
12. At the Center of the Storm (1947–1954) 259
13. Child Psychiatry 290
14. Retirement 310

Appendix

A. Diagram of Stanley Cobb's Ancestry; the Cobb Family Tree 340
B. Bibliography of the Published Writings of Stanley Cobb 342
C. Transcription of the Taped Reminiscences of D. Stafford Clark 371

Major Sources Employed in Compiling This Work 377

Notes 382

Index 424

Illustrations

Snapshot of Stanley Cobb at the Massachusetts General Hospital, taken by the author in 1938	Frontispiece
House on Oakland Street in Brookline, where Cobb was born in 1888	23
Cobb children in the early 1890s	23
Stanley Cobb in a sailor suit, early 1890s	24
Stanley Cobb as a young boy	25
Bust of Philip Sidney Smith (1887–1904)	25
Stanley Cobb's Massachusetts National Guard squadron, 1911	26
Cobb riding his favorite horse Omar	27
Stanley Cobb as a medical student at Harvard	28
Surgical staff of the Peter Bent Brigham Hospital, 1914–1915	29
Wedding picture of Stanley and Betty Cobb, July 10, 1915	30
North Broadway, Baltimore, Maryland	71
Staff of the Henry Phipps Psychiatric Clinic about 1917	72
Three generations of Cobbs	72
Duck blind on the Gunpowder River near Baltimore	73
Swans on the Gunpowder River, sepia wash, by Stanley Cobb	73
Lieutenant Stanley Cobb in uniform during World War I	74
Clinician Stanley Cobb in the early 1920s	75
The former Cherry Hill Tavern at Ponkapoag, the Cobbs' home between 1919 and 1929	76
Stanley Cobb at his desk at the Harvard Medical School, early 1920s	77
Water color by Stanley Cobb, 1924, of a village scene in Northern France	78
William Gibbs in 1930	127
James Lawrence Pool at the Boston City Hospital	127
Ivan P. Pavolv and Paul Yakovlev, 1929	128

Illustrations ix

Staff of the Boston City Hospital Neurological Unit about 1930	129
Staff of B.C.H. Neurological Unit circa 1931	130
Staff of the Boston City Hospital Neurological Unit about 1932	131
Stanley Cobb at the helm of his sloop *Fulmar*, late 1930s	132
Betty Cobb at the helm of a small sloop in the early 1920s	133
The Cobbs' sloop *Pamaho* setting out through the Cotuit Narrows	134
William Herman	261
M.G.H. Psychiatric Service in 1940	262
Some of Cobb's residents, 1934–1945	263
M.G.H. psychiatric staff in 1947	264
Some of Cobb's residents and fellows, 1946–1954	265
Staff of M.G.H. Psychiatric Service in 1953	266
Retirement party, 1954	267
Stanley Cobb's last lecture in neuropathology, Harvard Medical School, 1954	313
M.G.H. General Executive Committee, 1949	314
Medical Exchange Club circa 1930	315
Massachusetts General Hospital psychiatric staff, 1961	316
Stanley Cobb dissecting a bird brain during the later years of his retirement	317
Water color of the Himalayas, painted by Cobb, 1962	318

Figures

1. Floor plan of Cobb's Neuropathology Laboratory in Building D-2 of the Harvard Medical School in the 1920s	89
2. Floor plan of the Neurological Unit at Boston City Hospital.	162
3. Cobb's modification of Adolf Meyer's Life Chart, citing, under social data, "Fell in cesspool"	230
4. Illustration from *Emotions and Clinical Medicine*, showing Cobb's concept of the three main systems involved in emotional reactions	277
5. Cobb's observations on the brain-bill angle in three species of birds with different feeding habits	325

Preface

Why write a book about Stanley Cobb? A quarter of a century after his death in 1968 he is an almost forgotten figure, and outside the field of neurology the present generation of physicians hardly know him. He left no monumental discovery such as insulin or penicillin to establish him as a landmark figure in the annals of medicine, and no disease or syndrome distinguishes his name. His knowledge was broad, encompassing a number of modern medical specialties. Yet none of them claims him specifically as its own. Furthermore, many specialists among his contemporaries failed to understand his breadth of vision and consequently were critical of his contributions to their own narrow fields. They felt he would have achieved more had he restricted his interest to their discipline alone.

Nonetheless, Stanley Cobb was a seminal figure in several areas of neurology and psychiatry. He was not only one of the most important and influential teachers, researchers, and practitioners of these sciences in America; he was an important figure worldwide as well, enjoying an international reputation and commanding the respect of many of the greatest medical minds of his day. His reputation as a neuroanatomist and neuropathologist was especially high. Clinically, he was responsible for integrating the practice of neurology with psychiatry and for bringing psychiatry into the modern hospital environment. As a teacher, he not only introduced psychoanalysis into the medical school curriculum but directed the careers and research of scores of junior clinicians. From the soil he thus prepared there sprang up some of the forms of therapy that remain standard practice today.

Stanley Cobb was a uniquely creative man. Possessing the mind of a natural scientist, which in his youth had been formed through exposure to wildlife and by the study of ornithology, and with medical training in human and comparative anatomy, neuropathology, neurohistology, clinical neurology, and finally psychiatry, he was able to cross back and forth into all of these fields and piece together fragments of these sciences into an understanding of the nervous system that was imaginative and unique. In the doing, he added several important building blocks to the foundation structure of the modern neurosciences. Believing that all bodily functions were interrelated and that some somatic diseases had their origin in mental and emotional processes, he drew no narrow line between functional and organic illness. He recognized that in varying degrees all disturbances of the human brain demonstrated both tissue changes and some forms of dysfunction. As a result, he attempted to correlate the physical and the behavioral aspects of the human condition in order to understand better the underlying causes of disease and treat the patient as a whole.

The map of his interest was so wide that, admittedly, there were uncharted areas in his knowledge. However, his humility and honesty allowed him to recognize the boundaries between the known and the unknown and to differentiate data based on clinical observation from those grounded in scientific experiments. His breadth of knowledge and uncommon vision were important steadying forces in the evolving medicine of his era, and they remain models to be strived after in the future. While he may at first seem a dated personality, the comprehensive view he evolved has a staying power which transcends the limited parochialism that characterizes the medical specialties of the present day.

Hence, there is need to know about the life and work of this man and the lessons he learned and in turn taught to two generations of physicians. His students have not only continued his work but have taught it to a succeeding generation of medical men, many of whom now follow his precepts unwittingly aware of their origins. Thus, a book on Stanley Cobb not only contributes to a knowledge of the tangled paths that medicine has traveled from the recent past but it may help show its future branches. And, it also may prove the value of the occasional modern Renaissance medical man.

Acknowledgments

A great many people have contributed their time, energy and resources to make possible the publication of this book on the life and work of Stanley Cobb. Fifty-two such individuals—colleagues, students, friends and relatives of Cobb—who contributed significant information through personal interviews are listed on pages 380–381. Those who deserve special mention because they filled in especially large gaps in Dr. Cobb's story are, among the immediate family, Hildegarde Cobb Forbes, Dr. Cobb's sister, and Elizabeth Almy Cobb Hall, his widow. Hildegarde Forbes preserved the family history and provided many personal anecdotes, especially about Dr. Cobb's childhood. Mrs. Hall, who unfortunately did not live long enough to see this work in print (but who, fortunately, saw it through the final draft), furnished data on the Cobbs 1923–1925 European trip, on Dr. Cobb's early interest in analytic psychology and psychoanalysis, on his retirement years, and on many other aspects of his life as well. Both Mrs. Forbes and Mrs. Hall went over various drafts of this work and made important corrections and additions throughout.

The vivid memories of Phyllis Greenacre and Curt Richter greatly enriched the chapter dealing with Dr. Cobb's Baltimore years, and the interviews with Edwin F. Gildea and Margaret C.-L. Gildea were invaluable for recapturing the atmosphere of Cobb's neuropathology laboratory at the Harvard Medical School. Frederic and Erna Gibbs rounded out the epilepsy story, and Houston Merritt not only recalled many facts about the Neurological Unit at Boston City Hospital but also filled in details on the story of the discovery of Dilantin. Derek Denny-Brown furnished further data about the Neurological Unit at Boston City Hospital.

Much information on Cobb's years at the Massachusetts General Hospital came from John Adams Abbott, who vividly recalled the early years of the psychiatric service there. Maurice Greenhill, Avery Weisman, John Nemiah, Bernard Bandler, and Peter Knapp similarly served as authorities on the later years of Cobb's M.G.H. experience.

Harry C. Solomon and Oliver Cope contributed information on Cobb's effectiveness as a teacher at the Harvard Medical School. Mark D. Altschule recalled Cobb's interest in establishing a research laboratory under Jordi Folch-Pi at the McLean Hospital and contributed several personal anecdotes which help flavor the book. Suzanne Van Amerongen and Gregory Rochlin reviewed the stormy days of transition in child psychiatry from an initial Meyerian to a later psychoanalytic orientation, and Gaston Blum, Lucie Jessner and David Stafford-Clark also contributed significantly to the story of child psychiatry. Clorinda (Chloe) Binger recalled with élan vacations with the Cobbs during the nineteen twenties, thirties, and forties and filled in many revealing aspects of their personal and professional lives.

John Talbott remembered with great accuracy the work he did with Cobb on cerebral capillaries at the Harvard Medical School during the nineteen twenties and furnished much valuable information about Cobb's colleagues during this early period. Mary Dailey Irvine was able to portray many of Dr. Cobb's personal habits, idiosyncracies, and attitudes during the many years she worked with him at the Harvard Medical School and at Boston City Hospital. Charles Aring wrote about his memories as a resident at the City Hospital, revealing much about resident life there, and Mary A. B. Brazier furnished a critical review of Cobb's scientific contributions which proved to be invaluable for assesing his worth as a neuroscientist. Henry Brewster made insightful comments on the differences between Jacob Finesinger and Erich Lindemann, two of Cobb's closest associates and lieutenants. Harley Shands, Henry W. Miles, and William Trethowan wrote long letters detailing Cobb's research at the Massachusetts General Hospital in the post-World War II years. E. Peirson Richardson was most helpful in clarifying the work which Cobb carried on at the Warren Building of the M.G.H. during retirement, and Peter Dews discussed Cobb's work at the Massachusetts Institute of Technology during this same period. Finally Michael T. McGuire furnished reprints and protocols of work which Cobb conducted during his retirement, and Janice Stevens spoke of his attitude toward psychoanalysis at the very end of his life.

A number of professional historians reviewed the manuscript of this work in initial and later stages and made comments and suggestions which proved invaluable in restructuring it. These include Drs. Saul Benison of the University of Cincinnati, John C. Burnham of Ohio

Acknowledgments

State University, Gerald N. Grob of Rutgers University, and Nathan G. Hale, Jr., of the University of California. Drs. Charles Aring, Mary Brazier, Adam Moore, John Nemiah, David Satin, and Sanford Gifford read and commented on various drafts as well. As Librarian of the Boston Psychoanalytic Society and Institute, and as an historian of psychiatry and psychoanalysis, Dr. Gifford was particularly helpful in rounding out the psychoanalytic aspects of Dr. Cobb's background and interests.

The author is indebted to the staffs of a number of libraries and archival resources, in addition to those of The Francis A. Countway Library of Medicine, which holds the bulk of Dr. Cobb's manuscript correspondence and papers. Chief among these is the staff of The Alan Mason Chesney Medical Archives of the Johns Hopkins Medical Institutions, which preserves in the Adolf Meyer Papers a large and significant correspondence between Dr. Cobb and Dr. Meyer. Nancy McCall, Assistant Archivist at the Chesney Archives, was especially helpful and cooperative throughout. Similar assistance was rendered by the staffs of the American Philosophical Society in Philadelphia, the Rockefeller Archive Center in Pocantico Hills, New York, and the Rockefeller University Archives in New York City.

The contributions made by Richard J. Wolfe and Eugene Taylor to researching, rewriting and restyling this biography of Stanley Cobb have been acknowledged through the addition of their names to its title-page. Through the collaboration of the three of us, what started out as a family history has turned into a serious biography and, I believe, a history of academic neurology and hospital psychiatry in Boston, and to some extent in America, during the twentieth century as well.

Benjamin V. White, M.D.
North Easton, Massachusetts
June, 1984

Stanley Cobb: A Builder of the Modern Neurosciences

How many have lived for a while in those realms of gold? The boy in short trousers with his woods and hills and marshes to roam and his museum at home and long hours of quiet work had a marvelous chance to develop himself for medicine. Barnyard physiology and genetics left their marks; even the smells of the barnyard were good; the experiences with horses and farm animals were vital; and being much alone was salutary. Although the modern youth with competitive regimentation and more thorough grounding in physics and chemistry may go further, I doubt if he will be happier or wiser than he who came into medicine by way of biology.

—Stanley Cobb
From his Speech of Acceptance of the Kober Medal for 1956

1
Childhood

On December 10, 1887, Stanley Cobb was born at his parents' home on Walnut Street in Brookline, Massachusetts. He was the fourth child in the Cobb family, and there were three more to come. His well-to-do parents lived in a rather plain, large house of no particular architectural distinction (page 23), which was situated on a tract of several acres. It was about a half mile from Jamaica Pond, where members of the family used to row. By the standards of the times, it would barely have qualified as a "place," or an estate.[1] Stanley Cobb was only five years old when his family moved in 1893 from Bookline to Milton. However, his father's sister, Alice, and her husband, Uncle Alanson Bigelow, Jr., stayed on.[2]

Cobb was born into the late Victorian era—twenty-two years after the war between the states. It was the time of Grover Cleveland. The postbellum reconstruction was over, and the gay nineties were at hand. The great natural resources of the West were being developed. The mills of Lawrence and Lowell were humming and generating wealth for their owners from water power and cheap labor. House designs were influenced by the American Gothic trend. Although the light bulb had been invented, gas chandeliers were still the usual form of lighting. With inexpensive labor, extensive gardens were common. The customs of the time were formal and often rigid. Men practiced manly arts. Handlebar moustaches and spittoons were in vogue. Gentlemen's clubs were decorated with mounted elk heads and bearded portraits. Ladies were ladylike. They wore stiff-necked shirtwaists and whalebone corsets. They had tea wearing broad-brimmed hats. When making a formal call the husband would leave two calling cards, one for the host and one for the hostess. The wife would leave only one. She called only on the hostess. To call on the host would have transgressed the bounds of feminine modesty that then prevailed.

Although ancestry along other lines can be traced further back, the earliest direct Cobb relative with available family records was Stanley Cobb's great great-grandfather, Thomas. Thomas Cobb came to the United States from Nova Scotia (which at that time included New

Brunswick) at the age of seventeen and fought in the American Revolution. In 1788 he married Lucy Smith in Wiscasset, Maine. He was a farmer and lived in China, Maine, in Camden, Maine, and in Lynn, Massachusetts. He died prior to 1848. In colonial days there was a prominent Cobb family on Cape Cod, which included the shipowner, Elijah Cobb. Members of this family migrated to various seaports along the New England coast. It is probable that Thomas Cobb was descended from them.[3]

One of the more colorful ancestors on the paternal side of Stanley Cobb's family tree was Augusta Adams Cobb. Augusta Adams was born December 7, 1801, in Salem, and on December 22, 1822, married Thomas Cobb's son, Henry, in Charlestown. Augusta horrified the local community by deserting her husband and five children to become the fifth wife of the Mormon leader, Brigham Young. She moved to Salt Lake City, where she died on February 3, 1886. Augusta was apparently better educated than most of Brigham Young's wives, and, according to tradition, her task was to run the school for the Mormon community. It is also said that she and Brigham Young never lived as man and wife. There are two types of Mormon marriages, one for time and one for eternity. Apparently hers was for eternity. Augusta obviously was a person of strong convictions who had the courage to go against the disapproval of family and neighbors. Her independent frame of mind was shared by Stanley Cobb, too.[4]

Nor was Cobb's mother's line devoid of interesting characters. Stanley Cobb's maternal great great-grandfather, Archelaus Green Smith, was born in Otego, New York, on June 10, 1792, and died in Victor, New York, on June 19, 1850. He was married to Melania Boughton, in Victor, on February 3, 1814. He was an itinerant surgeon who operated in many communities of upstate New York. At one point he decided that he needed to learn more about anatomy and stole a cadaver. Where he got the cadaver is not recorded. However, his illegal act was discovered, and he was brought to trial in one of the small towns where the Smiths were living at the time. Apparently, Archelaus was expecting to be convicted, for on the last day of the trial he had horses posted at convenient distances between the courthouse and the Canadian border, so that he could make his escape. However, a dentist testified that the supposedly identified teeth on the right side of the cadaver's jaw were on the left side in the known deceased person. As a result, Dr. Smith was freed of all charges.[5]

Childhood 3

Cobb's father, too, had in him a streak of independence and adventure. He was born on May 10, 1858, in Brookline, Massachusetts, and reared there. On December 8, 1879, he married Leonore Smith in New York City. A mischievous boy, one Hallowe'en he turned all the street signs in his neighborhood so that they would be pointing in the wrong direction. Although he married Leonore Smith, he started his courtship by seeing her younger sister, Emma. The first time he took Emma out without a chaperone, he fixed the carriage so that it would break down. The carriage did break down, and after that she was either forbidden to go out with him again or refused to do so. Then he began to see Leonore. John Candler Cobb died in Milton on December 30, 1933. Emma's possible regrets and lingering affection were expressed when John Cobb's coffin was being lowered into the grave. At that time Emma went up to Leonore and gently put an arm around her.[6]

John Cobb had imagination and courage. For a number of years near the turn of the century he was engaged as an entrepreneur filling in the South Bay much as the Back Bay had been filled in earlier. Stanley Cobb's younger sister Hildegarde recalled walking over the area and seeing the fill brought in by horse-drawn wagon. Quite probably it was transported by horse and wagon from railroad cars. Mr. Cobb had a private railroad called the South Bay Wharf and Terminal Company. The tracks ran from a pier in the South Bay to the yards of the New York, New Haven, and Hartford Railroad Company near the South Station.[7] During the last years of his life John Cobb wrote a book on economics which was incomplete when he died. Stanley Cobb finished it and had it published after his father's death.[8]

Stanley Cobb's relationship with his father was open and businesslike. Mr. Cobb felt that Stanley's two older brothers might have profited from more parental support and encouragement than had been available to them and resolved to do better with Stanley. Mr. Cobb maintained a close interest in Stanley's activities at Harvard College, during his years of medical school and internship, and throughout the period of postgraduate study in Baltimore. During Cobb's third year at medical school he and Stanley conferred with Dr. David Edsall, then Jackson Professor of Medicine at the Harvard Medical School, about the most promising approach to an academic career in the neurosciences. At that time Mr. Cobb was doing well financially and was prepared to help Stanley survive the inevitable lean years. Correspondence between father and son was matter-of-fact, yet each appeared to have a real feeling of concern for the position of the other. When Mr. Cobb's real estate ventures bogged down during World War I, Stanley sensed that his father could no longer help materially and made every effort to become self-sufficient as rapidly as possible.

Stanley Cobb's mother, Leonore Smith,[9] was brought up in New York City. Her father was a prominent and financially successful New York attorney, and their home was on the south side of Fortieth Street overlooking the original Croton reservoir, where the New York Public Library now stands. Another house at Fort Washington, near the George Washington Bridge, remained in the family and was used as a weekend retreat. After their marriage John and Leonore Cobb settled in Brookline, moving later to Milton.

In Milton Mrs. Cobb maintained a home in opulent good taste with furnishings appropriate to the times, largely Victorian. Within this setting she raised a family of seven children, three boys and four girls. She was helped by a nursemaid named Mary Doyle and by other servants. She kept up with the social amenities of the community and attended the Unitarian Church. Her biggest problem was anxiety. For example, there had been seven wells on the property, and although all of them were securely covered and protected, she recurrently worried about children falling into one of them.

At the turn of the century, Milton Academy must have been a traditional and inflexible institution, unsuited to the growth and development of such individualists as the Cobb children. In any event, Leonore saw Milton in that light, as her daughter Hildegarde also did in later years. Mrs. Cobb did not believe in sending children off to school at the age of six or seven and kept several of them home for a year or two, so that Stanley started school at eight and Hildegarde at nine. When confronted with a child who for one reason or another was not doing well, it was characteristic of Mrs. Cobb to withdraw the child from school and engage a family tutor. She did this with Stanley, Florence, and Hildegarde—and possibly others.

Stanley Cobb had a very close relationship with his mother as indicated by his writing long letters to her on frequent occasions until the late twenties, when he was forty years old. According to his sister Hildegarde he could not have been regarded as a mother's boy, and he was not spoiled. As will be noted in detail later on, Stanley began to stammer early, and stammering may have been one reason for her keeping him out of school until the age of eight. In any event, he got off to a slow start in reading and writing. Later, Mrs. Cobb kept him out of school two more years because both the school boys and faculty members at Milton were teasing him about his stammer. Whenever Stanley was away from home in childhood or in adult life, he would write long letters to her with details of his day-to-day existence. Her letters to him were chatty, often telling about brothers' and sisters' activities. There was little exchange of philosophical concepts or of feelings in the correspondence.

Stanley Cobb's oldest brother, John Candler Cobb, Jr., was seven years his senior. John was left-handed and somewhat dyslexic. He studied at Harvard for two years and later at the Massachusetts Institute of Technology. Although he did not receive a degree from either institution, he mastered the art of working with and constructing extremely fine instruments. After college, he engaged in a number of business enterprises both in Kansas City and Chicago. During World War II he was able to use his skill with fine instruments as a contribution to the war effort. There is little evidence that Stanley Cobb and John were close pals in childhood. Correspondence at the time of John's wedding in 1909 refers mostly to shooting. In a letter dated January 25, 1911, John said, "There is no one I like to go hunting with as well as you. 'Cause we both like to chase them to their lair!"[10] In adult life Stanley Cobb saw John as a friend with similar interests in the manly art of hunting, but there is no evidence of great intimacy, and nothing to suggest that John was an important model.[11]

Emma May Cobb[12] was the oldest daughter in the Cobb family. She had extraordinary ability as an administrator and was vitally interested in Music Mountain in the Berkshires, where she was involved both musically and administratively. She stood out for her intelligence, her principles, and to some extent for her rigidity. Yet it is apparent that Stanley Cobb was very fond of her. Dr. Chandler Foot, whom she married in 1910, traveled and studied extensively in Europe, and they were in Munich when Louise, the first of their two daughters, was born in 1911. During their travels Emma sent Cobb postcards with references to Dr. Foot's professional activities. Dr. Foot and Cobb became mutual admirers and exchanged numerous long letters, mostly about scientific matters. Emma was Cobb's senior by five years and undoubtedly had a great impact on his life, primarily through her example of industry, integrity, and responsibility. Cobb had deep affection for her, yet there is little evidence of any real expression of feelings between them.

Cobb had a second older brother, Augustus Smith Cobb, who was born August 1, 1885, in Brookline and died February 27, 1971, in Tucson, Arizona.[13] Augustus attended Milton Academy after graduating from the Volkmann School and then went to Harvard. He graduated from Harvard College in three years and stayed a fourth for his M.A. His thesis was on railroads in New York State, and he was later consulted on railroad problems. In 1909 and 1910, Stanley's last two years at Harvard, Augustus was working out of his father's office for investment management at 60 State Street, Boston. He wrote letters signed "Dud" which largely dealt with preparations for hunting trips. He was glad to lend equipment to Stanley, yet he was very insistent that it be returned in good condition. It is fair to say that Stanley and Augustus never had an intimate relationship. They wrote to each other about hunting, shooting, riding, and the Massachusetts National Guard, of which they were both members. Augustus and Stanley had very different outlooks on life. Augustus was successful as a banker and became vice-president of the Bankers Trust Company in New York, but he had no interest in scientific matters. He and Stanley were both men of achievement along different lines of work. Their value systems differed, and their interests diverged as they grew older.

John, Emma, and Augustus were all older than Stanley. A sister, Florence, better known as "Polly," was two years Stanley's junior and his constant companion in childhood.[14] Stanley and Polly often rode their ponies together over Blue Hill or went on bird walks before breakfast. Polly did her school work with Stanley when both of them had a private tutor, between 1902 and 1904. They painted in watercolor and oils during that time under the tutelage of Elizabeth Taylor Watson, and Polly became an artist of considerable talent. Whereas Stanley became an accomplished amateur, Polly made a career of her painting. She sold paintings at times and even did some work on commission. She and Stanley maintained a close, affectionate relationship throughout the remainder of her life. Stanley had a constant concern for her because she was subject to severe mood swings of the manic-depressive type, being overactively in high spirits at times and deeply despondent at others. She depended upon him for help in finding the best available professional care. She required shock therapy at

Childhood

times, and in fact, shock therapy led to her death, for she died April 6, 1958, on the way home from the hospital after a treatment.

Beatrice, another sister, was four years younger than Stanley and also had a very special relationship with him.[15] The day of her birth was one of the most memorable in Stanley's life. In fact, he dated his stammering from that occasion. He was always fond of this sister, and she was devoted to him all her life. It is an odd coincidence that brother and sister both died on the same day. As a girl Beatrice enjoyed sports, especially tennis. She attended boarding school at Briarcliff Manor, New York, and when Stanley was at Harvard she wrote him many long letters. One, describing the family trip to Eastern Canada in August, 1909, gave an observant description of the countryside and customs and also expressed an awareness of the feelings of family members who were along. Another letter gave an account of a vacation at Isle-au-Haut in 1910. Two of Stanley's current flames, Katrine Amory and Elizabeth Bowdith, were to be there at the same time. Under the circumstances Beatrice was in a way relieved that Stanley was unable to come for a visit.

The youngest Cobb child was Hildegarde,[16] who as the baby of the family looked up to all her brothers and sisters. She was kept out of school by her mother, much as Stanley had been. Hildegarde did not start school until she was nine years old. After such a late start she did not do well academically and hesitated when reading aloud. Mrs. Cobb was afraid that Hildegarde, like Stanley, might become a stammerer and took her out of school when she was fifteen years old. Hildegarde never did become a stammerer. She was later found to be minimally dyslexic. For her senior year Hildegarde was transferred to Miss Windsor's School in Boston. She sometimes rode there on a dogcart drawn by the horse, Omar, which also transported Cobb to medical school each day. Hildegarde became a trained occupational therapist and was also a Red Cross nurse's aid. She obtained a position on her own credentials to do occupational therapy at the Henry Phipps Psychiatric Clinic of Johns Hopkins when Stanley Cobb was there in 1917 and 1918. Then from August, 1918, until July, 1919, she was on active duty as an occupational therapist at U.S. Army Hospital No. 6 in MacPherson, Georgia, where she did some emergency nursing during the influenza epidemic.

In 1920, when Cobb took over the neuropathology laboratory at the Harvard Medical School, Hildegarde learned from her brother-in-law,

Dr. Chandler Foot, then in the department of pathology, how to prepare slides for histopathological examination. She was taught neuropathologic staining methods by Dr. Myrtle P. Canavan, the neuropathologist at the Boston Psychopathic Hospital. She then became the first laboratory technician in Stanley Cobb's new laboratory, where Henry Stone Forbes was commencing his studies of circulation. After Hildegarde married Dr. Forbes in 1922 and was primarily occupied as a housewife and mother, she continued to come into the laboratory on a part-time volunteer basis and followed with interest the ongoing investigative work. She and her husband always lived in Milton, vacationing on Naushon Island, and they celebrated many holidays with Cobb and his family. When Cobb retired from his Harvard professorship in 1954, Hildegarde and her husband were the prime movers in forming a committee to raise funds for a Stanley Cobb professorship. Something of a pack rat, Hildegarde preserved all the letters that Cobb wrote home to his parents and all the correspondence incident to founding the Stanley Cobb professorship. With her sharp memory and her deep devotion to her brother, she became a most valuable resource in reconstructing Cobb's career.

Stanley Cobb's life was indelibly influenced not only by his inheritance, family traditions, parents, and siblings but also by two boyhood friends who shared his interest in nature and particularly in bird lore. One of these was his first cousin Philip Sidney Smith and the other Winthrop Sprague Brooks, his neighbor across Adams Street in Milton, who was generally known as "Nick."

Philip Smith (1888–1904), the same age as Stanley Cobb, was the son of Uncle Sidney Smith (1849–1922), the brother of Cobb's mother. Uncle Sidney, a prominent New York lawyer and the chairman of the board of trustees of Phillips Exeter Academy from 1903 until 1919, had a town house at 105 East Thirty-eighth Street in New York City, a country place in Greens Farms, Connecticut, and membership in the Balsam Lake Club in Hardenbergh, Ulster County, New York. He and his family frequented this fish and game club not only during the fly-fishing season but on weekends and holidays throughout the year. Philip's mother, Edith Cornell Smith, was Uncle Sidney's second wife. She was a fascinating, emotional, and sometimes difficult person. She was very possessive in bringing up Philip and coddled him. The Cobb children wondered how Philip could always be a free spirit and the master of his own soul when he was so smothered. One of the ways

Uncle Sidney compensated for Aunt Edie's limitations was to invite Stanley to New York and to Balsam Lake on frequent occasions, so that the boys became intimate friends. Philip Smith and Stanley Cobb had in common an interest in nature and in birds. They made a census of birds which, with additions, was later published by Cobb (16). Another interest the boys had in common was art. Philip studied sculpture with Gutzon Borglum, who carved the presidential heads on Mount Rushmore, and Gutzon Borglum made a bust of Philip (page 25). Whenever Cobb was visiting Philip, he would write home, and the letters were invariably illustrated with numerous small pen-and-ink sketches of birds, tennis games, and other appropriate themes. Philip died in 1904 of complications from Potts' disease (tuberculosis of the spine). He was only seventeen, and his death must have had a strong impact on Cobb's emotional life.

Winthrop Sprague Brooks (1887–1965) was always known as "Nick." Nick had a brother, Lawrence, eight years his senior, who had organized a small private museum in their home, just across Adams Street from where the Cobbs lived in Milton. By the time he was ten Nick, too, was interested in natural history and was making collections. Rather unconventional and in some ways crude, Nick had a quick wit, alert movements, and a whimsical smile. In his fiftieth Harvard class report Nick said, "Having learned as a youth the gentle art of catching things, I averaged seven or eight months a year doing zoological collecting for the Museum of Comparative Zoology, being able to handle the job of curator of birds at the Boston Society of Natural History between excursions." In later life Nick belonged to a number of important societies of natural history, geography, and ornithology.

His initial influence on Cobb was in Milton where the two boys engaged in nature study and the collection of specimens as well as the adoption of some wild animals as pets. In 1906 they made a trip together to Nova Scotia and the Magdalen Islands, and in 1909 they went on a junket in Eastern Alberta, which Nick Brooks later wrote up as his first published article (4). When Stanley Cobb was in medical school, he received numerous detailed letters from Brooks, who spent a winter frozen in the ice at Point Barrow, Alaska, surviving by virtue of food obtained from a nearby wreck. In correspondence Nick often addressed Cobb as "Sockamow" and sometimes signed himself "Odayi." The letters contained pithy bits of information expressed in his uniquely informal way. Cobb continued seeing Nick throughout his life. During his last years Nick lived with his wife in retirement at Eastham, on Cape Cod, where he had owned property for many years.[17]

In addition to family members and playmates there were at least two women who influenced Cobb in his childhood. One of them was the family nursemaid, Mary Doyle, who took care of Stanley Cobb in infancy and early childhood. The other, who came into his life later, was Cornelia Huntington, his tutor.

Mary Doyle, of Irish extraction and of limited education, came to the Cobb household when Stanley was a baby; she was in the Cobbs' employ as a nursemaid throughout the early years of his life. Mary Doyle was extremely fond of Stanley and appreciated his unusual talents. He also felt a strong pull toward her. Years later, when Cobb was on active duty with the Massachusetts National Guard in winter, Mary was concerned that he be warm enough and have enough to eat. In a letter to him from Milton on February 12, 1912, Mary mentioned that she had been seeing in the papers pictures of him on his horse. She said that she missed him and was worried. Then she added: "I hope they give you enough to eat and that you have a half-way decent place to sleep. I think of you these cold mornings and wish you could share in our nice breakfasts and comforts."[18] When Mary Doyle was told of Cobb's engagement to be married she threw her apron over her head, rocked back and forth, and began keening, sobbing and wailing a funeral dirge as Irish people often do at a wake. Cobb's impending wedding represented a loss for her which she could only express as grief.[19]

A severe handicap, which creatively motivated Stanley Cobb's entire life, was his stammering. There were in his family tree a large number of ancestors and living persons with speech disorders of one sort or another, so a genetic factor is a possible explanation. Too, Stanley Cobb was born left-handed and in infancy had his left arm bound in a sort of sling to encourage the use of his right. He was ambidextrous all his life; so mixed right-left cerebral dominance may have been a factor in causing the stammering. However, in his own mind the stammering clearly dated from the birth of his sister Beatrice on March 24, 1892, when he was four.

On that day strange happenings were taking place at the Cobb household on Walnut Street in Brookline. Stanley had not seen his mother that morning. She had retired to her bedroom, and an unfamiliar woman in a white uniform came and went with pitchers of hot water and other paraphernalia. A dignified older man with black bag had come and gone more than once. There was an uneasy feeling of excitement and expectancy from which Stanley felt that he was being excluded. His curiosity was piqued because on several occasions he thought he heard groans coming from his mother's room. Later in the day the children were all shooed out of the house to play. Stanley was on the lawn with his older brothers and sisters when he heard violent screams coming from his mother's room. His younger sister, Beatrice, was being born. Not knowing what was happening, Stanley stood transfixed with fear. His older brothers and sisters ran away, and he chased after them as hard as he could, but he could not catch up. At that point he felt a great rush of wind into his chest and was unable to catch his breath. From that day on he had trouble talking. He was a stammerer.

The stammering was such a source of embarrassment that not only was Cobb's schooling interrupted but his social life was limited as well. On the other hand his loneliness and free time in the country made it possible for him to develop his interest in nature. Moreover, it was his curiosity about the origin of his stammering that later led him into the medical neurosciences and particularly into analytic psychiatry. So, the entire course of his productive life may well have originated in this handicap. In any event, the handicap was not aggravated by lack of comforts in the home. A year after Beatrice was born the family moved to even more commodious surroundings.

The piece of property which the Cobbs settled upon when they moved from Brookline to Milton in 1893 was magnificently situated on the water side of Adams Street overlooking the Neponset Marsh and Dorchester Bay. The house, of late Victorian style, with wide verandahs and overhanging eaves, had large rooms with high ceilings and furnishings characteristic of the period. When the direction of the wind was right, the aroma of roasting chocolate wafted on the air from the Baker factory in Milton village and created an atmosphere which was homey and heartwarming. The woods behind the house, descending to the marsh below, afforded Stanley constant opportunity for the development of his interest in nature because plants, small animals, and birds abounded there. Stanley Cobb lived in Milton until he went to Harvard in 1906, and after that he was not far away. He was in Ponkapoag, right next to Blue Hill, from 1919 to 1928, and then built a house on a part of his parents' land in 1928, where he lived until after his retirement in 1954.

By any normal standards Stanley Cobb's early education was a disaster. In accordance with his mother's views on education he was not sent to school at all until he was eight years old.[20] At that time there did appear to be some improvement in his speech and he went to Milton Academy. However, reading aloud proved difficult for him, and he had trouble dealing with the peer pressures and faculty demands at a conventional school. The stammering became worse and by 1902, when Stanley was fourteen, not only the school boys but even members of the faculty were teasing him because of his impediment. It was then that Mrs. Cobb removed him from school, along with his sister Polly (Florence), so that he would have someone with whom to play.[21]

The tutoring at home was in some ways a blessing in disguise. The tutor whom Mrs. Cobb found was Cornelia Huntington, the daughter of the local Congregational clergyman. She was a very fine, bright woman who quickly developed an appreciation of Stanley's creativity and hence was exactly the teacher he needed at that time.

For Christmas in 1958, more than fifty years later, Cobb sent her a photograph of himself. At that time she was Mrs. Damon and was living in Worcester. The following excerpts from her thank-you letter give a sense of her appreciation for him.

> I wish that in your mature years my "lines" might have been cast nearer to yours. I selfishly feel that you could—and would—have given me something from the water of life which could have come from no one else.
>
> You were a marvelous boy, Stanley—delving into nature's ways and problems and purposes; within yourself searching out the deep things; holding a keen, eager disposition in an astonishingly steady leash and rarely letting it run away with you; always on the lookout to be helpful and kind. Everyone adored you for all this—and for the temper that could burst into a fury and come gently down into a song of living.
>
> Whenever I find myself reliving my young years it is with profound longing to return to the priceless opportunity of sharing in the flowering of boys such as you.[22]

Miss Huntington came for two hours each morning for two years and taught Stanley and Polly the traditional classroom studies appropriate to their respective ages.

However, Mrs. Cobb was wise enough to know that the children needed a form of self-expression, too. So she engaged Elizabeth Taylor Watson, a well-known artist, to teach them painting. During the summers they painted landscapes out of doors, and winters they worked in charcoal at the Museum of Fine Arts in Boston, making figure studies from statues. Stanley painted in oils in his early life but later switched to watercolor. Polly worked in both media.

During the period of withdrawal from school, Stanley learned to shoot ducks and also widely increased his knowledge of ornithology. And he used the knowledge of English acquired from Miss Huntington to write about it. His first magazine article was written at this time. In 1904 it was published in *American Ornithology* under the title "Nesting of a Golden Crowned Eaglet in Massachusetts." (1) Two years later there appeared in *Bird Lore* "A Little Black Rail in Massachusetts." (2) The following paragraph from "A Little Black Rail" gives a feeling for Cobb's literary style at that time.

> I saw a small bird come tumbling down through the soft pine tips, now and then clinging to one for a second. Finally he landed on the ground. Here he stopped for a minute on the wet pine needles as if to recover his balance, and then made for cover. While this was going on I had stood watching the proceedings with interest, but as soon as the bird started to run I saw at once by his diminutive size and peculiar shape that he must be something unusual. I quickly gave chase, and with the help of my terrier soon cornered the bird in some underbrush; but after getting close enough to touch him with my hand, he escaped to another hiding place. Knowing now that he was the rare Black Rail, I redoubled my zeal, and at last after an exciting quarter of an hour, I caught the little fellow.

In spite of the freedom from the academic demands and the peer pressure of Milton Academy, and his significant achievements in art, writing, and natural history, the stammering did not improve; so, after a heart-to-heart talk between father and son, the decision was made for Stanley again to return to school—but not to Milton Academy. This time he went to the Volkmann School, which later merged with Noble and Greenough. Stanley commuted each day to Boston to the school. He liked Mr. Volkmann, the headmaster. Stanley's speech did improve for a time. While at the Volkmann School, Stanley was thinking about his future and planning to become a field naturalist. He was adept with a scalpel and knew museum techniques for stuffing animals. He had learned taxidermy. Then one day he had an experience that altered the whole direction of his life. At the Balsam Lake Club a prominent surgeon observed him skinning a shrew, the smallest of American mammals. The surgeon looked over his shoulder and remarked, "My, I wish I had hands like that. Young man, you ought to be a surgeon." Cobb later said of this episode, "Although I did not go into surgery, this remark steered me toward medical school."

From February until June in 1906, Cobb was also enrolled at the New England Conservatory of Music studying voice.[23] He did not stammer when singing, and singing later became a major outlet for him. Mr. Volkmann still maintained an interest in Cobb even after his graduation in June of that year. In fact he visited Cobb in his room at Harvard the following fall and designed a school banner for him.

A fitting sequel to Cobb's periodically interrupted schooling was an invitation from Arthur Perry, the headmaster of Milton, to give the graduation day address in 1955. Had he not been withdrawn from Milton, Cobb would have been in the class of 1905, which was having its fiftieth reunion, and he was invited as a representative of that class. He did not know what to say or how to say it. The night before the lecture he was tossing about in bed searching for ideas when his wife suggested, "Stanley, why don't you tell them about the pranks you used to play?" Cobb brightened up and replied, "You mean all about the skunk at the post office and Malcolm Forbes's top hat?" Betty said, "Why not?"

The following day Cobb gave his address. He told the assembled alumni that he wanted to report on three areas of investigation he had pursued in his Milton days. One of them was *psychological*. He had studied the reaction on the face of one of the women teachers when her hand came upon a live mouse which he had put in her pocket. The second was *sociological*. He and a classmate observed the behavior of Mr. Malcolm Forbes whose high hat had mysteriously come off as he was walking up Adams Street. Stanley and a friend, secluded in some nearby bushes, had knocked the hat off with a long slender pole. The final investigation which Cobb reported that day was along *biological* lines. On a February afternoon he and his friend Nick Brooks caught a skunk in the woods. Like surgeons they carefully removed the sac containing the animal's odoriferous secretion and put the fluid in a bottle. With its odor removed the skunk was adopted as a family pet at the Cobbs' house. Nick and he then began to think about what to do with the prize in their bottle. They decided to take it to the Milton Post Office where they poured it all over the floor. Cobb later said that they had proved that a bad enough stink could close any U.S. Post Office for three days. Cobb did not mention in his address that the following week Maurice Pierce, the police chief, talked politely to

Childhood

Cobb's father and asked for money to pay for a new floor in the post office. Knowing nothing about what had happened Mr. Cobb initially said, "No!" and protested his son's innocence. However, Mrs. Cobb had smelled the aroma of skunk in the areaway, so Mr. Cobb agreed to pay for the new floor. Mr. Cobb never did tell Stanley about paying for the new floor, nor did he broadcast his knowledge of Stanley's mischief to other members of the family. The elder Cobb remembered the Hallowe'en night in his own youth when he had reversed the street signs in Brookline.

During Cobb's presentation at the graduation day luncheon, members of the Milton faculty looked a bit aghast, but the alumni listened with envy and enjoyment. In a thank-you note dated May 10, 1955, Arthur Perry said, ". . . All the fish came into your net, and so very willingly. You helped more than you would ever permit yourself to think to give us what seems to me to be the happiest Graduates' Day for ten years or so."

Of other mischief, it is told that one day, when Cobb was about thirteen years old, he brought his bow and arrow into the dining room where there hung a handsome oil painting of Cobb's mother, Leonore, standing beside her younger sister Emma. Cobb was angry at his mother at the time. He drew his bow, aimed at the maid, and let the arrow fly. Fortunately, it missed the maid, but it struck the portrait near the corner of his mother's mouth. The picture later became the property of Cobb's sister Beatrice, and the hole in the canvas was repaired. In later life Cobb learned to handle his anger less destructively.

Another insight into Cobb's boyhood mischief came from his long-time friend Alfred Redfield. Redfield said that in his adult life Cobb was looked upon by many of the proper Miltonians as a sort of father confessor, and he knew all the family skeletons on Adams Street. One day a troubled lady whose son had been apprehended for breaking into houses came to see him. Cobb's reassuring words to the mother were, "When I was your son's age I had broken into every house on Adams Street."

As he grew up Cobb developed a great love of animals. The private museum across the street from Cobb's house had been set up by Nick Brooks's older brother, Lawrence, who was eight years Cobb's senior. The museum's stationery had a very imposing letterhead. The Brooks boys advertised in nature magazines and were in the business of exchanging pelts for the eggs of various species of birds and retiles. Cobb said that when he was ten, to look over the shoulder of Lawrence Brooks at work was a tremendous stimulus to his own scientific interest. He said it led him at an early age into the museum game with all that was implied in terms of artistic constructiveness and manual dexterity, not to speak of its most important aspect, orderliness of thought and action.

There are many tales of Cobb's early interest in animals. His mother apparently understood the importance of animals in his life and demonstrated more patience and tolerance than one might expect of most mothers under the circumstances. For example, she permitted her son to bring home birds that had fallen from their nests, a mouse, a pig, and a fox, in addition to the aforementioned deodorized skunk. Once, when Cobb was away visiting his cousin, Philip Smith, at the Balsam Lake Club, he sent home a live porcupine, carefully packed in a barrel. Mrs. Cobb had the expressman deliver the barrel to the basement. Then she fed the porcupine every day until Cobb's return, even though she found the bristling animal distasteful.

On another occasion Cobb brought into the home a ball of nineteen snakes and put them in the bathtub. The outflow of the tub was designed in such a way that a piece of seven inch pipe inserted in the drain served as both a drain plug and an overflow. Stanley was told that Aunt Alice Cobb ("Lala"), a maiden lady petrified by the sight of snakes, was coming for a visit. He was instructed to remove the snakes from the house. Actually Mrs. Cobb and the three younger sisters gathered them up one by one, but there were only eighteen. Later, when Cobb himself was taking a bath in the tub, the nineteenth snake crawled out of the drain and looked him in the eye. Aunt Alice never knew how close she came to the fright of her life.

Alfred Redfield told another tale about a day when Cobb, wandering in the Neponset Marsh, came upon a canvasback duck in the rushes. He stalked the duck. Then just as the duck took off for flight Cobb lunged forward and caught it in his bare hands. Redfield said it was the first time he had ever heard of a person managing to catch a live wild duck in his hands.

Cobb loved to travel. Most of his traveling during his childhood was to New York City or to the Balsam Lake Club in Hardenbergh, New York, to visit with his cousin, Philip Smith. In order to reach the Balsam Lake Club, they would take a Hudson River steamer to Storm King

Childhood

Landing in the Catskills and then work their way to Ulster County by buckboard.

Stanley Cobb had an opportunity to visit Washington, D.C., in December, 1900, at the age of thirteen. In a letter to his mother he mentioned visiting the Smithsonian, the zoo, and the Library of Congress. He was impressed by the rows and rows of graves in Arlington National Cemetery and in youthful language commented on "those poor suckers" who were blown up on the battleship *Maine* at the start of the Spanish-American War. He was in Washington again in April, 1901.

In July, 1901, Cobb was on a trip to upstate New York with Lawrence Brooks and his brother Augustus. He was particularly impressed by Niagara Falls. He wrote to his mother, "We took a car over to the Canadian shore and saw the Horse Shoe Falls. I liked them best because of the shape and the deep green where the water was thickest." He spent hours studying, walking down the gorge by the whirlpool, and then up the other side. He said, "The water that had been sent down to the bottom by the force of the falls came up again and made the water some twenty feet higher in the middle than on the sides, while in the middle it was black and on the sides all white with foam."

After having graduated from the Volkmann School, Cobb had a summer of extensive wilderness travel in Canada before entering Harvard in the fall of 1906. In July of that year he went with his brother Augustus and other members of the family through Rochester, New York, to the shanty at Stony Lake, near Lakefield, Peterborough County, Ontario. Stony Lake is about thirty miles north of Port Hope on the north shore of Lake Ontario. At Stony Lake there was excellent muskellunge fishing.

He left Stony Lake toward the end of July and traveled to Nova Scotia, where he joined a number of friends including Nick Brooks and three other young men, named Walter, Louis, and Sam. They went on a canoe-and-portage trip through various estuaries of Lake Rossignol, which is in Queens County, almost due north of Shelburne and Lockport. Lake Rossignol has a finger, presumably Fairy Lake, extending to the northwest into Annapolis County. Cobb and his friends gathered at Annapolis Royal and then made their way inland to the "jumping off place," Milford, which is too small to be recorded in Rand McNally's World Atlas. They were on a trip through Fairy Lake to the

Indian Gardens, which also were off Lake Rossignol. They had two tents, one for the three guides, and one for the fishermen, as well as a fly over the dining table. They worked their way through Lake Rossignol to Loon Lake and then back again terminating their trip at Fairy Lake, where they had started. Just before leaving Milford on the way out, Cobb and his friend Sam spent a night on the edge of a beaver pond. On August 24, 1906, from the Queen Hotel in Annapolis Royal, Cobb wrote to his mother about the events.

> Sam and I started off to spend the night at a little pond six miles away where there are lots of beaver. The stunt is to get a good clear night and shoot them on the water, but after we started it clouded up. We walked the six miles with our light packs and then paddled across the lake and had a cold supper. From here we could see the beaver house across the lake and pulled the canoe up on a large, flat rock. Sam slept under this, and after arranging a sleeping bag, I went back to listen to the beasts. They were all around me. I could hear them in the house chewing bark and paddling about in the water. Every once in a while one would slap his tail as we approached.
>
> I stationed myself on one side of the house, Sam on the other. The first thing I knew, I saw what I thought was a small muskrat swimming fast about thirty yards away. I let it swim on, and when it was out of range it rose to the surface and proved to be a big beaver which had swum past me with just the top of its nose out. It grew dark quickly, and I had another come by which I shot at, but the beast saw the flash and was under before the shot reached him. . . . Early in the morning I got two more swimming shots, but they both dove before the shots reached them. However I had an extremely interesting time, and it was well worth it.[24]

At Annapolis Royal on August 24, 1906, Walter left the party and Louis joined it. Cobb wrote to his mother about the beaver pond. Then the group took the 12:30 train to Pictou, arriving there at 10:00 P.M. Pictou is on the north shore of Nova Scotia overlooking the eastern end of Prince Edward Island. From here Cobb and his friends took a ferry to Grindstone Island, the largest of the Magdalen group. In a letter to his father from Grindstone, Cobb indicated that the islands were beautiful, with rolling pasture land, high conical hills, and along the shore steep red sandstone cliffs eroded into round, deep caves. One day, when visiting a sand flat, they managed to get fifteen big birds but over across the bay they saw literally thousands of beetle-head plover and yellowlegs.

Before leaving the Magdalens, Cobb and Nick Brooks made a trip to the eastward where they had fine shooting. On September ninth

Childhood

Cobb wrote to his brother John describing in rather vivid language the house where they stayed.

> The only drawback was the quarters we had, and they certainly were the dirtiest, stinkingest accommodations I ever saw. The occupants of the house were two lazy Frenchmen, a nice French woman who ran the place, a slovenly girl with two kids, and an elderly consumptive hag who was the great feature. When we arrived and were eating our supper she sat close to the stove and spasmodically engaged in the act of hacking and spitting. The floor was none too good for her, and I nearly slid a lunch, as the idea of tubercle bacilli for a carpet is not attractive. However, we choked down our supper and had our meals in a separate room afterwards. The hag also had the habit of drinking water out of the tumblers on the table which were never washed; so I used my rubber cup the entire time.[25]

The letter continues with details of setting up decoys and enumerates the bag of birds as exemplified by the following paragraph:

> The next morning, however, was my big luck. We started out at 4:00 A.M., and I got set by about 6. Summer yellowlegs came first and a few beetles. At about seven a flock of 30 redbreasts came in and as they swerved over the decoys I knocked [down] five. They scattered and for the next hour kept coming back in singles and pairs. By 8:30 I had 16 of them and 32 birds in all. The first thing in the bag was an Eskimo curlew which lit about 100 yards away. I stalked him and shot him. I was tickled to death as it was a very rare bird.

It is paradoxical that Cobb, who demonstrably was such an animal lover, should have derived so much pleasure from killing birds for which he had no use.

During his years of primary and secondary education Cobb had become a proficient student of natural history and ornithology, had learned to express himself in English, and had made a few firm friends with whom to pursue his interests. He had learned to shoot and to camp in the wild. Nonetheless, deeper intellectual interests and social amenities were yet to be developed at Harvard.

2
Education at Harvard

There have been extensive changes in Harvard College since Cobb entered it in 1906. President Charles W. Eliot, who had done so much to raise academic standards and place the graduate schools on a firm footing, retired in 1909 and was succeeded by A. Lawrence Lowell, under whom the entire social and residential structure of the college was to change. When Cobb was there the dormitories in the Yard were reserved for seniors, while lower classmen lived in what they called "diggings," some of which were owned by the University and others privately maintained. Subsequently, with the house plan, introduced in the twenties, the Yard dormitories were reserved for freshmen, and the upperclassmen lived along the river.

There were also important changes in arrangements for meals. Even in Cobb's day the old fraternities were breaking away from their national ties, and the club system was evolving. Students could be elected to purely social waiting clubs such as the Phoenix, to which Cobb belonged. Those who wanted to eat together on a regular basis went on to join final clubs, which provided meals. Some of the final clubs served meals on their own premises, while others, such as D.K.E., had private rooms at the Hasty Pudding Club, where fare was available for a larger number of the student body. In his sophomore year Cobb was elected to the Zeta Psi final club, where he had his meals. Zeta Psi, originally a national fraternity, had broken away before Cobb entered Harvard and was colloquially known as the Spee. Subsequently Spee became its official name. The Spee Club had formal summer, fall, winter, and spring dinners, with elaborately printed menus, and the Phoenix Club also had formal dinners twice a year. The Spee was one of the most prestigious of the final clubs. Cobb's brother Augustus was also a Spee man. After the houses along the river were firmly established and provided all of a student's comforts and social needs, the clubs lost much of their appeal, and although many of them still exist, their importance has diminished to the point where most students feel no peer pressure to join them.

Education at Harvard

During his freshman year Cobb lived at 60 Mount Auburn Street.[1] According to the headmaster of the Volkmann School, who visited him one day, Cobb had a number of roommates. After calling on Cobb, Volkmann wrote a letter to his mother describing his visit and offering to have a school banner designed so that Cobb could have it in his room. In his letter to Mrs. Cobb, dated November 22, 1906, Volkmann said,

> I have a man who gets up flags and banners, and I shall be very glad to have him make one for Stanley if you will let me know the size approximately and if it is to be square or triangular. I am sure Stanley would like it and I shall be proud to have one in his room; for he is certainly a loyal boy and a joy in every sense. As I came home the other day after having seen him in Cambridge in a room with a lot of boys I remarked to Mrs. Volkmann that anybody would pick out Stanley as *the star* from a bunch of fellows after hearing them talk together for ten minutes. He has such good sense and such a directness of moral insight. He is always on the right side of the fence before anybody else.[2]

It is known that in his sophomore year, 1907–1908, Cobb was in Randolph Hall. His four permanent roommates, all members of the Spee,[3] were Gerard Gignoux, Raymond Emerson, Sigourney Olney, and Gordon Prince. In the fall of 1908 they were living at 7 Apthorpe House, a university-owned apartment building which later was joined with Claverly to form Adams House. They moved into 15 Holyoke Street for the remainder of the junior year and roomed at 20 Holyoke Street their senior year, rather than in the Yard as was customary for seniors at that time.

Raymond Emerson, an engineering student and a grandson of Ralph Waldo Emerson, was the most prolific correspondent among Cobb's roommates at Harvard College. On August 4, 1907, after Cobb's first year in college, Emerson wrote from the Harvard Engineering Camp at Squam Lake in New Hampshire. Cobb was in Minnesota and then Wyoming at the time, and in his letter Emerson was singing about the charms of the Bighorn Basin. In October, 1908, Emerson was working with the Stone and Webster Engineering Company at Hauser Lake in Helena, Montana. In July, 1909, he was back at the Harvard Engineering Camp again. Raymond Emerson was a great outdoors man. His letters are filled with descriptions of birds and of the countryside and of arrangements for shooting. From the sequence of his letters it appears that he took a year off from college, 1908–1909, in order to work and recoup his finances. Although socially a member of the Class of 1910, he received his B.S. in 1911. He later married Amelia Forbes (1888–1979). Emerson's letters to Cobb were profusely illustrated with pen-and-ink sketches of scenes related to duck hunting.

Girard Gignoux, informally known as "Gig," lived on Long Island. After college he married a French girl and bought a chateau in Champtoce, ten miles from Angers, on the lower Loire. In April, 1909, he visited his parents in Paris, after having made a trip down the Nile. In the summer of 1908 Gignoux was in Great Neck, Long Island, supervising the cutting of American chestnut trees that had been killed by the blight. He regretted that, because of this supervisory job, he would be unable to take part in the fall shooting in Eastham that September. In a letter dated July 8, 1908, from Minnamere, Great Neck, Long Island, he sent love to Beatrice and Florence Cobb and signed himself Gerard Christmas Gignoux, Vicompte de Ribaulet. In later years the Cobbs visited Gignoux at Champtoce and found him living in considerable luxury in the rebuilt chateau, situated in the middle of a great park with gardens and vineyards. The real work of the place according to Cobb was raising cattle, making wine, making butter, and keeping domestic animals.

Sigourney Olney lived in Lawrence, Long Island. He apparently was not a brilliant student. He wrote to Cobb in the summer after his graduation, elated over having received four B's and two C's, adding that he squeaked by and got his degree by the skin of his teeth. He graduated from the Harvard Law School in 1912 and eventually settled in Chicago. After completing law school he was working in the Office of General Counsel for the Brooklyn Rapid Transit Company. One New Year's Eve while there he wrote Cobb a nostalgic note about good times together. Cobb was in medical school at the time. Olney wrote, "Do you remember the day when the shooting was so good we got 12 or 13 and staid all day and having no lunch we became so ravenous we ate a slightly heated but absolutely uncooked duck . . . do you remember lying in at that first morning early and seeing the scamps and whistlers streaming by each side just out of gunshot? I remember the trip. It was just before midyear exams. . . . We were cramming for Bliss Perry's course." Later in the same letter he wrote, "Some day, Stan, when we are fat and bald and forty we'll go off again and shoot some more duck. I suppose we'll be so helpless then we'll have to have game keepers set out our decoys, wad our guns, light our

Education at Harvard

House on Oakland Street in Brookline where Stanley Cobb was born. In 1887 the property faced on Walnut Street. It was later subdivided.

Cobb children in the early 1890s. Left to right: Stanley, Emma, Polly, Hildegarde, John, Beatrice and Augustus

Stanley Cobb in a sailor suit, early 1890s

Education at Harvard

Stanley Cobb as a young boy

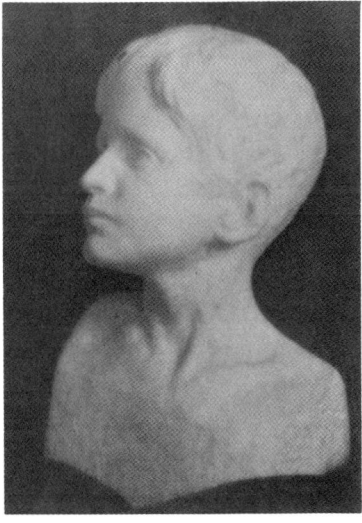

Bust of Philip Sidney Smith
(1887–1904), Cobb's first cousin and
intimate friend, by Gutzon Borglum

Stanley Cobb's Massachusetts National Guard squadron quelling a labor strike in Lawrence, Massachusetts, in 1911. Cobb is on his white horse Omar (lower left), serving as standard bearer

Education at Harvard

Stanley Cobb (right) on his favorite horse Omar. The accompanying rider remains unidentified but is thought to be the older brother of Nick Brooks

Stanley Cobb as a medical student at Harvard

Education at Harvard

Surgical staff of the Peter Bent Brigham Hospital, 1914–1915. Back row: Drs. Cutler, Horrax, Weed, Towne, Morton and Hurwitz; Middle row: Drs. Rand, Goetsch, Cushing, Homans and Jacobson; front row: Drs. Lehmann and Cobb

Wedding picture of Stanley and Betty Cobb, July 10, 1915

Education at Harvard 31

cigars, and uncork our bottles, but it will never be as good as when we did our own work." It is obvious from this letter that Olney was another outdoors man whom Cobb enjoyed in his hunting days. Olney also drew ducks at the end of his letters to Cobb.

Gordon Prince was a nephew of the well-known experimental psychopathologist, Morton Prince. The interest Cobb shared with Gordon Prince was riding. They were together in the Massachusetts National Guard cavalry. They enjoyed the riding and took part in its drills. Prince wrote,

> I don't see how I can ride the pony out on Wednesday as I can't very well get down until late Wednesday afternoon, and besides we have got to shoot on Thursday and have our horses shod on Friday. Friday night we have to go in to the troop armory and pack our stuff. What we want to do is meet somewhere Thursday . . . If you are out at Cambridge bring in my olive drab uniform as we are to wear the trousers they say. In the orders it says we have to send the overcoat and blouse but you had better ask Gus [Stanley's brother Augustus] if we can't leave them behind.

Another time Prince wrote suggesting that Cobb ride with him out to visit the Emersons in Concord.

Cobb was in college at the time when President Eliot had a profound influence in developing and expanding the elective system, whereby students were encouraged to till a wider field of knowledge than that provided by purely informational courses. The expanded elective system gave Cobb the opportunity for original research in comparative anatomy with Dr. William E. Castle, whom he came to view as one of his important life models.

The work which Cobb did with Castle was published by the Carnegie Institution of Washington in 1909 under the title "Studies of Inheritance in Rabbits" by W. E. Castle, in collaboration with H. E. Walter, R. C. Mullenix, and S. Cobb. (3) The monograph of seventy pages plus illustrations was divided into four parts, on ear size, weight, skeletal dimensions, and color. Cobb worked on color and with Castle designated eight hereditary traits responsible for the hue, chroma, value, and pattern of the rabbit's hair. In the monograph they went on to attempt classification of each as dominant or recessive in accordance with Mendelian principles.

Cobb's classroom work in college was better than respectable but not outstanding. The official transcript of his Harvard academic record indicates that on admission he was very weak in English, Latin, French,

German, history, algebra, plane geometry, and physics but had done well in elementary chemistry. Freshman year he did well in botany, zoölogy, and fine arts.[4] In his sophomore year he stood out in geology and zoölogy but was weak in chemistry, economics, and English. As a junior he continued his good work in botany and zoölogy and added an A in philosophy but did poorly in German, comparative literature, and physics. Again as a senior he did well in zoölogy and geology, both sciences, and less well in chemistry, comparative literature, and German. Throughout he distinguished himself in the nature studies, botany, zoölogy, and geology. He vacillated in philosophy between an A and a D. All his other marks were in the C to D range. When taking examinations Cobb used to outline the answers alongside the questions. On one of the preserved examinations in geology he actually drew pictures to clarify his thinking.[5]

Cobb was not elected to Phi Beta Kappa while he was in college. Rumor has it that he was not looked upon as a serious student. However, when he had established himself in medicine, he was belatedly taken into the Harvard chapter on his twenty-fifth anniversary in 1935. He did graduate with honors. A letter from Professor G. H. Parker in the Zoölogical Laboratory at Harvard dated April, 1910, speaks to this subject. It reads, "The list of courses, omitting Zoölogy 5, which you submitted in your note this morning seems to me to cover the necessary ground for the degree with distinction in Biology."[6]

When in college Cobb continued to be troubled by his stammering. He could sing without difficulty, but he had trouble with his spoken language, particularly when under stress. He was familiar with the work in hypnosis which was being carried out by Hugo Münsterberg, the professor of experimental psychology. Cobb asked Münsterberg to take him on for treatment in the hope of ameliorating the stammering. He wrote Münsterberg the following letter:[7]

Zeta Psi Club
Professor Münsterberg
Dear Sir:
   While listening to your courses in Philosophy E it has occurred to me that you might be able to relieve me from stammering, a problem which has bothered me for some twelve years. The reason I believe you would help me is that I know myself to be physically able to say any word I wish, but when the necessity arises a certain fear prevents the act. If my belief in my ability to speak could be strengthened by suggestion I think the trouble could be

Education at Harvard 33

overcome. If you are willing and in the habit of treating strangers, I should be very much interested in trying the experiment. Hoping this is not one of many bothersome letters I remain your sincerely,

Stanley Cobb

Münsterberg respectfully declined to take Cobb on as a subject for hypnosis. He wrote Cobb the following letter in which he stated that such treatment might help and suggested that Cobb look up any nerve specialist.[8]

Cambridge, Massachusetts
May 17, 1909

Dear Mr. Cobb:
Certainly there is the possibility of relieving stammering by hypnosis in cases like yours. You may find something about it in my "Psychotherapy." But, if I may remember rightly, I have already said in that book that I do not personally undertake the treatment of such cases. It fatigues me nervously in a considerable degree and thus I must beg you to excuse me. But any nerve specialist in town might be ready to undertake your treatment.

Sincerely yours,
Hugo Münsterberg

Cobb did eventually follow through on Münsterberg's recommendation and tried hypnosis elsewhere, but the treatment was not of lasting benefit. It is quite apparent, however, that Cobb looked upon his singing as therapeutic. He seized upon every opportunity to sing songs either solo or in groups such as choruses or operettas.

During the years at Harvard College Cobb's interests in birds, shooting, and travel were fulfilled simultaneously in hunting trips to various spots in the United States and Canada. Interest in the Balsam Lake Club waned after the untimely death of Philip Smith in 1904, but Cobb kept on receiving letters from George Owen, the caretaker, urging him to come back and describing the excellence of the hunting in the Catskill area.

In May, 1907, Cobb began making preparations for a trip that August to Wyoming and Minnesota. While there he sent some junco eggs to his friend Lawrence Brooks for the museum in his house in Milton. In September, 1908, with a number of friends, he went duck hunting in Eastham, Massachusetts, and in December of that year made the first of his trips to Muskeget Island with George E. Coffin of

Nantucket. He later owned a shack there which had belonged to Coffin, and made frequent landings at Muskeget Island with his own boat during the summers. For years hunting at Muskeget or adjacent Tuckernuck became a regular early December activity.

In the summer of 1909, Cobb and his naturalist friend, Nick Brooks, went on an extensive camping trip near Edmonton, Alberta, Canada. Preparations for the trip began in early spring with communications to and from the chief game warden of Canada about the best places for hunting and with the president of the Grand Trunk Railway about the transportation. Also one of Cobb's old friends, Rollins Maxwell of Duxbury, on a western trip himself, wrote a long letter containing all sorts of wisdom along these lines, but it was dated November 24, 1909, too late to be helpful.[9] Cobb, Nick Brooks, and another friend, Byam Whitney, were in Edmonton in August. From there they worked their way east to Birch Lake, which is near the villages of Ranfurly and Innisfree. They had a guide and companion named Emile Duplessis, who with his wife and child lived in Ranfurly. Innisfree was nearer the lake, and Nick Brooks's correspondence was postmarked there. Birch Lake, which covers an area of about twenty square miles, has an arm extending to the north. In 1911 Cobb and Brooks published in the ornithological journal, *The Auk,* under the title "Notes from Eastern Alberta," a census of birds seen within five miles of the upper arm of Birch Lake (4). Most of the birds must have been seen by Brooks, who remained in the Innisfree area much longer than Cobb and Whitney, who returned home in September. Brooks later wrote that he was tired of the long winter and was planning to come east in February.

The elegy to the trip was written by Emile Duplessis on March 11, 1910,[10] in a letter to Cobb with special greetings to him and Byam Whitney. Duplessis said that it had been the coldest winter ever, with temperatures of 60 below zero for a week and three feet of snow. He urged the boys, as he called them, to come back again for shooting and offered to build them a cabin, complete with bunks, between Island and Snowfall Lakes near the neck where they had seen the heron. Cobb went to Alberta again in 1911.

Cobb's interest in ornithology, exploration, and travel was recognized by some members of the faculty at Harvard, for he was one of the few undergraduate members, if not the only one, of the Harvard Travelers Club. Cobb preserved all the newspaper clippings he could find about Commodore Peary's discovery of the North Pole on April

Education at Harvard

6, 1909, and the controversy over Dr. Cook's claim to have been there on April 21, 1908. On March 31, 1910, the Travelers Club had a luncheon at the Harvard Union in honor of Sir Ernest Shackleton, the antarctic explorer. Cobb was asked by W. M. Davis, the president of the Travelers Club, to mention the event to members of his undergraduate circles in order to assure Sir Ernest of a fine crowd of men to talk with him in the living room after the luncheon.[11]

Cobb's interest and competence in ornithology and out-of-door life were recognized by his seniors in his undergraduate years not only by election to the Harvard Travelers Club but also by his membership in the American Ornithologists' Union and in the Boston Society for Natural History.[12]

On his next shooting venture in Eastham, Massachusetts, during September, 1910, Cobb was accompanied by his old college roommate, Raymond Emerson, and by his friend Byam Whitney. Emerson, who had taken a year out of college to work for Stone and Webster at Hauser Lake in Helena, Montana, was returning to Harvard for his final undergraduate year. Byam Whitney, who had gone on the trip to eastern Alberta with Cobb in August, 1909, was destined to become a frequent companion, because of his interests in horses and in hunting, during Cobb's medical school years, which were just commencing at this time.

Although the most important of Cobb's Harvard College clubs was the Spee, where he and his roommates all had their meals, his infrequent formal dinners at the Phoenix were pleasant social occasions. In addition to these organizations, D.K.E., and the Travelers Club, he also belonged to the Fencing Club, the Zoological Club, the Natural History Society, the Institute of 1770, and the Hasty Pudding Club. The last two were at that time separate organizations. The Institute had a broad membership and served meals to its members. The Hasty Pudding was a purely dramatic organization. After Cobb's day they merged into the Hasty Pudding Institute of 1770.

In his senior year Cobb was in the cast of the Hasty Pudding Club play, wearing a gown which from photographs looked like a cross between a clerical surplice and a Roman toga, with a Sherlock Holmes hat set transversely across his head. He was in a chorus of similarly attired males, while other members of the cast were decked out to look like Indian maidens. The Pudding show presented annually at the time of graduation was one of the great social attractions at Harvard for well-connected young ladies, and an invitation was a highly prized honor. Cobb had for guests at his table for the Hasty Pudding Club "spread" on Class Day, 1910, Katrine Amory, Elizabeth Bowditch, and Marion Weld, with all of whom he carried on a very low-key correspondence from time to time.

One would think that Cobb's social life in Harvard would have consisted of a continuous round of debutante parties. If so, the invitations were not preserved, and with one exception there are no references to debutante parties in his letter. What correspondence he had with Katrine, Elizabeth, and Marion was very superficial—in contrast to long letters from roommates. Emerson, Gignoux, and Olney communicated at great length, particularly about shooting, while Prince wrote about horses. Cobb's special friend, Nick Brooks, expounded in minute detail the observations made in his long explorations. It is of note that Cobb did have good communication with his sisters, especially Florence and Beatrice, who kept him well informed of their activities and occasionally their feelings.

It may be that he found communicating with his sisters was comparatively easy because of the family relationship. On the other hand, the young women Cobb knew socially were almost certainly seeking husbands, so that the intimate expression of feelings in letters to them would carry the risk of encouraging a deeper involvement for which he was not prepared at that time. While in college his emotional energy was directed primarily into his relations with his sisters and with men.

As a boy Cobb imagined that he would become a naturalist until the shrew-skinning episode during his senior year at the Volkmann School. From that day on, and throughout his college years, Cobb felt propelled in the direction of medicine. The Harvard Medical School, when Cobb went there in the fall of 1910, also was undergoing transition. The new quadrangle with its five classic marble structures had been completed in 1906 under the *aegis* of Dr. John Collins Warren and Dr. Henry Pickering Bowditch, and the school had moved there from its former building at 688 Boylston Street at that time. Because the expanding activities of the school had so rapidly overgrown the previous facilities, the new plant was planned on a grand scale to be used for decades; so at first the faculty were rattling around in the new structures. These buildings, constructed through the generosity of Mrs. Collis P. Huntington, J. Pierpont Morgan, John D. Rockefeller, David Sears, and other benefactors, included one for administration and four for laboratory sciences, each of the laboratory buildings consisting of

Education at Harvard

two wings connected by an amphitheatre. It was in Building D that Cobb was later to have a neuropathology laboratory.[13]

Admission to the Harvard Medical School was not highly competitive at that time. There were seventy-six men in the class of 1914, with a capacity for one hundred and twenty-five. In 1901 Charles W. Eliot, then president of Harvard University, in his effort to improve the academic standards of the graduate schools, had recommended to the medical faculty that all candidates for admission must have obtained the degree of Bachelor of Arts and also show evidence of knowledge of physics and chemistry. This academic restriction had grossly limited the number of qualified applicants.

Harvard Medical School had fared well in the Flexner report, written by Abraham Flexner of the Rockefeller Foundation and published in 1910. That report, which pointed to dismal teaching practices in medical schools throughout the country, commented favorably on the basic science courses at Harvard. The report was critical, however, of the policy of rotating service chiefs at the Massachusetts General Hospital.[14] The Peter Bent Brigham Hospital had been in its planning stages for ten years before opening its doors in 1913. At the Brigham, Harvard Medical School had an opportunity to experiment with full-time chiefs of staff who could carry their responsibilities year round on a continuous basis. The Peter Bent Brigham Hospital thus became a contained local version of the university hospitals growing up elsewhere.

The curriculum for the first two years of medical school in Cobb's day was quite traditional. Anatomy was taught in the fall of the first year along with histology and embryology. In the spring came physiology and biochemistry. The course of studies for the second year included bacteriology, pathology, preventive medicine with introductions to materia medica and therapeutics, theory and practice, clinical medicine, and surgery.

In the third and fourth years the method of teaching was vastly different from that of today and consisted to a large extent of lectures on clinical topics, often going on into the late afternoon. The fourth year was entirely elective, although most students took two months of medicine and two months of surgery. The work in fourth-year medicine and surgery included clinical clerkships in preparation for internship after graduation.

Several of the basic-science faculty and instructors had a direct impact upon Cobb's professional life, and others are worthy of mention because of their prominence. David Cheever, later on the surgical staff of the Peter Bent Brigham Hospital, was Cobb's demonstrator of anatomy, and Charles S. Minot, the professor of comparative anatomy, was a renowned embryologist. In physiology Cobb came under the influence of Walter B. Cannon, whose later work on the intermediary conduction of nerve impulses and on homeostasis led directly into Cobb's future interest in psychosomatic medicine. Also in the physiology department was Cobb's old friend Alexander Forbes, who acquired an Einthoven string galvanometer in 1911 and subsequently collaborated with Cobb in adapting it to function as an electromyograph for studies of disturbed muscular activity in various disorders of the nervous system. In biological chemistry were Otto Folin, a pioneer in simplifying biochemical techniques for clinical applications, and Lawrence J. Henderson, who was very much interested in the equilibrium between acids and bases in physiologic systems. It was Henderson who recognized that the concentration of hydrogen ions is proportional to the ratio between the concentration of carbonic acid ions and the concentration of bicarbonate ions.[15] The equation which he wrote was subsequently reduced to logarithmic terms by Hasselbalch and became the standard tool for clinical evaluations in later years. In bacteriology at the time was S. Burt Wolbach, who afterwards became professor of pathology and pathologist to the Peter Bent Brigham Hospital.

William T. Councilman, professor of pathology when Cobb was in medical school, became his adviser for independent work carried out in the summers of 1912 and 1913. Frank B. Mallory, who lectured in pathology, was pathologist to Boston City Hospital when Cobb subsequently was chief of the neurological unit there, and Elmer E. Southard, the Bullard Professor of Neuropathology, was in charge of the laboaratory in Building D-2, which Cobb eventually was to inherit. Milton J. Rosenau, professor of preventive medicine and hygiene, remained active for many years, and Franz Pfaff was professor of pharmacology and therapeutics.

Henry A. Christian, a former intern at Johns Hopkins under William Osler, was Hersey Professor of the Theory and Practice of Physic. Prior to the opening of the Peter Bent Brigham Hospital, where he became chief of medicine in 1913, Christian was dean of the Medical School. According to Francis M. Rackemann, Christian's lectures were outstanding. Christian was Harvard's first full-time professor of medicine. Previously, most of the clinical faculty practiced medicine or surgery and taught part time. Frederick Cheever Shattuck was Jackson Profes-

Education at Harvard 39

sor of Clinical Medicine at the Massachusetts General Hospital. According to David Cheever, "He was a picturesque figure as he drove about the city in an open victoria with a cigarette between his lips, a carnation in his buttonhole, a gaudy waistcoat, and with reading matter—medical journals or letters—piled up on the seat beside him, and attended by Hans, the dachshund."[16] Shattuck was an excellent clinically oriented diagnostician and teacher. Cheever went on to say, "His fundamental success as a teacher gave authority to his opinion that a full-time teacher, trained only in the laboratory and hospital ward, can impart only a partial knowledge of the practice of medicine." He was succeeded by David L. Edsall as Jackson Professor in 1912. Other prominent clinical teachers of medicine in Cobb's day were Elliott P. Joslin, Joseph H. Pratt, Francis W. Palfrey, William B. Robbins, Channing Frothingham, George Sears, Richard Cabot, William H. "Big Bill" Smith, Franklin White, William H. Robey, Edwin A. Locke, and Frederick T. Lord. In pediatrics, Thomas Morgan Rotch was departmental head, and John H. McCollom, professor of contagious diseases, was curing cases of diphtheria with massive doses of the newly developed diphtheria antiserum.

The Mosely Professor of Surgery during Cobb's first two years in medical school was Maurice Howe Richardson at the Massachusetts General Hospital, a man of many talents, who died at 61 in 1912. He was succeeded as Mosely Professor by Harvey Cushing, the neurosurgeon under whom Cobb subsequently interned in 1914 and 1915 at the Peter Bent Brigham Hospital. Other important surgical figures in Cobb's day were John Homans, who went with Cushing from Johns Hopkins to the Brigham; Robert B. Greenough, who went into oncology; Hugh Cabot, the urologist; Daniel F. Jones, who perfected techniques for colonic and ano-rectal surgery; and William J. Mixter, whose son, Jason later became chief of neurosurgery at the Massachusetts General Hospital.

Other clinical departments in the school were roentgen ray, then in its infancy, orthopedics, obstetrics, gynecology, dermatology, syphilis, neurology under James Jackson Putnam and E. W. Taylor, and psychiatry, taught by Edward Cowles, director of the McLean Hospital.

When Cobb entered the Harvard Medical School in 1910, the present dormitory, Vanderbilt Hall, did not exist. There were no dining or sleeping accommodations at the school. Most of the students lived in apartments or rooming houses and had to fend for themselves for meals. Some joined medical fraternities, of which Nu Sigma Nu and Alpha Kappa Kappa were perhaps the best known.

In 1912, after Cobb's second year, Dr. John Collins Warren, who had played a major role in bringing the quadrangle into existence, published a proposal in the *New England Journal of Medicine* for a dormitory and clubhouse near the quadrangle. He envisioned the dormitory on Longwood Avenue to the east of Avenue Louis Pasteur where the Boston Lying-in Hospital was later built, and a clubhouse to the west on the site of what is now Vanderbilt Hall.[17] (It was not until approximately a decade and a half later that a dormitory was built on the latter location.) Cobb's home in Milton was only about nine miles from the school, and he elected to commute from there. He occasionally used a Ford "tin lizzie," but he usually rode in on his three-fourths Arabian white horse, Omar.

The first concentrated course in medical school then, as now, was anatomy, and six students were assigned to each cadaver. How students were assigned cadavers is not clear. With a class of seventy-six members, alphabetical order might have thrown together Binger, Cheever, Cobb, and Gray. However, Lunt, and Millet, who was a friend prior to medical school, must have joined the other four through some kind of swap. Austin Cheever, who became a well-known Boston dermatologist, was on a different wave-length from the other five cadaver mates, all of whom in one way or another had a special interest in the central nervous system.

Of the remaining cadaver mates, Carl Binger was the closest to Cobb, both in terms of professional evolution and social intimacy. While Cobb was progressing from tissue neuropathology *via* neurophysiology and clinical neurology to dynamic psychiatry, Binger was moving from physiologic research, and through the practice of internal medicine, into psychoanalysis. On the social side, the Cobbs and Bingers cruised together every summer during the thirties and later set up adjacent homes in Little Compton, Rhode Island, in anticipation of retirement there.

After graduation from Harvard Medical School in 1914 Binger obtained a Sheldon Traveling Fellowship for two years. However, because World War I commenced that August, he was unable to travel in Europe; hence he spent the academic years from 1914 to 1916 at Johns Hopkins. He went to France with the Massachusetts General Hospital unit in 1917 and from 1918 after the armistice through 1919 was with

Education at Harvard

the Typhus Commission in Macedonia. On returning to the United States he joined the staff of the Rockefeller Institute, where initially, with a team of physiologists, he studied the effects of high altitude in the Peruvian Andes. Then he worked on gas-exchange problems in the laboratory for ten years and was viewed as an outstanding investigator.

In early 1928, for reasons not yet entirely clear, Binger began to lose interest in pure laboratory work and apparently was in need of a period of time for mid-life reorientation.[18] So, in August, 1928, he sailed for Europe and after an initial vacation spent the fall working under the distinguished physician, Ludolf Krehl in Heidelberg. That fall Binger did indeed become severely depressed and on January 15, 1929, went to Zürich for treatment with Jung. While working with Jung, Binger became convinced that he could no longer follow a purely intellectual laboratory pursuit, which allowed one-half to two thirds of his personality to remain fallow, and he began to contemplate resigning from the institute.[19] In the fall of 1929 he did so,[20] and on returning to New York set up an office for the practice of internal medicine and psychoanalysis.[21] From that beginning he went on to become one of the leading national figures in psychosomatic medicine.

In the relationship between Cobb and Binger it is a moot point as to who had the greater influence on the other. Binger looked upon Cobb as more a neurologist than a psychiatrist. From 1930 to 1934, however, when Binger was commencing practice of internal medicine and psychiatry in New York and had taken up psychoanalysis, Cobb was active in the Boston Psychoanalytic Society and the new Boston Psychoanalytic Institute. In 1942, after Cobb was established in psychiatry at the Massachusetts General Hospital, he was a founding member of the American Psychosomatic Society, and Binger became perennial editor of its journal. Then in 1955, after Cobb retired from the Massachusetts General Hospital, Binger moved his practice to Cambridge, became a psychiatrist to Radcliffe students, and joined the M.G.H. staff. It is only fair to say that the relationship was very close throughout the professional lives of both men without making a judgment as to whose impact was primary.

Horace Gray, of Nahant, was an old friend from the Spee Club at Harvard College, from which he graduated in the class of 1909. Before entering medical school with Cobb in September, 1910, Gray spent a year at St. John's University in Shanghai, China. On July 23, 1909, he sent Cobb a postcard from Nikko, in Japan,[22] indicating that he had been hiking and mountain climbing there en route to China. By August 29, 1909, he was established at St. John's University as a member of the faculty with three hundred students expected in two weeks.[23] Gray wrote again on February 28, 1910, during the new year recess, about entrance exams for the next year, and on May 16, 1910, congratulating Cobb on graduating *cum laude* from Harvard. Gray was one of the most brilliant men in the medical school class. Along with Cobb he was elected to Alpha Omega Alpha, the medical honor society, in the third year. Gray wrote Cobb a long letter from Germany in the summer of 1911 saying that Binger was studying in Frankfort; at Binger's suggestion he asked Cobb to check on whether they should apply for Hans Barkan, an assistant in pathology, as their section man the following year.

Gray and Cobb obviously had a close personal relationship which persisted through medical school. Both interned at the Peter Bent Brigham Hospital, Gray in medicine and Cobb in surgery. They were both brilliant students, and both of them ultimately became interested in psychiatry. Gray established himself in Santa Barbara, California, and in later years had little contact or correspondence with Cobb.

Lawrence K. Lunt knew Cobb at Harvard College and, before starting medical school in 1910, wrote from his home in Colorado Springs to ask whether he and Cobb could room together that year.[24] Inasmuch as Cobb was planning to live at home, rooming together was not practical, but Lunt worked on the same cadaver. Lunt must have had an emotionally dependent relationship with Cobb, for he wrote, especially in the summer, many long, meticulously detailed letters about the process of daily living. He had a camp at Haystack Gulch, Brookvale P.O., Colorado, just over the hill from Idaho Springs and approximately twenty miles west of Denver, and Cobb visited him there. After graduation from medical school in 1914, Lunt went into psychiatry and became the proprietor of a private sanatorium, Valley Head, in the vicinity of Concord, Massachusetts. Later, when Cobb was heading the psychiatric service at the Massachusetts General Hospital, Lunt had a clinical appointment there. Cobb enjoyed Lunt as a friend. However, he did not view him as a serious scholar, and it is doubtful that Lunt had any profound effect on the evolution of Cobb's professional life.

John A. P. Millet, along with Cobb, Gray, and Lunt, was one of the four Harvard College classmates who worked together in anatomy at medical school. Correspondence from Millet, though brief and infrequent, indicates a warm relationship with Cobb. Millet wrote from Camp Merryweather, North Belgrade, Maine, in the summer of 1913[25] about switching a rotation in gynecology at the Massachusetts General Hospital so that he could work on a project with Cobb. Millet was married while in medical school. He lived at 72 Pinckney Street third year and at 409 Audubon Road fourth year, where one night he and his wife had Cobb for dinner. Cobb was asked to resign from the Boylston Medical Society because of his irregular attendance. When he did so, Millet, as president, had the duty of informing him that his resignation had not been accepted.[26] After graduation from medical school in 1914, Millet interned at the Peter Bent Brigham Hospital and from 1923 to 1930 was a staff psychiatrist at the Austin Riggs Foundation in Stockbridge, Massachusetts. Still later, he took up psychoanalysis and practiced in New York City. Millet's parents owned a house at Broadway in the Cotswolds, where the Cobbs visited briefly while abroad in 1924.

Although Cobb's undergraduate grades were not outstanding, so that he only managed to graduate *cum laude* and narrowly missed election to Phi Beta Kappa, in medical school things were different. He took his work seriously from the beginning; yet he found time for horsemanship and other interests. He belonged to the Bolyston Medical Society, a group of high-ranking medical students who met from time to time to hear outstanding and sometimes illustrious speakers and discuss current developments in medicine, and he was elected in the third year, along with Horace Gray, Edwin P. Lehman, and Richard Ohler, to Alpha Omega Alpha, the national honorary society for medical men. One night the four members of Alpha Omega Alpha who had been elected in the third year held a meeting in Horace Gray's quarters to choose additional fourth-year members. With a class of seventy-seven, there were potential places for a total of twelve members, four of whom had been elected earlier. From a list of academic achievers it was decided to choose six at that time and to reserve two spots for possible late bloomers (as Cobb had been himself).

Just as in college Cobb had found a model in Professor William E. Castle, so in the medical school he found a model in W. T. Councilman. Councilman was a thickset, stoutish man, at that time in his fifties, with wisps of brown hair trying to cover his bald head. He had come from Johns Hopkins in the mid 1890s, where he had been associated with William Henry Welch, the pathologist, and William Osler, the clinician. He brought some Hopkins atmosphere with him and undoubtedly influenced Cobb in his decision to work there later. Councilman was a deliberate, careful worker. He gave the students relatively few slides and enough time to study them rather than a large collection to be gone through hurriedly.[27] According to Cheever, Councilman, when a farm boy in Maryland, made a collection of bones illustrating the comparative osteology of indigenous vertebrates,[28] reminiscent of Cobb's own boyhood nature studies. Councilman was effective in bringing about important changes. Prior to 1913 when he went to the Brigham, he was pathologist at Boston City Hospital, where he lured Frank B. Mallory from private practice into pathology. Earlier, in 1896, he had promoted the appointment of James Homer Wright as full time pathologist to the Massachusetts General Hospital. In 1912 Councilman became chairman of the board of trustees of the American Medical Association. Later on, after Cobb retired from his active professional life, he quoted some advice he had obtained from Councilman. Councilman had remarked that one of the most gratifying things a man can do in retirement is to choose a very small field and explore it in depth. That is precisely what Cobb later did, working on the comparative anatomy of bird brains.

Under Councilman's guidance when still in medical school Cobb spent two summers, 1912 and 1913, performing autopsies at the Boston Floating Hospital and correlating the findings. The work was published in the *Archives of Pediatrics,* June, 1915, by Richard M. Smith and Stanley Cobb under the title "A Clinical and Pathological Study of 100 Infants" and consisted of taking sections on the gastrointestinal tract, making urine and kidney examinations, and making evaluations of tuberculosis, fatty livers, lymph nodes, lung irregularities, and size of stomach. Smith later became a very prominent Boston pediatrician and during the Great Depression was an early advocate of national health insurance. Cobb's interests turned to neuropathology, clinical neurology, and psychiatry. In his liberal sociologic views Cobb undoubtedly had many common interests with Smith. However, their major *foci* of interest were different, and they worked in different institutions; hence they saw relatively little of each other in later years.

Councilman, as pathologist to the Boston Floating Hospital, encouraged Cobb to undertake his first teaching experience. In a letter to his mother Cobb described what took place:

I did a thing at the hospital the other night that now seems like some impossible dream. I lectured before thirty-five doctors on the pathology of cases infected with *Bacillus Aerogenes Capsulatus* and got through somehow without complete collapse. The way it came out was rather funny: Dr. Talbot [Fritz B. Talbot] called me up and asked if I would work up a paper to be read at a symposium of the staff at the Boston Floating Hospital, and I told him I wasn't much of a reader, but I could bring down some specimens and explain them so he said that was better and to come along.

I expected an informal smoke-talk effect. Imagine my surprise in getting there when I found a lot of visiting physicians from various cities and Dr. Bowditch presiding over the meeting with a pitcher of water on the table and a printed program with my name next to Dr. Smith's and Dr. Talbot's as "Dr. Stanley Cobb, on the pathological findings in cases, etc., etc. . . ." I was pretty weak in the knees when he called me up, but I got started by showing the specimens and then talked fairly briefly and answered questions for I don't know how long. It seemed like about two years and one half.

Afterwards I asked one of the men whom I knew well how it sounded, and he said it was perhaps a little slow in spots but perfectly connected and logical; and when I told him how scared I was he said, "Why, for heaven's sake, I thought you were enjoying yourself standing up holding onto the lapel of your coat, and cool as a cucumber."[29]

It is well known that anxiety and excitement often go together. Clearly Cobb was experiencing the combination of them both during the course of this presentation. Cobb later became very effective in speaking from a lectern. Because of his stammering he spoke slowly and was forced to construct his sentences clearly and to choose his words with care.

Councilman, Fritz Talbot, and Richard Smith were important in Cobb's life because all of them had energy and enthusiasms for pursuing knowledge beyond their regular work-a-day fields. Councilman followed comparative anatomy and was a trustee of the A.M.A.; Talbot branched into the study of epilepsy and chaired the department of pediatrics at the Massachusetts General Hospital; and Richard M. Smith, while conducting Boston's most fashionable pediatric practice, became concerned with plans for national health care. None of these men had a primary interest in the nervous system. They did not lead Cobb directly into his field, but by their example they inspired him to keep a wide view of medicine.

When still in Harvard College, Cobb and his roommate, Gordon Prince, were members of Squadron B in the Massachusetts National Guard, and Cobb's older brother Augustus was a member also. Several incidents are worthy of mention. Squadron B was a cavalry unit and Cobb, riding his white Arabian horse, Omar, was the standard bearer. Cobb's most serious service in the National Guard was to break up a strike of millworkers in Lawrence during February, 1912. (It was on this occasion that his former nursemaid, Mary Doyle, wrote to him about her concern that he be warm and have enough to eat.) As standard bearer he had to lead the squadron on horseback through the mob of workers who were picketing the mill. This had to be done twice, once at a walk for a warning and a second time at a trot or gallop. The second time through, some of the strikers were hurt, and Cobb felt distressed about the situation. He had not realized that anyone would be hurt. Furthermore, the millworkers were miserably paid, and Cobb believed they really had the right to strike. In his letters home he played down the violence of the episode and his misgivings about it. However, quelling the strike in Lawrence was the first of a series of episodes that led Cobb to a less militaristic viewpoint, and in later life he became a pacifist.

One night when returning from maneuvers Cobb and a number of other men from the squadron were seated at a table eating their meal in a restaurant. The door swung open and a group of friends, also from the National Guard, came in. Immediately, Cobb and those at his table jumped to their feet and started shooting blank ammunition at the intruders. The intruding guardsmen fired back, also with blank ammunition. There was panic in the restaurant, and the other customers, not knowing what was going on, all fell to the floor.[30]

One of Cobb's favorite activities in the company of the guardsmen was to engage in singing bawdy songs, which of course he did without stammering. In May, 1913, fifteen months after breaking the strike in Lawrence, Cobb was invited to a troop dinner. One of his guardsmen friends, G. Quincy Peters, wrote a letter asking him to sing on that occasion.[31] Peters wrote, "I hope you will be able to be at the troop dinner on Friday as it will be good fun. We want very much to have you sing a few of the old troopers' songs in your inimitable way, for instance, 'Black Sheep' and 'I learned about women from her.' Those are not the real names, but you know the ones I mean."

Cobb's interest in the fashionable art of riding to the hounds apparently commenced in the fall of his second year in medical school (1911–12) probably through the influence of his friend Byam Whitney. However, at that time Cobb was becoming acquainted with Dr. Alexander

Education at Harvard 47

Forbes of the physiology department at the medical school, and Forbes was also a hunter. Cobb was beginning to appreciate Forbes as a neurophysiologist and to form a lasting friendship with him as a collaborator and sort of senior adviser. However he got started, he received a letter written October 3, 1911, from Elizabeth Gardner of Jamaica Plain offering him the use of a horse at any time.[32] That fall he was invited by Madeleine T. Brewer, who later married Byam Whitney, Walter D. Brooks, who later married Cobb's sister "Polly," and Harvey Timmins, who later married Elizabeth Gardner, to paper chases scheduled for Saturdays in October and November at 9:00. In the fall of 1912 Cobb was a member of a group, with Madeleine T. Brewer and Walter Brooks, who invited people to a paper chase in Milton. On Saturday, October 18, he followed the drag hounds at Ipswich Trotting Park and on March 25, 1913, through his friend Gordon Prince, was elected an associate member of the Myopia Hunt Club, where he attended a number of hunting events without jumps.

The equestrian life brought with it some new friends, including ladies. Elizabeth Gilbert, who styled herself as secretary-pro-tem of the Tactful Club, wrote a number of very warm friendly letters during the winter of 1913[33] in which she mentioned among other things the nuptials of Madeleine Brewer and Cobb's longtime college friend Byam Whitney. The correspondence terminated some months later when Elizabeth announced her own engagement.

In addition to the pleasures that Cobb derived from the men and women he met through his horsemanship, there was also an active social life at the medical school and in the greater Boston community. In reminiscing on his Harvard Medical School years, Donald Macomber said that in the absence of a central dormitory there were few opportunities for men to meet students in classes other than their own.[34] There were, however, some student organizations in which members of the various classes did meet. Cobb enjoyed the Boylston Medical Society, the oldest of them, which combined professional and social activities. A member of the faculty was chosen to preside and each member of the society in rotation was required to write and deliver a scientific paper. The social part of the meetings was devoted to singing. Macomber remembered that the members entered every meeting in lockstep singing, "Good morning, Horace Greeley, does your mother know you're out?", embellishing their renditions with somewhat lewd emendations.

Cobb also belonged to the Innominate Club, which was largely social and rather exclusive. Some of these who failed to get in joined the national medical fraternity, Phi Rho Sigma, which later gave up its charter and became the Lancet Club. The Innominate Club ceased to exist but the Lancet Club survived. When in medical school Cobb wrote a paper for the Innominate Club entitled, "Proof that the head is the Butt End of a Goat." After graduation he was elected to the St. Botolph Club at 4 Newbury Street in Boston. He became well acquainted with various members of the Forbes family, which was based in Milton and spent summers on Naushon Island. On August 31, 1911, he was invited to take part in the annual sheeping there. His close friend and college roommate, Raymond Emerson, married Amelia Forbes in the spring of 1913. In thanking Cobb for his wedding present Amelia gave him a standing invitation to visit the island at any time. Later Cobb's sister Hildegarde married Dr. Henry Stone Forbes, the neurophysiologist who was one of Cobb's collaborators. And in September, 1913, Waldo Forbes invited Cobb cruising on the family yacht, *Black Duck*.[35]

In January, 1914, Cobb took his oral examination for internship in surgery at the Peter Bent Brigham Hospital. He must have had some elective courses in medical school during the spring of his fourth year, for he was permitted to commence the internship in early March, prior to formal graduation.

Cobb had given a great deal of thought to preparation for a career in the neurosciences. During his third year at the Harvard Medical School he had gone on long walks with his father and with David Edsall, later the dean but at that time the Jackson Professor of Medicine, talking about the desirability of some kind of neurosurgical experience, to be followed by physiology, pathology, clinical neurology, and psychiatry. When Cobb undertook the surgical internship under Harvey Cushing he knew that he was not going into surgery as a life work, and he talked about the future with Cushing. Cushing's ideas, partly expressed verbally and partly sensed "between the lines," were something like this: Take an internship and learn surgical technique; retain a state of blessed singleness; study neurology and physiology in Philadelphia and the laboratories of Europe; publish something before going to Europe then come back as a resident. In Philadelphia he recommended Spiller, in Paris, Pierre Marie, and in Freiburg, Aschoff.

Education at Harvard

On March 19, 1914, Cobb wrote his father a long letter describing in great detail the activities of one day in the life of a surgical intern:

> Things here are going very well. My ward is full & I can't [get] leave away until Saturday; so work will not be very heavy this week, as it is the arrival of new patients that makes the strenuous work.
>
> Today I gave two ethers & a chloroform, assisted at a major operation for gallstones (which were not found much to my joy as I had held out against the surgeons at the [undecipherable] & said it was only adhesions from a previous operation, & there were some adhesions which we cut loose); later I assisted at two smaller operations, then lunch at two, a little rest & then I took blood from 4 patients for tests, helped at a fracture setting, dressed some wounds, had supper, advised barrels of cathartics for my ladies & here I am at 9:30 about ready to scratch up a few notes & then bed.[36]

While at the Brigham Cobb prepared for publication one paper on hemangioma of the spinal cord. It came out in the *Annals of Surgery* in December, 1915.

In Cobb's day, and for twenty-odd years thereafter, interns at the Peter Bent Brigham Hospital were on call twenty-four hours a day and had no days or nights off. Marriage was strictly forbidden. Cobb was already engaged to Elizabeth Almy when he started internship and wanted to marry her. When he discussed the matter with Cushing, the reply was, "Can't she wait? My wife waited for me eight years."

When Cobb was appointed to the Brigham internship his prospective mother-in-law, Helen Cabot Almy, wrote him a congratulatory note in which she said, "It looks as if Dr. Cushing knew a good thing when he saw it—a characteristic I suppose of a good diagnostician. Well, I am not exactly surprised, but I am terribly pleased that you should have what you want, and that he should want to give it to you."[37]

However, asking for his daughter's hand in marriage was not Cobb's first contact with his future father-in-law, Judge Charles Almy. The first encounter had been in the Third District Court of Eastern Middlesex on Saturday, October 10, 1908, when Cobb appeared to answer unto one William A. Henderson of Cambridge in a matter of contract involving a sum of less than fifty dollars—probably as a result of property damage during some form of high jinx.

Then came Putnam Camp in Keene Valley, New York, the Adirondack retreat of Dr. James Jackson Putnam, the Boston neurologist who promoted Freudian psychoanalysis in this country prior to World War

I. It was here that in 1909 he entertained three renowned European psychoanalysts, Drs. Ferenczi, Freud, and Jung. A bill from Charles P. Putnam, treasurer of the camp, indicates that Cobb was there in August, 1913. He first met Elizabeth Mason Almy, whom he later married, on the railroad platform in Lake Placid. Knowing a good thing when he saw it, he was immediately attracted to her and became engaged later that year. In December 1913, Cobb received congratulatory notes from several of his friends, including his former college roommate, Gerard Gignoux.

In view of Cushing's prohibition of marriage, and the absence of nights off at the Brigham Hospital, Cobb and Betty Almy had a difficult year to weather. The marriage took place at Cotuit, on Cape Cod, July 10, 1915, and the couple departed for a nautical honeymoon. In a tiny cottage on the edge of Katama Bay, near Edgartown, on Martha's Vineyard, Cobb and his new wife painted some pictures and they spent a great deal of time cruising in a leaky catboat.

In August, 1915, after Katama Bay, the young couple went on an extended trip to the Pacific Northwest, country that Cobb had previously visited and wanted his wife to discover. They went west by train, visiting the Grand Canyon and taking in the San Francisco Exposition. They traveled by ship from Victoria to Prince Rupert, British Columbia. They took the Grand Trunk Railway from Prince Rupert to Jasper City, their base of operations for the ensuing three weeks. While based there they took a pack trip to Maligne Lake. One day they rowed a primitive boat half the length of the lake and spent the night on a tiny island in the midst of a summer snowstorm. Betty Cobb reported that the visibility was so poor that night that they saw almost nothing. The next morning dawned clear and they took in the beauty of the magnificent mountains around them. A month later they took a canoe trip down the Athebaska River with their guides, Mr. and Mrs. Bone, two Swiss boys, and a dog. In October they arrived at the Whitecourt Junction of two rivers and drove out to Edmonton over a twenty-five mile cordwood road. By that time Betty Cobb knew that she was pregnant. On the way east they stopped off in Chicago for the wedding of Cobb's cadaver mate, Horace Gray.

Elizabeth Almy was a helpful and supporting wife for Cobb. She had unlimited courage, and she was able to calm him down when he was flustered by excitement or fear. In a joking way Cobb wrote the following words to his mother:

I am most disgustingly under Betty's thumb, and if I get irritable and introspective, or blue, she quickly kicks it out of me and shows that I am lacking in common sense. I don't envy her her job, but she seems to like it.[38]

After his marriage, Cobb's stammering showed considerable improvement, but it was still enough of a handicap so that he wrestled with it for many years.

3
Baltimore and World War I

It was an exciting time when, after their four-month wedding trip, the Cobbs moved to Baltimore, where for the next three years Stanley was to work in physiology and psychiatry. With the deterioration of the Allied position in World War I, the future guaranteed only uncertainty. Yet Cobb had an inner conviction of being called to a career in the neurosciences, and there lay before him the almost unprecedented opportunity to work in neurophysiology under William Henry Howell and in psychiatry under Adolf Meyer. Howell, the professor of physiology at Johns Hopkins Medical School, was the author of a textbook used widely throughout the country and had a primary interest in neurophysiology. Meyer was professor of psychiatry at the new Henry Phipps Psychiatric Clinic, which had opened its doors on April 16, 1913. Meyer brought in as his chief aides two Scotsmen, C. MacFie Campbell as associate director of the clinic and David K. Henderson as senior resident. Both men had worked with Meyer previously in New York and were destined for important careers in psychiatry.[1]

Meyer had been developing a new approach to psychiatry that went beyond the traditional clinical study of mental illnesses.[2] In his former positions in Kankakee, Illinois, Worcester, Massachusetts, and New York City, he had worked out a new methodology incorporating tissue neuropathology, disturbed neurophysiology, social conditions, and psychological factors in the understanding of psychiatric disorders. He was to become for the next twenty years the most influential leader in American psychiatry.

Baltimore was exciting, too, because of the brilliant men in many departments of the Johns Hopkins Hospital and in the medical school laboratories. Years later Cobb said (373) that the time in Baltimore was the second golden age of his life.[3] Several of the renowned older staff were still there, including Halsted, Howell, Abel, Barker, Howland, Thayer, Janeway, Meyer, and McCollum. However, as he saw it, the younger teachers were the ones who made the time so exciting: Blackfan, Park, Gamble, Marriott, and Powers at the Harriet Lane in pediatrics; Bloomfield, Austrian, Levy, Thomas, Pincoffs, and King in medicine; Heuer, Reid, and Dandy in surgery; and at the Phipps, where he was working, Moore, Watson, Richter, Lewis, and Greenacre. Across the street in the medical school laboratories were Drinker, Lamson, Binger, Bayne-Jones, Rivers, H. B. Richardson, Wilson, Weed, and Clark. Cobb was welcomed by many of these great teachers and investigators who had their impact, however small or indirect, upon his yen to integrate pathology and physiology with disturbances of the mind. After World War I most of these men became professors and were widely dispersed across the United States.

For Cobb the period of transition was one not only of excitement but also of stress. Dr. Phyllis Greenacre, a resident physician on Meyer's service in 1916 and now a practicing psychoanalyst in New York City, recalled in 1978 that Cobb at that earlier time had many heavy folds in his face indicative of some form of tension, yet at the same time a great buoyancy. She remembered him as an enthusiastic, expanding person with a sparkle that seemed to transcend the serious handicap of his disordered speech.[4] One reason for Cobb's tension was his indecision about entering the military service, another the severe epidemic of poliomyelitis that summer when the Cobbs' son was an infant, and yet another, financial insecurity.

When the Cobbs arrived in Baltimore in November, 1915, they rented a row house at 206 East Chase Street and announced, "The lease is signed! We are Baltimoreans.'" However, they were not lonely in their new setting, for several old friends were nearby: Cecil Drinker, who was later at the Harvard School of Public Health; Henry B. Richardson, who subsequently worked on metabolic studies at Cornell; and Carl Binger, Cobb's former cadaver mate from medical school. Drinker and Richardson were married at the time and their wives were close friends of Mrs. Cobb. Binger was an inseparable companion to both of the Cobbs.

In November, 1915, Professor Howell was on leave of absence, so that Cobb had several weeks with no professional obligations. Much of his time was devoted to getting settled in the new house. However, Cobb's primary plan was to undergo some intensive psychotherapy with Meyer's associate director, MacFie Campbell. Campbell had adopted Meyer's integrative approach to psychiatry, often referred to as *psychobiology*, and he later espoused Meyer's views when he became professor of psychiatry at Harvard and director of the Boston Psychopathic Hospital.[5]

Campbell was glad to accept Cobb for psychotherapy. However, he did not want to do it on an intensive basis. He was aware of Freud's work, and he believed, as Meyer also did, that there was no magic in psychoanalysis. He did, however, see the value of mental catharsis. So he arranged to see Cobb on a regular basis two hours each week for several months in much the same manner as a Freudian psychoanalyst would do, and Cobb felt that the series of interviews was indeed helpful. In a letter to his mother Cobb said of the interviews:

> The stammering work is illuminating and I think will be useful in many ways even if I don't learn to talk. He (Campbell) is going at it slowly and thoroughly and I think in good time will get some results.

In another letter home two months later Cobb said that his speech was improving and he had hope of more marked improvement with the passage of time.

In January, 1916, when Howell returned from his leave of absence, Cobb went to work in the department of physiology at Johns Hopkins. One of the unanswered questions facing neurophysiologists at that time dealt with the sympathetic innervation of striated muscle. A key method of investigating this problem was the study of animal behavior after the surgical removal of varying amounts of cerebral cortex. Decerebrate animals demonstrated, among other manifestations, a marked spastic rigidity of the muscles, particularly of the back, neck, and extremities. In 1913 Dusser de Barenne had demonstrated relaxation of such rigidity in only five of nine decerebrate animals which had been subjected to unilateral interruption of the abdominal sympathetic chain. He concluded that the tonic impulses causing decerebrate rigidity did not reach the muscles of the hind leg by way of the sympathetic.[6] However, shortly afterwards evidence gained through experimental work by others[7] indicated that spastic rigidity was to be regarded as being mediated by fibers of the sympathetic nervous system. Cobb set out to confirm or disprove the role of the sympathetic nervous system in causing decerebrate rigidity. His protocols are recorded (10). He operated on seven cats between February 9—and May 14, 1916, and recorded his observations on each of them. He concluded that the abdominal sympathetic chains had no effect in producing decerebrate rigidity.

In the spring of 1916 Cobb, who had been attending lectures at the Phipps Clinic, was appointed as an assistant in neurophysiology with a stipend of five hundred dollars and was assigned a laboratory of his own, which later became known as the neurological laboratory of the Henry Phipps Psychiatric Clinic. During the academic year 1916–17, he did most of his work there. From June until August, 1916, he spent several weeks in the department of physiology at the Harvard Medical School learning about the use of the Einthoven string galvanometer, which his friend and former teacher, Alexander Forbes,[8] had brought back from Europe in 1911.[9] Cobb carried out work with Forbes on changes in the flexion reflex after spinal transection. This study, with additional observations by others, was published by Forbes in 1923. Forbes's report included a description in Cobb's own words of the work that he had done in 1916.[10]

During the summer of 1916 Cobb kept in touch with Meyer about his work and suggested the desirability of having a string galvanometer at the Phipps.[11] In early August of that year, Meyer returned from California, where a wealthy benefactor often provided for financial needs,[12] and wrote to Cobb, "At last I have found my way back from the Pacific Coast and am glad to find your interesting letter. We certainly must make plans to secure the string galvanometer apparatus to put you in the best possible position for work."[13] Soon thereafter Meyer authorized Cobb to order additional apparatus in Cambridge for use on his return in September.

When Cobb returned in the fall after his vacation on Cape Cod, he set up the galvanometer for use as an electromyograph to study the contractility of muscle fibers. From the Phipps Clinic he published two clinical papers with electromyographic observations on human beings. One of these, "Electromyographic Studies of Clonus," appeared in 1918 (9), and the other, "An Electromyographic Study of Chorea," came out in 1919 (11).

However, the major scientific *Arbeit* of 1916–1917 was carried out by Cobb, Albert A. Bailey, and Paul R. Holtz in the neurological laboratory on cats and was entitled "On the Genesis and Inhibition of Extensor Rigidity" (8). In this work the cats were rendered decerebrate by a surgical technique and were then suspended in a warm box with holes for the extremities to pass through. The extremities were connected to a Harvard Kymograph to record the degree of muscular contractility. Stimulation of remaining portions of the brain was carried out electrically. Cobb discovered that stimulation of a portion of the cerebellum in cats inhibited their extensor rigidity. He also observed an atypical form of extensor rigidity, differing from the usual decerebrate rigidity, in specimens transected below the red nucleus. Mary A. B. Brazier, afterwards Cobb's longtime associate, spoke of this observation in a recent critical review of his work as being one of his really important contributions to neurology, saying:

> In a series of intricate experiments on the role of the cerebellum in decerebrate rigidity he demonstrated for the first time the role of the red nuclei in the contrasting phenomena of Sherrington's "decerebrate rigidity" and the extensor tonus exhibited with more caudal transections. An original discovery at the age of only thirty.[14]

In Cobb's day there were two research laboratories at the Phipps Clinic in addition to his own. (Cobb's laboratory was in the west wing of the Phipps.)[15] In the Pavlovian laboratory studies of conditioned reflexes were carried out by Horsley Gantt, and the behaviorist, John B. Watson, had moved his laboratory into the Phipps, too. When Watson left Baltimore in 1920, Curt B. Richter took over his laboratory on the third floor and with it Cobb's equipment, including the Einthoven string galvanometer which he had used for his clinical studies on clonus and on chorea. By the spring of 1917 the pressure for military service built up to the point where Cobb had largely to abandon his investigative work. He was declared essential to the war effort and assigned to clinical psychiatry in the Phipps Clinic as an intern.

The Henry Phipps Psychiatric Clinic was in a new building on the grounds of the Johns Hopkins Hospital adjacent to the Harriet Lane Home, where the pediatric cases were housed. Meyer, who had come to Baltimore in 1909, was a Swiss innkeeper at heart. Under the influence of August Forel at the Burghölzli in Zurich, Meyer played an important role in designing the building with light, air, openness, and the comfort of the patients in mind.[16]

From the beginning of Cobb's stay in Baltimore Meyer was very supportive. He listened to Cobb's ideas attentively and helped to provide the space and facilities needed for his investigative work. And Cobb had been attending lectures and clinics at the Phipps, so that he had acquired a considerable understanding of psychiatry and Meyer's approach to it. Now a much more intimate phase in the relationship between the two men was about to come into being. Both of them were in a serious dilemma about Cobb's military future. Their relationship became something like that between father and son. Meyer wanted Cobb to do the right thing for him, yet needed his services.

Cobb was torn between his yen to carry on with his professional growth on the one hand and his sense of patriotism on the other. In view of the complexity of the relationship and the important influence that Meyer was destined to exert on Cobb's future life, it is desirable to look more closely at Meyer's personal life and personality.

A native of Switzerland, Adolf Meyer was born in 1866, the son of a Zwinglian minister. He gave up his inclination to follow his father's footsteps into the ministry because the ministry dealt with only part of a man.[17] Meyer wrote in his diary that he wanted to study the whole man and elected to follow his mother's brother into medicine. At the University of Zurich, where he studied medicine, Meyer came under the influence of August Forel, who was famous for his studies of brain anatomy and his contribution to the neuron theory. After passing his state examination in 1890, which entitled him to practice medicine, Meyer studied for a year in Paris, Edinburgh, and London. On returning to Zurich he worked primarily in neurology. After receiving his medical degree in 1892, he decided to come to the United States.

The first three years in this country were spent on an honorary fellowship at the University of Chicago with a position as pathologist to the Eastern Illinois State Hospital in Kankakee. At Chicago he gave a course in comparative anatomy of the nervous system, and at the hospital he induced the superintendent to make sweeping reforms in order to correlate his pathological findings with the clinical information about the patients, including adequate laboratory space and regular staff meetings. The clinical staff was small and its members were little interested in clarifying their knowledge. Meyer said of the situation, "... The worst and fatal defect was that I was expected to examine brains of people who had never been submitted to an examination." Although he was successful in bringing about a larger clinical staff, the situation was frustrating, and he welcomed the opportunity to play a more effective role at the Worcester State Hospital, where he relocated in 1896. In Chicago, through Paul Carus, editor of *The Monist,* then one of the leading philosophical journals in the United States, he became acquainted with the work of Charles S. Peirce, and he met John Dewey, who had gone to Chicago in 1894.

During the summer of 1896 Meyer spent six weeks in Kraepelin's clinic in Heidelberg. Kraepelin was renowned for his work in classifying the various psychoses on the basis of their clinical manifestations. Although Meyer decided to use Kraepelin's classification at Worcester, he was aware of its limitation in failing to convey a comprehensive understanding of the individual patient.

At Worcester, where he reported for duty in the fall of 1896, Meyer took charge of pathology and the clinical services at the hospital and became a docent at Clark University, which at that time had an internationally known department of psychology. At the time Meyer saw the basic need confronting psychiatry to be the systematic, open-minded collection of empirical data which could serve as the basis for a deeper analysis of the theoretical and practical problems posed by mental disease. To this end he worked closely with the hospital superintendent, Dr. Hosea N. Quinby, who was most cooperative. On Meyer's recommendation, even before his arrival, Quinby had advertised in professional journals for interns with such qualifications as a full collegiate and medical education, a reading knowledge of French and German, training in microscopic pathology, and the capacity to pursue independent work. Of the forty who applied four young men were chosen for these posts.

It was at Worcester that Meyer evolved his meticulously detailed pattern of study for each newly admitted patient. After the past history and the history of the present illness had been recorded and the mental status and physical examinations had been performed by one of the assistants, each case was presented at the daily staff conference. Thereafter, careful daily progress notes were taken on the wards and presented to a stenographer for typing. Thus at Worcester Meyer was able to implement his program for correlating carefully recorded clinical information with pathological findings at autopsy.

In 1901 Meyer was invited to become director of the New York Pathological Institute, then located on Manhattan Island and serving all the mental hospitals in the state. Meyer accepted the position after being assured that the laboratory would be moved to the Manhattan State Hospital on Ward's Island. Meyer was there for about a decade before moving to Baltimore. Twenty years after departing from Worcester Meyer wrote, "I cannot help considering my Worcester period as one of the soundest, and in a way the most solidly useful phase of my work—since I see in it the period during which I collected the most substantial material for work."[18]

When in 1911 Meyer was appointed professor of psychiatry at Johns Hopkins and director of the new Henry Phipps Psychiatric Clinic there, he came with a knowledge of psychiatry deeply rooted in neuropathology and a commitment to achieve a deeper understanding of clinical psychiatry through the analysis of carefully recorded data obtained during the examination and care of patients in the clinics.

In addition to the pattern of meticulous examination evolved at Worcester, Meyer developed a behavior chart on which nurses and physicians were to record day-to-day variations in the activities of the patients. Too, he worked out a chronological chart on which to record a patient's development along various lines from birth until the current illness. Meyer insisted that each of his interns and residents be firmly grounded in neuroanatomy by constructing a three-dimensional model of the human brain. He also required that every medical student write up his own psychiatric life history.

When Meyer commenced teaching in the Phipps he tried to give a formal course in medical psychology which grew out of a conference in 1911 at the Government Hospital in Washington, D.C.[19] Participants at this conference had included Elmer E. Southard of Harvard, Morton Prince of Tufts University, John B. Watson, and himself. In 1914 Meyer tried to implement the ideas from that conference through a panel teaching approach with Watson, a behaviorist, Knight Dunlap, an experimental psychologist, and himself simultaneously on a dais. The panelists failed to speak in a common language which students could understand, and some of them registered complaints in the dean's office. A year later Meyer tried again, this time giving the course alone, but he fared little better. Then he devised a new approach by having each student write out in detail his own psychiatric life history. These individual personality studies proved to be successful. As the program evolved, Meyer added the personality study to the first year's work. He had the students study complaints the second year, devote their attention to examination and formulation (diagnosis) the third year, and in the fourth year they followed six or more cases in treatment.

Partly as a result of the personality-study approach Meyer became very close to many of the students. One elective feature of the course was a supper conference at the home of Dr. and Mrs. Meyer. After dinner there was a time for discussion of psychiatric matters. Meyer said that the informality of seeing the students after dinner in his home was better than speaking from a platform because he could guide his comments by listening to the general conversation.

In describing his approach to psychiatry Meyer employed the term *psychobiology*. He tended to deemphasize the classification of mental diseases that had grown up in Europe under Kraepelin. Although he had worked with Kraepelin in Heidelberg and used a modification of Kraepelin's classification when in Worcester, Meyer looked upon many of the clinical states seen in psychiatry as reaction patterns rather than as disease entities. Hence, Meyer emphasized that each patient should be viewed as a whole person, taking into consideration a host of factors such as heredity, cultural background, nutrition, education, exercise, habits, temperament, intellectual capacity, and many others. Phyllis Greenacre said that in the beginning, at least, Meyer was tolerant of the work of Sigmund Freud. (Meyer was a member of the American Psychoanalytic Association.) However, Dr. Greenacre believed that Meyer could not go far with psychoanalysis because he was sex shy. As the son of a Zwinglian clergyman, Meyer believed that sex was basically sinful and acceptable only for the propagation of children. For many years he was a bitter opponent of birth control, but to his credit he once paid a visit to Margaret Sanger, the great birth control proponent, and after that he changed his attitude.

Henderson, Cobb's first senior resident at the Phipps Clinic, said that Meyer's finest teaching took place at the bedside.[20] He had great delicacy and was always able to probe into the most acute situations. Having acquired the patient's confidence, he could readily elicit the salient points of the life story. Henderson said he was more impressive under such circumstances than when presenting a formal lecture. He refused to differentiate between "interesting" and "noninteresting" cases, always looking upon the patient as a unique human being with an important message to convey.

Because he considered every patient as having a unique formulation, Meyer was not satisfied with the standard nomenclature of disease and devised one of his own. He differentiated and classified nervous and mental states as one or another forms of *ergasia,* a word for behavior reactions based upon his eclectic psychobiologic approach. He contrasted *merergastic* or part-reactions with *holergastic* or sweeping disorders. Among the latter he ranked disorders of mood as *thymergastic,* metabolic disorders as *dysergastic,* structural defects as *anergastic,* and states of mental deficiency as *oligergastic.* For the schizophrenic group he used the term *parergastic.* Curt Richter, who commenced service at the Phipps in 1919, said that Meyer originally introduced these terms for use at bedside rounds, so that the patients would not become aware of their diagnoses. The medical dictionaries and textbooks picked up the classification and perpetuated it.[21] However, none of the other major figures in the specialty used Meyer's scheme and it turned out to be an abortive effort.

Although Meyer was one of the most influential leaders in American psychiatry and made enormous contributions to its teaching and practice, he had three serious limitations. The accumulation of large quantities of undigested data proved cumbersome and less valuable as a research tool than Meyer originally had hoped. In fact one of his reasons for leaving Worcester had been his disagreement with Quinby over the administrative aspect of such a nondirective approach to research.[22] Moreover, many of Meyer's critics said that his confusing use of language made his work hard to understand except through interpretation by others.[23] More serious, Meyer was criticized because he never popularized a therapeutic method that could be widely adopted by the profession at large.[24]

At times Meyer became involved in the personal problems of his staff as indeed he did with Cobb over the dilemma about going into military service. Meyer was a charismatic person and, because of his beard, the patients often called him Christ. He had a custom of sometimes inviting a staff member to come to his house on a Sunday morning. Such invitations were looked upon as "command performances" and were universally dreaded. One Sunday morning, in apologizing for an outburst he made, Meyer said, "The Devil of negativeness got into me."

Meyer's judgment was sometimes overridden by loyalty to a former student. For example he was subjected to serious embarrassment when in the twenties he wrote the foreword to Henry A. Cotton's book, *The Defective Delinquent and Insane.* Cotton, a former resident from Worcester, had become overly enthusiastic about foci of infection as causes of mental disease, had removed patients' colons wholesale as a therapeutic measure, and had made unwarranted claims about recovery. Meyer's awkward position was highlighted by a formal investigation that discredited Cotton.[25]

However, Meyer's loyalty to his students and his involvement in their lives were generally of real and positive value. In Cobb's case, Meyer served as an important adviser for over fifteen years. The close relationship between Meyer and Cobb developed during the period of uncertainty over Cobb's military status. In a letter to his former medical classmate, Horace Gray, on April 1, 1922, Cobb recalled the timetable.²⁶ He went on the wards at the Phipps as an intern in the spring of 1917, and stayed on as assistant resident until August, 1918. He was commissioned a first lieutenant in August, 1917, but was not ordered to active duty until September, 1918. During this time he experienced a great deal of ambivalence about remaining in Baltimore and not entering the service, and he expressed this sense of confusion in communications with Meyer. One day Cobb received in the mail a white feather which had been sent by a woman in Boston to indicate his lack of patriotism. His father, too, was anxious to see him go into service, partly to lessen the financial burden of supporting him and his family. Moreover, Cobb had been urged by Colonel Charles Bagley, Jr., a neurologist stationed in Lakewood, New Jersey, to work with him in his department, and this opportunity would soon expire because Bagley was going to France. On the other hand Cobb really felt that he was of greater service in continuing on at the Phipps. On August 10, 1917, Adolf Meyer wrote to Major General William C. Gorgas, Surgeon General of the United States Army, on behalf of Cobb and said in part, "I hope very much it will be possible to reserve him for a continuation of the work at the Henry Phipps Psychiatric Clinic in view of the fact that out of ten available men five have already entered the service and two have their commissions."²⁷ Meyer's request was honored and Cobb had one more year in Baltimore.

During the winter of 1917–18 Cobb had, in addition to his care of patients on the wards, a heavy teaching load. On April 24, 1918, he sent Meyer a memo indicating that there had been fifty-five fourth-year students that year, and there would be ninety-two the following year, each of whom would have to work up six cases. He concluded that he would have to carry three cases a day just to cover the fourth-year students. In addition he proposed to Meyer that during the first trimester he work with third-year students and the third trimester with second-year students in the dispensary. Also, he was planning a probable anatomy course in the winter months.²⁸

Cobb also kept Meyer informed about the clinical work.²⁹ During the frightfully hot summer of 1918 Meyer was away. Cobb wrote to him about a report on teaching activities required by the Surgeon General's Office. Cobb also said that Campbell was making rounds on the wards. Harvey Wadsworth was running W1 and W2 under Cobb's supervision and Cobb himself was in charge of E2, a women's ward. Cobb also reported that Colonel Bagley had called to see Meyer about Cobb's military status. Although Bagley thought that Cobb's status on the essential list would keep him in Baltimore, he really hoped Cobb would go on active duty. Bagley said he expected to go to France soon and was reasonably certain he could get Cobb a good job in his department.

However, Cobb was soon informed that he would either have to go on active duty or resign his commission, and he could not do that because he had already been drafted. He was informed that his orders would arrive in mid-September and there would be a little time after that to complete his preparations.

Throughout the transition from work at the Phipps to active duty in the army, Cobb was in constant contact with Meyer over administrative matters, particularly the fate of his laboratory. Cobb departed from Baltimore on September 10, 1918, and reported for active duty later that month.

When Cobb gave up full time research in the spring of 1917 and became an intern on the psychiatric wards, he and his wife moved from 206 East Chase Street to another row house on State Street right across from the Phipps Clinic (page 71). The move was made so that he would be immediately available for emergency situations. The Cobbs had experienced a great deal of anxiety about the epidemic of poliomyelitis which broke out in the summer of 1916. Cobb's oldest son, Sidney, born in June of that year, was an infant. During June and July, while Cobb was working on the string galvanometer with Forbes at the Harvard Medical School, he and his family were living with his wife's parents on Brattle Street in Cambridge, and in August they vacationed on Cape Cod, where they thought they were relatively safe, but the epidemic dragged on into early October, and the new work in the laboratory was calling Cobb back to Baltimore.

The cause of poliomyelitis was not known in 1916. One theory, which impressed Cobb, linked it to a variant strain of streptococci, following the work of E. C. Rosenow in Rochester, Minnesota. As a precaution against young Sidney's contracting the disease from a bacterial contaminant, all four legs of the baby's crib rested in pots filled with water. Carl Binger, with whom Cobb had carried on dissections at medical school and who was now an intimate friend, laughed at the pots of water under the legs of the crib. However, Dr. and Mrs. Cobb did not think it was a funny, for one of the professors at Johns Hopkins had just had all four of his children taken with the disease and one had died. The baby was isolated in the third floor front room of the Cobbs' house and no one other than his parents was allowed to enter.

Dr. Rosenow's theory was not entirely fanciful because strains of streptococci had been linked to rheumatic fever, glomerulonephritis and the rash of scarlet fever. But Rosenow incorrectly rationalized the relationship between streptococci and a number of clinical disorders, and in the twenties all sorts of illnesses were attributed to focal infections.

There was some time for recreation, at least in the earlier part of the Cobbs' stay in Baltimore. The research work with Howell in early 1916 and in his own laboratory during the academic year 1916–17 afforded at least some free weekends when the family could get away from Baltimore. Accordingly the Cobbs, with Carl Binger and the Henry B. Richardsons, rented a small cabin on the Gunpowder River, which flows in a southeasterly direction and enters Chesapeake Bay only a few miles above Baltimore. There they spent weekends out of doors shooting ducks, swimming, and looking at the swans. The cabin was really a one-story bungalow and had bedrooms for the Cobbs and the Richardsons, but Binger had to sleep in an alcove off the living room. Binger's widow, Chloe, had in 1980 a sepia wash of whistling swans that Cobb had painted on the Gunpowder River (page 73) Cobb also shot ducks on various estuaries of Chesapeake Bay, for duck hunting was to remain an active interest for him throughout his life.

Opportunities to visit the Gunpowder River were few after Cobb gave up active investigation in the spring of 1917. After that he was firmly tied down by the demands of internship and residency at the Phipps along with his teaching responsibilities.

When he went into active duty in the army in September, 1918, Cobb made every effort to see that there were people available to take over his by then numerous activities. In a letter written to Dr. Meyer on August 27, 1918, Cobb crystallized the events leading to his departure:

> I went down to Washington and found Bagley at 3:00 P.M. He was much pleased, because it was his last afternoon on duty before sailing for France, and he was able to have me used in what he considers the most efficient and most immediate manner. By seeing Col. Arnold we arranged that my name would not be removed from the "essential list" until September 15th. The arrangements which Bagley has made will then be automatically put into effect and I will escape all the complications that are soon to descend upon the Surgeon General's office apropos of the new draft, the new policy towards the schools and the retirement of the Surgeon General himself. Bagley says that after the 15th my orders will probably not reach me for four or five days, so that I will have time to see my family before reporting for duty. If, however, this duty is to be overseas, he says that he will let me know in advance. In that case I should feel that I ought to leave the Phipps before

the 15th even if it shortens your vacation somewhat. This is the last thing I want to do because I realize how much you need the real relaxation.

I shall always be grateful that we have been able to settle this, at times, strained situation without resorting to the usual human antagonisms but with mutual understanding and regard.[30]

Then on September 3 he again wrote to Meyer stating that he was being sent to the Neurological Institute in New York to brush up on surgery and neurology. His friend Bagley had advised him, he wrote, to be ready for orders overseas at any time, because Bagley would send for him as soon as he found the right spot. Cobb went on to say in his letter:

Stevenson, Wadsworth, and Bowcock seem to be doing good work and I feel rather on the shelf as far as ward work is concerned, although I have 101 things I want to finish up in the lab, etc.

Chapman is interested to have the use of the galvanometer next winter and can easily put Holtz onto its curves. Chapman has been running the heart station all summer and feels quite grateful to me for getting him the job. I already have several records of Paralysis Agitans; and I might be able to enthuse them to make some more and do a piece of work describing the typical electromyogram of that disease.[31]

Cobb believed that the neurological research in the Phipps could be kept going by working out the typical electromyographic patterns of various neuromyopathies and establishing standards.

Cobb departed five days early on September tenth, because of the likelihood of orders overseas to be arranged by Bagley. After he had settled in at the home of his Uncle Sidney Smith at 105 East 38th Street in New York, Cobb again wrote to Meyer. In his letter, dated September 22, 1918,[32] he said that the previous Friday he had started the "neurosurgical course" at the Neurological Institute, which was then located at Sixtieth Street and Tenth Avenue. The course was directed by the neurosurgeon Charles A. Elsberg with the assistance of various members of the staff and several military men. One day, while stationed at the Neurological Instiute, Cobb made a one-day trip to Lakewood, New Jersey, where Bagley had been stationed. There he was treated royally by Dr. Penwood, who asked him to start off their galvanometer man in making electromyograms. They wanted to make tracings on neuromyasthenia which was a manifestation of neurocirculatory asthenia, or "Soldier's Heart," commonly observed in World War I. In the same letter Cobb told Meyer that in Boston he had seen Cecil Drinker, who, under Edsall, was chairman of a committee to study fatigue there and had concluded that it had to be investigated along holistic lines including adaptation to the environment.

The neurosurgical course at the Neurological Institute started with twenty-six students, mostly surgeons. Twenty of them were immediately detached for duty to care for victims of the 1918 influenza epidemic, and Cobb worried about the length of time they could keep the course in operation for the benefit of only six men. Cobb said in his letter to Meyer on October 6, 1918[33] that he had overheard an unofficial remark, which had originated in the Surgeon General's Office, to the effect that "Hopkins made a good fight to keep Cobb, and we owe it to them to see that he is put into efficient and fitting work." Weekly schedules for the second and eighth weeks of the neurosurgical course are on file in the Meyer papers at the Alan M. Chesney Archives of the Johns Hopkins Medical Institution in Baltimore.[34] Cobb said that the lectures, particularly those of Frederick Tilney, were brilliantly organized and presented; yet on the whole he found New York neurology, as presented in this course, to be quite dogmatic.

On November 11, 1918, the armistice was signed, and there was no longer any need for Cobb to go overseas. Instead, on November fourteenth, before the eight weeks' "neurosurgical course" could be completed, he was transferred to U.S.A. General Hospital Number 14 at Fort Oglethorpe, Georgia. On November 24 he again wrote to Meyer, reporting that he had been assigned to teach a four-week course in neurosurgery to medical officers. He said that he was quite excited because he had an opportunity to "try on the dog" all his pet theories, many of which he attributed to Meyer. He continued:

> I left my notes on your course in Baltimore by mistake, and at first was quite disgusted, but I have learned a lot by sitting down to the standard textbooks, gleaning the anatomical facts and brushing them up according to your ideas of integration. Preparing the lectures has certainly been most valuable to me. They wanted me to teach physiology and have someone else do anatomy, but I kicked and said the two were inseparable. I even got this sent in to the Surgeon General's Office as a feature of the course.... After my ... lecture on "The Nervous System as a Segmental Mechanism" a man from Oregon told me I ought to publish it, and one from Salt Lake said it was "the best thing he had ever heard"; so I felt quite set up.[35]

In the letter to Meyer he expressed his disappointment in having missed the opportunity to see fresh brain and cord wounds at the front. However, he was to see the end results in survivors on his next tour of duty at U.S.A. General Hospital Number 11 in Cape May, New

Jersey. In a subsequent letter to Meyer he reported that he had applied for discharge from the army while at Fort Oglethorpe and it had been denied even though he had called personally at the Surgeon General's Office; that his daughter, Helen, had been born on January 20, 1918; and that Mrs. Cobb and the two children spent Christmas that year with her parents in Cambridge.[36]

At this time David L. Edsall, now dean of the Harvard Medical School, sent a message that he would like to see Cobb as soon as possible. Cobb said in a letter to Meyer,[37] "I can only conjecture as to what he wants, but I suspect it is to offer me a job. Of course I still consider myself a member of your staff 'on leave'; so I will let you know what he wants of me if it takes any definite form."

On January 1, 1919, Cobb reported for duty at the U.S. Army General Hospital at Cape May on the head injury service of Lieutenant Colonel Charles Frazier, the Philadelphia neurosurgeon. He had just been preceded on Frazier's head service by two neuropsychiatric friends from Boston, Captain Donald MacPherson and First Lieutenant Harry C. Solomon, both affiliated with the Boston Psychopathic Hospital and both to be associated with Cobb on the Harvard faculty in later years. MacPherson was to work in Cobb's neuropathology laboratory at Harvard and to introduce psychiatry into the Peter Bent Brigham Hospital. Solomon was destined to become in 1943 professor of psychiatry and chairman of the department at Harvard.

In 1919 Cape May, the southernmost spot in New Jersey, had a population of only 2,471. On the ocean side of Cape May was a sandy beach, five miles long, where Cobb could observe marine life and shore birds. Arrangements were soon made for Cobb's wife and children to join him, and the family was quartered at the Victorian Windsor Hotel. The Windsor Hotel had a superb view of the ocean which was lighted in the winter mornings by floods of sunshine. Every morning Sidney Cobb, then two and a half years old, would exclaim, "See the sun roll out of the ocean, Daddy."

Lieutenant Cobb served as an instructor and also took care of patients with nerve injuries, some of which were severely incapacitating. Many had permanent brain damage, and others were paralyzed from neck or other spinal cord injuries. The tragedy of these permanently disabled men left an indelible mark on Cobb. When his children grew up he told them that after Cape May he no longer believed in war.

When at Cape May, Cobb, with C. C. Coleman of Richmond, Virginia, conducted a clinical study of recovery from spinal cord injuries in which tewenty cases were carefully followed and their courses tabulated over a period up to three hundred days after the injury. There was a wide spectrum of end results ranging between permanent quadriplegia (paralysis of all four extremities) to complete restoration of function. When the work was published in 1921 (23) the authors modestly stated that the paper was not written to present new facts but with the intention of illustrating by graphic methods the usual course of recovery in patients with cord injuries. Cobb was mustered out of the army on May 1, 1919, after which he returned to Boston.

An amusing epilogue to Cobb's Baltimore years took place later in his life when he returned there for a medical convention. William T. Councilman, who had come from Baltimore, may have been there, for he was a student of comparative anatomy, as were several of the others present. One evening at one of the better known Baltimore restaurants, Cobb and his friends ordered the specialty of the house, terrapin stew. It was not long before one of the party encountered a bone in his soup and carefully laid it on the tablecloth. A few minutes later another of the assembled physicians found a bone in his soup, and in due course there were several bones on the table. One of the anatomists appropriately arranged the bones and concluded that they had come from the skeleton of a rat. Through the offices of the head waiter, the owner of the restaurant was summoned and confronted with the discovery. He replied, "Yes, I have a rat farm in the penthouse on the roof. Would any of you gentlemen like to come upstairs and see it?"

Cobb's participation with Meyer in the dawning of a new age for psychiatry foretold later developments in the neurosciences in which Cobb was to play an innovative and integrating role. After working with Alexander Forbes in Boston and later with Sherrington and Vogt abroad, he would pioneer the direct application of research methods to human neurological problems and in the field of psychiatry would promote Freudian psychoanalysis as a university-based scientific discipline. The years of training at Harvard and Johns Hopkins had come to an end, and the war had given Cobb an opportunity to see some of the problems faced by practitioners of medicine. The future held a number of unexpected opportunities which Cobb was prompt to seize upon, and through these circumstances there lay ahead a brilliant academic career.

4
New Life in Boston

When Cobb returned to civilian life on May 1, 1919, he suffered from a state of confusion similar to that which after World War II was referred to as the separation syndrome. His conviction of being called to a teaching and investigative career in the neurosciences was stronger than ever; yet openings were few and he had no promise of an offer anywhere except with Meyer at the Phipps. Deliberations with Meyer began as early as December, 1918, when Dean Edsall's approach to Cobb through his friend Cecil Drinker indicated that there might be some kind of opportunity at Harvard. Cobb promptly called on Edsall and wrote to Meyer on January 13, 1919, about the possibilities.[1] Cobb said in his letter that, although Edsall made no specific offer, he did have money. He added that the opportunities for investigation and for clinical neurology in Boston were excellent. In psychiatry, on the other hand, all Edsall had to offer was consultation work in the general hospitals. Cobb wanted in a way to go back to Baltimore, but Meyer had only eighteen hundred dollars a year to offer him, and he had to weigh the pros and cons of both opportunities:

> It costs me $3500 a year to keep my family. I have an income of my own, now depleted to $600 a year. The $1800 you can give me in Baltimore makes $2400. The question is can I expect to get enough practice in spare time to make $100 a month without interfering with the full time basis I suppose I am [on] as "Associate in Psychiatry." I do not want to drop psychiatry at all—my hopes in Boston would be to get neurological and laboratory work on a half-time basis at the hospitals and school and do a practice in the other half time. The type of practice Dr. Putnam[2] had appeals to me, and the sort of life he led, I admire. But it isn't like the psychiatry at the Phipps.

In a letter he wrote to Meyer six days later[3] Cobb reviewed the same data and then went on to say that one thing which greatly attracted him toward Baltimore was the probability of being able to teach functional anatomy with Dr. Meyer to a group of good students. He doubted that he would find as good an opportunity in Boston. Moreover, he thought the laboratory facilities were better in Baltimore. He went on to say, "My New York work gave me many ideas, and my Oglethorpe experience showed me that I could lecture and demonstrate better than I ever thought possible. And I learned to enjoy the lecture room from the platform." Cobb thought that clinical neurology was stronger in Boston than in Baltimore and was leaning in the direction of Harvard. However, there were some other leads to follow before making a final decision.

Cobb afterward informed Meyer that Harvey Cushing wanted to see him before he made any final plans. Cushing then was contemplating the establishment of a national institute of neuropsychiatry in New York. However, he was having trouble getting the army to support it, and it looked as if any possibility there would be at least two years in the future. Cobb had to go to work at once, and he concluded that he would always be available if some remarkable opportunity developed with Cushing at a later date. Cobb also heard from Carl A. Elsberg, who had directed the neurosurgery course in New York the previous fall. Elsberg, too, wanted to see Cobb before he got out of the service, but nothing developed in the nature of a specific job offer. Cobb also considered working for Dr. Austin Riggs, who had established in Stockbridge, Massachusetts, an open sanitarium for treatment of psychoneuroses and other mental disorders of a manageable nature.

That Cobb was wavering in favor of Boston is indicated by another letter he sent to Meyer, dated March 10.[4] "The Baltimore situation strikes me in this way," he reasoned:

> You can give me, and have given me, exactly what I want as far as opportunities for hospital and laboratory work are concerned. I also believe that I could make enough money to bring the salary of $1800 up to a living wage. But, in looking over Baltimore as a place to start a practice, with opportunities for growing and getting into neurology as well as psychiatry— well the number of young men just older than me to perpetually keep me under is discouraging. And from the point of view of self-preservation I must look at that aspect of things. Boston looks better. The neuropsychiatrists are few and most of them twenty years my senior or practically in my class. Also I have family connections which are worth considerable hard cash.[5]

After considering all of these options Cobb finally decided upon Boston. On April 2, 1919, he informed Meyer[6] that he had written to Dean Edsall at Harvard, saying that he would definitely come provided that he could get the facilities to which Edsall had previously agreed. Cobb said he felt good about the decision. After the matter had been concluded, Cobb's remaining days at Cape May were rather kaleidos-

New Life in Boston

612 North Broadway, Baltimore, Maryland. The Cobbs lived in this row house across the street from the Johns Hopkins Hospital while Stanley was working at the Phipps Clinic

Staff of Henry Phipps Psychiatric Clinic about 1917. In the background from left to right are Drs. Aubrey Mussen, Harrington, Roscoe Hall, Joseph Moore, Nathaniel Brush, Clarence Neyman (one step down), Joseph Eidson, John Oliver, and Stanley Cobb. In the front row are Drs. Ruth Fairbank, Esther Richards, McFie Campbell, Adolf Meyer, Augusta Scott, and Phyllis Greenacre who made these identifications.

Three generations of Cobbs: John Candler Cobb (1858–1933), Stanley Cobb (1887–1968) and Sidney Cobb (born 1916)

New Life in Boston

Duck blind on the Gunpowder River near Baltimore, where the Cobbs vacationed before World War I

Swans on the Gunpowder River. A sepia wash, by Stanley Cobb, with an overlay of opaque white paint on the birds' wings. In the possession of Mrs. Carl Binger

Lieutenant Stanley Cobb in uniform during World War I

New Life in Boston

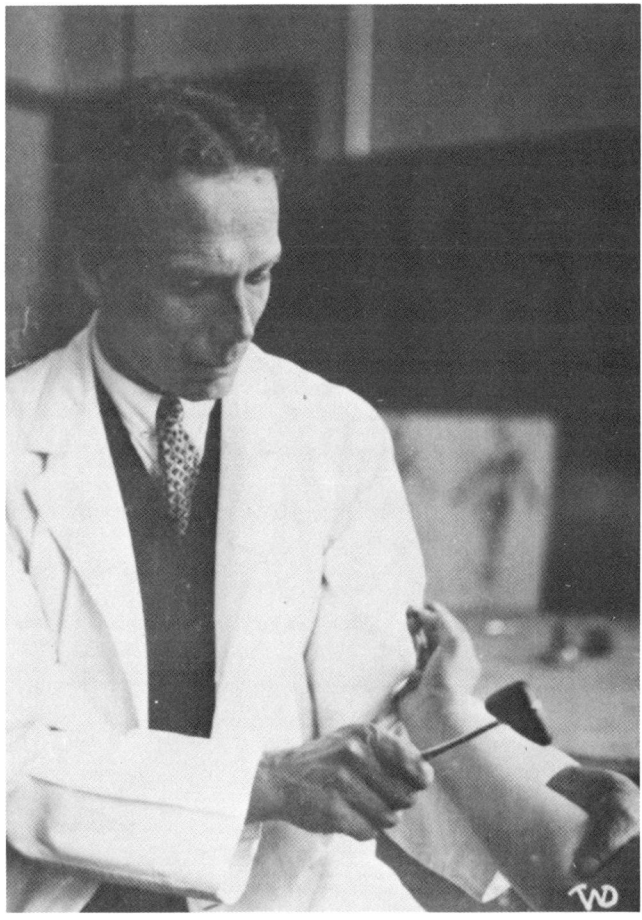

Clinician Stanley Cobb conducting a neurological examination in the early 1920s. The beginning of arthritic deformity of his fingers is evident.

The former Cherry Hill Tavern at Ponkapoag, Massachusetts, the Cobbs' home between 1919 and 1929

Stanley Cobb at his desk in his office at the Building D laboratory of the Harvard Medical School in the early 1920s. Note the filing baskets for "acute" and "chronic" matters.

Water color by Stanley Cobb, 1924, of a village scene in Northern France

New Life in Boston

copic. His interest had moved on; yet there were many things to be done. He applied for release from the army and obtained his discharge on April 30, 1919. He was also working on a paper on sensory examination and sent it to Meyer for his suggestions before completing the final draft (15). Cobb said he wrote that paper in self-defense to avoid some other pseudoscientific work which Major Frazier was trying to accomplish. Also at Cape May there was brief social contact with Cobb's old medical school classmate, Lawrence K. Lunt, who had been sent there for duty.

On April 23 Meyer wrote a very friendly letter in which he showed respect for Cobb's decision to go to Boston, yet at the same time indicating that things could have worked out well in Baltimore.[7] Nonetheless, he hoped that

> what you say at the end of your letter may prove true. The association has, I think, had all the personal elements that one could possibly look for both professionally, personally, and from the point of close relation to the families. I certainly hope to hear from you very often and I assure you that I shall always consider it a stimulation.

Meyer pointed out that in Boston Cobb would carry the full responsibility for integrating the opportunities available to him. The letter carried the implication that Cobb might need someone to lean on for reassurance and support. Meyer did not offer to function in that role, but it turned out that he did. Cobb continued writing to him as a father figure for many years.

The Cobbs lost no time in settling down in Boston. They visited Cobb's sister Polly (Mrs. Walter D. Brooks) for a few weeks and then went to the house in Ponkapoag where they were to remain for ten years. The house was the former Cherry Hill Tavern. It was on the property of Mrs. Cobb's Aunt Susan Cabot, who made it available rent free as an aid to meeting Cobb's financial needs while he was establishing himself as a neuroscientist. Aunt Susan Cabot was the widow of Dr. Arthur Tracy Cabot, a former surgeon at the Massachusetts General Hospital and Mrs. Cobb's uncle.[8] The low-ceilinged colonial house had been enlarged by the addition of a wing on the rear (page 76). It was located on the west side of Washington Street just south of the present intersection of Route 128 and Route 138. When Route 128 was constructed a section of the building was torn down, but the original part was preserved and moved across Washington Street into a secluded development. The site of the Cherry Hill Tavern can still be identified just north of an existing one-room schoolhouse and water tower. In 1919 Ponkapoag had its own post office, but it was really a section of Canton. As Cobb's wife put it, the family tumbled into Ponkapoag just before their youngest son, John Candler Cobb, was born on July 8th of that year.

His wife's delivery was one of Cobb's first professional activities in the Boston area. In a letter to her mother from Cherry Hill after the event he said that Betty seemed to be much less tired than after her previous children were born, but he was wary because he knew a slump could set in after a few days or weeks. He said that her labor lasted only three hours, and she said that she had no great pain. Cobb attributed her relative comfort to the anesthetizing he had done. John Candler Cobb II weighed nine and a half pounds at birth and had enormous hands. Cobb said in the letter, "On the whole she acted most coolly and with excellent judgment; I am rather proud of my wife."

The Cobb family was to remain in Ponkapoag until 1929, when they visited with Cobb's parents in Milton for a few weeks during the completion of the new home that they were building there. During the Ponkapoag years, Stanley Cobb commuted to Boston in a progressively more shabby Model T Ford.

When he arrived on the Boston scene in the late spring of 1919 Cobb had worked out with Dean Edsall a program of activities designed to support him financially. He had also developed a milieu that would allow for his own professsional growth and at the same time permit him to make a contribution to neurology and psychiatry at the Harvard Medical School. Cobb's base of operations was to be at the Massachusetts General Hospital, where he would have an office in which to see his private patients and an opportunity to study neurology under Edward W. Taylor and would be available as a psychiatric consultant in the hospital. In addition, he was to carry out investigations with Alexander Forbes and Walter B. Cannon in the physiology laboratories in the quadrangle of the Harvard Medical School and do some work in industrial hygiene with his old friend Cecil Drinker, who had also been working in Baltimore when Cobb was there.

Cobb informed Meyer on July 4, 1919, that he was getting started at the Massachusetts General Hospital in a rather scattered way.[9] However, the work there was shaping up very well. He said that Dean Edsall and Dr. Lee[10] had just the right attitude on psychiatric matters and on research, while many of the others did not; fortunately Edsall

New Life in Boston

and Lee were quite powerful. He went on to report that the wards were full of psychoneuroses with an occasional major psychosis, but he had not yet encountered a delirium. He added that he had hoped to see a lot of lethargic encephalitis but the cases had stopped coming in. Then followed, "What problems should you think most worth study in such a clinic as I have? From a teaching standpoint my first effort will be to give the staff a decent point of view on the psychoneuroses."

Cobb had a small office[11] and a Dalton Scholarship of five hundred dollars from the Massachusetts General Hospital. He also received a small stipend as assistant in neurology at the Harvard Medical School and another for his work in industrial hygiene. He had hoped that his father's friendship and his own previous conversations with Dr. Edsall would have led to some sort of full-time opening, but such an event was not to come to pass immediately. Cobb resented the time given to private practice and longed for the day when he could devote full time to teaching and research.

The teaching came fairly promptly through an opportunity in 1920 to take part in a course for graduates which was organized and administered by Richard Cabot, professor of clinical medicine.[12] Cabot was a second cousin of Mrs. Cobb, and although Cobb never listed him as one of the important models in his life, he had considerable influence because of his own holistic view of medicine. Cabot was a man intellectually honest to a painful degree. He was aware of the social problems of his day and their impact on medical care. He founded at the Massachusetts General Hospital the first medical social service department in 1905, and in 1907 Miss Ida Cannon became its director.[13] Convinced that reliable medical diagnosis was dependent on correlation between manifestations of disease during life and the tissue findings after death, he established the clinicopathological conferences which for many years were published in the *New England Journal of Medicine* under the heading "Cabot Case Clinics."

To Cabot the spiritual side of a patient's life was important too. With Dicks he wrote a book on pastoral care of medical patients.[14] He also wrote a classical text book on physical diagnosis, which, with the coauthorship of F. Dennette Adams, went through a long series of editions.[15] Cabot's intellectual honesty was demonstrated when he had congestive heart failure at the end of his life. One morning he awoke with cough and fever. His physician, Paul Dudley White said, "Richard, I think you have a touch of bronchopneumonia." Cabot replied, "Paul, you know on a statistical basis it has to be an infarct."[16]

In the spring of 1920 Cabot asked Cobb to take part in a course for graduates which was to run from June 1 to June 30 of that year, and Cobb was delighted to accept. He was anxious to get back into organized teaching. During the course, the participants spent the mornings examining patients on the wards, and at noon Cabot gave a lecture on a key medical topic. After lunch the doctors were offered a choice between a course in surgery or one in neurology. The neurology course, with special reference to the psychoneuroses, was given by Stanley Cobb and other members of the neurology staff under Edward W. Taylor. The audience turned out to be more sophisticated than Cobb had anticipated, and he was frightened. However, his presentation of neuropathological topics was well received, and he had for the first time the feeling that he had really begun to teach.

Other members of the Massachusetts General Hospital staff besides Cabot and Taylor were important in helping Cobb establish himself and his work there. James Howard Means was appointed Jackson Professor of Clinical Medicine in 1923, succeeding Edsall, who changed his status from half-time to full-time Dean. Although not a brilliant lecturer, Means had tact and imagination and was able to see the importance of psychiatry in a general hospital. He became one of Cobb's strong supporters. In fact he had considerable influence in establishing the psychiatric service at the Massachusetts General Hospital some years later. James B. Ayer, a budding neurologist, became internationally known because of his daring work in developing cisternal puncture and was destined to become Cobb's teaching arm at the Massachusetts General Hospital after the retirement of E. W. Taylor as chief of neurology in 1926.

However, the most influential person of all was William Herman, a medical intern who completed his service on July 1, 1922. Born to a Jewish family in Nashville, Tennessee, Herman was destined to become for Cobb a sort of junior Moses. Herman led Cobb through the maze of analytic psychiatry and paved the way at the Massachusetts General Hospital, encouraging him to establish his new service there. He died in January, 1935, with a binocular view of the promised land. In a letter to Adolf Meyer dated November 9, 1921, Cobb recommended Herman for a position as a resident in psychiatry:[17]

> He went through the school fairly well and has been doing good work as an interne. His strong suit is not scientific work but rather personal contacts and good judgment. He is rather older than most men in his position because

he entered medicine after having been in business several years. He is personally a very pleasing individual and good company, one whom we all like to have out over weekends and so forth.

Herman was not offered the residency then, but in the spring of 1923 he was interning with Meyer at the Phipps.[18] When he became qualified in psychiatry Herman undertook both Jungian and Freudian analysis and maintained his office in the Massachusetts General Hospital's Bulfinch Building under the *aegis* of Means. He was a pioneer Jewish staff member at the Massachusetts General Hospital and a pioneer psychiatrist. Moreover, he married Cobb's secretary, Susan Evarts Hale, and through close personal contact maintained a liaison during the years when Cobb was working elsewhere. He was an excellent lecturer. One of his gambits was to describe the physiologic manifestations of anxiety as he experienced them standing at the podium.

Even with the other demands upon his time Cobb was able to do some clinical investigation on the psychiatric patients whom he saw at the Massachusetts General Hospital. He published a paper in *Medical Clinics of North America* (17), reviewing three cases with somewhat different manifestations. The influence of Adolf Meyer was evident from Cobb's use of Meyer's life charts and from the formulations of the patients' illnesses. For example, instead of employing a brief diagnostic term Cobb formulated the second case as follows:

> We have, then, an individual with an inheritance of great energy from the maternal side, who develops an antagonism to the father, becomes ambitious, but breaks down under the strain of puberty. In spite of the decidedly ominous features of the psychosis into which he was plunged, he was able to recover, but the depression of the breakdown left its mark in the form of visceroptosis, which was perpetuated by the sedentary life. This organic defect (in my opinion secondary to the mood depression of the psychosis) caused constipation and intestinal stasis that may explain the neuritis. The present breakdown with its somatic symptoms is not bad, but can be seen to arise directly from the old unhygienic psychology of compensating for a feeling of inferiority, for it was the desire to rush into war work and not be considered a slacker that added the final burden which brought on the break.

Cobb went on to describe the advice given to the patient which included not only insight therapy but also medication for the bowels, an anteroposterior orthopedic abdominal pad, dietary instructions, and a program of regular exercise. Cobb was following Meyer's commonsense approach. For another issue of *Medical Clinics of North America*

Cobb reported on three cases of spastic paralysis in children, two from the pediatric service of Fritz B. Talbot, for whom he had worked during medical school at the Boston Floating Hospital, and the third from Jason Mixter's neurosurgical service (20). He also found time to complete observations with others that had been made at Cape May, New Jersey, when Cobb was still in military service (14, 18, 23). However, Cobb's actual investigative work following his arrival in Boston was primarily performed at the physiology department of the Harvard Medical School, where he worked once more in collaboration with Alexander Forbes—one of his declared life models.

Alexander Forbes was born in Milton on May 14, 1882. His father, William Hathaway Forbes, was a son of J. M. Forbes, the China trader and Mid-western railroad financier, and his mother, Edith Forbes, was the daughter of the poet and philosopher Ralph Waldo Emerson. Forbes was born into a world not only of economic security but also of intellectual, artistic, and spiritual stimulation. Endowed with a curious and incisive mind he developed a wide range of interests including deep-sea navigation, a study of the geography of Labrador, photogrammetry from the air, skiing, sailing, riding, and piloting his own plane. He wrote more than one hundred papers on neurophysiology. After graduation from Harvard in 1904, he received an M.A. in biology in 1905 and during that year learned the rudiments of electrophysiology. Following his graduation from Harvard Medical School in 1910 he became an assistant in physiology there and from 1911 to 1912, at the suggestion of Walter B. Cannon, he spent a year with Sir Charles Sherrington, then in Liverpool, working in the physiology of spinal reflexes. Later he worked with Keith Lucas and E. D. Adrian in Cambridge, England, on precise biophysical studies of peripheral nerves. With Adrian he described the all-or-nothing phenomenon in the transmission of an impulse along an individual nerve fiber.[19] Forbes died in Milton on March 27, 1965, and Cobb was one of the committee, headed by John R. Pappenheimer, which wrote the official memorial minute for the *Harvard Gazette*.[20]

In the physiology department Cobb was in contact with Walter B. Cannon, who was to become a lifelong faculty friend at Harvard; through Cecil Drinker he also became acquainted with Alfred Redfield, a physiologist with a longtime interest in birds.[21] A gentle man with a delicious sense of humor, Redfield became one of Cobb's closest friends and a companion for many years on hunting trips and cruises. Redfield

New Life in Boston

said that he and Cobb were already old friends because of the censuses of Christmas birds which even before 1910 they had submitted to *Bird Lore* magazine, he from Philadelphia and Cobb from Boston. However, Cobb did not work with Redfield professionally. The work Cobb did in the physiology laboratory was basically with Alexander Forbes.

With Forbes and Helen Cattell, Cobb completed and published the work on electrical studies of mammalian reflexes that he had commenced in the summer of 1916. From protocols of three experiments in 1916 and six more between March and May, 1921, with excellent galvanometer tracings, he concluded definitely that low spinal transection had no effect on the duration of the flexion reflex in decerebrate cats. The amplitude of the response was increased, however. Cobb said, "When the reflex arc of the flexion reflex is reduced to its simplest elements, the stimulus being applied to an afferent nerve and the response observed by recording the action current of a motor nerve, low spinal transection causes an immediate increase in the size of response to a single induction shock. There is no change in reflex time." (29)

Another project that Cobb carried out with Forbes at this time was on "Electromyographic Studies of Fatigue in Man" (30). Cobb demonstrated that when a muscle was exercised to the point of exhaustion the frequency of the action currents was diminished, whereas the amplitude of the currents was increased. As he said, "The study of muscular fatigue is so complicated by psychological factors that a method of recording any of its concommitant phenomena may be of value." In June, 1919, just after Cobb's return from Cape May, two Ringling Brothers circus elephants were outside the Boston Children's Hospital awaiting their turn for an exhibit. Cobb and Forbes saw the animals from the windows of the physiology laboratory next door, seized their opportunity, and obtained an electrocardiogram on one of the animals (21).

While still working in Baltimore with Meyer, Cobb had talked with his friend, Cecil Drinker, about the overlap between psychiatry and industrial hygiene. Drinker, who was going into applied physiology, and Cobb, whose interest was neuropsychiatry, decided to explore together the field of industrial hygiene, with special reference to contentment among workers and the phenomenon of fatigue. In a letter to Meyer dated September 22, 1918, from New York, where he was just commencing Elsberg's course in neurosurgery, Cobb wrote of his interest in neurasthenia and the need to study it in a comprehensive manner.[22] In the same letter he reported that he had just returned from Boston where his friend Drinker was chairman of the new committee on industrial hygiene. Cobb said that Edsall was head of the new department and that the point of view of these two men was excellent. He continued, "It was fine to hear a physiologist say that fatigue could not be studied by nerve-muscle preparations, that you had to go to the factory and size up the whole situation." In another paragraph Cobb went on to describe Drinker as enthusiastic and energetic, and he commented, "I think we will see big things from that Department. It is the influence of Edsall, I believe, acting on the keen material in Drinker."

Drinker came from a family of brilliant people. His father was president of Lehigh University. His brother, Philip, later invented the Drinker respirator, often referred to by the public as the "iron lung." Drinker's sister, Catherine Drinker Bowen, was a noted author who wrote among other things *Yankee from Olympus,* an incisive biography of the two Oliver Wendell Holmeses,[23] as well as a family history pointing out the brilliance and ideosyncrasies of its members.[24] As Mrs. Bowen stated, Cecil Drinker was an alcoholic, and Cobb found it very difficult to work with him. In fact he is quoted as saying, "I learned from Drinker that I can't work with an alcoholic."[25] It is of interest that when Cobb and Forbes completed their study on electromyographic findings in fatigue, it was published without any reference to a possible contribution by Drinker (30).

On his return from military service in 1919, Cobb was appointed psychiatrist in industrial hygiene by Edsall, who was both dean of the Harvard Medical School and chairman of the new department. Cobb's early interest in industrial hygiene is indicated by an article entitled "Applications of Psychiatry to Industrial Hygiene," which appears in the *Journal of Industrial Hygiene* in November, 1919 (13). In this published article he reviewed the case of a woman with numbness and pain in her thumb which had been diagnosed as an occupational neurosis but really was related to a number of personal problems outside the factory. He also went into fatigue as a subject of importance in the field of industrial hygiene. Additional work in industrial hygiene included a paper with D. C. Parmenter, an assistant in industrial hygiene at the Harvard Medical School, on headache (24) and another with B. C. Mitchell entitled "Social Work with Traumatic Neuroses" published in 1923 (31). With the appearance of these articles Cobb's

New Life in Boston

interest in industrial hygiene waned and he became fully occupied with other matters.

Cobb's great opportunity came with the dislocation of faculty jurisdictions that followed the tragic and untimely death of Elmer E. Southard from pneumonia in February, 1920. Southard, as the Bullard Professor of Neuropathology, held the very chair that Cobb was eventually to inherit, and he had an experimental laboratory in Building D-2 at the Harvard Medical School. However, his primary responsibility was in psychiatry as director of the Boston Psychopathic Hospital, a state institution. For political reasons, as well as convenience, most of Southard's laboratory work was conducted there, and the space in Building D-2 was used very little.[26] Southard's contributions to the Harvard Medical School were primarily his heading psychiatry at the Boston Psychopathic Hospital and secondarily his presentation each year of a course in neuropathology to the second-year medical students, a task that subsequently was to fall upon Cobb.

Donald J. MacPherson, an early staff member of the Boston Psychopathic Hospital, described Southard as a very brilliant man[27] whose early training had been in neuroanatomy. He was a philosopher, and he spoke several languages. His innate mathematical genius was indicated by his proficiency at chess. MacPherson said Southard could play twenty games at one time and sometimes played with him when blindfolded. MacPherson said that Southard's views on Freud were ambivalent. Southard was interested in Freud's observations. However, he felt that the theories were premature and required confirmation. MacPherson commented that Southard's viewpoint was to wait and see what would happen.

By the time of Southard's death, Cobb had already established himself as a person of importance in the neurosciences at Harvard, for he was consulted by Dean Edsall about finding a successor. In his letter of February 14, 1920, to Meyer[28] he asked for advice. Already the idea had dawned of freeing up the Bullard professorship for someone working primarily in neuropathology and of finding other funds for the new man in the chair of psychiatry.[29] Cobb listed a number of prominent psychiatrists who might qualify as candidates for the job. He said, "In other words I have an opportunity to give advice that will carry weight, and I don't know what advice to give." He also asked Meyer about someone to fill the Bullard position, which he later inherited himself, and commented, "We should get a good man to put his whole time into neuropathology at the School and give him the hospital connections in order to get material, but we do *not* want a man interested merely in pickled brain sections."[30] Meyer replied in a nine-page letter listing several possible candidates.[31] Among the names suggested was Meyer's associate, Dr. C. Macfie Campbell, who a few months afterward was appointed professor of psychiatry at Harvard and chief of service at the Boston Psychopathic Hospital. On June 20, 1920, Cobb wrote that he had been promoted to assistant professor of neuropathology with no full professor over his head.

Although Cobb maintained his office at the Massachusetts General Hospital for seeing his private patients and continued some teaching there, the focal point of his life for the next ten years was Southard's former neuropathology laboratory in Building D-2 of the Harvard quandrangle, to which he moved in September, 1920. In the neuropathology laboratory he directed his affairs from an office with a rolltop desk and in-baskets designated for "acute" and "chronic" matters (page 77).

The five principal buildings of the Harvard Medical School face on a rectangular lawn. If one stands on Longwood Avenue looking south the imposing classical columns of Building A occupy space at the far end, and there are two handsome marble buildings on each side of the quadrangle to the right and to the left. The building nearest to Longwood Avenue on the left is Building D, and the wing adjacent to Longwood Avenue is known as Building D-2. The space on the left side of the corridor just beyond the entrance was assigned to Dr. William A. Hinton, the serologist, and the entire remainder of the floor was assigned to Cobb (see Figure 1). Immediately to the right of the entrance was a room for experimental work on animals. Beyond this, under the stairway to the Building D amphitheatre, was a space which in the later years of Cobb's occupancy housed Southard's collection of pickled brain specimens in crocks and battery jars. Farther down the corridor on the right came a storage room, then the technical laboratory for cutting and staining neurological tissues, and finally another storeroom. Proceeding from the entrance along the left side of the corridor, after passing Dr. Hinton's laboratory, one came upon three private offices and then a large workroom occupied by secretaries and work tables for analysis of data and similar projects. The three private offices opened off a narrow hallway parallel to the main corridor. The

New Life in Boston

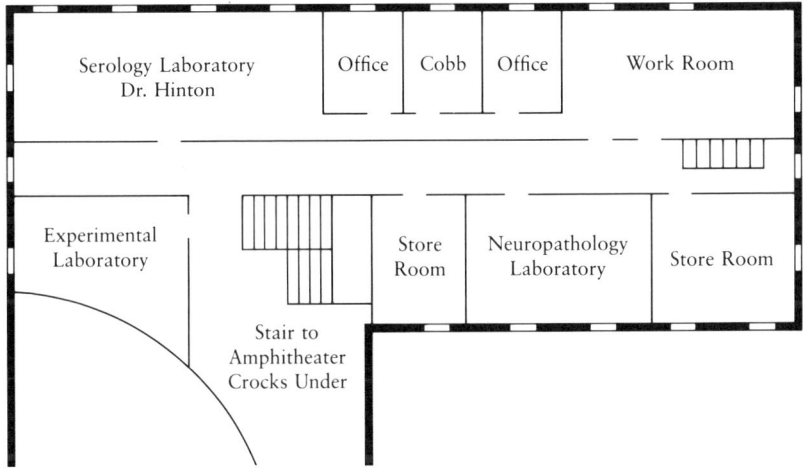

FIGURE 1.—Floor plan of Cobb's Neuropathology Laboratory in Building D-2 of the Harvard Medical School in the 1920s and throughout his professorship.

door between the hallway and the outside corridor was always kept closed, so that a secretary with her desk at the door of the large workroom could control the traffic to the doctors' offices and also keep an eye on the central hall. Cobb occupied one of the rooms personally and made the others available to various colleagues as they came along.

The first phase of the work in the neuropathology laboratory extended from September, 1920, when Cobb became its director, until June, 1923, when he went to Europe for a two-year period of study. The workers in the laboratory during this time, in addition to Cobb himself, were William Gordon Lennox in epilepsy, Henry S. Forbes in cerebral circulation, and Frank Fremont-Smith in studies of the cerebrospinal fluid, all of whom continued to be colleagues for many years. Edwin F. Gildea, as a medical student, studied vitamin deficiency, Maxwell E. MacDonald worked on experimental convulsions, Hugo Mella on manganese intoxication, and Schichi Uyematzu on experimental convulsions. Donald J. MacPherson, who had previously done work with the Einthoven galvanometer, was in the laboratory part time and carried some administrative responsibility. Paul Yakovlev, who originally had no official status in the University, came about 1922.

He made whole brain sections and helped translate articles from foreign journals.

William Gordon Lennox became Cobb's key collaborator in studies of epilepsy. Lennox, who was a graduate of the class of 1913 at the Harvard Medical School, had set out to become a medical missionary. After three years of postgraduate hospital work, mostly at the Massachusetts General Hospital, he went to Peking and joined the staff of the Rockefeller sponsored Peking Union Medical College and hospital. The first year he devoted to learning Chinese and then assumed his clinical duties. He came to Cobb's laboratory because his younger daughter developed epilepsy and he wanted to become an investigator of that disease. His early work in the neuropathology laboratory was on various metabolic aspects of epilepsy. Later he studied cerebral circulation, cerebral gas exchange, and the electrical discharges associated with epilepsy. He wrote exhaustively on the subject of epilepsy.

In terms of longevity of service and the importance of his work the next in line was unquestionably Henry Stone Forbes. Like his first cousin, Alexander Forbes, he was a grandson of J. M. Forbes, the financier. Henry Stone Forbes, always known as Harry, was graduated from the Harvard Medical School in 1911. After his hospital work and his World War I military service, mostly in what is now Yugoslavia,[32] Forbes volunteered his services at the neuropathology laboratory where he worked without a university appointment until Dean Edsall insisted that he have official status. It was in the neuropathology laboratory that he met Cobb's younger sister Hildegarde, whom he married in 1922.

The first paper that Forbes wrote with Cobb was on the swelling of brain tissue and headache following asphyxia from carbon monoxide (36). This article was favorably received and Cobb wrote to Forbes from Europe on July 3, 1924, "I was pleased to see the good write-up that the A.M.A. gave us. One paper that catches hold the way that one did probably does more good than a great many more abstract pieces of work."[33] The initial protocol on a cat was carried out in May, 1922, and there was later work in the spring of 1923. Forbes spent some time in New Haven and worked with a gassing machine designed by Yandell Henderson, professor of applied physiology at Yale. The work included opthalmoscopic examination of the retinal arteries in a human being after the inhalation of a low concentration of carbon monoxide.

New Life in Boston

Studies on a victim of illuminating gas asphyxiation were included in the article.

Forbes early began to work on cerebral circulation and evolved a method for studying, through a window artificially placed in a cat's skull, the flow of blood through the small arteries in the membranes covering the brain. By means of this method he and his collaborators over the years were to accumulate a vast amount of new information on cerebral circulation.

With the exception of four years from 1930 to 1934, spent at the Boston City Hospital, Forbes continued his work at the neuropathology laboratory until World War II. In 1937 the Association for Research in Nervous and Mental Disease published a comprehensive symposium on the circulation of the brain and spinal cord which was edited by Cobb and reviewed much of Forbes's most important work. By 1938 Forbes had published over fifty articles.[34] Forbes's studies of cerebral circulation dovetailed neatly into the work of Lennox on epilepsy.

A coauthor of the article on carbon monoxide asphyxia (36) and Cobb's right-hand man for many years was Frank Fremont-Smith, who graduated from Harvard College in 1915 and from the Harvard Medical School in 1921. After serving as an intern in pathology at the Brigham for a year (1921–22) Fremont-Smith was a medical intern at the Boston City Hospital under Francis Weld Peabody from 1922 through 1923. During his medical internship he collaborated with Harry Forbes in his work on carbon monoxide asphyxia (36). In January, 1924, Fremont-Smith went to the Massachusetts General Hospital, where he worked with James B. Ayer on the cerebrospinal fluid. By mid-1925 Fremont-Smith was occupied full time in Cobb's neuropathology laboratory, working on cerebrospinal fluid and cerebral circulation.

One of the very earliest workers in the laboratory was Hugo Mella, who commenced October 1, 1920. In a letter to Edsall, Cobb described Mella as a thirty-two-year-old married man with two children, living at 30 Prescott Street in Cambridge.[35] Mella had graduated from the medical department of the University of Georgia in 1916. After minimal hospital training in Augusta, Georgia, and in St. Paul, Minnesota, Mella practiced surgery in North Dakota until he entered the military service in 1917. Then, following a disability discharge from the army on January 31, 1920, he took a postgraduate course in neurology under

E. W. Taylor at the Massachusetts General Hospital. When the course was over he stayed on at the General with Taylor and worked with the psychoanalyst, Eugene Emerson, until he joined Cobb's staff at the neuropathology laboratory, initially part time, in September, 1920, prior to his full-time appointment on October first.

Mella helped Cobb with experimental work on basal ganglia. Mella and Cobb were successful in producing athetoid movements by the administration of manganese. In a letter to Edsall written December 22, 1922,[36] Cobb reported that he and Mella had brought about athetoid chorea in a monkey after six months of injecting manganese intraperitoneally, and in a letter to Meyer[37] he mentioned that he was working on basal ganglia. However, Cobb's name did not appear on Mella's paper.[38] Mella also worked on the treatment of paralysis agitans with sodium cacodylate. In a letter dated October 11, 1921, Cobb related that work was going on in the laboratory on the pathology and physiology of the disease.[39] Mella apparently had considerable administrative ability, for Cobb entrusted the management of the laboratory to him during his absence for study in Europe from 1923 to 1925.[40] Mella departed shortly after that and eventually settled in Colorado.

When Cobb inherited the neuropathology laboratory in September, 1920, after Southard had died, MacPherson came along with it. MacPherson was a bright, independent-minded physician who later made a most valuable contribution to psychiatry at the Peter Bent Brigham Hospital and also to the community through his office at 270 Commonwealth Avenue. He graduated from the Harvard Medical School in 1915, and while a student there had worked with Alexander Forbes on the Einthoven string galvanometer. It is said that MacPherson invented the electroencephalogram but was discouraged from going further by Forbes, who thought the vibrations of the string were artifacts.[41] After internship at the Brigham, MacPherson studied under Southard at the Boston Psychopathic Hospital and then went into the United States Army as a captain in the medical corps.

MacPherson for a time was second-in-command to Cobb in the supervision of the laboratory and he took an active part in teaching the neuropathology course each year. However, with the passage of time, he devoted more and more time to the liaison psychiatry that he was carrying out at the Brigham.[42] He and Mrs. MacPherson were social friends of the Cobbs but they saw less of each other as time went on. Mrs. Cobb said that MacPherson, who had an ambivalent

New Life in Boston 93

attitude toward Freud, used to tease Cobb about his interest in psychoanalysis. Sanford Gifford reported that although MacPherson was ambivalent toward analysis, he did have a sympathetic interest in it. He just did not think it was appropriate for him.

Another early worker in Cobb's neuropathology laboratory in Building D-2 at the Harvard Medical School quadrangle was Dr. Schichi Uyematzu, a Japanese physician who had been at the Massachusetts State Hospital in Danvers prior to joining Cobb's staff. Uyematzu worked with Cobb on experimental convulsion from wormwood oil and from thujone. They were trying to find the locus on the convulsive state. Cobb and Uyematzu presented a paper at the Boston Society of Psychiatry and Neurology entitled "Preliminary Report on Experimental Convulsions: Convulsions produced by Administration of Chemical Substances." In a letter to Dr. Bullard, the retired neuropathologist and a financial supporter, Cobb said:[43]

> Experimental work to determine the locus from which convulsions are discharged has been carried out on intact, decorticate, decerebrate and spinal animals. We have also been studying the effect on convulsions of basal metabolism by producing wormwood oil convulsions on rabbits which have been starved for a number of days, on rabbits intoxicated with thyroxin, and on thyroidectomized rabbits. We are repeating these same experiments with thujone, the dosage of which can be more accurately determined than that of wormwood oil.... We are planning to make a careful study of a series of fresh brains which Dr. Thom is getting for us from Monson.

Uyematzu came to grief in 1921 when he was convicted in court for attempting to bribe a police officer after a minor traffic violation. The case unfortunately received newspaper publicity, which was always regarded at Harvard as the one unforgivable transgression. Cobb wrote to President Lowell asking whether he should take any cognizance of the matter. Lowell replied that Uyematzu's appointment should not be renewed the following year. Uyematzu apparently did not bear resentment against Cobb as the result of his downfall, for he subsequently kept in touch through letters from Japan.[44] When Dr. and Mrs. Cobb were traveling around the world in 1962 they had an opportunity to visit Dr. Uyematzu, at that time a distinguished neuropathologist in Kyoto.

Also important in the early days of the laboratory was Edwin F. Gildea, who graduated from the Harvard Medical School in 1924. Throughout medical school he worked on vitamin deficiency in Cobb's neuropathology laboratory. Gildea said that in the beginning the work of the laboratory was almost exclusively investigational. Gildea recalled that Cobb was always interested in the brains from different species, including birds. According to Gildea, even at that time Cobb was making gross dissections of brains in his study of comparative anatomy. However, the principal modality of the laboratory was the microscopic examination of stained sections of neural tissue.

Gildea found Cobb extraordinarily hospitable and helpful.[45] He went out of his way to make neurological research understandable, interesting, and rewarding. Cobb made available space in which to work and assigned to Gildea the part-time services of Hannah Linden, a technician who did all of Cobb's scut work, cut sections for microscopy, and also helped Gildea in operating on animals. By microstaining techniques, Gildea studied the changes in the spinal cord that resulted when animals were maintained on vitamin-deficient diets. After graduation from medical school in 1924 Gildea interned in medicine for two years at Boston City Hospital, spent two years at the Boston Psychopathic Hospital, and then rejoined Cobb's staff. In 1928 Gildea became the first full-time resident physician on the clinical service that Cobb was developing at City Hospital. When there as a resident, Gildea completed his studies on vitamin deficiency and published them with Kattwinkel and Castle.[46] Gildea was to remain closely affiliated with Cobb for many years.

An outstanding example of Cobb's faith and his ability to seize a fortuitous opportunity was presented by the circumstances of Paul Yakovlev's introduction into the neuropathology laboratory. Yakovlev came to this country in an unusual way. He was an emigré Russian physican who had been living in Paris, and he had an opportunity to accompany from Europe to Providence, Rhode Island, as a sort of nurse or attendant, a neuropsychiatric patient who was being directed to Dr. George MacDonald there. Yakovlev came to Providence without a passport, the expectation having been that he would return promptly to France. Although in many ways eccentric, he was never shy, and he had a way of making his desires known. He indicated to MacDonald that he was a graduate of a Russian medical school and wished to enter the field of neurology in the United States. MacDonald had nothing to offer him and telephoned Cobb reiterating Yakovlev's background. Cobb said, "Send him up." So in 1921 Yakovlev came to Boston, unable to speak English, and destitute of funds. Cobb and his wife

New Life in Boston

welcomed him in their home in Ponkapoag, where he stayed for several weeks. He spent a year in Providence, and then through the efforts of Abraham Myerson a small niche was found for him at Boston City Hospital. Yakovlev also began working at the Neuropathology laboratory in Building D-2 at the Harvard Medical School without any formal appointment. Meanwhile Cobb resolved the passport problems and arranged for Yakovlev to remain in this country. Yakovlev subsequently became interested in a huge microtome which Southard had previously acquired. With this instrument, Yakovlev prepared sections of whole brains for microscopic examinations and over the years accumulated an outstanding collection,[47] which he eventually moved to the Armed Services Institute of Pathology in Washington, D.C.[48] Yakovlev, with his facile knowledge of languages, was of inestimable help in reviewing the world's literature on epilepsy with Lennox and Cobb. Later Cobb arranged a post for Yakovlev as pathologist to the Monson State Hospital, where he served from 1926 through the mid-thirties, always as an active participating member of Cobb's staff.

In addition to the physicians who were conducting studies in the neuropathology laboratory at the time, there was also a staff of women assistants who warrant mention. Cobb's younger sister Hildegarde, who in his medical-school days had commuted with him to Boston, became the first tissue technician in the laboratory. After her rapid preparatory study during the summer of 1920 at the Brigham and the Boston Psychopathic Hospitals, Hildegarde Cobb occupied the laboratory on the south side of the corridor in Building D-2. With her microtome and jars of stains she prepared all the slides needed for the second-year medical school class in neuropathology which Cobb had taken over after Southard's death. There were one hundred twenty students in a class, and two students shared a box of slides, so sixty slides were made from each specimen that was used for teaching. It was in this laboratory that Hildegarde Cobb was working when she met her future husband, Harry Forbes. One of the less inspiring tasks she had to perform was to maintain the level of preserving fluid on Southard's collection of pickled brains, which initially were in his laboratory and later were moved out into the corridor under the amphitheater stair landing. Because the entrance to her laboratory was just opposite to the door of the large workroom on the north side of the corridor, she was able to monitor the traffic when Cobb's personal secretary was absent.

In the early days Hildegarde Cobb's laboratory did not perform any routine neuropathological function for any of the hospitals, although at times Cushing would bring over a section from the Brigham for review. Even after her marriage to Harry Forbes in 1922, she continued to visit the neuropathology laboratory on frequent occasions because of her interest in the work her husband was doing there. Hildegarde Forbes's immediate successor in the tissue-preparation laboratory was Sadie Danziger, who had been the technician for Mrs. Forbes's brother-in-law, Dr. Chandler Foot, prior to his move from the Brigham Hospital to Cincinnati. She was followed by Sylvia Lovejoy, a very attractive recent high school graduate, who was responsible and effective. She married Dr. Maxwell MacDonald, who had worked with Cobb in the laboratory on intracranial pressure changes during experimental convulsions (34). MacDonald later practiced neuropsychiatry with Drs. Abraham Myerson and Harry C. Solomon. Another early member of Cobb's supporting staff was Mrs. Hannah Linden, who, as a general laboratory helper, assisted Gildea in his vitamin deficiency work. Mrs. Linden remained with Cobb for fifteen years.

When Cobb took over the neuropathology laboratory in 1920 he inherited Southard's secretary, Bessie Hamelin, who was quiet, efficient, and hardworking. However, not long after Cobb arrived, Miss Hamelin reached retirement age and was replaced by Susan Evarts Hale, who served for several years. Mrs. Hale developed a close friendship with Cobb's protégé, William Herman, and traveled with him in Europe when Cobb was there between 1923 and 1925. After she and Herman were married, they remained close friends of the Cobbs until Herman's untimely death in January, 1935.

Cobb was always interested in the personal growth of those who worked with him. He wanted everyone to understand the purposes of the laboratory. To this end he tried to educate the staff as much as he could. For example, he insisted that his sister, Hildegarde Forbes, and his secretary, Susan Hale, attend all the lectures in the neuropathology course, and he encouraged them to go to other Harvard Medical School lectures as well.

In addition to the medical school laboratory, Cobb's major responsibility was teaching the neuropathology course. Cobb had considerable anxiety when he took over that course. Initially, it did not fit in exactly with his style of teaching. So, over the years he modified it to suit his own scientific interests and outlook on neuropathology. He continued

New Life in Boston

to supervise the course throughout his entire professional career, even after becoming chief of psychiatry at the Massachusetts General Hospital.

Cobb was certainly best known to the majority of Harvard Medical School students through his personal teaching in the neuropathology course, which was given during the spring term of the second year. The compensation that Cobb made for the handicap of his stammering often greatly enhanced the effectiveness of his teaching. For example, he organized his material very crisply, so that he could present it with about one-third the number of words that other lecturers might employ. He chose simple words, when possible, presumably because of his difficulty in expressing complicated ones. When he did introduce a word that was not in common usage, he would write it on the blackboard so that the spelling would be absolutely clear. Medical students were impressed by his ambidexterity. He would often use both hands at once when drawing on the blackboard bilaterally symmetrical cross sections of the brain or spinal cord. Cobb also restated almost every point that he made during a lecture in the hope that at the end of the hour the average medical student would be able to remember at least two or three concepts. His stammering was at its worst in the lecture hall. Often, when lecturing, he would stumble over a word and build up a great sense of frustration. Then finally, with a stamp of his right foot on the floor, the desired word would issue forth from his mouth.

In 1922–23 the course was taught by Cobb with the assistance of James B. Ayer of the Massachusetts General Hospital, Harry C. Solomon from the Boston Psychopathic Hospital, and three members of his own staff, Drs. Hugo Mella, Donald J. MacPherson, and William Lennox.[49] Approximately fifty hours were allotted to the course, which consisted of lectures, laboratory work, review exercises, and periodic quizzes. The core of the course was neuropathology, but the content branched out to include the more commonly encountered neurological disorders, and there was even a lecture or two on psychiatric concepts.

In 1926 Cobb was later to publish a syllabus of the course entitled "An Outline of Neuropathology for Students of General Medicine." Emphasis was placed on the study of sections of nerve tissue from the more important functional portions of the brain, the spinal cord, and the peripheral nerves, as a basis for understanding disturbances in the working of these structures. Cobb pointed out the way in which even a minute focal injury might produce extensive complex and distant effects. He described the stains that were used to bring out the important features of nervous tissue, especially those that revealed minute structures within the nerve cells. He taught the rudiments of clinical examination and lectured at some length on the physiology of the cerebrospinal fluid and its importance as a diagnostic tool in various neurological disorders. He organized the neurological diseases as far as possible in terms of their causes. He talked of trauma and the rate of recovery after nerve injuries. He also took up infectious diseases such as encephalitis, meningitis, and syphilis; brain tumors; familial and hereditary disorders; and diseases with totally unexplained causation such as multiple sclerosis. Also included was a section on mental deficiency, epilepsy, psychosis, and psychoneurosis.

In Cobb's later psychiatric years Dr. Mandel Cohen took charge of the audiovisual aids needed in the course.[50] Cohen told a somewhat embarrassing and at the same time revealing story about Cobb. Each student had been given a slide box containing perhaps thirty stained sections of neural tissue and beforehand was told that nothing would appear on the examination that was not in the box. Then, in preparation for the examination Cobb discovered that some of the slides were in short supply. There were insufficient copies of one of the slides he wanted to use. So he substituted a slide of nerve tissue involved with leprosy. Cohen said, "Dr. Cobb, if you use that slide I will resign from the course, because I promised the students that they would have nothing on the examination except slides that were in the box." Cobb thought that Cohen was keeping his promise too literally, but when the examination came he did tell the students that there was, indeed, one slide which was not in the box, and not to take it too seriously. When the examination was given and the leprosy slide handed out, there were one or two students who recognized it correctly but most of them missed it completely and it made no difference in their grades.

Dr. Augustus S. Rose, later professor of neurology at the University of California in Los Angeles, audited the course more than once during his several years of study in Boston. Rose had a profound appreciation for the way in which Cobb tied together gross and microscopic neuropathology, neurophysiology, clinical neurology, and even some psychiatric knowledge. Rose recalled:[51]

> Cobb's brilliant lectures to medical students, coupled with my early interest in neurology, led me to sit in on these lectures several years in succession . . . I only wish that those in neuropsychiatry around the world who have

New Life in Boston

followed him could transmit to students in neurology and psychiatry the basic principles of the brain that he did so well.

With his supervisory work and investigation at the neuropathology laboratory, his neuropathology course, his fund raising for Lennox's work in epilepsy, and his teaching at the Massachusetts General Hospital, Cobb found the burden of private practice overwhelming. During the summer and fall of 1922 he was feeling physically and nervously exhausted, and on the advice of his physician, George Richards Minot, he decided to cut down on the teaching at the General. Then in December, 1922, he made arrangements to supplement his salary through the Epilepsy Committee in New York so that he could also give up the private practice that he had taken up as an economic necessity but never really had enjoyed. From then on he worked full time for over ten years and almost full time for the remainder of his professional life on teaching and research alone. He continued to see patients in consultation to help other doctors and to keep his own diagnostic acumen sharp, but he avoided as far as possible taking on patients for continuing care. The following paragraph from a letter to Edsall clearly expressed Cobb's distaste for practice:[52]

> Secondly, about this time, Mr. Howland had the annual meeting of the Epilepsy Committee. Previous to this I had talked to him about my desire to get rid of private practice and devote my energies to school and hospital without interruption. This is becoming increasingly irritating. I have restricted my hours to three mornings a week at the hospital, thus cutting down the number of patients, but their problems are urgent and interrupt my studies in a most disconcerting way. As a result the Committee are making me an offer of $3,000 a year (as noted in the copy of the minutes of the meeting, which I enclose). This salary, with my present school salary of about $4,500 would just about give me a living wage for the next two or three years. But it is not, perhaps, quite fair to my family to cut down on living expenses and savings as much as this $7,500 rate of income would necessitate. However, I want to do it very much.

The very responsibilities which led to Cobb's state of exhaustion in 1922 were also indications of his success and the degree to which he was permanently becoming established at Harvard. The children were six, four, and three years old. Mrs. Cobb's parents, Judge and Mrs. Charles Almy, owned approximately fifty acres of woodland with a thousand feet of shore front in Cotuit on Cape Cod. Sensing the ripeness of the moment, the Almys made available a fine tract of land overlooking Cotuit Harbor, and Mrs. Cobb's architect sister, Mary

Almy, was commissioned to design a cottage. During the winter of 1922–23 construction was accomplished, and the Cobbs had brief use of it the following summer before departing for two years of study in Europe.

Cobb's opportunity to study abroad came about through a series of coincidences stemming from the close relationship that he had maintained with Carl Binger, the old cadaver mate from medical school. Binger, doing physiological research at the Rockefeller Institute in New York in 1922, was sharing a bachelor apartment with Alan Gregg, who for many years dispensed medical grants for the Rockefeller Foundation.

One day, on the advice of Alan Gregg and Carl Binger, a depressed gentleman named Dr. Prudden came to Cobb, in Boston, for treatment. Subsequently, the depression lifted and Cobb received credit for the improvement. As a sequel to this happy episode, Cobb and his wife were invited to a supper party at Alan Gregg's and Carl Binger's apartment.

A letter from Binger to Cobb dated October 20, 1922, explained the circumstances that led to the invitation.[53] Binger said that Dr. Flexner[54] was very beholden to Cobb for his excellent treatment of Prudden who was well known to him. Binger went on to say that he had discussed with Flexner the importance of Cobb's work, and Flexner had expressed an interest in meeting him. Binger than made arrangements for the party later that fall.

The reception took place on Friday, November 24, 1922, the eve of the Harvard-Yale football game in New Haven. Binger had asked Cobb to give a talk at staff rounds the previous Wednesday, but that event did not take place. When Cobb and his wife entered Binger's and Gregg's apartment, they were overwhelmed. Both Dr. Simon Flexner and his brother Abraham, author of the Flexner Report, were there. Simon Flexner sidled up to Mrs. Cobb and said, "Tell me about yourself. Do you get to New York for the theatre very often? Do you keep up with the theatre world?" Overpowered, when she had an opportunity she asked Carl Binger, "Why are these people interested in me? What shall I say?" Binger replied, "Oh, just be yourself!" So Mrs. Cobb went on to describe her simple but hectic life in Ponkapoag and felt much more comfortable. The encounter with the Flexners led to a vast expansion of Stanley Cobb's world, through the European travel that was to follow and through financial support for his future work.

5
European Study, 1923–1925

By the time that he and his family sailed for England in October, 1923, Cobb had already demonstrated his ability as an investigator, clinician, teacher, and laboratory director. He had learned to seize the opportunities that came within his grasp and to pursue his objectives with an appropriate degree of flexibility. The trip to Europe was undertaken at the cost of some disruption of an established, well-coordinated program of activities in Boston, so that the period of time devoted to study abroad represented an act of faith. Cobb was not seeking a specific detailed field of knowledge or an immediately applicable technique but rather an opportunity to expand his horizon and to enrich his already demonstrated capacity for integrating bits of information acquired from a wide range of sources.

For Flexner, too, the venture was an act of faith. Flexner believed in Cobb's potential for further growth and for leadership in American medicine. Flexner thought that America was culturally behind the continent of Europe and that investigators here were severely handicapped by their comparative inability to communicate in foreign languages. So Flexner, who had limited knowledge of the opportunities in neuropathology abroad, was primarily interested in seeing his protégé master French and German, become familiar with the political scene, and saturate himself with exposure to art and music. Cobb readily accepted these objectives and added a few of his own. He wanted to make a wide range of professional contacts with neuropathologists, neurologists, and psychiatrists and to observe the differences in organization of the clinics and laboratories he was about to visit. Together with the challenge of attempting to master French and German, he had set for himself quite an assignment.

Cobb knew from the beginning that he wanted to spend some time in neurophysiology with Sir Charles Sherrington in Oxford, but it was obvious that he had to spend many months on the Continent in order to meet his language objective. Because there were limited clinical facilities in Oxford, it seemed wise to commence work in London, and Flexner wrote a letter to Sir Henry Head of Queen Square Hospital introducing Cobb. The letter, of September 26, 1923, was addressed to Head at his home, 4 Montagu Square, Hyde Park, and consisted only of the following paragraph:

> This letter will introduce to you Dr. Stanley Cobb of the Harvard Medical School who, as I wrote you, goes abroad for a long period of study in the field of neurology. Dr. Cobb will tell you what is on his and our minds. I shall be grateful to you beyond words if you will advise with him and give him such letters of introduction as he may need.[1]

A month later Head replied from his new house at 52 Montagu Square.[2] He said that Cobb had settled in for the winter and was already working at the National Hospital, Queen Square.

Flexner, who arranged to finance Cobb's trip,[3] gave Cobb letters of introduction also to Professor C. V. Ariens Kappers in Amsterdam[4] and Professor Heinrich Poll in Berlin.[5] During the entire two years when Cobb was abroad, he kept in close touch with Flexner, and Flexner continued to emphasize the importance of study in Berlin.

While he was studying in London, Cobb directed considerable energy into planning his course for the next two years, and he was helped in this by correspondence with his former chief, Adolf Meyer. In May, 1923, Cobb had written to Meyer outlining his trip as he then saw it, and he asked for Meyer's suggestions. The following paragraph indicates Cobb's ideas at that time:

> My first thought was to work a long period of time with Sherrington and then, after meeting and becoming familiar with the English neurologists, to go on the Continent. I have also thought of Amsterdam and of Cajal in Spain. Am I overlooking some good men in Switzerland or Italy? My tendency is to work on rather physiological problems in relation to neurology, and I would really rather work on the Continent than in England because I wish to become familiar with a language. Any hints . . . will be most helpful.[6]

When he received that letter, Meyer himself was about to set out on a trip to Europe. Later he wrote to Cobb recommending that he see Magnus and Winkler in Utrecht, Von Monakow in Zurich, and Oskar and Cecile Vogt in Berlin.[7]

On the other hand, Sir Henry Head at Queen Square was inclined to discourage study in Berlin. He said that three laboratories there had been combined and work was proceeding on a curtailed basis. So he recommended that Cobb go to Vienna instead. However, Cobb and Flexner both looked upon Vienna as too overrun by Americans and less suited to serious study than Berlin.

European Study

Cobb's trip was actually planned as it went along, with numerous changes in scheduling. However, in retrospect it encompassed five and one-half months in London, from mid-October, 1923, through March, 1924; several weeks in Puys, near Dieppe, during April, 1924; four months in Paris from May to August, with a side trip to Utrecht and Amsterdam; a three-week vacation near Angers from mid-August until early September; five and a half months in Berlin from September, 1924, through March, 1925; and then briefer stands in Florence, Zurich, Paris, and Oxford. The family embarked for home on the *S.S. Sachem* of the Furness Line on July 12, 1925.

The Cobbs' trip to England in October, 1923, was aboard the S.S. *Devonian* of the Leyland Line, which took them to Liverpool. The Cobbs were traveling *en famille* with their three children, Sidney, Helen, and John, as well as a nurse-companion named Miss Carroll.[8] On shipboard the Cobbs read Kipling's *History of England,* which, they felt, furnished a good general orientation. Cobb's first letter to his mother, written as they were gliding along the shore of Ireland, described the green sea and the enticing land half hidden in the haze.[9] The first week in London was spent at Worsley House, a sort of informal hotel made up of several old houses thrown together. Although it was not particularly attractive, it served as a base for seeking more satisfactory quarters, which Mrs. Cobb found at 28 Courtfield Gardens, South Kensington SW 5. This was a row house with a coating of stucco. Directly across the street was a triangular, secluded, fenced-in park where the children could play. The Cobbs were quite comfortable on a floor of this row house, where they lived until the end of March, 1924.

In London Cobb first met Henry Head, with whom he had previously corresponded. Head (1861–1940) was a physiologically oriented neurologist who had studied in the laboratories at Cambridge. His M.D. thesis in 1892 was on "Disturbances of Sensation, with Especial Reference to the Pain of Visceral Disease." Head's knowledge of pain, referred from deep structures, led him to study herpes zoster (shingles), and from there he proceeded to work on dermotomes.[10] Among other things, he studied sensory disturbances caused by disease processes within the brain, and he made significant contributions to knowledge of aphasia. Head was editor of the neurological journal *Brain* from 1910 to 1925. In 1927 the honor of knighthood was bestowed upon him. Although Cobb leaned heavily upon Head in planning his future course of study, the neurologist with whom he was most intimately associated was S. A. Kinnier Wilson (1878–1937).

Wilson was born in the state of New Jersey in America.[11] He was brought up and educated in Scotland and received his medical degree from the University of Edinburgh in 1902. After receiving a B.Sc. with honors from the University of Edinburgh in 1903 and completing a year of study abroad, he went to the National Hospital, Queen Square, as a house officer, and he spent the remainder of his fruitful career in that institution. In 1912, when he was thirty-three, he published his doctoral thesis on "Progressive Lenticular Degeneration: a Familial Nervous Disease Associated with Cirrhosis of the Liver," a disorder to this day known as Wilson's disease. When Cobb was at Queen Square in 1923 and 1924, Wilson was working on the "Old Motor System and the New." Cobb was assigned as a clinical clerk to Wilson and hence saw more of him than of any other neurologist.

Cobb repeatedly referred to Queen Square as a wonderful neurological museum. He said that it contained much that was hopeless and depressing, but if taken as a great collection of nature's experiments on the central nervous system it was a great place to learn in, and it gave one an idea of what the problems in neurology really were.

In a letter to his brother-in-law, Chandler Foot, dated March 12, 1924, Cobb summarized his experiences there.[12] He said that his work had been very worthwhile. He added that he had met a large number of clinical neurologists and a smaller number of laboratory workers. In addition to Wilson, he had been influenced at Queen Square by Gordon Holmes, with whom he had been making rounds once a week. A remarkably logical diagnostician, Holmes had just been made an editor of *Brain*. In his letter to Foot, Cobb said that he had also been impressed by Sir Farquhar Buzzard and James S. Collier. Collier was universally recognized as a great clinician, although he was one of the older staff members more interested at that time in his own patients than in teaching. In the same letter to his brother-in-law Cobb mentioned attending a meeting of the Physiological Society at which there were eight or ten physiologists of international reputation, including Charles Sherrington, John N. Langley, J. B. S. Haldane, A. V. Hill, and Cobb's own contemporary, Lord Adrian.

Cobb went on to describe the miserable state of general pathology in England. He said, however, that there were specialized clinics and laboratories where the pathology was outstanding. He mentioned in

European Study

particular the work of J. Godwin Greenfield at Queen Square. Cobb saw Greenfield as a quiet and unassuming man with good judgment and a wealth of rare pathological specimens to study. On February 8, 1924, Cobb wrote to his father about some of the work he had done in Greenfield's laboratory:

> At present there are a good many lectures by various good men to keep me busy. A new course is under way at Queen Square, and I attend some of the lectures and clinics, but mostly go around with Wilson and Holmes. I am writing up some cases for Wilson that he wants published, and in the laboratory with Greenfield I am cutting and staining some rat brains to study the effects of manganese. This work is for a man named Findlay at the Imperial Cancer Research, who was working along lines parallel to the work Mella and I did last year. If I get these two things done, I will leave England with a feeling of pretty well rounding off the job. Tell Hiddy [Mrs. Henry Forbes, Cobb's sister and technician at the Harvard Neuropathology Laboratory] that I am beginning to learn about technique, staining with Weigert, Victoria Blue, Bielschowsky, Nissl, etc. You see over here I can learn what I am already expected to know without damaging my precious prestige—there being nobody under me. It is a great chance.[13]

An incident of some interest during Cobb's stay in London was a visit to Cambridge which had been arranged by his double first cousin, Candler Cobb, at that time also in London with his wife, Beatrice. The invitation was to visit Dr. MacCurdy, a Canadian, who was a fellow at Corpus Christi College and a lecturer in psychopathology. In a letter to his mother, dated December 3, 1923, Cobb described the occasion:[14]

> So I went up Wednesday night and dined with him "in hall" at the "high table" on the right of the Provost. Then all retired to the combination room where the port was passed around for an hour and collegiate affairs discussed. While the port went around we ate nuts and apples, but no one smoked until the decanter was corked—it would have been an insult to the port. After they broke up MacCurdy and Adrian and I sat up in MacCurdy's rooms until after midnight and had the most interesting talk on nerves, brains, education, etc. Adrian is a delightful friend of Alexander Forbes and a well known authority on the physiology of the nervous system.

While Cobb was engaged in his studies at Queen Square, Mrs. Cobb and the children were maintaining a family life at 28 Courtfield Gardens. (When the author visited here in 1976, the house was in moderately good repair but situated in a deteriorating neighborhood.) Young Sidney Cobb, aged eight, was in a private school and the younger children were taught by their mother at home. Mrs. Cobb was involved in a good deal of entertaining, particularly having tea with the wives of Queen Square staff members. Moreover, the Cobbs frequently attended concerts, the opera, and visited museums. Writing to his father on January 20, 1924, Cobb said:

> Yesterday morning I sketched another bit of the Thames at Chelsea, and we also explored the Chelsea waterfront a bit. In the afternoon we took Helen to a picture gallery and showed her a few Landseers, etc. She has been asking to see pictures and is doing very good artistic work of the neolithic type; so we have hopes.[15]

In a letter to his mother a week later Cobb reported news of visits to still more art galleries and of his own tastes in art:

> We have made visits to the Tate Gallery and the collection at the Victoria and Albert Museum. I am trying to get ideas about water colors; so Turner interests me a good deal, but most of his oils are disappointing except one or two superb ones of Venice. Of the English painters I like Millais best; the brilliance of color and interest of subject is far ahead of any of the others. Perhaps I haven't seen enough Reynolds and Gainsboroughs yet, but I have not been much impressed by them.[16]

On Sundays the Cobbs often attended a worship service conducted by the feminist clergywoman, Maude Royden, at her Guild House. On January 15, 1924, Cobb had written to his mother about the services. He said that Maude Royden was the best preacher he had ever heard. (She would have liked to be ordained in the Church of England, but at that time was ineligible because women were not admitted to the ministry.) He went on to say in his letter:

> Most of her talk is a bit radical, but very humanely radical—and few people who mingle with the misery of the world remain in the ranks of the conservatives. This is another reason why she will find it difficult to get into the Church of England. But if the "Church" keeps up its attempts to join with Rome, there will be such a reaction that M.R. may well get her chance. In fact the whole scene over here is set for a fine turnover—they only lack Cromwell—and I certainly hope he won't turn up. Things will probably work out better without him.[17]

During the month of March, 1924, the Cobbs were busy "scoring off" their social obligations. They held a high tea one afternoon to repay a number of these debts. One night they invited MacPherson and his wife to dinner, along with Dr. and Mrs. Riddoch. George Riddoch, a Scotsman, had met Head during World War I when serving in a military hospital for traumatic paraplegias and head injuries. He

European Study

later became Head's favorite pupil and protégé and he wrote extensively on reflex functions of the completely divided spinal cord in men. And, with Head, in 1918 he published a famous monograph on the cord bladder.[18] It is of interest to note that MacPherson had preceded Cobb at U.S. Army General Hospital No. 11 in Cape May, New Jersey, before transfer to Europe with the head injury unit. Obviously MacPherson and Riddoch had many common interests and experiences.[19]

Before their departure from London, the Cobbs were also busy with trips to the countryside, catching up on places which they had wanted to visit. There were excursions to nearby landmarks such as Hampton Court and Windsor Castle. On a more ambitious outing they took in Stonehenge and Salisbury. One day Cobb went by himself to Oxford and had tea with Lady Osler, an American girl from Canton, Massachusetts, who remembered well the Cherry Hill Tavern, where the Cobbs lived in Ponkapoag.[20] She even showed Cobb a picture of the Blue Hill in Milton, which was visible from the tavern. That day Cobb spent the morning in Sherrington's laboratory, but Sherrington was ill. The afternoon was devoted to exploring some of the colleges before returning to London.

Perhaps the high point of the last-minute travel program was a visit to Mrs. Frank Millet at her home in Broadway, one of the most picturesque of the Cotswold villages.[21] Mrs. Millet, the mother of Cobb's medical school classmate, Jack, had invited the Cobbs for a weekend. After a train trip to Hingham the Cobbs walked six miles to Stowe-on-the-Wold where they had lunch and then went by auto to Broadway, a community of artists, where once Rossetti, Burne-Jones, and Morris lived together. Recent American artists there included LaFarge, Abbey, and Mrs. Millet's husband. Mrs. Millet's home, which she called Russell House, afforded the ultimate in luxurious living. On Sunday morning the Cobbs were awakened by maids in white caps with tea. The rolling hills and the bracing March air reminded Cobb of Stockbridge, Massachusetts, where Jack Millet and his wife, Alice, were living while on the staff of the Austen Riggs Foundation. Sunday afternoon the Cobbs walked across the flat garden country to Honey-Bourne and thence returned to London by train.

A letter to Cobb's father on April 2, 1924, indicated that the trunks were all packed and on the following day the family would cross the English Channel to Dieppe and then settle at the Hotel des Terraces in Puys.[22] The children were recovering from whooping cough, and Helen still was having some paroxysms, which added to the discomforts of the stormy channel crossing.

The Hotel des Terraces was a shabby old building. When the Cobbs arrived it had no other guests. However, during the two weeks of their visit others came in. The service and the atmosphere were good. It was a time of much needed vacation for Mrs. Cobb, who had been tied down in London with all the housekeeping and the care of her three children, who part of the time were ill. Cobb did some painting with his water colors (page 78) and spent a great deal of time making a census of the birds native to the area. He discussed these activities in a letter to Chandler Foot on April 16, 1924:

> The cliffs here are gorgeous, 150–200 feet high, of white and dry chalk with brown streaks. Naturally I have taken vigorously to sketching, and some of the results are favorable. I have advanced to water colors, and I think I will probably stay there because of the ease of transport and the greater speed with which one gets effect. Back of the cliffs are broad fields, with big horses dragging harrows, usually it seems in silhouette against the sky.
>
> The birds are quite exciting, everything new, and I have seen twenty-five species, or rather identified twenty-five, here. Many get by me, and it seems queer to hear songs and not be sure whether the voice originates from a wren, a redbreast, or a finch. . . . My list for this place reads: carrion crow 10, jackdaw 300, green finch 6, magpie 6, house sparrow 22, tree sparrow 10, chaffinch 60, brambling 1, skylark 200, yellow hammer (a sparrow) 15, blue tit 4, willow tit 2, blackcap 4, blackbird 6, wren 12, redbreast (locally "rouge gorge") 30, hedge accentor 6, green woodpecker 1, kestrel 30, cormorant 25, gannet 1, common scoter 150, herring gull 260, black headed gull 200, swallow 15, and of course many unidentified fellows.[23]

After a side trip to Rouen, where Joan of Arc was burned at the stake, the Cobbs moved on to Paris and initially stayed in an unattractive pension for several days. Then they moved to the home of a family named Seailles at 22 Rue de Verrières in Antony (Seine), a community twenty miles directly south of Paris, readily accessible in eighteen minutes on a fast train. The family with whom the Cobbs stayed was not dull. Mme. Seailles was a delightful Greek woman, who sang at times under the name Madame Sparanga Calo. Monsieur was a long-haired Ph.D. of uncertain occupation, and there were three children about the ages of the Cobb offspring. It was a great advantage that English was only used for emergency situations and never at meals.

In Paris Cobb did not have a Henry Head to guide his professional activities. He was much more responsible for his choice of work than had been the case in London. He knew about Jean L'Hermitte at *L'Ecòle de Médecine,* who was considered the leading neuropathologist in Paris. L'Hermitte welcomed Cobb and allowed him to work in the laboratory, which became his base of operations in Paris. Cobb spent most of his time there working up a single case. He cut the sections of brain tissue and did all the staining himself. He said it was not very advanced work, but he really needed the training in techniques and in straight pathology, and furthermore he wanted to know how the laboratory was organized and how the various functions were conducted. L'Hermitte planned to publish the work which Cobb did there, and Cobb did make an effort to prepare a manuscript. However, this research does not appear among Cobb's published works.

Cobb rounded out his work in Paris by spending two mornings a week at the Salpêtrière, a great almshouse where some seventy years earlier the famous neurologist, Charcot, had organized neuropathology, clinical neurology, and psychiatry into one of the most brilliant clinics to be found anywhere in the world. Jean Martin Charcot, himself a neuropathologist and clinician, had worked on the cerebral localization of Jacksonian [unilateral] epilepsy; had put his stamp on locomotor ataxia by describing the associated arthropathies now known as Charcot joints; and had made an outstanding contribution in sorting out the key triad of manifestations in multiple sclerosis. He attracted a strong group of students and followers at the Salpêtrière. However, he was best known during his lifetime for his outstanding work on hysteria. He made hypnosis respectable, and his work in psychopathology afforded a base for the subsequent studies of Pierre Janet (who later so powerfully influenced the Boston School) and the young neurologist Sigmund Freud. When Cobb was working at the Salpêtrière, Georges Guillain had just become the new professor. Guillain, perhaps most widely known for his contribution to understanding of the Guillain-Barré syndrome, was a good lecturer, but Cobb did not have as warm a relationship with him as he did with L'Hermitte.

Cobb later reviewed his professional experiences in Paris in a long letter he sent to Adolf Meyer in January, 1925. In addition to his work with L'Hermitte at *L'Ecôle de Médecine* and with Guillain at the Salpetrière, Cobb had visited other workers in their clinics and laboratories. He said he was a bit disappointed in the neuropathology. He thought L'Hermitte was probably the best, but occasionally he was hasty and slipshod in his methods. Next in line came Charles Foix, possibly outshining L'Hermitte as a clinicopathologist. However, Cobb said that both L'Hermitte and Foix were outstanding clinical neurologists, along with many others.

> In fact Paris is alive with clever diagnosticians. It certainly is a wit sharpening experience. L'Hermitte especially pleased me, for he reads extensively and is ever alert to bring up his new ideas on the ward. In this way I have been lucky in my two principal teachers, for Wilson has a similar mind—active and stimulating in the extreme—but inclined to jump uncritically into new ideas at times.[24]

Cobb said he had also seen Janet a few times but could learn little of his work because Janet mostly conducted a private practice from his own office.

The family life at Antony was generally happy with Mrs. Cobb and Sidney making great strides in learning French. Helen was slower but when angered she would express herself freely. Cobb said that the younger son, Jock, was behind and that he himself was quite handicapped by embarrassment over his speech disorder. In general the Cobbs and the Seailles got on well together, but a complication arose when the children had to be kept apart because of impetigo.

While living at Antony the Cobbs had a number of social engagements, mostly with old friends from the United States. One of the most significant was a visit from Abraham Flexner, who came for dinner one evening in May. He was extremely pleasant and the Cobbs related to him comfortably. However, Cobb became convinced that Flexner did not merely chat along but had a purpose behind his conversation. Flexner drew Cobb out on his reactions to the political situation in Europe and to the cultural opportunities there, and Cobb agreed that, in general, America was far behind the old world in popular appreciation of music, literature, and art. After Flexner went home Cobb began to mull over the effect of cheap magazines, newspapers, moving pictures, and radio broadcasting in diverting people from serious literature. He said that he personally never let a Sunday newspaper inside his house nor read a magazine story except on Christmas or the Fourth of July.

In mid-June Bill Herman, who had completed his internship with Meyer at the Phipps and his year with Campbell in Boston, made an appearance and obtained a room at the Seailles pension at Antony. He wanted to devote the summer to learning French. He and the Cobbs spent one delightful day going by rail to Chartres to see the cathedral. Cobb thought that the great rose window was the most beautiful man-

European Study

made thing he had ever seen. Toward the end of July he and Herman made a visit together to the Louvre, and Herman was able to point out a number of interesting features in the work of Monet, Degas, and Manet. Cobb liked Monet's paintings the best because of the use of color and light. Herman's path was to cross that of the Cobbs several times during the next year, with subsequent meetings in Brittany and in Amsterdam.

The day after Herman and Cobb visited the Louvre, there arrived in Antony for a walk and dinner Charles Hopkinson, the well-known Boston artist, and his family. Hopkinson later was commissioned to paint the portrait of Cobb which hangs in the Herman Room at the Massachusetts General Hospital.

In a letter to Chandler Foot dated September 21, 1924, Cobb colorfully described his impressions of the Seailles household:

> You would have enjoyed to the limit the pension we inhabited in the suburbs. It was a rule that we all talked French at meals. Usually the table consisted of our family, four other Americans, four or five Greeks, two Englishmen, one Spaniard, one Pole, and one real Frenchman. The Pole was a lady of eighty-five, who sat beside me and suffered from a senile psychosis which caused her to repeat one incident several times over—but that was excellent for my French. You can imagine the babel of the rest of the table. When Bill Herman arrived in July he was hopeless at French, but plunged in and talked loud and laboriously, recounting risque incidents to the huge delight of everybody. He did learn remarkably quickly, however, and by September was talking quite decently.[25]

Another social event during the time when the Cobbs were at the Seailles's was dinner once again with Cobb's colleague, MacPherson, and his wife. This time Herman was present along with Dr. Stack of London. And, one night the Cobbs dined out with James Howard Means, the new Jackson Professor of Clinical Medicine at Harvard, and Mrs. Means. In addition to the social and recreational activities which took place while Cobb was in Paris, there were two important professional trips. One was to visit the great neuroscientists of Holland and the other a preliminary visit to Professor Heinrich Poll in Berlin to sense what opportunity there might be for Cobb to work there for several months.

In early June Cobb sent a long and detailed account of his Dutch trip to his mother.[26] He went by way of Brussels, and because the railroad schedule had changed on June first, he missed his connection. Missing the train afforded him an opportunity to visit the Wiertz

Museum, the big general art museum, and the museum of natural history. The Wiertz Museum was what intrigued Cobb. It was a one-man show with three rooms of Wiertz's paintings. They were complicated, extensive canvases in the style of Rubens with many of the objects intentionally distorted. Cobb had with him on the trip Dr. Walter Kraus of New York, an old classmate from the Harvard class of 1910, who was also abroad at the time. After arriving in Amsterdam and bedding down for the night, Cobb and Kraus visited the Brain Institute the morning following. That afternoon Cobb went to hear a lecture by Professor Brouwer, who talked in Dutch. However, an intern served as a translator, so that Cobb knew something of what was said.

The following day Cobb went over to Utrecht where he spent the afternoon with Cornelis Winkler (1855–1941). Winkler had founded a school of neuroanatomy which afforded training for many renowned pupils including Brouwer, whom Cobb had heard lecture the previous day, and Ariens Kappers, to whom Flexner had written a note of introduction but whom Cobb did not actually see. Winkler was a man with a spectographic view of neurology, extending all the way from the simplest reflexology to the borderland of philosophy. Cobb described him as a most delightful man of sixty-seven or so. He headed a fine neuropsychiatric institute much like the Phipps in Baltimore, combining both neurology and psychiatry. Winkler was most cordial. He immediately took Cobb to his house for tea and then, after showing him the wards and laboratories, took him home again for dinner.

The next day Cobb made a second visit to Utrecht, this time to see Professor Rudolf Magnus (1873–1927), a man of gigantic intellect, who after obtaining a background in sophisticated physiological chemistry had worked with Sherrington in Liverpool on the neural regulation of bodily movement. He was then professor of pharmacology at Utrecht. His laboratory was in an old church. Magnus aroused more enthusiasm in Cobb than anyone else whom he had met. Magnus was relatively young at fifty-one. He had two assistants and some students working with him. Their work on the cerebellum and the basal ganglia particularly interested Cobb, who wanted very much to go back and spend an extended period of time there. However, he decided that his need to learn German took precedence. He returned to Paris with great admiration and respect for Brouwer, Winkler, and Magnus and the work that was being done in Holland.

At the end of July Cobb followed up a letter from Flexner introducing him to Professor Poll by making a quick journey to Berlin, and on the twenty-first he wrote to his mother about the trip.[27] The letter was mostly about the appearance of the city, art, and the political outlook of the citizens. The following day he met Poll, who was most cordial, and was introduced to the Vogts, who also were friendly. The Vogts devoted several hours to showing Cobb their laboratory and then took him to their home for lunch, during which he spoke a mixture of English, German, and French, but mostly French, for Mrs. Vogt had come from France.[28] Later Cobb told his brother-in-law, Harry Forbes, that Vogt was a strong drawing card for him.[29] He had a fine laboratory, with plenty of spirit, great precision, and conservatism. He told Forbes that the work was a little too much along his own line and in some ways he would have liked to branch out more. However, Cobb saw Vogt as the leader in neuropathology at the time and he made the decision to go to Berlin in September.

The die was cast, and plans were beginning to take shape. The family was to go to Rheims on August 10 for the day and then on August 16 was to move to Champtoce, near Angers (Marne-et-Loire), for a two-week visit with Cobb's college roommate, Gerard Gignoux, who (as was noted before) had married a French girl and had purchased a renovated twelfth-century chateau.

The last week in Antony was given over mostly to packing and working. Cobb finished writing up his case for L'Hermitte and left it with him to be gone over in the fall. The last evening, the Seailles opened champagne for a farewell party. Dining and singing went on until half after ten. The next day the Cobbs were on their way.

Gignoux's chateau had been substantially rebuilt and had four bathrooms. It was situated about ten miles from Angers in the midst of a great park in which there were gardens and vineyards. Gignoux and his wife lived quite simply amidst it all, enjoying the peacefulness and the ancient traditions. They devoted their time to making wine, raising cattle, churning butter, and keeping domestic animals. While visiting Gignoux the Cobbs had an opportunity to drive through some of the old roads and tiny villages in the area.

On September 1 Cobb and his wife took a private vacation, leaving the children with Miss Carroll at the Gignoux chateau. They went to Benodet, in the southwest corner of Brittany at the mouth of the river running up to Quimper. Cobb was impressed by the Celtic appearance of the peasants in Brittany. He said that with their brown eyes, high cheek bones, and long upper lips they might have come from Ireland very easily. He was impressed by the fishermen and their clumsy boats with orange, brown, and blue sails. The gorgeous colors made him want to paint. He said he thought the people must love color, "for the fishermen wore duck suits dyed magenta and orange, which fade and get streaky into the best color you ever saw."[30]

One day, after their return to Champtoce, the Cobbs and Gignoux made a motor trip to Mont Saint Michel, where on the causeway they came upon Herman with Cobb's secretary, Susan Hale, and Mrs. Cobb's close friend, Sarah Evarts, who was later to become head of Cobb's social service department at the Massachusetts General Hospital.[31] Herman and Susan were traveling together, although their marriage was still in the future, and Sarah Evarts, Susan's best friend, was along in a dual capacity as companion and chaperone. The Cobbs and Gignoux shared another happy day with Herman, Sue Hale, and Sarah Evarts. They went together on a trip to Caen, where they saw the Abbaye aux Hommes, the Abbaye aux Dames, and the Bayeux tapestry depicting scenes of the Norman Conquest.

The time for departure was soon at hand, and on September fourteenth the Cobbs boarded the H.M.S.P. *Ohio* at Cherbourg en route to Hamburg via Southampton. On the fifteenth Cobb wrote to his mother that the vessel was excellent and the channel crossing was calm.[32] In Southampton they were berthed next to the giant steamships *Leviathan* and *Majestic*. The trip through the North Sea was also smooth and pleasant. They docked at Hamburg in the afternoon of the sixteenth. The Cobbs stayed in Hamburg two days, during which Cobb visited the big psychiatric hospital. Then they moved on to Berlin, where initially they stayed at a small hotel frequented by Quakers. Soon, however, they moved to the home of Freifrau von Reibnitz in Grünewald, a suburb about three and a half miles from Vogt's laboratory.

Freifrau von Reibnitz was a femme fatale. She was a Junker and a nationalist, who correctly foresaw a future war of revenge. At one point she had a portrait of Kaiser Wilhelm II hanging in the Cobbs' room. Her first husband, a colonel, whom she married at sixteen, was a cousin of the Kaiser. However, eleven years later she separated from him and married the baron, with whom she lived for fourteen years before divorcing him, too. Even though she maintained friendly relations with both men and had them together at her parties, she referred to herself in conversation as a war widow.³³ She was an opinionated, overbearing, demanding, unreasonable woman, extremely difficult to get on with, yet she had a good heart which was manifested by the number of unfortunate people, sometimes known as "strays," whom she befriended. In time Mrs. Cobb became genuinely fond of her. Her home in Grünewald was not far from the Wannsee, a beautiful lake where the family had frequent afternoon outings. The Cobbs were comfortable at the Von Riebnitz home and remained there during the time they were in Berlin.

In his work at the Neurobiologischen Institut der Universität Berlin Cobb was associated with two men of great distinction: Vogt and Bielschowsky. From Weil's thumbnail sketch of Bielschowsky,³⁴ one gains the impression of Vogt as a plodding worker with a life-time project in mind, while Bielschowsky was more flexible, more open to human contact, and a better administrator. The Neurobiologischen Universitäts-Laboratorium, where Bielschowsky first went to work in 1904 when under the direction of Oskar Vogt, became in 1924 the Institut für Hirnforschung der Kaiser Wilhelm Gesellschaft, with Bielschowsky as its director. It is easy to understand from this reversal of responsibility why Henry Head tried to discourage Cobb from going to Berlin and why Cobb was, in fact, to encounter some uneasiness or friction in the relationship between these two men. With his work on the Myeloarchitektonik of the brain, Vogt was attempting to study the lamellae photographically in such detail that a relationship could be established between brain structure and psychiatric disorders. In fact, three years later, at the Deutsche Anstaltsforschung für Psychiatric in Munich, which grew out of a need to understand the types of mental disorders that Kraepelin had classified, Vogt was awarded the Kraepelin Medal for exactly this work. Vogt's approach, therefore, was of enormous importance to Cobb, who himself was trying to relate disturbances of function to tissue morphology.

The opportunity to work with Vogt and Bielschowsky simultaneously—even with the friction—was a happy one, for Vogt was primarily interested in stains for brain cells and nerve fibers, while Cobb was concerned with finding a microscopic method of visualizing the cerebral blood vessels. The work which Cobb did with Vogt was to study the Cytoarchitektonik and the Myeloarchitektonik of the area striata of three brains (39), yet his real interest, it has been noted, was in the blood supply. Bielschowsky was able to help because in his early work on multiple sclerosis he had studied with Weigert and had become an authority on staining techniques. He had made a number of studies on the silver impregnation of nerve fibers, and this knowledge was extraordinarily helpful. With Cobb, he worked out a method for intravital staining with silver ammonium oxide solution (39) which Cobb was able to put to use after his return to Boston in his studies of cerebral circulation.

The cultural activities in Berlin included the opera—*Meistersinger* was the favorite—, concerts, and brief trips to such places as Potsdam, Leipzig, and Dresden. Two social events are of interest. One night the Cobbs went to Bielschowsky's home for a musical evening. Bielschowsky and three other violinists played as a quartet. The playing was good and the evening delightful. Cobb said that when the conversations were brief, between the musical numbers, he could get on very well. On the other hand, a completely conversational evening would have overwhelmed him. Another evening, in February, the Cobbs dined with Oskar and Cecile Vogt, along with Herman, the MacPhersons and the Tracy Putnams who, providentially, were in town, having come up from Vienna where they were staying.

Before leaving Berlin, Cobb engaged in some correspondence about plans for life in Boston after the trip was over. He wrote a number of letters to James B. Ayer,[35] the associate professor in charge of the clinical work at the Massachusetts General Hospital, about utilizing Frank Fremont-Smith as his administrative assistant in place of Mella. In a letter on February 4, he indicated that he had received a noncommittal but encouraging letter from Flexner about continued funding after his return.[36]

Cobb was already feeling saltwater running in his veins. He wanted to get out onto Nantucket Sound after his return, and in a letter to his father at this time he recalled a comment his father had once made about possibly some day sharing the ownership of a boat:

> My only criticism of you is that you were too generous and have forgotten the relative importance of things. In a memorable letter to me, written on the Fall River boat last year, you said that the really worthwhile things in life lay between Monomoy Point and Cuttyhunk (including Muskeget) . . . that money ought to go into a boat for you to cruise on, and I'll come along (it will be a fight to see who is cook and who is captain). Perhaps we can let Betty be captain.[37]

When Mr. Cobb received the letter he enthusiastically offered to help with the financing. The yawl *Pamaho* was purchased and was used

European Study

every year from 1925 to 1935, though perhaps more by Cobb than by his father.

On about March 4 the Cobbs pulled up stakes in Berlin and went to Munich for a few days, while Cobb made flying trips to Copenhagen and Vienna. Mrs. Cobb wrote to her mother on March 10 from Munich that they had been there six days and that Cobb's father and mother had joined them for a period of several weeks.[38] On the agenda was a trip to Italy.

About March 15 the family group finally boarded the train for Florence and arrived at five forty-five the following afternoon. They spent eleven days there, largely exhausting their backs and lower extremities viewing the art and seeing the landmarks. On March 26, Mrs. Cobb informed her mother:

> I don't know where we are going from here yet. Mr. Cobb believes in endless contemplation over plans. The only difference between him and Stanley and me is that he contemplates and continues to contemplate because it is his philosophy of life, and we do it because we can't make up our minds.[39]

Actually they went to Interlaken, Switzerland, on about the twenty-seventh and were delightfully comfortable there. Charles Almy, Junior, Mrs. Cobb's brother, joined them for two days, on one of which they roped him to the crowd and walked over the upper glacier at Grünewald. The next day they climbed a mountain with him. On March 31, 1935, the family took an electric railway to Wengenalp at five thousand feet, and another to seven thousand feet, above the timber line. After returning to Wengenalp Cobb made a watercolor, while his wife wrote a letter to her mother.[40] Subsequently they took a railway to Sheidegg, the farthest point that service ran at that time of year. Mrs. Cobb said that they were within seven thousand feet of the summit of the Jungfrau. In a letter to his sister, Hildegarde Forbes, and her husband, Harry, Cobb described the outlook from there:

> Perhaps the most beautiful trip was the drive up Lauterbrunnen Valley; but the most awe inspiring was certainly that up to Sheidegg, at about 7,800 feet on the slope of the Jungfrau's shoulder; so you look across a great dazzling white amphitheatre, at the main peak about three miles away and seven thousand feet above us.[41]

The family drove from Interlaken to Zurich via Lucerne where they had lunch, and on April 6, when Cobb wrote the above letter, he went on to say that they had good accommodations and could see most of Switzerland from his father's window.

The key neuroscientists whom Cobb saw in Zurich were Constantine von Monakow, whom Meyer had recommended so highly, and his associate Minkowsky. In a letter that Adolf Meyer wrote to Cobb on February 19, 1925, he had described Monakow as a thorough worker much like Vogt, although more temperamental.[42] Monakow's longtime interest had been the choroid plexes. Among the psychiatrists, Meyer hoped that Cobb could see Eugen Bleuler, the chief at the Burghölzli, and his assistant, Maier, as well as Ulrich. Cobb replied to Meyer on April tenth about his experiences.[43] He spent two days in Monakow's laboratory and was truly impressed by the quality of the work and the cheerful environment. Then Maier, who had been away, came back and Cobb saw him and Ulrich too. Unfortunately Bleuler was away at the time. Of these encounters Cobb wrote:

> Ulrich is most cordial. I went to his hospital twice and had fine talks with him—or rather got him talking and sat back, for my German isn't equal to great reciprocity. . . . Professor Maier appealed to me, too. I like his keen, good sense; his ward rounds are excellent, and I picked up some good points from him.

In the same letter Cobb told Meyer about a dinner that he and his friend Harry Murray had with Jung. Murray at that time was an embryologist with the Rockefeller Institute in New York. He later succeeded Morton Prince as director of the Harvard Psychological Clinic. Moreover, Murray was the analytic psychologist with whom Bill Herman and Irmarita Putnam were associating during their Jungian days. Cobb and Murray both suffered from stammering, and they sought an opportunity to meet Jung and discuss this common problem with him. Cobb described the occasion:

> Through a friend who is working with Jung I had a prize dinner and evening. We three, Jung, Murray, and I, ate, talked, and imbibed local wine from eight until twelve-thirty. Jung opened up and was amusing, humorous, and interesting. He certainly is an attractive personality. Then by talking with Murray and discussing Psychological Types, etc., I feel as if I got a good picture of the man and his work.

Dr. Margaret C.-L. Gildea, later one of Cobb's associates, obtained the denouement of the story from Harry Murray.[44] According to her version Cobb and Murray did indeed talk with Jung about their stammering. Having spent a year in Zurich from 1930 to 1931, she knew well his humor and his warmth as well as his admiration for Americans and for professors. After Cobb and Murray had each developed their theme, she could well imagine Jung saying, "Don't at all costs give up stammering. It is most attractive to women." In Cobb's letter to Meyer, he did not mention the stammering. However, in a recent interview[45] Murray elaborated upon the story and remembered Jung's advice was "Don't at all costs give up stammering. It is most sexually exciting to women." Murray said that at the time the remark struck him as funny and he laughed, but Cobb was obviously embarrassed.

In a letter Cobb sent to Hildegarde and Harry Forbes he retold the story much as he did to Meyer.[46] He thought that Jung was indeed a most remarkable man, a bit too interested in dreams and world interpretation of neurotic phenomena, but very helpful to people in treatment and provocative of creative thinking. He went on to say that Jung was whimsical and humorous, saw the weaknesses in his own theories, and was delighted to discuss them—a rare personality. But Cobb did not mention a word about the discussion on stammering.

From Zurich the Cobbs departed for Paris on the night train on April 10.[47] They checked in the following day at the Grosvenor Hotel. While in Paris they saw several plays including *L'Aiglon* and *Macbeth*. Cobb's brother Augustus was there part of the time. One evening the people from Antony came in for a gala dinner, and one afternoon Mrs. Cobb went out there with the children. Then the Cobb parents fitted out her wardrobe as a gesture of appreciation for the two weeks together.

On April 17 the Cobbs crossed the channel and by the next day were safely in their new abode at 10 Lathbury Road, Oxford. The house, which had been engaged by correspondence, was a bit too snug to put up company. However, it came complete with the two servants of its owners, Mr. and Mrs. Steele. Sidney immediately started at the school, which had a fine reputation. By April twenty-seventh, when Mrs. Cobb wrote to her mother again, two bicycles and a punt had been acquired. The Cobbs had discovered a nearby riding stable where they could get good horses and ponies for three shillings, sixpence per hour.

Social life came promptly. Lady Osler had called and Jack Cabot, a cousin in Brasenose College, had been to dinner. The Cobbs had tea twice with the John Fultons of New Haven, and Dr. Lewis A. Bremer, the histologist from Harvard, came that same day.

The day that the Cobbs arrived in Oxford was a Saturday, and Cobb went immediately to the physiology laboratory, where he watched John Fulton conduct an experiment in muscle contraction. Later Cobb collaborated with Fulton on some work involving red (skeletal) muscle. The work did not get written up for four years and proved an embarrassment to both Fulton and Cobb, who in other writings had quoted it and inserted reference numbers which led nowhere. In 1928, Fulton decided the time had come to remedy the matter and took the occasion of Lady Osler's death to bring up the delicate situation with Cobb.

When writing to Cobb on September 11 about Lady Osler, Fulton closed his letter with the following paragraph:

> I am glad to have the notes concerning red muscle. Alas! I am a worse procrastinator than you. However, I shall try to make amends and put together a suitable note. As you referred to our forthcoming paper and I have also, in my book, we ought to do something albeit our original observations were meagre.[48]

Cobb's reply was brief and to the point:

> As to the paper on red muscle, go ahead in any way you believe wise and make it as brief as you wish. We merely ought to have a peg to hang the reference onto.[49]

John Fulton later worked mostly as a medical historian at Yale. He and his wife, Lucia, remained longtime friends of the Cobbs.

The work with Sherrington himself was exciting, although brief and punctuated with a number of interruptions. Cobb did not really have time to dig in and achieve a major piece of work. In fact, after the trip was over, Cobb observed that the best length of time to stay in a place was either six hours, in which one could meet the people and see the facilities, or six months, which can be long enough to become really involved. The brief stays in between proved frustrating. He discussed this subject in a letter to his sister Hildegarde:

> I find Sherrington's laboratory most ineresting.... The experiments are certainly most important neurologically. In fact, six months with Sir Charles is worth ten years in an out patient department. I wish I saw more of him, of course. He is very busy with his Royal Society but Wednesday I operated with him three times on three cats, two of which died—so now we feel quite comrade-like, and I'm not afraid of him any more. In fact, he is most shy and modest.[50]

In mid-May the Cobbs made a brief trip to Paris for the centenary of the birth of Charcot. One night during their stay in Paris they gave a dinner party for Professor and Mrs. L'Hermitte, Professor and Frau Brouwer from Amsterdam, as well as Gordon Holmes and Godwin Greenfield of London. Mrs. Cobb wrote, "I confess I was a good deal terrified of so many great people all at my table, but it went off well. They all knew each other by name and by writings, but had never met—so it was interesting."[51] On the way back to Oxford the Cobbs stopped over at Bruges, a walled city filled with early Flemish paintings. There was a little museum there, a room in an ancient hospital, with about ten Memlings, all perfectly superb, and exactly in their natural settings.

Before going back to the United States the Cobbs had an opportunity to make one more brief trip to Holland, from June 21 to June 25. After their channel crossing they were met by Bill Herman, who showed them around the Hague. He took them to the "Maurits House," a beautiful little museum, and then to a private collection where there were a number of Van Goghs. After lunch they went on to Amsterdam, where Cobb had an opportunity to chat with Cornelius V. Ariens Kappers, whom he had missed on his previous visit. Kappers was a brilliant comparative anatomist who had expanded Edinger's previous concepts about the neo-, archi-, and paleosubdivisions of the brain.[52] The relationship between these new and old parts of the brain to cerebral physiology was of particular interest to Cobb, especially in later life when he made comparative studies of avian anatomy. After his visit to Kappers, Cobb joined his wife who had gone ahead to the home of their host and hostess, Professor and Mrs. Brouwer. The Brouwers had a very old house on a canal. It was in spotless condition and Mrs. Brouwer, herself a physician, insisted that the Cobbs inspect every nook and cranny.

The next day, after a Dutch breakfast, with tea-to-raise-your-hair, eggs, toast, radishes, cheese, and grated chocolate, Cobb went to the hospital with Brouwer for rounds. Brouwer had four wards for neurology and a laboratory, more or less the kind of arrangement that Cobb wanted to develop in Boston after his return.

Tracy and Irmarita Putnam, who were working in Brouwer's laboratory at the time, joined the Cobbs and Herman for a peripatetic lunch.[53] The five of them took specialty items from three restaurants, one bar, and one raw-fish cart on the street. After a long discussion about psychoanalysis—Bill Herman and Irmarita Putnam being interested in Jung at the time—they went to the Ryks Museum, where Cobb was impressed by the Vermeers and the Rembrandts.

The following day, Betty went to Haarlem, and Stanley to Utrecht. Here he saw Professor Winkler in the morning and for lunch, and in the afternoon he visited the physiologist Dusser de Barenne, as well as

Professor Boeke, who had done anatomical work on nerve endings. After supper at Dusser de Barenne's house, Mrs. Cobb, who had been at the Franz Hals Museum in Haarlem, arrived, and Dusser de Barenne saw them off on the train for Hook of Holland. After their return to Oxford most of the Cobbs' time was spent in packing up for the trip home. In a letter to Stanley's mother postmarked in Halifax on July 12, 1925, Mrs. Cobb related:

> We have had calm seas and good weather all the way. The only drawback has been that Sidney seems to have developed German measles. He is not very sick, and so it really was a relief to have the rash break out this morning because the initial glands and fever came about six days ago.
>
> I don't know whether we are going to find you on the docks or not—so I thought I would write a line even though we may meet before this reaches you.[54]

Stanley wrote to his sister Hildegarde, "We approach Boston and I expect that you are at Naushon. If all goes well, we land early Thursday morning and go right down to Cotuit, part by auto and part by train. Here's hoping we can get together fairly soon."[55]

Abraham Flexner's view of Cobb's European travel has been recorded in a chapter of his autobiography entitled, "The Training of Men," from which the following paragraphs are quoted:[56]

> On one occasion Edsall [Dean of the Harvard Medical School] came to New York to talk to me about the possibility of developing a department of neurology at Harvard. I was, of course, thoroughly sympathetic. Dr. Edsall had a well-worked-out plan, calling for a clinic, laboratories, and an endowed staff, but his scheme made no appeal to me. "How else can it be done?" he asked. I replied, "Send the right man abroad to study and let him on his return to America gradually build up his clinic and his staff. Moreover, you are lucky, for you have the man in Stanley Cobb, a Harvard graduate and a pupil of Adolf Meyer's, who regards him highly." Dr. Edsall returned to Boston in the afternoon, and next morning when I reached my office Cobb was there waiting for me. "Dr. Edsall," he said, "has told me of his interview with you yesterday. It will be my salvation if it can be arranged." "There will be no difficulty about that. What is your salary at Harvard now?" He told me. "Will Harvard make you an allowance?" 'Yes, they will grant me leave of absence on half pay." "For how long?" "For an indefinite period." "Is your wife sympathetic?" "Yes, thoroughly." "Have you a family?" "Yes, one child."
>
> "How much do you think it will cost you yearly abroad?" We made a rough estimate, and Cobb added, "We have omitted our nurse, an Irish girl, who has been with us for years." "No," I said, "we will not send the Irish girl. This is your chance, your wife's, your child's, to learn French and

European Study

German. Get an English nurse in England, a French nurse in France, and a German nurse in Germany, and the whole Cobb family will come back polylingual." Laughingly Cobb assented. I added, "I will give you a letter to Dr. Henry Head of Queen Square Hospital in London. If you do well there, he will introduce you in Germany and France, for he is the most highly regarded of the English neurologists. Win him, and you win the rest."

Cobb went and remained abroad for a considerable period. When he decided to return home, he notified Dr. Edsall, and Edsall once more came to see me. I asked him what Cobb wanted. Cobb had said nothing on the subject. "Write him," I suggested, "and find out what he needs to begin with." His needs were extremely simple, a dozen beds in the Boston City Hospital, a laboratory assistant or two, and unrestricted use of clinical material. The entire sum needed was appropriated by the General Education Board.

Cobb returned and developed a splendid center of neurological study at Harvard. He has since repeatedly gone abroad to keep up the connections he formed during this period. We have never lost sight of each other.

The importance of the European trip to Stanley Cobb from a professional viewpoint is clearly expressed in Abraham Flexner's autobiography. Chloe Binger has added a more personal touch. In an interview she quoted her husband as saying that the European trip changed Stanley and Betty Cobb so much that for ever after they were free spirits and not just Bostonians going along the path expected of them.[57]

6
The Later Twenties, 1925–1930

Whereas prior to the European trip his principal focus of interest had been the laboratory, supplemented by his clinical work at the Massachusetts General Hospital, Cobb was destined after his return to assume a far wider range of responsibilities. David L. Edsall, who in 1923 had become the first full-time dean of the Harvard Medical School and who more than anyone else was responsible for raising it to its current preeminence, had been counseling Cobb on professional matters since the latter's medical school days. Edsall was fully aware of Cobb's capacities as a scholar and as an imaginative leader and obviously was planning to use him as a major instrument in advancing teaching and research in neurology at Harvard. Abraham Flexner, too, of the General Education Board of the Rockefeller Foundation, had a similar appreciation of Cobb and had kept abreast of his activities and professional growth through an exchange of letters with Cobb while Cobb was abroad. Edsall was delighted to get Flexner's assurances that he was on the right track in promoting Cobb's work at Harvard.

So, while Cobb was still in Europe, plans for his future were being laid, and Flexner agreed to provide some of the funding to develop them. This funding came in the form of a grant from the General Education Board of $350,000 to Harvard University in August of 1925, approximately one month after Cobb's return from abroad. The capital was to be held as an endowed fund, and the resulting income was to be used to support an academic department of neurology at the Harvard Medical School, with Cobb its head. To complete the necessary funding, the university would add a moderate amount to what it was already using annually for neurology, to equal the amount of income from the gift. Finally, Boston City Hospital, where the new department would be centered, was to provide space for special neurological wards and laboratories in a new building that was to be erected and would finance some of the services.[1] However, due to financial, administrative, and construction problems at the hospital, these new quarters did not come available until August 1930. As a

The Later Twenties

result, for the next five years Cobb divided his time between teaching and research at the Harvard Medical School and clinical work and research at Boston City Hospital.

After returning to Boston in July, 1925, Cobb resumed his activities at the neuropathology laboratory in the medical school quadrangle. Initially, he started out with his existing staff, comprising Mella, as administrative assistant, Henry S. Forbes, Lennox, and, as an adjunct teaching member, Dr. MacPherson. However, Cobb immediately added Frank Fremont-Smith, who had earlier worked with Forbes on the carbon monoxide asphyxia paper, and designated him first assistant to replace Mella. It is obvious that this move had been contemplated for some time, for Cobb had written to James Ayer from Europe a year and a half earlier about Fremont-Smith, who was then working under Ayer at the Massachusetts General Hospital on cerbebrospinal fluid.[2] In his letter Cobb said that he looked upon the position of administrative assistant as a two-year appointment. He felt that Mella's term of service was about over, and he wanted to appoint Fremont-Smith unless Ayer had other plans for him.

Although the neuropathology laboratory was to remain the focal point of his investigative work for another four years, Cobb was making plans concurrently to develop opportunities for clinical study and teaching at Boston City Hospital. As Knapp and Denny-Brown have pointed out in their successive discussions of the history of neurology at City Hospital,[3] neurological treatment had been carried on there for about fifty years prior to January, 1926, when Cobb assumed his responsibilities there. Starting with the appointment of Dr. Samuel G. Weber as "Electrician" in 1876,[4] who was charged with consulting the visiting staff as to the advisability of using faradism, the treatment of nervous disorders had developed to the point where wards were set aside for it and physicans had begun to specialize in it. A succession of such physicians over the years included, in addition to Weber, Robert Edes, and Drs. Philip Coombs Knapp, Morton Prince, and William Norton Bullard. By 1904 students from the Harvard and Tufts Medical schools were being taught neurological diagnosis in the clinic, which was equipped for massage, galvanism and faradism, high frequency treatment, and even x-ray and static electricity. Other physicians associated with the practice of neurology at Boston City Hospital after 1900 were John Jenks Thomas, Joseph W. Courtney, Isador Coriat (mainly a psychiatrist, who later espoused Freudian analysis), Arthur

Fairbanks, and Abraham Myerson. After the death of Knapp in 1920, Dr. Thomas became chief of the service. He was succeeded by Myerson in 1924.

According to John J. Byrne, as early as 1923 Thomas, who was nearing retirement, had approached Dean Edsall with a proposal to set up a Harvard service in neurology at City Hospital. While there exists no exchange of correspondence between Thomas and Edsall in the Dean's Papers in the Harvard Medical Archives, nor any memoranda or letters of understanding on this subject, it would appear that Thomas was impressed by Harvard's establishment of the Thorndike Memorial Laboratory at Boston City Hospital a year or so earlier,[5] and he wished to upgrade the teaching of neurology there and clinical research in a similar way. Although Thomas had been professor of neurology at Tufts Medical School from 1912 to 1916 and professor emeritus thereafter, he also had Harvard connections, having taught as associate in neurology at the Harvard Graduate School of Medicine and having served with the Harvard Unit at the English Base Hospital in 1915. He undoubtedly saw in the newly established Thorndike Laboratory a possibility to similarly upgrade teaching and clinical research in neurology at Boston City Hospital and came to realize that this goal could probably not be accomplished through Tufts. However, it could be achieved by Harvard, which, added to its resources, had the ability to raise the necessary funding for it. Additionally, Thomas must have heard of Harvard's designs to increase its teaching in neurology and wanted City Hospital to be part of them, for such plans were being considered shortly after Cobb's return from Baltimore; indeed, it may even have been part of Edsall's long-range calculations that Cobb be trained there and hopefully be lured back to Boston to become part of the grand design.

Although the circumstances indicate that informal talks had been going on between Dean Edsall and Abraham Flexner for some time, the first concrete documentation which thus far can be found on this matter comes from correspondence in the Dean's Files of the Harvard Medical School. And it is of interest to note that it is filed under the "Rockefeller Foundation—General Education Board" and not among files relating to Harvard's department of neurology or Boston City Hospital. The first relevant piece in the Rockefeller file is a letter from Cobb to Edsall, sent from Berlin on October 29, 1924, a little over five weeks after he had established himself and his family there.[6] Cobb

The Later Twenties

William Gibbs in 1930

James Lawrence Pool at the B. C. H. Neurological Unit where he worked with Harry S. Forbes

Ivan P. Pavlov and Paul Yakovlev, meeting at the time of thirteenth International Physiological Congress held in Boston in 1929

The Later Twenties

Staff of the Boston City Hospital Neurological Unit about 1930. Back row: [unidentified], Drs. Daniel Blain, Hans Molholm, and Walter Wegner. Front row: Drs. Antoine Schneider, Madelaine R. Brown, unidentified, Stanley Cobb, Abraham Myerson, Donald Monroe, Philip Solomon, and Merrill Moore.

Staff of B.C.H. neurological unit circa 1931. Back row: Mrs. Linden, Miss Madden, Miss Donohue, Miss Noonan, Miss Villa West, Miss Grady, Miss Gibson, Mrs. Secchino. Middle row: Miss Mary Dailey, Drs. Houston Merritt, Harry Forbes, Tracy Putnam, Frank Fremont-Smith, Stanley Cobb, Margaret Crane-Lillie, Jacob Finesinger, and Knox Finley. Front row: The Misses Frances Jefferson, Dorothy Miller (later Mrs. Robert S. Schwab), Margaret Doherty (later married Dr. Richard Chambers), Harriet Williams, Dorothy Sloane, Betty Fisher, Margaret Gray, Ruth Murphy, and Pierrot.

The Later Twenties

Staff of the Boston City Neurological Unit about 1932. Back row: Drs. Theodore Fender, Meyer Asekoff, Antoine Schneider, Martin Woodall, Robert S. Schwab, Hans B. Molholm, Simon Stone, Charles Aring, and Knox Finley. Front row: Drs. William Lennox and Houston Merritt, Miss Mary Dailey, Drs. Donald Monroe, Abraham Myerson, Stanley Cobb, Frank Fremont-Smith, and Jacob E. Finesinger.

Stanley Cobb at the helm of his thirty-foot, Crocker designed sloop *Fulmar*, late 1930s

The Later Twenties

Betty Cobb at the helm of a small sloop in the early 1920s

The Cobbs' sloop *Pamaho* setting out through the Cotuit Narrows

devoted the first page and a half of his five-page letter to a summation of his impressions and work to that date, noting the gist of what he had observed in England, France, Holland, and Germany. He then related that he had received a letter from Harry Solomon—"one of our really good men, I think"—who urged him to try to coordinate neuropsychiatry after his return to Boston.

Solomon, in his letter to Cobb, had stated that "in Boston we have the best group of neurologists and psychiatrists in the country. This, it seems to me, should be our aim, to build up a 'school' in the best sense of the word." Cobb told Edsall that he had replied to Solomon by saying that he was interested in doing everything that he could, "that my idea of a school was pupils—pupils who work intimately with us and go away with our points of view."

Cobb believed that it would be necessary to interest medical students in neurology and neuropsychiatry throughout their medical school training. In this way, some of them would come back for specialized training in these areas and all of them would take neurology into medicine. He also wanted to attract men from other schools to work with him as well as keep up the summer courses for graduates. Such was his general thinking. "Personally," he related, my desires are four:

(1) To investigate diseases of the nervous system,
(2) to teach students,
(3) to train house officers,
(4) to do enough clinical work to make me effective in 1, 2, and 3.

Cobb then told his dean that at present his facilities for 1 and 2 were good, provided he could get more room and more assistants at the school. At the Massachusetts General Hospital he had not, he confessed, made the most of his chance to work with house officers, and he stated that he wanted to do more in the future. "As for 4th item—clinical opportunity—," he advised:

> A neurological service is essential and at present entirely lacking. A ward should be arranged for neurological diagnosis and treatment.
> Incidentally I am convinced that, for me, a full-time basis is the only thing. My experience of the last four years has shown me that my "make-up" is such that I cannot subordinate practice; it must be my principal occupation or nothing. I don't seem to be able to get away from the responsibility it entails, especially with the type of patients I have.
> With these premises in mind it would seem timely to know what, if anything, the Rockefeller Foundation is going to do for neurology.

Cobb went on to tell Edsall that what was needed in Boston (and at Harvard) was a neurological institute in the German sense of the word, closely correlated with psychiatry and making use of the unexcelled neurophysiology and neurosurgery already existing at Harvard. The department of neuropathology, he observed, already had a good start in this direction, one which could be built upon. Cobb then surveyed the hospitals where such an enterprise could be developed: the M.G.H., the Brigham, and the Psychopathic Hospital. With regard to Boston City Hospital, he told Edsall that it

> can perhaps make the most immediate offer. It would be delightful to work there with Peabody, through him I could probably get the opportunity to work with good medical house-officers (but not so easily as at the M.G.H., perhaps). The neurological personnel there would have to be carefully re-organized, and the arrangement with Tufts clearly understood. An allotment of beds is not enough; there should be a modern neurological ward.

Shortly after Cobb wrote his letter to Edsall, the latter drafted a document entitled "Preliminary Memorandum on Neurology Department." Consisting of four pages, it is unsigned and undated, though it bears at the head of its title the pencil date "Oct. 31-24."[7] This report was completed about two weeks before Edsall received Cobb's December 29th letter and it summed up a lot of thinking that had been going on at Harvard about the establishment of a neurological service at Boston City Hospital. Edsall's memorandum looked into the number of neurological cases that would be expected at City Hospital and the clinical experience and teaching that would ensue. He then assessed the current hospital budget and concluded that with additional funding it was feasible to provide special neurological wards and services for forty beds. The dean noted that "Dr. Thomas, the head of the neurological service, is already beyond the retiring age and has merely held on, particularly because he hoped for some development such as I am suggesting. He must retire this winter, however."

Edsall suggested that the matter had to be taken up soon and then proceeded to assess the current neurological personnel at City Hospital. A long paragraph of the memorandum was devoted to Dr. Myerson, whom Edsall thought "an able man, an excellent clinical neurologist and teacher, and a very agreeable person." He then went into the relationship that would have to exist between him and Dr. Francis W. Peabody, who headed the Harvard Medical Service at the City. With regard to Tufts, and the teaching of Tufts students, Edsall concluded

The Later Twenties

that such an arrangement would not interfere, "for, in point of fact we have been actively endeavoring for some time to help Tufts in instances in which we can employ our clinical material to their advantage and without detriment to us." Finally, he looked into the possibility of establishing a really strong department and what costs would be involved, concluding that it would be better to attempt to make the department elaborate and not compromise.

On December 2, about two weeks after receiving Cobb's October 29th letter, Edsall responded.[8] Edsall told Cobb that his letter had stated very clearly the very things that he himself had in mind. He related that Flexner would be very glad to see him to discuss the matter, and he then reported that City Hospital presented a very good prospect to develop the type of situation they had in mind, afterwards going over pretty much the gist of his memorandum. Cobb replied to all of this on January 13, 1925,[9] telling Edsall that he would be deeply interested in hearing what takes place with Mr. Flexner, and adding that "American neurology is going to develop and we would hate to see the lead taken away from Boston. So let us not be too modest in our aspirations." He agreed with Edsall's plan of asking for $30,000.00 as an annual budget, saying that it fitted well with his idea of building up the department of neuropathology to the standard of a research institute in conjunction with a neurological service at Boston City Hospital. While he preferred to leave the negotiating for budget to Edsall's wiser head, he considered the following four points fundamental:

(1) A neurological ward need not be large, but it should have adjoining it a clinical laboratory with modern apparatus for diagnosis and investigation. I would rather have a 10 bed ward with adequate and convenient laboratory equipment, than 60 beds with scanty and scattered apparatus.

(2) 25% of the beds of a neurological ward should be in single rooms because neurology cannot be separated from psychiatry, many borderline cases need isolation, and psychoses often occur.

(3) The brains and spinal cords of patients dying on my wards (upon whom autopsy is allowed) may be removed by me, or according to my directions, and become the property of the Department of Neuropathology.

(4) My salary should be increased to $10,000, to deliver me from the temptation of practice.

Expressing the opinion that City Hospital seemed to present the most advantages and that he would gladly work with Dr. Peabody, he nonetheless had a warm feeling for the Massachusetts General Hospital and for its chief of medicine, James Howard Means. Means, he reported, had written to him the prior fall about his own hopes for developing neurology further at the M.G.H., and Means had asked Cobb to give him the first opportunity to say what inducement he could offer. Cobb then asked Edsall, "Could you talk the situation over with Howard? If it is decided that I had better work at the City Hospital I hope some money will be provided at the M.G.H. for Dr. Ayer, who has been doing some pioneering work of good quality."

Plans for Cobb's clinical work in neurology at Boston City Hospital were the subject of an exchange of letters between the Harvard Medical School and the hospital's representatives in the summer of 1925. William H. Robey, an outstanding internist, in his capacity as secretary of the hospital's senior staff, wrote on August 25, 1925, informing Cobb that he and Dr. Abraham Myerson had been recommended as joint heads of the neurological service.[10] In the staff hierarchy each would be a visiting physician. Robey was puzzled as to the best use of Arthur W. Fairbanks, who had been on the staff for many years, and he suggested that Fairbanks might be a visiting physician, too. Cobb's reply to the letter realistically appraised potential relations with Myerson, cast doubt on the feasibility of a third visiting physician, and then went on to crystallize his concepts of the embryonic neurological unit. Cobb responded to Robey on September 2, 1925, telling him that

> The personal relations between Dr. Myerson and myself, however, are such that I have perfect confidence that we can happily and effectively carry on the service to our mutual advantage. Any further splitting up of authority would be fatal.
>
> May I take this opportunity to state what I understand to be my relationship to the hospital? Dr. Myerson and I are to be joint heads of the Neurological Service, the one actually on service being the "acting chief." This service is to consist of a modern neurological ward, a research laboratory, and the Out-Patient department. The ward is to be constructed to care for 35 or more patients. The laboratory is to be built in connection with this ward, and, as soon as it offers me research facilities as good as I now enjoy at the Harvard Medical School, I am to transfer my research activity to the Boston City Hospital. The funds administered by me are Harvard funds and will be used to advance teaching and research in the wards and laboratories. Harvard has put me on a full-time salary and had assigned me to this work. The Ward and Out-Patient expenses are, of course, to be borne by the Boston City Hospital.
>
> If the above is in any way in disagreement with your ideas please set me straight about it, for now is the time to make a good start without misunderstandings.[11]

Following this exchange of letters Dr. Fairbanks was appointed to the consulting staff, where he was free of administrative responsibilities, while Cobb and Myerson took their turns in running the clinical service on Wards J and L. In addition to Myerson and Fairbanks, Cobb recommended for appointments to the staff William Gordon Lennox, whose primary work was in the neuropathological laboratory on epilepsy, and Maxwell E. MacDonald, who had done experimental work in the laboratory prior to Cobb's departure for the European trip (34). Percy L. Dodge rounded out the neurological staff.[12] In addition, Dr. Miner H. A. Evans was listed as an assistant visiting psychiatrist.

Although Cobb and Myerson were codirectors of the neurological service, Myerson left most of the administrative work to Cobb, who had a full-time salaried position. Myerson had a busy practice with Harry C. Solomon and MacDonald, and he was also deeply involved in his own Abraham Myerson Laboratory at the Boston State Hospital in Mattapan.

While relationships with the Boston City Hospital physicians were amicably and successfully established, and lines of authority and responsibility correctly outlined there, Cobb's sudden rise in Harvard neurology and the prospect of his special service caused ripples of concern within the Massachusetts General Hospital, where neurology had been carried on and taught for several decades previously. Understandably, M.G.H. personnel wondered where they would fit in the new scheme of things and who would exercise final authority for the teaching of neurology at Harvard. The two individuals most likely to be effected by the new service, and the rearrangement of teaching responsibilities along with it, were Edward W. Taylor and James B. Ayer.

Taylor had for several decades been responsible for the teaching of neurology at Harvard and was then in overall charge of the department. He particularly was concerned, especially since he was coming up for retirement in a few years and Harvard officials, including Cobb, felt that a place quickly would have to be made for Ayer. Furthermore, Taylor had been moved aside once before to accommodate a "comer," and it appeared to him that this was likely to happen once again. An 1891 graduate of the Medical school, Taylor had served as instructor in neuropathology at Harvard from 1896 until 1904. Then, his position was taken from him and bestowed upon Elmer E. Southard, who took on an important role in Harvard medicine and teaching for the next decade and a half until his untimely death in 1920. In 1906 Taylor was made instructor in neurology, a title he held until 1912, when he was promoted to assistant professor following the retirement from the M.G.H. service of James Jackson Putnam. In 1917 Taylor's rank was raised to professor of neurology, and in 1920, two years after the death of Putnam, he was made the first James Jackson Putnam Professor of Neurology at Harvard with overall direction of the department. Now, with the sudden rise of Cobb in the Harvard orbit, and his new teaching and clinical authority at Boston City Hospital, Taylor was understandably concerned about where he and the Massachusetts General Hospital would fit in the overall plans and exactly who would be in charge of teaching neurology in the future.

Edsall's files contain two letters which indicate Taylor's concern and which document meetings between them in early June of 1926.[13] As a result of plans that were actively being carried forward, Edsall informed Taylor in the second of these that

> The recommendation of the committee which was unanimous and with which I agreed and which I have taken up with President Lowell and in which he entirely concurs, was that Dr. Cobb should be advanced to full professor of Neuropathology and Dr. Ayer should be advanced from assistant professor to clinical professor of Neurology; that Dr. Cobb and Dr. Ayer should cooperate in the teaching of neurology; this situation to run for three years during which Dr. Ayer's appointment would last and then be subject to further consideration at the end of that time.

Taylor responded with a letter to Dr. Worth Hale, the assistant dean, on June 23.[14] He said that although he had not been directly informed, he assumed that his teaching had ended and that he would not be in control of the neurology department another year, for the work would more or less be changed with the implementation of the City Hospital idea. Whereupon Taylor started making arrangements to resign his professorship.[15] On June 24, at the suggestion of Cobb, Edsall wrote to William Norton Bullard, informing him that Cobb was to be made Bullard Professor of Neuropathology and would be the senior in charge of neurology:[16]

> The occasion for this is the prospective resignation of Dr. E. W. Taylor from the Chair of Neurology. The Plan is to have the neurological interests, namely neurology and neuropathology, in one division, with Dr. Cobb as head and Dr. Ayer as Clinical Professor of Neurology. This will not in any way encroach upon Cobb's time or his effectiveness in his studies, but will on the contrary make his opportunities for doing his work more effective and

The Later Twenties

will increase the force and prestige of his work in neuropathology. He will, as you know, continue on entire "full time" giving his attention altogether to the work he does in connection with the School. I shall be glad to know your feelings about this.

To which Bullard replied on the 29 that he was delighted to hear about these arrangements for Cobb. "I think it important that he should be on full time. He is an excellent man."[17]

Although James Ayer was being advanced under the new plan, it is obvious that Edsall and Cobb had to do some fence-mending at the Massachusetts General Hospital. As Cobb reported to the dean in a letter of July 12,[18] following a discussion of these new arrangements with Ayer, "I found there was a good deal of discontent and anxiety about the future at the Massachusetts General Hospital." This has even gone so far in the minds of some individuals, he reported to Edsall, as to make them fear that Dr. Ayer's three-year appointment is a scheme to transfer all neurology and teaching to City Hospital. Cobb felt that there was genuine fear that Ayer would not be reappointed at the end of his initial term and thus neurology at the Massachusetts General Hospital would be practically annihilated. After asking Edsall to allay Ayer's fears in August, Cobb proceeded to outline his own position in this new arrangement. He would be entrusted with the management of a large grant from the General Education Board of the Rockefeller Foundation, and other sources, to develop academic neurology at the Harvard Medical School. This money, he pointed out, was to be spent at Boston City Hospital because that hospital had offered remarkably good facilities. He believed, however, that in order to develop a well-rounded neurological department, both hospitals, the City and the General, would have to work cooperatively. Consequently, some of this money may well be spent at the Massachusetts General, and he did not believe that there was any need for the neurological unit at the M.G.H. to lose its autonomous control. Finally, he outlined the wording of the announcements of the departments of neuropathology and neurology for the forthcoming medical school catalog so that all parties would be satisfied.

Dean Edsall wrote a conciliatory letter to Ayer on August 4.[19] He assured Ayer that there was no idea in the new scheme for reducing the importance of the M.G.H. unit; on the contrary, he reasoned, the move—he claimed it was suggested by President Lowell, apparently to strengthen his argument—was designed to achieve more effective co-operation between the M.G.H., the B.C.H. and the Boston Psychopathic Hospital. "Your plans," he reassured Ayer, "have seemed to me to be entirely likely to make the unit at the M.G.H. not only more effective than it was but a very powerful unit." Edsall's letter had its soothing effect, for Ayer responded to it on August 11,[20] telling Edsall, "perhaps we of the neurological staff were over-alarmed, but in one way or another we seemed to be rapidly losing our identity. A definite word from you at the time would have been sufficient; now you have written and I see no reason for taking your valuable time for a conference. We will go ahead on any basis which seems best for the development of the general subject of neurology at the Harvard Medical School." Cobb and Ayer afterwards cooperated in their teaching efforts, and with that, the matter died accordingly.

While the General Education Board made its grant to the Harvard Medical School in 1925 for the establishment of the special neurological unit that Cobb and Edsall had proposed, and while the Harvard Medical School pledged considerable support on its own part, the final establishment of the new unit was incumbent upon the erection by Boston City Hospital of a new building to house it. However, as noted before, this took some years in coming about, for it was not until 1930 that Cobb had the new wards and new laboratories that had been promised to him five years before. In the meantime, he continued working in the neuropathology department of the medical school and at the same time began to establish himself on the neurological service at City Hospital, where he was titular head, dividing his time between both locations.

Members of Cobb's team at the neuropathology laboratory were added to the hospital staff at appropriate times during the next three years. In 1926 Bill Herman, whose wife was Cobb's secretary, came as a consultant in psychoanalysis. Harold G. Wolff, who for the next three years was one of the most important collaborators in the laboratory, worked primarily with Henry Stone Forbes. In 1927 Fremont-Smith, having recently returned from a year of study abroad, was added to the staff and helped Cobb with many of the administrative problems of running the service. Also that year came Dr. Samuel Epstein, initially as a member of the house staff. However, during the spring of 1929 he worked with Raymond Morrison in Cobb's neuropathology laboratory at the medical school quadrangle. He also published with Cobb a paper from Boston City Hospital on the use of salicylates in the treatment of chronic epidemic encephalitis (47). Epstein became a per-

The Later Twenties

manent staff member at City Hospital and proved to be a valuable and resourceful person in conveying the atmosphere that prevailed in Cobb's day.[21] Richard B. Easley of Richmond, a friend of C. C. Coleman, Cobb's collaborator on wartime spinal cord injuries (23), was also among those who came on the house staff at that time.[22] Easley indicated that he had a very happy experience at the City.[23]

Nineteen hundred and twenty-eight was a somewhat confused year at the neurological service at City Hospital because of Cobb's second trip for study in Europe. (This will be discussed shortly.) By that time Fremont-Smith had become firmly established, maintaining a laboratory in the Thorndike and serving also as Cobb's administrative assistant. Fremont-Smith held the service at the City together during Cobb's six-month absence. Also Gildea, who had worked with Cobb on vitamin deficiency while still in medical school and had been through four years of graduate training, took the new post of resident physician on Cobb's service, so things were left well in hand.

In spite of Cobb's absence there was a significant number of new appointments in 1928. That year John Jenks Thomas, who had formerly been chief of service, was appointed as a consultant. Gildea, of course, came as a resident. Tracy J. Putnam, a neurosurgeon of academic stature who had been trained by Cushing, was brought in to supplement the work of Donald S. Munro, the chief of neurosurgery.[24] Also, Guy C. Randall and Mark Wentworth both joined the staff to work primarily in psychiatry. Toward the end of the year H. Houston Merritt came up from Yale. He was destined to remain on the staff as acting director following Putnam in 1939. Several others joined the house staff or worked part time during the year.[25] Cobb returned from Europe in August, 1928, and was available thereafter, devoting much of his attention to plans for the neurosurgical unit which was in the final planning stages and under construction.

By 1928 the organization of the neurological service was almost complete. Psychiatry, on the other hand, had yet to be developed. When Cobb and Myerson took over the neurological service from Thomas in 1925 there were two staff members assigned to psychiatry. One was Arthur Fairbanks, who was placed on the consulting staff at that time, and the other was Miner H. A. Evans, who worked primarily in the outpatient department. Fairbanks was an old-fashioned psychiatrist whose principal function at Boston City Hospital was as an alienist committing patients to mental institutions. Evans, who was listed as an assistant visiting psychiatrist, shared with Fairbanks the work as an alienist. He also had a large private practice evaluating claimants for insurance companies. Evans must have felt a bit on the fringe of things and presumably tendered his resignation after a preliminary conference with Fremont-Smith and Harold G. Wolff. The following excerpt from a sensitive and appreciative letter from Evans to Cobb, written September 11, 1928, indicated that the resignation had not been accepted:

> I have felt for a long time that the best interests of the clinic would be served by having an all-the-year man who could give more to the Out Patient than I have to offer. I realize that I should have spoken to you or to Myerson rather than to talk it over with Dr. Fremont-Smith and Dr. Wolff. I am sorry for this breach of good taste, but it came out of a time when I really wanted their ideas in regard to the organization of the clinic.
>
> I am sure that both you and Dr. Myerson know without hearing me say it how happy I am to go on with the association which has always been a happy as well as a helpful one to me.[26]

William Herman, whom Cobb first met when an intern at the Massachusetts General Hospital and whom he appointed as a consultant in psychoanalysis in 1926, came to City Hospital about once a week for teaching and to help with the management of patients. After completing his psychiatric internship in Baltimore and studying further with MacFie Campbell at the Boston Psychopathic Hospital, he had worked with the Jungian analyst Dr. Van der Hoop. By 1928 he was moving toward Freud. In 1927 Campbell, then chairman of psychiatry at Harvard, had arranged a stipend for Herman to carry on his liaison psychiatry at the Massachusetts General Hospital, much as MacPherson was doing at the Brigham and Cobb at the City.[27] As pointed out earlier Herman felt very close to Cobb both professionally and socially, and in turn Cobb was moved by Herman's wisdom. The following letter of October 4, 1928, is entertaining and shows why Cobb found Herman's personality so fascinating.:[28]

> Dear Stanley,
>
> Do you know really whether you do things with your thalamus or your cortex and are you sure the best things you have done you have done with your cortex? Take your marriage, for example; how could you marry with your cortex alone and be very happy? Of course, some of us allow our thalami to rule our cortex and others our cortex to rule our thalami, and some of us, I fear, live by our spinal cords alone. But how can we ever know whether we are using our thalami or our cortexes in deciding what organ

The Later Twenties   145

the other fellow is using when we don't agree with him? That is a question which is going to form a chapter in my famous book written years after my death.

                                                                Affectionately,
                                                                W. H.

Another physician with a major interest in psychiatry who joined Cobb's staff in 1928 was Mark H. Wentworth, a relative of Tracy Putnam and a member of the class of 1905 at Harvard Medical School. Wentworth, who was also a personal friend of Cobb, had been in general practice in Concord, Massachusetts. He had developed an interest both in neurology and psychiatry. As a psychiatrist he was gentle, fatherly, and supporting. He did his work in the outpatient department where most of the problems were psychiatric and he made a real contribution, serving on the staff for many years. Psychiatry was to take on greater flair, however, with the arrival of Merrill Moore in 1929, but that is a story for another chapter (see chapter 7).

During the period of transition some of the laboratory work was done in space furnished by Peabody in the Thorndike. Fremont-Smith's spinal fluid laboratory was established there in 1927, and Erna Leonhart, Lennox's technician, had facilities there to make blood-gas analyses for the work on epilepsy.[29]

In 1927 Cobb published from Boston City Hospital with his neurosurgical colleague, Donald Munro, two cases on brain tumor (43), and the paper written by Samuel Epstein on the effect of salicylates in chronic encephalitis also was released from that institution (47). However, all Cobb's significant research and writing during the transition years came from the neuropathology laboratory at the Medical School.

In examining Cobb's scientific work at the neuropathology laboratory during the years 1925–1928, it is essential to restate his concept of a research laboratory as a place where investigators of ability are free to carry on their own projects in an atmosphere of helpful collaboration and understanding without the constraints imposed by a dominant controlling figure. All Cobb's associates did work that was at least tangentially related to the central themes of epilepsy and the cerebral circulation. However, much of each man's work was completed and published independently. By granting his colleagues such freedom Cobb was able to hold over the years persons of such remarkable talent as Lennox, Forbes, Fremont-Smith, Wolff, Talbott, and Gildea.

During the period after his first European trip, when Cobb was reorienting himself to investigative work in the neuropathology laboratory, his influence on these men was clearly colored by the experience of working with Vogt and Bielschowsky in Berlin. In a long letter to Meyer written January 2, 1925, Cobb described at some length what was taking place there. The following paragraph conveys the flavor of the atmosphere in Berlin and gives a notion of the techniques with which Cobb was becoming familiar.[30]

> Professor Vogt, as you probably know, seems to have some of the spark of divine enthusiasm that makes him an individual among a mob of the rest of us. His institute runs very well. The technique is fine, and I am plodding away at the "myeloarchitektonik" of the occipital lobe for him and trying to work in a few ideas of my own on "Vasoarchitektonik" that he doesn't think much of. But Bielschowsky (who works upstairs and is on not-too-good terms with the Chief) is my ally in this; so when I weary with looking through the microscope at laminae, I dabble my fingers in $AgNO_3$ and make them brown. The great thing that this contact has taught me is to have little respect for the "four-week researches" as Vogt calls them and for the men who put out fat and sudden monographs. Also Vogt's biological interests fall into my habit of mind, and I think his influence will direct my work at home a good deal.

Cobb was reorienting his own investigative approach from one of short-term independent studies to an ongoing accumulation of scientific knowledge related to specific themes in which, perhaps, cerebral circulation was the key. In fact, Cobb wrote to Vogt in October, 1925, and said that Forbes was devising a technique for studying cerebral vessels and Fremont-Smith was working on the cerebral circulation in embryos.[31]

In addition to those of Forbes and Fremont-Smith, the familiar faces in the laboratory belonged to Lennox, Yakovlev, MacPherson (in connection with the neuropathology course) and Gildea, particularly in 1928. John Hubbard[32] wrote one paper on cerebral hemorrhage with Cobb while still in medical school (33). However, the important new faces belonged to George Schaltenbrandt, Harold G. Wolff, and John H. Talbott. During early 1929 Raymond Morrison, a neuropathologist, and his assistant, John McKenna, were also there full time. Others, such as Jacob E. Finesinger, Houston Merritt, and Frederick Gibbs, either drifted in and out or were there only briefly. For purposes of presentation, Cobb's scientific work in the laboratory can be divided into three parts: that which he did with Forbes, Fremont-Smith, and Lennox; that which he did with Schaltenbrandt, Wolff, and Talbott; and finally the original research and writing that he carried on alone.

It was after Forbes had completed the article with Fremont-Smith and Cobb on carbon monoxide asphyxia, which included evaluation of arteries on the retina of the eye (36), that he set out to develop his new method for evaluating cerebral circulation.[33] In developing his skull-window technique Forbes derived some help from Harold G. Wolff. The first study that utilized this method and bore Cobb's name appeared in the *American Journal of Physiology* in 1929 (60). This article by Forbes, Wolff, and Cobb contains magnificent photomicrographs, showing the effect of histamine in dilating the pial arteries of cats under amytal anesthesia. Other work during the twenties was published by Forbes independently or with other collaborators. After the histamine study came out, a series of papers was published by Forbes and others using the skull-window method.

When Fremont-Smith became Cobb's administrative assistant following Mella's departure in 1925, plans were promptly made for him to go abroad for a year much as Cobb had done. In fact, Cobb broached this subject to Abraham Flexner in a letter written November 27, 1925,[34] and Fremont-Smith was away for the academic year 1926–27. In the fall of 1926 he was studying with Walther Spielmeyer in Munich and, as he reported in a letter to Cobb on October 7, he was planning to go at neurology from the biochemical angle.[35] He said that Spielmeyer was excited about the idea of a clinic with members having interest in special fields such as physiology, chemistry, and anatomy. Either Fremont-Smith was a procrastinator, or he went to Europe in haste, for he left on Cobb's hands considerable unfinished work. In the letter he said, "I am sorry you have so much trouble with my papers— more of my left-over work!" In the margin he scrawled, "Did Van Slyke accept the paper on knee-joint fluids for the *Journal of Biological Chemistry*? If so, let Miss Dailey do the proof reading." The net result of the situation was that Cobb published nothing with Fremont-Smith between 1924 (36) and 1930 (65).

However, a series of long letters during the fall of 1926 kept Cobb abreast of the ideas which were germinating in Fremont-Smith's mind for the new neurological unit at City Hospital and his role in developing his biochemical approach, especially through analyses of cerebrospinal fluid.[36] Fremont-Smith returned from Europe in the summer of 1927. He commenced work for Cobb in the outpatient department on Friday, September 9. Peabody had supplied a laboratory in the Thorndike and Mary Dailey was to be its technician.[37] In addition to his clinical and laboratory work, Fremont-Smith was to take on major responsibility for ironing out the structural details of the Neurological Unit then being built on the seventh to tenth floors of the new Medical Building.[38]

The remaining full-time worker with a familiar face was William Gordon Lennox. Lennox was concluding his work on diet and fasting as factors affecting the frequency of epileptic convulsions and was about to take a new tack based on the premise that localized deprivation of oxygen might be an important factor in bringing on seizures. Inasmuch as oxygen is carried in hemoglobin by the blood stream, this approach tied in well with Cobb's new interest in cerebral circulation. The story of Cobb's interest in Lennox and his work on epilepsy is recounted in chapter 8, along with Cobb's ongoing struggle for funds to support the project. However, during the late twenties Cobb worked very closely with Lennox and took part in three publications. The first of these was the epitaph to the study of fasting (50). Cobb and Lennox concluded that fasting might be helpful in some acute emergency situations but had no place in the long-term management of epilepsy. They also published in 1929 an article on the relationship between some physiological processes and epileptic seizures (56). At the end of their study of acidosis and oxygenation they concluded:

> Unfortunately it is not possible to maintain persons in an acidotic, dehydrated, and oxygenated condition. At the present time the only unusual therapeutic application of these observations is the use, in children, of a ketogenic diet.[39]

The big project on which Cobb and Lennox collaborated, with the help of Yakovlev[40] as a translator, was the compilation of a long review article summarizing the state of the art in epilepsy. This systematic review, with approximately six hundred references to the world's literature, first appeared in *Medicine* (50) and then was reissued in hardbound form as a *Medicine Monograph* (48). In what was essentially a two-hundred page book the authors reviewed all the current theories for the causation of epileptic convulsions. On page 143 they referred to the recent work of Forbes and Wolff which came from the cat-window experiments. The following paragraph is relevant to the direction of work then consuming the interest of those in the laboratory:

The Later Twenties

It will be seen that the procedures which tend to cause seizures in a patient are, in general, those associated with constriction of arteries, whereas many of the conditions which cause dilation tend to inhibit seizures. Some of the procedures mentioned above, such as clamping the trachea, involve a complicated series of factors which might influence conditions in the brain. Wolff and Lennox are analyzing the influence of the gaseous and other constituents of the blood on the cerebral circulation.

The possible role of impaired cerebral circulation as a factor in bringing on seizures remained a major interest of those in the laboratory for a number of years, and a variety of approaches in confirmation of the concept were made by various investigators.

A new face in the neuropathology laboratory in 1926 was that of George Schaltenbrandt, whose work, as a disciple of Sherrington, was primarily on decorticate or decerebrate cats and not primarily directed toward cerebral circulation. Schaltenbrandt came from Germany for a year's work in Cobb's laboratory before returning to his native land. He wrote three papers with Cobb. One on anesthesia in research on decerebrate animals appeared in 1927 (44). Another, observations on unilateral thalamus cats and striatum cats, after extirpation of the frontal or occipital poles, was published in 1929 (61), and a study of two cats deprived of their neocortex came out in 1931 (71). An exchange of letters with Schaltenbrandt in 1928 indicated that he was in Hamburg and on his way to join the staff of the Peking Union Medical College.

Without doubt, the most important new addition to the neuropathology laboratory during the period between 1925 and 1928 was Harold G. Wolff. Wolff, whom Cobb had known as a medical student, interned from 1923 to 1924 at Bellevue Hospital in New York with the distinguished neurologist Foster Kennedy and came to the neuropathological laboratory after Cobb's return from his European trip. Cobb later said that Wolff was the most valuable assistant he ever had, and indeed Wolff made great contributions in many ways. One was his collaboration with Forbes in working out the cat-window technique and in the initial experiments.[41] Another was to organize efficiently the clinical teaching at City Hospital while serving as Cobb's administrative assistant during 1926 and 1927 when Fremont-Smith was away in Europe. Of greater significance, however, was his work with Cobb and John H. Talbott, then a medical student, on changes in the capillary architecture of the brain following cervical sympathectomy (59), a study which had a dramatic impact on the epilepsy program by leading to human experimentation.[42] Wolff also carried on with Cobb a meticulous study of microscopically demonstrable changes in brain cells as a result of morphine intoxication (55). However, Wolff's greatest contribution was his wisdom. He had an outlook on neuropsychiatry much like Cobb's, and he repeatedly emphasized the importance of precise quantitative data to support clinical impressions, particularly in situations where bodily changes appeared to result from nervous tension or bodily stress. In fact, at a conference on psychosomatic medicine in 1929 Wolff said:[43]

> If our generation is to make any contribution to this subject, it would seem to me that it is in the direction of stating how much or how little or in what direction these bodily changes occur. If we repeat verbalizations and formulations of this relationship we add but little. If we actually devise means to study the amount of such changes we may be able to detect new relations not known to exist. Our job now, it seems, is to be creative in methods of producing various emotional states and using at the same time the tools that we have been given to measure accompanying bodily changes. If we do this, we will be able to say to what extent fear is related to ulcers of the stomach, to what extent Raynaud's Syndrome is associated with anxiety, to what extent Graves' disease is related to stress.

Cobb viewed Wolff as a man with rare imagination, vision, and technical knowledge and may even have been a bit envious of Wolff's success in this field. Cobb concluded his Lowell lecture on psychosomatic medicine in 1940 by quoting this paragraph which Wolff had written.

Cobb was quick to recognize Wolff as a potential leader in academic neuroscience and took upon himself an interest in making suitable opportunities available to him. He wanted Wolff to have a year abroad similar to the one which he personally had enjoyed and then to work with Meyer as an internist in the Phipps Clinic in Baltimore.[44] However, the latter plan did not work out. Cobb initiated the European trip in a letter to Abraham Flexner on May 21, 1927,[45] and Wolff went abroad for a year in July, 1928, where he worked primarily with Loewy in Graz.[46] On his return in the summer of 1929, Frederick Gibbs, who had just arrived from Johns Hopkins, met him briefly in the neuropathology laboratory, which at that time was still functioning in Building D-2 at the quadrangle.[47] Gibbs said that Wolff was packing his belongings in anticipation of his move to Cornell. Wolff's major scientific contributions to the laboratory had been his collaboration with

The Later Twenties

Forbes and his meticulous microscopic work on the changes in brain cells caused by morphine intoxication.

However, perhaps the most exciting study in which Wolff collaborated had to do with changes in the cerebral capillary bed following cervical sympathectomy (59). This meticulous study, with its far-reaching effects on neurosurgery,[48] was a direct outgrowth of the Vasoarchitektonik technique which Cobb had mastered when working in 1924 and 1925 with Vogt and Bielkschowsky in Berlin. The person most deeply involved with Cobb's project was John H. Talbott, who commenced working in the neuropathology laboratory in 1925 while a medical student at Harvard. In the spring of that year Cobb's friend Alfred Redfield, in the department of physiology, helped Talbott, who was in difficult financial straits, obtain a Charles Eliot Ware fellowship and directed him to Cobb's laboratory, where he worked during his second and third years of school. Relative to the study on cerebral capillaries, Talbott said:

> During my second and third year at school, I spent the two free afternoons a week in the experimental studies on cerebral circulation with Stanley. Our first study was on rabbits, measuring the vascularity of brain tissue. The second series was on cats following cervical sympathectomy. Stanley and I were essentially co-surgeons in each study. After injection with Berlin blue the tissues were handed over to the technicians and eventually the sliced tissues were returned to me to count and measure the injected capillaries.[49]

Talbott related that the first phase of the work on rabbits was reported at the meeting of the Association of American Physicians in the spring of 1927 by Cobb and himself. In the second phase, on cats, he received a great deal of editorial help from Wolff.

During 1927–28 Talbott was on leave from the Harvard Medical School and worked in the newly established Harvard Fatigue Laboratory.[50] After receiving his medical degree in 1929 and serving as a medical intern under Walter W. Palmer at the New York Presbyterian Hospital, Talbott worked for many years in rheumatology at the Massachusetts General Hospital. Later he became editor of the *Journal of the American Medical Association*. Although his time in the neuropathology laboratory was brief, he made a critical contribution to Cobb's study of cerebral circulation.

Aside from Cobb, the most sophisticated neuropathologist was Raymond Morrison, who came to Harvard in 1928 and spent a year with Fremont-Smith in the spinal fluid laboratory, at that time in the Thorndike. In 1929 he transferred his activities to the neuropathology laboratory in Building D-2. The new neurological unit at Boston City Hospital was then under construction, and Cobb must have been concerned about financing Morrison's future. In any event, he wrote the following recommendation to his friend Wilder Penfield in Montreal:[51]

> As for Raymond Morrison: he has been working here for about nine months, most of the time with Frank Fremont-Smith on spinal fluid. For the last [few] months he has been working in my laboratory doing some experimental work. He is an extremely good technician and knows his histology well. He is the kind of man that likes to be left alone to do his work with his own hands, and he works hard and long. He is a rather peculiar individual and more or less of a hermit, extremely shy, but he is one of those who wear well. He is about to get married and will need $3500 or so to live on. I should doubt if any ordinary scholarship would attract him.

The Montreal possibility apparently did not work out, and Morrison followed Cobb to Boston City Hospital and later to the Massachusetts General Hospital. He had serious health problems. While in the neuropathology laboratory he was bitten by a cat and had to undergo the Pasteur treatment to preclude the possibility of getting rabies.[52] Morrison was also a victim of tuberculosis and lost about seven years from his active professional life in "curing." At City Hospital, among other things, Morrison was to do routine neuropathology for the neurosurgeons there. Later, after recovering from tuberculosis, he worked on anoxemia problems with Cobb at the Massachusetts General. Much of this work, done during and after World War II, was buried in classified government publications; so in a way he felt that his work had not been fully appreciated. However, Cobb and Walter Bauer arranged to have his work published posthumously by the Commonwealth Fund.[53] The volume was extraordinarily well prepared and was appreciated by those who had known Morrison.

John McKenna was Morrison's assistant during 1929 at the neuropathology laboratory and later at Boston City Hospital. McKenna had an unsteady gait and had been told he had multiple sclerosis. Because of this health problem he gave up neuropathology and went into psychiatry. Whatever his neurological disorder was, it must have been relatively benign. McKenna moved to New Hampshire, where in time he became chairman of the department of psychiatry at the Hitchcock Clinic.

Several other members of Cobb's professional family worked briefly in the neuropathology laboratory in the final days before it was moved

The Later Twenties

to the new neurological unit at the City. In addition to Gibbs and Wolff, Edwin Gildea, Houston Merritt, and Jacob Finesinger came out to the laboratory to work during their City Hospital residencies. Gildea was winding up the study he had commenced in medical school on spinal cord changes resulting from vitamin deficiency. He also investigated with Cobb the effects of anemia on the cerebral cortex of the cat (66). The other recent arrivals were just beginning their careers.

During the late twenties, when based at the neuropathology laboratory in the quadrangle of the medical school, Cobb wrote a number of papers which bore his name alone without collaborators. Some were review articles, some addresses, and one was a report on the dedication of the Deutsche Forschungsanstalt für Psychiatrie in Munich (57). The most important piece of laboratory investigation that Cobb reported alone was a quantitative study of the capillaries in the hippocampus (58). One paragraph in this report reviews the relationship of Cobb's technique to his earlier experience with Vogt in Berlin:

> The great work of the Vogts on cerebral architecture aroused widespread interest in the laminations of the cerebral cortex. . . . Bolton even suggested reclassification of the psychoses on the basis of selective degenerations of certain cortical laminae. . . . From Vogt's laboratory one paper on vasoarchitecture has appeared, the great bulk of the work there having been concerned with cytoarchitecture and myeloarchitecture. The paper on brain capillaries is by Lorente de Nò;[54] it describes and pictures the capillary network of the area striata, area peristriata, and Ammon's horn. In the occipital cortex, the fourth layer is apparently the most vascular and in Ammon's horn, the pyramidal layer, but capillary measurements are not given.

Cobb acknowledged that he aimed to contribute to knowledge of cerebral circulation by giving quantitative data concerning the capillary blood supply of certain laminae of the rhinencephalon in the rabbit. Then he described the Berlin blue method that he had used with Talbott and Wolff (45, 59). It is apparent that with Bielschowsky's help, while in Berlin during 1924 and 1925, he had indeed worked out a method for studying vasoarchitektonik in spite of Vogt's disapproval of what he was doing.

One of his most important lectures, delivered at Yale on January 27, 1927, was entitled "Physiology, Psychiatry and the Inhibitions" (49). In this paper, which reviewed much of the then current physiological knowledge derived from the investigations of Pavlov, Sherrington, and others, Cobb first introduced his memorable triangular formulation of the relationship between physiology and psychiatry. At the base of Cobb's triangle was a bottom layer solidly on the ground composed of anatomy, flanked by physics and chemistry. The entire layer above, still with a rather firm foundation, was physiology, and above that with somewhat shaky underpinnings came experimental psychology. At the apex of Cobb's triangle were more esoteric aspects of knowledge. Most esoteric, at the very peak of the triangle, was philosophy. Below that came slightly-more-tangible theoretical psychology. Beneath that was analytical psychology—based on human experience—and one layer lower was a layer labeled psychiatry. Psychiatry, at least, was based on objective clinical observation. More than half the area of the triangle was totally blank. The blankness represented absence of knowledge. One of Cobb's great strengths was his ability to look at gaps in knowledge as fields for investigation rather than feeling a need to fill them with comfortable arm-chair hypotheses.

While Cobb was working with his collaborators, both those with familiar faces and new ones, and carrying on his own independent studies, he and his colleagues were dependent upon a rather remarkable supporting staff. Mrs. Linden, who cared for the animals, and Mrs. Herman, Cobb's secretary, had been on the payroll from the beginning in 1920. During the late twenties Mrs. Herman was replaced by Charlotte Temperley.[55] Alice Towne was Morrison's technician and was joined toward the end of the era by Margaret Doherty,[56] who subsequently was to supervise Morrison's laboratory at City Hospital. Betty Fisher,[57] the office manager, was about to direct the monumental task of moving the laboratory with all its equipment and files to the new neurological unit. Mary Dailey,[58] was not only the supervisor of Frank Fremont-Smith's spinal fluid laboratory; she also helped Cobb with his work in reviewing articles for the medical journals of which he was an editor.[59] Erna Leonhart, who has been noticed before,[60] had been doing gas analyses for Lennox in space provided by Peabody in the Thorndike Laboratory. However, toward the end of the twenties she set up Haldane apparatus in Building D-2. It was characteristic of Cobb to attract very able women, some of whom would have gone into medicine had the field been open to them at the time. With the talented staff he had gathered around him, and the support of these remarkable women, Cobb's achievements during the later twenties were truly significant.

During the European trip between 1923 and 1925, when he was attempting to master French and German, Cobb observed that his stammering became much worse. So, shortly after his return from

Europe he resumed treatment with the speech therapist, Samuel D. Robbins, whom he had consulted prior to departure.[61] Treatment with Robbins went on until February, 1927, when Cobb decided to discontinue his regular Thursday night classes.[62] The relationship with Robbins went beyond that of therapist and client. Through the intervention of Floyd H. Allport, instructor in psychology at Harvard, Cobb had arranged in 1921 for Robbins to have a speech clinic at the Massachusetts General Hospital on Saturday mornings.[63] Just at the time when Cobb was discontinuing his own treatment in 1927, Robbins received a letter from Douglas A. Thom, asking him to work at the Habit Clinic which Thom had established. Robbins asked Cobb's advice about giving up the work at the Massachusetts General in favor of Thom's clinic, a move with which Cobb agreed.[64] Cobb's advice to Robbins on the move to Thom's clinic was clearly motivated by consideration for Robbins's best interests. However, Cobb had by that time concluded that Robbins's approach was not helpful in his own case. Cobb's experience with treatment for his stammering is neatly summarized in the following paragraph from a letter to William Healy at the Judge Baker Foundation, then at 40 Court Street in Boston:[65]

> In 1910 I was helped temporarily by hypnosis. In 1916 I was helped very greatly by a psychoanalysis in the hands of Dr. Campbell. Immediately after this I went to a Mr. Robbins who gave me speech exercises, and these consolidated the work already started during my psychoanalysis. For the next five years things went along very well. Then with increasing work and anxiety the speech difficulty seemed worse and I tried Mr. Robbins again. This time I was not helped much. During my trip abroad learning new languages increased my difficulty conspicuously. During the last two years it has been rather bad. Then, with Dr. Seif, who was over here [from Munich] for about three months, I worked once more at psychoanalysis for about two months. This was of great and immediate benefit, and I am now better off than I was last spring, although I have relapsed more or less since coming back this autumn. Next March I plan to go over to Munich and work with Seif for about four months more.

This letter was written in response to a request for advice regarding a patient of Healy's named Tobey. Cobb's recommendation, on the basis of his own experience, was that Mr. Tobey undertake a psychological analysis with an Adlerian such as Seif. However, there was no Adlerian in Boston. Under these circumstances Cobb thought Mr. Tobey might undertake analytic therapy with Herman, who had been trained as a Jungian and later became a Freudian psychoanalyst.

Because of Cobb's disappointment in Robbins's treatment and the success of his brief taste of Adlerian analysis with Seif, Cobb determined to go to Europe again the following year. In Munich he could continue the analysis with Seif and also do valuable work in neuropathology with the great neuroanatomist, Walther Spielmeyer, at the Deutsche Forschungsanstalt für Psychiatrie. On April 27, 1927, Cobb proposed the venture to Dean Edsall[66] and on May 16, 1927, Edsall replied that the Corporation had approved the plan.[67]

The Cobbs sailed for Europe for the second time in February, 1928, and returned in August that year. They traveled to Munich by way of Naples. In Munich Cobb spent his mornings with Spielmeyer[68] and continued his analysis with Seif in the afternoons. Cobb was in Munich for the dedication of the Deutsche Forschungsanstalt für Psychiatrie on June 12–13, 1928. The institute, on Kraepelin Street in Schwabing, a suburb of Munich, represented the epitome of Emil Kraepelin's work. It provided extensive laboratories for neuropathological investigation of the human brain, directed in part to the hope of finding explanations for the psychoses. Professor Oskar Vogt, with whom Cobb had previously worked on the microscopic architecture of the cerebral cortex, was honored at the dedication ceremony as first recipient of the Kraepelin prize. In making the presentation Spielmeyer said:

> Thus has the first award of the Kraepelin Prize fallen to you, Dr. Vogt. You are known in the world as the founder of our knowledge of the architectural organization of the cerebral cortex. You have given us our first scientific orientation, so that we may find our way in the cortex, that complicated and psychologically important part of the central nervous system. Moreover, since the special morphology of these parts of the brain corresponds to special reactions, you have given us, by the areas and layers which you have outlined, the structural basis for the understanding of function.

Cobb's account of the dedication, translated into English, from which the above passage is quoted, appeared in the *Archives of Neurology and Psychiatry* (57).

In a letter to Meyer[69] Cobb referred to his analysis with Seif and said that his speech was already much improved. He also said he thought Seif was a better man than Adler. Of Adler, he said in his letter, "Adler has too much of a hobby and the more I read of his writings, the less I think of his mind." Cobb's disenchantment with Adler was already paving the way for his later interest in Freud.

In April, 1928, Cobb's friend Herman and his wife Susan were on their way to Zurich where Herman was to work with Jung. Herman, too, was about to change his allegiance to Freud.

The Later Twenties

Cobb and his family returned to the United States in August, 1928, in time for vacationing at Cotuit, on Cape Cod, before resuming the rigorous responsibilities at Harvard in September.

Cobb's domestic life during the latter half of the twenties had many delightful aspects. The parents and the growing children continued to live in the old Cherry Hill Tavern in Ponkapoag until 1929, when they moved to Milton. Summers were spent in the Cotuit cottage which had been built in the winter of 1922–1923, just before the Rockefeller trip to Europe. The cottage, situated on land given by Mrs. Cobb's parents, was built on a wooded knoll with a four-mile view down the harbor and across Nantucket Sound by Poponesset. Immediately in the foreground was a marsh with an almost land-locked salt pond where Cobb spent hours studying the vegetation, birds, and aquatic life. The family literally lived in their bathing suits.

A particularly joyous feature of the Cotuit vacations was sailing on *Pamaho*, the yawl that Cobb and his father bought in 1925 after the European trip. This boat, already old, had the spoon bow and overhang stern characteristic of early-twentieth-century yacht design. With a waterline length of twenty-three feet, it measured over thirty from stem to stern. One of the author's earliest recollections of the Cobb family was to see them reaching into Cotuit harbor before the waning southwest breeze at the tag end of the afternoon. The setting sun would brighten the orange-brown sails, dyed with tan bark in the tradition of fishermen in Brittany, and Mrs. Cobb would be wearing an orange bandana, which contrasted with the graceful, sleek, black hull. The heads of three children would be seen peering over the cockpit coaming.

Prior to 1930, the *Pamaho* was used primarily for day sailing and for brief cruises to nearby islands such as Martha's Vineyard, Tuckernuck, Muskeget, and Naushon, where Cobb's sister Hildegarde and her husband, Harry Forbes, spent their summers.

Cotuit remained the Cobbs' summer vacation spot for many more years, and exciting longer cruises on *Pamaho* and other boats lay ahead. However, many transitions in Cobb's life took place in the year or two following his return from Munich. The neuropathology laboratory found its home in the new neurological unit at Boston City Hospital. The family moved from the familiar rural environment in Ponkapoag to the suburbs in Milton. And Cobb himself began his gradual shift in interest from Adler to Freud, thus laying the groundwork for his eventual switch into the field of psychiatry.

One final incident of the 1925–1930 period is worthy of mention.

As the construction of the new medical building at Boston City Hospital dragged on, Cobb apparently became impatient about the delays and about adjustments in the space being allotted to his new neurological unit which would be housed there. He relayed his frustrations in a letter he sent Edsall on February 24, 1928,[70] just prior to embarking for Europe. He began by telling Edsall that he had just heard of big plans for developing neurology at Cornell and at Columbia, implying that there had been some thought of considering him for these possibilities, for he added in a note, "not to mention the Yale job I was offered last year."[71] However, he told Edsall, "But these things make it all the more important for us to stick out for all we asked at the B.C.H." The remainder of his letter was devoted to space problems and allotments in the new building and the difficulties that Dr. Dowling, the hospital's superintendent, was giving him in this regard.

Edsall sent a copy of Cobb's letter to George Sears, a trustee of Boston City Hospital, telling Sears that he was concerned about it. He reminded Sears that Harvard had made an agreement with the General Education Board, with Cobb, and with the hospital authorities conjointly, and he emphasized his concern by telling Sears:

> There is, of course, the other possibility that if Cobb becomes sufficiently convinced of the difficulties, he might be offered and might take a job at Cornell or Columbia, just as he was offered the job at Yale. There are few forcible men in this work in the country, and it would be practically impossible to replace Cobb effectively, particularly if he chose to go from here to another place. The black mark that would leave against things would be difficult to overcome.[72]

As will be shown in the following chapter, Cobb had a series of frustrations with Boston City Hospital officials over the construction of the new Medical Building and the layout of his neurological unit within it. That this continued right up to the completion of the building is shown by a piece of correspondence in Edsall's files indicating the concern of the General Education Board over these delays. Writing to Edsall in early March of 1929, Trevor Arnett of the board informed the dean that the Rockefeller authorities regretted that the City Hospital official had not seen their way clear to construct the new building, which was an important part of Edsall's overall plan for Harvard neurology and was needed to make the Rockefeller gift effective. Arnett concluded, "We are glad to note, however, that the building is being erected within the next two years. We sincerely hope that nothing further will intervene to prevent the carrying out of this plan."[73]

It is not known what specific effects these little pushes had. However, they must have done some good, for less than a year and a half later the new Medical Building had been completed and Cobb transferred his main activities to Boston City Hospital.

7
The Neurological Unit at Boston City Hospital (1930–1934)

Viewed from the perspective of Cobb's own life, completion of the neurological unit at Boston City Hospital represented the flowering of his ambition to be director of a laboratory devoted primarily to studying the anatomy, physiology, and tissue pathology of the central nervous system. From the time when he first talked with Edsall during medical school, Cobb's interest in the neurosciences had continued to expand.[1] While interning with Cushing, while undertaking studies in Baltimore, while tentatively orienting himself to life in Boston, and while on the European trip, Cobb's basic knowledge had been greatly enhanced, and during the years at the neuropathology laboratory he had learned to master the administrative details of directing a research unit. The earlier clinical work at City Hospital had afforded experience in dealing with the complexities of organization and logistics.[2] So by 1930 the growing bud of competence in the neurosciences was about to bloom.

The blooming of the flower in or about 1930 is indicated by Cobb's own statement when in 1956 he received the Kober Medal from the Association of American Physicians. The fourth and final golden age for neurology and neuropathology in his own words took place about 1930 and was epitomized by the neurological supper club to which he belonged (373). When he accepted the Kober Medal, Cobb said:

> Returning to Harvard, the years around 1930 produced one of those rare combinations of men, deeply interested and active in an advancing field; this concatenation was in Neurology. We spontaneously joined in a Neurological Supper Club and discussed at monthly meetings our current researches. From Physiology came Cannon, Alexander Forbes, Bard, Fulton, Rosenblueth, Davis; from Surgery Cushing, Tracy Putnam, Bailey, Mixter; from Clinical Neurology, Ayer, Viets, Crothers, and Solomon; and from my department of Neuropathology Lennox, Wolff, Harry Forbes, Morrison, Fremont-Smith, and Gildea. Some of the growing subjects under discussion were electroencephalography, epilepsy, homeostasis, cerebral circulation, the hypophysis, and sham range.[3] These fruitful investigations all developed into major fields

and spread over the country as these men were called to professorial posts in Baltimore, New York, Chicago, St. Louis, and New Haven.[4] Thus do the tides of Research rise, spread themselves, and ebb.

Teaching and research in clinical neurology and basic neuropathologic science remained in bloom at the neurological unit for many years under the leadership of Cobb, Tracy Putnam, Derek Denny-Brown, and recently Norman Geschwind. Some of the most notable work, particularly the discovery of Dilantin as an anticonvulsant, took place after Cobb's 1934 departure. The death knell of the neurological unit did not come until Harvard was forced to withdraw from Boston City Hospital in the seventies.[5]

On the other hand, even before August, 1930, when Cobb moved into the new quarters (68), events that would eventually change his course were beginning to make their appearance. One of these was the growing understanding of his own speech problem. When he realized the effectiveness of Adlerian analysis with Seif, in contrast to the speech exercises of Mr. Robbins, Cobb was on his way to an intensified interest in psychiatry. Moreover, because of his disillusionment in Adler as a thinker, Cobb was open to exploring other pathways in dynamic psychotherapy and developed a tentative interest in Freud. The interest in Freud was enhanced by Cobb's friend Herman, who had recently abandoned his Jungian studies in favor of Freudian psychoanalysis.

Cobb had experienced increasing friction in his relations with John J. Dowling, the administrator of Boston City Hospital. In April, 1929, when ground was finally broken for the new neurological unit, a situation arose which Cobb viewed as a crisis. An important aspect of Cobb's strategy in setting up the neurological unit was to incorporate neurosurgery, and Dowling had assured Cobb verbally that two operating rooms and other needed facilities for neurosurgery would be available on the eighth floor.[6] However, Dowling had been unwilling or neglected to give this assurance in writing. Now, at almost the last moment, Cobb wrote a letter to Edsall expressing his dismay and threatening to pull out at the last minute unless Dowling was willing to put his promise on paper.[7] Cobb continued to have trouble with the hospital administration and experienced it as an ongoing frustration. So, although the flower of Cobb's achievement continued to bloom, as measured by any objective observer, to Cobb himself the withering process was beginning to appear. Even though he may not have been aware of it, a shift in interest was already beginning to influence his future activities.

Meanwhile, as industrious as ever in pursuing his objective of a well-integrated neurological unit, Cobb, with his staff, went through the trying period of transition to the new accommodations on the seventh-to-tenth floors of the recently completed Medical Building at City Hospital. Cobb saw his new clinic as one of the few places in the world where serious neuropathological and physiological studies would be clearly and often directly related to human clinical problems. It was important to him, for example, that the observations made during neurosurgical procedures be integrated with those of the clinicians and the laboratory investigators. Indeed, such closely correlated studies were to come about, particularly in epilepsy (chapter 8). In fact, co-ordinated research efforts were to go beyond Cobb's own department and be correlated with work simultaneously under way in the Thorndike Laboratory.[8] With the physical move to the new facilities, Cobb's dream was brought to fruition.

The layout of the new unit was described by Cobb and Munro in the October issue of the *Harvard Medical Alumni Bulletin* (68). An on-site sketch of the ninth floor was made by the author during a visit in 1979 (Figure 2). It was the ninth floor that housed all the offices and laboratories. Cobb's own comfortable office occupied the southerly corner and was separated by a secretarial space from Fremont-Smith's office. Next in line along the southeast side of the building came the large neuropathology laboratory of Raymond Morrison,[9] followed by Lennox's area for the study of epilepsy and then on the east corner

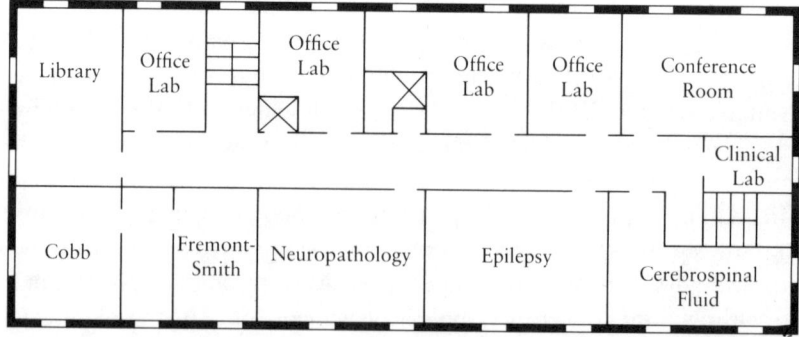

FIGURE 2.—Floor plan of the Neurological Unit at Boston City Hospital.

Fremont-Smith's work space for his spinal fluid studies. At the northeast end of the central corridor was a small laboratory for blood and urine studies. At the north corner was located the conference room, which in 1979 was hung with anatomical charts dating from Cobb's day. Then along the northwest side of the corridor were several rooms large enough to be used either as offices or laboratories. These rooms were assigned to various individuals from time to time. H. S. Forbes carried out his cat-window work in one of them. Munro had one. For a time Putnam and Merritt worked in one. The last of these offices, next to the library, was once occupied by Gibbs and later became the electroencephalographic laboratory. At one time Von Storch, of the Boston University faculty, was in that room. Taking up the westerly corner of the ninth floor was the library, a large room opening from the end of the hallway. To this day bound volumes of reprints and other old reference books are on the shelves alongside more recent acquisitions, and the wide central corridor has heavy wooden cabinets for storage along its walls.

According to Cobb and Munro, the plan of the seventh floor was modified slightly from that of a typical medical ward in order to make it appropriate for the care of male neuropsychiatric patients. The eighth floor was further modified to include the controversial neurosurgical operating rooms for Munro and Putnam. The remainder of the eighth floor was occupied by female patients. The tenth floor in Cobb's day was essentially a penthouse for the care of laboratory animals.[10] Relative to the purposes and direction of the neurological unit Cobb said, "The connotation no longer is 'morbid anatomy of the nervous system,' but 'study of the diseases of the nervous system' from any aspect—post mortem, clinical, or experimental."

In his *Alumni Bulletin* account Cobb classed those who participated in the professional work of the unit under three headings, laboratory, clinical neurology, and neurosurgery. The laboratory personnel included himself, Fremont-Smith, Putnam, Forbes, Lennox, Morrison, Finesinger (who had just completed his residency), and Mary E. Dailey. Miss Dailey held a position on the hospital staff and obviously was regarded as a collaborator rather than a secretary or technician. Gibbs's name is absent because that year he was in Philadelphia working on micropipette techniques with Professor Detlev W. Bronk at the University of Pennsylvania. As staff members in clinical neurology Cobb listed, in addition to himself, Myerson, Evans, Fremont-Smith, MacDonald, Lennox, Putnam, and Herman. In neurosurgery he recorded the names of Munro and Putnam. He recognized, of course, that some of the workers made contributions in more than one category. In addition, there were two residents, Merrill Moore and Houston Merritt, as well as six house officers with one-year appointments.[11]

During the next four years, prior to Cobb's departure for the Massachusetts General Hospital, a large number of promising young men and women were attached to the neurological unit in various capacities. Unfortunately their exact titles and terms of service are not available from official records.[12] Arranged in alphabetical order they were Aring, Asekoff,[13] Ask-Upmark,[14] Blain, Coggeshall, Craig, Fender,[15] Finley,[16] Margaret C.-L. Gildea, Irvine,[17] McNaughton,[18] Molholm,[19] Pool,[20] Rubin,[21] Schwab,[22] Slaughter,[23] Stone,[24] Von Storch,[25] and Woodall.[26]

H. Houston Merritt was an important addition to the staff even though Cobb never collaborated with him on a scientific publication. A Southern farm boy with a background of medical internship at Yale, Merritt came to City Hospital as a member of the house staff in 1928 and stayed on thereafter. He was described by Aring[27] as the most consummate neurological diagnostician he had ever met. When called upon by a junior member of the staff he would enthusiastically respond at any time of day or night and lend reassurance that nothing important had been overlooked. In a taped interview[28] Merritt recalled having been at the Cobbs' home in Milton one day when Finesinger literally sawed from a tree the branch on which he was sitting. Merritt was a rough diamond socially and even during the interview in late life had a somewhat gruff manner. At the neurological unit he worked principally with Putnam. When Putnam went to the New York Neurological Institute in 1939, Merritt was to become acting director of the neurological unit. However, probably because of what Cobb perceived as his lack of social grace, he was not even considered for the permanent position. Derek Denny-Brown was chosen, and Merritt went to New York, where a most distinguished career awaited him. He succeeded Putnam as the director of the Neurological Institute and was a phenomenal fund raiser. He reported in his interview that he was keeping in touch with a lady who had left in her will twenty-four million dollars for the study of Parkinson's disease. However, during the early thirties Merritt was indeed the clinical mainstay of the service in Boston, for Cobb was not always available and the other staff members were primarily involved in their research activities or special interests.

Some of those on the staff at the time, however, did work closely with Cobb, especially Charles D. Aring, Daniel Blain, Howard C. Coggeshall, Fremont-Smith, Jacob E. Finesinger, Margaret C.-L. Gildea, Lennox, and Morrison.

Charles D. Aring, who commenced work January 1, 1932, remained as resident until 1934. Aring was an outstanding figure on the service when he was there, and as professor of neurology and chairman of the department in Cincinnati he became one of Cobb's most appreciative, loyal, and effective disciples. Later in life Aring developed an interest in psychoanalysis and like Cobb bridged the gap between neurology and psychiatry. He and Cobb remained very close to each other. Cobb greatly admired Aring because he had "gone the whole route." Of his training at Boston City Hospital Aring said:[29]

> The three years in Boston were exciting and rewarding ones. We always had a complement of Harvard medical students to supervise and teach, an activity just as exciting as the patients we saw. It was also a privilege to instruct in neuroanatomy and in Cobb's course in neuropathology at the Harvard Medical School. Residents had the opportunity of attending all sorts of seminars and rounds on other services besides neurology.
>
> I departed from Boston assured that I could not have had better training. The company had been grand and established me on a course of looking for the best wherever I went. I was not about to settle for less. This questioning attitude was as much unconscious as not; certainly it played a role in my continuing education. The training at the Neurological Unit of the B.C.H. established me on the road to academic neurology from which I never deviated. Also, I was to keep in touch with the Boston crew, teachers and peers, for the rest of my professional career.

Aring expressed himself well in writing. The following words from a personal communication describe with appropriate humor the circumstances of his arrival for duty on New Year's Eve, his initiation to a city hospital atmosphere while making rounds on the alcohol ward with Cobb the following day, and what his experience with alcoholics had taught him about recognizing the clinical syndrome of subdural hematoma:

> Our introduction to life in Boston was curious. We had driven from Cincinnati toward the end of the year, as I was to begin work at the hospital on New Year's Day. I had word to proceed to the Charles Street Prison to be measured for hospital uniforms. Arriving there in the early afternoon of the final day of the year, we were greeted by a most pleasant tailor, who took my measurements and called them out to a "trusty" or two. The figures he obtained were much beyond my girth, length, etc., but he assured me that these allowed for the usual shrinkage, as indeed turned out to be the case.

> The uniforms were constructed of a material resembling sailcloth and were for all intents and purposes indestructible. . . .
>
> My initial meeting with Cobb was for rounds on New Year's morning. . . . After introductions we began a trek through the tunnels of the hospital, finally arriving at a door, of course unknown to me, which when flung open revealed as disheveled a scene as I ever witnessed before or since. We have arrived at the alcohol ward where our work was to begin. . . . The ward was taxed to capacity . . . what a stench it was, the delapidation of the guests, to say nothing of the ward personnel, defying description. Only a Hogarth could have done it justice. With care we picked our way among the clientele whose juices were exuding all over the place. My introduction to Harvard was that never-to-be-forgotten post Bacchanalia in the company of one of the most dignified gentlemen I have been privileged to know. . . .
>
> My final consultation nearly three years later, toward the end of my Chief Residency, was on this very ward [to see] a man battered by life's vicissitudes exhibiting the most severe trismus. I had him transferred to the neurology service with the diagnostic impression of tetanus. It turned out that he had bilateral subdural hematomas . . . and when these were removed he could chew about as well as the next. Whatever the cause of his locked jaw, this was a fitting finale to my neurological residency.

The respect and admiration which Aring and Cobb felt for each other led to their collaborating in a major review article on muscular atrophies and allied disorders that was published in *Medicine* in 1935 (101) with one hundred and thirty-two references. Aring and Cobb maintained correspondence until Cobb's death in 1968.

Another member of the house staff with whom Cobb collaborated in scientific work was Daniel Blain, who for a time was commissioner of mental health in California and later became director of the Philadelphia State Hospital. Blain was interested in the arteriosclerotic process. He and Cobb wrote the chapter on arteriosclerosis of the brain and spinal cord in a symposium edited by E. V. Cowdry (85), which appeared in 1933. This thorough review was illustrated with photomicrographs from Cobb's previous work, after Vogt and Bielschowsky, on Vasoarchitektonik of cerebral structures. Among other things Cobb and Blain quoted Haeckel's earlier work and clearly showed in diagrams how the aging process was already manifest in vertebral arteries at the age of thirteen. They went on to discuss the special physiology and the pathological histology of arteriosclerotic change and various clinical manifestations of the process. Cobb was always proud to have counted Blain among the members of his staff. However, there did not exist subsequently an intimate ongoing relationship between the two men.

Howard C. Coggeshall, who was a City Hospital intern under Cobb from 1932 to 1933, and at the Institute of Human Relations at Yale the following year, subsequently changed his field of interest from neuropsychiatry to internal medicine. After internship in medicine at the Massachusetts General Hospital from 1933 to 1934, he stayed on as a staff member for several years with a primary interest in rheumatology. He later settled in Dallas, Texas. Coggeshall and Cobb collaborated on and published a review article about the various forms of neuritis (97). In the article they cited the forms of neuritis caused by viral infections, those related to bacterial toxins, neuritides related to vitamin deficiency or metabolic disorders, polyneuritides caused by chemical substances, local nerve injury from pressure or trauma, and finally the very rare forms of neuritis related to specific infectious organisms such as diphtheria.

Of all the staff members Cobb's closest relationship was with Frank Fremont-Smith, whom he had been encouraging and helping since the early days in 1923 when Fremont-Smith and Forbes completed their paper with Cobb on carbon monoxide asphyxia (36). As told previously, Cobb had appointed Fremont-Smith as his administrative assistant in 1925, had arranged for Fremont-Smith's European trip in 1926, and had obtained a laboratory for Fremont-Smith at the Thorndike in 1927. Now in the new neurological unit he provided Fremont-Smith not only with a private office adjacent to his own but also with a well-equipped laboratory area for spinal fluid studies. Moreover, he had assigned to Fremont-Smith Mary Dailey, the most creative and entrusted member of the supporting staff. There can be no doubt that Fremont-Smith was bright and was dedicated to his objective of approaching neuroscience from a biochemical base. However, he was not a great clinician, and according to Gildea was a bit naive at times in his diagnoses.[30]

Gildea recounted the story, later substantiated with minor variations by Gibbs[31] and Merritt,[32] of a young woman who had been picked up on the Boston Common wandering about in a state of mental confusion. She exaggerated her multiple complaints and was prone to elaborating on totally improbable stories. Gildea said she really had the Baron Münchhausen syndrome, which is relatively rare in women. Fremont-Smith thought she had multiple sclerosis. She was examined by several members of the house staff. After swearing each of them to secrecy she made the claim that her real name was Lady Ann Courtney and that she had come to this country to escape her dictatorial parents who were forcing her to marry a French duke. When one of the house staff presented the case to Frank Fremont-Smith, the others discovered that they had all been sworn to secrecy over the same item and began to guffaw. Frank Fremont-Smith told them that they were not behaving in a professional manner, were acting unethically, and had violated the young lady's confidence. In Gibbs's version of the story one of the residents said to Fremont-Smith, "If this woman is telling the truth about being an English noblewoman, all of us will wear brown derbies for a month. If she isn't English, will you wear a brown derby?" Of course, to Fremont-Smith's embarrassment, she turned out to be a native American.

However, in addition to his own writings he did publish a second paper with Cobb (74). This article, the sixteenth in a series on cerebral circulation by Forbes, Wolff, and other members of the staff, was on changes in the human retinal circulation and in the pressure of the cerebrospinal fluid during the inhalation of a mixture of carbon dioxide and oxygen. Wolff and Lennox had previously demonstrated that an elevated concentration of carbon dioxide increased the volume of blood passing through the brain by increasing the systemic blood pressure and by dilating the cerebral arteries.[33] Moreover, Loevenhart and his co-workers had demonstrated that breathing mixtures of carbon dioxide and oxygen could arouse people from stupor.[34] Cobb and Fremont-Smith were interested in determining, if possible, what the mechanism of that phenomenon might be. Lumbar puncture and ophthalmoscopic observations on two humans before and during inhalation of the gas mixture demonstrated once again that cerebral vasodilation occurred. Cobb never published anything else with Fremont-Smith.

The Cobb and Fremont-Smith families were close, particularly in the twenties and the early thirties. Both families had summer cottages at Cotuit on Cape Cod. The friendship with Frank Fremont-Smith cooled somewhat later on after the divorce from his wife, Frances. However, Dr. and Mrs. Cobb remained in close touch with her for many years. Fremont-Smith went with Cobb to the Massachusetts General Hospital in 1934.[35] Mary Dailey Irvine said that Cobb gave emotional support to Fremont-Smith and appreciated his imaginative and constructive ideas as no other member of the department did.[36]

Another collaborator, of growing importance because of his subsequent role at the Massachusetts General Hospital, was Jacob Ellis

Finesinger, always known as Jake. After graduation from Johns Hopkins Medical School in 1929, Jake Finesinger came to the Boston City Hospital as a neurological house officer and in the spring of 1930 was promoted to resident. In 1931 he was dong investigative work on the neurological unit for a minuscule salary. In May, 1932, he obtained a Commonwealth Fellowship which enabled him to marry his wife, Grace, ending an engagement of seven years. The next academic year Finesinger continued to work part time on the neurological unit, but he was primarily engaged in psychiatry under Campbell at the Boston Psychopathic Hospital. That year, too, he undertook a psychoanalysis as the first analysand of Hanns Sachs, who had just come from Freud's circle in Vienna to succeed Franz Alexander as the training analyst of the Boston Psychoanalytic Society and Institute.[37] From June, 1933, until October, 1934, Finesinger and his wife were in Vienna, where Finesinger had training analyses with Anna Freud, Helene Deutsch, and Heinz Hartmann.[38] On his return from Vienna Finesinger went to work with Cobb at the Massachusetts General Hospital.

On the basis of the work that Finesinger did with Forbes's skull-window technique during 1931 and 1932, he published three papers on cerebral circulation as a coauthor with Cobb. It is of interest that Cobb shared with Forbes the laboratory where the skull trephines were carried out, yet the two usually published independently. The first of the three studies in which Cobb and Finesinger collaborated was on the vagal pathway of vasodilator impulses (84). This study was part of a collaborative effort with Wilder Penfield in Montreal to establish the pathway by which impulses from stimulation of the tenth cranial (vagus) nerve in the neck are transmitted to the pial membrane on the brain surface and dilate its arteries. The study was extraordinarily difficult to carry out because of the large amount of surgery needed to insert the skull window, to reach the vagus nerve in the neck, and to expose the origins of several cranial nerves beneath the medulla oblongata of the brain stem. Some of the work was done on cats and some on monkeys. Finesinger and Cobb concluded that nerve impulses may pass up either vagal nerve trunk to the medulla oblongata, leave the medulla along both facial nerves and travel as far as the geniculate ganglia, and thence along autonomic nerves to the cerebral vessels, where they cause vasodilation. This work was directly related to the research that Penfield was doing on epilepsy at the time (chapter 8). The other two studies that Cobb and Finesinger carried out together were technically less difficult. One had to do with the effect of such convulsive agents as caffeine, camphor, and picrotoxin on the pial arteries, all except camphor producing vasoconstriction (90). The third study showed that a variety of narcotic agents had different effects upon the blood vessels of the pia (100). Finesinger and Cobb collaborated on a number of subsequent projects at the Massachusetts General Hospital when Finesinger became Cobb's administrative right bower. Finesinger, like Aring, was a physician whom Cobb appreciated because he went the whole route from basic neuroscience through clinical neurology, and psychiatry to psychoanalysis.

Margaret Crane-Lillie was important not only for her scientific work but because of her contact with Dr. and Mrs. Cobb over a number of years and her marriage to Cobb's long-time collaborator, Edwin F. Gildea. Gildea had started working in the old neuropathology laboratory in Building D while still in medical school prior to 1924 and he was Cobb's first resident at City Hospital in 1928. He went first to Yale in 1929 and later to Barnes Hospital in St. Louis. Margaret Gildea said that in 1929, when a Ph.D. candidate at Radcliffe, she was working in S. Burt Wolbach's pathology department at the Harvard Medical School and at that time became acquainted with Cobb and some of the other persons in the neuropathology laboratory. After she got her Ph.D. she spent a year, from November, 1930, to November, 1931, in Zurich. Then on her return she commenced work in the neurological unit. She was there at the same time as Finesinger, who encouraged her to go into medicine. She went to Tufts Medical School in the fall of 1933. When she became engaged to Gildea in 1934 she transferred to Yale and by dint of working summers graduated there in 1936.[39] When at the neurological unit she finished some work that Gildea had been doing earlier with Cornelius P. Rhodes on black tongue in dogs. This work was published in collaboration with Cobb and William B. Castle (102). It was a meticulously controlled study of groups of dogs on diets deficient in the entire vitamin B complex and in Vitamin B_1 alone. In order to produce demonstrable cord lesions it was found necessary to keep the animals alive for a long time with periodic doses of vitamins. Otherwise the animals would die before the spinal cord lesions had time to develop.[40] Margaret and Edwin Gildea remained close personal friends of the Cobbs for many years.

Although Cobb's longtime associate, William Gordon Lennox, carried out most of his epilepsy work independently (chapter 8), he did occasionally collaborate with Cobb on a publication. During the early years of the neurological unit, when Gibbs was making his studies of cerebral circulation with their ultimate impact on the epilepsy program, Cobb and Lennox wrote three papers together. The first told of the founding of the Harvard Epilepsy Commission (81). The second was a twenty-page chapter on epilepsy for *Oxford Medicine* (82), and the third was a statistical analysis of the aura in epilepsy as observed in 1,359 cases. An aura was recorded in 764 of the patients. The auras were subdivided into categories dependent upon their clinical manifestations. Cobb's attachment to Lennox was close. When Cobb went to the Massachusetts General Hospital in 1934, Lennox, Gibbs, and Erna Leonhart remained at the neurological unit. However, in later years Cobb told his wife that he regretted not having taken Lennox along with him.

Raymond Morrison took charge of neurohistology in January, 1929, when he moved from the Thorndike to the neuropathology laboratory in Building D at the medical school. There, before completion of the City Hospital neurological unit, he became interested in the effect of electroshock on the brain substance and published with Weeks and Cobb an article on the effects of different types of electric shock on mammalian brains (69). The study was a meticulous one in which the effects of a high tension current from an induction coil, the electricity released by a condenser discharge, alternating current, and direct current were all evaluated in terms of the damage produced in cells of various parts of the brain. The effect of heat was also studied, with the conclusion that it had little to do with the observed lesions. Morrison continued at City Hospital to do routine neurohistology for the neurosurgeons Munro, Putnam, and their resident staff until 1934. At that time, Morrison departed with Cobb for the Massachusetts General Hospital, and the new director, Tracy Putnam, brought in Leo Alexander, a former student of Vogt in Berlin, to do the work in clinical neuropathology.

In addition to the work that Cobb did with Aring, Blain, Coggeshall, Fremont-Smith, Finesinger, the Gildeas, Lennox, and Morrison, he wrote an important paper on alcoholic polyneuritis in collaboration with George R. Minot and Maurice B. Strauss of the Thorndike staff (87). While not eliminating entirely the toxic effects of alcohol itself, the gist of this communication was to emphasize deficiency of the Vitamin B complex, and particularly Vitamin B_1, as the important causative factors in the polyneuritis associated with excess use of alcohol.

Also, during the early thirties at Boston City Hospital Cobb made a number of contributions to the literature alone, without collaborators. Several of these were review articles on very specific subjects such as the causes of epilepsy (80) and the clinical physiology of the cerebral circulation (89). He also wrote important chapters for two compendiums of medicine. The first was a beautifully illustrated review of the knowledge he had acquired over the years of the cerebrospinal blood vessels, which became a section in *Cytology and Cellular Pathology of the Nervous System,* edited by his friend Wilder Penfield (78). The second was a chapter for Blumer's *Practitioner's Library* (79). In 1932 Cobb also rewrote the outline for the second-year neuropathology course and made some miscellaneous contributions, including one on ornithology (91) and a poem (98).

Although Cobb's work at City Hospital was primarily in various aspects of neuropathology, it is important to note that the attention he gave to meeting the psychiatric needs of the institution afforded experience that would later be helpful in setting up the liaison service at the Massachusetts General. Prior to 1930, when Cobb moved into the new neurological unit, Arthur Fairbanks had been available for some kinds of consultations,[41] and Evans was working in the outpatient department with Wentworth. Herman's weekly visits for teaching and advice in the care of patients rounded out the psychiatric activities. Then, there came upon the scene one of the most colorful collaborators of Cobb's professional life, a Renaissance man named Merrill Moore.

Moore came on the service as an intern in 1929, was a resident in 1930, and then spent the remainder of his career at Boston City Hospital. He had a brilliant mind with rapid ideation and a host of variegated talents. When frustrated by stoplights or other traffic delays he wrote sonnets, and he published one thousand of them in a volume entitled simply *M.*[42] He had an infinite capacity for knowing people, including the minor details of their lives. He was able to induce people to work with him and for him. For example, in the days of Franklin D. Roosevelt's New Deal, he had about thirty WPA girls working on various hospital projects.[43] He was a universal consultant. He knew where to get anything. He built his house with his own hands. Each year he engaged in the annual swimming contest to the Boston Lighthouse. Metaphorically speaking, Moore had his fingers in about sixteen pies at one time. Often he would get others to finish his projects for him. After the death of William Herman in January, 1935, Moore became the central figure in psychiatry at City Hospital and the head of psychiatry within the neurological unit. Moore dreamed of an independent department of psychiatry, but that was not to come about in his day.[44]

While the psychiatric work at City Hospital was developing and expanding under the aegis of Moore, Cobb was devoting more of his own time to psychiatric activities. In the very early thirties he became involved with the young Boston psychoanalysts who, after training in Vienna, were reorganizing the Boston Psychoanalytic Society and developing the Boston Psychoanalytic Institute. He engaged in the struggle, against Freud's wishes, to establish psychoanalysis as a university discipline both in the department of psychology at Harvard and at the medical school. The story of his eventual success in this venture through the support of Alan Gregg is recounted elsewhere (chapter 10). In 1934 Cobb also undertook his own analysis with Hanns Sachs, the training analyst of the Boston Psychoanalytic Institute.

Cobb's stammering had greatly improved after his previous analytic work with Seif and was no longer a serious problem in conversation with individuals or in small groups, although it did interfere with public speaking. An amusing episode occurred on the ninth floor shortly before Cobb's departure for the Massachusetts General Hospital, an episode that brought into focus not only the stammering problem but also Cobb's liberal view on employing people with handicaps. One day a new neurosurgical resident named Samuel Weaver, who had come to Boston a few days early and was feeling homesick, came in to the ninth floor, hoping to get acquainted. Betty Fisher, the office manager, thought he should meet the director of the unit and brought him to Cobb's office. Dr. Cobb said, "Good morning, Dr. W-w-w-w-eaver." Dr. Weaver was a bit nonplussed to realize that his illustratious new mentor had a speech defect. Then Cobb took Weaver across the hall and introduced him to Von Storch. "Dr. W.-w-w-w-eaver, I want you to m-m-m-eet Dr. V-v-v-v-on Storch." Von Storch replied, "It's a p-p-p-pleasure to m-m-m-m-eet you, Dr. W-w-w-w-eaver." Then at Cobb's request Von Storch showed Weaver around the ninth floor. When they reached the spinal-fluid laboratory Von Storch introduced Weaver to a young volunteer who had a really severe speech disorder. She could hardly say "W-w-w-w-eaver" at all. Weaver was beginning to have acute anxiety about the kind of environment to which he had committed himself when he and Von Storch walked out into the corridor.

Von Storch commenced to introduced him to another young lady who was carrying a tray. She threw her arms up and said, "Oo-oo-uh." Then before she could complete saying the name, she dropped the tray, with all the things that were on it, and went into a grand-mal epileptic convulsion. Such was Dr. Weaver's introduction to the neurological unit.

Cobb's ready acceptance of people with ability, regardles of physical handicaps or other forms of minority status, led to an atmosphere on the neurological unit where the various workers had a feeling of being members of a large family. A number of those with technical, secretarial, or administrative positions took on with loyalty a great deal of responsibility.

Cobb used social gatherings at his home in Milton as a way of enhancing the morale of his staff. For example, he often invited staff members there for weekend afternoons. Many of the former staff members recall this hospitality with deep appreciation. The new house in Milton was on a part of Cobb's parents' property on the north side of Adams Street above the Neponset Marsh. The part of the land where Cobb built his house was heavily wooded; so cutting firewood and clearing brush were usual forms of entertainment. The other Cobb family activity which had a direct bearing on Cobb's professional life was cruising on the yawl *Pamaho* every summer with Binger and his wife, Chloe. During the long hours on a sailboat waiting for a breeze or for the tide to turn, Cobb and Binger were able to exchange ideas on neuropsychiatric topics. These cruises began approximately in 1929 and continued until the mid-thirties and spanned the period of time when Binger was experiencing the impact of giving up his metabolic research in favor of internal medicine and psychoanalysis. It was during the same years that Cobb was wrestling with the organization of psychoanalysis in Boston and laying plans for his new work in psychiatry at the Massachusetts General Hospital. An interaction between the two men was having an important influence on both their lives.

Amusing incidents from the days of cruising with the Cobbs have been told by Chloe Binger. Although there were occasional trips to Maine, most of the Cobbs' cruising was in the waters south of Cape Cod between Monomoy Point and Cuttyhunk with frequent visits to Muskeget, the little island where Cobb had so often gone duck hunting, and to the Elizabeth Islands, where his brother-in-law, Harry Forbes, had a summer place at Hadley's Harbor on Naushon. Chloe Binger told of two anxious moments aboard *Pamaho,* one of them in the

Boston City Hospital

waters near Muskeget and the other near the Elizabeth Islands. One afternoon in 1935 or 1936 after sailing in the vicinity of Muskeget, the Cobbs decided to enter Cape Pogue Pond on Chappaquiddick Island by way of a new artificial channel which had been dug as a WPA project during the Roosevelt administration.[45] The channel, or cut, only remained open for about two years, but the jetties that serve as its memorial are still visible.[46] The day the Cobbs went through, the wind must have been from an easterly or southerly direction. The story, undoubtedly with some hyperbole, is recounted here in Chloe Binger's own words:

> There was a channel from the eastern side of Cape Pogue Bay into Nantucket Sound. There was no way of knowing which way the sand was backed up, but at certain times with the tide and wind right you could cut through there into Cape Pogue Bay without coming in the regular channel on the Edgartown side. I remember Stanley's taking us around outside of the island in a gale of wind, just a rip snorter, and you could just see the waves pounding up all along the shore, and then a difference where the gap was. I can't remember whether it was more flat or more surfy, but he knew that was it. The wind was behind us and Stanley headed right at that thing like a man going over a stone wall on a hunter, shooting through. Betty and I were hanging onto everything. We came up like a cork on the inside perfectly safe. The motion was so fast that we didn't have time to be petrified, but we knew one just have to have confidence in the skipper or one would be petrified. He did that thing several times.

On another occasion when anchored in Quick's Hole, between Nonamessett and Pasque in the chain of Elizabeth Islands, Cobb nearly harpooned Binger. Binger, who had gone ashore for a swim at dusk, was swimming back to the *Pamaho* when Cobb, seeing something dark on the water, thought it was a big fish. He crawled out onto the bowsprit, harpoon in hand, but fortunately Binger saw him and just in time made his identity known.

The Cobbs and the Bingers cruised together on *Pamaho* from 1929 to 1935, at which time she was sold. The cruising in 1936 was aboard a rented catboat, and in 1937 the Cobbs' new cutter, *Fulmar,* was launched. Adventures aboard *Fulmar* are recounted in chapter 10.

Cobb and his wife decided to have a really good vacation in the summer of 1934 before commencing work on the new psychiatric service at the Massachusetts General Hospital. In the earlier part of the summer they spent some time at Alexander Forbes's ranch in Wyoming. While there the Cobb children sent one of their friends, a little girl, into the woods along a stream on a snipe hunt. Then they abandoned her, expecting that she would come home in tears after learning of their cruel deception in leading her to think she might be able to find a bird. Cobb, having learned what was going on, caught a duck, waded down the stream, and put it in the child's arms.

In early 1934 Cobb and his wife made their third trip to Europe. Hitler had come into power in 1933, and the atmosphere had dramatically changed from that of 1928. They were shocked, for example, to find that Cobb's former colleague, Schaltenbrandt, was a member of the National Socialist Party.

The neurological unit that Cobb had built at Boston City Hospital was a remarkable achievement. It had grown out of his own deep interest in the neurosciences, his imagination in seeing the creative possibilities of various situations as they arose, his unselfish dedication to the interests of students, house staff, and colleagues, and his manifold administrative talents. The neurological unit had become in all probability the leading center where scholars of varying disciplines could cooperate closely in studies of the nervous system. Charlotte Troutwine recalled receiving a letter from Alan Gregg, when she was Cobb's secretary, in which Gregg said that the Rockefeller Foundation funds awarded to Cobb had been the most gratifying of any of their grants.[47]

Why Stanley Cobb elected to abandon such an outstandingly successful venture is not entirely clear, but there were undoubtedly several factors that influenced his decision to move on to new activities. One of these was pragmatic. He never learned to work with the Irish politicians who controlled Boston City Hospital. Another factor, quite probably, was the influence of his friend William Herman. Bill Herman was a part-time staff member and a close personal friend. His office was at the Massachusetts General Hospital, and he could sense the atmosphere of that institution and the kind of reception that Stanley Cobb might find in attempting to set up a new psychiatric service there. Bill Herman encouraged him to come. Then, nationally, there was an awakening of a need for a liaison psychiatric service that would bridge the gap between acute general hospitals and crowded, often remote state psychiatric institutions. Pioneer efforts had been made, and the Rockefeller Foundation was interested in financing such ventures. Moreover, Stanley Cobb himself had become involved in Freudian psychoanalysis and was coming to think of psychotherapy in dynamic terms. He was becoming more aware of the role of emotions in his own stammering, and he was developing an interest in the importance

Boston City Hospital

of psychic factors in such illnesses as migraine headaches, bronchial asthma, Raynaud's phenomenon, duodenal ulcer, and rheumatoid arthritis. In fact, Houston Merritt criticized the Boston City Hospital service under Cobb's direction as having been too psychosomatic.

Among Dr. Cobb's preserved correspondence was found a letter to his old friend, Sir Charles Symonds of London, whom he had known even prior to his period of study there.[48] This letter, dated May 21, 1934, is reproduced below and summarizes in Cobb's own words his reasons for the move.

Dear Charlie:

I learn that gossip of my "change of life" has reached London. It's true. I am leaving the big Neurological Unit at the Boston City Hospital for a smaller Psychiatric Unit at the Massachusetts General Hospital. The M.G.H. has received money for a psychiatric development, and they asked me to take charge. My research will go along as before and on similar lines. My clinical work will turn to psychiatric problems, and I will have a small ward for ten or twelve psychiatric patients in the M.G.H. This will be in close connection with an O.P.D. and with the McLean Hospital and the General wards.

My reasons for accepting are varied. In the first place, I have been organizing too big a unit and I have become an administrator at the B.C.H. I want to get back into more intimate relation with patients and get my own hands into the experimental work. The new small unit gives me a chance for this. Secondly, the M.G.H. is a better milieu for trying to handle a few patients as nearly perfectly as possible. The B.C.H. is a great place for running through a lot of material and sifting out interesting cases, but I find that my desire is to do less and do it better, and have some leisure to think. (An impossible ideal, you will say—but why not strive for it?) I admit a certain degree of failure in my relationship to the big "Neurological Unit" at the B.C.H. I kept it running all right, but it finally got to running me! That was a situation that demanded radical treatment. If I had stayed on I hope I would have had the "guts" to cut the research staff in two and delegate most of the ward work; but I'm leaving the new problem to Tracy Putnam who will succeed me and has been made Professor of Neurology, while I retain my chair of Neuropathology.

In the research way I hope to go on with cerebral circulation and soon put it together and condense out ten years work into a monograph. Then I want to study some problems that have come to my attention in relation to cerebral circulation, i.e., sleep, coma, delirium. There is a good deal to do along these lines in a purely clinical way, applying some of the newer physiological techniques. In the O.P.D. I want to branch out a bit and see what can be done with the treatment of adolescents with "psychoneurosis." My belief is that a lot can be done by a psychiatrist with adequate help from the right sort of social service worker. If we can prove this, the set-up of

O.P.D.'s ought to be changed. The present system of a psychiatrist seeing one neurotic patient after another for a few minutes or a half hour once a week, is worthless.

Of course, a large part of the pleasure in the move to the M.G.H. will be the close association with Ayer (Neurologist-in-Chief) while I become "Psychiatrist-in-Chief." We will share a ward at first, and later hope to get a new separate ward, but close together.

What do you think of the idea? Am I dropping by the wayside, or forging ahead?

I had hopes of being able to spend about two months in England and France this summer, but I have had a mild arthritis for the last three months, so I have been advised to go to a high, dry climate. We are, therefore, all going out to Wyoming for July and August where I am hoping to roast the rheumatics out of my joints.

I am looking forward to a year from now when I hope to be on my way to Europe. If we are forehanded, we ought to be able to arrange a fishing trip in either Ireland or Scotland, or perhaps Scandinavia.

As ever yours,
Stanley Cobb

As indicated in his letter to Symonds, Cobb was really making the move to psychiatry as a manifestation of his own personal evolution and growth. If he had elected to remain at City Hospital, his department would undoubtedly have continued to make important contributions to the neurosciences, and with Merrill Moore's help he could have developed a psychiatric service. However, there were problems in dealing with the hospital administration. On the other hand, at the Massachusetts General Hospital he would be among friends with whom administrative problems could be worked out comfortably. Moreover, the neurological unit had grown to such proportions that Cobb was spending more time than he liked in his role as chairman, and he felt deprived of personal freedom for his own studies. Little did he know when he moved that the Massachusetts General service would become a veritable Goliath and that he would be busier than ever with administrative matters. In the long run, Cobb's decision was probably a wise one, for he was in many ways an ideal person to introduce psychiatry into a general hospital setting. Moreover, the high quality of the investigative work conducted there and the large number of prominent neuropsychiatrists whom he trained furnish resounding affirmation of Cobb's wisdom in making the move.

8
Epilepsy

A dominant theme at the neuropathology laboratory and later at the neurological unit at Boston City Hospital was research related to epilepsy. The evolving concern with epilepsy grew partially out of Cobb's own interest, for he and Uyematzu were working on experimental convulsions from the very beginning of his research in Boston in 1920 (26). However, as time went on, a complex sequence of financial needs, strong emotions, and intellectual decisions, some of them quite fortuitous, had their impact on the course of events, and one of the most important was availability of funding.

One of the largely fortuitous events that affected the direction of epilepsy research in Cobb's laboratory was the arrival of William Gordon Lennox in 1921. If Cobb profited from the untimely death of E. E. Southard, he was again blessed by Lennox's misfortune in having his younger daughter develop epilepsy. Lennox came to the laboratory in 1921, after having heard of the research that Cobb and Uyematzu were doing. Lennox's work on epilepsy became a point of focal interest in Cobb's laboratory thereafter. Lennox, who had been born in Colorado Springs in 1884, graduated from the Harvard Medical School cum laude in 1913 and married Emma Buchtel, daughter of the chancellor of Denver University. After three years of hospital work, he went to Peking with the newly established Peking Union Medical College and Hospital. When his younger daughter, Margaret, developed epilepsy, Lennox resolved to leave China and study that disorder. He applied for a research position in the neuropathology laboratory because he had been told that Cobb knew more about epilepsy than anyone else.

Lennox's first three papers, published in 1924, were about the metabolism of epileptic patients. He was seeking reasons to explain the beneficial effects of starvation and ketogenic diets in epilepsy. Lennox was neither a brilliant nor an innovative investigator. Rather his role was to study in a meticulous and thorough way factors that might be important in epilepsy and to make this basic knowledge readily available. He slowly gathered his data, while others made more imaginative contributions to the field. Yet he was dedicated and had irrevocably committed his life to the study of epilepsy.

For Cobb, another fortuitous event that for years colored the atmosphere of his interest in epilepsy was his father's friendship with Charles P. Howland, a New Haven financier on the board of the Rockefeller Foundation. Howland also had a heavy emotional stake in epilepsy research because his own son, Henry, was seriously affected by this disabling disease.

Both Lennox and Howland had been hard hit by the emotional burden of epilepsy. The disease affects one out of every two hundred people. Although many epileptics are affected by *petit mal* seizures, which may be almost imperceptible lapses of consciousness, even such persons are subjected to occupational and driving restrictions for fear of injury to themselves or others. However, to witness a *grand mal* convulsion, particularly in a loved one, is a most frustrating emotional trauma. Although half of those with *grand mal* seizures have a warning aura, usually a familiar but nonspecific and queer sensation, it does not ordinarily give the victim time to lie down or otherwise avert danger. The aura, if present, is followed by sudden complete loss of consciousness and a tightening or spasm of all the muscles, sometimes with the body thrown into distorted positions. There may be gurgling, groaning, or at times an actual cry. The victim falls, stops breathing, becomes a dusky color, and has saliva flowing between his lips. After a period of time, which seems like an age to the onlooker but is usually only a matter of seconds, the rigid contraction of the muscles changes to jerking movements. The arms, legs, and head jerk violently and simultaneously. However, at this point air begins to enter the lungs, and the color clears. Then the jerking movements subside and the victim lies relaxed, breathing heavily, sweating profusely, and insensitive to pain. Often he has lost control of the bladder or bowels and the tongue or lips may have been bitten. Many epileptics who have had large numbers of seizures experience significant loss of intellectual function.

Epilepsy is one of the few diseases still regarded as a family disgrace, and if possible it is often maintained as a closely guarded secret. Even with the knowledge acquired through electroencephalography and other tools of modern science, the cause of epilepsy (if, indeed, there is a single factor) remains obscure. It is not surprising, therefore, that until comparatively recent years epilepsy was often seen as a disorder caused by demonic possession, and one of the therapeutic modalities was the exorcising of evil spirits.

Epilepsy

Lennox's daughter actually had a good prognosis and became herself an important worker in the field. However, Howland's son, Henry, was really crippled, and the emotional strain under which his wealthy parents lived was unbearable. The major confluence of energy that launched the long-term program was rooted in the impact that epilepsy had had upon the Lennox and the Howland families. Both Lennox and Howland were driven by the hope of finding a cure for their own children. However, Lennox was prepared to make a life work of the project. Howland, on the other hand, like many business executives, had a task-force approach that aimed for quick results. He hoped that the investment of significant funds and the correlation of work in more than one institution would lead to a prompt reward.

But Cobb himself had an emotional stake, too. He had inherited Southard's neuropathology laboratory and a very meager budget. He was hoping that Howland would become interested in more basic studies and could be counted upon as a long-term benefactor. It was characteristic of Cobb, with his talent for integrating seemingly diverse opportunities, that he and Howland organized an epilepsy committee in New York.

Cobb's initial efforts to establish an epilepsy committee are discussed in a letter to Edsall written July 8, 1921. In this he reported that Dr. Washburn, the director of the Massachusetts General Hospital, where Cobb's office was at that time, had a capital fund of twenty-five thousand dollars, the income of which could be devoted to epilepsy.[1] Washburn suggested that half the twelve-hundred-dollar income could go to patient care and the other half to investigation. Cobb was clearly entertaining the hope that Howland might be willing to augment the fund. In his letter to Edsall Cobb said:

> My thoughts on the subject are as follows: 1) that I can mention this to Mr. Howland as a nucleus to which it would be worth while to add some more money; 2) that Dr. Talbot[2] and I might cooperate in the use of this in the hospital; 3) that we might use this as a nucleus around which to build the foundation for the much-needed neurological service, because with this ward started, the study of epilepsy could be carried on there with the epileptic money.

By August, 1921, with Lennox about to make his appearance on the scene, Cobb's thoughts had begun to crystallize. In a letter to William Norton Bullard, he indicated that he had found Howland very much in earnest about the work.[3] Cobb said that he and Howland had decided to go ahead and map out the organization, with a board of trustees to raise and distribute money and a medical board to advise how it should be used. After consulting Walter W. Palmer, professor of medicine at Columbia and physician-in-chief at the Presbyterian Hospital, a number of candidates were considered as possible members of the board of trustees. Dr. Walter James, a trustee of the College of Physicians and Surgeons at Columbia, had agreed to serve. Palmer was to be secretary and Howland, treasurer. Cobb was counting on Campbell and Edsall and in the letter invited Bullard to be a third Boston representative. The medical board consisted of Cobb and Henry Rawle Geyelin, who was working on epilepsy at the Presbyterian under Palmer. In the letter to Bullard Cobb said:

> The medical board we wish to have composed only of men who are actively working on Research in Epilepsy. Dr. Geyelin and I have both expressed a desire to devote ourselves to this problem.... The function of this medical board is: First, to work on research problems connected with epilepsy; Second, to watch the work of others; Third, to recommend to the trustees what work is worthy of support; Fourth, to write a report on the progress in epilepsy.

Bullard agreed to round out the committee.[4] In the letter to Bullard Cobb said that the hope of the committee was to raise about twenty thousand dollars annually, and Howland thought there would be no difficulty in getting fifteen thousand from sources already available.

Cobb was interested in factors influencing the susceptibility of animals to experimental convulsions and was working with Uyematsu along these lines. He reported this work to Meyer in November, 1921.[5] A month later, in a letter to Frederick Tilney in New York, Cobb agreed to discuss this subject at an oncoming meeting of the Association for Research in Nervous and Mental Diseases.[6] Among the factors which Cobb was studying at the time were thyroid feeding, thyroidectomy, acute infections, acidosis, and starvation. The growing edge of investigation at the time had to do with starvation and the known value of ketogenic diets as a limited therapeutic measure in epilepsy, and Geyelin was working in this field. Howland had in mind an organization that would make possible close cooperation between Geyelin in New York and the neuropathology laboratory in Boston.

Meanwhile Lennox had arrived in September, 1921, and because of the nature of the funding was pushed into undertaking chemical and metabolic studies that undergirded and supplemented Geyelin's dietetic studies in New York. Inasmuch as the body produces keto-acidosis

Epilepsy

during fasting, most of the work in the two laboratories was seen to be metabolic in nature. There was evidence that keto-acids, the end products of incomplete combustion of fat, had something to do with the effect of fasting in reducing the frequency of epileptic seizures. Some of the actual metabolic and biochemical studies were carried out in the internal medicine laboratory, which in 1921 was in the Harvard Medical School quadrangle but which moved in 1925 to the Thorndike Memorial Laboratory at City Hospital.

Even at the beginning Lennox published independently of Cobb, for Cobb always insisted that his associates be independent investigators and receive full credit for their work.[7] Lennox worked initially with O'Connor in biochemistry, and when clinical situations were being studied he collaborated with L. H. Wright at the Monson State Hospital. In 1924 Lennox, Wright, and O'Connor published an article on studies of metabolism in epilepsy,[8] and in 1925 Lennox and O'Connor reported a study of uric acid retention during fasting.[9] There was evidence that acidification of the blood during fasting was one reason for its effectiveness in reducing the number of convulsions. This notion was substantiated by a patient of Geyelin's who stopped having convulsions when taking large amounts of hydrochloric acid.[10]

The possible value of acidosis as an important adjunct to the management of epilepsy caught Howland's fancy, too. Howland knew an osteopathic physician in Battle Creek, Michigan, named Hugh W. Conklin, and Conklin was convinced that osteopathic manipulation was helpful in epilepsy. Howland wanted Conklin to set up a laboratory study to determine whether or not manipulations affected the acidity of the body, and Conklin wrote to Cobb for advice.[11] Cobb's letter to Conklin was very supportive and understanding. He said, "If your experiments show that osteopathic manipulations result in a decreased concentration of acetone bodies in the blood, as well as an increased concentration in the urine, that will be an important contribution to our knowledge of kidney function and a vindication of the manipulations." Lennox continued his clinical studies at Monson. These included an evaluation of potassium borotartrate, which had been introduced by E. J. Bigwood[12] as an acidifying agent of therapeutic value in epilepsy. Lennox and Wright published their work on borotartrate in 1926.[13] They found it no more effective than phenobarbital in controlling epileptic seizures.

At this point in time Cobb was about to depart for his Rockefeller sponsored two-year period of study in Europe. On June 16, 1923, he wrote a letter to Howland expressing the hope that the epilepsy work could continue in the laboratory during his absence.[14] Cobb suggested the following program:

> 1. Lennox to continue with chemical work on the effects of starvation, and also do salt metabolism work under the direction of Gamble. He can then be well guided and have both children and adults to work on.
>   Approximate cost: Lennox $2500, Gamble $1000.
> 2. Mella to take over my administrative work and carry on his researches in the study of involuntary muscular movements and in the pathology of senile epilepsy.
>   Expenses to be carried by the Department of Neuropathology.
> 3. Thom to go ahead with his studies of the relation of childhood convulsions to epilepsy.
>   Needs grant of $700 for this year.
> 4. Talbot to continue study of epileptic children.
>   He probably does not need money, since he can use the Fay Fund for beds and his own laboratory for research.[15]

So, Cobb went off to Europe having done his best to make sure things went well in his absence. In a series of letters to Meyer written during the European trip there was little mention of epilepsy. Cobb's interest at that time was absorbed by the excitement of meeting new people and being exposed to fresh ideas in England and on the Continent, as well as undertaking to learn a modicum of French and German. Then, too, he was stimulated by postwar politics and by the cultural patterns of the old world. The epilepsy work in the laboratory at Harvard was plodding along without any important discoveries.

On Cobb's return to Boston in 1925, the work on epilepsy took a new turn. Enthused by the knowledge of techniques that he had acquired from Vogt and Bielschowsky in Berlin, Cobb decided to tackle epilepsy from a circulatory point of view. Although microscopically demonstrable injuries to the brain were often seen in institutionalized victims of epilepsy, there were no consistent diagnostically significant findings, and the changes observed in such patients were thought to be the result rather than the cause of convulsions. In fact Kussmaul and Tenner in 1859 had written:

> Every physician of the present day who is at all judicious will relinquish the hope cherished with child-like confidence by certain schools and times, that pathological anatomy is destined to give an explanation of the nature and seat of epilepsy, and he will only expect that result from the progress of the experimental physiology of nerves.[16]

Epilepsy

Cobb thought the study of cerebral blood supply would be the most promising approach because a number of neurologists had observed pallor of the optic discs prior to convulsions, and many neurosurgeons had seen the exposed cerebral cortex undergo vascular changes during epileptic attacks on the operating table (48).

So, in October, 1925, Cobb wrote an enthusiastic letter to Howland, then with the Greek Refugee Settlement Commission in Athens. In the letter Cobb reviewed his enriching experience in Europe and referred to the depletion of the Epilepsy Committee's exchequer in New York, which had a balance of only five hundred dollars. However, the important message in the letter was Cobb's elaboration of plans for future work:

> In Berlin I learned a great deal from Professor Vogt that will be useful in our researches. I have for some time been dissatisfied with my plan of research—i.e., taking a disease and studying it is starting at the wrong end of things (when you have a life-time ahead of you). Taking a physiological problem that is interesting in itself, and will lead to a group of diseases that interest you, is a much more fundamental attack, and in the long run will go farther. Working with a man like Vogt showed me the truth of this theory. So after deliberation and discussion I have decided to outline a program covering several years for the study of cerebral circulation.[17]

He went on to discuss in more detail what his plans were, mentioning the development of Forbes's skull-window technique and Fremont-Smith's method of observing the circulation in the brains of living cat embryos. Cobb indicated that he would not only collaborate in those investigations but also would continue to study microscopically the finer anatomy of the cerebral circulation—the work he had commenced with Vogt and Bielschowsky in Berlin. Cobb indicated to Howland that these studies might well lead to a clearer understanding of convulsions and hence would correlate with the work of Geyelin and Lennox, which had been supported by the epilepsy committee.

Hoping for continued funding, Cobb reported to Howland the work Lennox was doing at that time. This included observations on the utilization of glucose by epileptic patients, measurement of the fibrin content of the blood, the collection of important clinical data, animal experimentation on factors affecting susceptibility to convulsions, and coöperation with other workers such as James Gamble at the Children's Hospital and Fritz Talbot at the Massachusetts General. None of this work that Lennox was doing was very promising except perhaps that on experimental convlusions. In the same letter Cobb pointed out to

Howland that the chemical laboratory for Lennox's work had just been transferred from the medical school quadrangle to the Thorndike Memorial building at City Hospital.

Between the lines in his letter to Howland, Cobb was saying that he was abandoning a patient-centered project in favor of more basic long-term research. Whether a more sensitive awareness of Mr. and Mrs. Howland's emotional desperation could have softened Cobb's ebullient declaration of new plans no one knows. However, it is easy to understand how Cobb, after two years of exciting new contacts abroad, could be swept up into unrealistic expectations of continuing interest and support from the Howlands. And there is the possibilty that with more expressed concern for the Howlands' anguish an ongoing relationship of some sort might have been preserved.

In any event, Cobb's new approach to epilepsy by way of studying cerebral circulation did not impress Howland as holding promise of early help for his epileptic son, Henry. Apparently it did not impress Mrs. Howland much either, for Cobb received a letter from her dated March 10, 1926, informing him that the period of time for investigation of epilepsy from the funds of the Epilepsy Committee was to expire July 1 of that year.[18] She asked Cobb for a detailed report, on the basis of which to decide whether such funding should be renewed. Cobb also received a letter from Howland mailed March 19, 1926, indicating that he thought the epilepsy work was not proceeding in such a way as to be fruitful of any definite results.[19] Howland reported:

> Mrs. Howland and I went over the whole subject before she left Oxford for New York in February. We have each taken it up with persons experienced in this sort of medical coöperation, and Mrs. Howland will get together in New York people who can best advise whether or not it is well to go on with the enterprise in its present form, and if not what ought to be done. The matter is now in her hands with that advice and assistance, and doubtless you have already been in direct touch with the whole situation. I cannot answer your letter, therefore, or make any promise for the future.

Mrs. Howland did gracefully acknowledge the material which Cobb sent in response to her earlier letter. Then on April 29, 1926, Howland wrote from Athens that Geyelin's suggestions of making a classification of epilepsy and searching for a toxic substance elaborated by intestinal bacteria[20] sounded rather nonspecific. He argued:

> The difference between what we expected to do and the exploratory character which the work has taken on is not unlike the difference between

sending a detective to make an arrest on well-founded suspicions and calling out the *posse comitatus* to hunt for an unknown murderer.

Cobb's ability to maintain his hope and genial manner in the face of such frustration is a tribute to his self-control as well as his imagination. On May 21, 1926, he replied to Howland that he had adequate funding for his own research; he was concerned about leaving some of Lennox's good work unfinished with "no visible means of support."[21] Cobb expressed his belief that Geyelin's and Lennox's work on acid-base changes was indeed relevant and important. Then in response to Howland's analogy to the detective arresting a suspected criminal, Cobb pointed out that in epilepsy there was in all probability a ring of criminals. He went on to say that staking everything on one point was like a get-rich-quick scheme in business. He said further that he and Lennox would be in New York for the meeting of the American Psychiatric Association from June 7 to June 10 and expressed the hope that they could spend an evening together to go over the whole situation at that time. It is of note that in this letter Cobb made no mention whatever of the Howland's personal exasperation over the gradual deterioration of their son's epilepsy. Cobb's letter was an intellectual argument which lacked any expression of empathy.

With the shift in Cobb's emphasis from a patient-oriented task-force approach to one of more basic science, through the study of cerebral circulation and oxygen supply, the Howlands did indeed lose interest and terminate their support. However, they were to appear again in Cobb's life some years later when, as told in a subsequent paragraph, young Henry had bilateral cervical sympathectomy carried out by Wilder Penfield in Montreal and Cobb served as one of his consultants.

While the Epilepsy Committee funding appears to have ceased altogether by July 1, 1926, Lennox kept in touch with Geyelin, who in October, 1927, was indeed seeking for the hypothetical toxic substance in the bowel. In a letter to Geyelin at that time Lennox said that Cobb was preparing an appeal through the National Research Council for adequate funds to carry on research on a more extensive scale. Gildea later said, "Stanley was always having trouble raising money for Epilepsy."[22]

Six months after Howland's Epilepsy Committee withdrew its support, Cobb organized a Harvard Epilepsy Fund. On January 24, 1927, he wrote in a letter to Bullard that he had received twenty-three hundred twenty-five dollars from five donors[23] and would need about three thousand more to see Lennox through to July 1, 1928, when most of his current work would be complete.

As summarized in the Medicine Monograph which Lennox and Cobb published that year, Lennox had continued to round out his series of papers on various aspects of metabolism in epilepsy (48). In addition, he had done some work on experimental convulsions with Beetham which was in press at the time. Most of Lennox's work was negative. In fact he is quoted as saying that epilepsy research is like exploring for oil. "You drill a lot of wells, and most of them are dry." Probably his greatest contribution at that time was completion of the monograph with its extensive review of the world's literature and of the various hypotheses for the origin of convulsions.

In the monograph Cobb and Lennox developed at greater length than previously the reasons for suspecting altered oxygen supply to localized areas of the brain as an important precipating cause of convulsions. Writing the monograph gave Lennox, and to some extent Cobb, the necessary springboard from which to launch studies of circulation and of gaseous interchange, studies which were to engage the interest of Forbes, Gibbs, Finesinger, and other collaborators during the next few years.

For a time it appeared that the epileptic work of the laboratory was falling together into a meaningful pattern related to what might be called the anoxemia theory. Initially Cobb's involvement with epilepsy had been primarily to obtain funding for Lennox's research, although other workers, such as Uyematzu and MacDonald, were in the field too. Now came the newer work on capillary circulation in the brain carried out by Cobb with the collaboration of Talbott (45), on increased capillary circulation after cervical sympathectomy with Talbott and Wolff (59), and on the increased cerebral circulation after administration of histamine by Forbes and Wolff with Cobb's collaboration (60). These studies reinforced the notion that localized changes in cerebral oxygen supply might well be important in bringing on the seizures in epilepsy. So in a way, although unrelated work was also in progress, the entire laboratory staff became oriented toward epilepsy. In 1929 Cobb wrote:

> There is good evidence that the cerebral vessels contract on stimulation of the cervical sympathetic nerve, that they lose their tone and dilate when the nerve is cut, and that they dilate when the central end of the vagus nerve is stimulated . . . according to Poiseville's Law (1842) the minute volume flow

Epilepsy

through a capillary tube of given length varies directly with the fourth power of the diameter of the tube. With a 22 per cent increase in diameter, therefore, there would be an almost 150 per cent increase in blood flow, that is the minute volume would become two and a half times as great.... Recent investigations . . . make vascular spasm a much more reasonable working hypothesis than it was thirty years ago (62).

On the basis of these studies and others to follow, Cobb entertained the idea of severing the sympathetic nerve in the neck as a therapeutic measure in epilepsy. He was in close contact over the years with Wilder Penfield, the neurosurgeon whom he had known since his days in Baltimore.[24]

When working in New York from 1921 to 1928 under Allen O. Whipple, the chief of surgery, Penfield devoted much of his time to microscopic neuropathology with William C. Clarke, who had a particular interest in the healing process as it affected brain tissue.[25] Out of this work on the healing process, Penfield became interested in posttraumatic epilepsy. He wanted to go beyond conventional neurosurgery, which dealt primarily with brain tumors and other space-occupying disease processes, and to develop a new field of his own. In 1928 he moved to the Royal Victoria Hospital in Montreal, and in 1933, with Rockefeller funding, founded the Montreal Neurological Institute. He perfected techniques for treating some forms of posttraumatic epilepsy in which a localized brain injury caused convulsions affecting one side of the body, but for the usual variety of epilepsy, the cause of which was unknown, there was no accepted surgical approach. Then, there occurred, almost fortuitously, a situation that led Penfield to a dramatic and intimate association with Cobb and his co-workers in Boston.

The situation involved Cobb's former benefactor, Howland, who was still seeking a cure for Henry's epilepsy, Alan Gregg, who dispensed funds for the Rockefeller Foundation, and a wealthy New Yorker named William Ottman, Senior, whose son, Bill, had severe epilepsy dating from childhood. Most of Penfield's contact was with Mrs. Ottman, who, divorced from her husband, first brought their son to Penfield as a patient when he was studying in Germany just prior to his move to Montreal. At that time Penfield refused to consider surgery.

Mrs. Ottman countered Penfield's refusal by making a ten-thousand-dollar gift to Penfield for neurological research in Montreal. Furthermore, the Rockefeller Foundation was becoming interested in Penfield's dream of a neurological institute in Montreal, and plans were beginning to crystallize. So, when Mrs. Ottman brought her son, Bill, to Montreal in 1929, still seeking help, Penfield felt obliged at least to carry out ventriculography. The ventriculograms did show significant atrophy of the left cerebral hemisphere; young Ottman had had a traumatic forceps delivery; and his seizures sometimes began with trembling of the right hand. There was at least the faint hope of finding a remediable process. Expense being essentially no consideration, Penfield asked Spielmeyer to come from Munich, Cobb to come from Boston, and Geyelin to come from New York as consultants. At operation a narrowed artery was found and tied off,[26] in the hope that new collateral circulation would improve the blood supply. Ottman was unable to talk for several days. Then his voice came back and his convulsions stopped. Ottman's surgery took place in 1930.

After Penfield's success with Ottman, Howland and his wife demanded that he perform surgery on their son, Henry. Howland was on the board of the Rockefeller Foundation, and Penfield was dependent upon Rockefeller funding for his new institute. But Henry Howland did not have posttraumatic epilepsy. He had the usual idiopathic variety for which there was no known effective surgical approach. Penfield was aware of Cobb's animal work, which indicated that stimulation of sympathetic nerves in the neck decreased cerebral circulation (59) (62). Accordingly, in 1931, after thoroughly explaining to the Howlands the risks and the improbability of dramatic improvement, Penfield proceeded to remove the periarterial sympathetic nerves from the carotid and vertebral arteries on one side of the neck. After that Henry's generalized seizures became unilateral. Then Penfield removed the sympathetic fibers from the other side of the neck, and although he encountered what he described as alarming complications at the time, Henry's epilepsy was dramatically improved. Penfield considered Henry Howland's operation frankly experimental and never wrote the procedure up in professional journals.

However, stimulated by the partial success of the experiment, Penfield decided to carry out the Howland operation on macacus rhesus monkeys under circumstances that would make it possible to study directly the effect on cerebral circulation. Accordingly, he, along with his co-workers, Lyle Gage and Jerzy Chorobski, took six monkeys to the neurological unit at Boston City Hospital and did the work reported

Epilepsy

by Cobb and Finesinger (84). An amusing incident took place while Penfield and his team were there. One of the monkeys got lost in the ventilation system for two days. Fortunately, the animal was recovered unharmed and so far as is known had not got into any significant mischief.

It is quite clear from the experimental surgery on Henry Howland and the supporting laboratory work that both Cobb and Penfield were adherents of the school which believed that depleted oxygenation of brain tissue was an important stimulus to the onset of convulsions. However, during the very same years that the work with Penfield was taking place, Gibbs was carrying on studies of cerebral blood and oxygen supply that tended to disprove the theory.

In Lennox's laboratory during the years between 1930 and 1934, much of the work had to do with blood gas analyses under the direction of Erna Leonhardt, who married Gibbs in late 1930. One of the projects that the Gibbses and Lennox worked on together was an attempt to determine what oxygen supply was necessary to maintain consciousness. They had volunteer human subjects lie on a tip table and inhale amyl nitrite, which is a vasodilating drug. Blood flow was estimated by analyzing expired air, which was collected in a Tissot bag, and relating it to the difference in oxygen concentration between arterial and venous blood. Blood gases were also studied on epileptics before, during, and after seizures in an attempt to confirm Kussmaul's theory of cerebral vascular spasm as an important precipitating factor in convulsions in accordance with Penfield's concept of the situation.[27] The Gibbses realized, however, that the methods they had employed thus far failed to measure instantaneous changes in cerebral circulation and devised other methods for recording blood flow in the carotid arteries of the neck, one using a Pitot tube[28] and the other one an electric thermocouple. In the fall of 1930, on a Macy Foundation grant, Gibbs went to Philadelphia, where he worked for a year with Detlev W. Bronk, learning micropipette techniques, and he returned to Harvard in the fall of 1931. Then he did experiments with artificially convulsed animals which failed to show any change in cerebral circulation.

One day, after their work had been published, Penfield came to Boston and gave a lecture on the mechanism of epilepsy. He failed to acknowledge Gibbs's work and reiterated the old Kussmaul theme.

There was an unpleasant exchange of views after the lecture. Cobb subsequently tried to mollify matters by writing a letter to Penfield. The following paragraph tells the story:

> Don't worry about Gibbs.... His paper in the *Archives* on cerebral blood flow in epileptics shows that in the eleven he studied there was no general vasoconstriction before the attack, and that is all it shows. I had quite a time convincing him that he must put in the possibility that there are various mechanisms of the fit. I liked your talk a lot. My only criticism is your title—"The Mechanism of Epilepsy." It might have been less specific, i.e., indicated that there might be others. But you adequately discussed this in the lecture.[29]

At the time when Lennox and the Gibbses had gone about as far as they could in studying the possible role of cerebral anoxia in epilepsy, another exciting topic engaged their interest. Their review of the literature led them to the work of Hans Berger, of Jena, Germany, who was interested in the electrical action potentials of the brain. Although the Liverpool surgeon, Richard Caton, had led off action potentials from the brains of animals in 1875, it was Berger who in 1929 demonstrated that such variations in voltage could be recorded through the intact cranium in humans.[30] Lennox said that Berger's breakthrough was made possible by use of vacuum tube amplification.[31] Lennox and Gibbs were also aware of work which had been done at the Kaiser Wilhelm Institute in Berlin demonstrating abnormal action-potential discharges in experimentally convulsed animals.[32] No one had demonstrated abnormal electrical potentials in human epilepsy. However, Gibbs and Lennox saw the possible implications of brain-wave research in the elucidation of epileptic convulsions. But the field was new, and Berger's pioneer work on electroencephalography had not as yet been generally accepted. Nevertheless, Cobb thought the project to be a worthwhile one, and with his backing Gibbs discussed with Hallowell Davis of the physiology department at the Harvard Medical School the possibility of studying the action currents of patients with epilepsy through the intact cranium in the manner of Berger.

Davis's response was enthusiastic. He said that William Derbyshire, a young Ph.D. candidate in the physiology department, had been recording brain waves through the intact cranium and had confirmed Berger's observations about the alpha waves, beta waves, and gamma waves.[33] Albert Grass, a technician in the department of physiology, assembled an instrument with multiple cranial leads suitable for Lennox's and Gibbs's purpose. Lennox advised that the initial clinical

Epilepsy

studies be made on patients with *petit mal* epilepsy because some of them are very quiet during their seizures. He was afraid that with *grand mal* seizures, the electrical disturbance from skeletal muscles would be confusing.

The initial studies were carried out on two staff members who suffered from *petit mal*. Gibbs and Lennox made prolonged tracings going on for hours at a time. One of the two patients, who could see the screen where the action potentials were recorded, recognized her own abnormal pattern. She said, "I wish you would stop showing that pattern. Every time one of those things comes across the screen I get a seizure." Gibbs said, "Of course she was seeing the electrical discharge itself. We knew that we had something all right, and Bill Lennox knew, but he couldn't believe it. It was just too astonishing to believe." The classical wave-and-spike pattern of *petit mal* was worked out initially. Later it was found that the tonic-clonic convulsions of *grand mal* also had a distinctive pattern as did some of the other types of epilepsy.

Nineteen hundred and thirty-four was the year of Cobb's departure for the Massachusetts General Hospital. It was in 1937 that a symposium on electrical activity in the nervous system was held by the Congress of Psychology in Paris. Lord Adrian and Berger were invited to preside at the conference and after that occasion electroencephalography became generally accepted as an investigative and diagnostic modality. Cobb had encouraged Gibbs and Lennox to go ahead with their investigations three years earlier. Cobb was always a courageous innovator. After their initial work the Gibbses became fascinated with the electrical storm recorded by the electroencephalogram in epileptic patients. After 1934 they invested most of their efforts in electroencephalography and published twenty-eight papers on the subject with Lennox. In later years, Lennox was joined in the work on epilepsy by his daughter, Margaret, the epileptic child whose illness had prompted Lennox's move to the neuropathology laboratory in 1921. By now, Margaret was a physician. Subsequently she married Fritz Buchthal, a neurophysiologist in Copenhagen, and continued her work there.

A direct outcome of the Gibbses' and Lennox's work on electroencephalography was the discovery by Putnam and Merritt in 1937 of Dilantin as a therapeutically valuable anticonvulsant. Merritt said in an interview that in the early thirties he shared a laboratory with Putnam, and Miss Jefferson was their assistant. Of course, when Putnam became director of the neurological unit in 1934, after Cobb's departure, he moved into Cobb's old office, but he and Merritt continued their experimental work, and Dorothy Miller Schwab joined them. Merritt referred to the experiments on artificially produced convulsions as the "cat-fit" work:

> It was work which Tracy and I did together. Howard [i.e. Albert] Grass, who invented the EEG machine, developed an instrument which would deliver a measured amount of induced electric current to the brain. We administered a measured current for an arbitrary two minutes and ten seconds. By that time we could tell whether a cat was going to have a fit or wasn't. Then we could run the rheostat up, so that the cat would get a larger amount of current next time. In this way we could find out the amount of current necessary to produce a convulsion in the animal. Then we tried a number of drugs, hoping that they would prevent the convulsions. We started with drugs that were known to have an analeptic effect, such as phenobarbital and other hypnotic drugs. Then we tried others that were not known to be hypnotic. We asked the pharmaceutical houses to send us some drugs which had been devised as hypnotics but had not been useful in that capacity. Parke-Davis was one of the first drug companies we asked, because the Director of Research there was a friend of Tracy Putnam. Parke-Davis sent about twenty-five drugs that had not worked as hypnotics. The first drug which they sent was diphenylhydantoin, and, by God, it worked. We tried about a thousand drugs after that. We found one or two which were more effective anticonvulsants than diphenylhydantoin, but they were too toxic to use.[34]

Dilantin took its place as the standard anticonvulsant for use in epilepsy. Other new agents gradually made their appearance. Some were better adapted to special situations, but to date none has displaced Dilantin. It is appropriate to say here that the introduction of diphenylhydantoin (Dilantin) was the greatest advance in treatment of epilepsy since the introduction of phenobarbital by Hauptmann in 1912. Dilantin was the first nonsedative drug to be useful, and it remains the cornerstone of therapy even to this day. If Howland had been more patient and had not stopped funding Cobb's work, he would indeed have seen a therapeutic achievement to reward him for the support that he withdrew ten years earlier.

Nineteen thirty-nine was an eventful year at the neurological unit. Putnam departed that year to become director of the Neurological Institute in New York.[35] Gibbs and his wife, Erna, moved to the Boston Psychopathic Hospital. So the epilepsy scene was to change somewhat. Lennox wrote a second book entitled *Science and Seizures*[36] which summarized his research and coordinated it with that of others. This book had a great influence on treatment and on a broader understanding of epilepsy both by patients' families and the medical profession. During the forties Lennox continued his studies and in 1944 with Cobb published a review of his work on cerebral circulation (181). Later, with the help of his daughter, Margaret, he completed a two-volume treatise entitled *Epilepsy and Related Disorders*.[37] This book brought together the endeavors of a lifetime and was published only a few weeks before his death in 1960.

In the maelstrom of research activities in epilepsy Lennox occupied the tranquil center. When writing his obituary in 1961, Cobb described him as modest, whimsical, and filled with quiet humor.[38] He was a careful, thorough worker, utterly dedicated to his life work. Cobb said, "No medical scientist has more successfully dedicated himself to the study of one disease." Yet Lennox was not a person who could engender in others excitement over what he was doing, and according to Gildea he was actually clumsy in working in the laboratory. However, the importance of his central role cannot be denied. His review of the literature, which culminated in the 1927 *Medicine Monograph*, established a base of information without which later, more exciting work would have been impossible (48). Yet, the really great advances in the twenties and thirties were only tangentially his. He undoubtedly served as a balance wheel for the boundless energy and enthusiasm of Frederick Gibbs. For example, he cautioned Gibbs to commence electroencephalographic studies on patients with *petit mal*. But it was Gibbs who assumed leadership in the initial work with Hallowell Davis on the instrument itself. Moreover, the work on experimental convulsions, which led to Dilantin, was carried out by Putnam and Merritt on the very same floor as Lennox's own laboratory. And the work on cerebral circulation was taken up by many different workers, including Forbes, Talbott, Wolff, Gibbs, Finesinger, and Cobb. Lennox established a milieu; he amassed enormous amounts of lackluster but essential knowledge; he focused his knowledge and he made it available. Yet, in terms of brilliant forward thrusts he appears to have been eclipsed by others in his own immediate environment.

In the epilepsy research Lennox was at the hub of the wheel. He occupied a central position. Yet the brilliant flashes of light appeared in the minds of those around him. Serendipity, too, played a crucial role. Although Cobb's ten-year project for the study of cerebral circulation encompassed many brilliant investigations, none of them made a direct contribution to the pathophysiology or the treatment of epilepsy. Moreover, it was because the studies of cerebral circulation had appeared to reach a dead end that Frederick Gibbs became an enthusiastic investigator of the electrical discharges in epilepsy as demonstrated by electroencephalography. And it was the new interest in brain waves that set the stage for Putnam and Merritt to make the discovery of Dilantin. Through all the work on cerebral circulation Cobb had the loyal support of a hand-picked team of competent investigators, some of them brilliant. But it was through his leadership, his sensing the creative moment in various situations, and his eclectic acceptance of new ideas from whatever source that the spirit grew which made the achievements possible.

9
Psychoanalysis

On Cobb's retirement from the Massachusetts General Hospital in 1954 the Harvard Medical School class yearbook, the *Aesculapiad*, was dedicated to him and Joseph Aub wrote the dedication to this volume.[1] Aub, who later published a biography of Dean Edsall,[2] commented on Cobb's shift of activities, noting that in making the transition from research in neuropathology and clinical neurology to the new field of psychiatry Cobb was fulfilling a precept of his former colleague and model, Richard Clarke Cabot. Cabot, an established clinician and teacher, developed a new field himself when in 1905 he founded at the Massachusetts General Hospital the world's first medical social service department. "Every man should change his job at fifty," Cabot said, and Cobb followed his injunction, whether he was aware of it or not.

Aub clearly showed his appreciation of Cobb as a growing being with new interests that had evolved during the course of his own maturation. After describing Cobb's earlier experiences with ornithology in childhood, as a medical student, as a surgical intern under Cushing, and subsequently as a serious student of the neurosciences in Baltimore and Boston, Aub went on to say, "It may well have been this [shift in interest] that maintained Dr. Cobb's enthusiasm during the intervening years. . . . His was a beautiful synthesis of anatomic, physiologic, and accurate psychologic and psychiatric training which made for sound progress." Aub then added that he saw Cobb's transition to the new work in psychiatry as a sort of anchor which tended to make him evaluate critically the many new-found approaches to psychiatry and to make him seek for scientific evidence.

Cobb's interest in dynamic psychotherapy can be traced to the days in Harvard College when he became familiar with the work in experimental psychology carried out by Hugo Münsterberg.[3] At that time Münsterberg was interested in hypnosis. Cobb's letter to him about the possibility of undergoing hypnosis as a form of therapy for his stammering indicated that he already had some awareness that the unconscious activities of the mind played an important role in human behavior.

In medical school Cobb came under the influence of James Jackson Putnam, whose professional career was a forerunner of his own in that Putnam, like Cobb, was a clinical neurologist who developed an interest in psychoanalysis. Putnam was born in 1846 and became Harvard's first professor of diseases of the nervous system in 1894. Putnam had already been experimenting with psychoanalytic methods for several years by 1909, when Freud, Jung, and Ferenczi came to the Clark University conference and he entertained them at his Adirondack Camp. Putnam was instrumental in founding the American Psychopathological Association in 1910, the American Psychoanalytic Association in 1911, and the Boston Psychoanalytic Society in 1914.[4] He was professor of neurology at the Harvard Medical School until 1905 and chief of neurology at the Massachusetts General Hospital until 1912, when he retired at the end of Cobb's second year in medical school. Cobb knew Putnam in medical school and was familiar with his way of life. In fact, after World War I, when Cobb was seeking an academic career in the neurosciences, he saw Putnam's association with Harvard and the Massachusetts General Hospital as an arrangement that he might well emulate.[5]

In 1913, when Cobb met his future wife on the platform of the Lake Placid railroad station, he was en route to Putnam's camp. Putnam's maiden sister, Lizzie, who lived with the Putnams, had a custom of arranging two-week houseparties where eligible young men and women could become acquainted with each other.[6] Although Cobb and Elizabeth Almy had not met previously, both of them were on the list for one of Lizzie Putnam's houseparties. So it was indirectly through Putnam that the two young people came to know each other and to start their life together in a union that was to be blessed with many coöperative ventures.

When he finished medical school Cobb was tied up in his surgical internship with Cushing and then busy in Baltimore; so he saw little of Putnam at that time. However, Putnam's daughter, Marian, after graduation from medical school became a child psychiatrist and psychoanalyst who worked in New Haven and in Boston. During the late forties, Betty Cobb worked under her at the James Jackson Putnam clinic in Roxbury. Marian and the Cobbs were close friends, with adjoining properties in Little Compton, Rhode Island, to which they contemplated retirement together.[7]

After graduation from medical school in 1914, Cobb's next important exposure to psychoanalytic theory and practice was in Baltimore, where he studied under Meyer and undertook analytic therapy with Campbell. After Meyer moved from the Manhattan State Hospital to Baltimore in 1911, he brought along as his right bower, C. Macfie Campbell, from the same institution. Psychotic patients at the Manhattan State Hospital on Ward's Island were the central focal point in New York City for early work in psychoanalysis, whereas in Boston emphasis was primarily on the treatment of psychoneurotic patients in the physician's office. At the Manhattan State Hospital between 1902 and 1910 Meyer encouraged the study of Freudian views, and a majority of the members of the New York Psychoanalytic Society were on his staff there. So Meyer and Campbell brought with them to the Phipps Clinic in Baltimore a substantial knowledge of psychoanalysis as it was understood at that time.

According to William Alanson White,[8] Macfie Campbell had written that Kraepelin's theory of an organic cause for dementia praecox was absurdly vague. Campbell had suggested a form of therapy best described as an attempt to give the patient gradual insight in an atmosphere of "warm enthusiasm." Above all, Campbell insisted, the physician must try to help the patient accept his sexual impulses, to which many symptoms were closely related. Campbell said that it was extraordinary how many people obtained relief from this kind of treatment. In his later life Campbell was not looked upon as a psychoanalyst, and it is doubtful that he was regarded as one in 1916, even though he had had a good deal of experience with treatment by mental catharsis. Sanford Gifford, present-day archivist of the Boston Psychoanalytic Institute, has stated that there have been three sequential standards for the recognition of a *bona fide* psychoanalyst. In the early phase, prior to 1930, it was sufficient to have studied and written on psychoanalysis, which Campbell had done. After 1930, to qualify as a psychoanalyst one required a training analysis, which Cobb later undertook. Then in the late thirties the American Board of Psychiatry and Neurology established more rigid criteria for recognition in psychiatry and indirectly limited the number of physicians eligible to become psychoanalysts.[9] So Campbell and Cobb in their respective days met the technical requirements for recognition as psychoanalysts, although in their basic thinking they were profoundly influenced by Meyer's psychobiological concepts rather than Freud's theories.

After Putnam's death in 1918 and during the early twenties there was a lapse of interest in psychoanalysis in Boston. During this fallow period Coriat maintained and regenerated interest in the subject. The initial Boston Psychoanalytic Society, founded in 1914 with Putnam as its president and Coriat as its secretary, ceased to function after Putnam's death.[10] Its activities were resumed in 1924, when Coriat invited a number of analysts to meet at his home for informal study. The group consisted of Jungians and Rankians, with Coriat perhaps the most orthodox Freudian. In the beginning of his career Coriat was somewhat eclectic.[11] First influenced by Prince and Janet, then Meyer, Coriat only became interested in Freud after 1913. He was attracted by Adler's concept of organ inferiority, which he saw as an explanation for amaurotic family idiocy, Kaiser Wilhelm's belligerent behavior,[12] and stammering, about which he wrote a book in 1928.

In that same year, 1928, Coriat's group of psychoanalysts was organized into the Second Boston Psychoanalytic Association, and Cobb became a member along with his friends William Herman, Irmarita Putnam, and Harry Murray, who had recently come to Boston from New York and was working under Morton Prince in the Harvard Psychological Clinic. It was in 1927 that Cobb had some analytic therapy for his own stammering with Leonhard Seif, the Adlerian from Munich, and in 1928 that he visited Munich for further analysis with Seif.[13] Cobb was to take an interest in the organizational aspects of Boston psychoanalysis for approximately ten years, particularly along the lines of insuring that the new science gain a place in university curricula.

Whereas Coriat's Boston Psychoanalytic Society had been quite liberal during the twenties and had included Jungians and Rankians among its members, the year 1930 saw a dramatic change. A number of Americans who had been analyzed in Berlin or Vienna commenced meeting at what was called the Freud Seminar in the home of Ives Hendrick. The members of the Freud Seminar in 1931 were Hendrick, M. Ralph Kaufman, John Murray, Leolia Dalrymple, and Margaret Ribble. Irmarita Putnam, then being analyzed in Berlin, subsequently joined, as did Isador Coriat and others. Through the influence of this

Psychoanalysis

group the Boston Psychoanalytic Association was reorganized along orthodox Freudian lines in September, 1930, with Cobb among its members.[14]

Thus, Cobb's interest in psychoanalysis preceded by several years his venture into psychiatry at the Massachusetts General Hospital. His interest in psychotherapy, first documented by his correspondence with Münsterberg when in college, was clearly related to his own stammering, and the comparative ineffectiveness of Samuel Robbins's speech therapy led to the helpful Adlerian analysis by Leonhard Seif in 1927 and 1928. What then were the factors that led Cobb to take an active interest in Freud? Undoubtedly the single most influential person was Herman, the M.G.H. medical intern whom Cobb had steered to the Phipps for training in psychiatry under Meyer. On returning from Baltimore, when a resident in psychiatry at the Boston Psychopathic Hospital, Herman had continued his Meyerian approach. Herman then undertook a Jungian analysis with Van der Hoop and subsequently, along with Irmarita Putnam, he abandoned Jung in favor of Freud. Herman, who had married Cobb's friend and secretary, Susan Evarts Hale, was serving as a consultant in psychoanalysis on Cobb's neurological unit at Boston City Hospital and was a neighbor at Cotuit. So, Herman almost certainly made Cobb aware of the excitement associated with Freud.

Another person who surely influenced Cobb was Binger. After his sabbatical from the Rockefeller Institute between 1928 and 1930, Binger devoted the remainder of his life to psychosomatic medicine. Like Herman, Binger had been well grounded in Jungian theory. He had had some therapy with Jung personally. Yet, on his return to New York he undertook a Freudian analysis with Fritz Wittels there. The Cobbs and the Bingers were very close friends. Betty Cobb reported that on their annual cruises together Binger tended to look upon Cobb as a neurologist and directed his psychoanalytic conversation to her. Cobb could not have avoided listening.

Three other people must have been influential. One was Putnam's daughter, Dr. Marian Putnam, who was undertaking a Freudian analysis prior to psychiatric work in pediatrics at Yale. A double second cousin of Betty Cobb, Marian Putnam was a neighbor at Cotuit and later at Little Compton, Rhode Island. Her colleague, Dr. Louise Jackson of New Haven, was a close friend of the Cobbs.[15] And finally,

Sarah Evarts, who later headed psychiatric social service at the M.G.H., a cousin of Mrs. Herman, was Betty Cobb's closest friend. Sarah Evarts was psychoanalyzed and became a well-spoken enthusiast.

Betty Cobb said in an interview that it was not the stammering which led Cobb to Freud. He had already been helped by Seif, the Adlerian. It was rather the conviction that Freudian psychoanalysis was something important, which he needed to understand in his search for knowledge of the human mind.

For a number of years Cobb took an active interest in the Boston Psychoanalytic Society. When the society was reorganized in 1930 its members proceeded to establish a training institute, such as that which Franz Alexander had conducted in Berlin. In the spring of 1931 the members of the institute were very active, and Cobb was crystallizing his own understanding of the subject.[16] They met at the Harvard Psychological Clinic on Friday afternoons throughout 1931. It was arranged that Alexander should come to Boston in September of that year. He worked part time on research at the Judge Baker Foundation and devoted the remainder of his energy to training analyses for members of the Boston Psychoanalytic Society who wished to qualify. These included Martin Peck, Harry Murray, William Herman, and Leolia Dalrymple. In addition, Alexander included Healy, the director of the Judge Baker, Catherine Bacon of Chicago, and Karl Menninger of Topeka. Irmarita Putnam was added later.

Although Cobb was not among those who had a training analysis with Alexander, his opportunity was to come later. Alexander remained in Boston only one year because he had an opportunity to establish a Chicago Psychoanalytic Institute supported by the Rosenwald Fund. On his recommendation and that of Irmarita Putnam, Hanns Sachs was invited to succeed him the following year. Hanns Sachs, a lawyer, had been one of the seven people closest to Freud who had agreed to resist psychoanalytic deviations, including university affiliation. Although Freud did not object to individual psychoanalysts receiving academic appointments, he wanted the psychoanalytic institutes to remain clear of university affiliations, and Sachs was the official teaching analyst of the Boston institute. Cobb had two important roles to play in his relationships with Sachs. One was his own training analysis. The other was the incorporation of Sachs, contrary to Freud's policy, into the teaching program at Harvard and into psychiatry at the Massachusetts General Hospital.

Although Cobb was a member of the Boston Psychoanalytic Society when it was reorganized by Coriat in 1928 and throughout the period from 1930 to 1932, he was later left out when the new American Psychoanalytic Federation, in the framing of whose constitution Boston had fully participated, required that all the members of each constituent society be fully qualified psychoanalysts. By the end of 1933 ten of Boston's twenty members had fulfilled this requirement and the others, including Cobb, resigned.[17] In December of that year the Boston Society became a member of the American Federation.[18] The Education Committee was incorporated as the Boston Psychoanalytic Institute, with the same members as the society, and in 1947 the two overlapping groups were combined as the Boston Psychoanalytic Society and Institute with quarters at 82 Marlborough Street.

Whereas Alexander had contributed greatly to the vitality of the Boston Psychoanalytic Society, Sachs was less interested in the creation of a new psychiatric specialty. He was much older than Alexander and physically unattractive with short stature, heavy features, thick lenses, and a black cigar. He was good in erudite discussions but aloof and intellectually austere. Moreover, when brought to this country by Irmarita Putnam, with Freud's blessing, he had made very clear his objection to affiliating psychoanalysis with academic psychiatry. He had also emphasized his objection and that of Freud to having the qualifications of psychoanalysts ruled upon by committees. It was their contention that the training analyst was the only one who really knew when an analysand was qualified.

However, Cobb made the best of the situation. Despite Sachs's lack of a medical degree, Cobb arranged a lectureship for him in psychoanalysis at the Harvard Medical School. With Cobb's support, Jacob E. Finesinger, who was to become a key staff member on Cobb's new service, was Sachs's first training analysand in 1932–33. Cobb was analyzed a year later, and after the psychiatric service at the Massachusetts General Hospital was established, Sachs made late afternoon rounds there with Cobb, Finesinger, and Erich Lindemann, the other psychoanalyst on the full-time staff. Although Sachs's afternoon rounds were valuable, Cobb saw them as making less of a contribution than William Herman would have made had it not been for his untimely death in January, 1935. It was Herman who had played a role in introducing Cobb to psychoanalysis; moreover, Herman had encouraged him to establish the Massachusetts General Hospital psychiatric service. In 1944, nine years after Herman's death, Cobb wrote with appreciation about the potential contribution that he might have made:

> Our first great loss was through the death of Dr. William Herman in January, 1935, when he had just begun his new responsibilities as Associate Psychiatrist, and had high hopes and good plans for the development of psychoanalysis in a university setting. This loss has been partly made good by Dr. Hanns Sachs, who conducts educational analyses for a number of younger members of the staff; but the close liaison that might have been developed between medicine, psychiatry, and psychoanalysis by Dr. Herman has not been possible with Dr. Sachs, because he is not a physician and therefore cannot work intimately with us at the hospital.[19]

When, in 1934, Cobb assumed directorship of the psychiatric service at the Massachusetts General Hospital, he became much less active in the Boston Psychoanalytic Society. The Boston Psychoanalytic Society had brought about the liaison between psychoanalysis and psychiatry at the cost of excluding lay analysts from becoming members. Cobb was glad to see psychoanalysis become a part of psychiatry; but he also wanted it recognized by universities as a science.

Cobb was a close friend of Henry A. Murray, the Rockefeller Institute embryologist, who in 1928 had come to Harvard as an assistant to Morton Prince in the Harvard Psychological Clinic and later had succeeded Prince as its director.[20] Whereas the Harvard students had found the clinical material presented by Prince as somewhat dull, their response to Murray was electrifying. His Psychology 24 became one of the most popular courses. Moreover, the discussions were brilliant, and often Murray had exciting visitors whom the students were invited to meet. The very popularity of Murray's psychological teaching was frowned upon by Edwin G. Boring, the chairman of the psychology department, who was the chief spokesman at Harvard for German laboratory psychology in the tradition of Wundt and Titchener.

In the beginning the income from Morton Prince's endowment barely carried the expenses of the clinic, but after the 1929 stock market crash the funds were totally inadequate, and Murray, although personally well off, had constant trouble in meeting the clinic's financial needs. Cobb, who wanted to see psychoanalysis become established as a recognized science, tried to help when, in 1933, Murray made an appeal to the department of neuropathology for funding. Although neuropathology had its financial troubles at the time and was unable to support Murray, Cobb's interest in the Harvard Psychological Clinic continued.

Psychoanalysis

Murray's difficulties were intensified in 1934 because James Bryant Conant, the new president of the University, placed much greater emphasis on published scientific work than his predecessor, Lowell, had done. Although Murray was engaged in a long-term treatise, he had published very little. Conant was indecisive about the future of the psychological clinic and even about the department itself. The psychological clinic was in limbo.

When working at the Rockefeller Institute Murray had known Alan Gregg, who was in charge of grants for medical institutions. Gregg had been interested in psychoanalysis since the time in 1909 when as a teen-age boy he had been at Putnam's Adirondack camp during the visit by Freud, Jung, and Ferenczi, who were in this country for the Clark University conference. Moreover, in 1933 Gregg had agreed to fund Cobb's new psychiatric service at the Massachusetts General Hospital.

During the three years from 1934 through 1937 Cobb was to play a significant if not vital role in the survival of Murray's clinic. In 1934 Murray applied to Gregg for funding. He had the permission of his departmental head, Edwin G. Boring, to seek outside funds. He had active support from other psychologists, as well as Alfred E. Cohn, the organic biochemist under whom he had worked at the Rockefeller Institute. Yet, Gregg was hesitant about making a grant without assurances as to the ongoing status of the clinic. It was Cobb who convinced Gregg in 1934 that Murray's clinic should be supported even though its future was uncertain. The strength of Cobb's recommendation is indicated by the following paragraph from a letter he sent to Gregg at the time:

> As to your inquiry about the committee on psychology, I went over to the University last week and talked to Professor Boring. He has heard from the President that I am to be on that committee and that there will be a preliminary meeting of it probably within the next month. I should think there would be *no* report until perhaps a month after that, but that is only my speculation. If you have to make any decision about aid for Dr. Murray, I for one, would urge that you go ahead and act on that as an individual item on its own merits. As you know, I rate these merits very highly. It would be fine if you could run up here, because we have much to talk about.[21]

The board of the Rockefeller Foundation subsequently made a grant of two thousand four hundred fifty dollars, and in a paragraph of supporting evidence for their decision, wrote:

Dr. Stanley Cobb, Dr. Alfred Cohn, and Dr. L. J. Henderson all have spoken of Dr. Murray and his work in terms of unusual earnestness and approval, and successive visits to the clinic show that it is composed of a group of workers within the field of psychology whose breadth of training and viewpoint, whose sincerity and modesty and whose common sense are not to be found easily elsewhere.[22]

Grants for the next three years were on an annual basis. However, aside from the small income from the Prince endowment, the clinic was to be totally funded by the Rockefeller Foundation until 1946, when it became a part of the new department of social relations.

Cobb not only contributed to the survival of Murray's clinic by urging Gregg to furnish funds in 1934 but he played an even more significant role in shaping psychology at Harvard.[23] After becoming president of the university in 1934, Conant made Cobb a member of a committee to review the status of psychology there. Later, when Murray's academic future at Harvard was under review Cobb sat on a committee which had very stormy sessions. The problem was intensified because Boring, the departmental chairman, had cooled in his enthusiasm for Murray, and because the new professor of experimental psychology, Karl T. Lashley, whose analysis by Alexander in Chicago had been a complete failure, was violently opposed to psychoanalysis. In the final vote of the committee, Drs. Cobb, Allport, and Burwell supported Murray, while Boring, Lashley, and Dean Birkoff of the faculty of arts and sciences, voted for his termination, and Conant had the power to break the tie. Lashley, who was Murray's most bitter opponent, and Allport, his strongest supporter, were chosen to write the report of the committee. In the end, at Boring's suggestion Murray was promoted to two five-year terms as associate professor without tenure. So, once again Cobb played an important role in preserving Murray's clinic and in supporting psychoanalysis as a university-based scientific subject.

Psychoanalysis, as such, was not one of Cobb's major problems when he opened the doors of the Massachusetts General Hospital psychiatric service in 1934. A much greater challenge was the monumental task of organizing a psychiatric service at that conservative institution where he encountered doubts and some overt hostility about the place of psychiatry in a general hospital setting. Some colleagues resented the number of Jews on the psychiatric service, and the neurologists, most of whom looked upon themselves as neuropsychiatrists, felt threatened by the competition from a new department of psychiatry. Psychoanalysis was not an immediate problem because James Jackson Putnam, it will be remembered, a very proper Bostonian, had experimented with psychoanalytic methods at the Massachusetts General Hospital as early as 1905.

When Putnam retired in 1912 he failed to leave behind an organized school of followers, and his successor, E. W. Taylor, by then was more interested in the organic aspects of neurology than in psychiatry. Nevertheless, a votive candle to psychoanalysis was kept burning by the clinical psychologist, L. Eugene Emerson. Emerson, a former student of William James, was appointed staff psychologist by Putnam in 1911.[24] When Putnam founded the first Boston Psychoanalytic Society in 1914, its most regular member was Eugene Emerson. Although Emerson did not take part in any of the subsequent Boston psychoanalytic societies, he continued to represent psychoanalysis at the Massachusetts General Hospital until his death in 1939. He was considered a member of Cobb's psychiatric service, which opened its doors in 1934, but actually was listed as a staff psychologist in neurology. Emerson was not the only person interested in psychoanalysis at the Massachusetts General Hospital, for Herman, who had a stipend from the Harvard Medical School to teach liaison psychiatry, was an active member of the Boston Psychoanalytic Society and, of course, had been influential in Cobb's personal life as well as in Cobb's decision to go into psychiatry.

Even before Herman's tragic death in January, 1935, Cobb felt a need to supplement the services of Sachs, and he was therefore receptive to opportunities, as they came along, to welcome other psychoanalysts on his staff. Chronologically, the very first was a young man named Erik Homburger, who had worked with children in Freud's home in Vienna. Homburger, who later became internationally known as Erik H. Erikson, arrived in Cambridge during October, 1933. He was heralded by Irmarita Putnam, who had just completed her own analysis with Freud. Erikson was also known to Hanns Scahs, whom he had met by accident on a street in Vienna earlier that year. Although Erikson had known Anna Freud and had been exposed to child analysis when living at Freud's home, he presented a problem for both Cobb and the Boston Psychoanalytic Society because he had no academic degree whatever. However, in 1934 Cobb was successful in obtaining for him an academic appointment at Harvard. Erikson reported that he was a research assistant in psychiatry at the medical school. (Actually he was a research fellow in psychology there).[25] Cobb assigned work for him with Frank Fremont-Smith on a project designed to investigate the importance of emotional factors in epilepsy. Erikson said that at the time he was so involved in settling in a new country and mastering a new language that he could not indulge in subtleties of conversation and hence did not know many of the other staff intimately.[26] Moreover, he was only at the General part time, for he also worked in the Harvard psychology clinic under Professor Harry Murray.

In 1936 Erikson moved to New Haven, where he continued his work in child psychology and frequently saw Louise Jackson and James Jackson Putnam's daughter, Marian. Partly because of the close relationship between Marian Putnam and the Cobbs, contact with Erikson was maintained over the years. It dated from the day in 1933 when the Cobbs were the first family to entertain the Eriksons in their home and was strengthened years later when Erikson returned to Harvard as a full professor. Erikson reviewed his relations with Cobb, both professional and social, in the following letter written from Cotuit in August, 1978, and signed Erik Homburger Erikson:

> Of Stanley Cobb I have two kinds of memories: professional and personal. The professional memories concern my personal fate; the more personal ones include both Betty and Joan. My first actual working contact with Stanley, in 1934, must be seen against the background of my immigration late in 1933. To be sure, I had arrived with Joan who, a Canadian, had lived and worked in the States—and who spoke English! But I was newly graduated from the Vienna Psychoanalytic Institute, had little academic experience, was told that I needed a Ph.D. to succeed in this country—and I mastered, at best, some "Basic English." How extraordinary, then, was Stanley's offer of a research assistantship in neuropsychiatry so I could work with Frank Fremont-Smith on his research in epilepsy. Unfortunately for this report, the manners and mores of the Harvard Medical School at that time were so new to me that I was not yet able to compare individuals in detail; but I will never forget Stanley at staff meetings, with his strongly chiseled face and his reassuring laughter.
>
> Yet, this decisive professional support alone would not have helped me to feel settled here had it not been for Stanley's and Betty's hospitality both to Joan and myself. From our first visits to Milton, to our (much later) reunion in Cotuit and our excursions to Little Compton, Stanley helped to explain to us not only the ethnic problems of the Boston area but also the ecology of the coast and the Cape, conveying his special delight in the wild swans of Little Compton and the wild geese of Cotuit. Of an evening, he would expand on his or my latest reading or writing, always holding our psychiatric

imaginations to sound neurological laws. Especially when, after two decades at Yale and in California, we returned for a Harvard professorship, the Cobbs helped us make Cotuit our Eastern home town, which it has remained even through our eventual California retirement. We never return here and drive down Main Street without a glance toward the Putnam and Old Post Roads and a warm and appreciative thought of Stanley.[27]

In the later years Erikson and Cobb did indeed spend evenings together expanding on their respective reading and writing. On December 8, 1964, Cobb, then in retirement, sat down and wrote Erikson a letter summarizing the high points of their discussion on the previous night which had been prompted by Konrad Lorenz's recent book on aggression. Much of Cobb's letter focused upon the semantics of the word *instinct*. However, the following paragraphs stand on their own feet and portray the flavor of the previous night's conversation:

Professor Erik H. Erikson
40 Robinson Street
Cambridge 35, Massachusetts

Dear Erik:
   Just to clarify my thinking, I am putting down some early morning notes on our enjoyable conversation of last evening about Lorenz and his recent book on *Aggression*.
   The most helpful phrase I picked up from you was "Psychoanalysis is a philosophy, not a science." This fits my loose definition of philosophy, that it is the bringing together of a body of observations into a reasonable whole. What Lorenz is trying to do is to put together two different bodies of observations. This interdisciplinary work is certainly important, but must be done critically and soberly. It strikes me that Konrad Lorenz has jumped on to a bandwagon with too much enthusiasm. Men who succeed in advancing to Philosophy of Science become great, e.g., Goethe and Darwin, and latterly Julian Huxley, Thorpe, and Brain are probably rising stars. Thorpe's little book approaches the same problems as Lorenz's fat volume; but (to my mind) more concisely and soundly. My one objection to Thorpe is that he is a dualist concerning the mind-body problem.
   Lorenz's main mistake in his book is his misunderstanding of *instincts*. For a man of his experience in animal behavior this is astonishing. He really knows animals and talks against anthropocentric thinking in his other books, but falls into the trap here. He tries to explain human psychology in terms of sub-human ethology. He does not know that Freud's early conception of instinct (his "instinctual theory") was greatly modified by Freud himself in later years and is not now considered by any scholar as a sound contribution.

Bon voyage.
Stanley Cobb, M.D.[28]

The evaluation in this letter of psychoanalysis as an art rather than a science is at variance with Cobb's earlier stand in the thirties and forties when he was trying to establish its scientific standing in the university. Janice R. Stevens, who shared an office with Cobb in the mid-sixties, recalled his "abhorrence of the impossibility of scientific tests of psychoanalysis."[29]

Erikson's early appointment to Harvard and his work with Fremont-Smith on epilepsy at the Massachusetts General Hospital exemplify Cobb's creativity in overlooking traditional academic standards and his interest in promoting the growth of promising students. Actually during the years from 1934 to 1936 Erikson's contributions to the psychiatric service were minimal.

Erich Lindemann was the first psychoanalyst to occupy a position of day-to-day importance in the activities of Cobb's psychiatric service. He was also to serve the longest, for when Cobb retired in 1954 Lindemann succeeded him as director of the psychiatric service until his own retirement in 1966. In 1935 Lindemann was brought to Boston by Cobb from the University of Iowa, where he had been studying the mental status of volunteers under the effects of various pharmacological substances, particularly sodium amytal.[30] Cobb arranged for Lindemann to work half time in Cannon's laboratory at the Harvard Medical School quadrangle and to spend the rest of his time on the psychiatric service at the General. However, Lindemann had not been in Boston many months before he realized that he was not cut out for the meticulous work of analyzing electroencephalograms but that he had an extraordinary capacity for conducting psychiatric interviews. Plans were, therefore, changed, and Lindemann became a full-time member of the staff on Cobb's service. During the thirties Lindemann continued his studies on changes in mental status under the influence of various pharmacological agents, among them acetyl choline. He was regarded as a master of the psychiatric interview and an excellent teacher. Lindemann's greatest contribution to psychiatric knowledge, however, grew out of his study of grief among the friends and relatives of victims of the 1942 Cocoanut Grove fire, work which he later published with Cobb (170). Lindemann was particularly interested in the limits of normal grief.

Lindemann was very active in the Boston Psychoanalytic Society and Institute. He served as a training analyst in the early forties and was president from 1944 through 1946.[31] At about the same time he was evolving a philosophy about what he called the normal patient, having in mind the medical or surgical patient without a previously recognized psychiatric problem. In the late forties Lindemann started a course for Harvard medical students in the department of social relations entitled "Normal Growth and Development." He was interested in the biology and physiology of growth, family structure, social change, and psychoanalytic concepts.

Lindemann's interests in community affairs and sociological concepts took him further from his primary responsibility at the Massachusetts General Hospital, and in 1948 he founded the Wellesley Human Relations Service, which is believed to have been the first community psychiatric clinic in the United States. Some years later he became involved in the displacement by urban renewal of the West End community near the Massachusetts General Hospital in Boston. He later had a hand in designing an institution there under the aegis of the Commonwealth of Massachusetts and in cooperation with the Massachusetts General Hospital. This facility in a new location is now known as the Lindemann Center.

Throughout his years as chairman of the psychiatric department, Cobb leaned heavily upon Lindemann, whose qualities as an investigator and teacher he fully appreciated, and on his retirement in 1954 he supported Lindemann as his successor. Throughout his days under Cobb Lindemann was regarded by those residents and fellows interested primarily in clinical psychiatry as the most important staff member to whom they could turn for help and advice. However, Lindemann was not a good administrator, and after Cobb's retirement, he demoralized his staff by making promises he was unable to fulfill and by assigning the same task to two or more staff members simultaneously.[32] Moreover, he was often away from his office because of the demands of his outside work in sociology.[33] Unfortunately, many of the nonpsychiatric members of the staff at the Massachusetts General Hospital attributed Lindemann's administrative faults to his being a psychoanalyst, and as he was nearing retirement, a neurosurgeon, Thomas Ballantine, circulated a petition among the staff recommending that Lindemann's successor not be a psychoanalyst.[34] The petition, with one hundred twenty-two signatures, was submitted to the executive board of the Hospital. So, for a time psychoanalysis was a topic discussed only in an atmosphere of strong emotions pro and con, and few of the staff members really knew the origin of their feelings.[35] After Lindemann retired in 1966, John Nemiah, a psychoanalyst and student of Cobb's, served as acting chairman for three years. Then the next chairman of the department was Leon Eisenberg, a nonanalyst[36] with a special interest in children. Despite his deficiencies as an administrator, Lindemann's contribution to psychiatry was important in terms of his research, his teaching, and his outreach into the community. He was obviously a creative man who was able to adapt his psychoanalytic knowledge to other fields of endeavor. Like Cobb he really undertook a new career in the middle portion of his life, when he extended his interest into sociology.

Another physician with full analytic training who served with Cobb over a long period of time was Jacob E. Finesinger. Finesinger had been a resident on the neurological unit from 1930 to 1931 and had done important investigative work on cerebral circulation (84). After he had completed his training analysis with Sachs in 1932–33, while doing clinical psychiatry under Campbell, and after eighteen months abroad, mostly doing control analyses in Vienna,[37] Finesinger returned to the United States and in 1935 rejoined Cobb on the new psychiatric service. Unlike Lindemann, Finesinger was a very practical man, and Cobb delegated to him much of the administrative work on the service. Moreover, he was helpful to residents and fellows who were interested in doing investigative work. From the Massachusetts General Hospital he collaborated with Cobb on four publications. The first was a description of the psychiatric unit (108), the second a review of psychoneurosis and psychosomatic disorders (191), and the other two were on original investigations. One, with Mary A. B. Brazier as a third worker, had to do with the contrast between the encephalograms in psychoneurotic patients and in normal adults (192). Psychoneurotic patients, they concluded, showed no gross abnormalities. The fourth paper was about the relationship between specific emotions and fatigue states (207). Finesinger's thinking was clearly along psychoanalytic lines, but he was less active in the Boston Psychoanalytic Society than Lindemann. As Paul Howard put it, "Finesinger was an analyst studying physiology.[38]

Finesinger remained with Cobb until January 1, 1950, when he moved to Baltimore to head the new Mental Health Center at the University of Maryland.[39] Cobb felt the loss acutely, because Finesinger's services over the years had been extraordinarily helpful in terms

Psychoanalysis

of teaching the resident staff, investigation, and administrative responsibilities.

Although available only on a part-time basis because of her busy analytic practice, another work-horse of Cobb's psychiatric service was Helene Deutsch, who came from Vienna in October, 1935, to be followed on the psychiatric service by her husband, Felix, the next January.[40] Helene Deutsch had been born on October 9, 1884.[41] She was the daughter of Wilhelm Rosenbach, an attorney in Przemysl,[42] a city in the Polish part of Austria-Hungary, and his wife, Regina. After graduation from the medical faculty at the University of Vienna in 1912, she married Felix Deutsch, whom she had met the previous year in Munich, and commenced work in the University of Vienna psychiatric clinic under Wagner Jauregg.[43] Then in 1918 she was psychoanalyzed by Freud, and after that she devoted her life to the practice of analysis, writing, and teaching.

After her arrival on Cobb's service in October, 1935, Helene Deutsch immediately established herself as a key member of the department. At fifty-one, she was a beautiful woman in the prime of life. She regularly attended the weekly staff conferences and was noted for the succinct manner in which she could summarize the psychodynamics of a case history. As a recognized European training analyst in Boston, she soon took on a number of the staff members for analysis. Moreover, as a physician, she was able to do hospital work and in later years made ward rounds on a regular basis.

When Helene Deutsch completed her volumes on *The Psychology of Women*, Cobb wrote a sympathetic and warm foreword. The book itself was later criticized by feminists because of the passivity of the feminine role as Deutsch saw it.

Helene Deutsch died in 1982 at the age of ninety-seven. In a 1978 interview she radiated her charm, vitality, and enthusiasm. She was no longer able to organize her thoughts effectively, but her responses to specific questions were often helpful. As a psychoanalyst, Helene Deutsch probably had more influence on Cobb and the psychiatric service than any other one person after Bill Herman's death.

Felix Deutsch, Helene's husband, who came onto the psychiatric service in January, 1936, had originally been trained in internal medicine. However, he became interested in psychoanalysis during World War I and in 1919 began to attend psychoanalytic meetings. In 1922 he had a didactic analysis with Siegfried Bernfeld, and he became Freud's personal physician. Felix Deutsch was the first to introduce the term "psychosomatic" in its present-day use at the 1927 General Medical Congress for Psychotherapy at Bad Nauheim.[44] It was because of Felix Deutsch's interest in psychosomatic medicine that Cobb invited him to come from Europe and join the Massachusetts General Hospital staff.[45]

However, Felix Deutsch's contribution to psychosomatic medicine was a disappointment to Cobb. Deutsch was extraordinarily gifted in the art of conducting psychiatric interviews.[46] He was particularly interested in asthma and enjoyed recounting the details of a patient's life, including the organic illnesses, such as whooping cough, with a thoroughness that would have pleased Adolf Meyer and his school of psychobiologists. However, Deutsch was not a laboratory man, and Cobb wanted to evaluate disturbed respiratory function biochemically. In 1937 Herrmann Blumgart and M. Ralph (Moe) Kaufman were planning a psychosomatic study of respiratory disturbances, with Felix Deutsch as a collaborator, and looking to Frank Fremont-Smith, by then president of the Josiah Macy Foundation, for funds. Fremont-Smith wrote to Cobb about Deutsch's qualifications,[47] and Cobb replied:

> As for Felix Deutsch, I told Blumgart that I would welcome an offer from the Beth Israel that would allow Felix more purely medical work. Here at the Massachusetts General he has a very minor position on the medical staff and there is no way of pushing him ahead of even the younger men. On our staff he is well satisfied, and he can go on using our laboratories and working here as long as he wants to. He is a remarkable therapist with extraordinary intuition and ability to help people rapidly. As a scientist he lacks training in fundamental knowledge of the value of evidence, but Blumgart and I can look after that and not allow him to publish anything until he has adequate controls.[48]

In 1939 Deutsch departed from Cobb's service and after a two-year sojourn in St. Louis spent the rest of his professional life working at the Boston Veterans Administration Hospital and at the Beth Israel. He wrote extensively with William Murphy. He was president of the Boston Psychoanalytic Society and Institute from 1951 through 1954. In the mid-fifties a series of papers on conversion were presented at the Boston Psychoanalytic Society, and a panel on the theory of the

Psychoanalysis

conversion process took place at the 1958 annual meeting of the American Psychoanalytic Association in San Francisco. Deutsch accumulated and edited the various papers in a volume entitled *On the Mysterious Leap from the Mind to the Body,* which was published in 1959.[49] Deutsch was more interested in psychosomatic medicine than in the practice of psychoanalysis per se. In fact, according to one commentator, he considered much of psychoanalytic theory farfetched, particularly his wife's interpretation of it.[50] However, although it was Felix Deutsch, with his interest in psychosomatic medicine, whom Cobb originally sought out as a collaborator, it was Helene who remained an effective staff member over a long period of years.

In addition to Sachs, who made late afternoon rounds, and Lindemann, Finesinger, and the Deutsches, who devoted a great deal of time to the inpatient service, there were others of importance. Eleanor Pavenstedt, a Meyerian who was later analyzed, and Edgerton Howard both worked primarily in the Outpatient Department. In a recent taped interview conducted by John Abbott and Eugene Taylor, Pavenstedt reported that she came up from Baltimore because she was interested in dynamic psychiatry and she wasn't getting any experience in it there. Cobb had heard her deliver a lecture in Baltimore in the early 1930s and invited her to join him at the Massachusetts General Hospital. Howard regularly took part in Cobb's weekly staff conference, until August, 1940, when he joined the staff of the Riggs Foundation in Stockbridge.[51] Others in regular attendance at Cobb's conferences during the thirties were Niels Anthonisen, who later became director of the Brattleboro Retreat, William G. Barrett, who settled in San Francisco, John C. Whitehorn, of the McLean Hospital staff, who subsequently succeeded Meyer as professor of psychiatry at Johns Hopkins and Director of the Phipps Clinic, and Edgerton Howard's younger brother, Paul, who was assistant resident in 1937. All of them made their contributions to Cobb's case presentations, as others did when they came along.

It would be an oversight in discussing psychoanalysis on Cobb's service to omit the experiences and views of Mandel Cohen, who like Lashley, director of the psychology laboratory at Harvard, had a training analysis which was totally ineffective. Lashley's was with Alexander and Cohen's with Sachs. Cohen was assistant resident on Cobb's service in 1935 and 1936 and then remained on the staff until 1950. He had worked with Soma Weiss on the Fourth Medical Service at Boston City Hospital in 1931–33 and later had been doing clinical investigation at the Boston Lying-In Hospital. In 1936 and 1937 Cohen was trying to determine cardiac output by the ethyl iodide method. Moreover, he was successful in demonstrating the anti-convulsive effect of neutral red and brilliant vital red dyes (126). Thus Cobb saw him as a valuable collaborator and one with a capacity to evaluate scientific data. However, he found it difficult to accept Cohen's rather rigid scorn for psychoanalysis, which Cobb viewed as an early science in the data-gathering stage of its development. In any event, Cohen said that during his analysis he had lain on the couch and free associated for an hour five days a week over a period of eight months without anything happening.[52] Cohen later said that in psychoanalysis an observation might mean what it appeared to mean, might mean its direct opposite, or might mean nothing at all.[53] With so many alternate interpretations, he said, it was possible to construct any kind of theory. As time went on Cohen devoted most of his time to projects such as neurocirculatory asthenia which required vascular studies, and he eventually transferred to the cardiovascular laboratory. He remained for years a devil's advocate on the subject of psychoanalysis.

In addition to Cohen and Paul Howard, several other residents during the thirties took up psychoanalysis, including Milton Rosenbaum and Maurice H. Greenhill. Then, during the forties a high percentage of the resident staff had analytic training. Along with the interest in psychoanalysis there developed a psychologically oriented psychiatric service, and as time passed there was less insistence that each man have a strong background of training in neurology and neuropathology.

After World War II, neurological training was no longer a prerequisite for service on the resident staff. With the passing of the neurology prerequisite there was also a loss of interest among the residents in caring for the emotionally disturbed patients on the nonpsychiatric services. The analytically trained staff was less skilled than the earlier residents had been in handling patients on the other clinical services. Greenhill, who later became director of the psychiatric service at Albert Einstein, also observed there that too intense an interest in prolonged analytic psychotherapy seemed to detract from the ability to handle psychiatric problems on a liaison service.[54]

Psychoanalysis

Psychoanalysis was an exciting field that gave promise of adding a powerful new dimension to psychiatry, and the aspiring young men returning from World War II were anxious for experience at this growing edge of knowledge. Cobb, too, saw psychoanalysis as important. He had been helped with his own speech defect by analytic therapy. He knew that it could be effective, and he wanted his resident staff to be analyzed and to plan their future lives in the light of what they learned.

However, in spite of his enthusiasm for psychoanalysis, Cobb remained at heart a disciple of Adolf Meyer, who insisted that the psychiatrist have a basic understanding of neuroanatomy and cerebral function. It is fair to say that during the later years of Cobb's chairmanship he was resisting a national trend toward the separation of psychiatry from its neuropathological underpinnings. When he was president of the American Neurological Association in 1949 an illustrated after-dinner skit was presented, and a lantern slide was shown of Cobb trying to ride two horses. He was standing with the reins in his hands and a foot on the saddle of each horse, one neurology and the other psychiatry. Cobb fought a losing battle in the effort to hold the team together.

Cobb's views on the importance of integrating psychiatry, including psychoanalysis, with basic neurophysiology and neuropathology, are brought into focus in a 1957 letter he wrote to his former City Hospital resident, Charles D. Aring of Cincinnati. Aring was professor of neurology there and very active in psychoanalysis. In the letter Cobb referred to a paper on senility that Aring had sent to him and pointed out that the psychiatric manifestations of senility were a classic example of multiple etiology:

> I have just read your paper on "Senility" with great pleasure and noted with even greater pleasure your inscription about pupil reflecting teacher—it is not "reflecting." It is that you have gone on and developed along lines of thinking similar to mine because we both had the guts to take the *whole* training! And it is quite a long job—but everlastingly worth it. With that behind us we may hope to use Trotter's "cool but imaginative attention" to some purpose. The psychiatrists with no training in neuropathology and neurophysiology are bigoted and those with no understanding of psychoanalysis are often worse. By the next generation I think much of the antagonism to psychoanalysis will have evaporated because the young are taking it in as a culture. What we can ever do about teaching all aspects of how

the brain works to students I do not know—probably we will have to look for professors with a flare for teaching rather than drive to laboratory research.

I am just now writing a chapter for the "American Handbook of Psychiatry" on "The Contribution of Neurology to the Theory and Practice of Psychiatry" (a horrid title) and I have just put in a lot about multiple etiology—I think I'll use "Senility" as an example. It is one of the best.[55]

One of the most significant things Cobb did for psychoanalysis was to view it as important. He gave psychoanalysis respectability at a time when it was almost an underground cult in Vienna. He saw psychoanalysis as one approach to the incredibly complex relations of mind, body, and environment. He was effective in establishing psychoanalysis as an academically recognized empirical science. With his impeccably proper Bostonian background he was able to introduce a number of talented foreign analysts into the conventional and ultraconservative Massachusetts General Hospital. He promoted psychoanalysis as an important new therapeutic and investigative method and looked upon it objectively. He never became entrapped in the quasi-religious fervor which, possibly because of their emotional rebirth experiences during analysis, took over many of his colleagues. He was not one to honor orthodoxy, whether in a conventional religious setting or in psychoanalysis.

10
Psychiatry at the Massachusetts General Hospital (1934–1939)

Cobb's reasons for changing his focus from clinical and investigative neurology to psychiatry are detailed in the long letter he wrote to his friend Charles Symonds in 1934 (chapter 7). In that letter Cobb told Symonds about the psychological forces at work within himself which prompted the change. Yet the change was symptomatic of more than Cobb's personal motivation.

New trends in psychiatry had been growing up throughout the country, and Cobb wanted to take an active part in these exciting developments. One powerful influence was the mental hygiene movement in the early twenties, which had grown out of Clifford Beers's book, *The Mind That Found Itself*. The new child guidance clinics that developed from the pioneer work of Healy and Bronner in Chicago had a constructive impact, as did the work of Samuel Orton and others on reading problems in children. Moreover, psychoanalysis was attracting the attention of intellectuals, both lay and professional, and it offered an approach to mental illness that could be effectively carried out on an ambulatory basis in the psychiatrist's office. Too, the state psychiatric hospitals were for the most part understaffed, overcrowded, and located in remote places far removed from medical centers. Out of these trends and others came an awareness of the need for psychiatry to join the mainstream of medicine.

There had been earlier attempts to integrate psychiatry into general hospital medical practice. In 1901 Jesse M. Mosher had established a psychiatric unit in the Albany General Hospital, but the time was not yet ripe for it to flourish.[1] There were also other settings in which psychiatric services were situated in close proximity to general hospitals and to some degree integrated with acute general medical care. Notable among these were the Henry Phipps Psychiatric Clinic at Johns Hopkins in Baltimore under Adolf Meyer, and the Institute of Human Relations, which was in the same building as the Yale Medical School. The Institute of Human Relations was directly across the street from the

New Haven Hospital and shared the same administration, the same dining facilities, and the same laboratories. Gillespie, one of Meyer's early residents, had established a psychiatric unit in a general hospital in Great Britain. There had also been, under the direction of Dean Clarke, a psychiatric service at the University of Rochester, with a few beds of acutely ill patients, and Nathaniel W. Faxon, the director of the M.G.H., who was promoting the psychiatric service there, had come from Strong Memorial. However, the Rochester beds were not in the Strong Memorial Hospital proper, and none of these earlier services insured the daily collaboration of psychiatrists and nonpsychiatrists in recognizing, studying, and treating the myriad of mind-body relationships that Cobb could envision in a general hospital. Moreover, Cobb was not without previous experience, for at Boston City Hospital he had been in a position to observe many interrelationships between the ills of the mind and the body.[2]

One of Cobb's own residents, Maurice H. Greenhill, published an in-depth study of psychiatric liaison programs in 1977.[3] Greenhill saw liaison psychiatry as an outgrowth of the psychosomatic movement which had originated in Germany and Austria in the second and third decades of the twentieth century. Greenhill correctly attributed great importance to the interest of the medical sciences division of the Rockefeller Foundation, under the direction of Alan Gregg, in furthering the development of psychiatry and in making funds available for full-time teachers of psychiatry in selected American medical schools. Grants for psychiatric development were given by the Rockefeller Foundation to Harvard (Massachusetts General Hospital) in 1934, the University of Colorado in 1934, the University of Chicago in 1935, Tulane University in 1936, Washington University in St. Louis in 1938, and Duke University in 1940. Greenhill pointed out that Gregg's foresight and that of his associate, Robert Lambert, set the course of psychiatry for a generation and put psychiatry squarely in the general hospital on course for impact with the rest of medicine.

Greenhill noted that the first of the Rockefeller-funded general hospital psychiatric units was at the University of Colorado under Franklin Ebaugh,[4] and the second was Cobb's service at the Massachusetts General Hospital. However, Ebaugh's service differed from Cobb's in having no hospital beds assigned to it and no specific niche in the outpatient clinic. At Colorado the patients were examined, treated, and utilized for teaching wherever they might be in the hospital. In contrast,

Cobb had twelve beds integrated with neurology and neurosurgery on the same floor and had two specifically designated outpatient services, one for children and one for adults. Cobb's was a more fully organized service than Ebaugh's, although both of them developed at about the same time.

During the thirties Cobb's psychiatric ward was on the third floor of the new semiprivate Baker Memorial Building. It was an open ward occupying the south wing. Although unlocked, the patients had some protection, for the ward was served only by an elevator within view of the nurses' desk. There was a small conference room of a size that might have resulted from removing the partition between two patient bedrooms. The location of the psychiatric ward, while remote from the medical and surgical wards of the Bulfinch Building, served to encourage badly needed contact with the neurologists and neurosurgeons, whose patients were also located on the third floor of the Baker. Faxon disliked the arrangement because the clinical orientation of the nursing service did not provide an appropriate atmosphere for psychiatric patients.[5] Yet, it was Cobb's very objective to integrate psychiatry with the other hospital services in order to avoid the stigma of isolation.

The offices of the full-time psychiatric staff members, the workrooms, the laboratory, and the library were off the main-floor corridor in the west wing of the Bulfinch Building itself, and Cobb's own office, under the portico, looked out upon the quadrangle. So during the late thirties Cobb's work area and staff were constantly on view to the medical and surgical staff members as they entered from the brick corridor into the Bulfinch Building, where at that time most of the general medical and surgical patients were treated.

The architectural arrangement of the psychiatric service at the very heart of the Massachusetts General Hospital complex was of inestimable value to Cobb in his effort to integrate treatment of the mind with treatment of the body, to bring psychiatry into the mainstream of modern scientific medicine and surgery. Cobb was also helped by his freedom in the use of funds from the Rockefeller Foundation. This support enabled him to initiate unanticipated projects that promised to improve relations with nonpsychiatric members of the profession. Cobb had the unqualified endorsement of Alan Gregg, who had supported his previous work in the neuropathology laboratory and at Boston City Hospital. Moreover, according to Wilder Penfield, who was also supported by Rockefeller funds, Gregg had said that in 1933 there were no institutions where psychiatrists had methods for investigating the causes of mental abnormality, not even at Johns Hopkins in Baltimore. So Gregg knew that Cobb was entering a new field of endeavor and needed a free rein in the use of funds. In his biography of Alan Gregg, Penfield made the following observation:

> Stanley Cobb remarked that in turning from neurology to psychiatry he moved the focus of his attention away from the smaller problems of brain physiology and pathology and directed it to the larger problems of human behavior. On the one hand he had been concerned with the musical instrument; on the other the music itself. The transition was not an impossible one, for the interrelationship of the two fields is so close.
>
> "Alan Gregg," Cobb observed, "was always interested in the work that I occasionally discussed with him, but he showed remarkable restraint in never asking me about the work. In other words, his skill in giving without strings attached was remarkable. I believe this freedom was a great thing in making a success of my bringing psychiatry to a general hospital, where one medical service after another had to be won over."[6]

Cobb's goals were clearly expressed in a report to the Rockefeller Foundation at a later date:

> When the Rockefeller Foundation made the grants to the Harvard Medical School and to the Massachusetts General Hospital in 1933, the aim was to aid psychiatric research and teachng in an excellent general hospital. As I understand the problem at that time the objectives were:
>   1. By group service to the medical, surgical, and special departments of the hospital, to educate the general staff and the social service workers in modern psychiatry.
>   2. By cooperation, seminars, informal meetings, and lectures, to educate the younger physicians and surgeons, especially the residents and interns.
>   3. To teach psychiatry to medical students and explain its place in general medicine.
>   4. To train a few assistants in advanced techniques.
>   5. To study psychotic patients in the early stages of their disorder.
>   6. To study the psychoneurotic patients so abundant in a general hospital clinic.
>   7. To carry on research in the clinic and laboratories.[7]

He pursued all of these aims, and in some areas achieved a remarkable degree of success. However, it is fair to say that his overriding objective—in line with his life-long effort to integrate the functions of mind and body—was to make psychiatry a respected integral part of the general medical scene, particularly at Harvard and in the Massachusetts General Hospital.

Activities of great importance to this end in the mid-thirties were the consultation service, which helped in the management of psychiatric problems throughout the hospital, emergency care, and investigative projects carried out in collaboration with physicians and surgeons in fields other than psychiatry. Other efforts that contributed directly or indirectly to the stature of the department were weekly staff conferences, work on the curriculum committee at the Harvard Medical School, continued direction of the second-year neuropathology course, publications of general interest to the medical profession, and even Cobb's eating lunch in the staff dining room, where he could talk with others about psychosomatic relationships.

Through his personal charm and his innate credibility Cobb was effective in overseeing, supervising, and often actually performing services for the nonpsychiatric staff members as well as his own residents, fellows, social workers, and medical students. The answering of consultations was of key importance, so that in the early days Cobb carefully reviewed the consultations carried out by his resident staff and actually made many of them himself. Greenhill pointed out in his monograph on liaison psychiatry that the rendering of consultations on a service such as Cobb's can be very difficult, because much of the time the psychiatrist is working in a part of the hospital over which he has no control. Moreover, nicety of judgment is required on the part of the psychiatrist to know whether in answering a consultation he is relating primarily to the actual patient, to a disturbed member of the family, to the anxieties of the patient's physician or surgeon, to the attitudes of nurses or other personnel, or to a crisis-intervention situation. In 1960, Avery Weisman, a staff member of the Massachusetts General Hospital, and Thomas Hackett, who later became chairman of its department of psychiatry, wrote:

> There are four phases to the work of therapeutic consultation: rapid evaluation, with special attention to the personal factors and the reason for consultation; psychodynamic formulation of the major conflict, predominant emotional patterns, ego functions, and object relationships; rational planning of a therapeutic intervention, based on formulation; and active information and implementation by the psychiatrist himself.[8]

There is no evidence to suggest that Cobb ever formulated the facets of consultation methodology so systematically. However, he was acutely aware of the resistance shown by patients, family members, and nonpsychiatric physicians to psychiatric consultations. It was also evident that nonpsychiatric nurses were easily upset by delirious, disoriented, unduly demanding, or obstreperous patients and hence often promoted the consultation in the hope that the patient might be transferred off their ward. Derek Denny-Brown, one of Cobb's successors as director of the Boston City Hospital neurological unit, said, "Stanley had to use very simple language.[9] He couldn't talk to Howard Means, Walter Bauer, or Oliver Cope[10] about libido, id, or pre-oedipal situations. Instead he had to point out the effect of 'worry' in aggravating arthritis or peptic ulcer." In Denny-Brown's opinion, "Stanley was a little naive in his psychiatric thinking. Only he could have introduced psychiatry into the Massachusetts General Hospital."

Earl Solomon, who was senior resident from 1950 to 1951, pointed out a related bugbear that Cobb and his staff had to face in answering consultations, namely the overwrought tendency of the predominantly Anglo-Saxon staff to reason intellectually from clear-cut premises through logical processes to crisp conclusions.[11] In psychiatry the expression of feelings and the establishment of relationships were often more important than crisp logic, and therapy, as in other branches of medicine, was often empirical. However, irrational suppositions and conclusions in psychiatric consultation notes only served to fortify the resistance of physicians and surgeons on other hospital services. Solomon thought that notes which could not be substantiated by logic might have been more prominent in the fifties than in an earlier day, because the service had grown so large that Cobb could no longer supervise all the consultation work personally. Also, there was a more widespread introduction of psychoanalytic terms into consultation notes because most of the staff members were actively interested in the subject, even if not personally analyzed. Solomon believed that psychoanalytic terms had no place in a clinical psychiatric consultation.

An area in which Cobb encountered less resistance was the handling of emergency situations on the nonpsychiatric services. Here, the physician or surgeon leaned heavily upon the liaison psychiatrist. Patients who were violent, delirious, suicidal, delusional, or even confused often presented more of a management problem than the nonpsychiatric staff of physicians and surgeons were prepared to handle. Often patients with problems of this nature became manageable with therapeutic measures that the consulting psychiatrist could prescribe on the patient's home ward. On the other hand, either because of the commotion produced by the patient or the technical nature of the indicated treatment it was sometimes more productive to transfer the patient to the psychiatric service either temporarily or until an appropriate disposition could be made elsewhere.

In the long run one of the most effective ways of integrating psychiatry into the mainstream of professional activities at the Massachusetts General was through clinical and laboratory studies carried out in collaboration with members of other departments. However, such collaborative efforts did not immediately come into being except on a very limited basis.

Although Cobb and his co-workers were interested in psychosomatic problems, the chiefs of other services such as gynecology, orthopedics, pediatrics, and even neurology were either blind or did not want to see. One of the earliest joint efforts was with Cobb's prior colleague from the old neuropathology laboratory, John H. Talbott. Talbott was associated with Walter Bauer in the rheumatology section of the department of medicine. In 1938 he and others published with Cobb a study of acid-base balance in the blood of a patient with hysterical hyperventilation (123). Another early interdepartmental collaborator was Robert Schwab, who had been one of Cobb's resident staff at City Hospital and in 1937 established the electroencephalographic laboratory at the General. Cobb and Schwab, then in the department of neurology, wrote about simultaneous electromyograms and electroencephalograms in paralysis agitans (136). Still another early study in collaboration with neurology was a review article with Edwin M. Cole on stuttering (135). The article emphasized familial incidence and the importance of mixed cerebral dominance. An interdepartmental study of wider general clinical interest was that of White, Cobb, and Jones on the irritable colon (138). Chester M. Jones was chief of gastroenterology in the department of medicine. Another internist, Walter Bauer, the rheumatologist, was also interested in psychosomatic relationships. He and his associate, Isabel Whiting, wrote a paper with Cobb on environmental factors in rheumatoid arthritis (139). That is all the work that Cobb published from the department of psychiatry during the thirties in collaboration with members of other clinical departments. However, later on, as psychiatry grew in importance, many collaborative studies were under way, some of them quite sophisticated. The investigative studies that Cobb carried out with members of his own department and the publications that he wrote alone are discussed elsewhere in this chapter.

The weekly staff conferences on the third floor of the Baker Memorial Building were primarily intended for members of Cobb's own department and others with a primary interest in psychiatry, some of whom came in from other institutions. At one such conference in about 1936 a patient with anorexia nervosa was presented, and Cobb in his summary concluded that anorexia nervosa was a disease entity in its own right, not a manifestation of schizophrenia.[12]

The conference was presided over by Cobb, then forty-seven years of age. He was strikingly handsome in his long white clinical coat with a Queen Square reflex hammer protruding from one of the pockets, yet the arthritic deformity of his hands could not be overlooked. Others who spoke one by one, beginning with the most junior, were Paul Howard, a gentle young man also in a white clinical coat; Sarah Evarts, the social worker, who was an extraordinarily handsome middle-aged woman with well groomed, wavy white hair; Finesinger; Lindemann; Mariana Taylor, and Helene Deutsch. Like Cobb, Finesinger was in a white coat. When Finesinger's turn to speak came, he had a cigarette with a long ash drooping from the corner of his mouth and apparently was just waking up from a snooze. Lindemann, similarly dressed, was slightly overweight and spoke very gently in a squeaky, high voice. Mariana Taylor was a stocky woman of middle age wearing a frumpy black Cambridge hat, while Helene Deutsch was a handsome, neatly attired woman of fifty who spoke with a heavy Middle European accent. At the end of the conference Cobb in his usual manner summarized the problem under discussion:

> The ordinary labels do not help in this case. She was called anorexia nervosa, and I don't see why this does not still fit. She was hurt in her relationship with her father, who died. She wants a man's affection but not sex. There are some anxieties about her becoming fat and therefore asexual and disgusting. She does not seem to be typically schizophrenic in her psychosis but is alert and reacts to people. . . .
> In the conference room here she seemed, with her choking and spitting, to be showing a reaction to swallowing. . . . Her reaction is a very special one, and I believe we should recognize it as an entity, anorexia nervosa, even though she looks to some extent infantile, hysterical, schizophrenic, and manic.[13]

When interviewed five years later the patient was warm and friendly, attractively attired in a black dress and hat, with red shoes which matched her red earrings. She said she felt completely well. She was seen again eleven years after leaving the hospital. At that time she had two children, seven and four years of age, ran her apartment easily, was active and happy. One of Cobb's later residents, John Nemiah, wrote a long paper on anorexia nervosa which was published in *Medicine*,[14] one of the most prestigious general medical review journals. So, in a indirect way Cobb's weekly conference led to widespread dissemination of knowledge about a psychosomatic disease.

Another channel used by Cobb in his struggle to bring psychiatry into the awareness of nonpsychiatric physicians was through the curriculum committee at the Harvard Medical School. One such effort involved Finesinger, who with Cobb devised a behavior sheet which they hoped would be adopted by the major clinical hospitals as an integral part of the history and physical examination forms then in use.[15] The surgeon, Oliver Cope, reported that the forms in use at the time were replete with spaces for information about family background, previous organic illnesses, surgical operations, exposure to industrial hazards, and for all the nuances of physical findings, including examination of the eyegrounds with an ophthalmoscope, the ear canals with an otoscope, the nasal passages with a speculum, and the oral cavity with a tongue depressor. The forms then in use had space for the lymphatic glands, the heart size and function, lungs, abdomen, genitalia including the female pelvis, rectum, reflexes, peripheral circulation, posture, and skin blemishes. For psychiatric observations the forms included only the words, "Mental status." Cobb and Finesinger's supplement was to include the apparent mood of the patient, whether outgoing or withdrawn, elated, depressed, or apathetic. It was also to contain references to acceleration or retardation of thought, speech, or bodily movements, as well as room for orientation as to time, place, and person. There was also to be room for notes about family history, traumatic past events, and current social or emotional difficulties. According to Cope, after many long-drawn-out battles in the curriculum committee, the behavior sheet was suitably condensed and was made an official part of the history and physical forms approved by Harvard for use in its affiliated hospitals.

Despite all of this, the behavior sheet was a dismal failure. Cope said it was used for a time on the surgical service at the Massachusetts General but was never adopted on any of the other services there or on any of the services at the Beth Israel, Boston City, or Peter Bent Brigham hospitals. Cope added that Finesinger attended most of the meetings of the curriculum committee when the behavior sheet was under discussion, and that he lacked the tact and persuasiveness that Cobb himself would have shown under the circumstances.

A more successful effort through the curriculum committee took place after Harry C. Solomon succeeded Campbell in 1943 as professor of psychiatry and director of the Boston Psychopathic Hospital.[16] Cobb and Solomon both wanted more time in the curriculum for fourth-year psychiatry. Prior to 1943 the Harvard medical students had a brief part-time exposure to psychiatry in the first and third years and were offered in the fourth year a month of full-time psychiatry as an elective course which was only infrequently chosen. Cobb, who was chairman of the departmental executive committee, and Solomon, the new professor of psychiatry, were determined to obtain more time in psychiatry for the fourth-year students. Cobb and Solomon argued, cajoled, and battled with the curriculum committee in order to obtain a full month of compulsory psychiatry in the senior year. At that time medical students as seniors were required to take one full month of medicine and one full month of surgery. Another month could be taken in either medicine or surgery, so that every Harvard medical student would have two months in one field or the other. When Solomon, a persuasive, warm man with a twinkle in his eye, pointed out that every medical student graduated with only one month in either surgery or medicine the curriculum committee gave in and planned a full month of psychiatry in the senior year.

At the Massachusetts General and the Brigham hospitals there was no difficulty about implementing the decision. However, at Boston City Hospital the situation was quite different. The most powerful men in the department of medicine there at the time were George Richards Minot and William B. Castle, both of whom were organically oriented and basically hostile to the notion of surrendering any of their time to psychiatry. One afternoon, after a long verbal battle, the cause seemed to be hopelessly lost, and the respective professors were about to go home. When they stood up and turned toward the door, Solomon said to Castle, "You know it is a shame the way parents know so little about bringing up their children these days." Castle instantly realized what Solomon was saying, and he replied, "Yes, you are absolutely right. Doctors have to know how to advise parents about bringing up their children. You can have your month." Castle, one of the most respected and loved of the professors in medicine, demonstrated his sensitivity and his flexibility in making this last-minute change in judgment. After that day Harvard medical students profited greatly from their increased exposure to psychiatry, and Castle became one of its strong supporters.[17]

In addition to influencing the nonpsychiatric members of the medical profession through psychiatric consultations, emergency care, joint research projects, clinical teaching, and work on the curriculum committee at Harvard, Cobb also directed some of his writing to the general medical reader. For example, from 1935 through 1959, he published each year a review of neuropsychiatry in the *Archives of Internal Medicine,* a specialty journal for internists.[18] Other writings for the general medical public which appeared during the thirties included an article on shock therapy in the *New England Journal of Medicine* (113) and a paper on the psychiatric approach to the treatment of epilepsy (147).

Much of the important clinical and investigative work carried on in the psychiatric department during the late thirties was published jointly by Cobb and a co-worker from his own staff. It is of note that at the time all of Lindemann's work was published independently of Cobb. However, Finesinger and Cobb wrote jointly for the *Bulletin of the Massachusetts Society for Mental Hygiene* a description of the Massachusetts General Hospital psychiatric service. Although Finesinger published most of his work independently of Cobb, his studies were nevertheless closely related to Cobb's overall plan. Cobb saw the need for an experimental laboratory for the study of conditioned reflexes in the manner of Pavlov, the Russian physiologist. Finesinger, who had visited Pavlov on the 1933–34 study trip in Europe, was in charge of the Pavlovian laboratory. The laboratory was located in temporary space during the thirties and moved to a fine new soundproof room in 1940. Work on conditioned reflexes was carried on by George Sutherland between 1939 and 1943 but had to be discontinued during World War II and was never seriously resumed.[19]

Over the years Mandel Cohen was one of Cobb's most consistent collaborators. During the thirties Cohen published with Cobb the first of two papers on the anticonvulsive effect of intravital dyes (126), and a sequel appeared in the early forties (156). Cohen also published with Cobb two papers on acid-base balance as affected by respiration. The first of these was on hysterical hyperventilation (123) and the second on the impact of hypnosis on the same disorder (140). The patient in

CASE V

NAME: The Girl Who Panted
HEREDITY: Alcoholic Father, Feeble Minded Mother
SIBLINGS: Third of Six
HOSPITAL # 352919
DATE: 1938

YEAR	MEDICAL DATA	ILLNESS	SOCIAL DATA	AGE
1915			Born in Maine	0
1916	Convulsions Pneumonia		Fell in cesspool	1
1917	Mumps		Brother born	2
1918				3
1919	Chickenpox			4
1920				5
1921	Measles			6
1922	Otitis Nail biting		Began school	7
1923				8
1924	Fractured arm. Sleep walking and talking.		Brother born	9
1925				10
1926	Menarche Strangling feelings			11
1927	Minor injury to knee Crutches for 3 months		Story of rape incident	12
1928	Menstrual cramps		Seventh grade	13
1929	Knee and crutches again			14
1930	Tonsillectomy Arm bandaged		Falling off at school	15
1931	Fainting spell		Scared by drunken father	16
1932	Vomiting "Nervous breakdown"		Father died Stopped school. Earns $4 a week	17
1933	"Kicked by a child" and on crutches		Another rape story. Earns $5 a week	18
1934	Fainting, blindness, paralysis		Caring for sick grandmother	19
1935	Headaches Choreic movements		Brother married Divine healing	20
1936	"Tetany" "Chorea"		Caring for asthmatic patient M.G.H.	21
1937	Improved		Discharged, back at work	22
1938	Hospital for tetany		Working again	23

FIG. 6

FIGURE 3.—Cobb's modification of Adolf Meyer's Life Chart, citing, under social data "Fell in cesspool."

the second study was worked up in the classical Meyerian manner with a life chart that recorded as a traumatic incident at age one, "fell in cesspool" (Figure 3). When hyperventilating the patient had tetanic contractions of the hands and feet which were aggravated by the hysterical features, and the blood pH and carbon dioxide studies were extremely disturbed. With hypnosis the tetanic contractures were controlled and the acid-base disturbances were greatly improved. When the case was reported at the Association for Research in Nervous and Mental Diseases in 1939, the point Cobb made was familiar. He had often said that the distinction between *functional* and *organic* disease was purely arbitrary. All illnesses have disturbances of both structure and function.

Another collaborator who worked on ventilation in the late thirties was William W. Sargant of London, England, who in 1939 was a Rockefeller fellow under Cobb. With Cobb and Schwab, who directed the electroencephalographic laboratory, Sargant made simultaneous electroencephalographic and spirometric studies of patients with *petit mal* epilepsy and found that in some instances hyperventilation preceded the seizure (142). Because of the outbreak of World War II Sargant returned to England in September, 1939.[20] He directed psychiatric treatment after the evacuation at Dunkirk and employed methods that he had learned with anorexia nervosa patients at the Massachusetts General Hospital. He was also one of the pioneers in the use of sodium amytal in interviewing for battle fatigue, a method he had learned in his work on hysteria with Cobb.[21] Sargant later had an illustrious career as a drug-oriented psychiatrist in England. For twenty-five years he was physician-in-charge of the department of psychological medicine at St. Thomas's Hospital in London.

With Clemens E. Benda, a research fellow from 1936 to 1937, Cobb collaborated in a monograph on the pathogenesis of paralysis agitans (159). When Benda completed his year at the Massachusetts General he continued his studies at the Wrentham State School. The monograph that he and Cobb wrote was based upon autopsy studies of eight cases obtained from several institutions in and near Boston. The monograph contained a discussion of the physiology and anatomy of the extrapyramidal system, suggesting that many so-called idiopathic cases of paralysis agitans were in all probability the result of encephalitis, and emphasized the lack of evidence of senility in most brain specimens from patients with this disease.

Neil T. McDermott and Cobb collaborated in a psychiatric survey of fifty cases of bronchial asthma. (137). They divided their cases into three groups. Thirty of the patients, or sixty percent, gave stories of clear psychological precipitation or aggravation of their attacks; seven, or fourteen percent, gave stories which strongly suggested such a relationship, and thirteen, or twenty-six percent, gave no such stories. The authors went on to discuss the importance of heredity, neurotic traits, family constellation, allergy, and other factors in the patients' susceptibility to anger and other manifestations of stress in relation to the wheezing and shortness of breath. Cobb's final collaboration with a staff member was the study of the irritable colon, with White and Jones, to which reference has already been made (138).

A number of persons who worked on Cobb's service during the late thirties played important parts in the growth of the department even though they did not collaborate with Cobb in any actual publications. The first resident was E. Murray Burns, from 1934 to 1935, and the assistant resident was John Adams Abbott. Burns subsequently practiced psychiatry in Portland, Oregon. He wrote to Cobb in 1966 to say that he had retired and was doing volunteer work in Vietnam.[22] Abbott, after further training in neurology, became a long-term member of the psychiatric staff and developed an interest in medical history. David A. Young, the psychiatric resident in 1935–36, later was clinical professor at the University of North Carolina, and at one time was state commissioner of health. Volta R. Hall, assistant resident in 1938, remained on Cobb's staff for a number of years. After that there were two very distinguished residents, Milton Rosenbaum and Maurice Greenhill. Rosenbaum (1938–39) worked for a time in Cincinnati and then joined John Romano in building up the active liaison service at the University of Rochester. He later headed the psychiatric service at Albert Einstein School of Medicine in New York. Maurice Greenhill followed Rosenbaum as resident and served from 1939 to 1940. After teaching psychiatry at Duke and elsewhere Greenhill also went to Albert Einstein and in 1971 became director of the psychiatry service there. It was Greenhill who wrote the study of liaison psychiatry which has already been discussed.[23]

In the 1934–39 era there were also a number of important research fellows. Russell Frazier from England was a Rockefeller fellow about 1939 and returned home because of the war. In England he became a leader of social medicine. Sargant wrote to say that after World War

II Frazier gave up psychiatry and become professor of endocrinology at the Royal Post-Graduate Medical School in Hammersmith.[24] Philip Buckley was another research fellow from England who had to return because of World War II. He had been at Balliol College and had worked at Queen Square before coming onto Cobb's service. He had a tomato red sports car when in Boston.[25] Sargant said that Buckley was later on the staff of the London Hospital, London East. Tsuneo Muramatsu was listed as a research fellow in 1935. After teaching for a time at Tokyo Medical College (1939–49) he became professor of neuropsychiatry at Nagoya National University in 1950 and served as its dean from 1960 to 1962. Donald B. Lindsley, Ph.D., was also a fellow in 1935. Lindsley later became chairman of the department of psychology at the University of California in Los Angeles, where in 1961 he established a new brain center with eight stories above ground and three below.[26]

There were also important workers in the outpatient department. In 1936 the head of the adult clinic was Maurice Fremont-Smith, a practicing internist, and the brother of Cobb's earlier associate, Frank Fremont-Smith, who had preceded him in that role. Maurice Fremont-Smith functioned in the outpatient clinic on a part-time basis. Child psychiatry under the direction of Eleanor Pavenstedt, assisted by Edgerton Howard and Robert A. Young, is discussed elsewhere (chapter 13).[27] In 1937 Lindemann took over both the adult and children's clinics.

Social service was directed by Sarah Evarts, a close friend of Betty Cobb. She had been psychoanalyzed and was able to take an active part in the discussion of cases at Cobb's weekly staff conference. She died prematurely in 1939, and after her death the psychiatric library in the Herman Room was named for her. Her successor in social service was Louise Silbert, a beautiful and very competent woman. She later married Bernard Bandler who was resident in 1941–42.

One of Cobb's major contributions during the late thirties, as had been the case in the City Hospital neurological unit, was the influence he had on young men going into the neurosciences. During the five-year period between 1934 and 1939, he assembled a group of residents and fellows whose subsequent accomplishments gave a hearty endorsement to his judgment in selecting them. The experimental nature of the new psychiatric service, with its emphasis on studying both the psychological and the physical manifestations of disease, afforded a wide range of approaches, which with Cobb's encouragement and support were open to these young men, many of whom had studied neurology and neuropathology before coming to the Massachusetts General Hospital.

While Cobb was carrying on the multitudinous tasks inherent in the building of his psychiatric service, he also had other interests that were important to him and broadened the scope of his knowledge and effectiveness. One of these interests had to do with the physicians, mostly Jewish, who were fleeing from European dictatorships, especially in Germany and Spain.

Hitler's evident intentions for expansion in Europe during the late thirties presented an opportunity for American medicine to attract some really great medical minds to this country. At the same time, it gave some of these people a chance to escape persecution in their dictator-ridden lands. The Boston Committee on Medical Emigrés was established in 1938 under the leadership of Jacob Fine, professor of surgery at Harvard and chief of surgery at the Beth Israel Hospital. The exectutive committee consisted of Dean Edsall as chairman, Stanley Cobb as vice-chairman, and Susan Herman as secretary. Five additional members were Oliver Cope, Fine, Tracy Putnam, Joseph H. Pratt, and Charles F. Wilensky. The executive committee was supported by a general committee of fifty-four physicians, all with imposing posts in Boston academic medicine. The object of the organization was to find employment for emigré physicians in the United States wherever this could be accomplished effectively. The Boston Committee on Medical Emigrés sought, through appropriate educational articles in professional and lay journals, to set before the public the plight of the emigrés, the American tradition of hospitality, and the possibility of mutual benefit through well-planned placements. The committee also set about seeking funds from foundations and individuals to maintain a registry of available foreign physicians and to establish contact with institutions and communities needing physicians.

Walter B. Cannon, professor of physiology at Harvard, was active in submitting names of appropriate emigrés. In a 1939 letter to Cannon, Susan Herman pointed out the difficulty in admitting a Spanish physician, because the quota was only two hundred fifty-two annually. In cases such as this it was sometimes necessary to arrange for immigration on a nonquota visa by getting an invitation from the dean of a medical school, in addition to finding funds for the man's support.[28]

Massachusetts General Hospital

Later in 1939 Fine became the official secretary of the executive committee, while Mrs. Herman continued to handle much of the correspondence. At one point Cobb pointed out in his realistic way that it was almost impossible to arrange for positions in advance except for men who were internationally known.

A review of Cobb's activities during the late thirties would be incomplete without mention of the honorary degree awarded to Jung by Harvard at the time of its tercentenary in 1936. To the department of psychology was delegated the authority to make one nomination for an honorary degree candidate. They would have liked to nominate Freud, but they feared he would decline, and they had no authority to make a substitute nomination. So they settled on Jung, who promptly accepted and visited the Cobbs when he came to this country for the presentation. Several amusing incidents occurred that June. When Jung arrived in the Boston area he called Mrs. Cobb to ask whether he could bring his secretary. Betty Cobb replied that there was only one guest room. Jung did not see that as a problem, but Betty Cobb did; so the lady made arrangements to stay elsewhere. The second night at the Cobbs' home Jung, in accordance with hotel custom both here and abroad, placed his shoes outside the bedroom door to be polished. Cobb polished the shoes. The most embarrassing incident, however, took place during a conference in the outpatient amphitheatre at the Massachusetts General Hospital, when after a long preamble about Jung's work in Zurich Cobb came to the final moments. Then, standing in front of the group he turned to Jung and said, "And now I have the pleasure of introducing to you Dr. Sigmund Freud." That faux pas was a Freudian slip that Cobb never lived down.[29]

There is a tradition at Harvard that recipients of honorary degrees wear either academic regalia or formal "morning" attire including a cutaway coat, striped trousers, and top hat. Apparently Jung had failed to bring academic regalia. He managed to find the necessary formal coat and trousers but did not have a top hat. Cobb rummaged through the attic and discovered his old collapsible opera hat, which was several sizes too small for Jung. However, Jung, who had a sense of humor, carried it along, so that it would seem as if he had just removed it, and handled the occasion with aplomb.

Unfortunately, there was a bitter side to Jung's visit. Jung had continued to see a number of prominent German patients during the prewar National-Socialist era, primarily in the hope of influencing favorably the course of events. He later said he was opposed to National Socialism but was often suspected of being a Nazi sympathizer because of his German contacts, and at the Harvard commencement exercises there were student demonstrations against him.

Although Harry Murray, Bill Herman, Irmarita Putnam, Carl Binger, and even Cobb himself had been attracted to Jung's work in the twenties, all of them had drifted off to the Freudian camp by the time of the tercentenary. Cobb enjoyed Jung's hearty warmth and humor but had little empathy with him on professional matters at that time.

The demands upon Cobb during the late thirties when he was establishing the new psychiatric service were taking their toll from his physical and emotional reserves. The rheumatoid arthritis, from which he had suffered for many years, gradually became more crippling, yet he continued to need the change of pace that he found in such activities as sailing, skiing, watercolor painting, and the study of nature.

Although Cobb had suffered from rheumatoid arthritis all his adult life—it was demonstrable on the group photograph taken during his internship—there was marked progression in its severity during the thirties. Still, Cobb remained active physically. He used his fingers deftly in the watercolor painting that he so greatly enjoyed and in other activities requiring manual dexterity. The arthritis was presumabley one important factor in making the decision to acquire a more stable and comfortable cruising boat. The old yawl *Pamaho,* leaky and uncomfortable, was sold in 1935. After a year of cruising on a chartered catboat, the Cobbs' new thirty-foot cutter, *Fulmar,* was launched in Saugus. It was a steady boat of rather broad beam and had full headroom; yet it sailed reasonably well to windward and very well on a reach. As in the past the Cobbs cruised mostly with Carl Binger and his wife, Chloe.

Chloe Binger told a tale[30] about a tug-of-war between two strong personalities, Cobb the skipper and Betty Cobb the cook. The story had to do with Cobb's fondness for old-fashioned pilot biscuits—the real water-thin type, not the crumbly, mealy, dry crackers one buys today. When cruising the Cobbs always stopped in a harbor at night and every two or three days had an opportunity to stock up with fresh provisions. Although they normally ate fresh food, under the berths in the bilge were stored enough rusty tins of corned beef, vegetables, and pilot biscuits for a year's cruise to the Galapagos Islands. Each day at about noon Betty Cobb would bring forth and place on deck an assortment of cheeses, fruits, and sandwich spreads for lunch, along with one or more half-finished loaves of bread. Also, every day Cobb would say to her, "How about some pilot biscuits?" Betty Cobb's reply would be, "We have all this opened bread. When that is gone we can have pilot biscuits." This familiar sequence took place every cruising day for years, and Cobb never had an opportunity to have his pilot biscuits for lunch. Then once when *Fulmar* was barging down Vineyard Sound with all sails set on a dusty southwest day, Betty Cobb brought up on deck the usual assortment of fruits, cheeses, and sandwich spreads. Cobb said, "How about some pilot biscuits?" Whereupon his wife brought on deck a fresh, unopened loaf of sandwich bread. Cobb grabbed the loaf of bread, stood up to his whole height, and with an arm motion similar to that of a World Series pitcher he hurled the bread down wind as far as it would travel. The Cabot in Betty Cobb was thunderstruck. She stood motionless for a moment or two and then went below and brought out a tin of pilot biscuits. For the first time in years she had met her master. The occasion was subsequently immortalized in a poem by Carl Binger entitled "Cast Not Thy Bread upon the Waters!"

Not only did the Cobbs and Bingers enjoy sailing, but they also took up skiing. It was in the early thirties when Americans were learning the Arlberg technique. With relatively short skis they could navigate trails, steering by the use of stem and Christiania turns. Inasmuch as people were no longer dependent upon finding open slopes, trail skiing in the White Mountains became *de rigeur*. Those were the days of Oscar Hambro's ski store behind the Copley Plaza Hotel in Boston and the ski trains, which ran to various places in New Hampshire on weekends. The Cobbs and the Bingers were hardly accomplished skiers, but they did enjoy the skiing weekends. There were some quaint aspects to the Cobbs' skiing. Chloe Binger said that each Washington's Birthday the Cobbs and Bingers visited a country hotel near Mt. Chocorua.[31] There they skied down an open slope on the premises and came to a halt by sitting down before reaching the fence at the bottom of the hill. For ski pants Cobb wore the pin-striped trousers of the cutaway suit in which he had been married. Binger pointed out that they were ideal for skiing because they were so closely woven that the snow stuck to them much less than it would have to a fuzzier surface. Under the cutaway trousers Cobb wore some red long johns that dated back to his days in the National Guard. On skiing weekends the Cobbs and the Bingers always shared a cottage with a living room, two bedrooms, and a bath. One day a Saint Bernard dog got into the Cobbs' bedroom. The lower drawer of the dresser was standing open, and Cobb's long johns were stretched out inside. The Saint Bernard sniffed around, lifted his leg, and drenched the entire contents of the bureau drawer.

A tale of domestic felicity in the living room of that cottage is also entertaining. A friend returning from China had brought Cobb a pair of hand-carved walnut talismans, which in China are used as worry beads. They were magnificently carved, much resembling an English walnut but considerably larger. Cobb's rheumatoid arthritis was becoming severe enough at that time so that he had been advised by his physician to exercise his fingers by flexing them around the wooden walnuts. One night after dinner when the two couples were sitting in the living room Betty Cobb said, "Carl, why don't you read to us aloud? Chloe and I can get on with our knitting and Stanley can play with his balls!"

In the late thirties the Cobbs' summer life was centered in the Cotuit house which was built in the winter of 1922–23, just prior to the Rockefeller-supported European study trip. With its gambrel roof and its location at the head of the harbor it was a delightful, semi-isolated situation for informal living. There was little contact with Cotuit neighbors, for the lot on which the house stood had belonged to Betty Cobb's parents, and relatives were close at hand. At the foot of the bluff was the salt pond where Cobb would sit by the hour studying the life patterns of the gulls, terns, and herons. His custom was to get up early and watch the birds while the rest of the family was still asleep. The cruising boat, *Fulmar,* was anchored at Cotuit half the summer. The rest of the time it was in front of Alfred Redfield's house in the salt pond at Woods Hole. At Cotuit Cobb spent much of his time in the bunk house, an outbuilding away from the telephone. He invariably had along a current project he was working on, often the completion of one of his scientific articles, or some aspect of science or history in which he was interested at the time. Because of his interest in birds, Cobb had strong feelings of distrust for cats. When the Cobb family had one for a time, he insisted that it be kept in the house in the early morning. Birds tend to alight on the ground at dawn seeking worms and insects for food. At that time they are easy prey for a cat, whereas later on, when actively flying about, they are better able to escape.

When in Cotuit, Cobb attempted to isolate himself from patients and from the other demanding aspects of his work, but he did make use of his time there for study and particularly for visits from friends and colleagues with whom he conversed at leisure about his various and manifold interests.

The close of the thirties was a time of incalculable transition both for the Cobbs and the world at large. In August, 1939, Hitler invaded Poland, and George VI made his classic address over the radio in which he announced the declaration of a war the end of which no man could foresee. With the beginning of the forties America was in a war economy that ended the Great Depression. Federal income taxes soared from modest to almost confiscatory levels. The sudden employment of women in the defense industries undoubtedly helped the war effort. It also gave many women a new sense of importance and independence. Because of the high taxes and the war work women were doing, domestic service went almost into oblivion, and many well-to-do families for the first time did their own cooking and housecleaning. With "lend-lease" and other forms of aid to Britain, the involvement of the United States in World War II became deeper, and the stage was set for our taking part as a belligerent after the Japanese attacked Pearl Harbor on December 7, 1941.

Anxiety about the war had its impact on the Cobbs, for their own children were of military age. Their son Sidney, who had finished Harvard College in 1938, was a student at the Harvard Medical School, from which he was to graduate in 1942. He later became a battalion medical officer during the Battle of the Bulge. Helen, Bryn Mawr 1940, was completing her college work, and John Candler Cobb II, better known as Jock, was due to graduate from Harvard College in 1941. In keeping with Cobb's own ambivalence about fighting, Jock became a conscientious objector and was an ambulance driver for the American Field Service Committee in North Africa during the battle for El Alamein. And Betty Cobb herself was going through psychoanalysis with Helene Deutsch.

So, not only in the world scene, but also in the Cobbs' own personal life an era was drawing to a close and a new one lay ahead. The new era was beset by frightening prospects and also by new opportunities. In summary, one might say that during the thirties Cobb brought about within himself the change to psychiatry from clinical and investigative neurology. During this time, too, he established a secure foothold for his new psychiatric service at the Massachusetts General Hospital. He attracted a number of able co-workers as visiting staff members, as residents, and as research fellows. He had begun to find a reasonable degree of acceptance from the physicians and surgeons on the non-psychiatric services. He had developed a working psychiatric unit of proven value in a large university teaching hospital. These achievements were apparent locally and were known nationally through professional publications, through presentations and discussions at national medical conventions, and through students and former staff members.

However, the full impact of Cobb's work was to be developed in the future, which was to see psychiatric wards in general hospitals throughout the country, widespread acceptance of psychiatry as a respected specialty of medicine, effective new forms of therapy, a marked decrease in the number of patients occupying state hospital beds, and vital new knowledge of neurotransmitters, which became important in psychiatric brain research. Cobb's work during the forties was destined to include a number of classified studies of direct importance to the war effort and, in spite of a limited staff, the expansion of cooperative studies with other hospital departments. In the late forties and fifties psychoanalysis assumed an increasingly important role and, with various forms of funding available, there was a vast increase in the number of residents and fellows in training. The psychiatric service was destined to become one of the largest and most important in the entire hospital.

11
Wartime Frustrations (1940–1946)

When Hitler danced a jig in a railroad car in Compiègne during the late spring of 1940, it became evident to all that Western civilization was seriously imperiled. France had been overrun by the Germans in only a few weeks, and the Battle of Britain was soon to follow. The evacuation of Dunkirk had made it clear that England would be heavily bombarded, and the threat of invasion aroused fears of ultimate defeat. Although the United States was not to become an active belligerent until December 7, 1941, Cobb had already lost his English research fellows, Sargant, Buckley, and Frazier. Soon to come was accelerated medical education, with nine-month internships and specialty training geared to immediate military needs. Fortunately for Cobb, there was a need for psychiatrists in the medical corps of the army and navy, so that the residency program was destined to continue during the war years. Research was also to be carried on but with more emphasis on its potential military value. With the one-by-one departure of staff members for active duty, research activities in progress were at times transferred from one worker to another for completion. Because the entire hospital was involved in the war effort, most of the clinical services were short-handed, so that the opportunity for coördinated studies was severely curtailed.

Moreover, at the end of the decade in 1940, Cobb was further frustrated by the necessity of moving the physicians' and administrative offices, laboratories, and psychiatric ward from their former locations to new space in the Bulfinch Building. Whereas the neurological and neurosurgical services were transferred from the Baker to the White Building on its completion in September, 1940, the psychiatric ward was separated from them and found its new home in the east wing on the third floor of Bulfinch. Cobb's new office was over the great stairway and under the ether dome. To the east of Cobb's office one came to the department offices and a work area before reaching D-7, the main psychiatric ward with fifteen beds, which was located along the east wall of the building. Two to four beds in direct view of the nursing station were set aside for the care of disturbed patients referred by other hospital services, and this area was referred to as D-8. Alongside D-7 a corridor ran in a northerly direction to what was then Allen Street and later became a right-angled extension of Blossom Street. The last door of this corridor opened on the right into a conference room, named for the late Dr. William Herman, which was used, among other things, for weekly staff rounds. In this room has been hung a portrait of Herman, as well as one by Charles Hopkinson of Cobb himself. In addition to the space in Bulfinch the psychiatric service also had use of facilities in the outpatient department and in various laboratories.

Along with the readjustments necessitated by the war effort and by moving from familiar surroundings into new quarters, Cobb had the perennial challenge of organizing his staff into many categories.[1] Cobb viewed staff categories as necessary to a table of organization; yet they conveyed little information about the work that individual members were doing. Many of the permanent staff members were primarily in practice or were actively working in other institutions. A number of them devoted essentially all their time to Cobb's service. Sometimes a person experienced frequent shifts from one category to another as in the case of Jurgen Ruesch, who was a research fellow in 1940, an assistant in psychiatry in 1941, and a psychologist in 1942.

During the wartime emergency there were relatively few projects carried out on a joint basis with members of other departments. By and large such coöperative efforts involved several workers, and the resulting scientific papers were published with three or more joint authors. There were, however, a number of papers on which Cobb's name appeared along with Lindemann, Finesinger, or Cohen. Some of these papers were purely intradepartmental, whereas others listed the names of staff members from other services.

The only work that Cobb wrote up with Lindemann was the psychiatric study of persons involved in the 1942 Cocoanut Grove fire (170). On the eighth day after the disaster an obviously psychotic woman in the Massachusetts General Hospital emergency room required the services of a psychiatric consultant. As a result of this encounter psychiatric evaluations were made of all the seventeen survivors in the emergency room at the time. Two of the patients had psychotic reactions, thought to have been basically psychogenic, and two had clear-cut past histories of psychoneurosis. However, the remainder appeared to be persons who had led relatively well-integrated lives prior to the accident. The patients were studied by the usual methods and also with the interaction chronograph, a device with which Lindemann had had previous experience. Designed by Eliot D. Chapple, it consisted of a revolving drum to which was attached a piece of graph paper on which a stylus recorded curves of behavior patterns. An observer behind a one-way glass screen controlled the stylus by pressing on appropriate keys.[2]

In their study of Cocoanut Grove victims the most significant observations Cobb and Lindemann made were on reactions to bereavement. These observations were on seven of the patients who had lost spouses or other family members. Cobb and Lindemann were able to describe the symptoms of acute grief, including sensations of somatic distress occurring in waves lasting from twenty minutes to one hour, a feeling of tightness in the throat, choking with shortness of breath, need for sighing, an empty feeling in the abdomen, lack of power in the muscles, and an intense subjective distress described as tension, lonesomeness, or mental pain. Lindemann and Cobb said that the grieving person could delay his grieving period but not avoid it. Depression during grief differed from states of morbid depression, in that much more muscular activity was present as indicated on the interaction chronograms.

John Nemiah, one of Cobb's later residents and colleagues, was in medical school at the time of the Cocoanut Grove fire. Nemiah said in an interview that Lindemann's work on the normal grief reaction was a real milestone.[3] However, he saw as an even more important outgrowth of the study Lindemann's concept of "loss" as playing an important role in psychosomatic illnesses. Nemiah believed that Lindemann's work on "loss" was an important influence on the well-known work of Engel in Rochester. Lindemann did not enjoy writing and when he did write was inclined to ramble. The medical care of the Cocoanut Grove victims was later described in detail in a Massachusetts General Hospital monograph,[4] and Oliver Cope, the surgeon, was its editor. Cope said that editing that book was one of the most embarrassing episodes in his life. The psychiatric portion was much too long as compared with the contributions from other specialties. In making the necessary condensation Cope was constantly mindful of the likelihood of hurting the feelings of his intimate friend Cobb.

A broad field that concerned Cobb during the early forties was neurocirculatory asthenia, a state characterized by fatigue, rapid heart rate, and often overt anxiety. Neurocirculatory asthenia had earmarks of a psychosomatic disorder. It was studied extensively during World War I by Sir Thomas Lewis and was believed to account for many cases of so-called shell shock.[5] A number of studies on various aspects of neurocirculatory asthenia were conducted by Cobb and his associates under a grant from the Office of Scientific Research and Development, through Paul D. White, the cardiologist (184). White requested the coöperation of the psychiatric service, and the main burden of the work was carried by Cohen, helped by Daniel W. Badal of the psychiatry service and William P. Chapman from medicine. Cobb and White served as consultants. Much of the key work was restricted, but papers bearing Cobb's name did appear on specific aspects of the work.

In a presentation at the annual meeting of the Association of American Physicians in 1944 White and Cobb, both members, presented a tabulation of signs and symptoms observed in patients diagnosed on medical wards as having neurocirculatory asthenia as compared with those on a psychiatric service diagnosed as having an anxiety neurosis. The two tabulations were identical (183). Cobb and his co-workers discovered that the configuration of the capillary loops in the nailbeds differed on a statistically significant basis in patients with neurocirculatory asthenia as compared with normal people (203) and that the reaction to painful stimuli was significantly more intense in many patients with neurocirculatory asthenia than in normals (184, 198). Studies on fatigue, an important manifestation of neurocirculatory asthenia, were initially carried out by Schwab and Finesinger. When Schwab went into the navy, his work was taken over by Mary E. Brazier, who had come to the electroencephalographic laboratory as a research fellow in 1941. Then in 1946 Harley Shands joined the service as a research fellow and engaged in the work on fatigue with Finesinger and Brazier.

Although Mary Brazier worked primarily as an electroencephalographer, she engaged in studies that made important experimental observations in disturbed physicochemical states affecting the brain. Cobb said of her work:

> When Dr. Schwab entered the Navy, Dr. Mary A. B. Brazier took over the research work and has carried forward several important investigations with Dr. Finesinger. It has been shown that low blood sugar goes with slow waves in the electroencephalogram and that hyperventilation enhances this effect. Low oxygen tension also causes these slow waves, and recent experiments by a team of workers (Finesinger, Brazier, Lindemann, and Chapple) have

Wartime Frustrations 245

shown by psychological tests carried out simultaneously with the encephalographic record that much less reduction in oxygen is needed to cause change in cerebral function than has ususually been supposed.[6]

Brazier's ability was recognized on Cobb's service by her promotion from research fellow on her arrival in 1941 to neurophysiologist in 1953, when she resigned and went to the Brain Research Institute at the University of California in Los Angeles. There she worked with H. W. Magoun on what he called the ascending reticular activating system.[7]

When in 1962 Brazier was promoted to a double professorship, Cobb wrote to Joseph F. Ross, the chairman, as follows:

> I am glad to hear that you are proposing Dr. Brazier for a professorship in both biophysics and anatomy. She worked with us here at the Massachusetts General Hospital for about twenty years and I have the highest regard for her originality and ability in research. She did a great deal to help in the development of the departments of neurology and psychiatry, especially the EEG laboratory. She has a great capacity for avoiding routine drudgery and doing the thing that really counts and advances scientific knowledge.[8]

Brazier was not only a distinguished neurophysiologist; she also became a medical historian.

The work on fatigue that Brazier, Finesinger, and Shands carried out was a joint project with Arthur Watkins, director of physical medicine, and much of the report was written in Cobb's terse, concise style (207). Although only eight pages long, it summarized a great deal of serious work, psychiatric, biochemical, and endocrine,[9] along with appropriate ergometric evaluation. The authors must have had difficulty finding a publisher, for the work came out in a physiatric journal as a preliminary report with the implication that more detailed studies would subsequently follow in print. It would appear that they never did. The project was important as a collaborative effort, for it brought together not only psychiatry, physical medicine, and cardiology but also Brazier's electroencephalography. Brazier demonstrated in the work she did in this study that her interests went beyond the technical aspects of electroencephalography and extended into physiological and biochemical areas. The comprehensive project included extensive psychiatric interviews with subjects complaining of fatigue and, as in the study of neurocirculatory asthenia, concluded that the predominant psychiatric diagnosis was anxiety state. Responses to work loads were measured by a number of ergometric methods utilized in physical medicine.

Determinations of such chemical substances as lactic acid, pyruvic acid, cholinesterase, and glucose were carried out and correlated with hyperventilation, tachycardia, and similar effects of exercise. The study of fatigue gives a notion of the comprehensive and thorough way in which Cobb tried to integrate emotional states with physical changes in the body.

Cobb and Finesinger also collaborated with others on a study of pain sensitivity in patients with psychoneuroses (210). William P. Chapman, a research fellow in the medical department working with Chester Jones, had a Wolff-Hardy apparatus which would apply a measured amount of heat to a 2.5 centimeter area of skin. Measurements of the threshold of perception for pain were made on a series of fifty psychoneurotic patients and on fifty-six normal controls, and there was no significant difference. However, the threshold values for motor reaction to pain were significantly higher for the control subjects than for the patients. A much smaller stimulus was required to evoke a motor response in the patients than in the controls.

Cobb and Finesinger also wrote together a chapter entitled "Psychoneurosis and Psychosomatic Disorders" for the *Manual of Military Psychiatry* (191). In twenty-nine pages, the annotated article set forth in a practical way clinical information hopefully of value to psychiatrists and other physicians in the armed services.

In the early forties Cobb wrote a number of papers with his former colleague, Lennox, on various aspects of epilepsy (161, 181), and one medicolegal article with H. W. Smith of the Harvard Law School (172). However, most of the writing Cobb did during the war years was done alone.

He continued to write his annual reviews of neuropsychiatry for the *Archives of Internal Medicine* covering such items as shock therapy, the Dunkirk evacuation, wartime brain injuries, theories of neurotransmission, experimental neuroses in animals, oxygenation of the brain, and motor areas of the cerebral cortex (149, 157, 162, 173, 190). From this yearly exercise it is apparent that Cobb was continuing his effort to keep psychiatry rooted in its organic matrix. Although Freud, who was originally a neurophysiologist, had limited his psychoanalytic principles to almost pure psychology, Cobb was ever involved in the struggle to integrate the functions of the mind.

Cobb never abandoned the approach he had learned in Baltimore from the psychobiologist, Adolf Meyer. In fact, two of Cobb's journal articles written during the wartime period emphasize the use of Meyer's life chart in taking and evaluating psychiatric case histories. One of them, entitled "Technic of Interviewing a Patient with Psychosomatic Disorder," written for general medical readers, appeared in *Medical Clinics of North America* (180). In this article Cobb pointed out how in history-taking "past history" and "present illness" often become blurred and that the orthodox lines between them are hard to draw. He also noted that psychiatric notes taken on a series of interviews are difficult to correlate. He then said:

> I, therefore, have had blank "life charts" printed on sheets that fit the hospital record [Figure 3]. They consist of horizontal lines making thirty spaces, each of which represents a year. At the left a column is ruled in which to put the years; at the right is another column in which is written the patient's age in each of these years. Near the middle of the sheet but somewhat to the left is ruled another narrow column. This is to be marked graphically and shows how much incapacity from illness the patient had in each year. A solid black square would indicate a year of complete disability, two or three lines would mean two or three months out of work, and so forth. The wide spaces to the left and right are the most important. The right side is taken for *social data* because more space is usually needed in which to write this. On the left are entered *medical data*.

Afterwards Cobb described the use of the life chart in unifying the data obtained from many sources when putting together an overview of a patient's illness. It afforded opportunities for introducing such therapeutic interventions as catharsis, ventilation, insight, suggestion, and (of temporary value) dependence. The persistence of Meyer's influence in Cobb's life and hence on his pupils is further emphasized by a later article entitled "Use of the Life Chart in Psychiatric Consultation," again written for general medical readers (201).

Cobb wrote a number of other papers on psychosomatic medicine (199, 206) and on psychiatry in a general hospital (200), as well as the decennial report of the psychiatric service at the Massachusetts General Hospital. This report contains a wealth of information about the work done there from 1934 to 1944 (182). In addition Cobb brought out a new edition of his classic volume, *Foundations of Neuropsychiatry* (184) and wrote a new book entitled *Borderlands of Psychiatry* (176). In this book Cobb developed a number of topics such as anorexia nervosa, which brought psychiatry together with other medical disciplines. During the early to mid-forties, several projects under way were related directly to the war effort. The work on neurocirculatory asthenia came under this classification, as did the studies of oxygen deprivation. There were also more specific tasks, such as devising a series of tests for the selection of aviators and evaluation of candidates for overseas service with the Office of Strategic Services.[10]

An amusing tale is told about Cobb's two-week visit to Washington, D.C., to inspect a camp where overseas intelligence personnel were being trained. According to the story, which was related by Dr. George Carter,[11] Cobb was unable to tell members of the family about his mission to Washington. He told his mother about the trip but not about the agenda. She went about Milton talking about her son's important assignment. One of her friends queried, "What is Stanley doing in Washington?" Mrs. Cobb replied off the top of her head, "Well, of course, he is seeing Roosevelt. Roosevelt is crazy, isn't he?" Cobb's sister Hildegarde confirmed the story when she wrote:

> The last sentence of George Carter's letter amused me. I am sure you know that Stan went to Washington on the business of the O.S.S. and, since he couldn't let on about it, he let his mother think what she wanted to. So since she didn't care much for F.D.R. she decided her beloved son was treating him for mental difficulties.
> The O.S.S. had a camp just outside Washington, D.C., where they trained people to go overseas. Stan went down to see how the candidates would do on their job. I suppose there is no reason to keep quiet about this any more.[12]

In addition to the investigative work and writing that Cobb carried out with his colleagues or on his own, he also had the numerous other responsibilities that go with chairmanship of a department. Even with his limited staff, teaching continued during the war years. Cobb said that when the service began in 1934 the only teaching was the informal instruction of the resident staff. As time went on, ten or twelve fourth-year medical students elected clinical clerkships in psychiatry, usually for a month, and voluntary seminar-type courses were offered each year. Whitehorn talked on interpersonal relations, Sachs on principles of psychoanalysis, Finesinger on physiological phenomena in the neuroses, and Lindemann on pharmacological effects.[13] In 1936 Cobb and Jones organized a course for students entitled "Psychological Symptoms in Medical Practice." Later the name of the course was changed to "Psychosomatic Medicine." From 1936 through 1942 the attendance grew slowly from fifteen to fifty students. Then in 1943 it suddenly jumped to one hundred thirty-five. Cobb said that apparently the importance of psychiatry in war medicine was becoming known to the

Wartime Frustrations

students, so they flocked in to learn a bit about what would soon affect them as military doctors.

In 1944 came the pay-off for the heroic struggle Cobb and Harry C. Solomon had carried on in the curriculum committee of the Harvard Medical School. As a result of that battle, psychiatry became a full-month required course in the senior year and students were coming onto the service every day. With this new burden and all the demands of the war effort, Cobb abandoned elective teaching for the duration of hostilities. However, two teaching conferences took place each week for students and staff, one for the ward and one for the outpatient department, and there were various specialty clinics, too.[14] Most of the conferences were held in the Herman Room on the north ell of the psychiatric unit in the Bulfinch Building.

The Herman room was convenient for inpatient conferences because of its location adjacent to the psychiatric wards D-7 and D-8. Cobb said that the types of patient treated on the service had changed somewhat over the years. Initially there was a tendency on the part of personal physicians to send in psychotic patients in order to save them from the stigma of being in a mental hospital. Cobb said that as time went on more patients with psychoneuroses were admitted, and the only psychotic patients were those presenting difficult diagnostic problems. From the beginning, however, an important function of the service had been the care of disturbed patients from other nonpsychiatric parts of the hospital. Although such patients were physically transferred to Ward 8 or less often Ward 7, they remained the primary responsibility of the original nonpsychiatric service and were therefore designated as boarders. In 1943 the number of boarders greatly increased because of a change in emergency room policy. Previously, the emergency room personnel had been able to keep disturbed patients overnight, but with the wartime shortage of nurses they were no longer able to do so.[15]

John Nemiah, who was familiar with Cobb's service from his medical school days on, said that the care of the patients was carried out almost exclusively by the resident staff.[16] He said that admissions to Bulfinch 7 were handled on a rotating basis. Thus, each resident would follow the cases that he had studied at the time of admission. In addition to the care of patients on Ward 7, there were three other important areas of service to be covered: Ward 8, with three or four beds occupied by patients with delirium tremens or other confusional states, the emergency ward with its challenging problems, and the off-service consultations. One of the residents was assigned to each of these areas, and of course the residents had to take turns covering nights. Nemiah said there were clinical and research fellows of various descriptions, but none of them took any part in patient care. So the resident staff was the backbone of the service in the clinical work of taking care of the patients.

From 1940 through 1943 there were two residents each year and from 1944 through 1946 there were three or more. Of the senior residents who served during this wartime period, Bernard Bandler and Avery Weisman became longtime staff members. Bandler, who departed about 1946 to head the psychiatric service at Boston University, was very sensitive to Cobb's unique creativity. He looked upon Cobb as one of his greatest teachers and was particularly impressed by Cobb's intellectual integrity. Cobb, according to Bandler, had an extraordinary degree of humility. In a taped interview Bandler said:

> His intellectual integrity and critical mind were such that he was very aware of his own ignorance. Knowing the bounds of his ignorance he could stimulate others to go beyond the cutting edge of knowledge.[17]

Bandler went on to say that Cobb was aware of his ignorance in every area, so that he was in a position to recognize advances in knowledge when confronted by colleagues who were following very different approaches to neuroscience. Bandler said that Cobb was more than just eclectic. He had an awareness for the possibility of putting together bits of information from various sources—a sense of "synthetic awareness" in Bandler's words. Hence, he welcomed suggestions and contributions from workers in various fields.

Bandler admitted that in earlier years he would not have immediately designated Cobb as his greatest teacher. However, when working on his forthcoming book *Residency Education in Psychiatry,* Bandler came to think more about Cobb as a teacher and to realize the important contribution made to his own life.[18] Bandler said that Cobb did not have the dazzling and flamboyant characteristics so often observed in brilliant teachers. Rather, he was a facilitator who helped his students find their own way and grow as individuals. Bandler noted in his interview:

> As soon as I began to think that way and see Stanley that way, I began to think of great teachers like Socrates. Stanley, I think, is of that order.[19]

Bandler recounted that in 1952 Cobb attended the Ithaca Conference on Psychiatric Education. That conference laid down the format that would be followed in graduate psychiatric training for the next twenty years. Cobb was afraid that rigid requirements for prescribed patterns of study and certifying examinations would stifle creativity on the part of the trainees. He said at the conference:

> If this conference ends up by pushing toward too much conformity, too many criteria, certification, recertification, studies, examinations, etc., it will have defeated the whole aim of psychiatric education. What we have to do is to produce creative, thoughtful, original people who will be adding to basic knowledge and research . . . and the worst thing you can do is to stultify that phase of life in their twenties and thirties.[20]

The other senior resident who remained on the long-time staff was Avery Weisman. Weisman continued as a member of the full-time staff of the psychiatric service throughout the remainder of his professional career, working under Cobb, Lindemann, Nemiah, Eisenberg, and finally Hackett. At the time of the present writing, Weisman was engaged in studies relating to death and dying, particularly with reference to cancer. Still other senior residents during the war era were Samuel P. Hunt, Burness Moore, George Saslow, James G. Miller, and Richmond Holder.[21]

Among the wartime assistant residents Daniel Badal remained on the staff as one of the team investigating neurocirculatory asthenia (183, 203). Later he became a psychoanalyst and moved to Cleveland, Ohio. Also Herbert Barry, Jr., an assistant resident in 1944, became an important longtime member of Cobb's staff. Barry, who had been a Ph.D. psychologist before going into medicine, joined Cobb as an assistant in psychiatry in 1943. When E. Peirson Richardson was called to active duty, Cobb offered his place as an assistant resident to Barry, who in spite of the financial sacrifice involved decided to take it. At the end of the year his running mate, Weisman, became the senior resident, and Barry went back on the attending staff. Barry said in an interview, "I was the cook and the captain bold and the mate of the Nancy Brig. I was giving one hour a day of psychotherapy to each of seven patients and doing all the consultations. I was the senior psychiatrist in the hospital."[22] Barry became an important colleague of Cobb's, for in 1950, when Finesinger went to Baltimore, Barry took over many of his administrative duties. Barry said that Finesinger and Lindemann were always at odds, partly because they were the two senior aspirants for

Cobb's professorship. Barry was critical of Cobb's lack of an organized approach to research. Barry said that his own projects had often been of the questionnaire type and had been carried out without specific funding. He said he had resisted Cobb's effort to lead him into research on genetics. When interviewed in 1980, Barry was actively practicing psychiatry from his office near the hospital.

Another assistant resident of the 1940–46 era who remained on the permanent staff was LeMoyne White, often known as "Lem." White became resident in 1947 and then was a member of the attending staff throughout Cobb's chairmanship but died shortly thereafter. Cobb looked upon White as a valuable teacher of the students and residents. Other assistant residents during the war time were N. B. Flanagan, Bruce H. Merrill, Eli Robbins, and Cecil Muschatt.[23]

There were a number of research fellows during the wartime years. In addition to Brazier, those who worked intimately with Cobb were Jurgen Ruesch and Harley Shands. Ruesch came from France on a Rockefeller fellowship in the fall of 1938 to work with Meyer at the Phipps Clinic in Baltimore. After three months he moved to the Massachusetts General Hospital with Cobb. In a letter Ruesch said:

> At first I had little contact with Stanley Cobb who was a much more remote person than Adolf Meyer, but as the months passed we had an occasional talk in his office, and in the spring of 1941 I was privileged to make rounds with him and to act as resident when he attended to his private patients. Most of the subject-matter teaching was left to Finesinger, while he himself [Cobb] was concerned with developing whatever creative qualities I might have had.[24]

Cobb for some reason looked upon Ruesch as more of a psychologist than a psychiatrist, possibly because one of Ruesch's major contributions was writing *The Medical Examiner's Handbook* with F. Lyman Wells as coauthor.[25]

In 1942 Cobb wrote to Karl Bowman, director of the Langley Porter Clinic in San Francisco, about Ruesch, and said:

> As a psychologist he is excellent, well trained and has original ideas. Moreover, he wants to go ahead with the application of psychology to psychiatry. In this field I would rate him high. As a psychiatrist his experience is somewhat limited, but he has learned a lot here and learns rapidly. He has adequate neurological training and is able to make a neurological examination.[26]

Ruesch took a position with Bowman (who had been Macfie Campbell's associate director at the Boston Psychopathic Hospital). The other

Wartime Frustrations

parts of Cobb's letter are of interest because they show not only Cobb's awareness of Bowman's needs in staffing a new clinic but also great sensitivity to Ruesch's hopes for his own future professional life, and in this setting he was utterly frank. It is easy to see why people placed so much trust in Cobb.

Ruesch told an entertaining story about the farewell party which the Cobbs gave for him at the Harvard Club:

> Unfortunately, a blizzard made traffic almost impossible that evening. Nonetheless, Stanley Cobb appeared in a fur coat, fishing boots, and dinner jacket, while Betty Cobb had on a long dress, shortened by a string fastened under the armpits, wearing boots. The place cards were made of pictures out of a book of mine, and witty verses were sung to the tune of "When I was a Lad" (H.M.S. Pinafore, Gilbert and Sullivan). After I had left Boston he [Cobb] wrote me one more letter to tell me that Lindemann had been appointed to succeed him. The last time I saw him was on the occasion of a party given in his honor at the Harvard Club.[27]

When interviewed in 1979 Ruesch indicated that he had indeed been interested in such topics as right versus left brain dominance, the mathematics of communications, cybernetics, and computer science. Cobb was probably right in emphasizing Ruesch's psychological bent.

If Ruesch was an atypical psychiatrist because of his interest in psychology, Harley Shands was also atypical, for he looked upon himself as an internist. Shands came to Cobb's department as a research fellow in 1946. It is reasonable to assume that in a way Shands was a replacement for Cohen, who had drifted away from psychiatry and was pursuing more purely cardiovascular studies. On his arrival in 1946 Shands was immediately assigned to the multidisciplinary study of fatigue that was under way at the time (207). However, from his background in internal medicine Shands developed a real interest in psychiatry and to some extent in psychoanalysis, although he always remained skeptical of the latter. He wrote a number of papers with Cobb and others on psychiatric subjects, culminating in a book entitled *Case Histories in Psychosomatic Medicine,* published in 1952 (303).

Shands, who graduated from Tulane in 1939, was clinical professor of psychiatry at Columbia College of Physicians and Surgeons in 1979, and he was director of the psychiatric unit at Roosevelt Hospital. Shands was a great admirer of Cobb and kept up a correspondence with him over the years. Shands's interest in psychosomatic medicine embraced arthritis in particular. He was also interested in linguistics and appreciative of the work done on Cobb's service in the early fifties by Maria Lorenz. These items are summarized in the following paragraph from a personal letter:

> His introduction to my book, *Thinking and Psychotherapy*, is one for which I remain very grateful. Since being at the General, my whole life has been involved in research in matters linguistic, and that interest was greatly encouraged by him. You probably also know that Maria Lorenz's several papers on the subject were directly related to Cobb's influence. I have never understood why she quit.[28]

One of Shands's greatest contributions to Cobb's service was introducing Henry H. W. Miles, who arrived in 1947 and probably did more research than anyone else in the later period after World War II. Shands himself was the last of the research fellows to join Cobb's staff in the era between 1940 and 1946. During those years Raymond Adams, Justin Hope, Else Neustadt, Robert A. Young, and James A. Meath also served Cobb in a research capacity.[29]

The attending staff showed relatively little change during the six-year period.[30] Raymond Morrison, the neuropathologist who had headed Cobb's histology laboratory at City Hospital, came on the service after a long illness with tuberculosis to work on problems in cerebral anoxia. Vernon Williams had been added to work in the outpatient department, and R. Barry Bigelow served from 1940 to 1951 in a more or less similar capacity. From time to time there were staff members, such as Williams and Bigelow, who were primarily engaged in private practice, had some outpatient responsibilities, and kept in touch with the remainder of the department through the weekly staff conferences. Dorothy McNaughton was added in child psychiatry. Two new psychologists, F. Lyman Wells and Frederick Wyatt, joined the staff as did Volta R. Hall, who had been an assistant resident in 1938 prior to the war. There were other additions and some departures, including Jurgen Ruesch and Mandel Cohen.

In addition to the work that Cobb and his staff did on the ward, in the laboratories, and on the consultation services, there was from the beginning an outpatient clinic under the supervision of a remarkable secretary named Dorothy Clark. The work in child psychiatry begun before Cobb's arrival by Margaret Anthonisen, Florence Clothier, and Robert Young, was carried on by Eleanor Pavenstedt and Dorothy McNaughton and later grew to enormous proportions under Lucie Jessner (chapter 13). In 1937 child psychiatry and adult psychiatry were integrated into one outpatient clinic, directed by Lindemann. During the war years, Cobb reported, there were seven hundred new

Wartime Frustrations

cases a year. Forty-six percent of them were consultations seen only once; the remainder had an average of seven visits.[31]

In addition to directing the routine operations of the psychiatric service in the outpatient department, on the wards, and in the other work areas, Cobb also brought his personality to bear on other hospital problems. For example, he became involved in the integration issue. It was during the war, and hospital personnel were limited. Ward 8, with its disturbed and at times violent occupants, some of whom were suicidal, had in charge only one female nurse. Cobb sought in vain to obtain from the hospital administration a male nurse or orderly to handle crises that might arise there at night. So he made an arrangement with the dean of the Harvard Divinity School, whose students were seeking opportunities to learn more about psychiatric care at first hand. The dean promised that he would furnish a divinity student to back up the nurse every night. In exchange Cobb agreed to give divinity students lectures and other opportunities to learn psychiatry during the day. It was not long before one night a black Harvard divinity student was scheduled to report for duty. Cobb had some misgivings, fearing that the nursing staff would rise up in open rebellion. However, he decided to take the chance because he knew that if trouble should arise, his surgical colleague, Oliver Cope, would shake the foundations of the hospital in the interest of racial fairness.

The story of the divinity students was recalled by Helen White, Cobb's daughter, who during the war was in charge of outpatient department volunteers. Helen White also observed at first hand in the Eye and Ear Infirmary what can only be described as the tonsillectomy horror. On several occasions she substituted for the volunteer regularly assigned to watch over children at the time of outpatient tonsillectomy. On the day of the procedure, each child, accompanied by his or her mother, would be taken to a small room while awaiting the results of a thymus X-ray and a urinalysis. Then the child, usually with no comprehension of what was about to happen, would be separated from the mother, undressed, and put to bed in an anteroom adjacent to the operating suites along with several other children who were also about to undergo tonsillectomy. When the first child was taken to the operating room the crying and screaming associated with open-drop ether could clearly be heard by the waiting children. After the tonsillectomy was accomplished each limp, ashen child, frequently vomiting blood, would be returned to the view of the other children in the anteroom. Helen White witnessed the increasing anxiety and at times panic experienced by those who were still to be taken to the operating room. When Cobb heard what was going on from his daughter, he worked through appropriate channels to effect a reorganization of procedure that would be less upsetting to the children. Psychological trauma from tonsillectomy is a well-known phenomenon.

In a paper which he later wrote with Miles, Cobb said that most children experience some anxiety at the time of tonsillectomy. However, sensitive children, with active fantasies, may experience an acute degree of panic. In his concluding remarks Cobb expressed the hope that parents, physicians, hospital administrators, and ward personnel would become more aware of the psychological implications of surgery in children.[32] Particularly, he hoped that hospital routines could be made more flexible in order to meet the needs of the individual child. (264) Cobb had a bit of the reformer in him. Here, he effected changes in the administrative environment.

During the war Cobb was also interested in McLean Hospital in Waverly, the psychiatric component of the Massachusetts General Hospital. McLean at the time was directed by Kenneth Tillotson. In collaboration with Tillotson, Cobb enlisted the support of his friend Ralph Lowell, then one of the directors, in establishing at McLean a new and badly needed biochemistry laboratory. The Mailman Laboratory, named after a benefactor who gave one million dollars, exists to this day under the direction of Seymour Kety. Along with neuropathology under Alfred Pope, it occupies a building separate from the wards and is devoted primarily to basic science. The first director of the laboratory was Jordi Folch-Pi as professor of biochemistry. Folch-Pi was a Spanish emigré who could not return home during the war. An excellent methodologist, his work was thorough and sound, but partly for geographic reasons, for the laboratory was separate from the hospital, it had no clinical orientation whatever. Mark Altschule, who directed the more clinically oriented former laboratory of Otto Folin in the main building, said that Cobb often came out for Thursday clinical conferences and would always drop in on Folch-Pi to see how work was progressing.[33]

Cobb was always reaching out to improve the world about him. Just as he did not shy away from the racial issue when he accepted the black divinity student for night coverage on the ward, similarly he set out to improve the atmosphere surrounding one-day tonsillectomies when his daughter reported her observations at the Eye and Ear Infirmary. He worked with Ralph Lowell to establish a first-class biochemical laboratory at McLean. Later, during the years of retirement, he was destined to harness the same sort of energy into writing about the physical environment and about such social problems as guns for children (482).

Directors of major hospital services during the war were subject to constantly changing government rules and regulations concerning the schedules of house staff, the availability of funds, and the requests for "classified research." Staffs were depleted and personnel for nonprofessional tasks were in short supply. Under the circumstances it was a great and frustrating responsibility to keep a clinical service operating at all.

From time to time Cobb needed to get away from the load he was carrying. He needed seclusion to be away from the telephone and to have time to think about his wider interests. One of the places where he could cogitate about such matters was in the "caboose" at his summer place at Cotuit. With grandchildren beginning to arrive on the scene the Cotuit cottage was less secluded and restful than it had previously been. The walls were only one board thick and, with the inevitable cracks between them, every sound penetrated the entire building. Cobb had many years before built a cabin about ten feet wide and eighteen feet long which was used as an overflow guest room. Now he and his wife bought a portable Hodgdon house of about the same size and set it up about twelve feet away from the cabin, leaving room for a most attractive deck between the two structures. This new living unit, on relatively low land as compared with the main house, looked out between the pine trees upon Mumichaug Pond with its geese, herons, and other bird life. The Cobbs abandoned the main cottage, allowing the children to take it over, and they took up residence in their new nest, sleeping in the cabin and using the deck and the caboose for meals, recreation, and study.

The new living unit in Cotuit was only in part generated by the children's need for the main house. Another factor unquestionably was the progression of Cobb's arthritis, which was beginnng to make stairs difficult. The impairment in the nimble use of his limbs was also a severe handicap in cruising, so the *Fulmar* was sold in 1946, and after that the summers were spent on land. The new arrangement at Cotuit was an ideal one, and the Cobbs made it their focus of vacation life until the purchase of property in Little Compton, Rhode Island, ten years later. It was in Cotuit that Cobb had the time and privacy he needed for puttering with tools, watercolor painting, enjoyment of nature, and his more philosophical thinking.

Cobb was making preparations in his mind for the transition to postwar psychiatry and the demands that it would make upon him and his service. The psychiatric problems of World War II had differed materially from those of the first World War. World War I had been fought in trenches along a relatively static front for four long years. Efforts to break the lines were made by sending more and more men into the rat-infested trenches, where most of them were destined to become casualties. The principal psychiatric diagnosis was "shell shock." World War II, on the other hand, was global in its scope, with numerous invasions of islands or other coastal areas from the sea. As always there were psychiatric casualties in combat. However, between invasions there were long periods in staging areas where the actual fighting seemed quite remote. Ennui and other frustrations often led to psychosomatic disorders, particularly in the intestinal tract. The psychiatrists in the services were dining in the mess halls and the ward rooms with other nonpsychiatric physicians and pointing out the obvious relationship between stress and bodily symptoms. So a new interest in psychiatry was growing up among the doctors on military duty. Along with this greater awareness of the importance of psychiatry came the G.I. Bill of Rights which insured financial aid for students during the early peacetime years. Hence, Cobb must have been developing some awareness of the ensuing rapid expansion of his department.

A change within him was taking place, too. He had surrounded himself with psychoanalysts. He recognized the importance of psychoanalysis as a therapeutic method and could see that it was having an enormous influence on many customs and social institutions. It was changing the rearing of young children in the effort to avoid unnecessary early traumas. It was infiltrating the ranks of teachers and social workers. In short, it was involved in a revolutionary change in society. Yet, it was a purely psychological discipline which had, at least in practice, abandoned its roots in the physiology of the body. Cobb was beginning to think that there must be some organic basis for feelings, a notion that William James had espoused some fifty years earlier and had been central to the thinking of Adolf Meyer. Cobb was about to undertake some studies of his own into this area. Such studies were destined to maintain for him a focal interest in the anatomy and physiology of the mind.

12
At the Center of the Storm (1947–1954)

The postwar years constituted for Cobb a period of rapid adjustment. Many of the physicians who had cared for psychiatric patients during the war wanted to enter psychiatry. Moreover, the enthusiasm of several key psychiatrists in military service for psychoanalysis and their active efforts to promote it in military manuals enhanced the desire of many young men to undertake psychoanalytic training when peace returned.[1] With the adoption of play therapy, child psychiatry was also becoming reorganized along psychoanalytic lines. The G.I. Bill of Rights and other forms of funding from federal and private sources greatly increased the number of candidates who could afford advanced training. The administrative problem Cobb faced in meeting the needs of his share of these trainees was overwhelming. And that burden fell on him just as the apogee of interest in psychoanalysis lay ahead, so that the entire teaching program required reorganization. Along with the emphasis on psychoanalytic teaching came new approaches to brain research with greater knowledge of neurotransmitters, cybernetics, and the limbic system. All these factors tumbled together in a kaleidoscopic way and continually reshaped the milieu in which Cobb found himself.

This period of rapid growth in the midst of multiple and conflicting factors was one in which Cobb's influence was widest because of the large number of young men who sought training under him and the impact he had upon their lives. On the other hand, it was a time of particular frustration for him, for the department was no longer neatly under his control. The clinical teaching became primarily oriented toward psychoanalysis and was carried out by various members of the departmental staff in their own particular jurisdictions, and the administrative functions were also divided among them. Moreover, with the bodily aches and pains from his progressive arthritis Cobb lacked the physical stamina to keep under control all the responsibilities that had devolved upon him.

The growing popularity of psychoanalysis in the postwar years led to a deeper dichotomy between neurology and psychiatry than had previously prevailed. It became apparent that the former requirement of thorough training in neurology as a prerequisite for psychiatric residency would have to be abandoned. During the war many physicians from other fields had been assigned to work as psychiatrists in the army and the navy. Some of these men had little interest in clinical neurology but wanted to continue their careers in psychiatry. Although Bandler, Weisman, Richardson, Barry, Knapp, and some of their successors had the basic neurological background, there was a major shift of emphasis to dynamic psychiatry in the Freudian tradition. Thus, most of the postwar residents lacked the full neurological prerequisite.

Freddy H. Frankel from South Africa, Cobb's next-to-last resident, who served in 1953 and 1954, wrote about the confusion he found on arrival and commented on some of Cobb's pithy expressions of wisdom. Frankel said that in some of the personal conferences he had with Cobb during his first few months on the psychiatric service he expressed his concern and confusion over the wide differences between the extravagant claims expressed by some of the psychoanalysts as well as the equally overdrawn views of the biological psychiatrists. Cobb's reassuring reply captured much of what Frankel came to admire not only about Cobb but also about the frank and open ways in this country. What Cobb said was, "We really don't know very much. We let them all shout and then hope that some truth will come out of it all."[2]

Frankel also described an incident in which he reported to Cobb his struggles with a newly admitted female patient who was accompanied by interfering family members. The woman, who had characterological problems and a psychopathic personality, was seen on Bulfinch 7 along with her husband and several of their grown children, all extraordinarily difficult to handle. Frankel had spent several hours on a Saturday morning trying to defuse the anger and sidestep the manipulativeness of the woman's relatives as they attempted to influence events in their own way. Somewhat wilted after all his travail, Frankel talked to Cobb, who told him within the privacy of his office, "If you don't watch out, people like that will just swallow you up." Frankel saw Cobb's admonition as the simple truth. He said that no amount of technical language could have been clearer, and he found the advice helpful. Frankel later joined the staff of the Beth Israel Hospital.

William Herman, 1891-1935

M.G.H. Psychiatric Service in 1940. From left to right, first row: Edgerton Howard, Niels Anthonisen, Eric Lindemann, Stanley Cobb, Jacob E. Finesinger, Helen Deutsch, William G. Barrett; second row: unknown, unknown, Norris P. Flanagan, Mandel Cohen, Samuel Hunt, Juntin Hope, Juergen Ruesch; third row: unknown, Marianna Taylor, Louise Silbert, rest of row unknown; fourth row: Harry Kozol, unknown, Dorothy Clark, unknown, Margaret Gray, Dorothy Adams.

Center of the Storm

From top to bottom row, left to right: E. Murray Burns, resident, 1934, Paul Howard, assistant resident, 1937, Milton Rosenbaum, resident, 1938, Maurice H. Greenhill, resident, 1939, Bruce H. Merrill, assistant resident, 1941, Burness Moore, resident, 1942, George Saslow, resident, 1943, James Grier Miller, resident, 1944, Eli Robbins, assistant resident, 1945.

M.G.H. psychiatric staff in 1947. 1. Suzanne Van Amerongen, 2. Cecil Mushatt, 3. Lucie Jessner, 4. Jacob Finesinger, 5. Jane Allen Hallenbeck, 6. Stanley Cobb, 7. Frances Bonner, 8. Eric Lindemann, 9. Martin Berezin, 10. Raymond Morrison, 11. Margaret Bullowa, 12. Harley Shands, 13. Henry Brewster, 14. Dorothy Adams, 15. Nicholas Rizzo, 16. Elliott Chapple or Marcel Verzeano, 17. Lemoyne White, 18. Barry Bigelow, 19. Herbert Barry, 20. Samuel Kaplan, 21. Vernon Williams, 22. Paul MacLean, 23. George Carter, 24. Mary A. B. Brazier, 25. James Skinner, 26. Dorothy Clark, 27. I. Paley Rak, 28. Consuela Tagiuri, 29. Bea Franseen, 30. Evelyn Stiles, 31. Ed Mason, 32. Sylvia Perry, 33. Henry H. W. Miles, 34. Paul Howard or Sam Waldfogel, 35. Peter Knapp, 36. Trudy Billings, 37. Claire Swift, 38. Diane Waldfogel

Center of the Storm

From top to bottom row, left to right: Robert Bruce Sloan, clinical and research fellow, 1953–1954, Peter M. Tow, assistant resident, 1954, William H. Trethowan, assistant resident, 1951, Charles P. Gore, assistant resident, 1952, David Stafford-Clark, clinical and research fellow, 1950, Harry Stockholm, clinical and research fellow, 1952, E. Peirson Richardson, assistant resident, 1946–1947, Harry Choa Hung Fang, assistant resident, 1952, Frederick E. Whiskin, Jr., resident, 1954.

Staff of M.G.H. Psychiatric Service in 1953. Back row left to right: Unidentified, unidentified, John Coolidge, Gardiner Quarton, unidentified, John Lamont. Third row: Dorothy Adams, Drs. Maria Lorenz, Morris Chafetz, Peter Sifneos, John Nemiah, and Vernon Williams. Second row: Unidentified, Avery Weisman, Lucie Jessner, Stanley Cobb, Mary A. B. Brazier, Abraham Fineman, and Lemoyne White. Front row: Drs. Herbert Barry, Norman R. Bernstein, Earl Wedrow, Robert B. Sloane, Ruth Weiss, Philip Margolis, unidentified

Retirement party, 1954. With Dr. Cobb are, left to right, Elizabeth Zetzel, Lucie Jessner and Eleanor Pavenstedt, all child psychiatrists

Until he departed for the University of Maryland in 1950, Finesinger continued to carry out the administrative aspects of the service. Finesinger's psychotherapeutic approach was predominantly Freudian, as was that of Lindemann, who ultimately became Cobb's successor. Henry H. Brewster, a clinical and research fellow in the immediate postwar period, stayed on until 1954, the year of Cobb's retirement, and eventually succeeded Lindemann as director of the psychiatric outpatient department. Brewster, who eventually settled in Stockton, California, returned after World War II as a Commonwealth fellow in psychiatry. Brewster later recalled that, to make it possible for him to have a psychoanalytic training analysis, Cobb arranged a scholarship which had been established in memory of the late Hanns Sachs. Brewster said that Cobb was an excellent person to work for, warm, charming, and imaginative, and commented in 1979 that Cobb had given him a good deal of room to utilize his own imagination.[3]

For Brewster, the word that best summarized Cobb's characteristics was *ambidextrous*. Not only did he continue to draw sections of the brain and spinal cord simultaneously with both hands in the second-year neuropathology course, but he also had interests that were set apart, namely the physiological and the psychodynamic approaches to psychiatry. Of Cobb's two subalterns, Brewster saw Finesinger as the more physiologically oriented and Lindemann as the one more concerned with psychodynamics. Brewster said that most of the residents and fellows tended to follow one or the other of them. Brewster noted that the dichotomy could be observed in Cobb himself, too. On the one hand Cobb was old Boston, genteel, charming, and warm; yet he could be a tough and successful politician, a pioneer, and a competitor—not to be outdone in struggles for space, power, and recognition among his colleagues at the Massachusetts General Hospital. Brewster, who came from Plymouth, was an old New Englander himself. Cobb had confidence in him and depended upon him.

Others upon whom Cobb depended for help in running the service after Finesinger's departure in 1950 were Daniel Dawes, Alfred O. Ludwig, Herbert Barry, and Gardiner Quarton. Dawes, who had been psychoanalyzed in Vienna during the mid-thirties, was the husband of Lydia Dawes, the child psychiatrist. After her own analysis with Anna Freud, Lydia Dawes was appointed an assistant in psychiatry in 1937 and remained on the staff for several years. Her husband became supervisor of the part-time staff. He was a great believer in physical fitness. Paradoxically, after Cobb's retirement he had a heart attack while riding his bicycle. He died about 1970.[4]

Alfred O. Ludwig was a psychoanalyst with a major clinical interest in rheumatoid arthritis. He served as an important visiting staff member during the postwar years.[5] Ludwig reported that Gardiner Quarton, who had been a resident in 1948 and 1949, took over much of the administrative work after Finesinger's departure for Baltimore in 1950. Quarton made important scientific contributions, too, so that Cobb looked upon him as most able and as a possible chief-of-service. After Cobb retired in 1954, Quarton remained on the service for four years and then took over the directorship of the new Stanley Cobb research laboratory. Later he became director of the Mental Health Research Institute in Ann Arbor, Michigan.

Not only did the administrative work on the service become more decentralized after Finesinger's departure, but the teaching was also reorganized and less directly controlled by Cobb. Barry reported that most of the teaching was being done by analysts, for almost all the residents were being analyzed, and he was in charge of scheduling the time they needed.[6] Bonner, who came on the service in 1946 as a clinical and research fellow and worked full time for several years in the postwar era, also indicated the importance of psychoanalytic training in the program.[7] She said, "Our teaching was mostly by analysts." Bonner began carrying out training analyses when she went on the part-time staff in the early fifties and in 1978 was still doing it from her home on the edge of the lake in Newton Center. Others engaged in teaching were LeMoyne White and John Nemiah.

According to Nemiah, who came on the service as an assistant resident in 1948 and remained in various capacities until 1969, the weekly teaching conferences continued to be held in the Herman Room, although they were later moved to the Ether Dome. Nemiah said that Cobb would "open" the blackboard behind him, thus making available a Meyerian life chart on which to make notes during case presentations. When the resident was making his presentation Cobb would be drawing lines across the central column of the chart to indicate the severity of the symptoms, would record highlights of the medical history on the left, and make notes on any traumatic experiences, such as the notorious "fell in cesspool at age three" under social events on the right. After running through a neurological examination and conducting a brief psychiatric interview with the patient, Cobb would call upon the staff members present in reverse order of seniority, as was customary in medicine, beginning with the most junior, for whatever comments they might care to make. Deutsch would summarize the case quite tersely in her psychoanalytic language. Barry would invariably ask for more information about early childhood, and Finesinger, appearing as usual to wake from a snooze, would make a comment indicating that he really had heard what was said.[8] Cobb would then summarize in Meyerian fashion what had gone on, invariably finding some nugget of anatomy, physiology, or neuropathology to drag in and round out the psychobiological picture. As Nemiah put it, "Each one had his ploy."

Oliver Cope, the endocrine surgeon who constantly supported Cobb in his work, reported that Cobb's rounds for the presentation and discussion of patients with psychiatric problems on the general wards of the hospital was another teaching activity of great value. Cope said that at these rounds in the early fifties Lindemann was clearly the star.[9] The clinics were enormously popular with the house staff, particularly on surgery. After a time Lindemann abandoned the conferences because he thought they were unfairly competing with the regular consultation services offered by the department of psychiatry. Lindemann in a way felt that he was stealing the show from the members of the department assigned to consultations. Cope said he regretted that the conferences were terminated, for Lindemann had an extraordinary capacity for drawing out a patient in the presence of a group and for demonstrating psychiatric factors at work. Walter Bauer, Cobb's close friend and the subsequent chief of medicine, was an active supporter of the clinics and with Cope also regretted that they were discontinued.

Of course, during these later years Cobb continued to teach the neuropathology course at the Harvard Medical School, and through their clinical work the members of his attending staff were constantly teaching the residents, fellows, and medical students.

The investigative work that Cobb personally carried out with staff members of the nonpsychiatric services in the postwar years was rather limited. It fell generally into three areas involving collaboration with neurosurgery, rheumatology, and pediatrics. In the neurosurgical field there was a paper with Bonner, in addition to the two neurosurgeons, White and Sweet, on frontal-lobe surgery in the treatment of pain (298). Bonner reported that she was rather disappointed in the outcome of the study, which indicated a rather high percentage of serious intellectual or emotional deficits in persons leucotomized for pain—more

Center of the Storm

so than in those who had the same treatment for depression. The collaboration in rheumatology, under Walter Bauer, had mostly to do with the psychiatric manifestations of ACTH.[10] The first of a series of papers appeared in 1952 under the names of Lincoln D. Clark, one of Cobb's assistant residents, Walter Bauer, and Cobb (295). It was a review of six major and four minor psychotic reactions observed during ACTH therapy; all the psychotic patients recovered. In 1953 these authors plus Quarton reported on thirteen more psychotic reactions in patients under treatment with one of these agents. Cobb and his associates observed that the psychotic reactions were likely to be prolonged in patients who had had previous psychotic episodes. They also observed that those with adrenal insufficiency were particularly prone to developing psychoses when treated with ACTH or cortisone (319). Cobb, Quarton, and Clark subsequently wrote a chapter on psychiatric disorders in a book published by the Harvard Medical School on the medical uses of cortisone (339), and additional studies appeared later (344, 359). The pediatric studies, all of which were carried out in collaboration with Miles and Butler, fall into the category of child psychiatry (chapter 13).

A study that drew upon the expertise of another clinical department, although not acknowledged in its title, was on the neuropsychiatric aspects of Cushing's syndrome (293). William H. Trethowan conducted this study when he was a resident and published it with Cobb. In a footnote the authors expressed their appreciation for the help they had received from the endocrinologist, Fuller Albright, in the department of medicine. In a retrospective study the authors reviewed a series of twenty-five patients with Cushing's disease who had been seen at the Massachusetts General over a period of sixteen years, and tabulated the significant clinical findings including emotional reactions as recorded on the charts. Mental disturbances were common, although quite variable in character, and usually cleared after definitive adrenal surgery.

In 1979, looking back on events of the past from his position as chairman of the department of psychiatry in Birmingham, England, Trethowan said that the work on Cushing's disease which he did with Cobb evoked more interest than any of his other writing. He reminisced:

> Another thing I remember well about the Massachusetts General was the extremely courteous treatment that those who were relatively junior received at the hands of their senior colleagues. This did not only apply to Stanley

Cobb himself but to a lot of the other revered consultants in the hospital. One never felt in any way looked down upon, and if one had an opinion to express about a patient, then one was encouraged to express it, whereupon it was listened to with genuine interest.

Although I have no doubt the hospital is as great now as it ever was, the days when I was there certainly seemed to be great days. I remember among others Walter Bauer, Oliver Cope—the endocrine surgeon, Sweet, the neurosurgeon—Molly Brazier, and of course the tragic figure of Fuller Albright, who was so severely struck down with Parkinsonism at that time. I shall always be grateful to him for making available to me his extensive case material on Cushing's Syndrome and thereby allowing me to write the paper.[11]

Albright probably withheld his name from the paper because of his lack of interest in psychiatry. Cope said that Albright had a seventy-five percent negative attitude toward psychiatry even though there was strong scientific evidence to suggest the importance of emotions on some endocrinological functions.[12]

The member of Cobb's own staff with whom he collaborated most frequently in the postwar years was Henry H. W. Miles. Miles had been attracted to Cobb's service by his friend Harley Shands. Miles worked on the psychiatric service from 1947 to 1952 and wrote many papers, mostly on clinical topics, and some of a more psychophysiologic nature with Shands and others. Cobb and Miles wrote thirteen papers as joint authors (237, 240, 242, 257, 262, 264, 273, 278, 279, 280, 290, 301, 302), and they collaborated with Shands on four more (274, 275, 294, 303). Miles became a psychoanalyst and practiced in New Orleans, where he was on the faculty in neurology and psychiatry at Tulane. Reminiscing in 1979, Miles made some observations about Cobb's relationship with students and fellows. In Miles's view Cobb's interest and generosity in helping young men and women achieve their goals were memorable characteristics. In fact, he said "We were always treated as respected colleagues and not as underlings who were on the staff to do menial jobs. Cobb devoted a lot of time to helping us select topics for clinical study and critically examining our research design." Miles went on to say, however, that Cobb expected his students and fellows to follow through on the work they had undertaken and he took pains to keep in touch with studies in progress. He was both helpful and critical in the preparation of manuscripts. Miles wrote, "He was not always easy to please because he set high standards. I recall writing and rewriting one paper through what seemed to be interminable sessions until finally he was satisfied." In jointly authored publications Cobb always insisted that Miles's name appear first.[13]

Miles also threw into focus the importance that he personally attached to Cobb's Meyerian psychobiological approach. Even though a psychoanalyst, Miles never forgot Cobb's emphasis on the physiological disturbances related in one way or another to emotions. Miles went on in the letter to say, "To this day I find myself telling students and residents not to think of diseases as *organic* versus *functional* but to consider the multiple factors involved in etiology and try to estimate how much of each is present." Miles attributed much of his clinical outlook to his work under Cobb. As Miles saw it, Cobb was a teacher of rare quality whose gifts, so freely given to his students, were passed on to succeeding generations. The students in Miles's view had become so imbued with some of Cobb's attitudes, values, and wisdom that it became a natural part of their own teaching. As Miles put it, "Thus what he gave us we have tried to give our students. Maybe this is the closest a man can come to immortality."

One of Miles's assigned tasks was the editing of case reports for publication in *The American Practitioner* and *The American Journal of Medicine*. The reports in many instances were based on clinical conferences jointly sponsored by the departments of psychiatry and of pediatrics, which was under the direction of Allan Butler (chapter 13). However, not all the case material involved children. Cobb and Miles, without the collaboration of Butler, published reports on rheumatoid arthritis (237), the differential diagnosis between hyperthyroidism and anxiety (240), anxorexia nervosa (242), ulcerative colitis (258) enuresis (262), convalescence (273), symptoms caused by withdrawal of barbiturates (278), hypertension (279), migraine (301), and other clinical topics.

As time went on Cobb collaborated with Miles on studies concerned with more fundamental issues. For example, they reviewed the work on neurocirculatory asthenia and were unable to equate it entirely with the anxiety state. They saw neurocirculatory asthenia as a clinical syndrome with the major symptoms centering around effort intolerance and breathing difficulties. They pointed out that there were two extreme prototypes: those patients whose effort trouble was largely due to inherited or developmental abnormality[14] and those whose symptoms were psychogenic, with, of course, a wide range of overlap (280). Perhaps the most ambitious study carried out with Miles and others was a psychosomatic study of young men with coronary artery disease (342). In writing several of their case reports Cobb and Miles collaborated with Shands, especially in one on asthma (276) and in one on the emotional significance of cancer (274), for Shands had been working with Finesinger and Cobb on that topic (281). In 1952 Miles, Cobb, and Shands summarized their experience in a volume entitled *Case Histories in Psychosomatic Medicine* (303).

Cobb did other important work with members of his own department. As was noted in the last chapter, he collaborated with Maria Lorenz on studies of language behavior. Lorenz first met Cobb at McLean Hospital conferences in 1946 when she was on the staff there. At Cobb's request she became a research fellow at the Massachusetts General Hospital in 1950 and remained for two years working with Samuel Waldfogel, the psychologist, on the structure of language. In 1952 with Cobb she published a study of language structure in manic patients. It was a technical analysis of several factors including the number of different words used in a conversation and the frequency with which such words were repeated. Cobb and Lorenz discovered that at this basic level of speech organization there was little difference between the psychotic patients and normal persons even though the context varied enormously (296).

Cobb and Lorenz subsequently wrote two more papers together. One on language behavior in psychoneurotic patients pointed out that although there were similarities between the behavior of manic and psychoneurotic patients, the latter paid more attention to the listener's side of the conversation (318). The other paper on language patterns in psychotic and psychoneurotic subjects came out in 1954 (343). Lorenz was married to Alfred Pope, the neuropathologist at McLean Hospital, who was associated with the research laboratory established during World War II under the directorship of Jordi Folch-Pi. In an interview on February 18, 1978, Lorenz said that she left Cobb's service and returned to McLean because she missed taking care of psychotic patients. She was critical of admission policy at the Massachusetts General Hospital, where an inordinate number of psychoneurotic patients were hospitalized on Ward 7. Lorenz was doing fundamental work, and her return to McLean was a loss for Cobb's service.

With Maria Bereday, Cobb wrote a paper on the relationship between hereditary optic atrophy and other familial degenerative diseases of the nervous system (299), particularly hereditary ataxia, from which his friend Bill Herman was said to have suffered.[15] Bereday was a diplomate in medicine from Poland. The work gave clear diagrammatic representations of the neuropathological changes noted in Leber's optic atrophy along with clinical observations on a number of other diseases at times associated with it. The article was published from the Department of Neurology and Psychiatry at the Harvard Medical School in the *Archives of Ophthalmology.*

Cobb was coauthor of several other publications that came from the psychiatric department in the early fifties. One of these, written with Harry Stockholm, was a review of Alexander's book, *Fundamentals of Psychoanalysis* (287). Stockholm, whose home was in Denmark, served as a clinical and research fellow in 1951 and 1952. He lived in the Cobbs' Milton house for a time, and Mrs. Cobb kept in touch with him after his return home. In their review, which appeared in *Psychosomatic Medicine,* Stockholm and Cobb concluded by quoting Alexander, who said, "Finally it should be emphasized that psychoanalytic theory and practice are in the process of development. To further this development a continuous revision of theoretical assumptions and generalizations, as well as experiments with therapeutic procedure, is imperative (287)." In another publication from his own department Cobb collaborated with Nemiah on one of the series of case reports usually edited by Miles (321). Cobb and Nemiah discussed a patient with pain in the low back and legs, which appeared to be complicated by psychological factors.

The writing Cobb did with others both in psychiatry and on other hospital services was helpful in extending his outreach, in supporting his colleagues, and in making contributions to scientific knowledge. However, it was the work he did by himself that he found most satisfying. When working alone he was free to explore his basic philosophic and physiologic approach to psychiatry and to cerebral function. Most important was the work he did on the anatomical and physiological basis for feeling. William James had emphasized that the bodily changes associated with a feeling often modified the quality of the feeling from which they arose. And Cannon had studied the importance of feedback from the viscera in such emotions as pain, hunger, fear, and rage.[16]

Cobb had a lifelong interest in the comparative anatomy and embryology of the brain and was intrigued by the sense of smell. In 1949 he delivered three Salmon lectures in New York, and he subsequently organized the material into his book entitled *Emotions and Clinical Medicine,* which was published by Norton in 1950 (261). Mark D. Altschule is the authority for an amusing incident which occurred during this presentation. As Cobb began his first lecture, Altschule recollected, he stammered noticably, due to nervousness. After stammering through a few sentences, he stopped, looked at his audience, and said: "I presume that you have noticed my speech defect." He then brought down the house (and took pressure off the situation as well) by adding, "I am not referring to my Harvard accent."

Cobb commenced his first lecture with a quotation from Kipling: "Smells are surer than sounds or sights to make your heart strings crack. . . ." It is common knowledge that smells often inexplicably give rise to powerful feelings. The primitive cortex of the brain in mammals was long looked upon primarily as an olfactory organ with elaborate receiving stations for smell. Cobb was particularly impressed by the work of J. W. Papez, who in 1937 published an article entitled "A Proposed Mechanism of Emotion."[17] Papez asked whether emotion was to be looked upon as a magic product, or as a physiologic process based on anatomical mechanisms. He suggested that the primitive cortex might not just be a specialized organ for receiving smell, but might also through connections with the hypothalamus and the pituitary body have an important visceral function. Cobb said, "I would now change my working hypothesis and say that the primitive cortex of the brain (archipallium) is largely visceral in function, having close connections with the autonomic nervous system and the sensation of smell and direct expression through the effector system of the hypothalamus."

Cobb went on to evolve a concept of the three main systems involved in emotional reactions as illustrated in figure 4. Figure 4A shows pathways of the stimuli from the outside world (except smell) and from the muscles, joints, and labyrinth of the ear. These pass through special sense organs and along spinal and brain-stem tracts to the thalmus in the mid-brain. From there they are relayed to the cerebral cortex (neocortex) and set up reverberating circuits. This part of the emotional reaction is very close to conscious awareness and was formerly considered to be the main mechanism for emotion. Figure 4B shows the part played by the old visceral brain or archipallium. This primitive cortex is vestigial in humans. It remains, and it is stimulated directly by smell and indirectly by the other senses. This visceral cortex discharges

Center of the Storm

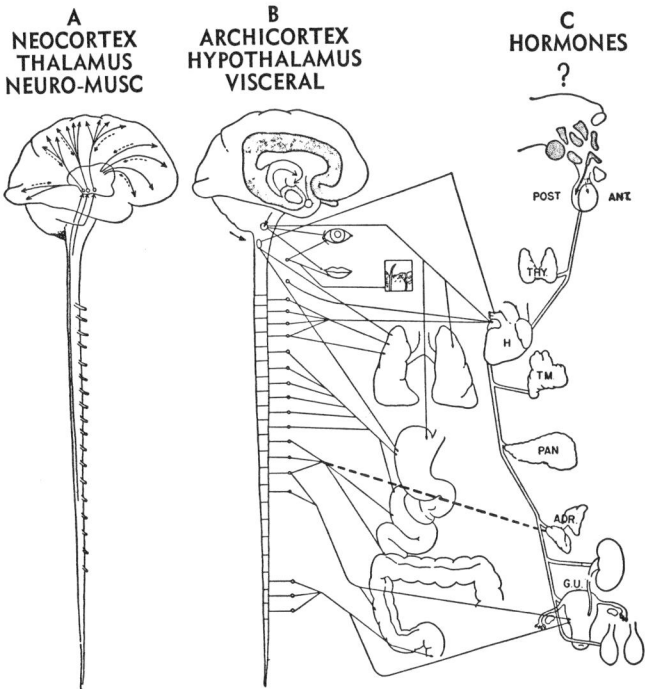

FIGURE 4.—Illustration from *Emotions and Clinical Medicine*, showing Cobb's concept of the three main systems involved in emotional reactions.

through the hypothalamus, where it has a great outflow into the autonomic system and the various viscera as shown. Figure 4C illustrates the important contribution of the endocrine glands as understood in Cobb's day. Only the posterior pituitary and the adrenal medulla (dark broken line) were known to be directly innervated. The others were activated by blood constituents or hormones pumped by the heart to the thyroid, thymus, pancreas, adrenal cortex, gonads, and other organs. In his book *Emotions and Clinical Medicine* Cobb said that all three systems worked together. They were inextricably connected. Emotions should be thought of as a reaction resulting from the interaction of all three.

One of Cobb's most creative clinical and research fellows, Paul MacLean, was working on psychomotor epilepsy at the Massachusetts

General Hospital in 1948. MacLean ran across Papez's writings in the library. A conversation with Cobb led to MacLean making a trip to Ithaca, New York, to become personally acquainted with Papez and his work. MacLean later wrote a chapter entitled "Challenges of the Papez Heritage" in the book *Limbic Mechanisms,* edited by Livingston and Hornykiewicz.[18] MacLean became director of the Laboratory of Brain Evolution and Behavior at the National Institute of Mental Health. It was he who in 1951 coined the term *limbic system* to include what Papez had called the limbic lobe and related structures. In recent years MacLean, through studying the brains of reptiles, has thrown light on primitive mammalian behavior patterns. There can be no doubt that MacLean influenced Cobb's work on the comparative anatomy of avian brains and that Cobb's encouragement and vision stimulated MacLean to pursue his highly imaginative work.

As an outgrowth of his work on the limbic system, Cobb became intrigued with the nature and locus of mind (292) and gave a paper under this title at the annual meeting of the American Neurological Association on June 18, 1951. In this presentation Cobb reviewed recent advances in knowledge of the human brain including those in anatomy, neurosurgery, learning, emotions (*vide supra*), neuron circuits, memory, feedback, as well as scanning mechanisms and the recognition of "Universals." Cobb concluded with a discussion inspired by a symposium paper he had read on the physical basis of mind.[19] He said it was almost impossible to conceive of a functioning mind without consciousness or without memory. A Dr. Slater, who was one of the contributors to the volume reporting the symposium supported Cobb's view of consciousness, emphasizing that it was not a matter primarily of being conscious or unconscious but of how conscious one was. Cobb saw a close parallel between consciousness and awareness. Prior to the development of cybernetics, Cobb believed that man had essentially no concept of memory storage mechanisms. Cobb saw the brain as the organ of mind, but mind as something greater, as an ever changing relationship between the functioning brain cells. In one of the concluding paragraphs he said:

> I would express it this way. The brain is the organ of mind; its great complexity in man makes his thinking possible, but no study of the anatomy and physiology of one brain will ever explain mind. Thinking is a sequence of events, depending on the interplay of messages from one part of the brain to another in response to external stimuli, including messages from other

brains. In other words mind is the relationship. If one takes the analogy of thought to a melody, it is obvious that no amount of histological study, no matter how advanced, could show in a brain more than the pattern left by one note. The sequence of the notes in time makes the melody. Ideas are such sequences.

Cobb concluded by saying that of all the anatomical and physiological properties of the brain touched upon in his review, the area most properly considered as mind was the integration itself, the relationship of one functioning part of the brain to another.

In a subsequent paper (300) Cobb enlarged on his understanding of consciousness and quoted at length from the Croonian lectures presented in 1884 by Hughlings Jackson, whose views on consciousness were similar to his own. Cobb was opposed to the notion that consciousness was a function of a specific area of the brain.

While chairman of his department during the postwar years Cobb published in the *Archives of Internal Medicine* his annual "Review of Psychiatry" (217, 241, 256, 277, 297). The reviews often were related to topics of a controversial nature, significant investigative work, or books that presented in a comprehensive way an important neuroscientific point of view. Some of the reviews contained comments about important figures in neuroscience who had recently died.

The 1950 review (277) contained a thorough analysis of Penfield and Rasmussen's book entitled *The Cerebral Cortex in Main; A Clinical Study of Localization and Function.*[20] Cobb had worked closely with Penfield in the past and disagreed with some of his basic concepts. According to Cobb the book contained the most important data ever presented on localization of function in the human brain. Cobb saw the first eight chapters as fine examples of the best sort of scientific reporting of clinical data. However, he viewed as more speculative the later chapters on "Memory, Sensory Perceptions, and Dreams," and the "General Conclusions." Specifically, he took exception to Penfield and Rasmussen's statement that the diencephalon contained "the essential neuronal mechanism upon which depends the very existence of consciousness; a mechanism which is able to employ the anterior frontal regions in the process of thinking and then to use them in the elaboration of thought."[21]

In his "Review of Psychiatry" for 1947 (217) Cobb outlined the work of the recently deceased Pierre Janet, who had visited the United States six times during his life and had made a signal contribution to the Boston school of psychotherapy at the turn of the century. In 1951 Cobb noted that the death of his former mentor, Sir Charles Sherrington, with whom he had worked briefly in Oxford many years earlier. Sherrington was one of the pioneers in the study of cerebral localization of function.

Important for our story are the remarks that Cobb made about his former teacher, Adolf Meyer, whose psychobiological approach had so deeply affected his own thinking and teaching. Cobb commenced his 1948 report (241) with a review of Lief's book, *The Common Sense Psychiatry of Adolf Meyer*, which was an authoritative exposition of Meyer's contribution to medicine.[22] Cobb described the book as a happy combination of long quotations from Meyer's papers with biographical material worked in chronologically. Cobb saw Meyer as the last of the distinguished group that brought about crucial psychiatric developments at the beginning of the century and as a leader in thinking about the dynamics of mental disorders. Cobb noted that forty years had elapsed before physicians took up Meyer's comprehensive approach and psychosomatic medicine had evolved.

Subsequently, when Cobb wrote Meyer's formal obituary (265), he referred the reader to Lief's book as the best source of material about Meyer's professional life. Cobb's own comments had to do with Meyer's human qualities and the gist of his message. Cobb wrote:

> Great as was Meyer's contribution by teaching individual assistants, even greater was his influence as a lecturer and writer. As early as 1897 his dynamic psychiatry was persuading psychiatrists to advance from the classic Kraepelinian point of view and look upon mental disease as a disorder of the person. To Meyer all life was reaction; the person was to be studied with the methods of anatomy, physiology, and psychology. One "cannot afford to disregard any side of the biological unit in the patient." Thus, before 1900 the basis for psychosomatic medicine was propounded, and the dynamic psychology of Meyer prepared America to understand Freud. Fifty years later Meyer was still insisting that psychiatrists take as their object of study the "he" and the "she," the person as a whole, without undue emphasis on any part such as the "ego" or the "unconscious." He appreciated Freud's great contribution pointing out that it was as important to psychopathology as dietetics was to medicine. But he considered psychoanalysis a partial and esoteric system, which engendered a spirit of denominationalism and bred controversy.

In his comments about Meyer, Cobb was undoubtedly reflecting his own views of psychoanalysis, which he, too, could accept as a valuable aspect of psychiatry without offering it religious homage.

Cobb served as one of the review editors of the journal *Psychosomatic Medicine* from the late 1940s until the mid 1960s. He obviously took his job seriously, for he not only wrote nearly one hundred and fifty reviews for the magazine during this time, but he was continually shuffling off recently published books to his residents, colleagues and former pupils to be reviewed by them also.

In all there were twenty-two senior residents on Cobb's service and a significant number of assistant residents as well (table 1). Between

Table 1. Residents and Assistant Residents, Massachusetts General Hospital

	Resident	*Assistant Residents*
1934	E. Murray Burns	John Adams Abbott
1935	David A. Young (1935–1936)	Mandel Cohen
1936	Neil T. McDermott	Paul Howard
1937	Sidney B. Maughs	Volta R. Hall
1938	Milton Rosenbaum	Maurice Greenhill
1939	Maurice H. Greenhill	
1940	Samuel P. Hunt	N. B. Flanagan
1941	Bernard Bandler	Bruce H. Merrill
1942	Burness Moore	Daniel W. Badal
1943	George Saslow	James G. Miller
1944	James G. Miller	Herbert Barry, Jr., Avery Weisman
1945	Avery D. Weisman	Eli Robbins, Richmond Holder
1946	Richmond Holder	Cecil Mushatt, LeMoyne White
1947	LeMoyne White	E. P. Richardson, Peter H. Knapp, James C. Skinner
1948	James C. Skinner, Archibald D. Leigh	George Carter, Gardiner C. Quarton, John C. Nemiah
1949	John C. Nemiah	Gardiner C. Quarton, Dorr G. Hollenbeck, Lincoln D. Clark
1950	Earl G. Solomon	Lincoln D. Clark
1951	Frank Egloff	Lyman C. Wynne, William H. Trethowan, Harry Choa-Hung Fang, John G. Gibson
1952	Peter Sifneos	Harry Choa-Hung Fang, Francis de Marneffe, Charles P. Gore
1953	Freddy H. Frankel	Earl M. Wedrow, Ruth S. Weiss, Norman R. Bernstein, Frederick E. Whiskin
1954	Frederick E. Whiskin	Norman R. Bernstein, Peter M. Tow, Jule P. Miller, Jr.

1947 and Cobb's retirement in 1954 there were twenty-six residents and assistant residents whose life stories are briefly summarized in table 12B. Cobb had personal contact with a number of them through joint research projects and the preparation of reports for publication, as already noted Quarton (319, 339, 344, 359), Nemiah (321), Lincoln D. Clark (295, 319, 339, 344, 359), and Trethowan (293). Cobb also knew Peter Sifneos well, for he wrote the foreword to his monograph on ulcerative colitis, entitled *Ascent from Chaos*.[23]

Table 2. Postwar Resident Staff Biographical Data

Norman E. Bernstein Assistant Resident 1953, 1954	Worked in child psychiatry at M.G.H. from 1954 until 1977, when he became professor of psychiatry at Abraham Lincoln School of Medicine in Chicago. He was a sculptor by avocation.
George Carter Assistant Resident 1948	Settled in Cambridge.
Lincoln D. Clark Assistant Resident 1949, 1950	Worked with Cobb on ACTH and cortisone. After further training at the Maudsley Hospital in London he became professor of psychiatry at the University of Utah in Salt Lake City.
Frank R. Egloff Resident 1951	After military service Egloff joined staff of Hartford Hospital. Later moved to Woods Hole. In 1969 he became a visiting professor of divinity at Vanderbilt and an adjunct professor at Hartford Seminary.
Harry Choa Hung Fang Assistant Resident 1951	Became professor of neuropathology at the University of California, Los Angeles.
Freddy Frankel Resident 1953	Born in South Africa, Frankel came to Cobb as resident in 1953. After returning to South Africa he came back to M.G.H. from 1963 to 1969. That year joined staff at Beth Israel.
John G. Gibson Assistant Resident 1953	Not listed in recent directories.
Charles P. Gore Assistant Resident 1951	Became medical director of the Menston Hospital in Menston Nr. Leeds in Yorkshire, England.

Dorr F. Hollenbeck Assistant Resident 1949	Hollenbeck was on the staff at MacLean for many years and has been on staff of Beaverbrook Guidance Clinic at the Waltham Hospital.
Peter H. Knapp Assistant Resident 1947	Interested in psychosomatic medicine, Knapp was president of the American Psychosomatic Association for one year. He became professor of psychiatry at Boston University.
Archibald D. Leigh Resident 1948	Generally known as "Denis," Leigh had a Nuffield fellowship in 1948 and served as assistant resident for six months. He later became director of Maudsley Hospital in London.
Francis de Marneffe Assistant Resident 1952	Joined the staff of MacLean Hospital and in 1962 became its director.
Jule P. Miller, Jr. Assistant Resident 1954	Was on staff of Austen Riggs Foundation in Stockbridge from 1956 to 1959 and practiced in Pittsfield, Massachusetts, until 1964.
John C. Nemiah Resident 1949	Wrote monograph on anorexia nervosa. Was acting chairman of department at M.G.H. from 1965 to 1967. Later chief of service at Beth Israel Hospital in Boston.
Gardiner C. Quarton Assistant Resident 1948, 1949	Published with Cobb on ACTH and cortisone; headed Stanley Cobb laboratories from 1957 to 1963; became director of Mental Health Research Institute in Ann Arbor, Michigan.
E. Peirson Richardson Assistant Resident 1947	Studied neuropathology with Charles Kubik and became head of neuropathology at the M.G.H.
Peter Sifneos Resident 1952	Served as head of the outpatient department for a number of years. Then moved with Nemiah to the Beth Israel Hospital.
James C. Skinner Resident 1948	Became chief of adult psychiatry at Boston University.
Earl G. Solomon Resident 1950	After neuropathological training with Raymond Adams Solomon came on service as resident in 1950 and remained a staff member with a private practice in Boston.

William Trethowan Assistant Resident 1951	Worked on Cushing's disease when at the M.G.H. He was chairman of psychiatry at Sydney University in Australia for several years and later at the University of Birmingham, England.
Peter M. Tow Assistant Resident 1954	Settled in Australia.
Earl M. Wedrow Assistant Resident 1953	Active member of the M.G.H. Staff Associates with office for practice of psychiatry in Boston.
Ruth S. Weiss Assistant Resident 1953	Living in Boston area, 1983.
Frederick E. Whiskin Resident 1954	Cobb's last resident, Whiskin, settled in Duxbury, where he conducts a private practice.
LeMoyne White Resident 1947	White remained on the M.G.H. staff until after Cobb's retirement. He was a key figure in teaching the resident staff.
Lyman C. Wynne Assistant Resident 1951	After stints at St. Elizabeth's Hospital in Washington, D.C., at the National Institute of Mental Health, and with the World Health Organization, Wynne became chairman at the University of Rochester. He was a pioneer investigator of family interactions.

Cobb took a personal interest in residents from foreign countries, including Leigh,[24] Gore,[25] and Tow.[26] Other native-born residents of the period carried on further studies abroad, notably Richardson, who worked both at Queen Square and Maudsley, and Lyman Wynne, who went to Queen Square and to Tavistock.

Several residents were attracted to Boston University, where Bernard Bandler, Cobb's 1941 resident, was chief of service. These included Knapp and Skinner, along with the child psychiatrist, Samuel Kaplan, who had been a research fellow at M.G.H. (chapter 13). In an interview on April 10, 1980, Knapp recalled with accuracy many events that took place during his residency in 1947.[27] He indicated, for example, that the consultation service was informal in his day, some of the work being done by residents and some by the visiting staff. Knapp also referred to Cobb's having to abandon the requirement of basic neurological training prior to residency on his service and to the exciting work that he and MacLean were doing on the relationship between smell and the feeling functions of the body. Peirson Richardson, who was also an assistant resident in 1947, did his stint in psychiatry because he saw it as an integral part of his training in the neurosciences. In later years, during retirement, Cobb was to work in Richardson's neurohistology laboratory.[28]

There were seventy-four clinical and research fellows on Cobb's service in the postwar years, some of them in child psychiatry. However, many of them were in adult psychiatry, and some subsequently had extraordinarily successful careers (table 3). A few have already been mentioned as collaborators with Cobb in scientific publications from the department. Among those who worked independently on adult psychiatry, or at least did not publish jointly with Cobb, were Marcel Verzeano, Franklin Carter, John R. Reid, Nozomi Suwa, Robert Cleghorn, Morris Chafetz, Philip Margolis, and Robert Sloane. Verzeano was brilliant in mathematics and electronics. He was not licensed to practice medicine when at the General from 1947 to 1949 but worked on such highly technical devices as the frequency analyzer for Brazier's electroencephalograph, Chapple's interaction chronograph, and other instruments. He later became a professor of biophysics at the University of California in Los Angeles.[29] Another fellow in whom Cobb took a personal interest was George Carter's brother, Franklin, who served from 1949 to 1950 and subsequently settled in Cambridge.[30] John R. Reid was professor of philosophy at Stanford University. In 1950 he was a visiting lecturer on psychiatry at the Harvard Medical School, and Cobb listed him as a clinical and research fellow. Reid had an interest in philology and was helpful to Cobb in semantics, particularly when he was writing *Emotions and Clinical Medicine* (262). Nozumi Suwa, who was a clinical and research fellow in 1952, subsequently settled in Tokyo, where the Cobbs visited him in 1964. He sent a photograph of Stanley and Betty Cobb standing on a pier overlooking Mount Fujiyama.[31] Cleghorn was on Cobb's service in 1953. In 1979 he wrote from Toronto expressing appreciation for his days with Cobb. Cleghorn recalled the work that Maria Lorenz had done in linguistics and gave an account of Lindemann's Wellesley project, which he visited. Cleghorn also said that he had written a book review for Cobb "on one of Gellhorn's tomes" but did not look back upon this effort

Table 3. Clinical and Research Fellows

Bandler, Bernard	1950	Mason, Edward A.	1949 C
Baumann, Herman H. W.	1952, 1953	McClellan, Samuel G.	1952 C
Benda, Clemens	1936, 1937	McDermott, Neil T.	1936, 1937
Blom, Gaston	1949 C	Meath, James A.	1945
Bonner, Frances	1946–1949	Miles, Henry H. W.	1947–1948
Brazelton, T. Berry	1949, 1950	Miller, Leon	1952, 1953
Brazier, Mary A.B., Ph.D.	1941–1950	Money, John William	1951
Brenner, Leon O.	1953	Muramatsu, Tsuneo	1934
Brewster, Henry Hodge	1946, 1947	Musnick, Henry	1949 C
Bullowa, Margaret	1948	Neustadt, Else	1938–1942 C
Carter, Franklin	1949, 1950	Painter, Paul H.	1952, 1953 C
Caulfield, Thomas	1949	Prentice, Norman M.	1953
Chafetz, Morris	1953, 1954	Reid, John R.	1950
Cleghorn, Robert A.	1953	Rickards, Winston J.	1952 C
Clement, Stephen M.	1947 C	Rizzo, Nicholas	1947–1948 C
Coolidge, John	1949–1951 C	Rollins, Nancy	1954 C
Crissy, William J., B.S.	1936	Rosenblum, Gershon	1953, 1954
D'Autremont, Chester C.	1953, 1954 C	Ruesch, Jurgen	1939–1942
DeBenedetti, Renata G.	1949 C	Sargant, William	1938
Doust, William C.	1953	Scoville, William Beecher	1937
Dwyer, Thomas F.	1949, 1950 C	Shands, Harley C.	1946, 1947
Fineman, Abraham	1952, 1953	Sharpe, William	1954 C
Fitzgerald, William E.	1953	Shippen, Eugene R.	1950–1952
Frazier, Russell	1939	Sloane, Robert B.	1954
Gilmore, Thomas H.	1953	Solomon, Earl	1951
Gruber, Sigmund	1953	Stafford-Clark, David	1950
Harris, Harold J.	1953	Stockholm, Harry	1951, 1952
Harvey, Harold I.	1941	Sutherland, George	1939–1943
Holder, Richmond	1950 C	Suwa, Nozomi	1952
Hollenbeck, Jane Allen	1948–1951 C	Tillman, William A.	1948, 1949
Holzer, Hedvig H.	1952 C	Tisza, Veronica	1949–1951 C
Hope, Justin	1940	Valanne, Eero H.	1951 C
Howard, Paul	1936	Van Amerongen, Suzanne P.	1946–1949 C
Jaffe, Ruth	1952	Verzeano, Marcel	1948, 1949
Johannet, Pierre	1953 C	Von Felsinger, John	1952
John, Clara R.	1950	Wahl, Charles W.	1952 C
Kagan, Robert	1953, 1954 C	Waldfogel, Samuel, Ph.D.	1948
Kaplan, Samuel	1948, 1949 C	Weisman, Avery	1948
Keuper, Charles S.	1952	Weiss, Ruth S.	1954 C
Knapp, Charles S.	1948	Wermer, Harry	1950 C
Lamont, John	1953, 1954 C	White, Benjamin V.	1936–1938
Lindsley, Donald B., Ph.D.	1934	Wolf, Irving	1954
Lorenz, Maria	1950	Wool, Max L.	1949
Macklin, Theodore O.	1953	Wyatt, Frederick, Ph.D.	1949
MacLean, Paul D.	1948	Young, Robert A., Ph.D.	1938–1944
Margolis, Philip	1952, 1953	Zahle, Vagn	1951
Martin, Charles	1948	Zucker, Joseph M.	1954 C

C Child Psychiatry with Jessner or prior to Jessner

as a great achievement. Cleghorn added that he had left McGill in 1978 and moved to Sunnybrook Hospital, a University of Toronto Clinic.[32]

Morris Chafetz, who served with Cobb as a clinical and research fellow in 1953–54, directed the alcohol clinic under the subsequent chairmen of the service until 1970. At that time he went to Washington and became the founding director of the National Institute on Alcohol Abuse and Alcoholism. In 1979 he was president of the Health Education Foundation in Washington.[33] Margolis, a clinical and research fellow in 1952–53, was chief of the psychiatric inpatient service at Billings Hospital in Chicago from 1955 to 1966 and after that was director of the Washtenaw County Mental Health Service in Ann Arbor, Michigan. In 1980 he was at the University Hospital there.[34] Sloane, who had been born in Harrowgate, England, and graduated from the University of London Medical School in 1950, worked with Cobb from 1953 to 1954. Three years later he was appointed professor at the University of Kingston, Ontario,[35] where he served until 1964, afterwards going to the staff of the Veterans Administration Hospital in Downey, Illinois.

An account of Cobb's staff in the kaleidoscopic years would be incomplete without mention of Jerome Weinberger, who joined the visiting staff in 1951 after previously working at the Massachusetts Mental Health Center under the psychoanalyst Ives Hendrick. After a verbal altercation with Hendrick over vacation dates, Weinberger resolved to leave the Massachusetts Mental Health Center and was invited by Cobb to join his staff at the Massachusetts General. Weinberger was an indefatigable worker. He helped Cobb with book reviews, as Cleghorn had done. He wrote on homosexuality and under the auspices of the American Psychoanalytic Association ran a workshop on the treatment of homosexuality for a number of years. Weinberger agreed with Bonner that under Cobb's direction the part-time members of the staff were indeed well integrated into the service as a whole. However, he later came to realize that, because of the rapid growth of the department, communication between the part-time and full-time people was deteriorating. He eventually organized them into the Psychiatric Staff Associates and arranged weekly meetings in the Herman Room independent of the official weekly staff conference.[36] Prior to the existence of the Psychiatric Associates, Weinberger had been an effective member of the part-time staff and served for many years under Cobb's successors.

As is apparent from the series of group photographs taken in 1940, 1947, 1950, and 1954, Cobb aged rapidly during the last few years of his chairmanship. His arthritis progressed, and he had severe trouble with his right knee, which eventually required above-the-knee amputation. He developed the Miculicz syndrome, which later proved to be a manifestation of Sjogren's disease. The dryness of his corneas required wearing glasses with flexible transparent windshields on the sides to contain whatever moisture was present. Because of the failing health and the stress of the burdensome final years there was inevitably some diminution of effectiveness toward the end.

His final year he served as chairman of the general executive committee of the hospital, and according to Cope,[37] frustration in that role was inevitable because of the dominant personality of Edward D. Churchill, the surgeon, who was somewhat junior to Cobb and retired several years later than he did. Cope said that Churchill got his way by the use of unpredictable ploys,[38] and he thought it unlikely that Cobb was very effective on that committee.

Cobb was not on the search committee when his successor was chosen. He thought Lindemann was a good choice and lent his name in support when consulted. However, he would have preferred to see Quarton, who later took over the Stanley Cobb laboratory, become the chairman or have someone imported from another institution.

There were very difficult days ahead, which form the basis for the chapter on retirement. Looking back over the postwar years it is apparent that what Cobb had hoped would be a small intimate service grew into a whirlpool of conflicting interests. As chairman of a relatively new department in a prestigious institution Cobb had enormous influence. The contributions that Finesinger and his successors made to psychosomatic medicine were outstanding, and Cobb's own interest in the anatomy and physiology of emotions was not only creative but for him therapeutic. It was a field that he could till independently of other permanent staff members, and it afforded respite from the maelstrom of activities in which he was almost involuntarily embroiled. His greatest contribution, perhaps, was in the field of education, for the influence he had on the lives of residents and fellows was limitless. A number of the residents and fellows enlarged upon the same theme. Although comparatively aloof, so that they had only infrequent talks with him, Cobb had their respective abilities, ambitions, and future welfare constantly in mind. He tended to imprart wisdom in the planning of experiments or in the future of a man's own life rather than to get into details that could be delegated to a colleague.

In an interview John Nemiah said that Cobb's greatest contribution to psychiatry was wisdom. One day Nemiah complained to Cobb that he was overwhelmed by the multiple approaches to the study of the nervous system and the complexity of the field. Cobb replied, "It is a huge field with many approaches. You just have to pick one field of interest to you and make it your own, but for God's sake, be tolerant of what the other person is doing!" Nemiah went on to say:

> His heart and his interest were in neurology and brain function; but he had tremendous curiosity about a wide variety of approaches. He was not only open minded about them. He actually fostered the development of individuals in their work. He was as responsible as anyone else for the ascendancy of the analytic movement, not only in Boston but nationally. He put his official stamp on his endorsement of psychoanalysis when he opened the Massachusetts General Hospital unit and asked Bill Herman to come. Bill unfortunately died but then he brought the Deutsches.[39]

Cobb was indeed tolerant of diverse views and approaches, but he was not tolerant of laziness. He expected his residents and fellows to work hard at their own projects, to obtain their detailed information from appropriate sources, and to develop their own native talents and interests. He was never one to subject his students or colleagues to rigid systems of thought or to inflexible established routines.

Milton Rosenbaum said that once when he was resident the secretary of a Boston political hack was admitted to the emergency room after a suicidal attempt, and Rosenbaum cared for her during the night. There were all kinds of pressures from members of her family and from political supporters for special services which Rosenbaum declined to provide because in his opinion they were not medically indicated. The following morning Rosenbaum reported to Cobb what had taken place and Cobb said, "Milt, *you* are the resident. Do what you think is right and I will back you up!"[40]

The loyalty Cobb showed in situations of this sort, his concern for the struggles and goals of his students, and the wisdom he so often imparted regarding matters of importance had an indelible effect on many of them. The distinguished careers they pursued after completion of their training were enhanced by that sense of values, which was thus passed down to generations of physicians, psychologists, social workers, and other key persons in the mental health professions.

13
Child Psychiatry

Although Meyer and others had previously done psychiatric work with children,[1] it was William Healy and his wife, Augusta Bronner, who firmly established the child guidance movement, primarily through their work in Boston. Healy had become well known after 1909 when he headed the Juvenile Psychopathic Institute in Chicago. Great impetus was added when he and Dr. Bronner were invited to head the Judge Baker Guidance Center toward the end of World War I.[2] Child psychiatry was also nourished by the development of well-baby clinics, where the notion arose that well children could be guided in health matters in order to avoid mental disease later, in a way parallel to the adult mental health movement. It was through his interest in well-baby clinics that Douglas A. Thom founded the Habit Clinic in 1921. This clinic was thought to be the third child guidance clinic in the United States.[3]

The clinic in child psychiatry at the Massachusetts General Hospital had been in existence several years before Cobb took over the psychiatric service there. It was started as a function of the department of neurology in 1931 by Dr. Margaret Anthonisen with the encouragement of Kenneth J. Tillotson, the director of McLean Hospital. Tillotson at that time was making an effort to expand psychiatry into the activities of the general hospital.[4] Margaret Anthonisen was assisted by Florence Clothier, later Mrs. George Wislocki, who had graduated from Johns Hopkins in 1930 and as a medical student had been well indoctrinated into Meyer's psychobiological approach. In fact she had had to prepare a personal life chart when she was there and had turned it in with a boy's number on many of the chapters. Later, when she was psychoanalyzed, Meyer asked her to compare the analytic material with the data she had already recorded.[5] She did not divulge the outcome of the comparison.

The influence of Meyer on the early work of the clinic was obvious. In fact Cobb said that in the beginning child guidance clinics basically followed the principles of Meyerian psychobiology. However, the influence of Healy's work at the Judge Baker was soon felt. There grew

Child Psychiatry

up a close relationship between the Judge Baker and the Massachusetts General Hospital, with M.G.H. appointments for some members of the Judge Baker staff and collaborative efforts in the training of child psychiatrists. Hence, the influences of Healy and Bronner, as well as those of Meyer, were important in shaping the trend of the child guidance clinics in their early years.

When Cobb became director of the psychiatric service at the Massachusetts General Hospital in 1934, Eleanor Pavenstedt was selected as head of child psychiatry, which at that time was primarily an activity in the outpatient department. Pavenstedt said in an interview that Cobb assumed responsponsibility for the psychiatric service on July 1, 1934, and on November 1 of that year she took over from Margaret Anthonisen the work in child psychiatry.[6] Like Clothier, Pavenstedt used the Meyerian approach, for she too had been trained in psychobiology at the Phipps Clinic in Baltimore. As late as 1936 she was ambivalent about Freudian psychoanalysis, even though she had become acquainted with the play therapy of Anna Freud through Erik Homburger Erikson when he was with Cobb from 1934 to 1936. Pavenstedt recalled that Erikson chaired meetings at the Judge Baker during those years. Of Cobb she said, "I wish I remembered more about Stanley. But I had relatively little contact with him in the outpatient there." Cobb was apparently quite happy to delegate child psychiatry to others, whereas other activities of greater interest received his meticulous personal attention.

Prior to 1934 George Gardiner was psychologist on the staff of the M.G.H. children's clinic. That year he left the M.G.H. to work with Healy at the Judge Baker Guidance Center and in 1941 became its director. The psychologist who worked with Pavenstedt in child psychiatry from 1934 through 1937 was Robert A. Young, Ed.D., who remained at the Massachusetts General Hospital until 1943, when he also joined the staff of the Judge Baker. One of the most exciting things Young did was to establish in 1935 a summer camp for neurotic children. A year later in a fund-seeking letter to Frank Fremont-Smith of the Josiah Macy Foundation, Cobb said that prior to 1934 emotionally disturbed children were often sent to existing summer camps, where they had to get along with predominantly healthy children. However, because of their poor social adjustment, many such children experienced an increased sense of isolation and failure in a traditional camp setting. The psychoneurotic ones needed help in establishing themselves as individuals in a group. Cobb said that this help could best be given by the therapists who knew the children's problem intimately from their work with them the previous winter. Young's camp set out to provide an environment for these children that was supervised and graded under controlled environmental conditions and in a holiday atmosphere. In his letter to Fremont-Smith Cobb wrote:

> The camp is, as far as I know, a unique experiment. It is not merely treating these children for a month and then leaving them alone; it is continuing their winter treatment (which has to be sporadic and more or less theoretical) by giving them a period of practice in living and reality. They have to learn to live with and cooperate with a group. The group activities are run by Mr. Wollan, who has had long experience with this type of social work. The children are supervised individually and helped in their attempts at socialization by Dr. Young and Dr. Pavenstedt. I was at the camp last summer and was astonished to see these children, whom I had known in the hospital clinic as individual "problems," forming an apparently homogeneous and happy group.[7]

Cobb requested fifteen hundred dollars, but did not get it from Fremont-Smith. Wherever the funds came from, the camp became a permanent institution. It was in Maine the first three years and then moved to Hillsboro Upper Village, New Hampshire. Although it was a function of the Massachusetts General outpatient department in the beginning, it later was annexed by the Judge Baker Guidance Center.[8] Pavenstedt looked upon the camp as an important achievement, and Cobb's widow said that Young was admired by all.[9]

In 1937 there was a reorganization of the outpatient department. Lindemann was assigned the task of integrating child and adult psychiatry into one clinic. Lindemann was attuned to the growing interest in child analysis. Hence, Pavenstedt, at that time a Meyerian undergoing psychoanalysis, resigned her post as head of the children's clinic, and Lydia Dawes, a child analyst, took over the therapy of children.

Lydia Dawes had had several years of work in child analysis with Anna Freud in Vienna. In late 1936 she came to the United States to join her husband, who had come to Providence from Vienna a year earlier and subsequently became a member of Cobb's staff in adult psychiatry. In Vienna the Daweses were good friends of Edward and Grete Bibring, who followed them to Boston several years later.[10]

The transition from Meyer's common sense psychiatry to the newer psychoanalytically oriented nonverbal techniques was brought into focus by Helen Witmer in her book *Psychiatric Interviews with Children*.

Child Psychiatry

In his 1947 review of neuropsychiatry Cobb quoted Witmer:

> By the end of the mid-nineteen thirties, however, a change in child guidance psychiatry was in progress. The stimulating conceptions derived from psychoanalytic work with young children were beginning to influence practice. Play was found to be an adequate substitute for discussion as a means of revealing young children's difficulties and giving help in overcoming them. Psychiatric interviews themselves became less intellectual, as the implications for the dynamic theory as well as for etiology became more apparent. Less emphasis was placed on symptoms, as expressed in behavior and personality traits, and more on feelings and desires. In short, psychiatric study and prescription gave way to psychiatric treatment.[11]

In the same review Cobb pointed out that the techniques of child psychiatry were necessarily different from those of an adult interview. As an illustration of this point Cobb quoted M. S. Mahler, another author, as saying:

> We have plenty of valuable substitutes for it in the use, as analytical material, of all productions and functions of the child: play, drawing, dramatic acting, competitive games, gymnastic stunts, handicraft, story telling, continual day dreams, fantasies, and the like are all our tools. We leave the initiative entirely to the child, and though we participate, we try to get the lead from the patient in order that we may avoid introducing elements into the situation not pertinent to the child.[12]

Cobb observed that although Freud had analyzed a hysterical boy as early as 1905, it was his schoolteacher daughter, Anna, who really introduced child analysis into the educational field (217). Because of the Nazis, Anna Freud and her father moved in 1938 from Vienna to London, where he died a year later. Anna had known Erik Erikson when he was a tutor in Freud's home in Vienna. Her influence on English-speaking psychiatrists was to become greater in London. Lydia Dawes visited London before Anna Freud's arrival, and child analysis was already rooted there, for after completing her analysis with Ferenczi in 1916 Melanie Klein had gone into the study of children.

Moreover, child analysis was already beginning to be recognized in this country. By the mid-thirties Putnam's daughter, Marian, was working as a pediatrician with Edith Jackson on child analysis in New Haven. Beata Rank, who had practiced child analysis in Paris from 1926 and was separated from her husband, Otto, came to Boston in 1935 and was working at the Judge Baker. Beata Rank was known to Marian Putnam and was asked to join her as one of the directors of the James Jackson Putnam Children's Center in 1942 before the clinic actually opened its doors. Thus, Lydia Dawes found a ferment of new interest in child analysis when she took over child psychiatry at the General in 1937.

As already indicated, when Tillotson set up the psychiatric outpatient service as a function of neurology in 1931, child psychiatry under Anthonisen and Clothier was separate from adult psychiatry. After Cobb came in 1934, the two clinics remained separate for three years with Fremont-Smith's brother, Maurice, in charge of the adult service and Pavenstedt working independently. Then, when in 1937 the outpatient department was reorganized under Lindemann, child psychiatry was absorbed into it. Cobb said in the Decennial Report that change was necessary because so many children from outside agencies had been referred for the treatment of behavior problems that the children on the pediatric service in the hospital were being neglected.[13] Cobb wanted to integrate child psychiatry with pediatrics and over the years because of resistance by the pediatricians had a varying degree of success. So, when Dawes arrived she worked in child psychiatry under Lindemann.

Dawes continued to have the loyal support of Robert A. Young, the psychologist who under Pavenstedt had played such an important role in establishing the summer camp for psychoneurotic children. Then from 1938 to 1942, Else Neustadt was listed as a clinical and research fellow. Neustadt, who presumably helped Dawes at the time, was also associated with the Habit Clinic of Dougas A. Thom. There was close cooperation with the Habit Clinic as well as with the Judge Baker Guidance Center in the early days and later with the James Jackson Putnam Children's Center as well. Dawes headed child psychiatry at the General on a part-time basis for several years. She was listed as a psychiatrist to the Judge Baker from 1938 to 1943, before going to the Children's Medical Center, where she served until 1950. At that time she became head of child psychiatry at the Beth Israel Hospital, under her old friend from Vienna, Grete Bibring. Elizabeth Hall, Cobb's widow, said it was customary for child psychiatrists to be affiliated with more than one institution and to have private practices in addition,[14] a pattern that persists to this day.

Lucie Jessner first came to the Massachusetts General Hospital from Baldpate, a private sanatorium in Georgetown, Massachusetts, in 1941 and served as an assistant in psychiatry for two years, working with children. Jessner was an extraordinarily sensitive, motherly woman, who in later years became the full-time director of child psychiatry and endeared herself to everyone. In the academic year 1942–43 she was joined by Gregory Rochlin. After one year at the M.G.H. and another at the Judge Baker, Rochlin moved on to the James Jackson Putnam Children's center in Roxbury, which opened its doors in January, 1943. It was at first an offshoot of the Judge Baker and became independent a year later. Marian Putnam was the founder, and she was promptly joined by Beata Rank as a director. Betty Cobb was on the initial staff, and Eleanor Pavenstedt came after completing her analysis. They were soon joined by Eveoleen Rexford, who had been working at the Judge Baker. Rochlin was the only male. The James Jackson Putnam Children's Center became very important as an affiliated institution in later years when under Jessner's chairmanship the child psychiatry service burgeoned to major proportions.

However, that was for the future. Nineteen forty-three was disappointing in many ways. It was in the middle of World War II. The James Jackson Putnam Center was becoming firmly established—it became independent of the Judge Baker in 1944—and good child psychiatrists were in short supply. Dawes had withdrawn from the General and was doing most of her work at the Judge Baker. Jessner left to become acting director of the Thom Habit Clinic. Rochlin went to the Putnam Center in Roxbury, and Robert Young also departed.

Gregory Rochlin[15] said that psychoanalytic child psychiatrists lost interest in the Massachusetts General largely because of the close association with pediatrics, which had come about after the adult and children's psychiatric clinics were merged under Lindemann in 1937. At that time Harold Higgins was the chief of pediatrics. He was a rather gentle, passive man primarily interested in clinical pediatrics. Hence, it is easy to imagine his ready assurance to Cobb of coöperation between the pediatric and psychiatric services. However, Allan Butler, who succeeded Higgins shortly thereafter, was primarily a laboratory man with a major interest in physiological chemistry. Intellectually he could understand the need for psychiatric care, and he loyally tried to help Cobb, but he had no real knowledge of psychiatry and he was strongly opposed to psychoanalysis. Moreover, at that particular time, Butler's opposition to psychoanalysis was particularly devastating to child psychiatry at the M.G.H. because of the active programs at the Judge Baker, the Thom Habit Clinic, and the new James Jackson Putnam Children's Center. The tense relationship with pediatrics persisted for many years, although there was improvement after 1950, when child psychiatry became centered in the Burnam Building and the child psychiatrists shared the same elevator with the pediatricians.

So, Cobb was shorthanded in staff for child psychiatry. Fortunately, Dorothy McNaughton arrived upon the scene. She was primarily attached to the Judge Baker, but she found time to work in child psychiatry at the General, overseeing the social workers, taking on a few cases herself and attending the psychiatric staff conferences. It was a makeshift arrangement, but Cobb was extraordinarily lucky to have her services, for as Betty Cobb Hall put it, she was a born psychotherapist—warm, sensitive, understanding, and professionally excellent.[16] McNaughton remained with Cobb through the war years and in 1946 joined the staff of the Putnam Center with Marian Putnam and Beata Rank.[17] In 1982 she was living in Edinburgh.

Susan Van Amerongen came to the M.G.H. in 1946. Prior to her arrival on Cobb's service she had had no experience with child psychiatry. When he greeted her Cobb asked, "Do you like children?" When she replied, "Yes," Cobb assigned her to McNaughton. Van Amerongen remained until 1949 and then joined Lindemann in his Wellesley Human Relations service. She said that initially in child psychiatry the trend was to have one worker see the mother and another work with the child. After a conference an effort would be made in the Meyerian tradition to tie the information together and formulate a reasonable approach. Then with the advent of nonverbal play therapy, it became possible to work with younger children, and at the Putnam Center the care of autistic children became a special interest. Van Amerongen noted that at the General, too, there was a trend toward seeing younger children and sicker children than in previous years. Through the symbolism expressed by the children in play therapy it soon became apparent that the father was an important figure; so the father was often invited to participate as well. With the passage of time the entire family became involved, and in this way family therapy had its beginnings. However, family therapy, as an organized approach, was not firmly established for another decade.

Child psychiatry at the Masscahusetts General Hospital took on an entirely new dimension in 1947 when Lucie Jessner came back from the Thom Clinic to be director of the as yet unorganized new child psychiatric service. Jessner reported that when Cobb offered her the

Child Psychiatry

position he discussed in his dry, understanding way what plans he had for the new service, indicating that he viewed child psychiatry not as a separate entity but as a part of general psychiatry. In a summary of her experiences with psychiatry at the General Jessner reviewed her reactions to what Cobb had said at the time. She agreed with him, because she had always seen child psychopathology as a part of development from the embryo through the life cycle. Jessner said in her summary that she always advised her fellows in child psychiatry to continue seeing some adults. She said of Cobb that he gave her a free hand but was always available for advice.[18] In her new position Jessner was essentially full time. Elizabeth Cobb Hall said that she was permitted time to see a few private patients, and she did some supervising work for fellows and other staff members.

Although the new child psychiatric service was officially listed in the annual reports of the Massachusetts General Hospital under psychiatry, there was a strong effort to tie it in with pediatrics as well. Initially Jessner met with little success, but in the course of time she was more successful. She thought that the initial difficulties arose in part because she was working from a base in the outpatient department and was further handicapped by being a woman. Jessner continued her summary of developments in child psychiatry, noting that

> service as well as research involved building up a liaison with pediatrics. This sounded easy, but it was not easy. Dr. Allan Butler, the chairman of pediatrics, had welcomed such a liaison and he consciously did his best to help it materialize, but ambivalence toward psychiatry and especially psychoanalysis made it difficult for him and for us. But when his staff and residents were against us, his empathy with the underdog drove him to fight for us valiantly and with mixed results. For example, he ordered his residents to attend our weekly conferences. They all came and then were called out by a nurse, one after the other, every five to ten minutes for this or that presumed emergency.

It is apparent that the resident staff in pediatrics was cool to Jessner's psychiatric service, even though Butler recognized its importance.

It was in 1950 that child psychiatry moved from the outpatient department to the top of the Burnham Building, which housed both pediatrics and gynecology. Gaston E. Blom, Jessner's first resident and her eventual successor as dircector of child psychiatry, said that they were assigned a relatively new wing on the sixth floor, in addition to an office for nine fellows around the corner and two overscheduled playrooms.[19] According to Jessner, in her 1979 report to John Abbott:

> The interpersonal relationships improved much after we moved into the same building as pediatrics, atop of them. Meeting daily in the elevator, being near and accessible, brought with it a change in atmosphere that led to discussion and collaboration. Geography plays a role in liaison services. Gradually we learned much from each other.

Jessner then added that her fellows had an opportunity, which the practicing child psychiatrist is likely to lose, of keeping in touch with medical problems. She said that the pediatricians and child psychiatrists began to enter each other's research projects. She mentioned a study of hermaphroditism with Nathan Talbot, a study of asthma with the allergists, and cooperation with Oliver Cope on a study of children with burns. Jessner also observed that one of the pediatric residents, Cornelius Lansing, had gone into psychiatric training with her and eventually joined the staff at Dartmouth. Gregory Rochlin, who had been at the General with Jessner in 1942–43, said that it was Butler and not Cobb who really kept child psychiatry alive.[20]

Jessner had been in her new position a year, from 1947 to 1948, when she undertook the training program for clinical and research fellows in child psychiatry. A number of the fellows had training grants from the United States Public Health Service. It was common at the time for a physician taking up child psychiatry to divide his time between the Massachusetts General Hospital and another institution, often the James Jackson Putnam Children's Center in Roxbury. Sometimes a fellow would be at the General for a year and later go to the Children's Center. Sometimes a physician would work in both places at once. However, Jessner said that most of the teaching on her service took place in the large outpatient department.[21]

As already mentioned Jessner reported that Cobb always gave her a free hand in academic matters. When in 1948 the time came to select the first fellow, Cobb's secretary, Dorothy Adams, showed her the applications for child psychiatric fellowships. According to Jessner, "It was a big bundle. Dorothy and I looked through them independently—both came up with Gaston E. Blom as first choice."

Blom said that his initial supervisors were Lucie Jessner herself and Samuel Kaplan,[22] both of them superb. Blom noted that Jessner had a special capacity for nourishing the positive qualities in her fellows and her staff. "I learned by observing her and by her emphasizing my positives," he said. "I recall being impatient at times that she was not more critical of my work. She was an elegant, lovely, insightful woman. . . . I think in the beginning I was often given too much responsibility too early."[23] In the early fifties Elizabeth Zetzel, wife of Louis Zetzel, gastroenterologist at the Beth Israel Hospital, joined Lucie as an assistant.[24]

Blom must have been well able to handle the responsibility. He worked closely with Jessner from the summer of 1948 until her departure for the University of North Carolina in 1955. After that he was director of child psychiatry at the General until his own departure for the University of Colorado in 1958.[25] Blom said that although conferences with Cobb were infrequent the few contacts he did have led to a growing admiration for Cobb's scholarship and for his open-mindedness to different theoretical views of behavior.

Blom also recalled the myna bird in Cobb's office, which would interrupt a serious conversation with a "What's up, Doc?" or a whistle. Cobb was studying neurological representation of language. "He intended to sacrifice the myna bird to study its brain," Blom said, "but I knew this would be a very difficult step for him to take."

Blom found it hard to talk with Cobb about money, particularly his own salary. Blom said there wasn't much money available. One had to do some private practice to make ends meet. Blom said that faculty ranks were low, too. He began as an assistant and became an instructor the last four years. When he moved to Colorado he became an associate professor right away.

The fellows in training saw many of their patients either in the high-ceilinged rooms of the outpatient department or at their bedsides in the hospital. It was therefore necessary to carry their toys and other paraphernalia to these locations from their base in the playrooms in Burnham. Blom said he recalled being teased at times by Walter Bauer, the physician-in-chief, concerning his equipment, which seemed remote from the ophthalmoscopes and stethoscopes of general medicine.

In table 4 are listed the clinical and research fellows from 1948 through 1954 whom Jessner recognized as participants in her formal program. There were several additional physicians who worked with children in pediatrics or in psychiatry under some special arrangement with Butler, Jessner, or Cobb. A number of these special fellows are discussed elsewhere in the text. The list of clinical and research fellows

Table 4. Clinical and Research Fellows in Child Psychiatry

Norman R. Bernstein	1954–1955	Professor of psychiatry and director of department, Abraham Lincoln School of Medicine, Chicago, Ill.
Gaston E. Blom	1948–1949	Professor of psychiatry, Michigan State University
Margaret Bullowa	1948–1949	Laboratory of medical electronics, Peter Bent Brigham Hospital
John Coolidge	1948–1951	Director of training, Judge Baker Guidance Center
Chester C. D'Autremont	1952–1954	Director of Walden Clinic, Concord, Ma.; Children's Medical Center, Boston
Renata G. DeBenedetti	1949	Professor of child psychiatry, University of Rome
Thomas F. Dwyer	1948–1950	Beth Israel Hospital; consultant to Massachusetts Institute of Technology
Harold J. Harris	1952–1953	Assistant professor of psychiatry, Duke University
Richmond Holder	1949–1951	Phillips Exeter Academy; McLean Hospital; Massachusetts General Hospital
Jane Allen Hollenbeck	1948–1951	Beaverbrook Guidance Center, Waltham Hospital
Hedwig H. Holzer	1952	Director, Paul A. Dever State School, Taunton, Ma. Died 1979
Pierre Johannet	1952–1954	Director of Nursery School, James Jackson Putnam Children's Center
Robert Kagan	1950–1952	Medical director, Psychiatric Clinic for Children, Long Beach, Ca.
Samuel Kaplan	1947–1949	Director of training in child psychiatry, Boston University School of Medicine
John Lamont	1953–1954	Director of child psychiatry, Massachusetts General Hospital, 1958–

Child Psychiatry

Edward A. Mason	1948–1949	Psychiatrist, Laboratory of Community Psychiatry, Boston
Samuel G. McClellan	1952	Danville, Kentucky
Henry Musnick	1948–1949	Assistant director, Beaverbrook Guidance Center, Waltham
Else Neustadt	1938–1942	Westwood Lodge, 1942–1945 Quincy Hospital, 1946–; deceased
Paul H. Painter	1951–1953	Assistant professor of child psychiatry and pediatrics, Washington University, St. Louis
Winston J. Rickards	1952	Settled in Australia
Nicholas D. Rizzo	1948–1949	Associate psychiatrist, Peter Bent Brigham Hospital; Phillips Academy, Andover
Nancy Rollins (McDonnell)	1953–1955	Children's Medical Center, Boston
William Sharpe	1954–1955	Albemarle Mental Health Center, Elizabeth City, N.C.
Veronica Tisza	1953–1955	Director of residents in child psychiatry, Children's Medical Center, Boston
Eero H. Valanne	1951	Founded a child psychiatric clinic in Finland, subsequently died
Suzanne Van Amerongen	1946–1949	Codirector of Thom Clinic with Eveoleen Rexford; Associate clinical professor of child psychiatry, Harvard
Charles W. Wahl	1951–1952	Chief of psychosomatic medicine, University of California, Los Angeles
Ruth S. Weiss	1954	Living in Boston area, 1979
Harry Wermer	1950	Deceased
Joseph M. Zucker	1953–1954	Director, psychiatric outpatient department, Rhode Island Hospital

in child psychiatry was culled from annual reports of the Massachusetts General Hospital, directories of medical specialists, and similar sources. It was submitted to Jessner during her lifetime and she made a few additions from memory. It is possible that some names were inadvertently omitted. In each case an effort was made to include at least one important professional appointment or activity.

While Lucie Jessner was not a brilliant lecturer, she was an extraordinarily competent psychiatrist. Her students unanimously testified that she was a sound and able teacher. Rochlin said that she was not a good administrator.[26] It was her warm, loving personality that held the service together and enabled it to grow, partly as Blom pointed out through her encouragement of the positive qualities which she found in her fellows. The warmth of her relationships is indicated by an incident when a number of them invited her to attend a night baseball game. Blom, in describing the event, said that Lucie knew nothing about professional baseball; so as an educational experience the fellows in child psychiatry decided to take her one evening to see the old Boston Braves. They coached Lucie in advance on the purpose of the game, its rules, and its special language, such as *southpaw*. They all piled into John Coolidge's Franklin car to go the game, meanwhile continuing to acquaint Lucie with baseball and its customs. Blom said the coaching went on throughout the game. Finally, somewhere about the fourth inning Lucie jumped up and exclaimed in her usual way, "Ah!" Blom said that the fellows were all puzzled by her excitement. On inquiry, she said, "I saw it!" It happened to be an easy pop fly into the infield.[27] Holder reported that Lucie Jessner was the most glamorous woman he had ever met.[28]

The teaching program at the Massachusetts General Hospital was no doubt strengthened by its association with the James Jackson Putnam Center, if only because Cobb's wife, Betty, worked there. Cobb told his wife that in child psychiatry he felt he had responsibility for a service in which his knowledge was sharply limited. In fact, he said, she knew more about child psychiatry than he did, and Holder, who had taken up child psychiatry after his residency, said Cobb looked upon the field as women's work. No doubt that view was held by others as well, for many of Cobb's former colleagues when reviewing staff photographs would dismiss the names of some of the fellows when they came to them with a comment such as "hmph, child psychiatry!" One of the later fellows in child psychiatry who did not know Cobb well was Sam McLellan. McLellan said that he saw the distinc-

Child Psychiatry

tion between child and adult psychiatry in terms of the spirit. Being relatively independent of Cobb with his monistic view of life, the child psychiatrists felt freer to look upon cerebral function and religious beliefs as they saw fit.[29]

Whatever Cobb's attitude toward child psychiatry may have been, the responsibility for a child guidance clinic was thrust upon him in 1934, and he felt a responsibility for adapting it to the psychiatric needs of the pediatric patients in the hospital. In this task Cobb found help in the rapidly growing experience with child psychiatry that was taking place at the James Jackson Putnam Children's Center.

The Putnam Center had wide recognition because Marian Putnam and Beata Rank were well-known child psychiatrists, and it gained even further reputation through the work at the Massachusetts General under the aegis of the Harvard Medical School and the direction of Stanley Cobb, whose reputation at the time was worldwide. Betty Cobb had an important role in integrating the programs of the two institutions. She was recognized as a psychotherapist and worked in the Putnam Center until 1955, when the Cobbs moved from Milton to Cambridge and commuting became more difficult than previously.[30] There is no doubt that Betty Cobb advanced the spirit of enthusiasm for the child psychiatry program and in that way had a hand in stimulating Cobb's interest. At the same time Cobb was influential in obtaining fellowships funds from various sources for the young physicians undertaking child psychiatric training on his service.[31]

In addition to the clinical work that contributed to Jessner's training program there was also a modest amount of investigation. Jessner responded to Cobb's attitude toward opportunities for clinical research in the following paragraph which she wrote as a part of her summary of child psychiatry:

> The training of child psychiatrists included, of course, diagnostic and therapeutic service to children and their families, as well as research. With our opportunities for observing children before, during, and after operations and in the course of illnesses, we felt that we might contribute to psychosomatic medicine. Right at the start Cobb gave me his unforgettable advice. He said there was pressure to be "scientific" in the sense of making quantitative, controlled observations. He also said that at that time much of psychiatric research could not meet those standards. He said he thought one should acknowledge this fact without being disconcerted. On the other hand, whenever something could be stated in numbers, it would be sloppy not to do so; there was no excuse for saying "several patients" or "frequently" instead of counting them.[32]

The informality of circumstances under which research projects were prepared for publication was described by Blom, who told of several hectic evenings prior to sending off the manuscript of the tonsillectomy study on which he had been working with Jessner and the psychologist, Sam Waldfogel, evenings at Jessner's home. Blom said the occasions were enriched by delicious pastries from the Window Shop and the ambience was delightful. He also admired Lucie's ability to recognize and deal with the complexities. However, he and Waldfogel became progressively more concerned about meeting the editor's deadline. Finally, after various delays the final deadline came, and Blom made a trip to the downtown post office about midnight to mail the manuscript. Mistakenly he put the empty envelope in a stamping machine and it was swept away, leaving him with the bare manuscript in his hand with no envelope and no change. After twenty minutes going to bars to obtain change and to acquire an envelope, the manuscript finally got off. Blom said in summarizing the episode, "Of course the mail which was received in New York the next day was the empty envelope!" Lucie's optimism prevailed—the manuscript was accepted and published.[33]

Blom went on to say that the location of the child psychiatric service within the pediatrics area of the Burnham Building afforded an opportunity to study reactions to hospitalization, illness, treatment procedures, and operations. He said that at the time the study of psychosomatic disorders was very much in vogue. So the interrelationships between illnesses and emotions were a natural focus for research.

At the beginning of Jessner's newly organized service in child psychiatry Cobb and Butler made a joint effort to promote the interdepartmental study of psychosomatic disorders. Cases were presented at conferences sponsored by pediatrics and psychiatry, and Miles wrote up the proceedings for publication in the *American Journal of Medicine*. Under the title of each article appeared a statement of purpose which in general read as follows:

> These clinics are designed to bring out psychosomatic relationships both in symptomatology of the patient and in the organization of the hospital. Reports are directed by Dr. Stanley Cobb and Dr. Allan M. Butler and are edited by Dr. H. W. Miles. This is a report from the Psychiatric Service of the Massachusetts General Hospital.

One of the joint conferences was about impulsive behavior in a crippled boy and the words were added, "in which the orthopedic service

Child Psychiatry

cooperated" (214). Cobb, Butler, and Miles published the proceedings of a number of such clinics including one on hysteria (215) and one entitled "Feeblemindedness or pseudoretardation?" in which they indicated that some children who appeared to be feebleminded actually had a disorder that could be helped by psychotherapy (218). Other topics included a case of duodenal ulcer with anxiety attacks treated by psychotherapy (238), and psychogenic deafness in a disturbed boy (243), which came out in 1949. Presumably Cobb and Butler stopped publishing together because Jessner's service was becoming well enough established to carry on without this form of support. The papers in the series all appeared in 1948 and 1949.

There were a number of physicians on Cobb's staff who worked with children or on children's problems, yet who were not formally in Jessner's training program. Foremost among these was David Stafford-Clark. Stafford-Clark was a resident on the psychiatric service from June through December, 1949, then became a clinical and research fellow. Holder said that Stafford-Clark was small of build and self-contained.[34] Holder looked upon him as one of his greatest heroes. In 1979 Stafford-Clark was living in retirement at Kantara in the Turkish part of the Island of Cyprus. Prior to his retirement he had served for twenty-five years as chief of service of the psychiatric division of Guy's Group and Medical School in London. In a most friendly and warm manner he dictated a tape describing a research project in child psychiatry and a personal experience with Cobb that led to another informal investigative study. Stafford-Clark's tape provided three stories of the way in which Cobb identified with his students and followed through in helping them meet their needs. This tape is so revealing that a transcript edited by Stafford-Clark personally appears in the appendix.[35]

The first of the three accounts has to do with a pilot research project in child psychiatry that Stafford-Clark conducted under Cobb's direct supervision. It was a study designed to explore the effect of the emotional ambience of a children's ward upon the health, happiness, and outcome of the patients. Stafford-Clark studied two groups of patients. The control group of twenty-five was composed of children with evident chronic illnesses who were necessarily aware of the need for bed rest and specialized forms of therapy. These children were treated in the usual manner as sick patients, and they responded by feeling that they were sick. The twenty-five experimental patients, matched as closely as possible to the controls for age and sex, were encouraged to pretend that they weren't patients and were getting better so fast that they would soon be all right. He called these children the *gung ho* group because of their high degree of optimism.

In fact, their overexuberance was often quite inappropriate as indicated by the second item on Stafford-Clark's tape which was the case history of a boy with bone sarcoma. This boy had been assigned to the *gung ho* group. His emotional support, fortunately in a hospital other than the M.G.H., was so great that the inevitable prognosis was withheld even from the parents, who were justifiably angry when the boy died. Stafford-Clark was abashed when he discovered that the boy's surgeon in his zealous enthusiasm had not discussed the implication of the illness with the parents. When Stafford-Clark reviewed the incident with Cobb, he experienced considerable guilt. He wondered whether inadvertently he had assumed responsibility for the boy and been derelict in not personally going over the situation with the surgeon. In replying, Cobb reassured Stafford-Clark that as a research investigator it would have been inappropriate to interfere with the surgeon's management of the case. Stafford-Clark's experience with this terminally ill child brought into focus the hazard of human experimentation twenty years before it became generally recognized as a major problem.

The third story recounted on the tape was a personal one about some coarse fibrillary twitches that Stafford-Clark developed when under the stress of separation from his family during his days as a fellow at the M.G.H. He had a mental image of falling victim to a progressive upper-motor-neurone disease. He finally screwed up his courage to discuss the matter with Cobb, who reassured him that coarse fibrillary twitching in the absence of muscular wasting was almost invariably benign. However, to provide additional reassurance he arranged for Stafford-Clark to have a myogram in the EEG laboratory. The myogram was normal, and Stafford-Clark was reassured. What impressed him was the empathic way in which Cobb had deliberately devised ways to reinforce his clinical evaluation and to make Stafford-Clark feel more comfortable.

Another prominent man whom Cobb knew and who worked on clinical problems in children was T. Berry Brazelton. Brazelton was a clinical and research fellow in psychiatry at the Massachusetts General Hospital in 1949–50, after having been a fellow in child psychiatry at

Child Psychiatry   307

the Putnam Center the previous year. Brazelton stated in an interview[36] that he technically spent half his time at the Putnam Center and the other half at the General. He said, however, in point of fact, that he learned much more child psychiatry at the center than he did at the hospital. He became a consultant to the center in pediatrics and retained that association for many years. In fact he looked upon himself as a pediatrician. He ran a clinic at the Children's Medical Center, where he studied the normal growth process. He published a number of books for parents and on the basis of his training and experience saw a need for pediatricians who would be aware of the stages of development, both physical and emotional, in young persons. Well-known, in 1979 he was an associate professor at Harvard.

Later Abraham Fineman was a clinical and research fellow (1952–53). Concurrently, he was a fellow in child psychiatry at the Judge Baker Guidance Clinic and at the James Jackson Putnam Children's Center, where he remained on the staff for many years. Fineman, as his name implies, was literally a fine man, an outstanding human being and highly regarded, although he was never in Lucie Jessner's program. Fineman's wife, Joanne, was also a child psychiatrist.

Cobb's own son John Candler Cobb, "Jock," had an interesting experience with child psychiatry when taking fourth-year psychiatry in medical school. Jock Cobb quoted his father as saying that interns and residents on the nonpsychiatric services of the hospital, such as medicine, surgery, and pediatrics, practiced what he called shoe-leather medicine, running about taking histories, making examinations, drawing blood, giving injections, and doing other forms of bustling activity. Such interns and residents were somewhat intolerant of their psychiatric counterparts whom they saw as sitting idly, listening to irrelevant stories told by their patients. As Jock saw it, the nonpsychiatric interns and residents were often buzzing about doing things without having listened to the nature of the real problem.

As an example of the way in which a well-taken and empathic history can clarify a difficult diagnosis, Jock Cobb told about a sixteen-year-old blind girl who was under his care on Bulfinch 7 when he was a clinical clerk. The girl had been referred from the Perkins Institute for the Blind, where she had been admitted because of blindness of rather sudden onset. The people at Perkins had recognized something atypical about the girl's blindness. Her awareness of the time of day had suggested to the personnel there that she could read clock faces. Jock spent many hours under the supervision of Lucie Jessner becoming acquainted with the girl and getting her to tell how she became blind. Finally the girl, designated as Jane, said that one day on entering her home she had discovered on the dining room table a sealed note from her adoptive mother saying that she had been unfaithful to her adoptive father and had left him for another man. Jane picked up the note, opened it, and read the contents. Her sudden blindness dated from that experience. In recounting the story later Jock Cobb quoted Jane as saying "what struck me between the eyes" was her adoptive mother's having been unfaithful and not wanting her to know. The key sentence in the letter had read, "But don't tell Jane." Being blind Jane could deny to herself having read the letter she was not supposed to see. Jock said that after that flash of insight the sixteen-year-old girl began to improve. At first she used her eyes only a little and had tunnel vision. Then Jock and she played games like checkers together, and finally, toward the end of her brief stay in the hospital she was playing ping-pong and her vision returned to normal. This case of hysterical blindness, because of its dramatic resolution, was an exciting case for presentation at various staff conferences and offered an extraordinary experience for a fourth-year medical student.[37] The story of the sixteen-year-old blind girl demonstrated in a most powerful way the value of the time taken for an adequate clinical history.

Although child psychiatry was a tangential interest for Cobb, thrust upon him by the necessity of carrying on a preexisting service and by the requirements of the Massachusetts General Hospital for psychiatric coverage of all age ranges, nevertheless, in some ways it was a satisfaction for him. One of his greatest contributions to medicine was through the values he imparted to the students, residents, fellows, and younger staff members who came under his influence. Jessner in a manner consistent with her own personality made a similar contribution to her own trainees.

Jessner and Cobb, with quite different personalities and methods, had in common their concern for the lives and careers of their students and colleagues. Cobb was more fatherly, more remote, and less accustomed to daily contact with his charges. He was more likely to have serious discussions at infrequent intervals and to review in depth major concerns at such times. Jessner, on the contrary, was motherly, warm, reassuring, and constantly available. She conveyed her sound knowledge through good personal teaching, without dependence upon an

Child Psychiatry 309

administrative organization. Cobb on the other hand had a large staff to supervise. He was eternally busy with long-range planning, investigative projects, budgets, teaching conferences, faculty reappointments, and similar responsibilities that fall upon a full-time service chief. Of necessity he had to delegate day-to-day matters to other members of his staff.

Although it would be unfair to enlarge upon a comparison between Cobb and Jessner, it is reasonable to conclude that Jessner's accomplishments were very rewarding to Cobb. Grounded in contemporary adaptations of psychoanalytic thought, her work was progressive yet clinically sound. After leaving her service, her graduates were in demand for important posts, many of them academic. Moreover, her trainees proved themselves in every way able to adapt to the evolutionary changes in the profession later brought on by group dynamics and family therapy.

14
Retirement

When Cobb retired in mid-1954 after twenty years as psychiatrist-in-chief at the Massachusetts General Hospital, he was faced with quandaries about the future. On the one hand he wanted to make a clean break with the psychiatric service in order to give his successor, Lindemann, freedom to make changes without feelings of criticism from a father figure looking down upon him. On the other hand, since his training in Baltimore, Cobb had never worked anywhere except at the Harvard Medical School and in Boston hospitals. His roots had been in greater Boston all his life. His friends were there, and it was for him the most comfortable and interesting milieu in which to live and work.

So Cobb made up his mind to remain in Boston. He established himself in a number of settings that would keep alive his interests in ornithology and in the human mind. He recalled his former pathology teacher, William Councilman, as having said in his old age, "When you have to retire, find a narrow field you love and till it extensively."[1] Having been an ornithologist and having spent most of his professional life trying to learn how the brain worked, it was natural that he chose avian neurology as his niche (511). However, he also felt a need to carry on some work in human psychiatry.

For his work in avian neurology, the most important setting was the tiny laboratory assigned to him by the department of neurology on the third floor of the Warren Building at the Massachusetts General Hospital. Here he had a small northeast corner room with a counter top for his microscope and a side annex for anatomical examinations and the storage of specimens. This small area in the experimental laboratory of histological neuropathology remained Cobb's personal base of operations until almost the end of his life, at first in association with the neuropathologist Charles Kubik and later with his own former resident, E. Peirson Richardson.[2] New laboratories under the department of psychiatry were established on the sixth floor in 1956 and were named for Cobb in 1959; yet he continued to work in the neuropathology area until 1965, when he finally moved upstairs.[3] The initial director

Retirement 311

of the psychiatric laboratories was Gardiner Quarton, followed by Frank R. Ervin, Seymour Kety, and Gerald Klerman.[4]

Cobb's next most important work area was the Museum of Comparative Zoölogy at Harvard, where the atmosphere and aromas brought back nostalgic memories of college days.[5] Here he worked once a week, primarily in paleontology with Dr. Tilly Edinger, and had stimulating contact with Professors Romer, Mayr, Simpson, Williams, and Griffin. Cobb observed that the long view of the paleontologist was fundamental to anyone interested in the philosophy of science. In his "Excursions Avian" Cobb said:

> The notions that "mind" and "consciousness" are attributes only of man and that "mental" can be separated from "physical" by naive dichotomy become unthinkable when one encompasses the sweep of geological time. Then, bickerings between neurologists and psychiatrists, between different psychiatric groups, between "organicists" and "psychoanalysts" become trivial indeed.[6]

Making a collection of brains adequate for studies in comparative anatomy took several years. Cobb wrote numerous letters to friends and institutions during that time in his effort to obtain specimens. A reply to one of Cobb's inquiries from Professor Carl L. Hubbs at the Scripps Institution of Oceanography in La Jolla, California, gives the flavor of the correspondence. Two paragraphs follow:

> Our mutual friend, Alfred Redfield, has told me something of your extremely interesting comparative work on the brains of birds and he has provided me with a copy of your letter to him of September 2, in which you list certain bird species of which you need brain preparations for your study.
>
> We should have no difficulty in obtaining the four marine birds that you mention, namely a Petrel, Shearwater, and a Fulmar, and also a Cormorant. We have no one here working on land birds particularly, but we might be able to pick up a couple of woodpeckers and an owl.[7]

Hubbs went on to say that he was planning a trip to Guadeloupe Island, where he might pick up some sea birds, and he asked Cobb technical questions about preserving the specimens in formalin.

An amusing incident in Cobb's quest for specimens followed a conversation with a navy physician after a talk that Cobb had given in Washington, D.C. The doctor told Cobb that at Midway Island albatrosses were so abundant that they were a hazard to airplanes landing and taking off. After that conversation Cobb wrote to the biologist at Midway asking him to preserve the heads of two albatrosses fixed in formalin solution and gave instructions for mailing the fixed preparations. On August sixth of that year, while relaxing on Cape Cod, Cobb heard the telephone ring and the operator read out the following message:

> NAVY OVERSEAS AIR CARGO TERMINAL, 01041Z YOUR ACTION, INFO:/ BUREAU AERONAUTICS, WASH. D.C./ OFFICE NAVAL RESEARCH, WASH. D.C./ FISH AND WILD LIFE SERVICE, DEPT. INTERIOR, WASH. D.C./ CITE SE-3 M.G.S. 231958Z/ TWO CRATES LIVE ALBATROSS DEPT. SAN FRANCISCO VIA AIRBORN FREIGHT THIS DAY/ BY GOVERNMENT BILL LADING N-3307299 AIRBORN AIRBILL SFO - 873981. (441).

After reading the cryptic message two or three times Cobb realized that he was the possessor of two crates of live albatrosses in "Wash. D.C." Without recounting all the ensuing telephone calls and air flights, it can be said the albatrosses went to Logan Airport and wound up in the Boston Zoo, sick. They were accordingly sent back to Washington, where two of them died and Cobb eventually received the brains. In time Cobb had a large collection of avian brains and many of them became the property of the Museum of Comparative Zoology at the time of his death.

Cobb's third work area was the department of student health at the Massachusetts Institute of Technology. He was a psychiatrist to students three days a week for several years. His work was predominantly clinical, for he did not publish with any of the faculty members there. However, he did have stimulating contact with a number of them, including Dr. Hans Lucas Teuber, who prior to his death in 1977 was the first to establish psychology as a respectable science at the institute. Teuber, a former psychology student of Gordon Allport at Harvard, set up the psychology department in a small factory building during the early sixties. Walle Nauta in Teuber's laboratory was one of the foremost neuroanatomists in the United States and was in charge of neurophysiology at that time. Cobb was helpful in obtaining specimens of bird brains for one of Nauta's associates, Harvey Karten.[8] After Cobb's death his entire collection of brain slides was contributed to Nauta's laboratory through Karten.[9] Another person with whom Cobb had close contact at the Massachusetts Institute of Technology was Dr. Jerry Lettvin, a psychiatrist who worked in the clinic there and also on the psychiatric service at the Massachusetts General Hospital. A massive man with a shock of black hair, Lettvin was not only brilliant as a scientist but was also gifted with the talents of an actor. His wife

Retirement

Stanley Cobb's final lecture in neuropathology in the amphitheater of Building D of the Harvard Medical School, 1954. Individuals identified are: Joseph Aub (third from left), Carl Vernlund (sixth from left), Harry C. Solomon (eighth from left), Betty Cobb (eleventh from left), Stanley Cobb (in white coat, twelfth from left), Samuel A. Levine (thirteenth from left), possibly Dean Clark (sixteenth from left), Howard B. Sprague (seventeenth from left), and possibly Franz Alexander (twentieth from left and farthest right).

M.G.H. General Executive Committee, 1949. Back row: Mr. Wood, Dr. McKittrick, Dr. Cobb, Mr. Robinson, Dr. Bland. Front row: Dr. Mallory, Dr. Dean Clark, Dr. Means, Dr. Faxon, and Dr. Churchill.

Retirement

Medical Exchange Club *circa* 1930. Back row. Drs. J. H. Means, Richard Miller, George R. Minot, James L. Gamble, Watson Sellards, Cecil K. Drinker. Front row: Drs. E. Granville Crabtree, Kenneth Blackfan, Frank Rackemann, Fritz Irving, and Stanley Cobb.

The psychiatry staff of the Massachusetts General Hospital in 1961. Left to right, front row: Daniel Dawes, Gardiner Quarton, Carl Binger, Stanley Cobb, Erich Lindemann, John Nemiah, Avery Weisman, Morris Chafetz; second row: Peter Sifneos, Fred Dohl, Richard Peebles, George Talland, Jack Rice (in white coat), William McCourt, Norman Bernstein, Gerald Davidson, Harry Olin, Lloyd Caplan; third row: unidentified, unidentified, Captaine Thompson, Ann Overbeck, Dorothy Clark, unidentified, unidentified, John Li, Manuel Hernandez, Ed Messner; fourth row: all unidentified; fifth and last row: unidentified, unidentified, unidentified, Nancy Durant, Herbert Barry, John Baldwin, unidentified, Philip Boyd, Thomas Hackett, John Lamont, Harold Williams, George Perrin

Stanley Cobb dissecting a bird brain in the Warren Building laboratory at the Massachusetts General Hospital during the later years of his retirement. The advanced deformity of his fingers is obvious

Watercolor of the Himalayas, painted by Dr. Cobb through an airplane window on a round-the-world trip during retirement in 1962

Retirement

was a ballet dancer and he himself sometimes appeared on television. So, although Cobb's collaboration with his colleagues at the Massachusetts Institute of Technology was not extensive, he found them exciting and the work rewarding.

Cobb's fourth work area, the Massachusetts General Hospital, presented, at least to some extent, the awkwardness of too close an association with his own former psychiatric service. Although he made strong resolutions about noninterference, propinquity made it very difficult for him to divorce himself entirely from the evolution of hospital policy.

An example of Cobb's continued interest in policy matters is indicated by a letter written to Raymond Adams, the antipsychiatric chief of neurology, after a joint conference on mentally retarded children in which psychiatric factors had been shown to be important. Cobb wanted to improve relations between neurology and psychiatry. In the letter, which was written in December, 1959, Cobb suggested better coöperation between the two departments and reëmphasized the importance of emotional factors at least in some retardates. In the letter Cobb said:

> I was much pleased with the conference on "Memory" today and learned much from your presentation. But what struck me most, afterwards, was that by such meetings we were accomplishing what you, Erich, and all of us desire—a drawing together of mental and neurological sciences.[10]

Cobb remembered that at a recent conference on child psychiatry he had seen an autistic, pseudoretarded child whose illness had been clearly shown to have important psychogenic factors.

Also, almost certainly because of Lindemann's ineffectiveness as an administrator, Cobb engaged in an exchange of letters with George Packer Berry, then dean of the Harvard Medical School, about the desirability of maintaining an old tradition of rotating departmental chiefs. In a letter to Berry in August, 1963, Cobb reflected his uneasiness about the appointment of permanent departmental chairmen and reminded Berry of an old Harvard Medical School policy of making such appointments open-ended. Cobb wrote:

> I have been told that the policy of *not* appointing permanent chairmen of departments in the Medical School no longer holds. If this is true, I would be greatly troubled, because I have always believed that one of the reasons for the superiority of the Harvard Faculty was that in each department there were several full professors equal in standing. The rotation of the chairman-

ship among them emphasized this equality and kept anyone from becoming too fond of power or too much burdened with administration. Both power and administrative duties are to my mind enemies of real scholarship.[11]

Berry's reply to the letter indicated that times had changed and that it was often difficult to obtain a departmental chairman from another institution without some assurance of tenure. Cobb was apparently grinding his teeth over the state of affairs in his former department and frustrated over being unable to do anything about it.

A third interchange of letters again points to Cobb's motherliness in being concerned about what might be called the "neurological situation" at the Massachusetts General Hospital. In 1965 William Sweet, the chief of neurosurgery, was seriously considering a professorship in California because the neurological service was so conservative in consulting neurosurgeons. James C. White of the neurosurgical service and Cobb spent a noon hour one day discussing the situation and then White wrote a letter to John H. Knowles, the hospital director, emphasizing the potential danger to the hospital in the event that Sweet should depart. In his letter White warned Dr. Knowles:

> I realize the difficulties involved but want to point out that if Bill accepts the appointment at the University of California you will never be able to persuade any other neurosurgeon of his caliber to replace him as Chief unless these difficulties with the Neurological Service can be corrected.[12]

White sent Cobb a copy of the letter that summarized their deliberations. In a covering letter he said to Cobb:

> In line with our conversation at lunch about Bill Sweet I had an idea which I thought was important and am therefore sending the enclosed note to John Knowles. I think the problem must really be faced or else no top-notch neurosurgeon will care to remain here.[13]

Cobb had an enormous emotional investment in the neurosciences at the Massachusetts General Hospital, and with his office and laboratory so close at hand it was inevitable that he should become aware of problems whether they affected psychiatry, clinical neurology, or neurosurgery. Although he had retired from his official duties as chairman of psychiatry in 1954, he found it emotionally impossible to stay entirely on the sidelines. It is of interest that in a group photograph of the 1961 psychiatry staff Cobb is shown occupying the revered central position in the front row (page 316). Furthermore, Cobb's emotional attachment to the department is indicated by an episode that took place in 1967 after the arrival of Leon Eisenberg as chairman. Cobb attended one of the weekly staff conferences in the ether dome and sat in the first row. Eisenberg studiously avoided recognizing his presence, and Cobb's feelings were deeply hurt.[14]

During retirement Cobb published more than sixty papers from his office and laboratory in the Warren Building. Those on the anatomy of bird brains were enriched by his weekly contact with Edinger at the Museum of Comparative Zoölogy in Cambridge and by the correspondence that he carried on with friends and others about ornithology. In addition there were collaborative studies with members of the staff at the Massachusetts General Hospital and with other members of the Harvard faculty. However, many of Cobb's publications during retirement were book reviews, obituaries, and brief tracts or letters to editors about his various social concerns.

Most of the work Cobb published in the early years of retirement was actually on subjects other than ornithology. In collaboration with the neurosurgeon James C. White, he wrote on psychological changes associated with giant pituitary neoplasms. It was a study of intellectual deficits and emotional instability observed in five cases (224). He wrote a chapter on cerebral circulation for a German handbook of special pathological anatomy and histology (225). Of interest are his comments on the role of oxygen deprivation in bringing on epileptic seizures. He supported Gibbs in stating that there was no evidence for generalized vascular spasm as a cause for fits but left open the possibility that small vessel contraction in critical areas might be significant.

He wrote reviews of neurology and psychiatry for the *Archives of Internal Medicine* covering 1955 (374), 1956 (391) and 1958 (424). The review for 1955 was largely concerned with neuropharmacology and the clinical effects of new pharmacological agents, particularly meprobamate, Rawolfia, and chlorpromazine. He cited Magoun's work on relating levels of awareness in anesthesia to his ascending reticular activating system. Cobb also wrote at some length about brainwashing, which he saw as primarily a psychological phenomenon. The remainder of the 1955 review had to do with genetics and its importance in instinctive behavior.

In the review for 1956 (391) Cobb commented upon the retirement of his friend Sir Charles Symonds, after twenty-five years of service, from Guy's Hospital. Then he discussed the growing importance of neurochemistry and commented upon the appointment by the Harvard

Medical School of Folch-Pi to head the new laboratory at MacLean. Folch-Pi had done fundamental research on the proteins and lipids of the brain. There followed a long section on such confusing terms as *cybernetics, communication, information theory, behavioral science, entropy,* and *feedback*. Although unable to unravel the confusion introduced by such terms, Cobb acknowledged the possibility that a major breakthrough in psychiatric research might be at hand. He concluded his report with a long review of Judson Herrick's five-hundred-six-page book *The Evolution of Human Nature,* a comprehensive volume analyzing some forms of human behavior in terms of animal and human development with particular reference to psychobiology.[15]

During the early years of retirement, from 1954 through 1958, while assembling his collection of bird brains, Cobb's principal interest in ornithology had to do with instincts. Cobb's interest in instincts was not new, for in 1938 he had thought deeply about the subject when reviewing two of Konrad Lorenz's writings, a monograph in German and a review article in English (129). In 1955 Cobb wrote a review on instincts, comparing the points of view of ethologists,[16] behaviorists, and psychiatrists (362). He said, "Ethologists believe that innate behavior patterns ('instincts') are laid down in the neurological pattern of the brain; that their motor patterns are inhibited by higher nervous mechanisms until the appropriate stimulus ('releaser') is applied to the brain," and added that many American psychologists and zoologists had taken exception to the view of the ethologists. The American workers believed that the concept of instincts as innate was no longer tenable. In his 1955 review Cobb summarized the situation in the following paragraph:

> Many psychologists and zoölogists believe that the concept that "instinctive acts" are innate hereditary forms of behavior is no longer tenable. They believe that the ethologist's description of neuronal patterns, inhibitory mechanisms and releasers is too schematic. They point out that modern students of embryonal development show that from the very beginning the development of the embryo is greatly influenced by environment (374).

On July 3, 1957 the Foundations' Fund for Research in Psychiatry in New Haven made a grant to Cobb for the "Study of the Neurology of Instinctive Behavior." One of the projects he undertook under that grant was physiological work on whether or not pigeons had a sense of smell. In 1826 Audubon had shown that vultures were attracted to dead animals by sight and not by smell, and Darwin's evidence also supported the notion that birds lacked a sense of smell.[17] The plan for studying the sense of smell in pigeons was worked out with Professor B. F. Skinner of the psychology department at Harvard[18] and was carried out in Skinner's laboratory[19] by Wolfgang J. Michelsen, as an honors thesis at Harvard University. Following a plan of study largely laid out by Cobb, Michelsen clearly demonstrated that a pigeon could differentiate between smell and no smell.[20]

Cobb's other writings during his early retirement from 1954 through 1958 dealt either with material already familiar to the reader or were brief expressions of concern regarding social customs. Cobb received the Samuel W. Hamilton award for a prepared lecture on awareness, attention, and the physiology of the brain stem (388). He discussed the importance of monism in his presidential address before the American Psychosomatic Society in 1956 (390). He talked about contemporary developments in the theory and treatment of psychoses at the dedication of the Renard Hospital in St. Louis (375). He published the report of a clinic at which he discussed a patient with persistent ankle pain after orthopedic treatment (361) and he expressed his views on peace of mind (389), the death penalty (401), and admirable qualities of horses (399). He also wrote a poem entitled "Psychosomatic Meteorologist" which read as follows:

> The weather is a living part of me;
> It gets me in the heart and bones and guts.
> A winter rainstorm breaking in the west
> With driven clouds and streaks of sunset sky
> Raises my heart with reminiscences
> Of days on sea and marsh when northers blew
> And brought the wild fowl scudding to the lee.
> Doldrums before a southern hurricane
> With soggy softness make my bowels sink.
> One inhalation of keen mountain air
> Sets me atop the world, inspirited.
> Sometimes in cities, insulated well
> Unknowing of the sky and wind I dwell.
> But even there a storm I can foretell
> Because it makes my old bones ache like hell.

During the second trimester of Cobb's retirement years, from 1959 through 1963, enough specimens of bird brains had been accumulated so that he could make some meaningful studies of comparative anatomy. The work on comparative anatomy occupied him for the remainder of his life and was largely devoted to studies contributing to knowledge of the olfactory system. The first paper to appear in print was on the cerebral axis of the woodcock (421). In his "Excursions Avian" Cobb commented on the brain of the woodcock. He said that Dr. Walter J. Bock, then at the Museum of Comparative Zoölogy at Harvard, had led him to understand that there was a close relationship in any species of bird between the shape of the bill and the rest of the skull related to the posture of the bird when feeding. When Cobb removed the frontal bones of a woodcock at first he found no brain! Later he came upon the brain, almost upside down according to one's ordinary ideas. As he said, "No wonder the folklore in Europe had branded the woodcock as a brainless bird!"

Cobb's experience with the woodcock led to a study of bird postures in relation to the brain-bill angle.[21] The brain-bill angle seemed to indicate a significant phylogenetic change in those shore birds that became progressively more specialized in probing for food with a long bill in wet ground. The eye apparently moved backward as the bill lengthened and the nostril approached the base of the bill. As the eye developed its large size and posterior position it gained space at the expense of the forebrain which tipped backward causing the midbrain and hindbrain to push downward and even slightly forward. Cobb said that the woodcock fed chiefly at night and the eye was relatively enormous. According to Cobb the location of the woodcock's eye had two advantages for the bird. Its posterior location enabled the bird to see better above and to the rear, and it also minimized the risk of the eye getting into the mud. The brain-bill angle of the American woodcock is one hundred seventeen degrees, as compared with forty-seven degrees for the owl, which is a nocturnal predator, and only fifteen degrees for the cormorant, which dives and swims under water for its food (Figure 5).

Cobb's next ornithological publication was on the size of the olfactory lobes in specimens from forty-six species of birds. The study was stimulated by Audubon's and Darwin's belief that birds could not smell and Michelsen's demonstration that at least the pigeon could. Relatively large bulbs tended to correlate with large hippocampal areas in the brain and aquatic habitat. Small olfactory lobes, contrariwise, went with small hippocampal areas and tree living (436). A subsequent article on the comparative anatomy of the avian brain was basically a recapitulation (439).

Retirement

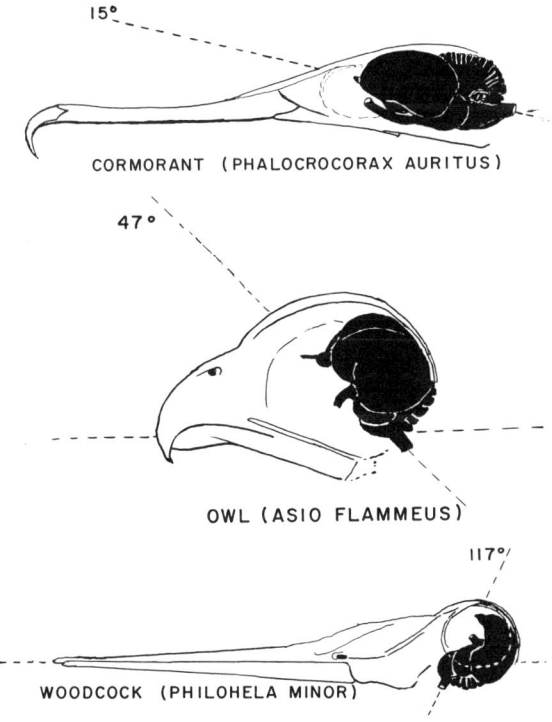

FIGURE 5.—Cobb's observations on the brain-bill angle in three species of birds with different feeding habits.

The final ornithological study published during the mid-period of Cobb's retirement life was on the brain of the hummingbird (465). The study was carried out on a specimen that had been sent from Colorado by Walker Van Riper. Van Riper had conducted an ingenious series of experiments in which he fed a natural population of hummingbirds from specially designed bottles containing syrup that was either pure, contaminated by various flavors, or masked by strong odors. After observing some seven hundred visits to the feeders van Riper concluded that the responses of the species of hummingbird he studied (*Selasphorus platycercus*) in its search for food utilized the senses of sight and taste but not of smell.[22] When Cobb dissected the hummingbird's brain he discovered a well-developed olfactory chamber in the beak and a comparatively small olfactory bulb. Although Cobb did not draw any conclusions from this observation he did note that a wine taster knows whether a wine is sweet or sour by means of his glossopharyngeal nerve complex but he recognizes the vineyard and the vintage through his olfactory nerve.

Other publications in Cobb's mid-retirement period included an obituary of Finesinger (422), an article on behavior in endocrine disorders (438), two papers on psychosomatic medicine (453, 464), and his address at the dedication of the Stanley Cobb laboratories (441), in which he reviewed the reasons for his change of focus from neurology to psychiatry. He said the change had not been difficult because his interest had always been *to study how the brain works and why it often does not work* (Cobb's italics). He remarked, "To me the mind and brain are one: if you study the violin, you must also study the music it makes."

In the same address Cobb recounted his fruitful and largely satisfying years at the Massachusetts General Hospital and attributed the idea of a psychiatric ward to J. Howard Means, the former chief of medicine, adding:

> And now the service is taking on new expansion under Dr. Lindemann, who sees psychiatry with a broad and fresh vision. Problems I was never able to meet are being taken up. There is a remarkable new service for the alcoholic patient; important relationships with the community are being made, and, last but not least, there is this new laboratory for research in psychiatry which is already an active and productive institute under the direction of Gardiner Quarton. Here I am fortunate in being generously given a warm nook in the sun for my old age.

Cobb concluded by discussing his interest in ornithology and recalling the story of the two crates of live albatrosses that had mysteriously arrived in Washington, D.C.

During the final trimester of retirement, from 1964 until his death in 1968, Cobb continued to write primarily on ornithological topics. He collaborated with Frank R. Ervin, Quarton's successor as director of the Stanley Cobb laboratories, and Nancy K. Mello in a study for the navy entitled "Intertectal integration of visual information in pigeon electrophysiological and behavioral observations" (485). Cobb's comments about this paper follow:

> In our laboratory, Dr. N. K. Mello and Dr. Frank R. Ervin were studying sensory physiology by means of electrodes implanted in living brains. The visual system of the pigeon seemed an easy approach to certain problems of learning and memory.[23]

Cobb described the experiments in greater detail, commenting that it was possible with the implanted electrode to pick up responses to a sudden flash of light.[24]

Although Ervin and others in the laboratory were busy with such modern quantitative experimental techniques, Cobb continued to work with what he could learn from comparative anatomy, and he published a number of papers. The first of these was on the avian optic lobe (474). The optic lobe in birds is enormous as compared with that in mammals. It occupies the *tectum mesencephali,* which is the roof of the mid-brain and has a laminated structure. Cobb said, "The fact that such a structure has developed in the avian mid-brain, taken with the fact that birds seem to have little or no neocortex in their forebrains, may help to explain the functional significance of the laminated arrangement." Actually Cobb said that the number of layers and their complex interconnections resembled the arrangement of neurons seen in the visual neocortex of mammals.

In another ornithological study Cobb compared the size of the auditory nucleus with the size of the optic lobe in twenty-seven species of birds (488). The auditory nucleus, or *Torus,* is a part of the optic lobe. Cobb measured the volumes of the auditory nucleus and the entire optic lobe and established ratios for various species. The highest ratio was found in the cave-dwelling oil bird which hardly uses its visual apparatus at all. The lowest ratio was found in birds like the falcon with very highly developed eyesight. Cobb published in the *Archives of Neurology* an article on brain size in which he indicated that the size of the brain was more definitely related to the complexity of an animal's life than to the size of its body (502). Then there were two papers on the brain of the emu. The first was written with Tilly Edinger at the Museum of Comparative Zoölogy in Cambridge (466) and the second by Cobb alone (505). Next to the ostrich the emu is the largest extant bird. It is flightless, lacks a keel on the sternum, and is regarded by many as primitive. Cobb's study of the emu's brain was exhaustive. For the second paper showing the nerve tracts within the brain, he enlisted the help of his former colleague, Yakovlev, in preparing microscopic sections cut across the entire brain. Cobb said he also obtained help from Yakovlev in identifying and naming some of the structures. Cobb did not think that the emu's brain was very compact; so he made comparisons with brains of smaller birds including the tiny hummingbird. He decided that the emu's brain was indeed less compact. Both of the emu papers were published in *Breviora*, the journal of the Museum of Comparative Zoology.

With B. C. Bang of the Johns Hopkins School of Hygiene and Public Health in Baltimore Cobb collaborated on an important comparative study of the olfactory bulb in one hundred eight species of birds (508). Bang had already made a study of the olfactory chambers in the nasal fossa[25] and Cobb had carried out work on the comparative size of the olfactory lobe in forty-six species (436). Bang and Cobb were able by pooling their collections to correlate data on the one hundred eight species. They measured with a millimeter rule the greatest diameter of an olfactory bulb and the greatest diameter of the corresponding cerebral hemisphere. From these figures they established a ratio expressed as percent. Bang and Cobb were cautious in drawing conclusions from their findings. However, in general the higher ratios were in tube-nosed marine birds and the evidence suggested that water birds, marsh dwellers, and waders had a useful olfactory sense. Cobb had a capacity for sifting through masses of data and organizing the material in clear and readable form. He showed this talent in a letter to Betsy Bang written on April 20, 1967:

> I have at last been through the unbelievable mess of data and letters which we have accumulated concerning this paper. I have done my best to boil things down to what is significant. I have rewritten the text in accordance with your corrections and I hope made a satisfactory amalgamation.[26]

Cobb commented on the arrangement of the tabulated data and indicated what observations would be appropriate. It is obvious that he made a great contribution to the paper in its final form.

In his unpublished "Excursions Avian" Cobb reviewed his experiences with research in ornithology.[27] Fortunately, the factual material was preserved in the abridged version which appeared in print (511), but many more personal, yet important, thoughts and feelings were omitted. A final ornithological paper on the swans at Little Compton was edited posthumously by Cobb's friend Alfred Redfield and was submitted to the Rhode Island Audubon Society for publication.[28]

The most widely read article Cobb ever wrote was "Death of a Salt Pond," which appeared in *Audubon Magazine* in May, 1963. It was one of his writings on social issues and more particularly on protection of the environment. He was concerned with the use of insecticides, especially DDT. In 1962, as a mosquito control measure, ponds and marshlands on Cape Cod were sprayed with this insecticide, which

Retirement

proved fatal to crustacea such as fiddler crabs as well as to insect arthropods.

When his own salt pond was sprayed Cobb was furious. His wife wrote the story of his anger and how he transformed it into the most widely read publication of his life:

> Nineteen sixty-two was the summer that Stanley lost his eyesight.[29] We had a great Scandinavian doctor who kept saying, "You will get your vision back. I have seen many cases like this at home in Scandinavia." Stanley did not believe him and was very depressed.
>
> Then came the day at Cotuit when an airplane flew over and sprayed us and the salt pond in front of our cottage with DDT. Stanley was furious. He asked me to call various governmental agencies until we located the person responsible for the spraying. We then left word for him to call back. The call came as evening approached. Sparks flew, and we had our dinner. After dinner, two men arrived and asked to see Stanley. I told them he was not seeing anyone now because of his bad eyes. They told me who they were. Immediately I let Stanley know and he came in. I did not hear the conversation that followed, but I am sure that Stanley did not mince words. When the men departed an hour later all they could say was that they had agreed to disagree about the wisdom of the spray.
>
> Next day Stanley took pen and paper in hand and began to write in letters one-half inch high, carefully keeping the sheets of paper in sequence. I remember Aunt Helen came in, and because I was busy, she undertook to write for him, just what I don't recall. Gradually, during the next few days Stanley discovered that he could write his thoughts in large letters and see what he had written. Then he decided that he needed someone to whom he could talk or even dictate. Finally, I found a Cotuit woman who had previously done secretarial work for Erik Erikson. She was just right, silent when she needed to be, but very attentive, having taken in at one swallow—as it were—my few words about the situation—Stanley's eyes, his strong feelings, and his need to write about the spraying situation. I drove Stanley to the lady's house on several different days. She took much of what Stanley dictated directly on the typewriter. Stanley then took her rough drafts home and edited them. I had no function in this. Stanley and his amenuensis understood each other perfectly.
>
> And so, to make a long story short, Stanley decided to publish what he had written in the Barnstable *Patriot*.
>
> I was in the local grocery in Marston's Mills the night the article came out. When I asked for a copy of the paper the girl who sold it said, "Read that first article. It is very good." She had no notion of why I wanted the paper.
>
> The article was reprinted or quoted all over the Cape and later in Audubon Society publications across the country as far away as Texas. There were more requests for reprints than for anything else Stanley had ever written.
>
> *The Death of a Salt Pond* was not the last thing Stanley wrote, but it was something of vital importance into which he put his whole self.[30]

As a sequel to "The Death of a Salt Pond" Cobb wrote a brief commentary entitled "Death by Poison—One Year Later" (476). It was not until the nineteen eighties that fiddler crabs reappeared in significant numbers.

Because of Cobb's longstanding interest in nature and in conservation of natural resources, he had deep admiration for the pioneer environmentalist, Rachel Carson, whose *Silent Spring* aroused widespread interest and concern. When Rachel Carson died in 1964 Cobb wrote a tribute to her:

To Rachel Carson, who died April 14, 1964

Silent and cold this April dawn for you
No robins pipe the coming of the sun.
Gulls cry, a mourning dove complains.
I'm glad you cannot sense this from your bier.
Your foresight and your courage wakened us
To dedicate our anger and our strength
Against shortsighted poisoners of life,
To resurrect a glorious, singing dawn (483).

Cobb wrote a tract on social problems entitled "Guns for Children" (482) and still another entitled "Human Values and Culture" (489). He also wrote a brief note on the seasons of the year (490) and a prologue for a biography of Austen Fox Riggs which was compiled by the old cadaver-mate from medical school, J. A. Millet, but which was never published. In addition he wrote a number of obituaries including those for his old friends Winthrop Sprague Brooks (499) and Alexander Forbes (506).

Cobb's active and productive life as a departmental chairman, investigator, and teacher, and his continued intellectual activity during retirement were recognized by a number of organizations that bestowed appropriate honors upon him. Because of his breadth of interests and his achievements he was a member of many societies.[31] One would anticipate his membership in the neurological and pathological societies and in the American Medical Association with its component, the Massachusetts Medical Society. However, some of the other memberships were distinct honors, notably the American Society for Clinical Investigation and its august parent organization, the Association of American Physicians. It was also an honor to belong to the Interurban Clinical Club, a small group of highly placed academicians, and the

Medical Exchange Club (page 315). The Medical Exchange Club was a group of twenty very distinguished Boston physicians and surgeons who met monthly at each other's homes for the presentation of scientific papers and for mutual entertainment. It was customary for the host to provide dinner for his guests and to speak on a prepared medical topic afterward. Most of the members were well-to-do, with servants, so that the preparation of the meal presented no particular difficulty. Cobb's gambit was to produce wild duck, which he had shot personally.

Five of the societies to which Cobb belonged honored him with their presidency, the Boston Society of Psychiatry and Neurology in 1938, the Association for Research in Nervous and Mental Diseases in 1941, the American Association of Neuropathology in 1942, the American Neurological Association in 1948, and the American psychosomatic Society in 1955. Cobb was also honored by two medical societies of which he was not president. In 1955 the American Psychopathological Association presented to him their Samuel W. Hamilton Award.[32] As his acceptance address Cobb gave a scholarly paper on "Awareness, Attention, and the Physiology of the Brain Stem" (388).

In Cobb's opinion the greatest honor he ever received was the Kober Medal of the Association of American Physicians. The presentation address at the annual meeting in May, 1956, was given by Cobb's former student and colleague, Harold G. Wolff of Cornell. Wolff reviewed in a sensitive way the many experiences to which Cobb had reacted in working out the various approaches to his extraordinarily creative life (373).

There were other honors that did not come from medical societies.[33] On November 17, 1952, while still chairman of psychiatry at the Massachusetts General Hospital, Cobb was awarded the honorary degree of Doctor of Science at the opening ceremony of the Psychiatric Institute at the University of Maryland. The presentation was made by Cobb's former colleague and the director of the Institute, Jacob E. Finesinger, who, too, reviewed salient aspects of Cobb's life. In summary Finesinger said, "To me, in addition to his other attainments, he is eminent in being a rare human being who has the unique faculty of finding and bringing out the best in those associated with him."

Cobb's next great honor was the Albert Einstein award from Yeshiva University in 1956. He later received a folder of fan mail from all over the world. The actual presentation was something of a disaster. It took place at a fund-raising banquet in New York, and most of the activity of the evening had to do with obtaining substantial pledges from the guests. Cobb had prepared an appropriate acceptance speech, but by the time his turn came, the evening had worn on, and he was asked only to stand up and take a bow. Governor Lehmann of New York was sitting next to him at the head table and saw the work that had gone into preparing the speech. He instantly took in the situation and reassured Cobb with an understanding comment, "It's tough, but these things always happen." Cobb was greatly honored by the award, which carried with it a stipend of one thousand dollars, later used to build an additional room on the house at Little Compton. The medal was embedded in a recess on the closet door, and the addition became known as the Einstein room.

Other honors were the General Leonard Wood Memorial Medal, presented at the seventieth Alumni Day Dinner of the Boston City Hospital Association at the Harvard Club April 25, 1958, and the Salmon Medal, awarded in 1967. It was presented on the occasion of one of the Salmon lectures on December sixth of that year at the New York Academy of Medicine. Cobb's daughter, Helen, represented him at the ceremony.

Mention has already been made of the Stanley Cobb laboratories for research in psychiatry, which were dedicated in October, 1959. Another great memorial was the Stanley Cobb professorship in psychiatry. The Stanley Cobb Fund came into being in 1955 and over a five-year period grew to five hundred thousand dollars.[34] At the Harvard University commencement in 1960 the professorship was formally announced and Cobb received a congratulatory note from President Pusey.[35] In 1962 Peter Booth Dews was appointed as the first occupant of the chair.

The numerous activities, ornithological, investigative, and clinical, with which Cobb filled his retirement years necessitated his living close to his work. Accordingly, he and Betty sold their house in Milton and moved to a modest apartment at 34 Fernald Drive in Cambridge. It was at this time that they also built a small house on a body of water in Little Compton, Rhode Island, adjacent to Carl Binger and his wife and Marian Putnam, their intimate old friends. Although they had originally thought of Little Compton as an ultimate retirement home, Cobb's life was much too active for that. The house there was used almost every weekend spring and fall and twice a month during the winter. Summers were spent in the bunk house and caboose in Cotuit.

The house at Little Compton was planned with economy, comfort, and simplicity in mind. It nestled into the landscape with almost all the fenestration on the south side to obtain a maximum amount of solar heat. Built entirely on one floor, it was an ideal place for Cobb to live when he became progressively more crippled with arthritis. However, the apartment on Fernald Drive in Cambridge was less satisfactory because there were steps in the entry. A chronic infection in Cobb's right knee eventually necessitated an above-the-knee amputation. After that, in 1967, Cobb and his wife moved to a high-rise apartment at 1010 Memorial Drive in Cambridge, but they still continued their frequent visits to Little Compton.

Binger's wife, Chloe, reported on both Cobb's love of nature and his readiness for experimenting with unusual items of food. Chloe Binger said that on one occasion Cobb and his wife Betty had the pleasure of making a game pie. It was at the time when Route 24 between Boston and Fall River was just being opened. A woman, a friend of the Cobbs, driving on the new highway, accidentally ran into a pheasant and killed it. The lady felt guilty about having hit the pheasant, but she thought little was to be gained by allowing it to disintegrate by the side of the road, so she picked it up and took it to Cobb to put in the refrigerator. At about the same time, one of the residents of Little Compton was trying to naturalize the Chukka partridge, a strikingly beautiful and extremely tame bird, which had probably originated in India. The Chukka partridges were so tame that they danced around in people's birdbaths and seemed to have inadequate anxiety for their own protection. One day a Chukka partridge entered the Cobbs' living room, and Stanley Cobb saw that its lower jaw had been shot away. Inasmuch as the bird had no chance of survival, Cobb wrung its neck and put it in the refrigerator alongside the pheasant. Another day a starling flew down the chimney. Cobb ran for his crab net and pranced around the living room in hot pursuit, finally entrapping the starling. He wrung its neck and put the starling in the refrigerator, too. Then Cobb and his wife proceeded to make a game pie out of the three birds that had arrived under such unusual circumstances.

Chloe Binger related another incident concerning Cobb's broadminded eating habits. She told a story about finding a snapping turtle in her driveway. Snapping turtles were a menace at Little Compton, being so numerous that one had to be careful about trailing one's fingers in the water when rowing or canoeing. She said she saw a brown living object in her driveway one day and knew it could not be a raccoon or a woodchuck because those animals would go on across the road quickly. It turned out to be a snapping turtle. She covered it with a bushel basket, weighted down with a large rock, then called Stanley Cobb. Cobb showed up with a shotgun and shot off the snapping turtle's head. After that he carried the body to the garbage ditch and covered it over lightly with earth. The following morning, when the Bingers' son, David, took the family garbage to the pit, he discovered that during the night the snapping turtle had turned a circle, partly uncovering itself, and had laid an egg. David covered it again and went on his way. By the following morning the snapping turtle had made a full circle and laid a total of thirteen eggs. When Cobb was told about it, he came over, amazed, picked up the eggs, took them home, and ate them.[36]

Even as Cobb's health deteriorated he was able to continue his frequent trips to Little Compton. There he could sit in his living room, looking out over the pond, and with his telescope study the swans, geese, and herons. However, during the last few months of his life he was aware of some intellectual deficits and was careful not to publish anything he might regret. He had a prostate operation in the spring of 1967 and later a small stroke. After that he asked Seymour Kety, who came to Boston to head the Stanley Cobb laboratories at that time, if he would review and critique any papers that Cobb wrote, and Kety agreed.

When Cobb died on February 8, 1968, he was in a delirium. His wife, who was sitting near him, asked, "How are you feeling, my dearest?" Cobb's reply was, "Can't you see I am delirious?" In his delirium he kept calling, "Pull me out." It seemed to one who was there with him that he felt as if he were falling down a hole.[37] He was temporarily reassured by holding on to the hands of a family member, but then again, after a time, he would cry, "Pull me out!" When Cobb was young, his mother, an anxious woman, had been afraid of the dark and had forbidden her children out of the house after dark. Also, there were seven shallow wells on the property where the family lived, and all these wells had been covered over, so that the children could not fall down them. It seemed possible that fear of falling down a well had been instilled by his mother when Cobb was a very small child.

After Cobb's death, his body was examined by autopsy at the Massachusetts General Hospital.[38] The examination revealed in addition to advanced rheumatoid arthritis a diffuse disorder of supporting con-

Retirement

nective tissue called Sjøgren's disease, which is often seen as a complication of arthritis but may give rise to arthritis as one of its own manifestations. Examination of the kidneys revealed anyloidosis, a waxy degeneration which sometimes follows a long-standing chronic infectious process and which undoubtedly contributed to Cobb's mental confusion at the end.

A service was held in the Memorial Chapel in the Harvard Yard. Officiating were the Reverend Ralph D. Helverson, minister of the First Parish (Unitarian) Church in Cambridge, and the Reverend Charles P. Price, the University Chaplain. Cobb's old friends, Penfield and Binger, gave prepared addresses about Cobb's life. The ushers for the service were all grandchildren: John Stanley Cobb, Peter Cobb, Elijah Cobb, Lauren Cobb, Nathan Cobb, Stanley Cobb Solomon, and John Cobb Solomon. Nineteen hundred sixty-eight was just before the peak of the hippie movement in this country. Cobb's daughter, Helen, was embarrassed because she could not get her Solomon sons to wear appropriate clothing for the service. They did manage to wear jackets over their blue jeans. Imagine her relief at the service when she discovered that her brothers' sons were even more casually attired than her own.

The service was conducted at the university chapel in part, no doubt, because of Cobb's widespread recognition in the academic world, but in part, too, because he had no strong roots in any denominational religious organization. He and his wife were nominal members of the First Parish Church in Cambridge (Unitarian) but he rarely attended religious service.

In the fiftieth anniversary report of his Harvard class Cobb said that he had seen a good deal of suffering from the disheartening diseases encountered in neurology yet somehow had been borne up by the satisfactions of research and teaching. He commented, "Passing on this experience to young men gives a joy akin to parenthood. Matching wits with them keeps one young." He then recounted once again his understanding of monism, the unitary concept of the universe. He emphasized that monism left room for such concepts as order and directiveness, which could not yet be explained.

In the field of religion per se, he said that with the passage of time he had become more definite. In the fiftieth anniversary report he wrote:

> In all humility, facing the vastness of the universe, I believe that the *directiveness* which I see in the evolutionary drive toward making whole organisms and whole societies is God. I appreciate the forms and rituals of religion;

> they give solace and solidarity. It is enough immortality for me if I may become even a very small part of advancing wisdom, hoping that I have done my bit to make the world a better place.[39]

Although intellectually Cobb saw religion in terms of the brain and the mind, he also had in him a touch of Eastern mysticism. All his life he experienced from to time a sense of oneness with nature akin to Zen.

Betty Cobb reported that one night about three years before Cobb died, she and he attended a small dinner party in Cambridge to meet a Zen Buddhist Master. The Zen Master was invited to tell the guests something about his experiences and Cobb listened attentively all evening. The next day, when driving to Little Compton, Betty asked Cobb what he thought of the Zen Master's comments.

> Hell, he said, I've known all about that for years. I've known about it *first* hand since I was a kid—when I've been alone in the woods or marsh—everything quiet around us—the feeling comes of really being *one* with nature—almost a part of it—sounds, smells, sights. Sometimes even now at sunset in Little Compton when I go down to the marsh and sit there quietly alone—listening—I still can get that feeling—the *oneness of nature*—being a part of it, sights, sounds, and smells.[40]

Mrs. Cobb went on to say that her experience in the car that day left an indelible impression on her mind. She did not put Cobb's comments on paper, however, until several years later when something she read reminded her of the incident. She said Cobb spoke from the very pit of his being and his voice cracked in trying to tell of his intense feelings. She recalled that the last previous occasion when she had heard in Cobb's voice the expression of that emotion was when he was delivering the acceptance speech of the Kober Medal after Harold Wolff's presentation. It was a crowded occasion, and Mrs. Cobb sat in a chair which had been slipped in so that she could be very near to her husband. She said she was afraid that he would break down.

Betty Cobb said that Wordsworth's poem, "The Rainbow," was one of Stanley's favorites and often he would be heard reciting to himself the first six lines:

> My heart leaps up when I behold
> A rainbow in the sky:
> So was it when my life began;
> So is it now I am a man;
> So be it when I shall grow old,
> Or let me die![41]

Mrs. Cobb said that when her husband was a boy his mother often saw him sitting silently before a sunset. Cobb told his wife that at such times he felt he was becoming a part of the world of nature. The great blue heron would be crossing the marsh and other birds would be returning to their nests. Although she had been married to him for fifty years, Mrs. Cobb said she never previously recognized the parallel between his need for closeness to nature and the Zen Buddhist tradition.

Cobb's retirement years, particularly because of his failing health, had their frustrations, and at times he had a sense of failure because he did not feel that his psychiatric service had been fully integrated into the mainsream of medical practice. On the other hand, he took delight from ornithology, which was both his occupation and his hobby, and he continued his watercolor painting, usually making pictures of birds or other natural themes. Correspondence with old friends and the enjoyment of family life were also rewarding compensations. Moreover, he had an inner faith, though not always expressed in traditional religious terms, of accomplishment along the lines determined by his true self. There was no sham about him.

Appendixes

Major Sources Employed
in Compiling This Work

Notes

Index

APPENDIX A

Diagram of Stanley Cobb's Ancestry
The Cobb Family Tree

Albert Adams Cobb
B. Apr. 12, 1830, Boston
M. Aug. 28, 1851, Brookline
D. July 6, 1900, Brookline
R. Brookline

John Candler Cobb
B. May 10, 1858, Brookline
M. Dec. 9, 1879, New York City
D. Dec. 30, 1933, Milton
R. Brookline, Milton

Mary Russell Candler
B. Feb. 26, 1830, Boston
D. Dec. 25, 1911, Brookline

Stanley Cobb, M.D.
B. Dec. 10, 1887, Brookline
D. Feb. 25, 1968, Cambridge

Augustus F. Smith
B. Oct. 3, 1819, Victor, N.Y.
M. May 22, 1844, New York City
D. July 6, 1876, Fort Washington, N.Y.
R. Rochester and New York City

Leonore Smith
B. June 16, 1858, Ft. Washington, N.Y.
D. April 30, 1947, Milton

Lucy Ann Elliot
B. Sept. 26, 1819, Woodstock, N.Y.
D. Nov. 8, 1870, Ft. Washington, N.Y.

Henry Cobb
B. June 23, 1798, Camden, Me.
M. Dec. 22, 1822, Charlestown
D. Aug. 20, 1872, Amherst
R. Lynn, Boston, Amherst

Thomas Cobb
B. about 1762
M. 1788 Wiscasset, Me.
D. before 1848
R. Camden and China, Me., Lynn, Ma.

Lucy Smith
B. probably 1770
D. April 23, 1848, aged 78.
R. Lynn, Ma.

John Adams
Birthdate unknown
M. Feb. 11, 1798
D. Before 1804
R. Beverley

Augusta Adams
B. Dec. 7, 1802, Beverley
D. Feb. 3, 1886, Salt Lake City, Utah

Mary Ives
B. June 2, 1775, Beverley
D. Dec. 22, 1816, Beverley

John Candler
B. Nov. 3, 1764
M. Feb. 11, 1790
D. Sept. 26, 1848, Marblehead

John Candler, Jr.
B. Feb. 12, 1792, Marblehead
M. (2) Nov. 4, 1824, Boston
D. Aug. 23, 1842
R. Boston and Marblehead

Abigail Hulin (Russell)
Baptized Nov. 14, 1758
D. June 21, 1830, Marblehead

Lot Wheelwright
B. June 17, 1770
M. Dec. 10, 1793
D. Sept. 2, 1848
R. Boston

Susan Wheelwright
B. Oct. 23, 1798, Boston
D. Aug. 23, 1882, Brookline

Susanna Wilson
B. April 18, 1771, West Cambridge
D. May 30, 1830, Newton

Gilbert Smith
B. Jan. 7, 1756
M. Jan. 3, 1783
D. Mar. 10, 1795
R. Otego and Salem, N.Y.

Dr. Archelaus Green Smith
B. June 10, 1792, Otego, N.Y.
M. Feb. 3, 1814, Victor, N.Y.
D. June 19, 1850, Victor, N.Y.
R. Rochester and New York City

Delilah Bundy
B. Sept. 7, 1758, Preston, Conn.
D. Mar. 24, 1846, Victor, N.Y.

Jared Boughton
B. Feb. 19, 1766
M. 1787
D. Feb. 10, 1852
R. Stockbridge, Ma. and Victor, N.Y.

Melania Boughton
B. Oct. 11, 1789, Stockbridge
D. July 7, 1888, Shrewsbury, N.J.

Olive Stone
B. Jan. 2, 1790
D. Jan. 17, 1849
R. Stockbridge

David Eliot
B. June 8, 1752
M. Nov. 19, 1789
D. Jan. 11, 1793
R. Mason and Dublin, N.H.

Dr. Daniel Elliot
B. Oct. 10, 1792, Dublin, N.H.
M. Oct. 6, 1818, New York City
D. Mar. 30, 1868, New York City
R. Woodstock, N.Y. and N.Y.C.

Lucy Emery (Campbell)
No genealogical data

Samuel Greeley
B. Sept. 29, 1752
M. Nov. 9, 1779
D. Sept. 26, 1798
R. Hudson, N.Y. and Wilton, N.H.

Abigail Greeley
B. May 12, 1793, Wilton, N.H.
D. Mar. 3, 1878, Stonington, Conn.

Olive Reed
B. July 23, 1757
D. Feb. 23, 1811, Wilton, N.H.

APPENDIX B

Bibliography of the Published Writings of Stanley Cobb

(Unsigned articles and reviews have been verified from manuscripts in Dr. Cobb's papers in the Harvard Medical Archives.)

1. Cobb, S. "Nesting of a golden-crowned kinglet in Massachusetts." *American Ornithology*, IV (1904) 138–140.
2. Cobb, S. "A little black rail in Massachusetts." *Bird-Lore*, VIII (1906) 138–140.
3. Castle, W. E., Walter, H. E., Mullenix, R. C. and Cobb, S. *Studies of inheritance in rabbits*. (Washington, Carnegie Institution, 1909, Publication no. 114).
4. Brooks, W. S. and Cobb, S. "Notes from Eastern Alberta." *The Auk*, XXVIII (1911) 465–469.
5. Cobb, S. "Egrets (Herodias egretta) in Massachusetts." *The Auk*, XXVIII (1911) 482.
6. Smith, R. M. and Cobb, S. "A clinical and pathological study of 100 infants." *Archives of Pediatrics*, XXXII (1915) 434–451.
7. Cobb, S. "Hemangioma of the spinal cord associated with skin naevi of the same metamere." *Archives of Surgery*, XXXVII (1915) 641–649.
8. Cobb, S., Bailey, A. A. and Holtz, P. R. "On the genesis and inhibition of extensor rigidity." *American Journal of Physiology*, XLIV (1917) 239–258.
9. Cobb, S. "Electromyographic studies of clonus." *Johns Hopkins Hospital Bulletin*, XXIX (1918) 247–266.
10. Cobb, S. "A Note on the supposed relation of the sympathetic nerves to decerebrate rigidity, muscle tone and tendon reflexes." *American Journal of Physiology*, XLVI (1918) 478–482.
11. Cobb, S. "An electromyographic study of chorea." *Johns Hopkins Hospital Bulletin*, XXX (1919) 336–341.
12. Cobb, S. "Theories of muscle tone." *Neuro-Surgical Exchange*, I (1919) 5.
13. Cobb S. "Applications of psychiatry to industrial hygiene," *Journal of Industrial Hygiene*, I (1919) 343–347.

Appendix B: Bibliography 343

14 Cobb, S. "Cutaneous sensibility in cases of peripheral nerve injury: epicritic and protopathic hypothesis of Head untenable." *Archives of Neurology and Psychiatry,* II (1919) 505–517.
15 Cobb, S. *Notes on sensory examinations.* Cape May, N.J., January 30, 1919.
16 Cobb, S. "Midsummer birds in the Catskill Mountains." *The Auk,* XXXVII (1920) 46–49.
17 Cobb, S. "The treatment of the psychoneurotic." *Medical Clinics of North America,* III (1920) 1137–1155.
18 Cobb, S. and Scarlett, H. W. "A report of eleven cases of cervical sympathetic nerve injury, causing the oculopupillary syndrome." *Archives of Neurology and Psychiatry,* III (1920) 636–653.
19 Cobb, S. "Electromyographic studies of muscles during hysterical contraction." *Archives of Neurology and Psychiatry,* IV (1920) 8–15.
20 Cobb, S. "Spastic paralysis in children." *Medical Clinics of North America,* IV (1920) 417–436.
21 Forbes, A., Cobb, S. and Cattell, M. "An electrocardiogram and an electromyogram in an elephant." *American Journal of Physiology,* LV (1921) 385–389.
22 Cobb, S. "Some neurologic aspects of chorea." *Medical Clinics of North America,* IV (1921) 1863–1870.
23 Cobb, S. and Coleman, C. C. "The course of recovery following trauma of the spinal cord." *Archives of Surgery,* III (1921) 132–139.
24 Cobb, S. and Parmenter, D. C. "Headache." *Journal of Industrial Hygiene,* III (1921) 173–178.
25 Cobb, S. "A report on the brief neuropsychiatric examination of 1,141 students." *Journal of Industrial Hygiene,* III (1922) 309–315.
26 Uyematzu, S. and Cobb, S. "Preliminary report on experimental convulsions." *Archives of Neurology and Psychiatry,* VII (1922) 660–663.
27 Cobb, S. "Electromyographic studies of paralysis agitans." *Archives of Neurology and Psychiatry,* VIII (1922) 247–264.
28 Cobb, S. "A case of epilepsy with a general discussion of the pathology." *Medical Clinics of North America,* V (1922) 1403–1420.
29 Forbes, A., Cobb, S. and Cattell, H. "Electrical studies in mammalian reflexes: III. Immediate changes in the flexion reflex after spinal transection." *American Journal of Physiology,* LXV (1923) 30–44.
30 Cobb, S. and Forbes, A. "Electromyographic studies of muscular fatigue in man." *American Journal of Physiology,* LXV (1923) 234–251.
31 Mitchell, B. C. and Cobb, S. "Social work with traumatic neuroses." *Journal of Nervous and Mental Disease,* LVIII (1923) 105–123.
32 Cobb, S. "Studies in mammalian neuropathology. I. Cerebral cholesteatoma in the horse." *Journal of Mammalogy,* IV (1923) 221–223.
33 Cobb, S. "A fee list from the papers of Archelaus Green Smith, M.D. (1792 to 1850)." *Boston Medical and Surgical Journal,* CLXXXIX (1923) 641–645.

34 MacDonald, M. E. and Cobb, S. "Intracranial pressure changes during experimental convulsions." *Journal of Neurology and Psychopathology,* IV (1923) 228–235.
35 Cobb, S. "Electromyographic studies of experimental convulsions." *Brain,* XLVII (1924) 69–75.
36 Forbes, H. S., Cobb, S. and Fremont-Smith, F. "Cerebral edema and headache following carbon monoxide asphyxia." *Archives of Neurology and Psychiatry,* XI (1924) 264–281.
37 Wilson, S. A. K. and Cobb, S. "Mesencephalitis syphilitica." *Journal of Neurology and Psychopathology,* V (1924) 44–60.
38 Cobb, S. "On the application of micrometry to the study of the area striata." *Journal für Psychologie und Neurologie,* XXXI (1925) 261–274.
39 Bielschowsky, M. and Cobb, S. "A method for intra-vital staining with silver ammonium oxide solution." *Journal für Psychologie und Neurologie,* XXXI (1925) 301–304.
40 Cobb, S. "Review of the tonus of skeletal muscle." *Physiological Reviews,* V (1925) 518–550.
41 Cobb, S. *Outline of neuropathology for students of general medicine,* (Boston, Department of Neuropathology, Harvard Medical School, 1926).
42 Forbes, A. and Cobb, S. "Physiology of sympathetic nervous system in relation to certain surgical problems." *Journal of the American Medical Association,* LXXXVI (1926) 1884–1886.
43 Cobb, S. and Munro, D. "Two cases of brain tumor." *Boston Medical and Surgical Journal,* CXCVI (1927) 772–773.
44 Schaltenbrandt, G. and Cobb, S. "Bulbokapninkatalepsie und Lokalanästhesie bei Grosshirnoperationen im Tierversuch." *Pflügers Archiv für die gesamte Physiologie,* CCXVIII (1927) 475–476.
45 Cobb, S. and Talbott, J. H. "Studies in cerebral circulation. II. A quantitative study of cerebral capillaries." *Transactions of the Association of American Physicians,* XLII (1927) 255–262.
46 Cobb, S. Review of *Epilepsie—vergleichende Pathogenese, Erscheinungen, Behandlungen,* by L. J. J. Muskens. *Archives of Neurology and Psychiatry,* XVII (1927) 714–717. Unsigned.
47 Epstein, S. H., Farnham, R. K. and Cobb, S. "The use of salicylates in the treatment of chronic epidemic encephalitis." *Boston Medical and Surgical Journal,* CXCVII (1928) 1552–1556.
48 Lennox, W. G. and Cobb, S. "Epilepsy, from the standpoint of physiology and treatment." *Medicine,* VII (1928) 105–290. Published also as Medicine Monographs, XIV (Baltimore, Williams and Wilkins, 1928).
49 Cobb, S. "Physiology, psychiatry and the inhibitions." *Archives of Neurology and Psychiatry,* XIX (1928) 981–996.
50 Lennox, W. G. and Cobb, S. "Studies in epilepsy. VIII. The clinical effect of fasting." *Archives of Neurology and Psychiatry,* volume XX (1928) 771–779.

Appendix B: Bibliography

51 Cobb, S. "Cerebellar atrophy in cat." *Archives of Neurology and Psychiatry,* XIX (1928) 931–932.
52 Pressey, H. E. and Cobb, S. "Observations on the spinal cord of phocaena." *Journal of Comparative Neurology,* XLVII (1928) 75–83.
53 Wolff, H. G., Keutmann, H. and Cobb, S. "The electromyogram in myasthenia gravis." *Brain* (1928) 508–519.
54 Cobb, S. "The cry of the geese." *The Open Road,* November, 1928, p. 17.
55 Wolff, H. G., Reed, W. P. and Cobb, S. "Changes in interstitial cells of the brain with morphine intoxication." *Archives of Neurology and Psychiatry,* XXI (1929) 1387–1399.
56 Lennox, W. G. and Cobb, S. "The relation of certain physicochemical processes to epileptiform seizures." *American Journal of Psychiatry,* VIII (1929) 837–847.
57 Cobb, S. "Kaiser Wilhelm Society for the advancement of science; dedication of the Institute for Research in Psychiatry in Munich." *Archives of Neurology and Psychiatry,* XXI (1929) 704–710.
58 Cobb, S. "The cerebral circulation. VIII. A quantitative study of the capillaries in the hippocampus." *Archives of Surgery,* XVIII (1929) 1200–1209.
59 Talbott, J. H., Wolff, H. G. and Cobb, S. "The cerebral circulation. VII. Changes in cerebral capillary bed formation following cervical sympathectomy." *Archives of Neurology and Psychiatry,* XXI (1929) 1102–1106.
60 Forbes, H. S., Wolff, H. G. and Cobb, S. "The cerebral circulation. X. The action of histamine." *American Journal of Physiology,* LXXXIX (1929) 266–272.
61 Schaltenbrandt, G. and Cobb, S. "Beobachtungen an halbseitigen Thalamuskatzen und Striatumkatzen sowie nach halbseitiger Extirpation des Frontal- oder Occipitalpoles." *Pflügers Archiv für die gesamte Physiologie des Menschen und der Tiere,* CCXXII (1929) 589–612.
62 Cobb, S. "The cerebral circulation. IX. The relationship of the cervical sympathetic nerves to cerebral blood supply." *American Journal of the Medical Sciences,* CLXXVIII (1929) 528–535.
63 Cobb, S. and Hubbard, J. P. "Cerebral hemorrhage from venous and capillary stasis; a report of five cases with autopsy." *American Journal of the Medical Sciences,* CLXXVIII (1929) 693–708. Published also in the *Transactions of the Association of American Physicians,* XLIV (1929 349–377.
64 Cobb, S. *An outline of neuropathology for students of general medicine* (Cambridge, Harvard University Press, 1929).
65 Fremont-Smith, F., Putnam, T. J. and Cobb, S. "Forced drainage of the central nervous system, its effect on the blood and on the cerebrospinal fluid." *Archives of Neurology and Psychiatry,* XXIII (1930) 219–226.
66 Gildea, E. F. and Cobb, S. "The effects of anemia on the cerebral cortex

of the cat." *Archives of Neurology and Psychiatry*, XXIII (1930) 876–903.
67 Crothers, B. and Cobb, S. "Report of a case of progressive athetosis with lesions in the basal ganglia." *New England Journal of Medicine*, CCIII (1930) 213–218.
68 Cobb, S. and Munro, D. "The Neurological Unit, Boston City Hospital." *Bulletin of the Harvard Medical Alumni Association*, V (1930) 3–8.
69 Morrison, R., Weeks, A. and Cobb, S. "Histopathology of different types of electric shock on mammalian brains." *Journal of Industrial Hygiene*, XII (1930) 324–337, 364–380.
70 Cobb, S. "The cerebral circulation. XIII. The question of 'end-arteries: of the brain and the mechanism of infarction'." *Archives of Neurology and Psychiatry*, XXV (1931) 273–280.
71 Schaltenbrandt, G. and Cobb, S. "Clinical and anatomical studies on two cats without neocortex." *Brain*, LIII (1931) 449–488.
72 Cobb, S. "A report of plans and progress in the investigation of convulsions at the Harvard Medical School." In *Epilepsy and the Convulsive State*, published by the Association for Mental and Nervous Diseases (Baltimore, Williams and Wilkins, 1931, v. VII, pp. 176–181).
73 Cobb, S. and Lennox, W. G. "The non-institutional epileptic. A preliminary report." In *Epilepsy and the Convulsive State*, published by the Association for Mental and Nervous Diseases (Baltimore, Williams and Wilkins, 1931, v. VII, pp. 358–372).
74 Cobb, S. and Fremont-Smith, F. "The cerebral circulation: XVI. Changes in the retinal circulation and in the pressure of the cerebrospinal fluid during inhalation of a mixture of carbon dioxide and oxygen." *Archives of Neurology and Psychiatry*, XXVI (1931) 731–736.
75 Finesinger, J. E. and Cobb, S. "Demonstration of cerebral circulation; effect of caffeine sodiobenzoate on the diameter of the pial vessels during amytal anesthesia." *Transactions of the American Neurological Association*, LVII (1931) 441–443.
76 Cobb, S. *Neuropathology Outline. I. Anatomical and Physiological Review. II. Principal Disorders of the Nervous System.* (Boston, Harvard Medical School, 1932).
77 Yakovlev, P. I. and Cobb, S. "Hepato-lenticular degeneration. Report of a case with autopsy." *New England Journal of Medicine*, CCVI (1932) 207–211.
78 Cobb, S. "The cerebrospinal blood vessels." Section XII in *Cytology and Cellular Pathology of the Nervous System*, edited by Wilder Penfield (New York, P. B. Hoeber, 1932, v. II, pp. 575–610).
79 Cobb, S. "Pathological physiology of the nervous system." Chapter XIX in Blumer, G., *Practitioner's Library of Medicine and Surgery* (New York, D. Appleton, 1932, v. I, pp. 1029–1071).
80 Cobb, S. "Causes of epilepsy." *Archives of Neurology and Psychiatry*, XXVII (1932) 1245–1256.

Appendix B: Bibliography

81 Cobb, S. and Lennox, W. G. "The work of the Harvard Epilepsy Commission." *Harvard Medical Alumni Bulletin,* VI (1932) 55–58.
82 Cobb, S. and Lennox, W. G. "Epilepsy." Chapter XXX of *Oxford Medicine* (New York, Oxford University Press, 1932, v. VI, pp. 893–916).
83 Cobb, S and Wolff, H. G. "Muscle tonus. A critical review based on work presented at the International Neurological Congress, Bern, Switzerland, 1931." *Archives of Neurology and Psychiatry,* XXVIII (1932) 661–678.
84 Cobb, S. and Finesinger, J. E. "Cerebral circulation. XIX. The vagal pathway of the vasodilator impulses." *Archives of Neurology and Psychiatry,* XXVIII (1932) 1243–1256.
85 Cobb, S. and Blain, D. "Arteriosclerosis of the brain and spinal cord." Chapter 14 in *Arteriosclerosis, a Survey of the Problem,* edited by Edmund V. Cowdry (New York, Macmillan Co., 1933, pp. 397–429).
86 Cobb, S. "Az agy vérkeringése és az u.n. agyi végartériák és az erek elágazasanak kérdese." *Vidéki Orvosok és Gyógyszerészek Lapja,* II (1933) 1–10.
87 Minot, G. R., Strauss, M. B. and Cobb, S. "'Alcoholic' polyneuritis: dietary deficiency as a factor in its production." *New England Journal of Medicine,* CCVIII (1933) 1244–1249.
88 Lennox, W. G. and Cobb, S. "Epilepsy. XIII. Aura in epilepsy; a statistical review of 1,359 cases." *Archives of Neurology and Psychiatry,* XXX (1933) 374–387.
89 Cobb, S. "The cerebral circulation. XXV. Remarks on clinical physiology." *Annals of Internal Medicine,* XII (1933) 292–302.
90 Finesinger, J. E. and Cobb, S. "Cerebral circulation. XXVII. Action of the pial arteries of the convulsants caffeine, absinth, camphor and picrotoxin." *Archives of Neurology and Psychiatry,* XXX (1933) 980–1002.
91 Cobb, S. "Golden eyes." *The Hartford Daily Courant,* March 12, 1933, p. 2.
92 Cobb, S. and Morrison, L. R. Review of *Die Schädigungen des Nervensystems durch technische Elektrizität,* by Friedrich Panse. *Archives of Neurology and Psychiatry,* XXIX (1933) 682. Unsigned.
93 Cobb, S. "The cerebral circulation. XXVI. Cerebral anemia: a discussion of the mechanism and a case report." *American Journal of Psychiatry,* XIII (1934) 947–955.
94 Canavan, M. M., Cobb, S., and Drinker, C. K. "Chronic manganese poisoning; report of a case, with autopsy." *Archives of Neurology and Psychiatry,* XXXII (1934) 501–512.
95 Canavan, M. M., Cobb, S. and Drinker, C. K. "Mangen-vergiftung, chronische, gewerbliche." In *Sammlung von Vergiftungfällen* (Berlin, F. C. W. Vogel, 1934, v. V, pp. 197–198).
96 Cobb, S. "Problems in cerebral anatomy and physiology." Section III, chapter I in *The Problem of Mental Disorder,* a study undertaken by the

Committee, Psychiatric Investigations, National Research Council (New York, McGraw-Hill, 1934, pp. 111–119.)

97 Cobb, S. and Coggeshall, H. G. "Neuritis." *Journal of the American Medical Association,* CIII (1934) 1608–1617.

98 Cobb, S. "On first opening Gordon's package." *The Lyric,* XIII (1934) 55.

99 Cobb, S. and Mixter, W. J. "Lingual spasm." *Annals of Surgery,* CI (1935) 49–55.

100 Finesinger, J. S. and Cobb, S. "The cerebral circulation. XXXIV. The action of narcotic drugs on the pial vessels." *Journal of Pharmacology and Experimental Therapeutics,* LIII (1935) 1–33.

101 Aring, C. D. and Cobb, S. "The muscular atrophies and allied disorders." *Medicine,* XIV (1935) 77–118.

102 Gildea, M. C-L., Castle, W. B., Gildea, E. and Cobb, S. "Neuropathology of experimental vitamin deficiency; a report of four series of dogs maintained on diets deficient in the B vitamins." *American Journal of Pathology,* XI (1935) 669–680.

103 Cobb, S. "The material dealt with by the neurophysiologist in the study of personality." *American Journal of Psychiatry,* XCII (1935) 301–312.

104 Cobb, S. "Review of neuropsychiatry." *Archives of Internal Medicine,* LVI (1935) 1287–1297.

105 Cobb, S. "Integration in the nervous system, as exemplified by locomotion." *Proceedings of the California Academy of Medicine,* V (1935–1936) 111–123.

106 Cobb, S. "Concerning fits." *Medical Clinics of North America,* XIX (1936) 1583–1595.

107 Cobb, S. *Neuropathology outline* (Boston, Harvard Medical School, 1936).

108 Cobb, S. and Finesinger, J. E. "The psychiatric unit at the Massachusetts General Hospital." *Monthly Bulletin of the Massachusetts Society for Mental Hygiene,* XV (1936) 1–3.

109 Cobb, S. "Review of neurology and psychiatry for 1935–1936." *Archives of Internal Medicine,* LVIII (1936) 1111–1123.

110 Cobb, S. *A Preface to Nervous Diseases* (Baltimore, William Wood, 1937). Published in 2d ed. under title *Foundations of Neuropsychiatry* (Baltimore, Williams & Wilkins, 1941).

111 Cobb, S. and Forbes, H. S. "The cerebral circulation." *New England Journal of Medicine,* CCXVI (1937) 99–102.

112 Forbes, H. S., Nason, G. I., Cobb, S. and Wortman, R. C. "Cerebral circulation. XLV. Vasodilation in the pia following stimulation of the geniculate ganglion." *Archives of Neurology and Psychiatry,* XXXVII (1937) 776–781.

113 Cobb, S. "Shock therapy." *New England Journal of Medicine,* CCXVII (1937) 195–196.

114 Forbes, H. S. and Cobb, S. "Vasomotor control of cerebral vessels." Chapter III in *The Circulation of the Brain and Spinal Cord,* edited by

Appendix B: Bibliography 349

Stanley Cobb (Baltimore, Williams and Wilkins, 1938, pp. 201–217; Volume XVIII of the *Proceedings of the Association for Research in Nervous and Mental Diseases,* 1937).

115 Cobb, S. "Integración en el sistema nervioso, demonstrada por la locomoción." *Archivos Argentinos de Neurologiá,* XVII (1937) 45–55. A translation of no. 105.

116 Cobb, S. "Review of neuropsychiatry for 1937." *Archives of Internal Medicine,* LX (1937) 1098–1110.

117 Cobb, S. Abstract of "Differential oxygen uptake of regions of limulus optic nerve as related to distance from the sense organ," by Rita Gutman. *Archives of Neurology and Psychiatry,* XXXVIII (1937) 143.

118 Cobb, S. Abstract of "The changes in the cells of the striated ducts of the cat's submaxillary gland after autonomic stimulation and nerve section," by H. E. Rawlinson. *Archives of Neurology and Psychiatry,* XXXVIII (1937) 1070.

119 Cobb, S. Abstract of "The caudal level of termination of the spinal cord in American whites and American negroes," by J. H. Needles. *Archives of Neurology and Psychiatry,* XXXVIII (1937) 667.

120 Cobb, S. Review of *Die Epilepsie des Kindesalters,* by Eugen Schreck. *American Journal of Psychiatry,* XCIV (1937–1938) 1474.

121 Cobb, S. and Forbes, H. S. "Cerebral circulation. A critical discussion of the symposium." Chapter XXVII in *The Circulation of the Brain and Spinal Cord,* edited by Stanley Cobb (Baltimore, Williams and Wilkins, 1938, pp. 710–752; Volume XVIII of the *Proceedings of the Association for Research in Nervous and Mental Diseases,* 1937).

122 Cobb, S. and McDermott, N. T. "Postoperative psychosis." *Medical Clinics of North America,* XXII (1938) 569–576.

123 Talbott, J. H., Cobb, S., Coombs, F. S., Cohen, M. E. and Consolazio, W. V. "Acid-base balance of the blood in a patient with hysterical hyperventilation." *Archives of Neurology and Psychiatry,* XXXIX (1938) 973–987.

124 Forbes, H. S. and Cobb, S. "Vasomotor control of cerebral vessels." *Brain,* LXI (1938) 221–233.

125 Cobb, S. "Review of neuropsychiatry for 1938." *Archives of Internal Medicine,* LXII (1938) 883–899.

126 Cobb, S., Cohen, M. E. and Ney, J. "Anticonvulsive action of vital dyes." *Archives of Neurology and Psychiatry,* XL (1938) 1156–1177.

127 Cobb, S. Draper, G. and Meyer, A. "James Ramsay Hunt, 1894–1937." *Transactions of the Association of American Physicians,* LIIII (1938) 12–13.

128 Cobb, S. Abstract of "The chromatophorotropic hormone of the crustacea: standardization, properties and physiology of the eyestalk gland," by A. A. Abramowitz. *Archives of Neurology and Psychiatry,* XXXIX (1938) 1316.

129 Cobb, S. Review of "Der Kumpan in der Umwelt des Vogels," by Konrad Lorenz. *Archives of Neurology and Psychiatry,* XXXIX (1938) 430–432. Unsigned.

130 Cobb, S. Review of *To Drink or Not to Drink*, by C. H. Durfee. *Archives of Neurology and Psychiatry*, XXXIX (1938) 654. Unsigned.
131 Cobb, S. Review of *Reading, Writing and Speech Problems in Children*, by S. T. Orton. *Archives of Neurology and Psychiatry*, XXXIX (1938) 1373. Unsigned.
132 Cobb, S. Review of *Correction of Speech Defects of Early Childhood*, by Robbins and Robbins. *Archives of Neurology and Psychiatry*, XXXIX (1938) 1123–1124. Unsigned.
133 White, B. V. and Cobb, S. Review of *Digestion and Health*, by W. B. Cannon. *Archives of Neurology and Psychiatry*, XXXIX (1938) 884. Unsigned.
134 Cobb, S. Review of *Kraempfe in Kindesalter*, by Hans Bischoff. *Archives of Neurology and Psychiatry*, XL (1938) 226. Unsigned.
135 Cobb, S. and Cole, E. M. "Stuttering." *Physiological Reviews*, XIX (1939) 49–62.
136 Schwab, R. S. and Cobb, S. "Simultaneous electromyograms and electroencephalograms in paralysis agitans." *Journal of Neurophysiology*, II (1939) 36–41.
137 McDermott, N. T. and Cobb, S. "Psychiatric survey of fifty cases of bronchial asthma." *Psychosomatic Medicine*, I (1939) 203–244.
138 White, B. V., Cobb, S. and Jones, C. M. *Mucous colitis; a Psychological Medical Study of Sixty Cases* (Washington, National Research Council, Committee on Problems of Neurotic Behavior, 1939; Psychosomatic Medicine Monograph I).
139 Cobb, S., Bauer, W. and Whiting, I. "Environmental factors in rheumatoid arthritis; a study of the relationship between the onset and exacerbations of arthritis and the emotional or environmental factors." *Journal of the American Medical Association*, CXIII (1939) 668–670.
140 Cohen, M. E. and Cobb, S. "The use of hypnosis in the study of the acid base balance of the blood in a patient with hysterical hyperventilation." Chapter XX in *The Inter-relationship of Mind and Body*, edited by F. Kennedy *et al.* (Baltimore, Williams & Wilkins, 1939, pp. 318–332; *Association for Research in Nervous and Mental Disease, Research Publication*, XIX).
141 Cobb, S. "Review of neuropsychiatry for 1939." *Archives of Internal Medicine*, LXIV (1939) 1328–1339.
142 Cobb, S., Sargant, W. W. and Schwab, R. S. "Simultaneous respiratory and electroencephalographic recording in cases of petit mal." *Archives of Neurology and Psychiatry*, XLII (1939) 1189–1191.
143 Cobb, S. Abstract of "A physiological and histological study of the frontal cortex of the seal (phoca vitulina)," by D. M. Rioch. *Archives of Neurology and Psychiatry*, XLI (1939) 379.
144 Cobb, S. Abstract of "The action of certain drugs on the insect central nervous system, by K. D. Roeder. *Archives of Neurology and Psychiatry*, XLII (1939) 919.
145 Cobb, S. Review of *Physiology of the Nervous System*, by J. F. Fulton. *Archives of Neurology and Psychiatry*, XLII (1939) 973–975. Unsigned.

Appendix B: Bibliography

146 Cobb, S. Review of *Clinical and Experimental Studies in Personality*, by Morton Prince (edited by A. A. Roback). *American Journal of Psychiatry*, XCVI (1939–1940) 755–756.

147 Cobb, S. "Psychiatric approach to the treatment of epilepsy." *American Journal of Psychiatry*, XCVI (1940) 1009–1021.

148 Finley, K. H. and Cobb, S. "The capillary bed of the locus coeruleus. *Journal of Comparative Neurology*, LXXIII (1940) 49–58.

149 Cobb, S. "Review of neuropsychiatry for 1940." *Archives of Internal Medicine*, LXVI (1940) 1341–1354.

150 Cohen, M. E. and Cobb, S. Anti-convulsive action of disodium 4-sulfamidophenyl-2-azo-7-acetylamino-1-hydroxynaphthalene 3, 6 disulfonate (neoprontosil) in epileptic patients." *Transactions of the American Neurological Association*, LXVI (1940) 199–202.

151 Cobb, S. Abstract of "Clinical mediation in crustations: III. Acetylcholine and autonomy in petrolisthes armatus (Gibbes)," by J. H. Welsh and H. H. Haskin. *Archives of Neurology and Psychiatry*, XLIII (1940) 817.

152 Cobb, S. Review of *The Genetics of Schizophrenia*, by F. J. Kallman and S. T. Rypins. *Archives of Neurology and Psychiatry*, XLIII (1940) 857–858. Unsigned.

153 Cobb, S. Review of *Explorations in Personality: a Clinical and Experimental Study of Fifty Men of College Age*, by H. A. Murray *et al*. *Archives of Neurology and Psychiatry*, XLIV (1940) 1152–1153. Unsigned.

154 Cobb, S. "Sir Henry Head, 1861–1940." *Transactions of the Association of American Physicians*, LVI (1941) 20–21.

155 Ruesch, J., Cobb, S. and Finesinger, J. E. "Studies on muscular tension in neuroses." *Transactions of the American Neurological Association*, LXVII (1941) 186–189.

156 Cohen, M. E. and Cobb, S. "Anticonvulsive action of azosulfamide in patients with epilepsy." *Archives of Neurology and Psychiatry*, XLVI (1941) 676–694.

157 Cobb, S. "Review of neuropsychiatry for 1941." *Archives of Internal Medicine*, LXVIII (1941) 1232–1245.

158 Cobb, S. *Foundations of Neuropsychiatry*. (2nd revised and enlarged ed. [of *A Preface to Nervous Diseases*, 1936]. Baltimore, Williams and Wilkins, 1941).

159 Benda, C. E. and Cobb, S. "On the pathogenesis of paralysis agitans (Parkinson's disease)." *Medicine*, XXI (1942) 95–142.

160 Cobb, S. "Psychosomatics and psychoneurosis." *Journal of Aviation Medicine*, XIII (1942) 245–255.

161 Lennox, W. G. and Cobb, S. "Employment of epileptics." *Industrial Medicine*, II (1942) 571–575.

162 Cobb, S. "Review of neuropsychiatry for 1942." *Archives of Internal Medicine*, LXX (1942) 1017–1032.

163 Cobb, S. "Anatomical Basis of the emotions." Lecture XXI in *Collected Lectures of the Seventh Postgraduate Seminar in Neurology and Psychiatry, Including a Course in Military Neuropsychiatry, Oct. 3, 1941–*

April 10, 1942 (Waltham, Mass., Metropolitan Hospital, 1942, pp. 266–273).

164 Cobb, S. "Relationship between psychology, neurology, and psychiatry." *Lecture XXII in Collected Lectures of the Seventh Postgraduate Seminar in Neurology and Psychiatry, Including a Course in Military Neuropsychiatry, Oct. 3, 1941–April 10, 1942* (Waltham, Mass., Metropolitan Hospital, 1942, pp. 274–281).

165 Cobb, S. Abstract of "The response of catfish melanophores to ergotamine," by G. H. Parker. *Archives of Neurology and Psychiatry*, XLVII (1942) 1039.

166 Cobb, S. Review of *Epilepsy and Cerebral Localization*, by Wilder Penfield and T. C. Erikson. *Science*, n.s. XCV (1942) 577–579.

167 Cobb, S. Review of *Science and Sanity*, by Alfred Korzybski, 2d ed. *Archives of Neurology and Psychiatry*, XLVII (1942) 877–878. Unsigned.

168 Cobb, S. Review of *The Creative Unconscious; Studies in the Psychoanalysis of Art*, by Hanns Sachs. *Archives of Neurology and Psychiatry*, XLVIII (1942) 864. Unsigned.

169 Cobb, S. "Speech disorders and their treatment." *Bulletin of the New York Academy of Medicine*, XIX (1943) 34–46. Reprinted in Doherty, W. B. and Runes, D. D. *Rehabilitation of the War Injured* (N.Y., Philosophical Library, 1943, pp. 71–84).

170 Cobb, S. and Lindemann, E. "Neuropsychiatric observations" [of Cocoanut Grove disaster]. *Annals of Surgery*, CXVII (1943) 814–824. Reprinted also in *Management of the Cocoanut Grove Burns at the Massachusetts General Hospital*, by J. C. Aub *et al.*, (Philadelphia, Lippincott, 1943, pp. 14–24).

171 Cohen, M. E., Coombs, F. S., Cobb, S. and Talbott, J. H. "Metabolic studies of epileptic patients receiving azosulfamide and phenobarbital." *Archives of Neurology and Psychiatry*, L (1943) 149–161.

172 Smith, H. W. and Cobb, S. "Relation of emotions to injury and disease: a call for forensic psychosomatic medicine." *Annals of Internal Medicine*, XIX (1943) 873–908.

173 Cobb, S. "Review of neuropsychiatry for 1943." *Archives of Internal Medicine*, LXXII (1943) 795–806.

174 Solomon, H. C. and Cobb, S. "Charles MacFie Campbell, 1876–1943." *Transactions of the American Neurological Association*, LXX (1944) 189–192. Published also in the *Archives of Neurology and Psychiatry*, L (1943) 711–714.

175 Cobb, S. and Ruesch, J. "Series of tests for measurement of disturbed consciousness." *Transactions of the American Neurological Association*, LXIX (1943) 113–119.

176 Cobb, S. *Borderlands of Psychiatry* (Cambridge, Harvard University Press, 1943).

177 Cobb, S. Review of *Unconsciousness*, by J. G. Miller. *Archives of Neurology and Psychiatry*, XLIX (1943) 320–321. Unsigned.

Appendix B: Bibliography

178 Cobb, S. Review of *Lectures on Conditioned Responses*, by I. P. Pavlov. Vol. 2, *Conditioned Reflexes and Psychiatry*, translated by W. H. Gantt. *Archives of Neurology and Psychiatry*, XLIX (1943) 637. Unsigned.

179 Cobb, S. Foreword to *The Psychology of Women; a Psychoanalytic Interpretation*, by Helene Deutsch (New York, Grune & Stratton, 1944, pp. vii–viii).

180 Cobb, S. "Technique of interviewing a patient with psychosomatic disorder." *Medical Clinics of North America*, XXVIII (1944) 1210–1216.

181 Cobb, S. and Lennox, W. G. "Cerebral circulation—intrinsic control and clinical phenomena." *Federation Proceedings*, III (1944) 151–158.

182 Cobb, S. *Decennial report of the Psychiatric Service of the Massachusetts General Hospital, 1934–1944*. [Boston, 1944].

183 White, P. D., Cobb, S., Chapman, W. P., Cohen, M. E. and Badal, D. W. "Observations on neurocirculatory asthenia." *Transactions of the Association of American Physicians*, LVIII (1944) 129–136.

184 Cohen, M. E., Johnson, R. E., Cobb, S., Chapman, W. P. and White, P. D. "Studies of work and discomfort in patients with neurocirculatory asthenia." *Journal of Clinical Investigation*, XXIII (1944) 934.

185 Cobb, S. *Foundations of Neuropsychiatry* (3rd revised and enlarged ed., Baltimore, Williams and Wilkins, 1944).

186 Cobb, S. Abstract of "Independent differentiation of the sensory areas of the avian inner ear," by H. J. Evans. *Archives of Neurology and Psychiatry*, LI (1944) 89.

187 Cobb, S. Review of *The Psychiatric Novels of Oliver Wendell Holmes*, by C. P. Oberndorf. *Archives of Neurology and Psychiatry*, LI (1944) 301.

188 Cobb, S. Review of *Experimental Basis of Neurotic Behavior*, by W. Horsley Gantt. *American Journal of Psychiatry*, CI (1944–45) 565–566.

189 Cobb, S. "Psychiatric Service Affairs." *Massachusetts General Hospital News*, No. 29, February, 1945, pp. 1–2; No. 30, March, 1945, p. 1.

190 Cobb, S. "Review of neuropsychiatry for 1944." *Archives of Internal Medicine*, LXXV (1945) 65–71.

191 Finesinger, J. E. and Cobb, S. "Psychoneurosis and psychosomatic disorders." Part IV, Topic 15 in *A Manual of Military Psychiatry*, edited by H. C. Solomon and P. I. Yakovlev (Philadelphia, W. B. Saunders, 1945, p. 128–159).

192 Brazier, M. A. B., Finesinger, J. E. and Cobb, S. "A contrast between the electroencephalograms of 100 psychoneurotic patients and those of 500 normal adults." *American Journal of Psychiatry*, CI (1945) 443–448.

193 Cobb, S. "A comparison of the summer resident birds today and forty years ago in a small area in Massachusetts." *The Auk*, LXII (1945) 606–610.

194 Cobb, S. Review of *Introduction to Physical Methods of Treatment in Psychiatry*, by E. Slater. *American Journal of Psychiatry*, CII (1945–46) 141.

195 Cobb, S. Review of *Embryology of Behavior*, by Arnold Gesell. *The Yale Journal of Biology and Medicine*, XVIII (1945–46) 124–125.
196 Cobb, S. "The psychiatric case history of Isabella Shawe Thackeray." In *The Letters and Private Papers of William Makepeace Thackeray*, collected and edited by Gordon N. Ray (Cambridge, Harvard University Press, 1945–1946, v. IV, pp. 453–459, Appendix 28).
197 Cobb, S. "Review of neuropsychiatry for 1945." *Archives of Internal Medicine*, LXXVII (1946) 576–591.
198 Chapman, W. P., Cohen, M. E. and Cobb, S. "Measurements related to pain, neurocirculatory asthenia, anxiety neurosis, or effort syndrome: levels of heat stimulus perceived as painful and producing wince and withdrawal reactions." *Journal of Clinical Investigation*, XXV (1946) 890–896.
199 Cobb, S. "Psychosomatic medicine." *Bulletin of the Harvard Medical Alumni Association*, XX (1946) 50–52.
200 Cobb, S. "Psychiatry in a general hospital." *Bulletin of the New York Academy of Medicine*, 2d ser. XXII (1946) 137–146.
201 Cobb, S. "Use of the life chart in psychiatric consultation." *Clinical Medicine*, LIII (1946) 254–256.
202 Cobb, S. "David Lynn Edsall, 1869–1945." *Medicine*, XXV (1946) 111.
203 Cobb, S., Cohen, M. E. and Badal, D. W. "Capillaries of the nail fold in patients with neurocirculatory asthenia (effort syndrome, anxiety neurosis)." *Archives of Neurology and Psychiatry*, LVI (1946) 643–650.
204 Cobb, S. Abstract of "Neurosecretion: VI. A comparison between the intercerebralis-cardiacum-allatum system of the insects and the hypothalamo-hypophyseal system of the vertebrates," by B. and E. Scharrer. *Archives of Neurology and Psychiatry*, LV (1946) 143.
205 Cobb, S. "Review of neuropsychiatry for 1946." *Archives of Internal Medicine*, LXXIX (1947) 113–126.
206 Cobb, S. "Psychosomatic medicine." In Cecil, R. L., McDermott, W. and Wolff, H. G. *A Textbook of Medicine* (7th ed., Philadelphia, W. B. Saunders, 1947, pp. 1646–1650).
207 Watkins, A. L., Cobb, S., Finesinger, J. E., Brazier, M. A. B., Shands, H. C. and Pincus, G. "Psychiatric and physiologic studies on fatigue." *Archives of Physical Medicine*, XXVIII (1947) 199–206.
208 Cobb, S. "Amnesia for the left limbs developing into anosognosia." *Bulletin of the Los Angeles Neurological Society*, XII (1947) 48–52.
209 Cobb, S. "Photic driving as a cause of clinical seizures in epileptic patients." *Archives of Neurology and Psychiatry*, LVIII (1947) 70–71.
210 Chapman, W. P., Finesinger, J. E., Jones, C. M. and Cobb, S. "Measurements of pain sensitivity in patients with psychoneurosis." *Archives of Neurology and Psychiatry*, LVII (1947) 321–331.
211 Cobb, S. "Integration of medical and psychiatric problems: a report of progress." Chapter III in *Psychiatric Research; Papers Read at the Dedication of the Laboratory for Biochemical Research, McLean Hospital, Waverly, Massachusetts, May 17, 1946* (Cambridge, Harvard University Press, 1947, pp. 39–66).

Appendix B: Bibliography

212 Cobb, S. and Butler, A. M. "Child Psychiatry Training and Research Unit." *The Massachusetts General Hospital News*, No. 62, November, 1947, p. 1.
213 Cobb, S. "One hundred years of progress in neurology, psychiatry and neurosurgery." *Archives of Neurology and Psychiatry*, LIX (1948) 63–98.
214 Cobb, S. Butler, A. M. and Miles, H. H. W. "Impulsive behavior in a crippled boy." *American Journal of Medicine*, IV (1948) 588–593.
215 Cobb, S., Butler, A. M. and Miles, H. H. W. "A case of hysteria." *American Journal of Medicine*, V (1948) 272–276.
216 Cobb, S. "Psychiatric conference: a case of hysteria." *American Practitioner*, III (1948) 58–60.
217 Cobb, S. "Review of neuropsychiatry for 1947." *Archives of Internal Medicine*, LXXXI (1948) 381–396.
218 Cobb, S., Butler, A. M. and Miles, H. H. W. "Feeblemindedness or pseudoretardation?" *American Journal of Medicine*, V (1948) 891–897.
219 Finesinger, J. E., Cobb, S., Chapple, E. D. and Brazier, M. A. B. "The Squantum study." Part I in *An Investigation of Prediction of Success in Naval Flight Training*, prepared by the National Research Council Committee of Aviation Psychology (Washington, Civil Aeronautics Administration, Division of Research, 1948, pp. 1–155 Research Report No. 81).
220 Finesinger, J. E., Cobb, S., Chapple, E. D. and Brazier, M. A. B. *Appendices to an Investigation of Prediction of Success in Naval Flight Training* (Washington, Civil Aeronautics Administration, Division of Research, 1948; Research Report No. 82).
221 Cobb, S. *Foundations of Neuropsychiatry* (4th revised and enlarged ed., Baltimore, Williams and Wilkins, 1948).
222 Cobb, S. *Five Year Report of the Hall-Mercer Hospital. For the Period January 1, 1942–December 31, 1946* (Philadelphia, 1948).
223 Cobb, S. Review of *Paravertebral Block in Diagnosis, Prognosis and Therapy*, by F. Mandl. *Psychosomatic Medicine*, X (1948) 65–66. Unsigned.
224 Cobb, S. Review of *Studies in Genius*, by W. G. Bowerman. *Psychosomatic Medicine*, X (1948) 67–68.
225 Cobb, S. Review of *Dr. Kirkbride and His Mental Hospital*, by Earl D. Bond. *Psychosomatic Medicine*, X (1948) 68.
226 Cobb, S. Review of *Medical Addenda: Related Essays on Medicine and the Changing Order*. *Psychosomatic Medicine*, X (1948) 123–124.
227 Cobb, S. Review of *New Fields of Psychiatry*, by David M. Levy. *Psychosomatic Medicine*, X (1948) 124–125.
228 Cobb, S. Review of *Introduction to Clinical Neurology*, by Gordon Holmes. *Psychosomatic Medicine*, X (1948) 184.
229 Cobb, S. Review of *How Life is Handed On*, by Cyril Bibby. *Psychosomatic Medicine*, X (1948) 188.
230 Cobb, S. Review of *Practical Clinical Psychiatry*, by E. A. Strecker *et al.* *Psychosomatic Medicine*, X (1948) 252.

231 Cobb, S. Review of *A Textbook of Clinical Neurology*, by Israel S. Wechsler, 6th ed. *Psychosomatic Medicine*, X (1948) 252.

232 Cobb, S. Review of *The Place of Psychology in an Ideal University; the Report of the University Commission to Advise the Future of Psychology at Harvard*. *Psychosomatic Medicine*, X (1948) 380–381.

233 Cobb, S. Review of *The Case of Rudolf Hess; A Problem in Diagnosis and Forensic Psychiatry*, by Henry V. Dicks et al. *Psychosomatic Medicine*, X (1948) 381–382.

234 Cobb, S. Review of *Personality in Nature, Society and Culture*, by Clyde Kluckhohn. *Psychosomatic Medicine*, X (1948) 387–388.

235 Cobb, S. Review of *Psychobiology and Psychiatry*, by Wendell Muncie. *American Journal of Psychiatry*, CV (1948–1949) 239.

236 Cobb, S. "Human nature and the understanding of disease. Chapter 3 in *The Hospital in Contemporary Life*, edited by N. W. Faxon (Cambridge, Harvard University Press, 1949, pp. 109–136).

237 Cobb, S. and Miles, H. H. W. "Psychiatric conference" [a case of arthritis]. *American Practitioner*, III (1949) 407–411.

238 Cobb, S., Butler, A. M. and Miles, H. H. W. "A case of duodenal ulcer with anxiety attacks treated by psychotherapy." *American Journal of Medicine*, VI (1949) 368–374.

239 Cobb, S. "Presidential address." *Transactions of the American Neurological Association*, LXXIV (1949) 1–8.

240 Miles, H. H. W. and Cobb, S. "Hyperthyroidism or anxiety neurosis?" *American Practitioner*, IV (1949) 86–91.

241 Cobb, S. "Review of neuropsychiatry for 1948." *Archives of Internal Medicine*, LXXXIII (1949) 454–469.

242 Cobb, S. and Miles, H. H. W. "Anorexia nervosa." *American Journal of Medicine*, VII (1949) 819–824.

243 Cobb, S., Butler, A. M. and Miles, H. H. W. "Psychogenic deafness in a disturbed boy." *American Journal of Medicine*, VII (1949) 221–227.

244 Cobb, S. Gefässerweiternde Therapie Cerebraler Gefässerkrankung." Article published in an unidentified journal, 1949. Headed, Lz. 3429, Festschrift B (Cobb), Spalte 1. Filed under 1949 in the bound set of Dr. Cobb's reprints in the Countway Library, and included in index at front under the year 1949. Translated by P. J. Jossman.

245 Cobb, S. Review of *Take Off Your Mask*, by Ludwig Eidelberg. *Psychosomatic Medicine*, XI (1949) 132.

246 Cobb, S. Review of *Clinical Examination of the Nervous System*, by G. H. Monrad-Krohn. *Psychosomatic Medicine*, XI (1949) 184.

247 Cobb, S. Review of *Fundamentals of Psychiatry*, by E. A. Strecker, 4th ed. *Psychosomatic Medicine*, XI (1949) 184.

248 Cobb, S. Review of *Modern Clinical Psychiatry*, by A. P. Noyes. *Psychosomatic Medicine*, XI (1949) 184.

249 Cobb, S. Review of *Intracranial Tumors*, by P. Bailey. *Psychosomatic Medicine*, XI (1949) 185.

250 Cobb, S. Review of *The Commonsense Psychiatry of Dr. Adolf Meyer*, by Alfred Lief. *Psychosomatic Medicine*, XI (1949) 185–186.

251 Cobb, S. Review of *The Mentally Ill in America*, by Albert Deutsch, 2d ed. *Psychosomatic Medicine*, XI (1949) 186.
252 Cobb, S. Review of *Cybernetics or Control of Communication in the Animal and the Machine*, by Norbert Wiener. *Psychosomatic Medicine*, XI (1949) 242–243.
253 Cobb, S. Review of *Motivation in Health Education; the 1947 Health Education Conference of the New York Academy of Medicine. Psychosomatic Medicine*, XI (1949) 321.
254 Cobb, S. Review of *You and Psychiatry*, by W. C. Menninger and M. Leaf. *Psychosomatic Medicine*, XI (1949) 321–322.
255 Cobb, S. "The psychosomatic dilemma." *American Journal of Psychiatry*, CVI (1949–1950) 789–790.
256 Cobb, S. "Review of neuropsychiatry for 1949." *Archives of Internal Medicine*, LXXXV (1950) 998–1009.
257 Cobb, S. and Miles, H. H. W. "Ulcerative colitis." *American Journal of Medicine*, VIII (1950) 789–793.
258 Cobb, S., Pool, J. L., Scarff, J., Schwab, R. S., Walker, A. E. and White, J. C. "Section of U fibers of motor cortex in cases of paralysis agitans (Parkinson's disease)." *Archives of Neurology and Psychiatry*, LXIV (1950) 57–59.
259 Cobb, S. Foreword to *The Biology of Mental Health and Disease*, the Twenty-seventh Annual Conference of the Milbank Memorial Fund (New York, P. B. Hoeber, 1950, pp. xix–xxi).
260 Cobb, S. "Treatment of Psychoneurosis and results of follow-up study." *Monatsschrift für Psychiatric und Neurologie*, CXX (1950) 316–326.
261 Cobb, S. *Emotions and Clinical Medicine*. (New York, W. W. Norton, 1950; Salmon Memorial Lectures of the New York Academy of Medicine, 1949).
262 Miles, H. H. W. and Cobb, S. "A case of enuresis; psychiatric conference." *American Practitioner and Digest of Treatment*, I (1950) 812–815.
263 Cobb, S. and Miles, H. H. W. "A child's reaction to adenoidectomy." *American Journal of Medicine*, IX (1950) 242–246.
264 Cobb, S. and Shands, H. C. "Psychiatric conference" [a case of recurrent depression]. *American Practitioner and Digest of Treatment*, I (1950) 1292–1295.
265 Cobb, S. Obituary [of] Adolf Meyer, M. D., 1866–1950." *Archives of Neurology and Psychiatry*, LXIV (1950) 879–881.
266 Cobb, S. "Treatment of psychoneurosis and results of follow-up study." *Monthly Review of Psychiatry and Neurology*, CXX (1950) 316–326.
267 Cobb, S. Review of *More About Psychiatry*, by Carl Binger. *Psychosomatic Medicine*, XII (1950) 401–402.
268 Cobb, S. Review of *Practical and Theoretical Aspects of Psychoanalysis*, by L. S. Kubie. *Psychosomatic Medicine*, XII (1950) 402–403.
269 Cobb, S. Review of *Killers of the Dream*, by Lillian Smith. *Psychosomatic Medicine*, XII (1950) 406–407.

270   Bonner, F. J., Cobb, S. and Sweet, W. H. "Orbital gyrectomy for intractable pain." *Archives of Neurology and Psychiatry*, LXVI (1951) 238–259.
271   Cobb, S. "Too scientific." *American Journal of Psychiatry*, CVII (1950–1951) 935–936.
272   Cobb, S. "Psychosomatic Medicine." In Cecil, R. L. and Loeb, R. F. *A Textbook of Medicine* (8th ed., Philadelphia, W. B. Saunders, 1951, pp. 1513–1517).
273   Cobb, S. and Miles, H. H. W. "Convalescence in a patient with permanent neurologic disability." *American Journal of Medicine*, X (1951) 386–392.
274   Shands, H. C., Miles, H. H. W. and Cobb, S. "The emotional significance of cancer." *American Practitioner and Digest of Treatment*, II (1951) 261–265.
275   Cobb, S., Shands, H. C. and Miles, H. H. W. "A case of asthma treated with psychotherapy." *American Journal of Medicine*, XI (1951) 117–122.
276   Cobb, S. "Lawrence Raymond Morrison, M.D., 1897–1950." *Archives of Neurology and Psychiatry*, LXV (1951) 788–791.
277   Cobbs, S. "Review of neuropsychiatry for 1950." *Archives of Internal Medicine*, LXXXVII (1951) 889–898.
278   Cobb, S. and Miles, H. H. W. "Symptoms due to withdrawal of barbiturates." *American Practitioner and Digest of Treatment*, II (1951) 768–771.
279   Cobb, S. and Miles, H. H. W. "Psychotherapy of a psychosomatic illness: essential hypertension." *American Journal of Medicine*, XI (1951) 381–386.
280   Miles, H. H. W. and Cobb, S. "Neurocirculatory asthenia, anxiety and neurosis." *New England Journal of Medicine*, CXLV (1951) 711–719.
281   Shands, H. C., Finesinger, J. E., Cobb, S. and Abrams, R. D. "Psychological mechanisms in patients with cancer." *Cancer*, IV (1951) 1159–1170.
282   Cobb, S. Review of *Brucellosis (Undulant Fever): Clinical and Subclinical*, by H. J. Harris, 2d ed. *Psychosomatic Medicine*, XIII (1951) 206–207.
283   Cobb, S. Review of *The Cerebral Circulation in Health and Disease*, by C. F. Schmidt. *Psychosomatic Medicine*, XIII (1951) 207.
284   Cobb, S. Review of *The Clinical Examination of the Nervous System*, by G. H. Monrad-Krohn. *Psychosomatic Medicine*, XIII (1951) 207.
285   Cobb, S. Review of *New Discoveries in Medicine: Their Effect on Public Health*, by L. B. Murphy and H. Ladd. *Psychosomatic Medicine*, XIII (1951) 207.
286   Cobb, S. Review of *the Yearbook of Psychoanalysis*, Vol. IV. *Psychosomatic Medicine*, XIII (1951) 207.
287   Stockholm, H. and Cobb, S. Review of *Fundamentals of Psychoanalysis*, by Franz Alexander. *Psychosomatic Medicine*, XIII (1951) 267–269.

288 Stockholm, H. and Cobb, S. Review of *Psychosomatic Medicine,* by Franz Alexander. *Psychosomatic Medicine,* XIII (1951) 320–332.
289 Cobb, S. Review of *Schizophrenic Art: Its Meaning in Psychotherapy,* by Margaret Naumberg. *Psychosomatic Medicine,* XIII (1951) 406.
290 Cobb, S. and Miles, H. H. W. "Diagnostic and therapeutic problems in a patient with epilepsy, psychosis and temporal lobe abnormality." *American Journal of Medicine,* XII (1952) 238–243.
291 Cobb, S. *Foundations of Neuropsychiatry* (5th revised and enlarged ed., Baltimore, Williams and Wilkins, 1952).
292 Cobb, S. "On the nature and locus of the mind." *Archives of Neurology and Psychiatry,* LXVII (1952) 172–177.
293 Trethowan, W. H. and Cobb, S. "Neuropsychiatric aspects of Cushing's syndrome." *Archives of Neurology and Psychiatry,* LXVII (1952) 283–309.
294 Miles, H. H. W., Shands, H. C. and Cobb, S. "Clinical implications of the 'infantile personality'." *American Practitioner and Digest of Treatment,* III (1952) 280–284.
295 Clark, L. D., Bauer, W. and Cobb, S. "Preliminary observations on mental disturbances occurring in patients under therapy with cortisone and ACTH." *New England Journal of Medicine,* CCXLVI (1952) 205–216.
296 Lorenz, M. and Cobb, S. "Language behavior in manic patients." *Archives of Neurology and Psychiatry,* LXVII (1952) 763–770.
297 Cobb, S. "Review of neuropsychiatry for 1951." *Archives of Internal Medicine,* XC (1952) 410–421.
298 Bonner, F., Cobb, S., Sweet, W. and White, J. C. "Frontal lobe surgery in the treatment of pain." *Psychosomatic Medicine,* XIV (1952) 383–405.
299 Bereday, M. and Cobb, S. "Relation of hereditary optic atrophy (Leber) to other familial degenerative diseases of the central nervous system." *Archives of Ophthalmology,* XLVIII (1952) 669–680.
300 Cobb, S. "Consciousness and cerebral localization." *Epilepsia* 3rd ser. I (1952) 17–20.
301 Cobb, S. and Miles, H. H. W. "Migraine and character neurosis." *American Practitioner and Digest of Treatment,* III (1952) 985–990.
302 Cobb, S. and Miles, H. H. W. "Hyperventilation in a patient who stammered; methedrine as an adjunct to psychotherapy." *American Journal of Medicine,* XIII (1952) 777–781.
303 Miles, H. H. W., Cobb, S. and Shands, H. C. *Case Histories in Psychosomatic Medicine* (New York, W. W. Norton, 1952).
304 Cobb, S. Review of *The Biology of Human Starvation,* by A. Keys *et al. Psychosomatic Medicine,* XIV (1952) 65.
305 Cobb, S. Review of *Treatment in Psychiatry,* by O. Diethelm, 2d ed. *Psychosomatic Medicine,* XIV (1952) 147–148.
306 Cobb, S. Review of *Psychiatric Sections in General Hospitals: An Architectural Record Book,* by P. Haun. *Psychosomatic Medicine,* XIV (1952) 148.

307 Cobb, S. Review of *Emotions and Memory*, by David Rapaport, 2d ed. *Psychosomatic Medicine*, XIV (1952) 148.
308 Cobb, S. Review of *Textbook of Abnormal Psychology*, by C. Landis and M. M. Bolles, 2d ed. *Psychosomatic Medicine*, XIV (1952) 235–236.
309 Cobb, S. Review of *The Neurologic Examination: Incorporating the Fundamentals of Neuroanatomy and Neurophysiology*, by R. N. De Jong. *Psychosomatic Medicine*, XIV (1952) 237.
310 Cobb, S. Review of *Bases of Human Behavior: a Biological Approach to Psychiatry*, by L. J. Saul. *Psychosomatic Medicine*, XIV (1952) 322–323.
311 Cobb, S. Review of *Manual of the International Statistical Classification of Diseases, Injuries, and Causes of Death* (Sixth Revision of the *International Lists of Diseases and Causes of Death*). *Psychosomatic Medicine*, XIV (1952) 327.
312 Cobb, S. Review of *Freud or Jung*, by Edward Glover, *Psychosomatic Medicine*, XIV (1952) 505.
313 Cobb, S. Review of *Principles of Abnormal Psychology*, by A. H. Maslow and B. Mittelmann. *Psychosomatic Medicine*, XIV (1952) 512.
314 Cobb, S. *Ten Year Report of the Hall-Mercer Hospital. For the Period January 1, 1942–December 31, 1951* [Philadelphia, 1953].
315 Cobb, S. "For a general classification of certain psychoses." *American Journal of Psychiatry*, CIX (1953) 869–870.
316 Cobb, S. and Bereday, M. "Familial system diseases of the neuraxis; the relation of the neural muscular atrophies to other heredodegenerative diseases of the nervous system." *Transactions of the American Neurological Association*, LXXVIII (1953) 12–14.
317 Cobb, S. "Anaclitic treatment in a patient with ulcerative colitis." *American Journal of Medicine*, XIV (1953) 731–735.
318 Lorenz, M. and Cobb, S. "Language behavior in psychoneurotic patients." *Archives of Neurology and Psychiatry*, LXIX (1953) 684–694.
319 Clark, L. D., Quarton, G. C., Cobb, S. and Bauer, W. "Further observations on mental disturbances associated with cortisone and ACTH therapy." *New England Journal of Medicine*, CCXLIX (1953) 178–183.
320 Cobb, S. "Review of neuropsychiatry." *Archives of Internal Medicine*, XCII (1953) 273–283.
321 Cobb, S. and Nemiah, J. C. "A case of low back and leg pain complicated by psychologic factors." *American Journal of Medicine*, XV (1953) 391–398.
322 Cobb, S. "Walther Spielmeyer." In *The Founders of Neurology*, edited by Webb Haymaker (Springfield, Ill., C. C. Thomas, 1953, pp. 214–219).
323 Cobb, S. "James Jackson Putnam." In *The Founders of Neurology*, edited by Webb Haymaker (Springfield, Ill., C. C. Thomas, 1953, pp. 350–353).
324 Cobb, S. Review of *From a Doctor's Heart*, by E. F. Snyder. *Psychosomatic Medicine*, XV (1953) 94.

Appendix B: Bibliography

325 Cobb, S. Review of *Frontal Lobotomy and Affective Behavior,* by J. F. Fulton. *Psychosomatic Medicine,* XV (1953) 184–185.
326 Cobb, S. Review of *Annual Report on Stress,* by Hans Selye. *Psychosomatic Medicine,* XV (1953) 267–268.
327 Cobb, S. Review of *Practical Clinical Psychiatry,* by E. A. Strecker *et al. Psychosomatic Medicine,* XV (1953) 272.
328 Cobb, S. Review of *Mental Hygiene,* by L. P. and Alice Crow. *Psychosomatic Medicine,* XV (1953) 273.
329 Cobb, S. Review of *An Analysis of the Multi-Test Clinic of Richmond, Virginia,* by W. E .Boek. *Psychosomatic Medicine,* XV (1953) 274–275.
330 Cobb, S. Review of *King Solomon's Ring,* by K. Z. Lorenz. *Psychosomatic Medicine,* XV (1953) 549–550.
331 Cobb, S. Review of *Visceral Innervation and Its Relation to Personality,* by A. Kuntz. *Psychosomatic Medicine,* XV (1953) 550–551.
332 Cobb, S. Review of *The Autonomic Nervous System: Anatomy, Physiology, and Surgical Application,* by J. C. White *et al.,* 2d ed. *Psychosomatic Medicine,* XV (1953) 551.
333 Cobb, S. Review of *Physical and Mental Stress and Consequential Development of Atherosclerosis within the Jewish Population of Denmark,* by G. Hartmann and F. Schulsinger. *Psychosomatic Medicine,* XV (1953) 554.
334 Cobb, S. Review of *The Untouchables,* by Alfred Maund. *Psychosomatic Medicine,* XV (1953) 562.
335 Cobb, S. Review of *Problems of Consciousness: Transactions of the Second Conference, March 19–20, 1951. Psychosomatic Medicine,* XV (1953) 638.
336 Cobb, S. Review of *Four Prophets of Our Destiny,* by William Hubben. *Psychosomatic Medicine,* XV (1953) 638–639.
337 Cobb, S. "I wish my hands were as skillful as that." Chapter 33 in *Why We Become Doctors,* edited by Noah D. Fabricant (New York, Grune and Stratton, 1954, pp. 127–128).
338 Cobb, S. "Psychiatric research, 1934–1953." *Massachusetts General Hospital News,* No. 130, January, 1954, pp. 1–2.
339 Cobb, S., Quarton, G. C. and Clark L. D. *Neuropsychiatric disorders. The Medical Use of Cortisone* (New York, Blakiston Press, 1954).
340 Cobb, S. and Sloane, B. "Depersonalization simulating epilepsy." *American Practitioner and Digest of Treatment,* V (1954) 425–429.
341 Cobb, S. "Psychiatric service." *Massachusetts General Hospital News,* No. 136, July–August, 1954, pp. 1–2.
342 Miles, H. H. W., Waldfogel, S., Barrabee, E. L. and Cobb, S. "Psychosomatic study of 46 young men with coronary artery disease." *Psychosomatic Medicine,* XVI (1954) 455–477.
343 Lorenz, M. and Cobb, S. "Language patterns in psychotic and psychoneurotic subjects." *Archives of Neurology and Psychiatry,* LXXII (1954) 665–673.
344 Cobb, S., Quarton, G. C. and Clark, L. D. "Neuropsychiatric disorders."

Publication 132 of *Robert W. Lovett Memorial Foundation for the Study of Crippling Disease,* 1954, pp. 506–518).

345 Cobb, S. Review of *A Textbook of Clinical Neurology,* by I. S. Wechsler, 7th ed. *Psychosomatic Medicine,* XVI (1954) 83.

346 Cobb, S. Review of *History of American Psychology,* by A. A. Roback. *Psychosomatic Medicine,* XVI (1954) 90.

347 Cobb, S. Review of *Totem and Taboo: Some Points of Agreement between the Mental Lives of Savages and Neurotics,* by Sigmund Freud (translated by James Strachey). *Psychosomatic Medicine,* XVI (1954) 180.

348 Cobb, S. Review of *The Anatomy of the Nervous System. Its Development and Function,* by S. W. Ranson, 9th ed., revised by S. L. Clark. *Psychosomatic Medicine,* XVI (1954) 180–181.

349 Cobb, S. Review of *Psychoanalytic Explorations in Art,* by Ernst Kris. *Psychosomatic Medicine,* XVI (1954) 181.

350 Cobb, S. Review of *Mental Prodigies,* by Fred Barlow. *Psychosomatic Medicine,* XVI (1954) 181–182.

351 Cobb, S. Review of *Fundamental of Psychiatry,* by E. A. Strecker, 5th ed. *Psychosomatic Medicine,* XVI (1954) 184.

352 Cobb, S. and Cleghorn, R. A. Review of *Physiological Foundations of Neurology,* by Ernst Gellhorn. *Psychosomatic Medicine,* XVI (1954) 274–275.

353 Cobb, S. Review of *Frontal Lobes and Schizophrenia,* by M. Greenblatt and H. C. Solomon. *Psychosomatic Medicine,* XVI (1954) 353.

354 Cobb, S. Review of *The Living Brain,* by W. G. Walter. *Psychosomatic Medicine,* XVI (1954) 354–355.

355 Cobb, S. Review of *The Conception of Disease: Its History, Its Versions and Its Nature,* by Walther Riese. *Psychosomatic Medicine,* XVI (1954) 355–356.

356 Cobb, S. Review of *On Dreams,* by Sigmund Freud (translated by James Strachey). *Psychosomatic Medicine,* XVI (1954) 363–364.

357 Cobb, S. Review of *The Autonomic Nervous System,* by Albert Kuntz, 4th ed. *Psychosomatic Medicine,* XVI (1954) 366.

358 Cobb, S. "Review of neuropsychiatry." *Archives of Internal Medicine,* XCV (1955) 129–136.

359 Quarton, G. C., Clark, L. D., Cobb, S. and Bauer, W. "Mental disturbances associated with ACTH and cortisone: a review of explanatory hypotheses." *Medicine,* XXXIV (1955) 13–50.

360 Cobb, S. Discussion on genetics and inheritance of neuropsychiatric patterns. In *Genetics and the Inheritance of Integrated Neurological and Psychiatric Patterns,* edited by Davenport Hooker (Baltimore, Williams and Wilkins, 1954, pp. 316–318; Research Publication of the Association for Research in Nervous and Mental Disease, v. XXXIII).

361 Cobb, S. "A case of persistent ankle pain in spite of adequate orthopedic treatment." *American Journal of Medicine,* XVIII (1955) 653–658.

362 Cobb, S. "Comment: instincts." *American Journal of Psychiatry,* CXII (1955) 149–151.

363   White, J. C. and Cobb, S. "Psychological changes associated with giant pituitary neoplasms." *Archives of Neurology and Psychiatry,* LXXIV (1955) 383–396.

364   Cobb, S. "Physiological observations on disturbances of the cerebral circulation." In *Handbuch der speziellen pathologischen Anatomie und Histologie,* edited by O. Lubarsch (Berlin, Springer-Verlag, 1955; v. XIII; *Nervensystem,* edited by W. Scholz, pp. 1165–1179).

365   Cobb, S. "Psychosomatic medicine." In Cecil, R. L. and Loeb, R. F., *A textbook of Medicine.* 9th ed., Philadelphia, W. B. Saunders, 1955, pp. 1645–1649).

366   Bonner, F. and Cobb, S. "Psychiatric considerations." In *Pain,* by J. C. White and W. H. Sweet (Springfield, Ill., C. C. Thomas, 1955, Chapters IV and X, pp. 99–120, 287–339).

367   Cobb, S. Review of *The Six Schizophrenias: Reaction Patterns in Children and Adults,* by S. J. Beck *et al. Psychosomatic Medicine,* XVII (1955) 170.

368   Cobb, S. Review of *Recent Developments in Psychosomatic Medicine,* by E. D. Willkower and R. A. Cleghorn. *Psychosomatic Medicine,* XVII (1955) 247–248.

369   Cobb, S. Review of *Nature and Nurture: a Modern Synthesis,* by J. L. Fuller. *Psychosomatic Medicine,* XVII (1955) 254.

370   Cobb, S. Review of *Problems of Consciousness,* by H. A. Abramson. *Psychosomatic Medicine,* XVII (1955) 333–334.

371   Cobb, S. Review of *Freedom from Fear,* by L. L. Coleman. *Psychosomatic Medicine,* XVII (1955) 336.

372   Cobb, S. Review of *Cerebral Vascular Diseases (Transactions of a Conference Held under the Auspices of the American Heart Association),* by I. S. Wight and E. H. Luckey. *Psychosomatic Medicine,* XVII (1955) 486.

373   Cobb, S. "Acceptance of the Kober Medal for 1956." *Transactions of the Association of American Physicians,* LXIX (1956) 40–43.

374   Cobb, S. "Review of neuropsychiatry, 1955." *Archives of Internal Medicine,* XCVII (1956) 610–617.

375   Cobb, S. "Contemporary problems in psychiatry." In *Theory and Treatment of the Psychoses; Some Newer Aspects. Papers Presented at the Dedication of the Renard Hospital, St. Louis, October, 1955* (St. Louis, Washington University Press, 1956, pp. 15–27).

376   Cobb, S. Review of *Needed Research in Health and Medical Care: A Bio-Social Approach,* by C. G. Sheps and E. H. Taylor. *Psychosomatic Medicine,* XVIII (1956) 98.

377   Cobb, S. Review of *Heredity in Health and Mental Disorder,* by F. J. Kallmann. *Psychosomatic Medicine,* XVIII (1956) 99.

378   Cobb, S. Review of *Das Zwischenhirn: Syndrome Lokalisationen Funktionen (The Diencephalon: Syndrome Localization Function),* by W. R. Hess, 2d ed. *Psychosomatic Medicine,* XVIII (1956) 100.

379   Cobb, S. Review of *Cultural Differences and Medical Care,* by L. Saunders. *Psychosomatic Medicine,* XVIII (1956) 100.

380 Cobb, S. Review of *Expression of the Emotions in Man and Animals*, by Charles Darwin. *Psychosomatic Medicine*, XVIII (1956) 274–275.

381 Cobb, S. Review of *Studies of the Cerebral Cortex*, by S. Ramón y Cajal. *Psychosomatic Medicine*, XVIII (1956) 275.

382 Cobb, S. Review of *Problems of Consciousness (Transactions of the Fifth Conference*, March 1954). *Psychosomatic Medicine*, XVIII (1956) 275–276.

383 Cobb, S. Review of *On Aphasia: A Critical Study*, by Sigmund Freud (translated by E. Stengel). *Psychosomatic Medicine*, XVIII (1956) 276.

384 Cobb, S. Review of *The Therapeutic Community: A New Treatment Method in Psychiatry*, by M. Jones. *Psychosomatic Medicine*, XVIII (1956) 276.

385 Cobb, S. Review of *Bertrand Russell's Dictionary of Mind, Matter and Morals*, by L. E. Denonn. *Psychosomatic Medicine*, XVIII (1956) 276.

386 Cobb, S. Review of *Psychosurgery and the Self*, by M. F. Robinson and W. Freeman. *Psychosomatic Medicine*, XVIII (1956) 517–518.

387 Cobb, S. Review of *Religion, Healing and Health*, by J. D. Van Buskirk. *Psychosomatic Medicine*, XVIII (1956) 519.

388 Cobb, S. "Awareness, attention & physiology of the brain stem." Chapter 12 in *Experimental Psychopathology*, edited by P. H. Hoch and J. Zubin (New York, Grune & Stratton, 1957, pp. 194–204).

389 Cobb, S. "Comment: Peace of mind." *American Journal of Psychiatry*, CXIII (1957) 663–664.

390 Cobb, S. "Monism and psychosomatic medicine." *Psychosomatic Medicine*, XIX (1957) 177–178.

391 Cobb, S. "Review of neuropsychiatry." *Archives of Internal Medicine*, C (1957) 998–1006.

392 Cobb, S. Review of *Medical Research: A Midcentury Survey*, by E. E. Lape. *Psychosomatic Medicine*, XIX (1957) 83–84.

393 Cobb, S. Review of *Hypothalamus and Thalamus*, by W. R. Hess. *Psychosomatic Medicine*, XIX (1957) 86.

394 Cobb, S. Review of *Culture and Mental Disorders*, by J. W. Eaton and R. J. Weil. *Psychosomatic Medicine*, XIX (1957) 174–175.

395 Cobb, S. Review of *The Evolution of Human Nature*, by C. J. Herrick. *Psychosomatic Medicine*, XIX (1957) 350–351.

396 Cobb, S. Review of *The Evaluation of Therapeutic Agents with Special Reference to the Tranquilizing Drugs*, by S. Wolf. *Psychosomatic Medicine*, XIX (1957) 440.

397 Cobb, S. Review of *Das Zwischenhirn-Hypophysensystem, The Diencephalic-Hypophyseal System*, by W. Bargmann. *Psychosomatic Medicine*, XIX (1957) 503.

398 Cobb, S. Review of *College Men at War*, by J. P. Monks. *Psychosomatic Medicine*, XIX (1957) 505.

399 Cobb, S. "Comment: Equus et machina." *American Journal of Psychiatry*, CXIV (1958) 759.

400 Cobb, S. "Psychosomatic meteorologist [poem]." *New England Journal of Medicine*, CCLVIII (1958) 845.

401 Cobb, S. "Comment: The death penalty." *American Journal of Psychiatry,* CXV (1958) 559–560.
402 Morrison, L. R., Cobb, S. and Bauer, W. *The Effect of Advancing Age upon the Human Spinal Cord* (Cambridge, Harvard University Press, 1958).
403 Cobb, S. *Foundations of Neuropsychiatry* (6th revised and enlarged ed., Baltimore, Williams and Wilkins, 1958).
404 Cobb, S. Review of *The Riddle of Stuttering,* by C. S. Bluemel. *Psychosomatic Medicine,* XX (1958) 83.
405 Cobb, S. Review of *Chronic Illness in the United States,* Commission on Chronic Illness. *Psychosomatic Medicine,* XX (1958) 84.
406 Cobb, S. Review of *Mastery of Stress,* by D. H. Funkenstein, *et al. Psychosomatic Medicine,* XX (1958) 84.
407 Cobb, S. Review of *Meprobamate and Other Agents Used in Mental Disturbances,* by J. G. Miller *et al. Psychosomatic Medicine,* XX (1958) 85–86.
408 Cobb, S. Review of *Emotional Hazards in Animals and Man,* by H. S. Liddell. *Psychosomatic Medicine,* XX (1958) 169.
409 Cobb, S. Review of *Physiology of the Nervous System,* by E. G. Walsh. *Psychosomatic Medicine,* XX (1958) 169–170.
410 Cobb, S. Review of *Matter, Mind and Man,* by E. W. Sinnott. *Psychosomatic Medicine,* XX (1958) 251–252.
411 Cobb, S. Review of *Prescription for Survival,* by Brock Chisholm. *Psychosomatic Medicine,* XX (1958) 253.
412 Cobb, S. Review of *Ten Million and One: Neurological Disability as a National Problem* (An Arden House Conference Sponsored by the National Health Council). *Psychosomatic Medicine,* XX (1958) 256.
413 Cobb, S. Review of *Disorders of Character,* by J. J. Michaels. *Psychosomatic Medicine,* XX (1958) 257–258.
414 Cobb, S. Review of *Psychobiology of Adolf Meyer.* Compiled and edited by E. E. Winters and A. M. Bowers. *Psychosomatic Medicine,* XX (1958) 339–340.
415 Cobb, S. Review of *Fundamentals of Clinical Neurophysiology,* by P. O. Chatfield. *Psychosomatic Medicine,* XX (1958) 340.
416 Cobb, S. Review of *Learning and Instinct in Animals,* by W. H. Thorpe. *Psychosomatic Medicine,* XX (1958) 420–421.
417 Cobb, S. Review of *Psychosomatics: A Series of Five Lectures,* by J. Booij. *Psychosomatic Medicine,* XX (1958) 421.
418 Cobb, S. Review of *Instinct in Man: In the Light of Recent Work in Comparative Psychology,* by Ronald Fletcher. *Psychosomatic Medicine,* XX (1958) 425–426.
419 Cobb, S. Review of *Instinctive Behavior,* by C. H. Schiller. *Psychosomatic Medicine,* XX (1958) 495.
420 Cobb, S. "Neurology." Chapter 81 in *American Handbook of Psychiatry,* edited by S. Arieti (New York, Basic Books, 1959, v. II, pp. 1639–1647).
421 Cobb, S. "On the angle of the cerebral axis in the American woodcock." *The Auk,* LXXVI (1959) 55–59.

422 Cobb, S. "Jacob Ellis Finesinger, 1902–1959." *Journal of Nervous and Mental Diseases*, CXXIX (1959) 415–419.
423 Cobb, S. Book review of *The Excitable Cortex in Conscious Man*, by Wilder Penfield. *Electroencephalography and Clinical Neurophysiology*, XI (1959) 621–623.
424 Cobb, S. "Review of neuropsychiatry." *Archives of Internal Medicine*, CIII (1959) 981–990.
425 Cobb, S. Review of *Live at Peace with Your Nerves*, by W. C. Alvarez. *Psychosomatic Medicine*, XXI (1959) 75–76.
426 Cobb, S. Review of *Mental Symptoms in Temporal Lobe Epilepsy and Temporal Lobe Gliomas*, by Torsten Bingley. *Psychosomatic Medicine*, XXI (1959) 81
427 Cobb, S. Review of *Clinical Neuroanatomy, Neurophysiology and Neurology*, by Louis Hausman. *Psychosomatic Medicine*, XXI (1959) 82.
428 Cobb, S. Review of *Interdisciplinary Team Research*, by M. B. Luszki. *Psychosomatic Medicine*, XXI (1959) 84.
429 Cobb, S. Review of *Ego Psychology and the Problem of Adaptation*, by Heinz Hartmann (translated by David Rapaport). *Psychosomatic Medicine*, XXI (1959) 87.
430 Cobb, S. Review of *Autonomic Dyspraxia: An Hypothesis for the Mechanism of Psychosis, Neurosis and Psychosomatic Disease*, by B. G. Haynes. *Psychosomatic Medicine*, XXI (1959) 88.
431 Cobb, S. Review of *Modern Trends in Neurology*, by Dennis Williams. *Psychosomatic Medicine*, XXI (1959) 174.
432 Cobb, S. Review of *The Clinical Examination of the Nervous System*, by G. H. Monrad-Krohn, 11th ed. *Psychosomatic Medicine*, XXI (1959) 261.
433 Cobb, S. Review of *The Anatomy of the Nervous System*, by J. W. Ranson (revised by S. L. Clark), 10th ed. *Psychosomatic Medicine*, XXI (1959) 436.
434 Cobb, S. Review of *Emotional Problems of Adolescents*, by J. R. Gallagher and H. I. Harris. *Psychosomatic Medicine*, XXI (1959) 502.
435 Cobb, S. "A psychobiologist in retirement." *Psychosomatic Medicine*, XXII (1960) 247–248.
436 Cobb, S. "A note on the size of the avian olfactory bulb." *Epilepsia* ser. 4, I (1960) 394–401.
437 Cobb, S. "Brain and personality." *American Journal of Psychiatry*, CXVI (1960) 938–939.
438 Cobb, S. "Some clinical changes in behavior accompanying endocrine disorders." *Journal of Nervous and Mental Disorders*, CXXX (1960) 97–106.
439 Cobb, S. "Observations on the comparative anatomy of the avian brain." *Perspectives in Biology and Medicine*, III (1960) 383–408.
440 Cobb, S. "A pain in the neck." *Harvard Medical Alumni Bulletin* XXXIV (1960) 8–12.
441 Cobb, S. [Address at the dedication of] "The Stanley Cobb Laboratories

for research in psychiatry." *Massachusetts General Hospital News*, No. 199, December, 1960, pp. 3–4.

442 Cobb, S. Foreword to *Thinking and Psychology; an Inquiry into the Process of Communication*, by Harley C. Shands (Cambridge, Harvard University Press, 1960, pp. vii–x).

443 Cobb, S. "A Salute from Neurologists." Introduction to *The Neurophysiology of Lashley; Selected Papers of K. S. Lashley*, edited by Frank A. Beach ed al. (New York, McGraw Hill, 1960, pp. xvii–xx).

444 Cobb, S. Review of *The Neurological Basis of Behavior: a CIBA Foundation Symposium*, edited by E. E. W. Wolstenholm and C. M. O'Connor.*Psychosomatic Medicine*, XXII (1960) 159–160.

445 Cobb, S. Review of *The Central Nervous System and Behavior*, edited by M. A. B. Brazicr. *Psychosomatic Medicine*, XXII 1960) 160–162.

446 Cobb, S. Review of *Insulin Treatment in Psychiatry*, edited by M. Rinkel and H. E. Himsich. *Psychosomatic Medicine*, XXII (1960) 234.

447 Cobb, S. Review of *J. M. Charcot, His Life and Works*, by G. Guillain *Psychosomatic Medicine*, XXII (1960) 240–241.

448 Cobb, S. Review of *Sigmund Freud: Collected Papers*, volumes 1 thru 5, edited by E. Jones and J. Strachey. *Psychosomatic Medicine*, XXII (1960) 246.

449 Cobb, S. Review of *Behavior and Evolution*, by A. Roe and G. G. Simpson. *Psychosomatic Medicine*, XXII (1960) 488–489.

450 Cobb, S. Review of *Comparative Morphology of the Forebrain of Birds*, by W. Stingelin. *The Auk*, LXXVIII (1961) 284.

451 Cobb, S. "Obituaries: William Gordon Lennox." *Archives of Neurology*, IV (1961) 463–465.

452 Cobb, S. "Correspondence [John Farquar Fulton, 1890–1960]. *Psychosomatic Medicine*, XXIII (1961) 77.

453 Cobb, S. "Mind and body." *The Atlantic*, CCVIII (1961) 63–67.

454 Cobb, S. "The comparative anatomy of the avian brain." *Midway*, VII (1961) 23–52.

455 Cobb, S. Review of *The Case Against Adolf Eichmann*, by H. A. Zeiger. *Psychosomatic Medicine*, XXIII (1961) 86.

456 Cobb, S. Review of *From Death Camp to Existentialism*, by Victor E. Frankl. *Psychosomatic Medicine*, XXIII (1961) 86–87.

457 Cobb, S. Review of *Experiment Perilous: Physicians and Patients Facing the Unknown*, by Renee C. Fox. *Psychosomatic Medicine*, XXIII (1961) 180.

458 Cobb, S. Review of *Blood Pressure and Subarctic Climate in the Soviet Union*, by Bruno Hoffmann (translated by E. A. White). *Psychosomatic Medicine*, XXIII (1961) 181–182.

459 Cobb, S. Review of *The Phenomenon of Man*, by Pierre Teilhard de Chardin. *Psychosomatic Medicine*, XXIII (1961) 269–270.

460 Cobb, S. Review of *The Mother-Child Interaction in Psychosomatic Disorders*, by A. M. Garner and Charles Wenar. *Psychosomatic Medicine*, XXIII (1961) 272.

461 Cobb, S. Review of *Significant Trends in Medical Research: CIBA Foundation Tenth Anniversary Symposium*. Psychosomatic Medicine, XXIII (1961) 365–366.

462 Cobb, S. "Comments: Psychiatric implications of the Eddington lecture." American Journal of Psychiatry, CIX (1962) 273–275.

463 Cobb, S. "Literary and scientific publications of Carl Binger." Psychosomatic Medicine, CIX (1962) 4–9.

464 Cobb, S. "Psychosomatic medicine today." Journal of Nervous and Mental Diseases, CXXXIV (1962) 299–304.

465 Cobb, S. "Notes on the brain of the hummingbird." Archives of Neurology, VI (1962) 43–48.

466 Cobb, S. and Edinger, T. "The brain of the emu (dromaeus novaehollandiae lath). I. Gross anatomy of the brain and pineal body." Breviora, Museum of Comparative Zoology, No. 170, (November 16, 1962) 1–18.

467 Cobb, S. Review of *The Torch*, by Wilder Penfield. Psychosomatic Medicine, XXIV (1962) 114.

468 Cobb, S. Review of *The Central Nervous System and Behavior, Transactions of the Second Conference, February 22–25, 1959*, by M. A. B. Brazier. Psychosomatic Medicine, XXIV (1962) 423–424.

469 Cobb, S. Review of *The Central Nervous System and Behavior, Transactions of the Third Conference, February 21–24, 1960*, by M. A. B. Brazier. Psychosomatic Medicine, XXIV (1962) 424.

470 Cobb, S. Review of *The Central Nervous System and Behavior: Translations from the Russian Medical Literature*. Psychosomatic Medicine, XXIV (1962) 424.

471 Cobb, S. "Doggerel" [poem]. New England Journal of Medicine CCLXVIII (1963) 1239.

472 Cobb, S. "Zoologist claims action on pesticides is urgent." Vineyard Gazette, August, 1963.

473 Cobb, S. "Death of a salt pond." Audubon Magazine, LXV (1963) 70–72.

474 Cobb, S. "Notes on the avian optic lobe (tectum and nucleus mesencephalicus lateralis)." Brain, LXXXVI (1963) 363–372.

475 Cobb, S. "Mind-body relationships." Chapter 3 in *The Psychological Basis of Medical Practice*, edited by H. I. Lief et al. (New York, Harper & Row, 1963, pp. 36–43).

476 Cobb, S. "Death by poison—one year later." Massachusetts Audubon Newsletter, III (August–September 1963) 2.

477 Cobb, S. Review of *Somatosensory Changes after Penetrating Brain Injuries in Man*, by Josephine Semmes et al. Psychosomatic Medicine, XXV (1963) 402.

478 Cobb, S. Review of *Mental Abnormality and the Law*, by H. J. Wily and and K. R. Stallworthy. Psychosomatic Medicine, XXV (1963) 503.

479 Cobb, S. Review of *Electrical Stimulation of the Brain: An Interdisciplinary Survey of Neurobehavioral Integrative Systems*, by D. E. Sheer. Psychosomatic Medicine, XXV (1963) 586–587.

480 Cobb, S. Review of *Textbook of Psychiatry for Students and Practitioners*, by Henderson and Gillespie (revised by Sir D. Henderson and I. R. C. Batchelor). *Psychosomatic Medicine*, XXV (1963) 587–588.
481 Cobb, S. Foreword to *Ascent from Chaos, a Psychosomatic Case Study*, by P. E. Sifneos (Cambridge, Harvard University Press, 1964, pp. xi–xiii).
482 Cobb, S. "Guns for children." *Parents' League Letters*, March, 1964, p. 12.
483 Cobb, S. "To Rachel Carson, who died April 14, 1964." *Vineyard Gazette*, April 16, 1964.
484 Cobb, S. "Comments: thoughts on schizophrenia." *American Journal of Psychiatry*, CXX (1964) 707.
485 Mello, N. K., Ervin, F. R. and Cobb, S. *Intertectal Integration of Visual Information in Pigeon; Electrophysiological and Behavioral Observations* (Washington, Office of Naval Research and the Air Force Office of Scientific Research, 1964).
486 Cobb, S. "In Memoriam: Walter Bauer, M.D., 1893–1963." *Psychosomatic Medicine*, XXVI (1964) 103.
487 Kury, G. and Cobb, S. "Epileptic dementia resembling schizophrenia: clinico-pathological report of a case. *Journal of Nervous and Mental Disease*, CXXXVIII (1964) 340–347.
488 Cobb, S. "A comparison of the size of an auditory nucleus (n. mesencephalicus lateralis, pars dorsalis) with the size of the optic lobe in twenty-seven species of birds." *Journal of Comparative Neurology*, CXXII (1964) 271–280.
489 Cobb, S. "Human values and culture." *Christian Science Monitor*, June 13, 1964 (in "Features-Readers Write" section).
490 Cobb, S. "Calendar no gauge for winter." *Christian Science Monitor*, December 20, 1964.
491 Cobb, S. "A review of three books on evolution of interest to neurologists and psychiatrists: *Darwin's Biological Works: Some Aspects Reconsidered*, by P. R. Bell; *Behavior and Evolution*, by A. Rae and G. G. Simpson; *The Phenomenon of Man*, by P. Teilhard de Chardin." *Archives of Neurology*, X (1964) 533–534.
492 Cobb, S. Review of *Die Wahnwelten (Endogene Psychosen)*, by Erwin Straus and Jurg Zitt. *Psychosomatic Medicine*, XXVI (1964) 195–196.
493 Cobb, S. Review of *Civilization and Its Discontents*, by Sigmund Freud. *Psychosomatic Medicine*, XXVI (1964) 296.
494 Cobb, S. Review of *Theories of the Mind*, by J. M. Scher. *Psychosomatic Medicine*, XXVI (1964) 296–297.
495 Cobb, S. Review of *The Life of Birds*, by J. C. Welty. *Psychosomatic Medicine*, XXVI (1964) 298.
496 Cobb, S. "Machines, medicine and morals." *American Journal of Psychiatry*, CXXI (1964–1965) 1212–1213.
497 Cobb, S. Review of *The Disorganized Personality*, by G. W. Kisker. *American Journal of Psychiatry*, CXXII (1964–1965) 234.

498 Cobb, S. "Norbert Wiener, 1894–1964." *Journal of Nervous and Mental Disease,* CXL (1965) 3–16.
499 Cobbs, S. [Obituary of Winthrop Sprague Brooks]. *The Auk,* LXXXII (1965) 684–685.
500 Cobb, S. "Reverence for life—is the extinction of life a prerogative of brash, arrogant men?" *Vineyard Gazette,* August 13, 1965.
501 Cobb, S. "Brain size." *Archives of Neurology,* XII (1965) 555–561.
502 Cobb, S. Review of *Wild Heritage,* by Sally Carrighar. *Psychosomatic Medicine,* XXVII (1965) 584.
503 Cobb, S. "Science and ecology." *Christian Science Monitor,* January 10, 1966, p. 18.
504 Cobb, S. "Only a stamp profile?" *Massachusetts Audubon Newsletter,* V (February, 1966) 1.
505 Cobb, S. "The brain of the emu dromaeus novaehollandiae. II. Anatomy of the principal nerve cell ganglia and tracts." *Breviora, Museum of Comparative Zoology,* No. 250 (November 4, 1966) 1–27.
506 Cobb, S. "Alexander Forbes, 1882–1965." *Journal of Nervous and Mental Disease,* CXLI (1966) 609–614.
507 Cobb, S. "Brain size." *C M D* (August, 1966) 1225–1228. Condensed from *Archives of Neurology* article of 1965 (no. 501).
508 Bang, B. G. and Cobb, S. "The size of the olfactory bulb in 108 species of birds." *The Auk,* LXXXV (1968) 55–61.
509 Cobb, S. "On the size of the auditory nuclei in some apodiformes and caprimulgiformes." *The Auk,* LXXXV (1968) 132–133.
510 Cobb, S. Book review of *Brain Mechanisms Underlying Speech and Language,* by F. L. Darley. *New England Journal of Medicine,* CCLXXVIII (1968) 55–61.
511 Cobb, S. "Adventures in avian neurology." Chapter 1 in *Modern Neurology; papers in tribute to Derek Denny-Brown,* edited by Simeon Locke (Boston, Little Brown, 1969, pp. 1–13).

APPENDIX C

Transcription of the Taped Reminiscences of D. Stafford-Clark

"After my residency at M.G.H. I was appointed to a Clinical Fellowship at Harvard Medical School and M.G.H. for six months. I had a pilot project for which Cobb helped me with funds and which he thought had possibilities. This is how we set it up: I should see, if possible, a maximum of fifty children in the M.G.H. during the six months of the project. These fifty children would be divided into two groups, the first made up of kids suffering from some disorder such as cardiac impairment due to rheumatic fever which required not only a lot of nursing but a lot of restrictions on the child's movement, so that he or she wouldn't suffer permanent cardiac damage. We wanted about twenty-five such kids who were, in fact, in hospital under the stress, not only of separation from their parents, who were allowed to visit frequently, but also the stress of being made aware, long before they were able to take it in, that they were sick patients and not ordinary kids. The other twenty-five were patients who, for one reason or another, in the same age group and matched as far as possible for age and sex, were being encouraged to pretend that they weren't patients and were getting better so rapidly that they would be soon O.K.

"What we wanted to find out was the effect on the child, on the staff, and on the parents of the two totally different approaches. In order to find our fifty children within the six months we had to call on other Boston pediatric departments as well as M.G.H., including the Boston City Hospital and the Peter Bent Brigham Hospital.

"In the end we got about twenty-two of each group: the so-called invalid children who were made to feel invalids because everyone was scared that if they did get up and run about, they might get permanent mitral damage; and by contrast, those kids who, whatever their real prognosis, were encouraged to be as lively and active as possible. Some of these, in fact, had a terrible prognosis, one of whom exemplifies the irony of what we learned.

"I don't remember exactly what the results were except that there was a very heavy preponderance of overt anxiety (and all the symptoms of severe latent anxiety that children between the ages of five and fifteen, which I think was our age limit, might show) in those who were invalids; whereas in the sort of *gung-ho* kids who were being encouraged to be active, there was practically no anxiety at all.

"Anxiety was also apparent in the staff caring for the invalid group in contrast to the enthusiasm of those looking after the *gung-ho* brigade. This contrast was reflected among the parents who immediately took the cue from the staff; so if a little fellow or girl was running about the ward and appearing to be recovering and thereby encouraged, they felt good, and they gave the child added security.

"On the other hand, if the child was kept in bed continuously, and being fed reclining, parents became terribly anxious and guilty too, so that this all rubbed off on the kid. This all came through very clearly. We had a whole battery of psychological tests. The findings were consistent, written up in the pilot project and left at the M.G.H. My own copy unfortunately was destroyed in my home in Cyprus in the 1974 war; but that is another story. I don't have a single record of those days left, except a picture on the wall of myself in the 1949 residency group and my memory of that research, although I think you will find there are records of it at M.G.H., because I did write it up."

Having discussed the protocol and the general findings, Stafford-Clark went on to tell about the tragic impact of the study on one boy. He then presented the story of Billy.

"The psychological tests bore out exactly what we found clinically, and this anecdote shows what an interesting and in a way ironic study it turned out to be. The most *gung-ho* patient of the lot among the children was a little boy of about eight, whom I will call Billy. I don't remember his real name. He had sarcoma of the femur for which his left leg had been amputated above the knee. The sarcoma was near the knee, and I think Billy was left just enough stump to have a prosthesis fitted, but you know what the prognosis is in such sarcomas in children. He was almost certainly going to die in six months from multiple secondaries. But having removed his leg and got the dreaded neoplasm out of the way, the surgeons and the nurses got instructions from the

Appendix C: Reminiscences of D. Stafford-Clark

Chief to make this kid as happy and as excited and as cheerful about his future as possible. This was the word which went out, and everybody carried it out. And this was the word which the parents got, although nobody told them the kid had less than a one-in-twenty chance of surviving a year, yet alone longer. By the time I went to interview him, as one of my *gung-ho* group, if you like to call it that, he was hopping about the ward on one leg without crutches, like a little bird, and he had already constructed a personal fantasy of how he was going to be the greatest baseball player ever when he grew up.

"One of the things that I had to find out was how these children envisaged their future. Practically all the invalids expected to die, and they mostly thought they had cancer of the heart. No one had told them this, of course, but it represented for them about the worst thing you could have, you see. You know your heart is somehow bad, and cancer is the worst thing you can have, and in their vague way, they mostly thought that cancer must be what they had. They thought that this was why they were invalids, why they had to lie in bed, and why they were going to die. Not so Billy. Billy, who was undoubtedly going to die, thought he was going to live to a ripe old age, and he was going to be a baseball star like Joe DiMaggio of the New York Yankees and Ted Williams of the Boston Red Sox.

"I remember asking Billy, among the things that I had on my check list, 'Well, Billy, if you make it as a great baseball star, how will you do it? Are you going to be a pitcher or a hitter, which?' He said, 'Oh gee, I don't think I can stand up to pitching all day on one leg. I think I will be a hitter, and I can have a guy run for me. On one leg I'll be able to hit enough home runs to make myself as great as Joe DiMaggio or Ted Williams.' So I said, 'Well, that's fine.' He asked, 'Would you like to join my fan club?' I said, 'How do I do that?' 'Well,' he said, 'all the nurses and doctors I have seen are members. They type out a piece of paper saying, "You are a member of the Billy Smart Fan Club for baseball," and I write my name on it.' He was going to play for the Red Sox. So I obliged him, and I went away thinking to myself, 'What an extraordinary thing! Here is this child full of enthusiasm and hope for the future, without a future really, and there are all these invalid kids with an ultimately better prognosis racked with anxiety that they have cancer of the heart.'

"Before I even left M.G.H. in June, 1950, Billy was dead. A terrible thing about this now emerges. I had simply seen him as one of my research-project candidates, and I had not interfered with his treatment, nor had I spoken to the Chief of Surgery, where he had been operated on, about the fact that the parents should surely be told the almost inevitable prognosis: that child was not likely to live. I discovered, quite by accident after he was dead, that the parents had never been told, so that they, as innocently enthusiastic members of his fan club, had had no chance to prepare themselves for his death. Their reaction was one of outrage; they became bitterly incensed against the hospital. I can't remember which one it was, but in fact I don't think it was M.G.H. Anyway, I was supposed to do a follow-up just before I left, but because I had seen their Billy even once, they wouldn't see me. They were really badly hurt people. It was one of the many things which taught me how much we had to learn, how much we had to teach our colleagues about handling relatives of sick children.

"I discussed my uneasiness with Stanley Cobb, and he said to me, 'I think that you were absolutely right on a research project to stay clear of clinical involvement if you weren't specifically invited to give your views.' This was invaluable support to me at a difficult time, because by then I was naturally feeling guilty too, although I had played no part in the management of the case other than this one interview, and the non-existent follow-up, because the kid was dead and the parents had turned completely off. But Stanley Cobb thought the whole concept of the project was good, right from the beginning, and the results that we got were worth while."

Stafford-Clark's third story about his own benign fasciculation illustrated the concern with which Cobb offered reassurance when he was suffering from anxiety about his health.

"I went to the Massachusetts General, as I have said, in June '49 to start as a resident on the exchange program with Nuffield Fellows in Psychiatry from the University of London. I was the second one to go. Dennis Leigh was the first, and Bill Trethowan was about fourth or fifth. Now I had been away in the war, for most of the time separated from my wife. Being away from my wife and children in the war seemed natural. Being away in peace time, in America particularly, seemed totally unnatural, the more so because nobody else was away from home that I knew, except Kenny Nash, my fellow resident who lived in Pasadena, and had come almost as far to the Massachusetts General as I had. I missed my wife terribly, partly because of the enormously warm hospitality and kindness which everybody showed the residents, the nurses, the wives of the residents, and the husbands of the nurses. I had about six invitations at Christmas, 1949, and I remember feeling, in a way it made it all the more tough to be away from my own family. I wished I could afford to fly back to England just to be with them, but I couldn't. There was basically a terrible conflict between being lonely and yet being among friends. I learned to love America with a love that has lasted a lifetime; but I am sure that young husbands and wives and children should not be separated for a year as the price of an invaluable traveling fellowship.

"Just after I finished my residency, or maybe, even before, I began to get fasciculation in the small muscles of my hand, and this worried me to death, because I thought I had upper-motor-neurone disease. I thought, 'What the hell am I going to do, if I have? This is going to kill me, maybe before I see my wife and children again.' In fact, it was purely an anxiety state. I had tense muscles which can cause benign fasciculation, but I didn't know that at the time. I didn't know what to do, and I didn't know whom to tell. I mentioned it to Kenny Nash, and he said, 'Why don't you tell Stanley Cobb?' So I screwed up my courage and I arranged to see Stanley on a personal matter. I showed him the muscle between my right thumb and first finger fasciculating, and I told him all my anxieties, and I asked him whether I should fly back to England. Should I get my wife out? What should I do? He listened perfectly. In the end he said, 'Look, David, I am quite sure that you have nothing to worry about. That's coarse fasciculation. It's not the fine fibrillation that you get in upper-motor-neurone disorders. You do sometimes see fine fasciculation after wasting and fibrillation, but coarse fasciculation in the absence of wasting is almost certainly benign. There is no waste in your hands. What I am going to do is, I am going to arrange for Bob Schwab, who is our electromyographic specialist, to make some electromyographic tracings.' I had horrible visions of needles being stuck into my hand. I must have been looking a bit sad, and he said, 'It is quite all right. He will put plates on your muscles and will take readings, and these will confirm, I am sure, that you have coarse fasciculation and that really this is anxiety, separation, loneliness, all the things that you have told me about.'

"And so it proved; later Bob Schwab and I wrote a paper together on this phenomenon, because we found that it was by no means so uncommon as we had thought. We dug up about a dozen doctors and nurses who had the same thing under the same kind of circumstances.

We found that the benign fasciculation which we had all experienced was quite a common thing. That paper was published in the *British Medical Journal* by Bob Schwab, John Stobe Pritchard, and myself: B.M.J. July 28, 1951, Vol. 2, p. 209. Stanley Cobb, generous as ever, refused to have his name on it, even though it was due to his effort that the paper got written at all.

"I think those two stories, the story of Billy, the kid with the sarcoma, and the story of my benign fasciculation and later collaboration with Bob Schwab on the paper, show something of the kind of man Stanley Cobb was, the kind of research he inspired doctors to do, and the kind of gratitude and admiration with which I and other former students and colleagues will always remember him."

Major Sources Employed in Compiling this Work

Information documenting this book on the life and work of Stanley Cobb was derived mostly from manuscript and archival sources as well as from personal and taped interviews with friends, colleagues, students, members of Cobb's family, and others who touched his life. In reconstructing his earliest years the author relied to a large extent upon family letters—letters to parents, sisters, and brothers—which Dr. Cobb's sister Hildegarde Forbes gathered together over the years. This material was supplemented by interviews and discussions with Cobb's immediate family, especially Hildegarde Forbes and his widow, Elizabeth Almy Cobb Hall. These last two sources not only furnished facts and details on the earlier part of Cobb's life, but added valuable information about his later years as well. Additionally, they continually provided a check on the reliability of information gathered from other sources, cleared up ambiguities, and assisted in establishing a proper chronology.

Most of Cobb's early manuscript papers and correspondence were long ago deposited in the Harvard Medical Archives and are now in the Francis A. Countway Library of Medicine. This mass consists mainly of drafts of his research papers, speeches, and similar materials as well as his office and sometimes personal correspondence and covers the period from 1906 until 1934, but mainly the years from 1920 to 1930. (These Countway files contain mostly papers and correspondence accumulated by Dr. Cobb prior to his transfer to the Massachusetts General Hospital in 1934 when he established the psychiatric service there.) Included within these Countway holdings, fortunately, are two files labeled "1906–1911" and "1911–1914" respectively. These letter cases contain family and other letters written to and from Cobb during the years he was attending Harvard College and afterwards the Harvard Medical School, as well as academic grades, invitations of a social nature, and programs at various events. The material in these cases was invaluable for documenting the most formative period of Cobb's education.

The office files dating from 1934 when Cobb moved to the Massachusetts General Hospital until 1954, when he retired, were designated at that time for deposit among his earlier papers in the Harvard Medical Archives. Unfortunately, because of an administrative or custodial error at the hospital, they were trashed instead and lost forever. In order to overcome the information gap caused by this unfortunate accident, the author and his wife undertook in 1977 a lengthy series of taped interviews with more than fifty of Dr. Cobb's relatives, friends, students, and others who were acquainted with him or his field. These persons provided essential information on Cobb's years at the M.G.H. during the period for which manuscript sources were lacking, and they divulged a rich store of anecdotes and reminiscences about Cobb's everyday life and the lives of many of the talented and exceptional people with whom he interacted. Fortunately, the letters and papers which Dr. Cobb accumulated following his retirement in 1954 and up to his death in 1968 have been for the most part preserved. These served as one of the important sources for sketching out the final years of his life.

Most of the materials gathered together by Hildegarde Forbes and put into the author's hands for the writing of this book, as well as the letters and manuscripts dating from 1954 through 1968, are at the time of the writing of this resumé of sources being readied for deposit among Cobb's papers in the Harvard Medical Archives in the Countway Library. Therefore, all such letters and manuscript papers, including family and other correspondence assembled by the author in the course of compiling this work, as well as the earlier Countway file, have been referenced in the notes with the simple designation "Cobb Papers." Unfortunately, when the author changed his residence during the compilation of this book, one box containing family letters, including letters exchanged between Cobb and his mother, became lost. Letters from that box are designated in the notes as "Cobb Papers, Lost Family Correspondence." Fortunately, abstracts had been made of many of these letters prior to the move, so that part of this material remains among Cobb's Countway files as a permanent record of his earlier life.

Several other large manuscript resources were utilized for discovering facts about Cobb's life and the lives of others in his milieu. Most important in this category are the files of Cobb's correspondence with his teacher Adolf Meyer, which are now preserved in the Meyer Papers in the Alan M. Chesney Medical Archives of the Johns Hopkins Medical Institution in Baltimore. Materials from this important resource are cited as "Meyer Papers" in the notes. The correspondence of Abraham Flexner and other officials of the General Eduction Board of the Rockefeller Foundation also provided important information about Cobb, particularly on his first European trip and on the funding of his activities thereafter. This material, now preserved in the Rockefeller Archives in Pocantico Hills, New York, is cited in the notes as "Rockefeller Archives." Manuscript letters and papers of David L. Edsall, Dean of the Harvard Medical School from 1918 until 1937, also divulged important facts about Cobb's professional life, especially at Harvard. These papers form part of the Dean's Files in the Harvard Medical Archives and are therefore designated "Dean's Files, Harvard Medical Archives."

In addition to the above sources, which were the chief ones used, information came from a variety of other manuscript collections, some of which are in the Boston area and others elsewhere. For instance, the manuscript papers in the Countway Library of Joseph Aub, Walter B. Cannon, Alexander Forbes, Frank Fremont-Smith, and others furnished crucial pieces of information about various aspects of Cobb's life, as did, for example, the papers of Simon Flexner and Rufus Cole of the Rockefeller Foundation, now in the collections of the American Philosophical Society. Notes concerning these collections are cited with the name of the collection and the repository which holds it, *viz.*, "Aub" ("Cannon," "Forbes," "Fremont-Smith") Papers, Countway Library," or "Simon Flexner" (or "Rufus Cole") Papers, American Philosophical Society."

As noted before, the large gap that was created in documenting Cobb's life in the 1934–1954 period by the loss of his files at the Massachusetts General Hospital was made up for by taped interviews with more than fifty of Cobb's family, co-workers, and friends. The indexed tapes of these interviews, which are listed alphabetically by interviewee at the end of this résumé, are also being deposited among Cobb's Papers in the Countway Library. It must be noted here that this program was undertaken at just the proper time, for many of those interviewed have passed away since, and a great deal of important information on Cobb and Boston medicine would otherwise have been lost.

Finally, to document what Cobb was doing as a research scientist along the way, great reliance was placed on his published writings of about 500 books, papers, and other materials in all. A complete bibliography appears in the volume as Appendix B. References in the text to items in the bibliography are designated with the bibliographic entry number in parentheses.

Recordings of Tape Interviews on File in The Francis A. Countway Library of Medicine

John Adams Abbott, M.D.
February 16, 1978

Leo Alexander, M.D.
February 14, 1978

Bernard Bandler, M.D.
February 19, 1978

Herbert Barry, M.D.
April 8, 1980

Clorinda (Chloe) Garrison Binger (Mrs. Carl Binger)
July 24, 1977

Frances Bonner, M.D.
April 16, 1978

George Carter, M.D.
December 2, 1979

Mandel Cohen, M.D.
February 22, 1978

Oliver Cope, M.D.
February 23, 1978

Derek Denny-Brown, M.D.
December 10, 1978

Helene Deutsch, M.D.
February 16, 1978

Peter B. Dews, M.D.
December 4, 1979

Samuel Epstein, M.D.
August 10, 1979

Erik Erikson
July 22, 1978 (notes from memory)

Grace Finesinger (Mrs. Jacob E. Finesinger)
February 22, 1978

Knox Finley, M.D.
March 27, 1979

Elizabeth Fisher
August 21, 1977

Hildegarde Forbes (Mrs. Henry Stone Forbes)
August 11–12, 1977; February 13, 1979

Frederic Gibbs, M.D., and Erna Leonhard Gibbs
December 30, 1977

Sanford Gifford, M.D.
February 19, 1978; May 8, 1982

Edwin F. Gildea, M.D., and Margaret C.-L. Gildea, M.D.
April 16, 1977

Margaret Gray
July 28, 1978

Phyllis Greenacre, M.D.
January 5, 1978

Maurice Greenhill, M.D.
April 27, 1978

Thomas Hackett, M.D.
February 21, 1978

Elizabeth Almy Cobb Hall (Mrs. Stanley Cobb)
April 18, 1977

Sources

Richmond Holder, M.D.
February 15, 1979

Elizabeth Lindemann (Mrs. Eric Lindemann)
April 16, 1978

Maria Lorenz, M.D.
February 18, 1978

Alfred O. Ludwig, M.D.
August 3, 1979

Gladys Nason Lothrop
June 24, 1978

H. Houston Merritt, M.D.
June 1, 1978

John Nemiah, M.D.
April 4, 1977

Eleanor Pavenstedt, M.D.
July 23, 1978 (tape of poor technical quality)

Alfred Pope, M.D.
February 18, 1978

Alfred Redfield
July 16, 1977

E. Pierson Richardson, M.D.
April 10, 1980

Curt Richter
August 18, 1977

Jurgen Ruesch, M.D.
March 27, 1979

Gregory Rochlin, M.D.
April 8, 1980

Milton Rosenbaum, M.D.
July 25, 1978

Earl Solomon, M.D.
February 28, 1978

Harry C. Solomon, M.D.
February 14, 1979

David Stafford-Clark, M.D.
August 4, 1979 (taped submitted by mail)

Eugene Taylor
April 28, 1981

Charlotte Richards Troutwine
July 5, 1977

Suzanne Van Amerongen, M.D.
February 14, 1979

Jerome Weinberger, M.D.
August 27, 1977

Avery Weisman, M.D.
February 15, 1978

Florence Clothier Wislocki, M.D.
July 18, 1978

Notes

Chapter 1

1. Personal visit to the homestead in 1977.
2. The property was subdivided. The old driveway became Oakland Street. Two very well constructed, handsome row houses were built on the corners of Walnut and Oakland Streets. As one entered Oakland Street, the large, nondescript house which had served as the Cobbs' home was on the left. Between the house and the row house on the corner, the driveway led to a stable with a cupola on top. There is a legend that one moonlight night during World War I Uncle Al Bigelow and his wife observed the cupola to be ever so slowly ascending toward heaven. They nudged each other to be sure that they were not imagining the phenomenon. Then, on a subsequent clear night, they noticed the same thing happening again. These observations were reported to the police, and later study revealed that the old Cobb home was occupied by German sympathizers, who in some way were using the elevated cupola to communicate with ships in the harbor. Hildegarde Forbes tape, August 22, 1977. Continuous wave radio was not in commercial use during World War I but was presumably available for intelligence purposes.
3. Hildegarde Forbes to Benjamin V. and Helen White, January 30, 1978, Cobb Papers.
4. Information on Augusta Adams Cobb comes from papers accumulated by Hildegarde Forbes.
5. This story was recounted in Cobb's article "A Fee List from the Papers of Archelaus Green Smith, M.D. (1792 to 1850)," *Boston Medical and Surgical Journal*, CLXXXIX (1923) 641–645 (Entry 33 in Cobb's Bibliography).
6. This story was recorded verbatim during an undated interview with Hildegarde Forbes.
7. A U.S. Government chart of Boston Harbor published in 1904 shows drawn in lightly a railroad spur running from the New York, New Haven and Hartford tracks along the east side of the South Bay and terminating on its southern shore. The South Bay, now entirely filled in, was an extension of the Fort Point Channel, as far south as Boston City Hospital with wharves along the east side of Albany Street. The Southeast Expressway now crosses the area. There is no evidence presently at hand to prove that the spur on the chart was in fact the South Bay Wharf and Terminal Company. The U.S. Government chart is on file in the Archives of the Massachusetts State House as Map No. 4398.
8. John Candler Cobb (1858–1933), *The Application of Scientific Methods to Sociology* (Boston, Chapman and Grimes, 1934). "Editorial Note" signed Stanley Cobb.

Notes

9. Leonore Smith Cobb was born at Fort Washington, New York, June 16, 1858, and died in Milton, Massachusetts, April 30, 1947. She was a daughter of Augustus F. Smith (1819–1876) and Lucy Ann Elliott (1819–1870).

10. John Candler Cobb to Stanley Cobb, January 24, 1911, Cobb Papers.

11. John Candler Cobb, Jr., was born in 1880 in Brookline and died in 1948. He was married in the fall of 1909 to Mary Louise King, who died in 1977. The couple is survived by two children, Mrs. Margaret Gessel of San Diego, California, and Kenneth Wilson Cobb of Silver Spring, Maryland.

12. Emma May Cobb was born November 12, 1882, in Brookline, Massachusetts, and died May 3, 1975, in Southport, Connecticut. On January 11, 1910, she was married to Dr. Nathan Chandler Foot (1881–1958). They had two daughters, Louise Foot Besson (1911–   ) and Ellen Foot Neumann, M.D. (1913–1945).

13. Augustus Smith Cobb had three marriages. The first was in Newton, Massachusetts, on June 9, 1915, to Mary Christine Converse. There were three children, Jean Cobb Moore of Prescott, Arizona, and New London, New Hampshire, Virginia Cobb Heywood of Tucson, and Mary Christine Cobb Ming of Tucson. The marriage of Augustus Cobb to Christine Converse was terminated by divorce, and on February 14, 1929, in New York City, he married Dorothy Harvey Thompson. He was later married to Eleanor Brown Stevenson.

14. Florence Smith Cobb was born January 6, 1890, and died April 6, 1958. On June 3, 1911, she married Walter Dennison Brooks, a Milton neighbor; they had three children, Florence Cobb Brooks (1912–1918), Walter Dennison Brooks, Jr., and Stanley Brooks, all of Milton.

15. Beatrice Cobb was born March 24, 1892 in Brookline and died February 25, 1968 in Peru, Vermont. On June 18, 1920, in Milton, she married Bruce Smart. Three children issued from the marriage, Stephen Bruce Smart, Jr., Leonore Smart, and Katherine Smart.

16. Hildegarde Boughton Cobb was born November 7, 1893 in Milton and on September 23, 1922, again in Milton, she married Henry Stone Forbes. Their four children were Hildegarde Green of Providence, Elizabeth Candler Gordon of Cambridge, Marjorie Elias of Cambridge, and Beatrice Cobb Forbes of Vermont.

17. Cobb's widow recalled that the September hunting, when Cobb was in medical school, took place here.

18. Mary Doyle to Stanley Cobb, February 9, 1912, Cobb Papers.

19. Later on when Mary Doyle was terminally ill with cancer she was a patient at the little Milton Hospital. She refused to pay her bill although she had funds in the bank which the Cobb family knew about. Hildegarde convinced the hospital superintendent that it was all right to extend credit because Mary had the money. When Mary died, however, she left her money to various Cobb children. To compensate for Mary's financial delinquency, Hildegarde and her husband, Dr. Henry S. Forbes, gave the hospital a new delivery table, which settled the account.

20. Hildegarde Forbes said in November, 1981, that Mrs. Cobb believed in keeping children home until they were eight years old or so.

21. Although Mrs. Cobb's frequent withdrawal of children from school has been viewed by many as a behavior pattern for dealing with frustration, Hildegarde Forbes cited in November, 1981, the faculty teasing as evidence that Mrs. Cobb was right in removing Stanley from Milton Academy.

22. Cornelia Huntington Damon to Stanley Cobb, December, 1958, Cobb Papers.

23. Registration card preserved in the papers accumulated by Hildegarde Forbes; she confirmed in 1981 that Cobb was studying voice.

24. Stanley Cobb to Leonore Smith Cobb, August 24, 1906, Cobb Papers.

25. Stanley Cobb to John Candler Cobb, Jr., September 9, 1906, Cobb Papers.

Chapter 2

1. Harvard College Catalog, 1906–1907.

2. D. L. V. Volkmann to Leonore Smith Cobb, November 22, 1906, Cobb Papers.

3. Essentially all the information about Cobb's roommates was assembled from preserved correspondence in two files labeled "1906–1911" and "1911–1914" in the Cobb Papers.

4. Volkmann School grades are included in the Harvard transcript and were as follows: Elementary: English D, Latin C, German D, French D, History D+, Algebra C, Plane Geometry D, Physics C, and Chemistry B. Advanced: Latin D, German C, and French D. His Harvard record reads as follows: Full courses freshman year: English C+, Government C−, Fine Arts B, Chemistry C. Half courses: Botany A, Zoology B. Full courses sophomore year: Economics C, English C. Half courses: Chemistry C, Geology A, Zoology B, A, and B. Full courses junior year: German C, Physics C, Zoology A. Half courses: Botany B, Comparative Literature C, and Philosophy A. Full courses senior year: Chemistry C. Half courses: Comparative Literature C, Geology B, German D, Philosophy B, Zoology A and B.

5. On the final examination in Geology 4 at the end of senior year in 1910 appeared question 6, "How do you determine the relative ages of rocks and rock structures? What evidence does the earth present to show the lapse of time?" Cobb drew a sketch showing superimposed layers of the earth's crust labeled "fresh water," "coal," "marine," "desert," "red sandstone," "petrified trees," "sandstone," "igneous," and in a more or less parallel column wrote "position in crust," "fossils," "structure."

6. G. H. Parker to Stanley Cobb, undated, but probably April, 1910, Cobb Papers.

7. Stanley Cobb to Hugo Münsterberg, May, 1909, Cobb Papers.

8. Hugo Münsterberg to Stanley Cobb, May 17, 1909, Cobb Papers.

9. Rollins Maxwell to Stanley Cobb, November 24, 1909, Cobb Papers.

10. Emile Duplessis to Stanley Cobb, March 11, 1910, Cobb Papers.

11. W. M. Davis to Stanley Cobb, March 23, 1910, Cobb Papers.

12. The Boston Society of Natural History operated the Museum of Natural

Notes

History, which later became the Museum of Science. When Cobb was elected to it there were only three other members, including Penelope Noyes.

13. *Official Register of Harvard University,* Vol. VII, No. 45, December 15, 1910.

14. Francis M. Rackemann, *The Inquisitive Physician* (Cambridge, Harvard University Press, 1956) p. 33. The problem of clinical teaching at Harvard is summed up in a recent article by Dr. Kenneth M. Ludmerer, "Reform at Harvard Medical School, 1869–1909," *Bulletin of the History of Medicine,* LV (1981) 343–370.

15. Rackemann, *op. cit.,* p. 38.

16. David Cheever, "The Turn of the Century—and After," *New England Journal of Medicine* CCXXII (1940) 1–11.

17. John Collins Warren, "The Social Side of Student Life," *Boston Medical and Surgical Journal,* CLXVI (1912) 875–876, 895–896.

18. Dr. Saul Benison, medical historian at the University of Cincinnati, reported that Binger became depressed after the sudden death of a patient to whom he was administering anesthesia in the Rockefeller Hospital. According to Benison, Binger was granted a year's leave of absence for restoration of his health. A search of Rockefeller correspondence in the Rockefeller Archives, in the Rockefeller University Archives, and in the Simon Flexner Papers and the Rufus Cole Papers in the American Philosophical Society has failed to reveal an account of this death from anesthesia, though it turned up much of the material on Dr. Binger that is revealed here.

19. Carl Binger to Rufus Cole, April 4, 1929, Cole Papers, American Philosophic Society. In this letter to Cole, Binger explained at great length the principles of Jung's psychology and expressed the hope that he could work on psychosomatic problems when he returned. He said he saw psychological aspects of organic and functional disease as the "coming field" in medicine. He told Cole, who was director of the Rockefeller Institute at the time, that he would like to have his leave extended for an extra six months if possible, and it was extended until February 1, 1930.

20. Carl Binger to Rufus Cole, October 12, 1929, Cole Papers, American Philosophical Society. The Rockefeller Institute had made clear to Binger that his opportunity there was for work on organic disease, and at Cole's request to brush up on clinical medicine, he spent the fall of 1929 under Francis Fraser at St. Bartholomew's Hospital in London. However, Binger saw more clearly than ever that he really wanted to get into psychosomatics. So at this time he tendered his resignation to the Institute.

21. Chloe Binger, taped interview, July 24, 1977. Mrs. Binger quoted her husband as saying that he realized he had a calling for some form of counseling work because so frequently strangers on trains had opened up to him and talked about their intimate personal problems. The practice of internal medicine and psychoanalysis presented some problems. Even though Binger had a Freudian analysis with Fritz Wittels, the psychiatrists disclaimed him as an internist, and the internists were inclined to dismiss him as a psychiatrist. Initially he paid the price so often exacted of those who cross two academic disciplines.

However, after 1939, he was nationally recognized as the perennial editor of the journal *Psychosomatic Medicine*.

22. Horace Gray to Stanley Cobb, July 23, 1909, Cobb Papers.
23. Horace Gray to Stanley Cobb, August 29, 1909, Cobb Papers.
24. Lawrence K. Lunt to Stanley Cobb, September 11, 1910, Cobb Papers.
25. John A. P. Millet to Stanley Cobb, August 17, 1913. Cobb Papers.
26. John A. P. Millet to Stanley Cobb, October 26, 1913. Cobb Papers.
27. Rackemann, *The Inquisitive Physician*, p. 39.
28. Cheever, "The Turn of the Century—and After," p. 4.
29. Stanley Cobb to Leonore Smith Cobb, date unknown, Cobb Papers, Lost Family Correspondence.
30. Alfred Redfield, taped interview.
31. G. Quincy Peters to Stanley Cobb, May 20, 1913, Cobb Papers.
32. Elizabeth Gardner to Stanley Cobb, October 3, 1911, Cobb Papers.
33. Elizabeth Gilbert to Stanley Cobb, October 24, 1913, Cobb Papers.
34. Donald Macomber, "Medical Education at Harvard at the Turn of the Century," unpublished typescript, Harvard Medical Archives.
35. Waldo Forbes to Stanley Cobb, August 14, 1913, Cobb Papers.
36. Stanley Cobb to John Candler Cobb, March 19, 1914, Cobb Papers.
37. Helen Cabot Almy to Stanley Cobb, dated "Friday" only, but certainly 1913, and after July. Cobb Papers.
38. Stanley Cobb to Leonore Smith Cobb, date unknown, Cobb Papers, Lost Family Correspondence.

Chapter 3

1. While there appears to be no documentation in Cobb's or the Cobb Family's papers on the subject of his choice of Baltimore as the place to further his education in the neurosciences, available information indicates that Dean Edsall was greatly instrumental in directing him there (see footnote 2 of Chapter 9). The Johns Hopkins Medical School was still in its initial bloom and its reputation was large, and with the addition of Adolf Meyer to its staff it had begun an innovative program in psychiatry. In addition, many of Cobb's teachers at the Harvard Medical School had come up from Baltimore and now staffed the recently opened Peter Bent Brigham Hospital, where Cobb was serving his internship—Drs. Cushing, Christian, and Councilman, to name but three—and they too must have encouraged him in that direction. Indeed, it is likely that they and Edsall made the necessary contacts and arrangements for him to continue his postdoctoral training there.

2. While a full-dress biography of Adolf Meyer remains to be written, his philosophy and important papers and work are summed up in two studies on him, which also contain much biographical information. These are *The Commonsense Psychiatry of Dr. Adolf Meyer; Fifty-two Selected Papers Edited, with Biographical Narrative*, by Alfred Lief (N.Y., McGraw-Hill, 1948) and *Psychobiology, a Science of Man; Compiled and Edited by Eunice S. Winters and Anna Mae Bowers* (Springfield, Thomas, 1957). Much information on Dr.

Notes

Meyer's career, particularly on his Worcester years, which he himself considered especially important in his overall development, can be found in Gerald N. Grob's *The State and the Mentally Ill; a History of Worcester State Hospital in Massachusetts, 1830–1920* (Chapel Hill, University of North Carolina Press, 1966). Information on Dr. Meyer here has been drawn from all of these sources. Meyer's manuscript papers, which have been preserved practically *in toto,* also provide detailed sources on his life and work. These may be found at the Alan M. Chesney Archives of The Johns Hopkins Medical Institution. In 1980 a typescript guide of the Adolf Meyer Archive was completed. Finally, Adolf Meyer's *Collected Papers* were edited by Eunice Winters and published in four volumes by the Johns Hopkins Press in 1950 and 1951.

3. In his acceptance speech when presented the Kober medal in 1956, Cobb said he had lived through four golden ages. The first was his childhood nature study; the second was the time spent in Baltimore; the third was the opportunity between 1923 and 1925 to work with the great neurologists of Europe; and the fourth was epitomized by a neurological supper club in Boston around 1930. He said he could also almost see a fifth, at least silver age dawning for psychiatry in his later years at the Massachusetts General Hospital.

4. Dr. Phyllis Greenacre, taped interview.

5. The name of the Boston Psychopathic Hospital was later changed to the Massachusetts Mental Health Center, by which it is presently known.

6. J. G. Dusser de Barenne, "Über die Enthirnungsstarre (Decerebrate Rigidity Sherrington's) in ihrer Beziehung zur efferenten Innveration der quergestreiften Muskelatur," *Folia Neuro-Biologica* VII (1913) [651]–654.

7. J. W. Langelaan, "Über Muskeltonus und Sehnenreflexe im Zusammenhang mit der doppelten Innervation quergestreifter Muskeln," *Neurologisches Centralblatt* XXXIII (1914) 1140–1151; S. de Boer, "Die Bedeutung der tonischen Innervation für die Function der quergestreiften Muskeln," *Zeitschrift für Biologie* LXV (1915) [239]–354.

8. Alexander Forbes lived in Milton, enjoyed horseback riding, and had taken part in paper chases with Cobb.

9. Judith H. Goetzl, memorandum to Richard J. Wolfe, November 3, 1981. Mrs. Goetzl inventoried and put in order the papers of Alexander Forbes, which are now in The Francis A. Countway Library of Medicine. Mrs. Goetzl's memorandum can be found in the Forbes archive.

10. *Ibid.* Judith Goetzl said, "Half the experiments for 'Electrical Studies in mammalian reflexes, III, Immediate changes in the flexion reflex after spinal transaction' were carried out in the summer of 1916 and written up by Cobb. Additional data was collected in the spring of 1921 with Edith Heizer Cattell and published with the first in 1923. It appears to be Cobb's holograph and typed MS for each version." (Forbes Papers, Box 33, 1433–34).

11. Stanley Cobb to Adolf Meyer, June 7, 1916, Meyer Papers.

12. Curt Richter, taped interview. Henry Phipps's donation of $580,000 was to cover cost of construction of a building with sixty beds and maintenance for ten years, along with a professorship and assistants, but it did not include the support of laboratories for either neurology or psychiatry. Lief, pp. 336, 339.

13. Adolf Meyer to Stanley Cobb, August 1, 1916. Meyer Papers.
14. Mary A. B. Brazier to Benjamin V. White, April 18, 1979, Cobb Papers.
15. Curt Richter, taped interview.
16. *Ibid.*
17. Grob, *The State and the Mentally Ill*, p. 271.
18. Adolf Meyer, "The Integrative Function of a Hospital Laboratory—Retrospect and Prospect," *State Hospital Quarterly* VI (1920–1921) 445–451, in Adolf Meyer, *Collected Papers* II, 80ff.
19. David Henderson, introduction to *The Collected Papers of Adolf Meyer*, I, xiii.
20. *Ibid.*, p. xiv.
21. Curt Richter, taped interview.
22. Grob, *The State and the Mentally Ill*, p. 312.
23. Curt Richter, taped interview.
24. Meyer's common sense approach to the individual patient with evaluation of assets and liabilities, and the piecing together of understandings was sometimes designated "Distributive Analysis and Synthesis." It by no means had the dramatic appeal of Freud's Psychoanalysis.
25. Dr. Phyllis Greenacre, taped interview.
26. Stanley Cobb to Horace Gray, April 1, 1922, Cobb Papers.
27. Adolf Meyer Papers.
28. Stanley Cobb, Memo on Teaching, April 24, 1918, Meyer Papers.
29. Stanley Cobb to Adolf Meyer, August 12, 1918, Meyer Papers.
30. Meyer Papers.
31. Meyer Papers.
32. Meyer Papers.
33. Meyer Papers.
34. New York Neurosurgical School, Charles A. Elsberg, Director. Fourth Course, Eighth week, September 16–21, 1918, and Fifth Course, Second Week, October 21–October 26, 1918.
35. Meyer Papers.
36. Stanley Cobb to Adolf Meyer, December 20, 1918, Meyer Papers.
37. Stanley Cobb to Adolf Meyer, December 30, 1918, Meyer Papers.

Chapter 4

1. Stanley Cobb to Adolf Meyer, January 13, 1919, Meyer Papers.
2. James Jackson Putnam, a pioneer in Freudian psychoanalysis, was professor of neurology at Harvard and chairman of neurology at the Massachusetts General Hospital until his retirement in 1912. He died in 1918.
3. Stanley Cobb to Adolf Meyer, January 19, 1919, Meyer Papers.
4. Meyer Papers.
5. Cobb was undoubtedly referring to an offer by his wife's Aunt Susan, the widow of Dr. Arthur Tracy Cabot, to live rent free in a house in Ponkapoag, near Milton, Massachusetts, next door to her own house.
6. Meyer Papers.

Notes 389

7. Adolf Meyer to Stanley Cobb, April 23, 1919, Meyer Papers.

8. John Homans, "Reminiscences 1, The Life of a Surgical Interne at the Turn of the Century." *Harvard Medical Alumni Bulletin*, XXIV (1950) 35. Homans, who graduated from Harvard Medical School in 1903, said that during his internship on the South Surgical Service at the Massachusetts General Hospital the three visiting surgeons, each of whom took charge four months a year, were Dr. H. H. A. Beach, Dr. Arthur T. Cabot, and Dr. William M. Conant. Homans continued, "I have since realized that Dr. Cabot was not only a very progressive and enterprising surgeon but conscientious to an unusual degree, a New Englander of the New Englanders."

9. Stanley Cobb to Adolf Meyer, July 14, 1919, Meyer Papers.

10. Roger I. Lee headed the East Medical Service at the Massachusetts General Hospital.

11. Joseph Aub reported that Dean Edsall, who spent only half of his time at the Massachusetts General Hospital and the other half at the Medical School as Dean and consequently was no longer seeing many patients at the hosopital, allowed Cobb to use his little office in the small red building by the Blossom Street gate to the Bulfinch Building. (Memorandum in the Cobb File of the Aub Papers, Countway Library.) The building was moved from its Blossom Street site to its present location on Cambridge Street on May 21, 1982.

12. That same year Cabot was appointed professor of social ethics at Harvard University. He was chief of the West Medical Service from 1912 until his retirement.

13. Ida Cannon was the sister of Walter B. Cannon, professor of physiology at the Harvard Medical School.

14. Richard Cabot and Russell Dicks, *The Art of Ministering to the Sick* (New York, Macmillan, 1936).

15. Richard Cabot, *Physical Diagnosis*. The first edition, limited to diseases of the heart, was published in 1900. By the time that Adams's revision came out (thirteenth edition, N.Y., W. Wood & Co., 1942), the work was more comprehensive, covering many areas beside diseases of the chest.

16. In the clinicopathological conferences at the Massachusetts General Hospital it had been clearly demonstrated that infarcts were repeatedly diagnosed clinically as bronchopneumonia.

17. Stanley Cobb to Adolf Meyer, November 9, 1921, Meyer Papers.

18. William Herman to Stanley Cobb, March 12, 1923, and April 16, 1923. Cobb Papers.

19. E. D. Adrian and A. Forbes, "The All or Nothing Response of Sensory Nerve Fibers," *Journal of Physiology LVI* (1922) 301–330.

20. John R. Brooks, Stanley Cobb, Hallowell Davis, William H. Forbes, Eugene M. Landis, John R. Pappenheimer (Chairman), John F. Perkins, Jr., and George Wald, "Memorial Minute on the Life of Alexander Forbes." *Harvard Gazette*, LXI (October 16, 1965) 32–33.

21. Alfred Redfield, taped interview.

22. Meyer Papers.

23. Catherine Drinker Bowen, *Yankee from Olympus* (Boston: Little, Brown and Company, 1944).

24. Catherine Drinker Bowen, *Family Portrait* (Boston: Little, Brown and Company, 1970).

25. The author has been unable to locate the source of this quote, but it is well known by members of Cobb's family.

26. In a letter to Adolf Meyer dated February 14, 1920, Cobb wrote, "Dr. Southard filled the chair of neuropathology and did practically nothing with his school laboratory but transferred his work to the psychopathic hospital and the new Psychiatric Institute. (This institute was an organization to carry on research in all the state hospitals and raise the standards, its central laboratories to be at the psychopathic hospital.) Meyer Papers.

27. Sanford Gifford, taped interview of Dr. MacPherson in Dr. Gifford's possession.

28. Meyer Papers.

29. Southard's former associate, Dr. Herman Adler, had been an assistant professor at Harvard, and the funds for his position were available.

30. This comment was undoubtedly a jibe at Southard who left jars and jars of pickled brains in the neuropathology laboratory at the school. The jars occupied space under the stairs during Cobb's subsequent era, and one of his technicians had to maintain the fluid levels in them.

31. Adolf Meyer to Stanley Cobb, February 10, 1920, Meyer Papers. The names Meyer mentioned in this letter, which replied to a previous one from Cobb, were Adler, Barrett, Schwab, Kirby, Ebaugh, Stevenson, and Campbell. Adler, he said, was not trained broadly enough; Barrett was a man who had outgrown his good start twenty-five years earlier; Schwab (father of Cobb's colleague, Robert) would be Cushing's first choice but was a nice fellow better adapted to pioneer work in St. Louis than to a headship. Meyer left the other four in the running.

32. Hildegarde Cobb and Hildegarde Greene, *Letters of Henry Stone Forbes* (Privately published, 1981). Forbes served with Dr. Strong's clinic in the Balkans during 1916 and 1917. Later he joined the Brigham Unit in the European Theatre.

33. Cobb Papers.

34. In 1968 Edwin Clark and C. D. O'Malley published a tome entitled *The Human Brain and Spinal Cord, a Historical Study Illustrated by Writings from Antiquity to the Twentieth Century* (Berkeley and Los Angeles, University of California Press, 1968). In this massive volume there is a section which places in perspective the work of Forbes and Cobb. A part of one paragraph reads, "This new concept of cerebral blood vessels, and thus of the control of cerebral circulation, was the work of many men, but the most active and significant group appeared in Boston in the 1930s. Henry S. Forbes was the most important contributor to the sequence of papers that resulted."

35. Stanley Cobb to David L. Edsall, September 9, 1920. Cobb Papers.

36. Cobb Papers.

37. Stanley Cobb to Adolf Meyer, March 17, 1922, Meyer Papers.

38. H. Mella, "Experimental Production of Basal Ganglion Symptomatology in Macacus Rhesus." *Archives of Neurology and Psychiatry,* XI (1924) 405.

39. Stanley Cobb to Mr. L. S. Campbell, October 11, 1921, Cobb Papers.

40. Stanley Cobb to Charles P. Howland, June 16, 1923, Cobb Papers.

41. Sanford Gifford, taped interview of Dr. MacPherson in Dr. Gifford's possession. In his *Encephalography in Clinical Practice* (Philadelphia, W. B. Saunders, 1951, p. 2), Robert Schwab relates that in 1918, when a young medical student working in the physiological laboratories of the Harvard Medical School under Alexander Forbes, McPherson, in the course of some experiments, put two electrodes on the exposed brain of a cat and led these to the input of an amplifier and ran the output into a string galvanometer. Much to his surprise, when the film was developed he noted regular 10-per-second waves that were unlike the spikes and paroxysmal bursts that he had picked up from the muscles. He showed the tracing to Forbes, who felt that even if it was unusual, it was possibly an artifact and was out of line with the investigation assigned to McPherson, and the matter was summarily forgotten.

42. *Ibid.* In the interview with Gifford, MacPherson said, "I was inducting—moving around talking to the patients where I might pick up a sense of emotional distress and then giving the individual a chance to air or ventilate the area that seemed to be sensitized. Often in just a very brief contact the patients would open their hearts and comment on distresses that they had retained or felt were not primarily of medical interest, but which very critically influence the nature of their illnesses."

43. Stanley Cobb to William N. Bullard, March 13, 1922, Cobb Papers. Cobb said the article would appear in the *Archives of Neurology* under "Society Transactions."

44. Schichi Uyematzu to Stanley Cobb, July 5, 1922, and July 20, 1922. Cobb Papers.

45. Edwin F. Gildea, taped interview.

46. E. F. Gildea, E. E. Kattwinkel, and W. B. Castle, "Experimental Combined System Disease." *New England Journal of Medicine,* CCII (1930) 523–527.

47. Dr. Knox H. Finley, who worked with Cobb and Forbes in 1932, said in a taped interview on March 27, 1979, that Yakovlev's brain collection was of inestimable value. He said that Yakovlev had a deep interest in the ontology and phylogeny of the brain—i.e., its development in the embryo and in the species. In 1952 an epidemic of encephalitis hit the central valley of California. It was benign in adults but left infants practically decerebrate. Sections of the brain of a twenty-one year old who had acquired Western Encephalitis at four months were prepared and examined by Yakovlev. They showed, as expected, clearly marked atrophy of those portions which were youngest in their development.

48. In August, 1979, there was still an enormous floor-mounted microtome in a laboratory on the tenth floor of the City Hospital neurological unit along with a sizable collection of Yakovlev's whole brain sections.

49. The following description of the course and faculty was sent to Dean Edsall on June 6, 1922, for inclusion in the 1922–1923 Harvard Medical School Catalogue:

Diseases of the Nervous System
(Composed of the departments of Neuropathology,
Neurology, and Psychiatry)

NEUROPATHOLOGY

Stanley Cobb, M.D., Assistant Professor of Neuropathology.
James B. Ayer, M.D., Instructor in Neuropathology and in Neurology.
Harry C. Solomon, M.D., Instructor in Psychiatry and in Neuropathology.
Hugo Mella, M.D., Assistant in Neurology and Instructor in Neuropathology.
Donald J. MacPherson, M.D., Assistant in Neuropathology and in Medicine.

(William Lennox, M.D., Research Assistant in Neuropathology. This appointment will be confirmed later before the catalogue goes to print.)

Second Year.—The course consists of lectures, laboratory work, and demonstrations, with tests, review exercises, and quizzes as required, amounting to approximately 50 hours. Some of the exercises are appropriately integrated with the course in General Pathology. The more special diseases of the nervous system are treated in a series of twelve consecutive morning exercises. A brief review is given of the anatomy required for grasping the pathological physiology of the nervous system. The lectures introduce conceptions of value for the third-year courses in neurology and psychiatry and for the neurological parts of courses in internal medicine and in surgery. The histopathological part of the laboratory work deals with the inflammatory reactions, the classical degenerations, and (in brief) with important entities such as general paresis of the insane and tabes dorsalis. Gross pathological specimens are also shown and physiological demonstrations are given to illustrate living pathological processes.

SECOND YEAR

Lectures and laboratory work. Dr. Cobb and assistants.
April 4–May 9, Wednesday and Friday: 9–12:30

50. Mandel Cohen, personal communication.

51. Augustus S. Rose, personal communication to Benjamin V. White dated July 21, 1978.

52. Stanley Cobb to David L. Edsall, December 22, 1922, Cobb Papers.

53. Carl Binger to Stanley Cobb, sent from the Hospital of the Rockefeller Institute. Rockefeller Archives.

54. Dr. Simon Flexner, whose brother Abraham Flexner was not a physician. Simon Flexner expressed his gratitude for Cobb's care of Prudden in a letter dated September 14, 1922, Cobb Papers.

Chapter 5

1. Abraham Flexner to Henry Head, September 26, 1923, Rockefeller Archives.

2. Henry Head to Abraham Flexner, October 30, 1923, Rockefeller Archives.

3. The details of the Rockefeller Foundation's support of Cobb's European trip are outlined in a letter of understanding from David L. Edsall to Abraham Flexner of September 23, 1923. Rockefeller Archives.

Notes

4. Abraham Flexner to C. V. Ariens Kappers, December 26, 1923, Rockefeller Archives.

5. Abraham Flexner to Dr. Heinrich Poll, December 26, 1923, Rockefeller Archives.

6. Stanley Cobb to Adolf Meyer, May 23, 1923, Meyer Papers.

7. Adolf Meyer to Stanley Cobb, January 29, 1924, Meyer Papers.

8. Flexner was reluctant to finance Miss Carroll's expenses, thinking that on the continent it would be better to employ girls who spoke the native language. However, the strong-willed Cobbs prevailed and Miss Carroll went along.

9. Stanley Cobb to Leonore Smith Cobb, October 19, 1923, Cobb Papers.

10. When sensory nerves emerge from the spinal cord they fan out along more or less parallel pathways to the skin from which they convey sensory impulses toward the spinal cord and brain. However in the neck and shoulder area (brachial plexus) and in the lower spinal region (lumbar plexus) they become interwoven into the major peripheral nerves, so that the sensory innervation of the spinal nerves (dermatomes) may be quite different from that of the peripheral nerves.

11. Stanley Cobb to Abraham Flexner, December 1, 1923, Cobb Papers.

12. Stanley Cobb to Chandler Foot, March 12, 1924, Cobb Papers.

13. Stanley Cobb to John Candler Cobb, February 8, 1924, Cobb Papers.

14. Stanley Cobb to Leonore Smith Cobb, December 3, 1923, Cobb Papers.

15. Stanley Cobb to John Candler Cobb, January 20, 1924, Cobb Papers.

16. Stanley Cobb to Leonore Smith Cobb, January 27, 1924, Cobb Papers.

17. Stanley Cobb to Leonore Smith Cobb, January 15, 1924, Cobb Papers.

18. Henry Head and George Riddoch, "The Automatic Bladder, Excessive Sweating and some other Reflex Conditions in Gross Injuries of the Spinal Cord", *Brain* XL (1917) 188–263. It was republished in book form in the next year.

19. Riddoch's life is abstracted in Haymaker, *Founders of Neurology*, p. 362.

20. Ponkapoag was a part of Canton but had its own post office.

21. Stanley Cobb to Leonore Smith Cobb, March 31, 1924, Cobb Papers.

22. Stanley Cobb to John Candler Cobb, April 2, 1924, Cobb Papers.

23. Stanley Cobb to Chandler Foot, April 16, 1924, Cobb Papers.

24. Stanley Cobb to Adolf Meyer, January 2, 1925, Meyer Papers.

25. Stanley Cobb to Chandler Foot, September 21, 1924, Cobb Papers.

26. Stanley Cobb to Leonore Smith Cobb, June 9, 1924, Cobb Papers.

27. Stanley Cobb to Leonore Smith Cobb, July 21, 1924, Cobb Papers.

28. Stanley Cobb to Leonore Smith Cobb, July 30, 1924, Cobb Papers.

29. Stanley Cobb to Henry S. Forbes, August 3, 1924, Cobb Papers.

30. Cobb and his father were to buy a yawl in 1925 and name her *Pamaho*. Cobb lost no time in dyeing her sails a brownish orange after his experience in Brittany.

31. Miss Dorothy Clark in a personal communication on June 14, 1983, said that Sarah Evarts was social worker to the psychiatric outpatient department prior to Cobb's era and was employed there since 1932.

32. Stanley Cobb to Leonore Smith Cobb, September 14, 1924, Cobb Papers.
33. Stanley Cobb to John Candler Cobb, November 20, 1924, Cobb Papers.
34. Haymaker, *Founders of Neurology*, pp. 168–171.
35. There is a file of letters from Stanley Cobb in the Ayer Papers in the Countway Library.
36. Stanley Cobb to James B. Ayer, February 4, 1925, Ayer Papers, Countway Library.
37. Stanley Cobb to John Candler Cobb, December 11, 1924, Cobb Papers.
38. Elizabeth Almy Cobb to Helen Cabot Almy, March 10, 1925, personal collection in the possession of the Almy Family.
39. Elizabeth Almy Cobb to Helen Cabot Almy, March 26, 1925, personal collection in the possession of the Almy Family.
40. Elizabeth Almy Cobb to Helen Cabot Almy, March 31, 1925, personal collection in the possession of the Almy Family.
41. Stanley Cobb to Henry Stone Forbes and Hildegarde Cobb Forbes, April 6, 1925, Cobb Papers.
42. Adolf Meyer to Stanley Cobb, February 19, 1925, Meyer Papers.
43. Stanley Cobb to Adolf Meyer, April 10, 1925, Meyer Papers.
44. Margaret C. L. Gildea, personal communication to Benjamin V. White, March 22, 1978.
45. Eugene Taylor, personal communication to Benjamin V. White, April, 1982. Mr. Taylor has carried on extensive conversation and interviews with Dr. Murray over several years.
46. Stanley Cobb to Henry Stone Forbes and Hildegarde Forbes, April 6, 1927, Cobb Papers.
47. Elizabeth Almy Cobb to Helen Cabot Almy, April 7, 1925, Cobb Papers.
48. John Fulton to Stanley Cobb, September 11, 1928, Cobb Papers.
49. Stanley Cobb to John Fulton, September 21, 1928, Cobb Papers.
50. Stanley Cobb to Hildegarde Cobb Forbes, date uncertain, but probably April 19, 1925, Cobb Papers.
51. Elizabeth Almy Cobb to Leonore Smith Cobb, May 29, 1926, Cobb Papers.
52. Haymaker, *Founders of Neurology*, pp. 7–10.
53. Stanley Cobb to Leonore Smith Cobb, June 28, 1925, Cobb Papers.
54. Elizabeth Almy Cobb to Leonore Smith Cobb, June 12, 1925, Cobb Papers.
55. Stanley Cobb to Hildegarde Cobb Forbes, July 14, 1925, Cobb Papers.
56. Abraham Flexner, *I Remember, the Autobiography of Abraham Flexner* (N.Y., Simon and Shuster, 1940) p. 312.
57. Chloe Binger, taped interview.

Chapter 6

1. Details of the Rockefeller grant can be found in the files of the General Education Board in the Rockefeller Archives. Other material on it exists in

Notes

President Lowell's Papers in the Harvard University Archives in the Pusey Library in Cambridge and still more in Dean Edsall's Papers in the Harvard Medical Archives, now in the Countway Library.

2. Stanley Cobb to James B. Ayer, January 1, 1924, Ayer Papers, Countway Library.

3. *A History of the Boston City Hospital from Its Foundation until 1904. Authorized by the Trustees and Edited by a Committee of the Hospital Staff* (Boston, Municipal Printing Office, 1906). Dr. Knapp compiled the chapter, XXII, on the Department of Neurology (pp. 364–368); John J. Byrne, *A History of the Boston City Hospital, 1905–1964* ([Boston] Boston City Hospital [1964]). Dr. Derek Denny-Brown was responsible for writing up the Department of Neurology in this continuation (pp. 110–122).

4. In this stage of development, physicians who were in charge of the electric and magnetic apparatus that was employed in the treatment of nervous and hysterical disorders were referred to as "Electricians." Similarly, James Jackson Putnam was appointed "Electrician" at the Massachusetts General Hospital in 1872 and put in charge of its magnetic and electric apparatus.

5. The Thorndike Laboratory, Harvard's great experiment in clinical research and teaching, was brought into being with the appointment on July 1, 1921 of Dr. Francis Weld Peabody as its director. In early August of 1921 the contract for the Thorndike Building was awarded, and toward the end of August, 1923 Dr. Peabody and his staff began to occupy these new quarters. For a detailed history of this effort see Max Finland's *The Harvard Medical Unit at Boston City Hospital; History of the Thorndike Memorial Laboratory and the Harvard Medical Services from Their Founding until 1974* (Boston, Countway Library of Medicine, 1982–1983), 2 v. in 3.

6. Stanley Cobb to David L. Edsall, October 29, 1924, Dean's Files, Harvard Medical Archives (filed under Rockefeller Foundation, General Education Board).

7. Copies of this unsigned memorandum can be found in the Dean's Files in the Harvard Medical Archives, filed both under the Department of Neurology and the Rockefeller Foundation, General Education Board. It is obvious that this was circulated to senior staff in the neurosciences, for a responding letter from Harvey Cushing is attached to the copy filed under the Department of Neurology.

8. David L. Edsall to Stanley Cobb, December 2, 1924, Dean's Files, Harvard Medical Archives (under Rockefeller Foundation, General Education Board).

9. Stanley Cobb to David L. Edsall, January 13, 1925, Dean's Files, Harvard Medical Archives (under Rockefeller Foundation, General Education Board).

10. William H. Robey to Stanley Cobb, August 25, 1925, Cobb Papers.

11. Stanley Cobb to William H. Robey, September 2, 1925, Cobb Papers.

12. There was also a house staff comprised of Morris Yorshis, Julius Lohman and Jacob Chayet. Dr. Yorshis worked for many years at the Worcester State Hospital and later practiced neuropsychiatry in Lawrence. Dr. Lohman worked briefly in Cobb's neuropathological laboratory and then went into

practice, affiliated primarily with the Beth Israel Hospital. Walter B. Seelye served as a senior intern for part of 1926 and later went into pediatrics.

13. David L. Edsall to Edward W. Taylor, June 1 and June 5, 1926, Dean's Files, Harvard Medical Archives (under Department of Neurology).

14. Edward W. Taylor to Worth Hale, June 23, 1926, Dean's Files, Harvard Medical Archives (under Department of Neurology).

15. While no official resignation from Dr. Taylor can be found in the Harvard Medical Archives, on August 14, 1926, Edsall wrote to Mr. F. W. Hunnewell, the secretary of Harvard University, informing him that he was forwarding Dr. Taylor's resignation as James Jackson Professor of Neurology, which would become effective on September 1. Edsall also told Mr. Hunnewell that James B. Ayer had been appointed in his place and that he should be called the "James Jackson Putnam Clinical Professor of Neurology." Dean's Files, Harvard Medical Archives (under Department of Neurology).

The members of the department of neurology at Harvard must have been well aware of the awkward circumstances that led to Taylor's premature resignation. A dinner in his honor on May 7, 1926 was attended by the key members of the department and was accompanied by a masque. In attendance were James B. Ayer, Stanley Cobb, James Courtney, Bronson Crothers, Harvey Cushing, Henry S. Forbes, Frank Fremont-Smith, Maurice Fremont-Smith, Frederick Lund, Tracy Putnam, George Schaltenbrandt, Edward Wyllis Taylor, Henry R. Viets, and possibly others. The masque with overtones reminiscent of a Gilbert and Sullivan operetta began when Tracy Putnam, clothed in resplendent academic regalia, entered the banquet room and took over the presiding role as dean. He was followed by Cobb as executioner, Frank Fremont-Smith and Schaltenbrandt as heralds, and Maurice Fremont-Smith as musician, all attired in medieval costumes, along with Henry S. Forbes as a sacrificial bull.

A raucous evening followed. The Dean paid Taylor a poetic tribute which concluded with the verses,

> The pen is mightier than the sword
> Is a saying often heard—
> I've an idea, if one knew
> How the others talked of you,
> What they say behind your backs—
> Well—
> The tongue is mightier than the axe.
> So let us while the hour away
> And tell what other people say.

Cobb, the executioner, then went around the table singing verses that pointed out the foibles of his colleagues who in turn were awarded by the dean honorary degrees of a humorous and sometimes lurid nature. The final degree of the evening was awarded to James B. Ayer, who had distinguished himself by his introduction of the cisternal puncture. When the heralds began to escort Dr. Ayer, the Toreador music from Carmen started to play. The bull rushed in and charged at the executioner who neatly pricked him in the *cisterna magna.* Cerebrospinal fluid rushed forth and the bull died. The executioner then sang

> James Bourne Ayer, Toreador,
> Pierces the cistern, makes fluid pour,
> But he never, never gets a bloody tap,
> Only makes the fluid pour . . . .
> Makes the fluid pour—or—or
> Never got no gore—
> No gore!

Then the dean presented Ayer's degree with the words, "in recognition of your great contribution to hydro-rachido-encephalodynamics we honor you with the degree of D.A., Doctor of Aquaphilics." He then quoted from scripture

> Yea verily he feared not water, neither the
> Raging ocean; nor the deep flowing river;
> Nor even human waters, polluted and corrupt,
> That flow from the body of man.
>
> Mark: NE by N ½ E.

The dean, turning to the assembly, closed the evening's entertainment with these words,

> So ends our masque; no more degrees to give,
> No bulls to kill, no pock to let live.
> We know our Wyllis knows what deeper lies;
> Just that we all seek favor in his eyes—
> Just that we love him well, and gather here
> To wish him happiness another sixty year.
>
> ———
>
> Now let more sober tongues take up our task
> And sing his praises; for so ends our masque.

The entire masque is recorded in a volume of Stanley Cobb's published papers, 1921–1926, which is now part of the Countway Library's collection.

Taylor was obviously touched by the tribute made to him, and harbored no resentment about his impending retirement, for in the Cobb papers, in a file containing a typescript copy of the masque, there is a letter of thanks from Taylor to Cobb dated May 8, 1926. Taylor referred to the wonderful performance which made the dinner a success and thanked Cobb for his and Tracy Putnam's roles in it. The senior neurologist concluded by telling Cobb that he wanted to talk to him about the possibility of doing some work at the laboratory again, "now that I presumably will have more time." He asked to be allowed to keep his little room, where he could go over his specimens and do what else was desirable to make them more available for general use.

16. David L. Edsall to William N. Bullard, June 24, 1926, Dean's Files, Harvard Medical Archives (under Department of Neurology).

17. William N. Bullard to David L. Edsall, June 29, 1926, Dean's Files, Harvard Medical Archives (under Department of Neurology).

18. Stanley Cobb to David L. Edsall, July 12, 1926 Dean's Papers, Harvard Medical Archives (under Department of Neurology).

19. David L. Edsall to James B. Ayer, August 4, 1926, Dean's Files, Harvard Medical Archives (under Department of Neurology).

20. James B. Ayer to David L. Edsall, August 11, 1926, Dean's Files, Harvard Medical Archives (under Department of Neurology).

21. Dr. Milton Rosenbaum, who in the thirties was a resident in neurology at City Hospital, described Samuel Epstein as the Walter Winchell of Medicine, aware of all the gossip in academia. His knowledge of other people's lives adequately supported the use of the epithet. From 1932 to 1936 Epstein ran the neurosyphilis clinic, after which on a Rockefeller fellowship he studied at Queen Square Hospital in London. He wrote extensively on neurosyphilis, and he continued the private practice of neuropsychiatry in Boston. When interviewed on August 10, 1979, Epstein was alert, helpful, and in apparent excellent health.

22. Those who commenced as house officers in 1926 included Edwin M. Deery and Raymond K. Farnham. Those who came in 1927 were Epstein, Easley, Porter S. Dickinson, and John S. Roach.

23. Richard B. Easley to Stanley Cobb, November 12, 1928, Cobb Papers.

24. Tracy Putnam was to succeed Cobb as director of the neurological unit in 1934 and to play a major role in the discovery of Dilantin as an anticonvulsant drug in 1937. In the late twenties, when the neurological unit was being planned, Donald Munro was already ensconced as the neurosurgeon at Boston City Hospital. He had been a classmate of Stanley Cobb in the class of 1914 at the Harvard Medical School and he had already acquired a reputation as an authority on traumatic neurosurgery.

25. New members of the house staff in 1928 were Houston Merritt, Roderick Heffron, Leopoldo Pardo, and Paul C. Dozier. Short-term workers were Thomas L. Fentress, later a prominent Chicago psychiatrist, and Frank C. D'Elseaux, who worked for many years with Harry C. Solomon in the laboratories of the Boston Psychopathic Hospital and later went into psychoanalysis. In 1979 D'Elseaux was living in Marblehead.

26. Miner H. A. Evans to Stanley Cobb, September 11, 1928, Cobb Papers.

27. C. MacFie Campbell to Stanley Cobb, March 31, 1927, Cobb Papers; C. MacFie Campbell to David L. Edsall, March 1, 1927, and David L. Edsall to C. MacFie Campbell, Dean's Files, Harvard Medical Archives (under Department of Psychiatry).

28. William Herman to Stanley Cobb, October 4, 1928, Cobb Papers.

29. Erna Leonhard subsequently married Frederick Gibbs and the couple devoted their lives to epilepsy with especial reference to electroencephalography.

30. Stanley Cobb to Adolf Meyer, January 2, 1925, Meyer Papers. Vogt was a withdrawn, lonely man. The quoted paragraph goes on to say, "Of course he is not easy to get on with, he is lonely, a bit suspicious, and his wife so guards him that the amount of personal contact I get is almost nil. They are a strange couple. . . . I think he would enjoy admiring pupils, but he doesn't attract them."

31. Stanley Cobb to Oskar Vogt, October, 1925, Cobb Papers.

32. Hubbard went into pediatrics. Later in life he became director of the National Board of Medical Examiners.

33. Forbes inserted a window in the skull of a cat, so that he could observe the dilation and contraction of the arteries in the pial membrane covering the brain surface. Gladys Nason Lothrop (Mrs. Quincy Adams Lothrop, Jr.), who was Forbes's technician for many years in the thirties and forties, accurately described the procedure as it finally evolved. In a personal communication she wrote as follows: "The work in H. S. F.'s laboratory was done mainly on anesthetized cats. (Follow-ups were done on Rhesus monkeys.) The head was held firmly in a clamp. A window was screwed into a trephine hole in the left parietal region. The *dura* was carefully removed with a cautery. Air beneath the window was driven out with cerebrospinal fluid or Ringer's solution. Blood vessels in the *pia* were studied. Usually a suitable *pial* artery was selected. The artery was measured through a microscope with a micrometer eye piece. Photomicrographs were also taken.

"The effects of various forms of nerve stimulation (sympathetic and vagal) were noted; also the effect of drugs such as epinephrine and pitressin. Some studies were also made in the vessels of the *dura mater*.

"A series of papers on cerebral circulation was published in the Archives of Neurology and Psychiatry."

34. Stanley Cobb to Abraham Flexner, November 27, 1925, Rockefeller Archives.

35. Frank Fremont-Smith to Stanley Cobb, October 7, 1926, Cobb Papers.

36. Frank Fremont-Smith to Stanley Cobb, October 22, 1926, Cobb Papers.

37. Stanley Cobb to Frank Fremont-Smith, May 28, 1927, Fremont-Smith Papers, Countway Library.

38. Frank Fremont-Smith to Stanley Cobb, March 23, 1928, Cobb Papers.

39. A ketogenic diet is one containing much fat and so little carbohydrate that the fatty acid chains are only partially combusted and leave residues of acetone, diacetic acid, and similar end-products in the body.

40. There is no available record of Yakovlev's being on the payroll at the neuropathology laboratory. In 1926, through Cobb's intervention, he became pathologist at the Monson State Hospital. Prior to that, Mrs. Cobb believes he had a small stipend, arranged for by Dr. Abraham Myerson, at City Hospital.

41. Forbes's widow, Hildegarde, said that her husband was fond of Wolff and found him to be a stimulating collaborator. However, Wolff had one quality which drove Forbes to distraction. Wolff, young, active, and free of family ties, would spend his evenings thinking up new ideas and then unfold them to Forbes the next morning. Forbes, on the other hand, went home each evening to a wife and a family of small children who claimed much of his attention. Sometimes he dreaded meeting Wolff the next morning because he knew he would have to decide which of Wolff's ideas were worth following up and which were merely fanciful.

42. Reference is made to Wilder Penfield's surgery on Henry Howland, which is discussed in Chapter 8.

43. These words were written at a time when he at Cornell and Cobb in Boston were both working in the field of psychosomatic medicine. Wolff's classical work with Stewart Wolf on gastric changes in varying emotional states achieved precisely the goal set here.

44. Stanley Cobb to Adolf Meyer, October 25, 1927, Meyer Papers. Although there was an exchange of correspondence with Meyer, Wolff already had an offer at Cornell, which he eventually accepted.

45. Stanley Cobb to Abraham Flexner, May 21, 1927, Cobb Papers.

46. Stanley Cobb to Adolf Meyer, February 21, 1928, Meyer Papers.

47. Frederick Gibbs, taped interview.

48. See footnote 42.

49. Personal communication of John H. Talbott to Benjamin V. White.

50. A native of the Midwest, Talbott had learned about Harvard from faculty members at Grinnell College. In the spring of 1925 Redfield was tutor of physiology for his group of eight which included Miles Baker, Charles Short, Marshall Bartlett, Magnus Gregerson, and Philip Bard. Talbott worked in the neuropathology laboratory from the spring of 1925 until the end of his third year in 1927. He then took a year out of school and worked in the fatigue laboratory at the Harvard Business School which was being established by L. J. Henderson, the biochemist, Arlie Bock, a Massachusetts General Hospital clinician, and Bruce Dill. Cobb played no role in establishing the fatigue laboratory. During the academic year 1928–1929, Talbott returned to Harvard Medical School and obtained his medical degree while continuing to work part time in the fatigue laboratory. Personal communication of Dr. Talbott to Benjamin V. White.

51. Stanley Cobb to Wilder Penfield, April 30, 1929, Cobb Papers.

52. The Pasteur treatment in 1929 took approximately six weeks, and each injection into the abdominal wall produced a reaction larger and more frightening than the one before.

53. Joseph P. Evans to Stanley Cobb, February 23, 1959, Cobb Papers.

54. R. Lorente de Nò, quoted in Cobb's "A Quantitative Study of Capillaries in the Hippocampus" (58).

55. Charlotte Temperley became Mrs. Richards while still working for Cobb and later took the name Charlotte Troutwine, from a subsequent husband. She was a brilliant woman who later headed the graduate education program of the Massachusetts Medical Society.

56. Margaret Doherty later married Richard Chamberlin, professor of neurology at Thomas Jefferson University and head of the department there.

57. Betty Fisher was in charge of office affairs for years on the new neurological unit at the City Hospital. She moved with Tracy Putnam to the New York Neurological Institute, and after his departure was secretary for the new director, H. Houston Merritt. She was a woman of extraordinary ability.

58. Mary Dailey married S. Rodman Irvine, one of Cobb's residents on the neurological unit. Irvine went into ophthalmology and became a professor at the University of California in Los Angeles.

59. The *Archives of Neurology and Psychiatry, Medicine, Psychosomatic Medicine, American Journal of Psychiatry,* and others.

Notes 401

60. See footnote 29.
61. Stanley Cobb to Samuel D. Robbins, March 25, 1922, Cobb Papers.
62. Samuel D. Robbins to Stanley Cobb, February 10, 1927, Cobb Papers.
63. Floyd H. Allport to Stanley Cobb, October 21, 1921, Cobb Papers; Stanley Cobb to Edward W. Taylor, November 10, 1922, Cobb Papers.
64. Stanley Cobb to Samuel D. Robbins, May 28, 1927, Cobb Papers.
65. Stanley Cobb to William Healy, October 10, 1927, Cobb Papers.
66. Stanley Cobb to David L. Edsall, April 27, 1927, Cobb Papers.
67. David L. Edsall to Stanley Cobb, May 16, 1927, Cobb Papers.
68. Spielmeyer was what Hitler called an Aryan, and Mrs. Spielmeyer was Jewish. As long as Spielmeyer was alive Hitler left Mrs. Spielmeyer alone. The Rockefeller funds supporting the Anstalt protected her from the stormtroopers. However, when Spielmeyer died in 1934, Alan Gregg of the Rockefeller Foundation sensed Mrs. Spielmeyer's danger and arranged to bring her and her daughter to the United States.
69. Stanley Cobb to Adolf Meyer, April 22, 1928, Meyer Papers.
70. Stanley Cobb to David L. Edsall, February 24, 1928, Dean's files, Harvard Medical Archives (under Rockefeller Foundation, General Education Board).
71. There is no documentation in Cobb's personal files, in the Dean's files at Harvard, or in the Dean's files at Yale concerning the offer of a Yale position to Cobb. There is at Yale a folder for Cobb in Box 2 of the Dean's files, now in the University Archives, which has 1926–1927 correspondence about his participation in a lecture series there. On January 27, 1927 Cobb delivered a talk entitled "Neurophysiology and Psychiatry," and the file related to this talk and its subsequent publication. There is no mention of an offer at all. On the other hand, the annual reports of the Yale Medical School in the late 1920s indicate that the departments of neurology and psychiatry were being built up, and it is possible, perhaps even likely, that Cobb was approached and sounded out for a position there. In 1928–1929 money was finally obtained from the Rockefeller Foundation and from the Commonwealth Fund to establish the Yale Institute of Human Relations, which was to cover many disciplines, including psychiatry. If a contact was made with Cobb in regard to a job at Yale, it was probably done on the personal and verbal level, most likely at the time of or after his January, 1927 talk. Indeed, it is possible that he may have been invited to deliver this talk as a way of looking him over for a position at Yale.
72. David L. Edsall to George Sears, February 25, 1928, Dean's Files, Harvard Medical Archives (under Rockefeller Foundation, General Education Board).
73. Trevor Arnett to David L. Edsall, March 5, 1929, Dean's Files, Harvard Medical Archives (under Rockefeller Foundation, General Education Board).

Chapter 7

1. At the time when Cobb first talked to Edsall, Edsall was Jackson Professor of Clinical Medicine at Harvard. In 1918 he became part-time dean and in 1923 full-time dean.

2. In their description of the new neurological unit (67), Cobb and Munro documented the financial assistance afforded by the Rockefeller Foundation. They said, "Coincidentally, the General Education Board of the Rockefeller Foundation had shown an interest in Neurology and sent Stanley Cobb for two years to study European methods. By 1925, when he was about to return to America, the negotiations between Hospital, School, and Foundation came to a head, and the Education Board offered Harvard University a substantial gift 'to establish an academic department of Neurology' if the University would add a very moderate amount to what it was already using annually for Neurology, to equal the amount of income from the gift. This was accepted, and on Cobb's arrival in Boston in August, 1925, he was asked to organize a new unit at the Boston City Hospital."

3. The work on electroencephalography and epilepsy, to which Cobb referred, was carried on by Lennox and Gibbs; homeostasis was the purview of Cannon and his staff at the department of physiology; Bard, also in physiology, was working on sham rage; Cushing at the Brigham was a student of the hypophysis; and, of course cerebral circulation was a major topic of study in Cobb's own department.

4. After Princeton, and a return to Harvard, Bard became professor of physiology at Johns Hopkins in Baltimore. Wolff and Putnam went to New York; Gibbs to Chicago; Davis and Gildea to St. Louis; and Fulton to New Haven.

5. The background and facts of Harvard's loss of its facilities at the Boston City Hospital are summed up by Robert H. Ebert, "The Termination of Harvard Medicine at Boston City Hospital: a Personal Account," which appears on pp. 745–767 of Volume I of Maxwell Finland's *The Harvard Medical Unit at Boston City Hospital*. Ebert was dean of the Harvard Medical School during this period of crisis.

6. Practically unknown before 1900, neurosurgery had by 1920 become an indispensable part of the neurological armamentarium, particularly through the influence of Harvey Cushing and other pioneers.

7. Stanley Cobb to David L. Edsall, April, 1929, Dean's Files, Harvard Medical Archives. A visit in 1979 to the space formerly occupied by the neurological unit revealed the remnants of these two operating suites at the northeast end of the eighth floor. The eastern corner room, with its large no-shadow operating-room light still in place, was being used as a conference room. The north corner room was being used for gastrointestinal endoscopy.

8. After the death of Francis Weld Peabody in 1927 the Thorndike was directed by George R. Minot, who with William B. Castle was studying nutritional aspects of anemia. Other important teachers and investigators there at the time were Chester Keefer, Soma Weiss, Clark Heath, and Henry Jackson, Jr.

9. According to Houston Merritt, in a taped interview on June 1, 1978, the neuropathology for Munro's and Putnam's neurosurgery was carried out here and prior to 1930 had been done by Morrison on the Building-D laboratory.

10. In 1951 the tenth floor was extended, with a special grant for the

Notes

purpose from the office of Mayor James M. Curley, to include three new laboratories at the east end.

11. The list is incomplete. Philip Solomon interned in 1930, and Eugene C. Eppinger, later a dean at the Harvard Medical School, was there part of the year. McKenna, who had worked with Morrison a year earlier, was a clinical intern, as was George R. Lavine. Wilfred Bloomberg, later Commissioner of Mental Health for Connecticut, was on the house staff that year. Also, in 1930 the neurological unit had for the first time a neurosurgical house staff. Walter Wegner was the resident neurosurgeon, Antoine Schneider, the senior house officer, and Madelaine R. Brown was designated as a house surgeon.

12. As an economy measure in the Great Depression, the staff list was omitted from the annual report of the Boston City Hospital after 1930.

13. Meyer Asekoff spent many years at the Metropolitan Mental Hospital in Waltham. Later he took up psychoanalysis and settled in Marblehead.

14. Erik Ask-Upmark was at the neurological unit in 1932. According to Finley his interests were in clinical neurology and neurophysiology. People at Boston City Hospital had great difficulty with his name, which they assumed was only "Upmark." "Ask Upmark," they would say. Ask-Upmark later became professor and chairman of the department at the University of Upsala. When at City Hospital he worked with Tracy Putnam on the living choroid plexus of the cat. In 1963 Ask-Upmark was living at Ramlösa Brunn, Sweden.

15. Theodore Fender was a young man from California who served on Cobb's service for only one year. In a taped interview on July 28, 1978, Margaret Gray said he had osteomyelitis of the hip. She said he had adopted one of her father's old suits and had it cut to fit.

16. Knox H. Finley worked with H. S. Forbes during the academic year 1931–32. On March 24, 1979, at the San Francisco Yacht Club, overlooking the lights of the Golden Gate Bridge and the Sausalito shore, Finley recalled in an interview some of his memories of Boston, including details of his work with Forbes and Gladys Nason, his assistant. Finley had a deep feeling for Cobb's struggle to promote a broad concept of the nervous system. In a previous personal communication he had said:

> The advances in our knowledge of the human brain both in normal and diseased state, particularly for the past fifteen to twenty years, have thoroughly established the justification for Dr. Cobb's basic concept that structure and function cannot be dichotomized. They are closely interrelated and clearly interrelate the clinical disorders of psychiatry and neurology. The academic division of the conventional clinical disorders of neurology and psychiatry had been and is an academic scientific artefact.

Finley became the director of the Institute of Neurological Sciences at 2200 Webster Street, San Francisco, and also maintained a private office there.

17. S. Rodman Irvine became an ophthalmologist and taught at U.C.L.A. He married Mary Dailey. It was in his office that ZaZa Gabor, gazing at a

picture of Cobb, remarked to Mary, "My how handsome he is. You must have fallen in love with him!"

18. Francis McNaughton became the senior neurologist at Penfield's Montreal Neurological Institute.

19. Hans B. Molholm followed Cobb to the Massachusetts General Hospital and did work on the psychology of eye movements. He died young from coarctation of the aorta.

20. James Lawrence Pool, professor of neurosurgery at Columbia-Presbyterian Medical Center in New York. Pool worked with H. S. Forbes briefly in approximately 1932.

21. Dr. Rubin, who was a house officer from 1933 to 1934, followed Cobb to the Massachusetts General and changed his name to I. Paley Rak.

22. Robert S. Schwab had his medical internship at Boston City Hospital and served on the neurological unit. He became interested in electroencephalography and went with Cobb to the Massachusetts General Hospital, where he set up, with Margaret Gray as his assistant, the first clinical electroencephalographic laboratory in the United States. He married Dorothy Miller, who was working as a technician with Merritt and Putnam on experimental convulsions in cats.

23. Frank Slaughter died prematurely of a brain abscess shortly after leaving the neurological service.

24. Simon Stone. Margaret Gray recalled him as a very shy person.

25. Theodore Von Storch, generally known as "Connie," was a neurologist. He went to Montefiore Hospital in the early forties and subsequently settled in Florida.

26. Martin Woodall became director of the Adams Nervine, which as Adams House subsequently became a part of the Faulkner Hospital complex.

27. Charles D. Aring to Benjamin V. White, October 26, 1978.

28. H. Houston Merritt, taped interview.

29. Charles D. Aring to Benjamin V. White, October 26, 1978.

30. Edwin F. Gildea, taped interview.

31. Frederick Gibbs, taped interview.

32. H. Houston Merritt, taped interview.

33. Harold Wolff and W. G. Lennox, "Cerebral Circulation: XII, The Effect on Pial Vessels of Variations in the Oxygen and Carbon Dioxide Content of the Blood." *Archives of Neurology and Psychiatry* XXIII (1930) 1097–1120.

34. A. S. Loevenhart, W. F. Lorentz, and R. M. Walters, "Cerebral Circulation." *Journal of the American Medical Association*, XCII (1929) 880–883.

35. Fremont-Smith's brother was later head of the psychiatric outpatient department at the M.G.H., and his son, Eliot, became editor of the *Village Voice*, a liberal New York newspaper.

36. Mary Dailey Irvine, personal communication.

37. Grace Finesinger, taped interview.

38. Freud was ill with cancer of the mouth. However, he did accept Roy Grinker for analysis; Grinker was Freud's only analysand at the time.

39. Edwin F. Gildea and Margaret C. L. Gildea, taped interview, April 16, 1977, and subsequent personal communications.

Notes

40. Margaret Gildea's accomplishments were all the more remarkable in that by a previous marriage she had two young children at home. One of them, Frank R. Egloff, was resident in psychiatry on Cobb's service at the Massachusetts General Hospital in 1951.

41. Arthur W. Fairbanks mostly committed patients to state hospitals.

42. Merrill Moore, *M* (New York: Harcourt, Brace and Co., 1938).

43. Works Project Administration, a federally supported agency, furnished emergency employment during the Great Depression.

44. A psychiatry department was formed in 1952 by Dr. Philip Solomon. Solomon was a very personable and able young man who interned in neurology at City Hospital in 1930. For many years he lived in California, where he shared an office with Tracy Putnam. When Solomon returned to the City in 1952 he established the first residency program in psychiatry.

Putnam became director of the New York Neurological Institute in 1939. That position did not work out well for him, and he later moved to the Los Angeles area where he was a neurosurgeon at the Cedars of Lebanon Hospital.

45. Chloe Binger, taped interview.

46. Dr. Arthur T. Phinney, personal communication. Dr. Phinney lives on Chappaquiddick summers with a view directly across the pond.

47. Charlotte Troutwine, taped interview. Mrs. Troutwine was Mrs. Richards when serving as Cobb's secretary.

48. In his *Review of Neuropsychiatry* for 1956 (234) Cobb wrote of Symonds's retirement from Guy's Hospital in London where he had served for twenty-five years. Symonds's principal scientific contributions were in the field of demyelinizing diseases. However, he had been an early pupil of Adolf Meyer in Baltimore and shared with Cobb the belief that neurology and psychiatry were part of the same field.

Chapter 8

1. Stanley Cobb to David L. Edsall, July 8, 1921, Cobb Papers.

2. Fritz B. Talbot, Chief of the Children's Medical Service at the Massachusetts General Hospital.

3. Stanley Cobb to William Norton Bullard, August 10, 1921, Cobb Papers.

4. The epilepsy committee consisted of William N. Bullard, the retired Boston City Hospital neuropathologist, after whom the chair later occupied by Cobb had been named; C. MacFie Campbell, the new professor of psychiatry at Harvard; David L. Edsall, dean of the Harvard Medical School and still Jackson Professor of Medicine at the Massachusetts General Hospital; Dr. Walter B. James of New York, a trustee of Columbia; Walter W. Palmer, secretary; and Charles P. Howland, treasurer.

5. Stanley Cobb to Adolf Meyer, November 9, 1921, Meyer Papers.

6. Stanley Cobb to Frederick Tilney, December 31, 1921, Cobb Papers.

7. Lennox published 233 papers during his professional career. Mary Dailey Irvine, for many years one of the most responsible and effective members of Cobb's technical and secretarial staff, said in a letter dated December 8, 1978, "In thinking about Dr. Cobb and my experience in his department, in contrast

to other departments, I felt I must ask you to be very sure that you state how admirably he credited co-workers with any contributions they made in teaching or research, even if he were the major inspiration for the work. . . . There are professors across the country who like to see their names on all publications coming from their departments. Dr. Cobb always preferred to have the co-workers get the credit, leaving his name off many articles of which he could claim to be the author." Mary Dailey Irvine to Benjamin V. White, December 8, 1978.

8. W. G. Lennox, L. H. Wright, and M. O'Connor, "Studies of the Metabolism in Epilepsy, I, Non-protein constituents of the blood," *Archives of Neurology and Psychiatry*, XI (1924), 54–63.

9. W. G. Lennox and M. O'Connor, "A Study of the Retention of Uric Acid during Fasting," *Journal of Biological Chemistry*, LXVI (1925) 521–572.

10. Henry Rawle Geyelin to Stanley Cobb, April 18, 1922, Cobb Papers. The patient was taking 1200 cc. of tenth normal hydrochloric acid a day. It had to be discontinued because it gave him pain in the stomach and nausea.

11. Hugh W. Conklin to Stanley Cobb, January 11, 1923, and March 2, 1923, Cobb Papers.

12. E. J. Bigwood, "Perturbation d'l'équilibre acid-base du sang dans l'épilepsie," *Comptes Rendus des Scéances de la Societé de Biologie*, LXXXIX (1923) 839–841.

13. W. G. Lennox and L. H. Wright, "Comparative Effects of Borotartrate and of Luminal on the Seizures of Epilepsy." *Boston Medical and Surgical Journal*, CXC (1926) 1199–1202.

14. Stanley Cobb to Charles P. Howland, June 16, 1923, Cobb Papers.

15. James Gamble was a clinical biochemist at the Children's Hospital. Douglas A. Thom worked in the outpatient department at the Boston Psychopathic Hospital.

16. Adolf Kussmaul and Adolf Tenner, "On the nature and origin of epileptiform convulsions caused by profuse bleeding, and also those of true epilepsy." Translated by Edward Bronner in the New Sydenham Society *Select Monographs* v. 5, 1859, 1–109.

17. Stanley Cobb to Charles P. Howland, October 29, 1925, Cobb Papers.

18. Virginia Howland to Stanley Cobb, March 10, 1926, Cobb Papers.

19. Charles P. Howland to Stanley Cobb, March 19, 1926, Cobb Papers.

20. The reference is to the work of Henry A. Cotton, of Trenton, N.J., who was removing the colons from patients with schizophrenia and other mental troubles as a therapeutic measure (chapter 3).

21. Stanley Cobb to Charles P. Howland, May 21, 1926, Cobb Papers.

22. E. F. Gildea, taped interview.

23. Ralph Lowell $1000, Godfrey Cabot $500, Charles C. Jackson $500, Miss M. C. Jackson $250, and Mrs. Greeley S. Curtis $75. Cobb Papers.

24. Wilder Penfield was at Johns Hopkins School of Medicine when Cobb was working at the Phipps Clinic in 1916.

25. Wilder Penfield, *No Man Alone* (Boston and Toronto, Little, Brown, 1977).

26. Removal of brain tissue was impossible because of proximity to the speech area.

27. Frederick Gibbs and Erna Leonhardt Gibbs, taped interview.

28. A "T" shaped tube, utilizing the Venturi principle. Measurement of pressure in the side arm indicates velocity of flow through the tube proper.

29. Stanley Cobb to Wilder Penfield, October 27, 1934, Cobb Papers.

30. Haymaker, *The Founders of Neurology*, p. 105.

31. W. G. Lennox, *Science and Seizures* (New York: Harper and Brothers, 1941), p. 86.

32. Frederick Gibbs and Erna Leonhardt Gibbs, taped interview.

33. The first tracings which Derbyshire made were on Hallowell Davis himself and have been preserved. The original electroencephalograph used at the time is at the Francis A. Countway Library of Medicine. At a meeting of the Eastern Electroencephographic Society in recent years the old machine was dusted off and put into operation again to record the brain waves of Hallowell Davis, who was present for the occasion. An historical summary of the early attempts to investigate the electrical properties of the central nervous system, including the work of Berger and others and the experiments and eventual discovery in 1934 of the electroencephalograph at the Harvard Medical School, forms Chapter I of Robert S. Schwab's *Electroencephalography in Clinical Practice*.

34. H. Houston Merritt, taped interview.

35. An amusing and tragically prophetic story is told about Donald Munro's comments at a farewell dinner in Putnam's honor. Munro told the guests that Putnam was making a mistake in going to New York. Then he recounted the story of a farmer who called his veterinarian one night because the cat was sick. The veterinarian advised castor oil, which the farmer dutifully administered to the cat. The next morning the veterinarian met the farmer and asked how the cat was doing. The farmer said that he had trouble getting two teaspoonfuls down the cat's throat. The veterinarian replied, "Two teaspoonfuls! I said two drops. Is the cat all right?" The farmer said that she had diarrhea all night, but she had friends. "Twelve neighborhood cats showed up. Six of them were digging holes and the other six were covering them up." Munro went on to say, "Tracy, here you have friends to dig and cover up for you; you won't have friends like that in New York."

36. W. G. Lennox, *op. cit.*

37. W. G. Lennox and M. L. Buchthal, *Epilepsy and Related Disorders* (Boston, Little, Brown, 1960), 2 v.

38. Stanley Cobb, "William Gordon Lennox M.D." Obituary, *Archives of Neurology*, IV (1960) 463–465.

Chapter 9

1. Joseph C. Aub, "Dedication," *The Aesculapiad* (Boston, Harvard Medical School, 1954), p. 7.

2. Joseph C. Aub and Ruth K. Hapgood, *Pioneer in Modern Medicine:*

David L. Edsall of Harvard (Cambridge, Harvard University Press, 1970). In his biography of Edsall, Aub referred to Cobb's youthful appointment to the Harvard faculty, noting that "This is a nice example of how Edsall nursed a young man along. He picked them well when they were young and then placed them strategically around the medical school, often in primary posts." Aub's annotated draft of *The Aesculapiad* dedication is in the Cobb folder among Dr. Aub's papers in the Countway Library. Also in this folder is a memorandum marked "For Saul Benison," who at that time was conducting an oral history on Dr. Aub for the Columbia University Oral History Program. Aub's memorandum reads:

> A good example of how Edsall developed his young promising people until they were ready to direct a well integrated unit is shown in the story of Stanley Cobb. Edsall met Stanley as a 4th year medical student, partly because of his friendship with Carl Binger. Carl at that time was quite intrigued by one of the Tileston girls and was out at the Tileston house frequently, and Stanley got to know David Edsall who was married to an older Tileston sister; they were living in Milton.
>
> Edsall saw the promise in Stanley Cobb and advised him as a 4th year student to take an internship with Cushing, even though Cobb had no intention of becoming a surgeon. Cobb, therefore, spent a year with Cushing, and still following Edsall's advice then went to Hopkins where he studied physiology for a year with Howell, and continued at Hopkins for two more years with Meyer in psychiatry. This was his training before he came back to MGH.

3. In Cobb's day Münsterberg was professor of philosophy, and the Harvard Psychological Laboratory was administered by the department of philosophy.

4. Nathan G. Hale, "James Jackson Putnam and Boston Neurology, 1877–1918," in *Psychoanalysis, Psychotherapy, and the New England Medical Scene, 1894–1944*, edited by George Gifford (New York, Neal Watson, 1978) p. 149.

5. Cobb knew Putnam socially, both at Cotuit on Cape Cod, where Putnam spent his summers, and at his Adirondack Camp in Keene Valley, New York. The camp in Keene Valley had been built as a joint venture with Henry Pickering Bowditch, the professor of physiology, but Bowditch had given up his interest in it. In the foreword to Hale's *James Jackson Putnam and Psychoanalysis,* Putnam's daughter, Marian, also a psychoanalyst, wrote very sensitively about some of her father's characteristics, views, and customs. She said her father was a poor sleeper and did most of his reading and writing between three and seven or eight in the morning. She described his busy practice as seen through her eyes as a child. Everyone in the house was forbidden to use the word "nervous," an invidious term which Putnam believed described neither the patients nor their problems. Marian Putnam related that Putnam's family and close friends knew him as a charming, gentle, overconscientious person—though by no means without humor—slow to anger, public spirited, thoughtfully purposeful in every undertaking whether personal or professional.

Even while gardening or sailing on summer weekends with his family in Cotuit on Cape Cod, or mountain climbing, reading and conversing in his beloved Adirondacks during the month of September, he was constantly thinking about problems philosophical, social, or artistic. Marian C. Putnam, foreword to *James Jackson Putnam and Psychoanalysis,* edited by Nathan G. Hale, Jr., (Cambridge: Harvard University Press, 1971).

6. Putnam married Marion Cabot, eleven years his junior, with whom he had shared years of work in the Associated Charities of Boston. Putnam himself and Marion Cabot were both second cousins of Cobb's mother-in-law, Helen Jackson Cabot, who married Judge Charles Almy of Cambridge.

Putnam's wife had nothing in her background that prepared her for his interest in psychoanalysis. When he accepted the validity of this new science she reacted with tragic bitterness. Yet, Putnam did not accept all of Freud's psychoanalytic theory. Beginning in 1905, he had experimented with Freud's analytic method. However, Putnam could not divest himself of the idealism and the emphasis on free will which had come down to him through his religious tradition as well as that of James, whose thoughts on psychoanalysis paralleled and to a considerable extent colored his own. After Freud's visit to the United States in 1909, when Putnam entertained him at the camp, there ensued a long correspondence between the two men in which Putnam tried to convince Freud that an American form of idealism should find a place in psychoanalytic theory. Sanford Gifford, "Psychoanalysis in Boston: Innocence and Experience," in *Psychoanalysis, Psychotherapy and the New England Medical Scene, 1894–1944.*

7. Marian Putnam, Stanley Cobb, and Carl Binger acquired homes on a tract on Quoquonsett Lane about one mile south of Little Compton common. The land looked across a marsh and pond to the ocean beyond. Although all three intended to retire there none of them actually did so.

8. William A. White and Smith Ely Jelliffe, *The Modern Treatment of Nervous and Mental Diseases by American and British Authors* (Philadelphia, Lea and Febiger, 1913).

9. Sanford Gifford, personal communication to Benjamin V. White.

10. As its secretary Coriat was vital to the 1914 Boston Psychoanalytic Society, which Putnam had described to Freud as "A small group that meets at my house every Friday afternoon, and although we are not geniuses, yet we do fair work and I think keep our heads level." During the twenties, although still leaving some room for eclecticism, Coriat became much more orthodox as a Freudian. He made the psychologists L. Eugene Emerson and Frederick Lyman Wells quite unwelcome in his group, yet he accepted some of the frank Jungians.

11. Barbara Sicherman, "Isador H. Coriat," *Psychoanalysis, Psychotherapy, and the New England Medical Scene 1894–1944.*

12. William Hohenzollern II, the Kaiser of World War I, had a withered arm presumably resulting from a birth injury at the hands of Queen Victoria's obstetrician. Hence, according to this theory, his antagonism against Great Britain.

13. Sanford Gifford said, after a taped interview with Cobb's wife in 1977, that she recalled Seif as a gentle elderly man whom Cobb and she often saw together. Cobb would go in first, then after a time she would enter, and a sort of family therapy would follow. Gifford presented material from the taped interview on February 10, 1982, at a historical colloquium sponsored by the Harvard psychiatric department in the Countway Library.

14. Members of the reorganized Boston Psychoanalytic Society in 1930 were S. Spafford Ackerly, George E. Clark, Stanley Cobb, Isador H. Coriat, Leolia Dalrymple, Julia Deming, William Healy, Ives Hendrick, William Herman, Jacob Kassarin, M. Ralph Kaufman, Henry A. Murray, John Murray, Martin W. Peck, Irmarita Putnam, Margaret A. Ribble, David Rothschild, Harvey Sanborn, John Taylor, and George Wilbur. Ives Hendrick, *The Birth of an Institute* (Freeport, Maine, Bond-Wheelwright, 1958) p. 17, footnote.

Of the new approaches to which Aub referred in *The Aesculapiad*, Freudian psychoanalysis was the most exciting and the most controversial, and Cobb was gradually attracted to it. After approximately 1930, when the Boston Psychoanalytic Association was limited to Freudians, the term "psychoanalysis" was used only to refer to a most orthodox application of the free association technique by a therapist trained by one of Freud's school. However, earlier, "psychoanalysis" was used in a more eclectic way to include the work of Jung, Adler, and others.

15. In the spring of 1936 the author and his wife accompanied Betty Cobb on a call to Jackson and Putnam in New Haven. They had with them their one-year-old son, who was given a cubical box and a ball to play with. When the child failed to place the ball in the box, all three ladies looked aghast, as if the failure presaged a disastrous psychiatric prognosis. They were experimenting with one of their new play-therapy techniques.

16. In September, 1931, Cobb wrote down for his own use and not for publication a statement about his comprehension of psychological analysis as he saw it at that time. He scrawled on the manuscript, "This is a rough draft of my attempt to clarify my own attitude toward psychoanalysis. It is written as if for an editorial but will never be published until ripened and peeled." It was written before Cobb had his own analysis with Sachs in 1933 and 1934, hence presumably before he had a first-hand experience with the transference situation, a key aspect of psychoanalytic therapy.

The statement which Cobb wrote included references to the well known terminology used by Freud, Jung, and Adler. Cobb expressed his conviction that analytic therapy could indeed change personalities—with a good therapist for the better—but sometimes with unfortunate results. Because analytic therapy could change personalities Cobb saw it of such enormous importance that it merited all possible study. Dismissing Jung's and Adler's contributions as elaborations, Cobb saw Freud as the true pioneer, yet he could not accept the concepts of any of the three as of specific significance in the illness of any one human being. Instead, he returned to the Meyerian emphasis on studying the patient as a whole. In summary, Cobb said, "From the medical point of view self understanding is the essence of psychoanalysis . . . let us honor the analytic psychologist, whatever his creed, who with painstaking endeavor and wise restraint learns to understand his patient." Stanley Cobb, "Human Motives," unpublished manuscript, Cobb Papers.

17. The ten qualifying members of the Boston Psychoanalytic Society were Isador H. Coriat, Leolia A. Dalrymple, William Healy, Ives Hendrick, William J. Herman, M. Ralph Kaufman, Henry A. Murray, John M. Murray, Martin W. Peck, Irmarita Putnam. Ives Hendrick, *Birth of an Institute,* p. 39, footnote.

18. Sanford Gifford, "Psychoanalysis in Boston—Innocence or Experience," p. 335.

19. Stanley Cobb, Decennial Report of the Psychiatric Service of the Massachusetts General Hospital (1934–1944), p. 3.

20. Rodney Triplet, "Henry A. Murray and the Harvard Psychological Clinic, 1926–1938; the struggle to expand the Disciplining Boundries of Psychology," Unpublished, Ph.D. dessertation, University of New Hampshire, 1983.

21. Stanley Cobb to Alan Gregg, September 24, 1934, Rockefeller Archives.

22. "Grants-in-Aid, New York," Rockefeller Foundation Archives, Series 200, Box 91, Folder 1095.

23. Rodney Triplet, *op. cit,* chapter 6, p. 13.

24. Sanford Gifford, *op. cit,* p. 331.

25. Collected Papers, Department of Diseases of the Nervous System, Harvard Medical School, N.S. vol VI, 1936.

26. Erik H. Erikson, notes recorded after a personal interview, July 22, 1978.

27. Erik H. Erikson to Benjamin V. White, August, 1978, Cobb Papers. Erikson's reference to the Putnam Road refers to Putnam Avenue, which was named after James Jackson Putnam.

28. Stanley Cobb to Erik H. Erikson, December 8, 1964, Cobb Papers.

29. Janice R. Stevens to Benjamin V. White, June 24, 1982, Cobb Papers. Dr. Stevens in 1982 was professor of neurology and psychiatry at the Oregon Health Sciences University in Portland.

30. Intravenous sodium amytal was later popularized as "truth serum" and was used as a short cut in the ventilation of repressed memories.

31. Ives Hendrick, *op. cit.,* p. 162.

32. In a taped interview on April 16, 1978, Frances Bonner said that Lindemann had a way of dividing people. Jerome Weinberger on August 27, 1977, described Lindemann as a "yes" man who could not say "no," yet failed to live up to his promises, and Alfred O. Ludwig on August 3, 1979, said, "Lindemann had the unfortunate custom of promising everybody everything." Ludwig added that Lindemann would delegate the same task to two or more people and then concluded, "He was a master of creating trouble."

33. In a taped interview on April 8, 1980, Herbert Barry told a tale he had heard from Lemoyne White. During the late forties Lindemann was failing to

attend many of the weekly staff conferences. Cobb and Finesinger warned him that if he did not attend the conferences he would have to resign from the staff.

34. John Adams Abbott, taped interview, February 16, 1978. The petition was got up in 1964.

35. Jerome Weinberger, taped interview, August 27, 1977.

36. Eisenberg served from 1969 through 1976 and was succeeded by Thomas Hackett who, with his eclectic background, restored a balance between psychoanalysis and clinical psychiatry.

37. Finesinger's control analyses were with Anna Freud, Helene Deutsch, and Heinz Hartmann.

38. *Psychoanalysis, Psychotherapy and the New England Medical Scene, 1894–1944*, p. 372. The statement is attributed to Edgerton Howard, but from the context it must have been made by his brother, Paul, who was a resident under Cobb in 1937.

39. Cobb would undoubtedly have encouraged him to remain at the Massachusetts General Hospital but he did not believe that at that time the General Executive Board would consider a Jew as his successor. Personal communication from Mrs. Jacob Finesinger.

40. It was Felix Deutsch whom Cobb originally attracted to Boston. In a conversation on June 16, 1982, Cobb's widow said that Felix Deutsch came to the United States on Cobb's invitation in early 1935 and stayed at the Cobbs' home for a period of weeks to evaluate the move, while Helene was making up her mind about whether or not to come over herself. Actually Helene came earlier, in October, 1935, so that their son, Martin, could commence study at the Massachusetts Institute of Technology.

41. Suzanne Gordon, "Helene Deutsch and the Legacy of Freud," *New York Times*, Magazine Section, July 30, 1978.

42. There was a World War I limerick about Przemysl which ran as follows:

> There was an old man from Przemysl
>   [pronounced to rhyme with chisel]
> Who cut off his toe with a Czemysl.
> When asked, "Did it bleed?"
> He replied, "Yes, indeed."
> And peroxide caused it to Szemysl.

43. *Psychoanalysis, Psychotherapy and the New England Medical Scene, 1894–1944*, p. 419.

44. Helene Deutsch, in *Psychoanalysis, Psychotherapy and the New England Medical Scene*, p. 420.

45. Elizabeth Almy Cobb, personal communication, June 16, 1982.

46. Sidney Kligerman, personal communication. Kligerman, a Hartford psychoanalyst, had his training analysis with Felix Deutsch.

47. Frank Fremont-Smith to Stanley Cobb, June 14, 1937, Fremont-Smith Papers, Countway Library.

48. Stanley Cobb to Frank Fremont-Smith, June 16, 1937. Fremont-Smith Papers, Countway Library.
49. Felix Deutsch, *On the Mysterious Leap from the Mind to the Body* (New York, International Universities Press, 1959).
50. Mark D. Altschule, personal communication to Benjamin V. White.
51. Edgerton Howard was assistant director of the outpatient department. He later played a very influential role at the Riggs Foundation by laying the plans to develop the center into a truly psychoanalytic institution. *Psychoanalysis, Psychotherapy and the New England Medical Scene, 1894–1944*, p. 274.
52. According to Cobb's wife, Cohen and Sachs gave up the analysis by mutual consent. Personal communication.
53. Mandel E Cohen, personal communication.
54. Maurice Greenhill, taped interview.
55. Stanley Cobb to Charles Aring, from Little Compton, R.I., undated, 1957 retirement correspondence. Cobb Papers.

Chapter 10

1. G. H. Sweeney, "Pioneering General Hospital Psychiatry," *Psychiatric Quarterly Supplement*, XXXVI (1962) 209–268, relates that Mosher's unit, established at the Albany General in 1902, was the oldest psychiatric unit in an American hospital.
2. Merrill Moore, "Review of Neuropsychiatric Development at Harvard," *Harvard Medical Alumni Bulletin*, VIII (1934) 61–70.
3. Maurice H. Greenhill, "The Development of Liaison Programs," in *Psychiatric Medicine*, edited by Gene Usdin (New York, Brunner Mazel, 1977).
4. E. G. Billings credited Franklin Ebaugh with influencing Alan Gregg's decision to establish psychiatric services in general hospitals. Greenhill, *op. cit.*
5. John Adams Abbott, personal communication, June 14, 1983.
6. Wilder Penfield, *The Difficult Art of Giving* (Boston, Little, Brown, 1967).
7. Decennial Report of Psychiatric Service of the Massachusetts General Hospital (1934–1944), Appendix A.
8. Greenhill, *op. cit.*, p. 136.
9. Derek Denny-Brown, taped interview.
10. Means was Jackson Professor of Clinical Medicine and head of the medical department; Bauer headed rheumatology at the time and later succeeded Means; Cope was an outstanding endocrinological surgeon.
11. Earl Solomon, taped interview.
12. In later years one of Cobb's residents, John Nemiah, made a comprehensive study of this disorder. See footnote 14.
13. Stanley Cobb, *Emotions and Clinical Medicine* (New York, W. W. Norton, 1950).
14. John C. Nemiah, "Anorexia Nervosa: A Clinical Psychiatric Study." *Medicine*, CXXIX (1950) 225–268.

15. By "behavior sheet" Cobb and Finesinger meant an abbreviated psychiatric history and mental status sheet. Adolf Meyer had used the term "behavior sheet" in reference to daily progress notes by nurses on hospitalized patients.

16. The Boston Psychopathic Hospital later became a part of the new Massachusetts Mental Health Center and came to be conveniently referred to as "Mass. Mental."

17. Harry C. Solomon, taped interview.

18. The *Archives of Internal Medicine* is published monthly by the American Medical Association. The references to Cobb's reviews are in Appendix B.

19. Sutherland had worked with Howard Liddell on conditioned reflexes at Cornell University in Ithaca, New York, before joining Finesinger. Dr. Mandel Cohen referred to him as the "pig psychiatrist." Cohen said that Sutherland produced a neurosis in a six-hundred-pound hog. One night the hog got loose and smashed a great deal of valuable equipment in the laboratory.

20. Maurice H. Greenhill, taped interview.

21. Jurgen Ruesch, taped interview, March 27, 1979. Ruesch said that Sargant was interested in brainwashing and examined Patricia Hearst, who had presumably been brainwashed. However, at the time of her trial, according to Ruesch, the testimony was not introduced in court.

22. E. Murray Burns to Stanley Cobb, September 5, 1966, Cobb Papers.

23. Maurice H. Greenhill, taped interview.

24. William W. Sargant to Benjamin V. White, June 7, 1979. In this letter Sargant, while he held Cobb in high regard, was quite critical of the widespread interest in psychoanalysis on the part of his staff. In the letter Sargant referred to his early interest in drug therapy, which he said antedated Lindemann's, and referred to his budding interest in brainwashing, which he said was inspired by Helene Deutsch.

25. Mandel Cohen, taped interview.

26. Donald B. Lindsley to Stanley Cobb, January 10, 1961, Cobb Papers.

27. Decennial Report of the Psychiatric Service of the Massachusetts General Hospital (1934–1944). Child Psychiatry is taken up in chapter 13.

28. Susan Herman to Walter B. Cannon, May 16, 1939, Cannon papers, Countway Library.

29. The source of these stories is Cobb's widow, the late Mrs. Elizabeth Cobb Hall.

30. Chloe Binger, taped interview.

31. *Ibid.*

Chapter 11

1. The staff in 1940 comprised the following members: psychiatrists: Cobb, Finesinger, Tillotson; associate psychiatrists: Anthonisen, Barrett, Helene Deutsch, Lindemann; neuropathologist: Charles S. Kubik; assistant psychiatrists: R. Barry Bigelow, Edgerton Howard, Martin Peck, Taylor; assistants in psychiatry: Abbott, G. Burnham Beaman, Cohen, Lydia Dawes, Raymond

Duffy, Molholm, Marian Putnam, Sutherland, John W. Thompson, J. Kendall Wallis, Vernon P. Williams; research fellows: Raymond D. Adams, Justin M. Hope, Else Neustadt, Jurgen Ruesch; psychologist: Robert A. Young; assistant psychologist: Elizabeth M. Hincks; resident: Samuel P. Hunt; assistant resident: Norris P. Flanagan.

2. E. D. Chapple and E. Lindemann, "Clinical Implications of Measurements of Interaction Rates in Psychiatric Interviews." *Applied Anthropology* I (1942) 1–11.

3. John C. Nemiah, taped interview.

4. J. C. Aub; H. K. Beecher; Bradford Cannon; Stanley Cobb; Oliver Cope; N. W. Faxon; Champ Lyons; Tracy Mallory; and Richard Schatski, *Management of the Cocoanut Grove Fire at the Massachusetts General Hospital* (Philadelphia, Lippincott, 1943). Reprinted from *Annals of Surgery* CXVII (1943).

5. Sir Thomas Lewis, *The Soldier's Heart and the Effort Syndrome* (London, Shaw and Sons, 1918).

6. Decennial Report of the Psychiatric Service of the Massachusetts General Hospital, 1934–1944, p. 13.

7. J. D. French, F. K. Amerongen, and H. W. Magoun, "An Activating System in the Brain Stem of Monkeys," *Archives of Neurology and Psychiatry*, LXVIII (1952) 577. In an untaped interview on December 9, 1979, Peter B. Dews, the Stanley Cobb Professor of Psychiatry, said that the basic idea for the ascending reticular activating system was derived from work by Robert S. Morison and Edward Dempsey in Alexander Forbes's laboratory.

8. Stanley Cobb to Joseph F. Ross, November 2, 1961, Cobb Papers. Cobb was replying to a letter from Ross dated October 17, 1961.

9. It had been shown that an adrenal cortical hormone, presumably 11-oxygenated corticosteroid, regulated the production of circulatory lymphocytes resulting from a variety of stress situations which were attributed to increased adrenal cortex activity.

10. Earl Solomon, taped interview.

11. George Carter, taped interview.

12. Hildegarde Forbes, personal communication to Benjamin V. White.

13. Decennial Report, p. 10.

14. Lindemann gave a series of exercises to students from the Harvard School of Public Health, and Dr. Elizabeth Hincks gave a course on mental testing. Also there were talks for divinity students and student nurses.

15. Decennial Report, p. 7.

16. John Nemiah, taped interview.

17. Bernard Bandler, taped interview.

18. Bernard Bandler, "Residency Education in Psychiatry."

19. Bernard Bandler, taped interview.

20. *Ibid.*

21. Hunt became a psychoanalyst and practiced in New Haven, Connecticut; Burness Moore after seven years at Yale settled in New York City; George Saslow became chairman of the department at the University of Oregon; James

Grier Miller became president of the University of Louisville; and Richmond Holder was at Phillips Exeter Academy from 1951 to 1960 and later became a member of the McLean Hospital staff.

22. Herbert Barry, Jr., taped interview.

23. Flanagan remained on the staff for several years with a designation that he was on active duty; Cecil Muschatt became a professor at Boston University.

24. Jurgen Ruesch to Benjamin V. White, November 20, 1978, Cobb Papers.

25. F. Lyman Wells, Ph.D., was appointed a Psychologist in 1941. He had been a student of psychoanalysis during the twenties.

26. Stanley Cobb to Karl M. Bowman, September 16, 1942, Cobb Papers.

27. In a taped interview on March 27, 1979 Ruesch cited some other associations he had had with psychological studies when working with Cobb. Before the United States entered World War II, he was working part time with Harry Murray on the question, "Can you figure out who will make a good spy when dropped over enemy lines in Europe?" Ruesch said it was Chapple, the anthropologist, who wrote *An Investigation of Success in Naval Flight Training*. Ruesch had a copy of the volume, which was published under the authorship of Cobb, Finesinger, Chapple, and Brazier. Ruesch believed that the only test of a good flier was motivation.

28. Harley C. Shands to Benjamin V. White, February 6, 1979, Cobb Papers. Lorenz said she went back to McLean because she enjoyed caring for psychotic patients.

29. Raymond Adams took one year in psychiatry with Cobb before going into neuropathology at City Hospital in 1942. He later became chief of neurology at the General. Justin Hope worked on neurocirculatory asthenia with Cohen and later went to the Pratt Diagnostic Hospital with him. He died prematurely in an automobile accident. Neustadt was designated as a research fellow from 1938 through 1942. Her work was actually at Thom's Habit Clinic. She later was on the active staff of the Quincy Hospital and died in 1980. Robert A. Young, Ed.D., worked in child psychiatry under Pavenstedt. Meath, an internist who later settled in Dublin, New Hampshire, worked with Brazier in 1945.

30. Chief of service: Cobb; psychiatrists: Finesinger, Tillotson, Lindemann; neuropathologists: Charles S. Kubik, L. Raymond Morrison; assistant psychiatrists: Bandler, Barry, Bigelow, Williams; assistants in psychiatry: Beaman, Benda, Raymond T. Duffy, Flanagan (on military leave), McNaughton, Neustadt, I. Paley Rak (Rubin), John B. Tomkins; psychologists: Hincks, Wells, Wyatt; resident: Richmond Holder; assistant residents: Cecil Muschatt, LeMoyne White; clinical and research fellows: Brazier, Shands, Weisman.

31. Decennial Report, p. 10.

32. At Hartford Hospital about 1947 the author found his six-year-old son, scheduled for herniorrhaphy the next day, tied down in a crib with a strait jacket. The strait jacket was too small, so that the boy could not move at all. When asked the reason for the strait jacket, which was promptly removed, the nurse said, "Oh, nothing. It is just a hospital routine."

Notes 417

33. Mark D. Altschule, personal communication, July 20, 1982. Altschule, who also came to Folin's laboratory at McLean during World War II, was doing clinical work. He started by studying patients before and after electroshock therapy and later worked into neurotransmitters and drug therapy. In 1982 he was a full time executive officer for the Boston Medical Library, one of the components of the Countway. Altschule said that Folch-Pi had for an assistant a Turk named Lahut Uzman. Folch-Pi, a devout Roman Catholic, Uzman, a Muslim, and Altschule, a Jew, used to have religious conferences. Uzman embarrassed Folch-Pi by having a greater knowledge of Catholicism than he did himself. One day Folch-Pi asked Uzman how he acquired so much knowledge. Uzman replied, "I am looking forward to being Pope some day."

Chapter 12

1. William Menninger had responsibility for procuring psychiatric medical officers for the army and John Murray for the air corps. M. Ralph Kaufman was in charge of psychiatric casualties in the Pacific theater. All of these men were Freudian analysts. Henry Fox, later MacPherson's successor at the Peter Bent Brigham Hospital, gave up his Meyerian background and became a psychoanalyst because he observed that Kaufman's psychoanalytic approach, in contrast to Meyer's psychobiology, was effective therapeutically in treating psychiatric casualties. The chief naval procurement officer was Francis J. Braceland, who later directed the Institute of Living in Hartford.

2. Fred H. Frankel to Benjamin V. White, June 26, 1979, Cobb Papers.

3. Henry H. Brewster to Benjamin V. White, February 10, 1979, Cobb Papers.

4. Jerome Weinberger, taped interview.

5. Alfred O. Ludwig, taped interview.

6. Herbert Barry, taped interview.

7. Francis Bonner, taped interview. Bonner said that Finesinger could actually take in a case presentation when to all observers he appeared to be sound asleep.

8. John Nemiah, taped interview.

9. Oliver Cope, taped interview.

10. Anterior Corticotropic Hormone.

11. William H. Trethowan to Benjamin V. White, May 30, 1979, Cobb Papers. Trethowan was professor of psychiatry and chairman of the department at the University of Sydney in Australia for seventeen years from 1956 to 1973.

12. Oliver Cope, taped interview. Cope said that in 1933 Dale demonstrated the need for a stimulus from the hypothalamus to evoke ovulation in the ferret.

13. Henry H. W. Miles to Benjamin V. White, June 18, 1979, Cobb Papers.

14. Arthur M. Master, who during World War II was cardiologist-in-chief at the National Naval Medical Center in Bethesda, Maryland, repeatedly pointed out the asthenic build and the vertical "broomstick" heart observed in sailors with neurocirculatory asthenia.

15. In a personal interview Richard L. Day, Harvard Medical School, 1931, quoted Herman as saying during a lecture in the second year neuropathology course, "I have Friedreich's ataxia; my son has Friedreich's ataxia."

16. Walter B. Cannon, *Bodily Changes in Pain, Hunger, Fear, and Rage* (New York, Appleton, 1915).

17. J. W. Papez, "A Proposed Mechanism of Emotion," *Archives of Neurology and Psychiatry*, XXXVIII (1937) 725.

18. *Limbic Mechanisms*, edited by Kenneth Livingston and Oleh Hornkiewicz (New York, Plenum Publishing Corporation, 1978).

19. *Physical Basis of Mind: A Symposium*, edited by P. Laslett (Oxford, Basil, Blackwell and Mott, 1950).

20. Wilder Penfield and T. Rasmussen, *Cerebral Cortex in Man: A Clinical Study of Localization of Function* (New York, MacMillan, 1950).

21. In the light of more recent knowledge of the ascending reticular activating system, Pope has taken the position that Penfield may have been nearer the truth than Cobb. Alfred Pope, taped interview.

22. *The Commonsense Psychiatry of Adolf Meyer, Fifty-two Selected Papers Edited, with Biographical Narrative, by A. Lief.*

23. Peter Sifneos, *Ascent from Chaos* (Cambridge, Harvard University Press, 1964).

24. Archibald D. Leigh, telephone conversation with Benjamin V. White from Maudsley Hospital, May 19, 1977.

25. Charles P. Gore to Stanley Cobb, June 26, 1957, Cobb Papers.

26. William Trethowan to Benjamin V. White, May 30, 1979, Cobb Papers. Trethowan wrote that when he was in Australia he had seen Tow, who was seeking a position at the time.

27. Peter H. Knapp, taped interview. Of psychoanalysis Knapp said, "By 1950 everyone was taking up psychoanalysis. It was a national wave. In order to be a chief of service one had to be analyzed. Tremendous impetus was given to psychoanalysis by World War II. Will Menninger, Jock Murray, 'Mo' Kaufman, and Roy Grinker, all analysts, were the outstanding psychiatrists in the armed services." Knapp omitted Francis J. Braceland, a non-analyst, who was in charge of procurement of psychiatrists for the navy.

28. E. Peirson Richardson, taped interview.

29. Joseph F. Ross to Stanley Cobb, October 7, 1963, Cobb Papers.

30. Franklin Carter to Benjamin V. White, March 18, 1978, Cobb Papers.

31. Nozumi Suwa to Dr. and Mrs. Benjamin V. White, June 11, 1980, Cobb Papers.

32. R. A. Cleghorn to Benjamin V. White, May 25, 1979, Cobb Papers.

33. Morris Chafetz to Benjamin V. White, July 27, 1979, Cobb Papers.

34. Philip Margolis to Benjamin V. White, January 28, 1980, Cobb Papers.

35. Stanley Cobb to R. Bruce Sloane, April 24, 1957, Cobb Papers.

36. Jerome Weinberger, taped interview.

37. Oliver Cope, taped interview.

38. *Ibid.* Cope reported that when the new White Building was being completed it was to have been shared equally by medicine and surgery. Churchill

took the stance that seventy percent of the patients in the hospital were surgical, and after all it was the surgeons who supported the hospital financially. Therefore, Churchill said, the surgeons should have seventy percent of the space in the building. Churchill badgered Means, the chief of Medicine, to the point where his exasperation reached the breaking point. In the crunch Means said, "Take the whole G-- D--- building. We will get along in the Bulfinch." In reply Churchill said, "All right. I will." And so it turned out that the only part of the White Building occupied by medicine was one-half the eleventh floor, which clinical neurology shared with neurosurgery.

39. John C. Nemiah, taped interview.
40. Milton J. Rosenbaum, taped interview.

Chapter 13

1. H. L. Witmer, *Psychiatric Interviews with Children* (New York: Commonwealth Fund, 1946), p. 6.
2. With funds raised by Judge Frederick P. Cabot, the Judge Baker Foundation came into being in 1917, and Healy was appointed its first director at that time. The name was changed in 1931 to the Judge Baker Guidance Center.
3. Suzanne Van Amerongen, taped interview. See also J. G. Orne and P. Stuart, "The Habit Clinics: Behavioral Social Work and Prevention in the 1920s." *Social Service Review*, LV (1981) 242–256.
4. Although located in Waverly, McLean Hospital is a part of the Massachusetts General Hospital.
5. Florence Clothier Wislocki, in *Psychoanalysis, Psychotherapy, and the New England Scene*, p. 381. Mrs. Wislocki is a big, strong, muscular woman. Meyer reported to her that some of the installments of her life history were submitted with a boy's number. She said that she had a habit of reversing digits and apparently did so inadvertently.
6. Eleanor Pavenstedt, taped interview.
7. Stanley Cobb to Frank Fremont-Smith, November 14, 1936, Fremont-Smith Papers, Countway Library.
8. Eleanor Pavenstedt, taped interview. Today the camp is associated with McLean Hospital and is known as Camp Weideko.
9. Elizabeth Cobb Hall, marginal note on manuscript.
10. Edward and Grete Bibring were psychoanalysts. Edward held a part-time teaching position at Tufts, but he was primarily a full-time analyst and an excellent teacher at the Boston Psychoanalytic Society and Institute. Grete was invited by Herrmann Blumgart to reestablish at the Beth Israel Hospital the department of psychiatry which had remained dormant during the early war years after the departure of M. Ralph Kaufman. (*Psychoanalysis, Psychotherapy, and the New England Medical Scene*, p. 417). She eventually became the first woman to hold a full professorship at the Harvard Medical School.
11. H. L. Witmer, *Psychiatric Interviews with Children*, p. 12.

12. M. S. Mahler, "Child Analysis", in N. D. C. Lewis and B. L. Pacella, *Modern Trends in Child Psychiatry* (New York, International Universities Press, 1945), p. 275.

13. Decennial Report of the Psychiatric Service of the Massachusetts General Hospital 1934–1944, pp. 9, 10.

14. Elizabeth Cobb Hall, personal communication, August 8, 1982.

15. Gregory Rochlin, taped interview, April 8, 1980, and subsequent conversation.

16. Elizabeth Cobb Hall, personal communication, August 8, 1982.

17. Suzanne Van Amerogen, taped interview.

18. Lucie Jessner. Unpublished report prepared for Dr. John A. Abbott at Massachusetts General Hospital, 1979. In November 1947 the *Massachusetts General Hospital News* (212) described a new cooperative unit of Child Psychiatry growing out of the existing liaison between the Children's Medical Service and the Department of Psychiatry. After reviewing the history of child psychiatry nationally and at the M.G.H., the article told about Lucie Jessner's new assignment as chief of the unit and mentioned as clinical fellows Dr. Jane Allen, Dr. Margaret Bullowa, Dr. Samuel Kaplan, and Dr. Nicholas D. Rizzo. It also indicated that the new cooperative unit was made possible by a grant from the Public Health Service under the Mental Health Act of 1947.

19. Gaston E. Blom to Benjamin V. White and John Adams Abbott, August 25, 1979 including "Memoir Notes," Cobb Papers.

20. Gregory Rochlin, taped interview.

21. Lucie Jessner to Benjamin V. White, August 7, 1979, Cobb Papers.

22. Samuel Kaplan came from the Judge Baker to the Massachusetts General Hospital in 1947, prior to development of the formally organized service, and served as a clinical and research fellow for two years until 1949. He later worked for years at the James Jackson Putnam Children's Center. Then he became affiliated with Boston University, where in 1979 he was cochairman of child psychiatry, along with Steckler, and was director of training in child psychiatry.

23. Gaston E. Blom to Benjamin V. White, August 25, 1979, Cobb Papers.

24. Annual Report, Massachusetts General Hospital, 1953.

25. In 1979 Blom was professor of psychiatry at Michigan State University in East Lansing.

26. Gregory Rochlin, taped interview.

27. Gaston Blom to Benjamin V. White and John Adams Abbott, August 25, 1979, Cobb Papers.

28. Richmond Holder, taped interview.

29. Samuel G. McLellan to Benjamin V. White, September 22, 1979, Cobb Papers.

30. There is reason to believe that Betty Cobb fell out of favor with Beata Rank and was encouraged to go elsewhere.

31. The comment beneath the title of a clinic on hysteria indicated that the preparation of the report was aided by a grant from the Josiah Macy, Jr., Foundation.

Notes 421

32. Lucie Jessner, Unpublished report to John Abbott, 1979.
33. Gaston E. Blom to Benjamin V. White, August 25, 1977, Cobb Papers.
34. Richmond Holder, taped interview.
35. David Stafford-Clark, taped communication from Cyprus, July/August 4, 1966.
36. T. Berry Brazelton, personal interview, 1979 (untaped).
37. John Candler Cobb, personal communication.

Chapter 14

1. Stanley Cobb, "Excursions Avian," preliminary draft of "Adventures in Avian Neurology," unpublished manuscript, Cobb Papers. The published version (284) is abridged.
2. E. Pierson Richardson, taped interview.
3. Cobb moved upstairs to Room 601 in 1965. Stanley Cobb to E. P. Richardson, November 16, 1965, Cobb Papers.
4. Quarton directed the psychiatric laboratories from 1956 until 1961. He was followed by Frank R. Ervin who served until 1967. Irvin was followed by Seymour Kety until 1976 and then by Gerald Klerman. Klerman, who had been a resident in psychiatry at the Massachusetts Mental Health Center and for a time was director of the Drug Abuse and Mental Health Administration in Washington, D.C., was clinical director of the Lindemann Center from 1970 to 1976.
5. Stanley Cobb to Peter French, May 3, 1961, Cobb Papers. In the letter Cobb said, "At the museum I began my career in studying how the brain works in 1908 under G. H. Parker, then Professor of Zoology.... It has a strong romantic and emotional value that I now return to the same old museum once a week and smell the same smells and see the same rooms although much changed and improved."
6. Stanley Cobb, "Excursions Avian," preliminary draft.
7. Carl L. Hubbs to Stanley Cobb, January 10, 1957, Cobb Papers.
8. Peter B. Dews, personal interview.
9. Frank R. Ervin to Mrs. Stanley Cobb, May 10, 1968, Cobb Papers.
10. Stanley Cobb to Raymond Adams, December 18, 1959, Cobb Papers.
11. Stanley Cobb to George Packer Berry, August 15, 1953, Cobb Papers.
12. James C. White to John H. Knowles, March 16, 1965, transmitted copy in Cobb Papers.
13. James C. White to Stanley Cobb, March 16, 1965, Cobb Papers.
14. Elizabeth Cobb Hall, personal communication.
15. C. Judson Herrick, *The Evolution of Human Nature* (Austin, Texas, The University of Texas Press, 1956).
16. According to Cobb, Lorenz, the director of the Max Planck Institute for Ethology in Westfalen, Germany, was largely responsible for developing the new field in zoölogy called ethology, which is essentially the study of animal behavior.

17. F. R. P. Grant 56-156. Foundation Fund for Research in Psychiatry to Stanley Cobb, July 3, 1957, Cobb Papers.

18. Stanley Cobb to B. F. Skinner, February 20, 1958, Cobb Papers.

19. "Study of the Neurology of Instinctive Behavior," Progress Report to Foundation Fund for Research in Psychiatry, March 27, 1959, Cobb Papers.

20. Wolfgang J. Michelsen, "Procedure for studying olfactory discrimination in pigeons." *Science,* CXXX (1959) 630–631.

21. The brain-bill angle is defined as the number of degrees between the axis of the bill and the long axis.

22. Walker van Riper, "Does a Hummingbird Find its Way to Nectar by a Sense of Smell?" *Scientific American,* CCIII (1960) 1571.

23. Stanley Cobb, "Excursions Avian," preliminary draft.

24. Cobb went on to say, "Flash-evoked responses can be recorded from both optic tecta in the normal and unilaterally enucleated pigeon. Electrical stimulation of the optic nerve yields similar results."

25. B. G. Bang published four articles between 1960 and 1966 on the olfactory apparatus of birds. The most recent was "The Olfactory Apparatus of Tubenosed Birds," *Acta Anatomica,* LXV (1966) 391–415.

26. Stanley Cobb to B. C. Bang, April 20, 1967, Cobb Papers.

27. Stanley Cobb, "Excursions Avian," preliminary draft.

28. Alfred Redfield to Elizabeth A. Cobb, March 20, 1968, Cobb Papers.

29. Cobb's health was deteriorating. His generalized rheumatoid arthritis was progressively more crippling, and his eyes were becoming a serious problem. In fact, he experienced that summer a period of temporary blindness. These factors undoubtedly contributed to a latent sense of anger and frustration.

30. Elizabeth Cobb Hall to Benjamin V. White, personal communication, undated.

31. Memberships in professional and other societies:
    Alpha Omega Alpha
    American Association of Neuropathology (president, 1942)
    American Medical Association
    American Neurological Association (president, 1948)
    American Ornithologists Union
    American Psychiatric Association
    American Psychosomatic Society (president, 1955)
    American Society for Clinical Investigation
    Association of American Physicians
    Association for Research in Nervous and Mental Diseases (president, 1941)
    Boston Society of Natural History
    Boston Society of Psychiatry and Neurology (president, 1938)
    Cruising Club of America
    Interurban Clinical Club
    Massachusetts Medical Society
    Medical Exchange Club

Neurological Societies of France, Germany, Brazil, Japan (honorary member)
Royal Medico-Psychological Association (honorary member)
Royal Society of Medicine, London

32. Cobb is not listed as a member of the American Psychopathological Association.

33. "Honors," *Harvard Medical Alumni Bulletin,* XXXII (1958) 40.

34. The members of the Stanley Cobb Fund committee were Mr. Charles P. Curtis, Mr. Ralph Lowell, Dr. Harry C. Solomon, Dr. LeMoyne White, Dr. Henry S. Forbes, Chairman, and Mrs. Henry S. Forbes, Secretary.

35. Nathan M. Pusey to Stanley Cobb, June 21, 1960, Cobb Papers.

36. Chloe Binger, taped interview.

37. Helen C. S. White, personal communication.

38. Case Records of the Massachusetts General Hospital, founded by Richard C. Cabot, Benjamin Castleman, Editor, Case 42-1968, *New England Journal of Medicine,* CCLXXIX (1968) 876–883.

39. Harvard University. Fiftieth Annual Report, Class of 1910, (Cambridge, 1960), p. 79.

40. Elizabeth A. Cobb to Benjamin V. White, quotation obviously paraphrased, undated, Cobb Papers.

41. The final three lines of the poem read:

> The Child is father of the Man;
> And I could wish my days to be
> Bound each to each by natural piety.

Index

Abbey, E. A., 107
Abbott, John Adams, 215, 232, 281, 298, 420
Abel, John J., 52
Acidosis, 148, 182, 183
Ackerly, S. Spafford, 410
ACTH, 271, 282, 283
Adams, Dorothy, 298
Adams, F. Dennette, 81
Adams, Raymond, 254, 283, 319, 416
Adler, Alfred, 155, 156, 157, 161, 200, 201, 202, 410
Adler, Herman, 390
Adrian, E. D., 84, 104, 193
L'Aiglon, 119
Albany General Hospital, 219, 413
Albert Einstein Award, 331–332
Albert Einstein School of Medicine, 216, 232
Albright, Fuller, 271, 272
Alcohol, Cecil Drinker's problem with, 86; Clinic at Massachusetts General Hospital, 287, 326; And polyneuritis, 171–172; Ward at Boston City Hospital, 165–166
Alexander, Franz, 169, 202, 203, 206, 215; *Fundamentals of Psychoanalysis,* 275
Alexander, Leo, 171
Allan, Jane, 420
All-or-nothing law, 84
Allport, Floyd H., 155, 206
Allport, Gordon, 312
Almy, Elizabeth, *see* Cobb, Elizabeth Almy
Almy, Charles, 49, 99, 119, 409
Almy, Charles, Jr., 117
Almy, Helen Jackson Cabot, 49, 99, 119, 409
Almy, Mary, 99–100
Alpha Kappa Kappa, 40
Alpha Omega Alpha, 42, 43
Altschule, Mark D., 256, 276, 417
American Association for Research in Nervous and Mental Diseases, 331
American Board of Psychiatry and Neurology, 199
American Field Service Committee, 239
American Handbook of Psychiatry, 218
American Journal of Medicine, 273, 304
American Journal of Physiology, 147
American Medical Association, 44, 45, 90, 330; *Journal,* 151
American Neurological Association, 217, 278, 331
American Ornithologists' Union, 35
American Ornithology, 13
American Practitioner, 273
American Psychiatric Association, 187
American Psychoanalytic Association, 60, 215, 287
American Psychoanalytic Federation, 203
American Psychopathological Association, 198, 423; Hamilton Award, 323, 331
American Psychosomatic Association, 283, 321
American Psychosomatic Society, 41, 331
American Society for Clinical Investigation, 330
Amory, Katrine, 7, 36
Amsterdam, Cobb's visit to, 111–112, 121
Amyl nitrite, 191
Anemia, 153
Annals of Surgery, 49
Anorexia nervosa, 226–227, 231, 247, 273
Anthonisen, Margaret, 254, 290, 291, 294
Anthonisen, Niels, 215
Anti-Semitism, 206
Anxiety, 150
Archives of Internal Medicine, 229, 246, 279, 321
Archives of Neurology, 327
Archives of Neurology and Psychiatry, 156
Archives of Ophthalmology, 275
Archives of Pediatrics, 44
Aring, Charles D., 164, 165–166, 170, 171, 217–218

Index

Armed Forces Institute of Pathology, 95
Arnett, Trevor, 158
Arteriosclerosis, 166
Arthritis, 177, 225, 269, 273; Stanley Cobb suffers from, 178, 236, 238, 257, 288, 333, 334
Aschoff, Ludwig, 48
Asekoff, Meyer, 164, 403
Ask-Upmark, Erik, 164, 403
Associated Charities of Boston, 409
Association for Research in Mental Diseases, 91, 182, 231, 331
Association of American Physicians, 151, 244, 330; Kober Medal, 160, 331, 336
Asthma, 177, 214, 232, 274, 298
Ataxia, 274, 418
Aub, Joseph, 197, 410
Audubon, John James, 322, 324
Audubon Magazine, 328
The Auk, 34
Austin Riggs Foundation, 43, 70, 215, 283, 413
Austrian, Charles R., 52
Autism, 296
Ayer, James B., 97, 116, 138, 160, 178; Shows concern over Cobb's Neurological Unit, 139–140, 141–142; Work on cerebrospinal fluid, 91, 125; Work on cisternal puncture, 82

Bacon, Katherine, 202
Badal, Daniel W., 244, 251, 281
Bagley, Charles, Jr., 62, 64, 65
Bailey, Albert A., 55
Bailey, Percival, 160
Ballantine, Thomas, 211
Balsam Lake Club, 8, 9, 13, 16
Bandler, Bernard, 233, 250–251, 260, 281, 284, 286
Bang, B. C., 328, 422
Bang, Betsy, 328
Barbituates, 273
Bard, Philip, 160
Barkan, Hans, 42
Barker, Lewellys F., 52
Barnes Hospital, 170
Barnstable *Patriot*, 329
Baron Münchausen Syndrome, 167
Barrett, Albert M., 390
Barrett, William G., 215
Barry, Herbert, Jr., 251–252, 260, 268, 269, 270, 281, 411–412
Bauer, Walter, 224, 225, 270, 271, 272, 299, 413
Baumann, Herman H. W., 286

Bayne-Jones, Stanhope, 53
Beers, Clifford, *The Mind That Found Itself*, 219
Behavior chart (sheet), 59, 227–228, 414
Bellevue Hospital, 149
Benda, Clemens E., 231, 286
Bereday, Maria, 274–275
Berger, Hans, 192, 193
Berlin, 192, 200, 202; Stanley Cobb's visit to, 113, 114–117, 151, 153, 185; Stanley Cobb's experiences in, 146
Bernfeld, Siegfried, 214
Bernstein, Norman R., 281, 282, 300
Berry, George Packer, 319–320
Beth Israel Hospital, 214, 227, 234, 260, 282, 283, 294, 299, 300, 419
Bibring, Edward, 292, 419
Bibring, Grete, 292, 294, 419
Bielschowsky, Max, Stanley Cobb's work with, 115–116, 146, 151, 153, 166, 184, 185; Staining technique of, 105
Bigelow, Alanson, Jr., 1
Bigelow, Alice, 1
Bigelow, R. Barry, 254
Bigwood, E. J., 183
Binger, Carl, 42, 53, 63, 123, 335, 408, 409; Early career, 40–41; Psychotherapy with C. G. Jung, 41, 385; Relationship with Stanley Cobb, 40–41, 42, 53, 63, 64, 100, 174–175, 201, 204, 236, 332; Reorientation from physiology to psychiatry, 41, 201, 385–386; Vacations with the Cobbs, 64, 174–175, 236–238
Binger, Chloe, 64, 123, 174–175, 236, 333–334
Binger, David, 334
Bird Lore, 13, 85
Birkoff, Dean, 206
Black tongue, 170
Blackfan, Kenneth D., 52
Blain, Daniel, 164, 166, 171
Bleuler, Eugen, 118
Blom, Gaston E., 286, 297, 298–299, 300, 302, 304
Bloomfield, Arthur L., 52
Blumer, George, *Practitioner's Library*, 172
Blumgart, Herrmann, 214, 419
Bodysnatching, 2
Boeke, Jan, 122
Bolton, Joseph S., 153
Bone, Mr. & Mrs., 50
Bonner, Frances, 269, 286, 287

Borglum, Gutzon, 9
Boring, Edwin G., 204, 205, 206
Borotartrate, 183
Boston City Hospital, 38, 44, 91, 94, 95, 136, 140, 141, 143, 164, 165, 169, 170, 172, 190–191, 216, 224, 227; Administrative problems of, 158, 161, 176; Alcohol ward, 165–166; Clinical teaching at, 149; Early teaching of neurology at, 125–126; Facilities for Neurological Unit, 124, 142, 145, 147, 158, 162–163, 171; Neurological Unit at, 94, 123, 124–125, 126, 136–139, 147, 152, 154, 157, 158–159, 160–178, 179, 201, 212, 221, 233; Neuropathology laboratory at, 154, 162, 254; Neurosurgical facilities, 161, 163; Psychiatry at, 143–144, 145, 172–173, 178, 201, 220; Residency program in psychiatry, 405; Spinal fluid laboratory at, 145, 147, 151, 173; Thorndike Memorial Laboratory at, 126, 143, 145, 147, 151–152, 154, 162, 167, 183, 186, 395
Boston City Hospital Association, 332
Boston Committee on Medical Emigrees, 234–235
Boston Floating Hospital, 44, 45, 84
Boston Lying-in Hospital, 40, 216
Boston Psychoanalytic Association, 200, 201
Boston Psychoanalytic Institute, 41, 173, 199, 202, 203
Boston Psychoanalytic Society, 41, 173, 198, 200, 202, 203, 204, 207, 210, 214, 409, 410, 419
Boston Psychoanalytic Society and Institute, 169, 202, 203, 214
Boston Psychopathic Hospital, 8, 53, 67, 87, 88, 94, 95, 97, 136, 141–142, 169, 194, 201, 228, 252, 387, 414
Boston Society of Natural History, 9, 35, 384–385
Boston Society of Psychiatry and Neurology, 93, 331
Boston University, 163, 250, 283, 284, 300, 420
Boughton, Melania, 2
Bowcock, Harold M., 65
Bowditch, Elizabeth, 7, 36
Bowditch, Henry I., 45
Bowditch, Henry Pickering, 36, 408
Bowen, Katherine Drinker, 86
Bowers, Anna Mae, 386
Bowman, Karl, 252, 253
Braceland, Francis J., 417, 418

Brain, Russell, 209
Brain, 103, 104
Brain tumors, Cobb's publications on, 145
Brainwashing, 321, 414
Brattleboro Retreat, 215
Brazelton, T. Berry, 286, 306–307
Brazier, Mary A. B., 56, 212, 244–245, 252, 272, 285, 286, 416
Bremer, Lewis A., 119
Brenner, Leon O., 286
Breviora, 328
Brewer, Madeleine T., 47
Brewster, Henry Hodge, 268, 286
Bronk, Detlev W., 163, 191
Bronner, Augusta, 219, 290, 291
Brooklyn Rapid Transit Company, 22
Brooks, Lawrence, 9, 15–16, 17
Brooks, Walter D., 47, 79
Brooks, Winthrop Sprague ("Nick"), 8, 9–10, 14, 15–16, 17, 18, 34, 36, 330
Brouwer, Bernard, 112, 120, 121
Bryn Mawr College, 239
Buchtel, Emma, 179
Buchthal, Fritz, 193
Buchthal, Margaret Lennox, *see* Lennox, Margaret
Buckley, Philipa, 233, 241
Bullard, William Norton, 93, 125, 140–141, 181, 182, 187
Bulletin of the Massachusetts Society for Mental Hygiene, 229
Bullowa, Margaret, 286, 300, 420
Burghölzli, 118
Burne-Jones, Sir Edward, 107
Burns, E. Murray, 232, 281
Butler, Allan, 271, 273, 295, 297, 298, 299, 304, 305
Buzzard, Sir Farquhar, 104

Cabot, Arthur Tracy, 79
Cabot, Frederick P., 419
Cabot, Hugh, 39
Cabot, Jack, 119
Cabot, Richard Clarke, 39, 81, 82, 197; Clinico-pathological conference, 81
Cabot, Susan (Mrs. Arthur Tracy Cabot), 79
Cajal, Santiago Roman y, *see* Ramon y Cajal, Santiago
California Mental Health Department, 166
Calo, Madame Sparanga, 108
Cambridge, England, Cobb's visit to, 105
Camp Weideko, 419

Index

Campbell, C. MacFie, 52, 62, 182, 212; Attitude toward psychoanalysis, 54; Becomes Professor of Psychiatry at Harvard, 88; Director of Boston Psychopathic Hospital, 144, 169, 228, 252; Performs psychotherapy on Stanley Cobb, 53, 54, 155, 199; Qualifications as psychoanalyst, 199–200
Canavan, Myrtle P., 8
Cancer, 274
Cannon, Ida 81
Cannon, Walter B., 38, 80, 84, 160, 210, 234, 275
Capillaries, cerebral, 153
Carbon monoxide asphyxia, 147, 167
Carnegie Institution of Washington, 31
Carroll, Miss, 103, 113
Carson, Rachel, *Silent Spring,* 330
Carter, Franklin, 285, 286
Carter, George, 248, 281, 282, 285
Carus, Paul, 57
Case Histories in Psychosomatic Medicine, 274
Castle, William B., 94, 170, 228–229
Castle, William E., 31, 43
Caton, Richard, 192
Cattell, Helen Heizer, 85, 387
Caulfield, Thomas, 286
Cerebral anoxia, 254
Cerebral circulation, 160, 168, 195, 212; As factor in epilepsy, 147, 148, 171, 184–185, 186, 187, 188–189, 190, 191, 195–196; Henry S. Forbes' work in, 81, 89, 91, 146, 148, 149, 163, 168, 169, 185, 188; Skull-window technique for investigating, 91, 147, 148, 149, 169
Cerebrospinal fluid, 91, 125, 147. *See also* Boston City Hospital, Spinal fluid laboratory
Cervical sympathectomy, 149–150, 151, 169, 187, 188–189, 190–191
Chafetz, Morris, 285, 286, 287
Chapman, Leland S., 65
Chapman, William P., 244, 246
Chappaquiddick Island, 175
Chapple Eliot D., 243, 244; *An Investigation of Success in Naval Flight Training,* 416
Charcot, J. M., 109
Charles Street Jail, 165
Chartres, France, 110–111
Cheever, Austin, 40
Cheever, David, 37, 39, 44
Cherry Hill Tavern, 79–80, 107, 157
Chicago Psychoanalytic Institute, 202

Child guidance, 219, 290, 293
Child psychiatry, 207, 271; At Massachusetts General Hospital, 233, 254, 290–291, 294–309; Beginning of, 290; And clinical research, 303–304, 305–306; Differs from adult psychiatry, 293; Eleanor Pavenstedt's involvement in, 233, 254; Interview methods in, 296; Play therapy in, 291, 293, 296, 410; Psychoanalytic orientation, 293–293; Role of father and family in, 296; Stanley Cobb's attitude toward, 297, 302–303; Summer camp for, 291–292
Children's Hospital, 85
Children's Hospital Medical Center, 294, 298, 301, 307
Chlorpromazine, 321
Chorobski, Jerzy, 190
Christian, Henry A., 38
Church of England, 106
Churchill, Edward D., 288, 419
Cisternal puncture, 82
Clark, Admont H., 53
Clark, Dorothy, 254
Clark, George E., 410
Clark, Lincoln D., 271, 281, 282
Clark University, 58, 198, 205
Clarke, Dean, 220
Clarke, William C., 189
Cleghorn, Robert A., 285, 286, 287
Clement, Stephen M., 286
Clothier, Florence (Mrs. George Wislocki), 290, 291, 294, 419
Cobb, Alice, 16
Cobb, Augusta Adams, 2
Cobb, Augustus Smith, 6, 17, 20, 31, 45, 119, 383
Cobb, Beatrice (cousin by marriage), 105
Cobb, Beatrice (sister), 7, 10–11, 15, 22, 383
Cobb, Candler, 105
Cobb, Elijah (shipowner), 2
Cobb, Elijah (grandson), 335
Cobb, Elizabeth Almy ("Betty" Cobb, later Mrs. Elizabeth Hall), 14, 81, 100, 108, 110, 115, 117, 119, 120–121, 122, 123, 157, 175, 201, 202, 233, 234, 253, 294, 296, 297, 333, 334, 336–337, 410; Birth of children, 63, 67, 80; And "Death of a Salt Pond" article, 329–330; Influence on Stanley Cobb, 50–51, 236–237; On London trip, 105–106; Marriage to Stanley Cobb, 49–51; Psychoanalyzed

Cobb, Elizabeth Almy (continued)
by Helene Deutsch, 239; As psychotherapist at the Putnam Center, 198, 295, 302, 303, 420
Cobb, Emma May (Mrs. Chandler Foot), 5–6, 15, 383
Cobb, Florence ("Polly," later Mrs. Walter D. Brooks), 4, 6–7, 12–13, 22, 47, 79, 383
Cobb, Helen (Mrs. Lester Solomon, later Mrs. Benjamin White), 67, 103, 106, 107–108, 110, 239, 255–256, 332, 335
Cobb, Henry, 2
Cobb, Hildegarde (Mrs. Henry S. Forbes), 3, 4, 117, 119, 120, 122, 157, 248, 383; Marriage to Henry S. Forbes, 8, 48, 90, 96; Work in Harvard Neuropathology Laboratory, 8, 90, 95–96, 105
Cobb, John Candler, 3–4, 6, 48, 49, 81, 106, 107, 116, 117, 180
Cobb, John Candler, Jr. 5, 6, 383
Cobb, John Candler III ("Jock"), 80, 103, 110, 239, 307–308
Cobb, John Stanley, 335
Cobb, Lauren, 335
Cobb, Leonore Smith, 3, 4, 15, 21, 50–51, 106, 111, 114, 117, 119, 122, 383, 384
Cobb, Nathan, 335
Cobb, Peter, 335
Cobb, Sidney, 63, 67, 103, 105, 110, 119, 122, 239
Cobb, Stanley, Abraham Flexner's opinion of, 122–123; Academic record, 31–32, 42, 43; On alcohol ward of Boston City Hospital, 166; Ambidexterity, 10, 97, 268; Anxiety about World War II, 239; Appointed Bullard Professor of Neuropathology at Harvard, 140; Appointed to General Executive Board of Massachusetts General Hospital, 288; Assessment of Adolf Meyer, 280; Attempts to interrelate neurology and psychiatry at Massachusetts General Hospital, 319; Attempts to interrelate child psychiatry and pediatrics at Massachusetts General Hospital, 271, 294, 295–296, 297–298, 304–306; Attitude toward child psychiatry, 297, 298, 302–303, 308; Attitude toward the handicapped, 173–174; Birth, 1; Birth of children, 63, 67, 80; And cervical sympathectomy, 149–150, 151, 169, 187, 188–189, 190–191; Collaboration with non-psychiatrists, 223–225, 240, 244, 248, 270–271; Concern about Eric Lindemann as successor, 319–320, 337; Contacts with C. G. Jung, 118–119, 235–236; Courtship and marriage; 49–51; Death, 334; Designs behavior sheet, 227–228, 414; And development of encephalography in epilepsy; 192–193; Directs child psychiatry at Massachusetts General Hospital, 290–291, 294–309; Donates brain slide collection to Massachusetts Institute of Technology, 312; Early clinical investigation at Massachusetts General Hospital, 83–84; Early interest in medicine, 13–14, 36; Early neurological research, 55–56, 64, 65, 85; Early psychiatric interests, 80, 83–84; Early schooling, 4, 5, 6, 12, 13, 384; Early work at Massachusetts General Hospital, 80–81, 83, 88, 124; Eating habits, 333–334; Education at Harvard College, 20–21, 31–33, 34–36; Education at Harvard Medical School, 36–45, 47–49; Effect of wife on, 50–51, 236–237; Effect of World War II on research, 242, 244–246, 247–248, 257; Effect of World War II on staff, 241, 242, 257; Epilepsy research, 90, 91, 95, 148, 172, 179–192; European trips, 89, 92, 100, 101–123, 124, 143, 146, 149, 154, 155, 156–157, 158, 160, 176, 178, 183–184, 238; Evaluates candidates for Office of Strategic Services, 248; Finances, 53, 69, 70, 80, 81, 137; First teaching experience, 44–45; Frustrations with administrators at Boston City Hospital, 158, 161, 176; Growing interest in psychiatry, 173, 201, 217, 219; Honors bestowed upon, 330–332; Independent spirit of, 2; Influence of Oscar Vogt on, 115, 116, 146, 151, 184, 185; Influence of Paul McLean on, 278; And the integration of psychiatry with neurology, 216–218, 289; Interest and work on cerebral circulation, 91, 146, 147, 148–149, 151, 153, 172, 177, 184–185, 186, 187, 188–189, 190, 191, 195–196, 321, 390; Interest in comparative anatomy of bird brains, 44, 94, 121, 275, 278, 299, 310–312, 321, 322, 323–328, 421; Interest in Freud, 201, 202; Interest in horses

Index 429

and riding, 6, 31, 35, 36, 46–47, 323; interest in hunting and shooting, 5, 6, 13, 16, 18–19, 22, 31, 33–34, 35, 36, 64, 174, 331; Interest in instinct, 322–323; Interest in language behavior, 274; Interest in nature study and wildlife, 9, 11, 15–16, 337; interest in ornithology, 6, 9, 13, 19, 33, 34–35, 85, 108, 172, 197, 238–239, 334, 337; Interest in psychoanalysis, 68, 121, 173, 174, 176, 200, 201–204, 217–218, 258, 280, 289, 410–411, 414; Interest in sailing, 116–117, 157, 174–175, 257; interest in sense of smell, 276–277, 322–323, 328; Interest in skiing, 237–238; Interest in social problems, 257, 328–330; Internship at Peter Bent Brigham Hospital, 42, 48–49; Kober Medal awarded to, 160, 331, 336, 387; Member of Boston Psychoanalytic Society, 41, 200, 202, 203, 204, 410; Member of Massachusetts National Guard, 6, 10, 31, 45–46; Member of Medical Exchange Club, 330–331; Member of Neurological Supper Club, 160–161, 387; Membership in learned and professional soccieties, 422–423; Memorial service for, 335; Military research during World War I, 67–68, 79, 84, 143; Military service during World War I, 53, 56–57, 61–63, 64–68, 79; And Neurological Unit at Boston City Hospital, 136–139, 143, 158–159, 160–178; Neurophysiological research at Johns Hopkins University, 54, 55–56, 64, 65; As a neurologist, 80, 81, 82, 83, 88, 124; Objectives of his psychiatric service at Massachusetts General Hospital, 222; Obtains electrocardiogram of elephant, 85; Office at Massachusetts General Hospital, 81, 88, 181, 388; Pacifistic viewpoint, 46, 67; As painter and watercolorist, 6, 9, 12–13, 108, 236, 337; Physical and health problems, 259, 287, 329, 333, 334–335, 337, 422; Poetry of, 172, 323, 330; Portrait pointed by Hopkinson, 111, 242; Preference for full-time teaching, 81, 99, 135; Private practice, 80, 99; Problems in post World War II era, 259–260; As psychiatrist at Massachusetts General Hospital, 42, 97, 174, 175, 176, 193, 204, 240; Publications on brain tumors, 145; Publishes annual reviews of psychiatry, 229, 246, 279, 293, 321–322; Publishes *Borderlands of Psychiatry*, 247; Publishes *Case Histories in Psychosomatic Medicine*, 253, 274; Publishes *Emotions and Clinical Medicine*, 276, 277, 285; Publishes *Foundations of Neuropsychiatry*, 247; Publishes *Outline of Neuropathology*, 97, 174; Qualifications as a psychoanalyst, 199–200; And racial integration, 255, 256; And relationship between functional and organic disease, 231; Relationship with James B. Ayer, 97, 116, 138, 139, 142, 178; Relationship with Clemens E. Benda, 231; Relationship tith Maria Bereday, 274–275; Relationship with Carl Binger, 40–41, 42, 53, 63, 64, 100, 174–175, 201, 204, 236, 332; Relationship with Gaston E. Blom, 299; Relationship with Mary A. B. Brazier, 56, 212, 244–245; Relationship with Mandel Cohen, 215–216, 229, 231, 242, 244; Relationship with Helene Deutsch, 213; Relationship with Cecil K. Drinker, 53, 65–66, 69, 80, 84, 85–86; Relationship with David L. Edsall, 3, 48, 69, 70, 80–81, 122, 123, 124, 126, 136–139, 408; Relationship with Erik H. Erikson, 207–209; Relationship with Miner H. A. Evans, 144; Relationship with father, 3–4, 14–15; Relationship with Jacob E. Finesinger, 169–170, 212–213, 229, 242, 244–246, 252, 260; Relationship with Alexander Forbes, 38, 46–47, 55, 63, 68, 80, 84–85, 86, 90, 387; Relationship with Henry S. Forbes, 48, 90–91, 95, 113, 146, 147, 168, 169, 185, 188; Relationship with Freddy H. Frankel, 260; Relationship with Frank Fremont-Smith, 89, 91, 116, 125, 142, 143, 147, 163, 164, 165, 167, 168, 171, 185, 208; Relationship with William Herman, 82–83, 144–145, 176, 201, 203–204, 213; Relationship with William G. Lennox, 89, 90, 95, 97, 99, 125, 139, 146, 147, 148, 163, 164, 165, 170–171, 179, 184, 185, 188, 195, 246; Relationship with Eric Lindemann, 210–212, 239, 242, 243, 319–320, 337, 412; Relationship with Maria Lorenz, 274; Relationship with Neil T. McDermott, 232; Relationship with Adolf Meyer, 56–57, 61–62, 63, 83, 217, 246–247, 410; Relationship

Cobb, Stanley (continued)
  with Henry W. H. Miles, 272–274;
  Relationship with mother, 4, 5, 16;
  Relationship with Abraham Myerson, 138–139; Relationship with John Nemiah, 212, 243, 275, 289; Relationship with Marian Putnam, 198–199, 201, 208, 332; Relationship with Gardiner Quarton, 269, 288; Relationship with Alfred Redfield, 84–85, 151, 311, 328; Relationship with Jurgen Ruesch, 252–253; Relationship with Harley Shands, 253–254; Relationship with sisters and brothers, 5, 6, 12–13, 36; Relationship with David Stafford-Clark, 306, 371–379; Relationship with Harry Stockholm, 275; Relationship with students and fellow investigators, 145–146, 253, 272–273, 288–289, 405–406; Relationship with William Trethowan, 271–272; Relationship with Schichi Uyematzu, 89, 93, 179, 182; Relationship with Harold G. Wolff, 147, 149–151, 153, 188, 331, 336; Relationship with women, 36, 47; Relationship with women workers, 154; Reorganizes tonsillectomy procedures, 255–256; And research in neuropathology, 89–96; Research on carbon monoxide asphyxia, 147; Resettlement in Boston, 79–80; Resident training at Johns Hopkins University, 53–57, 61–65, 386; Residents and fellows in child psychiatry, 233, 282, 284, 285, 298–302; Residents and fellows in psychiatry, 232–233, 250–254, 281–284, 285, 305–307; Resignation from Boston Psychoanalytic Society, 203; Retirement from Harvard and Massachusetts General Hospital, 197, 257, 285, 310; Retirement homes, 332–333, 409; Review editor of *Psychosomatic Medicine*, 281; Reviews literature of epilepsy, 148; Role models of, 43, 45, 81, 84, 198; Salmon Lectures delivered by, 275–276; Samuel W. Hamilton award to, 323; And signing, 14, 46; And shaping of psychology at Harvard, 206; Shift from neurosciences to psychiatry, 176–178, 197, 219, 222, 240, 326; And social gatherings of staff, 174, 253; Social writing of, 323, 328–330; Staff conferences of, 226–227, 233, 269–270; And staining techniques, 105, 116, 153; Stammering problem, 4–5, 7, 10–11, 12, 13, 14, 32–33, 51, 53, 54, 97, 110, 118–119, 154–156, 161, 173–174, 176, 197, 200, 201, 202, 217, 276; And structure of cerebral capillaries, 153; Study of avian brain size, 327–328; Study of Cocoanut Grove fire victims, 243; Suffers from arthritis, 178, 236, 238, 257, 288, 333, 334, 422; And support of epilepsy research, 99, 181–182, 184, 185–188; And support of Henry A. Murry's psychology clinic, 204–206; And support of Robert Young's camp for psychoneurotic children, 291–292; Summer home at Cotuit, 99–100, 157, 168; Taste in art, 106, 111, 112, 121; As teacher, lecturer and advisor, 97, 98–99, 250–251, 272–273; Teaching at Johns Hopkins University, 62, 64, 70; Teaching during military service, 66, 67–68; Teaching of neurology at Harvard, 126, 135–136, 161; Teaching of neuropathology at Harvard, 67, 69, 70, 79, 87–88, 92, 95, 96–99, 125, 142, 143–144, 270, 391–392; Teaching of psychiatry at Harvard, 227–228, 248–249, 259, 269–270; Tolerance of diverse approaches, 289; Trip to Niagara Falls, 17; Trip to Washington, D.C., 17; Trips to Canada, 9, 17–19, 34, 35; Undergoes psychoanalysis, 155, 156, 161, 173, 199, 200, 201, 202, 203, 410; Undergoes psychotherapy, 53–54, 155, 156, 199; Use of Adolf Meyer's life chart, 83, 247, 269; Use of behavior sheet, 227–228, 414; Vacationing of, 64, 108, 113–114, 117, 157, 174–176, 236–239, 257; Views of consciousness, 279; Views of the emotions, 276–277, 278–279; Views of Eastern mysticism and Zen Buddhism, 336–337; Views on localization of function, 279; Views of the locus of the mind, 278–279; Views of psychiatric education and training, 251; Views of religion, 106, 335–336; Views on successor at Massachusetts General Hospital, 288, 319–320, 337; Work at Boston Floating Hospital, 44; Work at National Hospital, Queen Square, London, 102, 104; Work in laboratory of E. P. Richardson, 285, 310; Work in Harvard Physiology Department, 55, 63, 80, 84; Work in in-

Index

dustrial hygiene, 80, 81, 85–87; Work in Student Health Service at Massachusetts Institute of Technology, 312, 319; Work on anorexia nervosa, 226–227, 247; Work on basal ganglia, 92; Work on behalf of Jewish emigrees, 234–235; Work on behalf of World War II war effort, 240, 241, 244–246, 247–248, 257; Work on neurocirculatory asthenia, 65, 243–244, 247–248; Work on wards at the Phipps Clinic of Johns Hopkins University, 62; Work with Max Bielschowsky, 115–116; Work with John Fulton on red skeletal muscle, 119; Work with Charles Sherrington, 120; Work with Oscar Vogt, 68, 113, 115, 146, 151, 153, 166, 184, 185; Writes "Death by Poison," 330; Writes "Death of a Salt Pond," 328–330; Writes "Excursions Avian," 311, 324, 328; Writing style, 245; Yale lecture on "Physiology, Psychiatry and the Inhibitions," 153–154, 401; Youthful pranks, 14–15, 46, 49; Youthful publications, 9, 13, 31
Cobb, Thomas, 1–2
Cocoanut Grove fire, 210, 242–243
Coffin, George E., 33–34
Coggeshall, Howard C., 164, 165, 167, 171
Cohen, Mandel, 98, 215–216, 229, 231, 242, 244, 253, 254, 281, 413, 414
Cohn, Alfred E., 205, 206
Cole, Edwin M., 225
Coleman, C. C., 67, 143
Colitis, 273
Collier, James S., 104
Columbia University, 158, 182; College of Physicians and Surgeons, 182
Commonwealth Fund, 152, 169
Conant, James Bryant, 205, 206
Congress of Psychology, Paris, 193
Conklin, Hugh W., 183
Consciousness, 279
Coolidge, John, 286, 300, 302
Cook, Dr., 35
Cope, Oliver, 224, 227, 234, 243, 255, 270, 272, 288, 298, 413
Coriat, Isador, 125, 200, 203, 409, 410, 411
Cornell University, 150, 158, 331, 414
Coronary artery disease, 273
Cotton, Henry A., 61
Councilman, William T., 38, 43–45, 68, 310
Courtney, Joseph W., 125

Cowdry, E. V., 166
Cowles, Edaward, 39
Craig, Dr., 164
Craine-Lillie, Margaret, *see* Gildea, Margaret Craine-Lillie
Crissy, William J., 286
Croonian Lectures, 279
Crothers, Bronson, 160
Croton Reservoir, 4
Cushing, Harvey, 39, 48, 49, 70, 96, 143, 160, 197, 198
Cushing's Syndrome, 271–272, 284
Cybernetics, 278, 322

Dailey, Mary E. (Mary Dailey Irvine), 147, 148, 154, 163, 167, 168, 400, 405–406
Dale, Sir Henry H. 417
Dalrymple, Leolia, 200, 202, 410, 411
Dandy, Walter E., 53
Danvers State Hospital, 93
Danziger, Sadie, 96
Darwin, Charles, 209, 322, 324
D'Autremont, Chester C., 286, 300
Davis, Hallowell, 160, 192, 407
Davis, W. M., 35
Dawes, Daniel, 268–269, 292
Dawes, Lydia, 268, 292, 293, 294, 295
DDT, 328–329
"Death by Poison," 330
"Death of a Salt-Pond," 328–330
Death penalty, 323
DeBenedetti, Renata G., 286, 300
Degas, H. G. E., 111
de Marneffe, Francis, 281, 283
Dementia praecox, 199
Deming, Julia, 410
Dempsey, Edward, 415
Denny-Brown, Derek, 125, 161, 164, 224
Denver University, 179
Derbyshire, William, 192
Deutsch, Felix, 213–215, 289, 412; *On the Mysterious Leap from the Mind to the Body*, 215
Deutsch, Helene, 169, 213, 215, 226, 239, 270, 289, 412, 414; *The Psychology of Women*, 213
Deutsch Anstaltsforschung für Psychiatrie, 115, 153, 156
Devonian (S.S.), 103
Dewey, John, 57
Dews, Peter Booth, 332, 415
Dicks, Russell L., 81
Diet, In epilepsy, 148, 179, 182–183, 184

Dilantin (Diphenylhydantoin), 161, 193–194, 195
D.K.E. Club, 20, 35
Dodge, Percy L., 139
Doherty, Margaret, 154, 400
Doust, William C., 286
Dowling, John J., 158, 161
Doyle, Mary, 4, 10, 46, 383
Drinker, Cecil K., 53, 65–66, 69, 80, 84, 85–86; Alcohol problem, 86
Drinker, Philip, 86
Duke University, 220, 232
Dunkirk evacuation, 231, 241, 246
Dunlap, Knight, 59
Duplessis, Emile, 34
Duodenal ulcer, 177
Dusser de Barenne, J. G., 54, 121–122
Dwyer, Thomas F., 286, 300

Easley, Richard B., 143
Eastern Illinois State Hospital at Kankakee, 57
Ebaugh, Franklin, 220–221, 390, 413
L'Ecole de Médecine, 109
Edes, Robert, 125
Edinger, Ludwig, 121
Edinger, Tilly, 311, 321, 327
Edsall, David Lynn, 65, 87, 90, 91, 92, 140, 156, 161, 181, 182, 388, 401; Chairman of Boston Committee on Medical Emigrees, 234; Chairman of Committee on Industrial Hygiene, 86; And Cobb's advancement at Harvard Medical School, 80–81, 122, 123, 124, 126, 135–136, 158, 407–408; Confer's on Cobb's career in the neurosciences, 3, 48; And the establishment of a neurological unit at Boston City Hospital, 136–139; Jackson Professor of Medicine at Harvard, 39, 48, 82; Offers Cobb a job at Harvard, 67, 69, 70; And the teaching of neurology at Massachusetts General Hospital, 140–142
Egloff, Frank R., 281, 282, 405
Einthoven string galvanometer, see String galvanometer
Eisenberg, Leon, 212, 251, 321, 412
Electroencephalograph, 92, 160, 210, 225, 244–245, 285, 391, 407; In epilepsy, 192–193, 194, 195, 196, 231; Laboratory at Massachusetts General Hospital, 231, 245, 306; And psychoneurotic patients, 212
Electromyograph, 38, 55, 65, 180, 225; see also String galvanometer

Electroschock, 6–7, 171, 246
Eliot, Charles W., 20, 31, 37
Elsberg, Charles A., 65, 70, 85
Emerson, L. Eugene, 92, 207, 409
Emerson, Ralph Waldo, 21, 35, 84
Emerson, Raymond, 21–22, 31, 36, 48
Encephalitis, 145
Emotions, Cobb's concept of, 276–277, 278–279
Engel, George L., 243
England, Cobb's experiences in, 103–107, 119–120; State of pathology in, 104–105
Enuresis, 273
Epilepsy, 45, 98, 160, 162, 277; Acidosis in, 148, 182, 183, 187; Aura of, 171, 180; Blood gas analysis in work on, 145, 154, 191; Brainwave measurements in, 192–193, 194, 195, 196, 231; And cerebral circulation, 148, 149, 184–185, 186, 187, 188–189, 190, 191, 195–196, 321; Cervical sympathectomy as treatment for, 149–150, 169, 187, 188–189, 190–191; Stanley Cobb's research in, 90, 91, 95, 148, 172, 179–192; Diet and fasting as factors in, 148, 179, 182–183, 184; Dilantin as anticonvulsant in, 161, 193–194, 195; Emotional factors in, 208, 210, 229; Frequency of seizures, 183; Funding for research on, 148, 181–182, 184, 185–188; Jacksonian type, 109; W. G. Lennox's work in, 89, 90, 91, 99, 139, 148, 170–171, 179–180, 181, 183, 184, 185, 187, 188, 192, 195, 246; Literature review of, 95, 148, 172; Nature of, 180; Oxygen deprivation in, 148, 191, 192, 321; Therapeutics in, 183; Wilder Penfield's interest and views on, 189, 191–192
Epilepsy Committee, 99, 181–182, 185, 186, 187, 405
Epstein, Samuel, 142–143, 145, 398
Eric Lindemann Center, 211, 421
Erikson, Erik Homberger, 207–210, 291, 293
Erikson, Joan, 208
Ervin, Frank R., 311, 326, 327
Evarts, Sarah, 114, 202, 226, 233, 393
Evans, Miner H. A., 139, 143–144, 164, 172

Fairbanks, Arthur W., 125–126, 138, 139, 143–144, 172, 405
Family therapy, 296, 309

Index

Fang, Harry Choa-Hung, 281, 282
Fasting, In epilepsy, 148
Fatigue, 244, 253
Faxon, Nathaniel W., 220
Fender, Theodore, 164, 403
Ferenczi, Sandor, 50, 198, 205, 293
Fine, Jacob, 234
Fineman, Abraham, 286, 307
Fineman, Joanne, 307
Finesinger, Grace, 169
Finesinger, Jacob E., 146, 153, 163, 165, 168–170, 171, 188, 191, 195, 212–213, 215, 226, 244, 245, 246, 248, 270, 274, 288, 326, 331, 417; And behavior sheet, 227–228, 414, 416; Departure from Massachusetts General Hospital, 268, 269; Freudian approach to psychiatry, 260; Physiological orientation, 268; Psychoanalysis of, 169, 203, 212, 412; Relationship with Stanley Cobb, 169–170, 212–213, 229, 242, 244–246, 252, 260; Relationship with Eric Lindemann, 251–252, 412; Saws self off tree, 164
Finley, Knox H., 164, 391, 403
Fisher, Betty, 154, 173, 400
Fitzgerald, William E., 286
Flanagan, N. B., 252, 281, 416
Flexner, Abraham, 100, 110, 122–123, 124, 126, 137, 147
Flexner, Simon, 100, 101, 102, 112, 113, 116
Flexner Report, 37, 100
Florence, Italy, Cobb's trip to, 117
Foix, Charles, 109, 110
Folch-Pi, Jordi, 256, 274, 322, 417
Folin, Otto, 38, 256, 417
Foot, Chandler, 5, 8, 96, 104, 108
Foot, Emma May Cobb, *see* Cobb, Emma May
Foot, Louise, 5
Forbes, Alexander, 84, 105, 160, 175, 415; Friendship with Stanley Cobb, 38, 47, 330, 387; Interest in hunting, 46–47; Work with Stanley Cobb, 55, 63, 68, 80, 85, 86; Work with Donald MacPherson, 92, 391
Forbes, Amelia, 22, 48
Forbes, Edith, 84
Forbes, Henry Stone ("Harry"), 8, 95, 113, 125, 142, 146, 157, 160, 174; Develops skull-window technique for study of cerebral circulation, 91, 148, 149, 163, 169, 399; Marriage to Hildegarde Cobb, 8, 48, 90, 96; Relationship to Stanley Cobb, 48, 90–91, 95, 113, 146, 147, 168, 169, 185, 188; Work on carbon mynoxide asphyxia, 90–91; Work on cerebral circulation, 81, 89, 91, 146, 148, 163, 168, 169, 185, 188, 390; Work on morphine intoxication, 151
Forbes, Hildegarde Cobb, *see* Cobb, Hildegarde
Forbes, J. M., 84, 90
Forbes, Malcolm, 14
Forbes, Waldo, 48
Forbes, William Hathaway, 84
Forel, August, 56, 57
Foundations' Fund for Research in Psychiatry, 321
Fox, Henry, 417
Frankel, Freddy H., 260, 281, 282
Frazier, Charles, 67, 79
Frazier, Russell, 232–233, 241, 286
Fremont-Smith, Frances, 168
Fremont-Smith, Frank, 116, 144, 146, 152, 160, 162, 165, 210, 233; Director of Josiah Macy, Jr. Foundation, 214, 291–292; European travel, 142, 147–148, 149, 167; Naiveté of, 167–168; Relationship with Stanley Cobb, 89, 91, 116, 125, 142, 143, 147, 163, 164, 167, 168, 171, 185, 208; Spinal fluid laboratory at Boston City Hospital, 145, 147, 151, 163, 167; Tendency to procrastinate, 147
Fremont-Smith, Maurice, 233, 294
Freud, Anna, 169, 207, 268, 291, 292, 293, 412
Freud, Sigmund, 49–50, 54, 60, 68, 83, 87, 93, 109, 125, 155, 156, 157, 161, 169, 173, 176, 198, 199, 200, 201, 202, 205, 207, 209, 235, 236, 268, 291, 293, 404, 409, 410–411; opposed to academic affiliations for psychoanalysis, 202–203; Psychoanalyzes Helene Deutsch, 213
Freud Seminar, 200
Frothingham, Channing, 39
Fulmar (cutter), 175, 236–237, 238, 257
Fulton, John Farquar, 119–120, 160
Fulton, Lucia, 119, 120

Gage, Lyle, 190
Gamble, James L., 52, 184, 185, 406
Gantt, Horsley, 56
Gardiner, George, 291
Gardner, Elizabeth, 47
Gellhorn, Ernst, 285
General Leonard Wood Memorial Medal, 332

George VI, 239
Germany, Cobb's visit to, 113, 114–117; Emigrees from, 234
Geschwind, Norman, 161
Geyelin, Henry Rawle, 182, 183, 185, 186, 187, 190
G.I. Bill of Rights, 258, 259
Gibbs, Erna Leonhard, *see* Leonhard, Erna
Gibbs, Frederick, 146, 150, 153, 163, 167, 168, 171, 188, 191, 192, 195, 321; And encephalography in epilepsy, 193, 194, 196
Gibson, John G., 281, 282
Gifford, Sanford, 93, 199
Gignoux, Gerard, 21, 22, 36, 50, 113–114
Gilbert, Elizabeth, 47
Gildea, Edwin F., 89, 93–94, 96, 143, 146, 153, 160, 167, 170, 171, 187, 195
Gildea, Margaret Crane-Lillie, 118–119, 164, 165, 170, 405
Gillespie, R. D., 220
Gilmore, Thomas H., 286
Goethe, J. W. von, 209
Gore, Charles P., 281, 282
Gorgas, William C., 62
Government Hospital, Washington, D.C., 59
Grand Trunk Railway, 34
Grass, Albert, 192, 194
Gray, Horace, 40, 41–42, 43, 50, 61
Greek Refuge Settlement Commission, 185
Greenacre, Phyllis, 53, 60
Greenfield, J. Goodwin, 105, 120
Greenhill, Maurice H., 216, 220–221, 223, 232, 281
Greenough, Robert B., 39
Greeg, Alan, 100, 173, 176, 189, 205, 206, 220, 221, 222, 401, 413
Griffin, Donald R., 311
Grinker, Roy, 418
Group dynamics, 309
Gruber, Siegmund, 286
Guillain, Georges, 109
Gun control, 330
Gunpowder River, 64

Hackett, Thomas, 223, 251, 412
Haeckel, E. H. P., 166
Haldane, J. B. S., 104
Hale, Susan Evarts (Mrs. William Herman), 83, 96, 114, 142, 154, 156, 201, 202; Secretary of Boston Committee on Medical Emigrees, 234–235
Hale, Worth, 140
Hall, Volta R., 232, 254, 281
Hamburg, Stanley Cobb's visit to, 114
Hamelin, Bessie L., 96
Harris, Harold J., 286, 300
Hartmann, Heinz, 169, 412
Harvard College, 3, 5, 6, 9, 11, 14, 19, 42, 45, 84, 91, 197, 239; Changes in, 20, 31; Clubs, 20, 35–36; Stanley Cobb's education at, 20–21, 21–33, 34–36
Harvard Divinity School, 255
Harvard Epilepsy Commission, 171, 187–188
Harvard Gazette, 84
Harvard Law School, 22
Harvard Medical Alumni Bulletin, 163
Harvard Medical School, 3, 37–40, 41, 48, 68, 84, 90, 91, 92, 93, 95, 96, 99, 102, 112, 122, 138, 145, 146, 148–149, 150, 151, 152–153, 157, 160, 170, 198, 208, 239, 275, 285, 303, 307, 310, 419; Admission standards, 37; *Aesculapiad*, 197, 410; Archives, 126; Boylston Medical Society, 43, 47; Bullard Professorship of Neuropathology, 38, 87; Changes in, 36–37; Stanley Cobb as student at, 36–45, 47–49; Cobb's early research at, 80; Cobb's teaching of neuropathology at, 69, 70, 87–88, 125, 223, 270, 391–392; Course for Graduates, 82; Curriculum, 37; Curriculum Committee, 227–228, 249; Department of Neurology, 124; Department of Neuropathology, 136; Department of Psychiatry, 67, 144; Dormitory, 39, 40; Establishes Neurological Unit at Boston City Hospital, 126, 135–139, 140, 141, 142, 158; Graduate School of Medicine, 126; Industrial hygiene research at, 80, 86; Innominate Club, 48; Jackson Professorship, 38–39, 48, 82, 111; James Jackson Putnam Professorship of Neurology, 140; Lancet Club, 48; Layout of, 88–89; Mosley, Professorship, 39; Neuropathology at, 139–140, 165; Neuropathology Laboratory, 7–8, 37, 87, 90, 105, 125, 142–143, 145, 151, 161, 170, 171, 179, 181, 182, 184, 188, 322; Physiology Department, 55, 63, 80, 84, 192, 204; Publishes book on medical

Index

uses of cortisone, 271; Rotation of department heads, 319; Sheldon Travelling Fellowship, 40; Social life at, 47–48; Stanley Cobb Professorship, 8, 332, 423; Teaching of neurology at, 122–123, 124–125, 126, 135–136, 140, 141; Teaching of psychiatry at, 222, 227–230, Teaching of psychoanalysis at, 202, 203, 207–208; Thorndike Memorial Laboratory, see Boston City Hospital; Vanderbilt Hall, 39, 40

Harvard School of Public Health, 53

Harvard University, 93, 155, 209, 210; Charles Eliot Ware Fellowship, 151; Department of Social Relations, 211; Fatigue Laboratory, 151; Fencing Club, 35; Harvard Engineering Camp, 21; Harvard Travelers Club, 34–35; Memorial Chapel, 335; Museum of Comparative Zoology, 9, 311, 312, 321, 327, 328, 421; Psychological Clinic, 118, 200, 202, 204–206, 208; Psychology Department, 173, 204, 206, 215, 235, 323; Tercentenary celebration, 235–236

Harvey, Harold I., 286

Hasselbalch, Karl, 38

Hasty Pudding Club, 20, 35; Annual play, 35–36

Hauptmann, Alfred, 194

Head, Sir Henry, 101–102, 103–104, 107, 108, 115, 123

Health Education Foundation, 287

Healy, William, 155, 202, 219, 290–291, 410, 411, 419

Hearst, Patricia, 414

Helverson, Ralph D., 335

Henderson, David K., 52, 60

Henderson, Lawrence J., 38, 206

Henderson, Yendell, 90

Hendricks, Ives, 200, 287, 410, 411

Herman, William J., 116, 144–145, 155, 156, 233, 242, 249, 289, 410, 411; Appointed consultant in psychoanalysis, 142, 144, 172; Courtship and marriage, 83, 96, 114, 201; Death, 96, 173, 203, 204, 207, 213; Interest in C. G. Jung, 118, 121, 201, 236; Interest in psychoanalysis, 83, 200, 202, 207; As lecturer, 83; Relationship with Adolf Meyer, 82–83; Relationship with Stanley Cobb, 82–83, 144–145, 176, 201, 203–204, 213; Reorientation towards Freudian analysis, 156, 161, 201; Suffers from ataxia, 275, 418; Vacationing with Stanley Cobb, 110–111, 121

Herman, Mrs. William, see Hale, Susan Evarts

Hermaphroditism, 298

Herrick, Judson, *The Evolution of Human Nature*, 322

Heuer, George J., 53

Higgins, Harold, 295

Hill, A. V., 104

Hincks, Elizabeth, 415

Hinton, William A., 88

Histamine, 147, 188

History taking, 247, 308

Hitchcock Clinic, 152

Hitler, Adolf, 176, 234, 239, 241, 401

Hogarth, William, 166

Holder, Richmond, 251, 281, 286, 300, 302, 305, 416

Holland, Stanley Cobb's trips to, 111–112, 121–122

Hollenbeck, Dorr, G., 281, 282

Hollenbeck, Jane Allen, 286, 300

Holmes, Gordon, 104, 105, 120

Holmes, Oliver Wendell, 86

Holtz, Paul R., 55

Holzer, Hedvig H., 286, 300

Homans, John, 39

Homberger, Erik, see Erikson, Erik Homberger

Homeostasis, 160

Homosexuality, 287

Hope, Justin, 254, 286, 416

Hopkins, Dr., 66

Hopkinson, Charles, 111, 242

Hornykiewicz, Oleh, 278

Howard, Edgerton, 215, 233, 413

Howard, Paul, 212, 215, 216, 226, 281, 286

Howell, William Henry, 52, 53, 54, 64

Howland, Charles P., 99, 180, 181, 183, 185–187, 189, 190, 194

Howland, Mrs. Charles P., 186, 187, 190

Howell, Henry, 180, 181, 186, 187, 189, 190

Howland, John, 52

Hubbard, John, 146

Hubbs, Carl L., 311

Hunt, Samuel P., 251, 281, 415

Huntington, Mrs. Collis P., 36

Huntington, Cornelia, 10, 12

Huxley, Julian, 209

Hydrochloric acid, 183

Hypertension, 273
Hyperthyroidism, 273
Hypnosis, 32, 33, 155, 197, 229, 231
Hypophysis, 160
Hysteria, 229, 231
Hysterical blindness, 307–308

Industrial hygiene, 80, 81, 85–87
Influenza, Epidemic of 1918, 66
Instinct, 209, 322–323
Institut für Hirnsforschung der Kaiser Wilhelm Geschellschaft, 115
The Institute of 1770, 35
Interurban Clinical Club, 330
An Investigation of Success in Naval Flight Training, 416
Ipswich Trotting Park, 47
Irritable colon, 225, 232
Irvine, Mary Daily, *see* Dailey, Mary
Irvine, S. Rodman, 164, 403–404
Ithaca Conference on Psychiatric Education, 251

Jackson, Hughlings, 279
Jackson, Louise, 201, 208, 293, 410
Jacksonian epilepsy, 109
Jaffe, Ruth, 286
James, Walter, 182
James, William, 207, 258, 275
James Jackson Putnam Children's Center, 198, 293–294, 295, 296, 300, 306–307, 420; Cooperation with Massachusetts General Hospital, 294, 298, 302, 303; Work with autistic children, 296
Janet, Pierre, 109, 110, 200, 279–280
Janeway, Theodore C., 52
Jauregg, Wagner, 213
Jefferson, Miss, 193
Jessner, Lucie, 254, 286, 294–295, 296–299, 302, 303, 304, 305, 307, 308–309, 420
Joan of Arc, 108
Johannet, Pierre, 286, 300
John, Clara R., 286
Johns Hopkins University, 39, 40, 43, 44, 68, 150, 222, 290; Alan M. Chesney Archives, 66, 387; Harriet Lane home, 52, 56; Henry Phipps Psychiatric Clinic, 7, 52, 53, 54, 55, 56, 58–59, 60, 62, 63, 64, 65, 69, 83, 110, 150, 199, 201, 215, 219, 252, 291, 387; Lack of dynamic psychiatry at, 215; Medical School, 38, 52–53, 169; Pavlovian Laboratory, 56; School of Hygiene and Public Health, 328; Stanley Cobb's residency at, 53–57, 61–65
Jones, Chester M., 225, 232, 246, 248
Jones, Daniel F., 39
Joslin, Eliott P., 39
Journal of Biological Chemistry, 147
Journal of Industrial Medicine, 86
Journal of the American Medical Association, 151
Judge Baker Foundation, 155, 202, 419
Judge Baker Guidance Center, 290–291, 295, 420; Collaboration with the James Jackson Putnam Center, 295; Collaboration with Massachusetts General Hospital, 291, 294, 307
Jung, Carl Gustav, 41, 50, 83, 121, 144, 155, 156, 161, 198, 200, 201, 205, 385, 410; Accused of being a Nazi sympathizer, 235–236; Advises Cobb and Murray on stammering problem, 118–119; Awarded honorary degree by Harvard, 234–235
Juvenile Psychopathic Institute, 290

Kagan, Robert, 286, 300
Kaiser Wilhelm Institute, 192
Kaplan, Samuel, 284, 286, 298, 300, 420
Kappers, C. V. Ariens, 102, 112, 121
Karten, Harvey, 312
Kassarin Jacob, 410
Kattwinkel, E. E., 94
Kaufman, M. Ralph ("Moe"), 200, 214, 410, 411, 417, 418, 419
Kennedy, Foster, 149
Kety, Seymour, 256, 311, 334, 421
Keuper, Charles S., 286
King, John T., 52
Kipling, Rudyard, 276; *History of England*, 103
Kirby, George H., 390
Klein, Melanie, 293
Klerman, Gerald, 311, 421
Knapp, Charles S., 286
Knapp, Peter H., 260, 281, 283, 284–285, 418
Knapp, Philip Coombs, 125, 126
Knowles, John H., 320
Kober Medal, 160, 331, 336, 387
Kraepelin, Emil, 57, 60, 115, 156, 199, 280
Kraus, Walter, 112
Krehl, Ludolf, 41
Kubik, Charles, 283, 310
Kussmaul, Adolf, 184, 191

Index 437

LaFarge, John, 107
Lambert, Robert, 220
Lamont, John, 286, 300
Lamson, Paul D., 53
Langley, John F., 104
Langley Porter Clinic, 252
Landseer, Sir Edwin H., 106
Lansing, Cornelius, 298
Lashley, Karl T., 206, 215
Leber's optic atrophy, 275
Lee, Roger I., 80–81
Lehman, Edwin P., 43
Lehmann, Herbert, 332
Leigh, Archibald D., 281, 283
Lennox, Margaret (Margaret Lennox Buchthal), 179, 181, 193, 195
Lennox, William Gordon, 89, 91, 154, 160, 181, 183, 187, 192, 405; And encephalography in epilepsy, 193; Nature and method of working, 179–180, 195; Publishes *Epilepsy and Related Disorders*, 195; Publishes *Science and Seizures*, 194–195; Relationship with Stanley Cobb, 89, 90, 95, 97, 99, 125, 139, 146, 147, 148, 163, 164, 165, 170–171, 179, 184, 185, 188, 195, 246
Leonhard, Erna (Mrs. Frederick Gibbs), 145, 154, 171, 191, 192, 193, 194, 398
Lettvin, Jerry, 312, 319
Levy, Robert L., 52
Lewis, David S., 53
Lewis, Sir Thomas, 244
L'Hermitte, Jean, 109, 110, 113, 120
Liddell, Howard, 414
Lief, Alfred, *The Common Sense Psychiatry of Adolf Meyer*, 280, 386
Life chart, 83, 231, 247, 269
Limbic Mechanisms, 278
Limbic system, 278
Lindemann, Eric (Erich), 203, 210–212, 215, 226, 248, 251, 411–412, 415; In charge of children's clinics at Massachusetts General Hospital, 223, 254, 292, 294, 295; Establishes Wellesley Human Relations Service, 211, 285, 296; Freudian approach to psychiatry, 268; Ineffectiveness as an administrator, 211, 319–320; Pharmacologic studies, 210, 243, 414; Psychodynamic orientation, 268; Relationship with Stanley Cobb, 210–212, 229, 242, 243, 319–320, 337, 412; Relationship with Jacob E. Finesinger, 251–252, 412; Retirement, 211–212; Sociologic interests, 211; Succeeds Cobb as director of psychiatry at Massachusetts General Hospital, 210, 211, 288, 310, 326; And study of grief, 210; As teacher and lecturer, 210, 270; And West End renewal project, 211; Writing ability, 243
Linden, Hannah, 94, 96, 154
Lindsley, Donald B., 233, 286
Linguistics, 253–254, 274, 285
Livingston, Kenneth E., 278
Locke, Edwin A., 39
Localization of function, 279, 280
Loevenhart, Arthur S., 168
Loewy, Otto, 150
London, Stanley Cobb's study in, 103–107
London Hospital, 233
Lord, Frederick T., 39
Lorente de Nò, *see* Nò
Lorenz, Konrad, 329, 421; *Aggression*, 209
Lorenz, Maria (Mrs. Alfred Pope), 254, 274, 285, 286, 416
Louvre, 111
Lovejoy, Sylvia, 96
Lowell, A. Lawrence, 20, 93, 140, 141, 205
Lowell, Ralph, 256
Lowell Lectures, 150
Lucas, Keith, 84
Ludwig, Alfred C., 268, 269
Lunt, Lawrence K., 40, 42, 79

Macbeth, 119
McClellan, Samuel G., 286, 301
McCollom, John H., 39
McCollum, Elmer V., 52
MacCurdy, Dr., 105
McDermott, Neil T., 232, 281, 286
MacDonald, George, 94
MacDonald, Maxwell E., 89, 96, 139, 164, 188
McKenna, John, 146, 152
Macklin, Theodore O., 286
MacLean, Paul, 277, 285, 286
McLean Hospital, 39, 177, 215, 274, 283, 290, 300, 416, 419; Cobb's interest in, 256, 257; Mailman Laboratory, 256, 322
McLennan, Sam, 302–303
McNaughton, Dorothy, 164, 254, 296
McNaughton, Francis, 164, 404
Macomber, Donald, 47

MacPherson, Donald J., 67, 87, 107, 144, 391, 417; Relationship to Stanley Cobb, 89, 92–93, 97, 106, 111, 116, 125, 146
Macy Foundation, 191, 214, 291
Magnus, Rudolf, 102, 112
Magoun, H. W., 245, 321
Mahler, M. S., 293
Maier, H. W., 118
Mallory, Frank B., 38, 44
Manet, Édouard, 111
Manhattan State Hospital, 58, 199
Manual of Military Psychiatry, 246
Marie, Pierre, 48
Margolis, Philip, 285, 286, 287
Marriott, McKim, 52
Martin, Charles, 286
Mason, Edward A., 286, 301
Massachusetts Eye and Ear Infirmary, 255, 256
Massachusetts General Hospital, 39, 41, 43, 44, 45, 79, 91, 92, 99, 116, 125, 137, 151, 152, 167, 173, 176, 181, 193, 198, 210, 211, 220, 252, 268, 271, 274, 277, 310, 321, 331; Alcohol clinic, 287, 326; Antisemitism at, 206; Baker Memorial Building, 221, 226, 241; Bulfinch Building, 22, 241, 249, 260, 419; Burnham Building, 296, 297, 299, 304; Child psychiatry at, 233, 254, 290, 291, 294–309, 420; Children's clinics, 233, 290; Clinico-pathological conference, 81, 389; Cobb organizes psychiatric service at, 42, 97, 172, 240; Cobb's early neurological work at, 80–81, 88, 124; And Cocoanut Grove fire, 242–243; Collaboration of psychiatric and non-psychiatric services, 223–225, 229, 244, 270–271, 273, 420; Collaboration with James Jackson Putnam Center, 294, 298, 302, 303; Collaboration with Judge Baker Guidance Center, 291, 294, 307; Collaboration with Thom Habit Clinic, 294; And concern about Neurological Unit at Boston City Hospital, 139–142; Criticized in Flexner Report, 37; Dalton Scholarship, 81; Department of Neurology, 290, 310, 416; Department of Pediatrics, 271, 294, 295–296, 297–298, 304, 420; Department of Social Services, 81, 114, 197, 202, 233; Encephalographic Laboratory, 231, 245, 306; General Executive Committee, 288; Herman Room, 233, 241, 249, 269, 287; Integration of neurology and psychiatry at, 221; C. G. Jung at conference at, 234; Pavlovian Laboratory, 299; Psychiatric Outpatient Department, 291, 292, 294; Psychiatric rounds, 270, 273; Psychiatric Staff Associates, 287; Psychiatric Service, 221, 222, 229, 233–234, 240, 241–242, 247, 249–250, 254–255, 326; Psychiatric staff, 210, 212–216, 232–233, 287; Psychiatry at, 82, 83, 144, 174, 177, 178, 201, 202, 203–204, 205, 220–229, 231–236, 414–415, 416; Psychoanalysis at, 206–207, 218, 269, 289; Relationship between neurological and neurosurgical services, 320; Residents and fellows in child psychiatry, 282, 284, 285, 298–302; Residents and fellows in psychiatry, 281–284, 285; Speech Clinic, 155; Staff conferences at, 226–227, 269, 270; Stanley Cobb Laboratories, 310, 326, 332, 334, 421; Surgical Service, 227; Teaching of neurology at, 135, 136, 138, 139; Teaching of psychiatry at, 228, 248–249, 269; Teaching of psychosomatic medicine at, 248; Warren Building, 310, 321; White Building, 241, 418; World War I unit, 40
Massachusetts Institute of Technology, 5, 300; Cobb works in Student Health Service, 312, 319
Massachusetts Medical Society, 330
Massachusetts Mental Health Center, 287, 387, 414
Massachusetts National Guard, 6, 10, 31, 45–46
Master, Arthur M., 417
Maughs, Sidney B., 281
Maxwell, Rollins, 34
Mayr, Ernst, 311
Means, James Howard, 82, 83, 111, 138, 224, 326, 413, 419
Meath, James A., 254, 286, 416
Medical Clinics of North America, 83, 247
Medical Exchange Club, 330–331
The Medical Examiner's Handbook, 252
Medicine, 148, 166, 227
Medicine Monographs, 148, 195
Die Meistersinger, 116
Mella, Hugo, 89, 91–92, 97, 116, 125, 147, 184
Mello, Nancy K., 326
Menninger, Karl, 202
Menninger, William, 417, 418

Index

Mental Health Research Institute, 269
Mental hygiene movement, 219
Meprobamate, 321
Merrill, Bruce H., 252, 281
Merritt, H. Houston, 146, 153, 163, 164, 167, 177; Acting director of Neurological Unit at Boston City Hospital, 143, 164; And discovery of Dilantin as anticonvulsant in epilepsy, 193–194, 195, 196; As neurologist, 164
Meyer, Adolf, 52, 53, 55, 56, 62, 64, 65, 66, 67, 68, 69, 70, 80–81, 85, 102, 110, 118, 146, 150, 182, 184, 199, 200, 201, 214, 215, 219, 252, 258, 270, 296, 386–387, 388; Advises on neuropathology position at Harvard, 87–88, 390; Assessed by Stanley Cobb, 280; Attitude toward birth control, 60; Attitude toward psychoanalysis, 54, 60, 280; Behavior chart of, 59, 414; *The Common Sense Psychiatry of,* 280; Directs Phipps Clinic, 58–59; Directs New York Pathological Institute; 58; Education and early career, 57–58; Influence on child psychiatry, 290, 291; Life chart of, 83, 231, 269, 290; Limitations of methods of, 61, 417; Nomenclature and terminology of, 60–61; Psychiatry of, 52, 58, 59–60; Psychobiology of, 53, 59, 200, 273, 280, 290, 322; Relationship with Florence Clothier, 290; Relationship with Stanley Cobb, 56–57, 61, 62, 63, 79, 83, 122, 217, 246–247, 273, 410; Relationship with William Herman, 82–83; Relationship with Eleanor Pavenstedt, 215, 291, 292; Relationship with students and staff, 59, 61; Teaching methods of, 59, 60; At Worcester State Hospital, 57, 58
Michelsen, Wolfgang J., 323, 324
Migraine, 273
Miles, Henry H. W., 254, 256, 271, 272–274, 275, 286, 304, 305
Millais, Sir John E., 106
Miller, James Grier, 251, 281, 415–416
Miller, Jule P., Jr., 281, 283
Miller, Leon, 286
Millet, Mrs. Frank, 107
Millet, John A. P. ("Jack"), 40, 42–43, 107, 330
Milton Academy, 4, 5, 6, 13, 14–15, 384
Mind, Locus of, 278–279

Mind-body problem, 209
Minkowsky, Miechel, 118
Minot, Charles S., 38
Minot, George Richards, 99, 171, 228
Miss Windwor's School, 7
Mitchell, B. C., 86
Mixter, Jason, 39, 84, 160
Mixter William J., 39
Molholm, Hans B., 164, 404
Monakow, Constantine von, 102, 118
Monet, Claude, 111
Money, John William, 286
The Monist, 57
Monson State Hospital, 93, 95, 183
Montreal Neurological Institute, 189
Moore, Burness, 251, 281, 415
Moore, Joseph, 53
Moore, Merrill, 145, 164, 172–173, 178
Morgan, J. Pierpont, 36
Morison, Robert S., 415
Morphine intoxication, 150, 151
Morris, William, 107
Morrison, Raymond, 142, 146, 151–152, 154, 160, 162, 163, 165, 171, 254
Mosher, Jesse M., 219, 413
Münsterberg, Hugo, 32–33, 197, 201, 408
Mullenix, R C., 31
Multiple sclerosis, 115, 167
Munich, 147, 155, 156, 213; Cobb's visits to, 115, 117, 200
Munro, Donald S., 143, 145, 163, 164, 171, 398, 407
Muramatsu, Tsuneo, 233, 286
Murray, Henry A., 118–119, 200, 202, 204–206, 208, 236, 410, 411, 416
Murray, John M., 200, 410, 411, 417, 418
Muschatt, Cecil, 252, 281, 416
Museum of Fine Arts, Boston, 13
Muskeget Island, 33, 34, 157, 174, 175
Musnick, Henry, 286, 301
Myerson, Abraham, 95, 96, 126, 136, 138–139, 143, 144, 164
Myopia Hunt Club, 47

Nagoya National University, 233
National Hospital, Queen Square, London, 102, 104, 105, 106, 123, 284
National Institute of Mental Health, 278, 284
National Institute of Neuropsychiatry, 70
National Institute on Alcohol Abuse, 287

National Research Council, 187
National Socialist Party (Nazi), 176, 236, 293
Naushon Island, 8, 48, 157, 174
Nauta, Walle, 312
Nemiah, John, 212, 227, 243, 249–250, 251, 269, 270, 275, 281, 282, 283, 289, 413
Neuritis, 167
Neuroanatomy, 217
Neurobiologischen Universitäts-Laboratorium, 115
Neurochemistry, 321
Neurocirculatory asthenia, 65, 243–244, 247–248, 251, 273, 416, 417
Neurological Supper Club, 160–161, 387
Neurology, 170; In Boston, 70; Cobb's early practice of, 80–81, 83, 88, 124; Early teaching of at Boston City Hospital, 125–126; At Harvard Medical School, 122–123, 124–125, 140; Integrated with psychiatry at Massachusetts General Hospital, 221; In Paris, 109–110; As prerequisite for psychiatry, 216; Separation from psychiatry, 217–218
Neuropathology, 217; At Harvard Medical School, 139–140
Neuropharmacology, 321
Neuropsychiatry, 135, 150, 167
Neurosurgery, 151, 221; At Boston City Hospital, 161, 162; In epilepsy, 189; At Massachusetts General Hospital, 320; see also Cervical sympathectomy
Neustadt, Else, 254, 286, 294, 301, 416
New England Conservatory of Music, 14
New England Journal of Medicine, 40, 81, 229
New Haven Hospital, 220
New York Academy of Medicine, 332
New York, New Haven, and Hartford Railroad Company, 3, 382
New York Neurological Institute, 65, 66, 164, 194
New York Pathological Institute, 58
New York Presbyterian Hospital, 151, 182
New York Psychoanalytic Society, 199
New York Public Library, 4
Nissl, Franz, 105
Nò, R. Lorente de, 153
Noble and Greenough School, 13
Nu Sigma Nu, 40

O'Connor, M. F., 183
Office of Scientific Research and Development, 244
Office of Strategic Services, 248
Ohio (H.M.S.P.), 114
Ohler, Richard, 43
Olney, Sigourney, 21, 22, 31, 36
Orton, Samuel, 219
Osler, Grace Revere, 107, 119, 120
Osler, Sir William, 38, 43
Ottman, William, 189, 190
Ottman, Mrs. William, 189, 190
Ottman, William, Sr., 189
Oxford, Cobb's visits to, 107, 119–120, 121, 122, 280
Oxford Medicine, 171
Oxford University, 105
Oxygenation, 246, 248; In epilepsy, 148, 191, 192

Painter, Paul H., 286, 300
Palfrey, Francis W., 39
Palmer, Walter W., 151, 182
Pamaho (yawl), 116–117, 157, 174–175, 236
Papez, J. W., 276, 277
Pappenheimer, John R., 84
Paralysis agitans, see Parkinson's disease
Paris, Cobb's opinion of neurology in, 109–110; Cobb's visit to, 103, 108–110, 112, 119, 120
Park, Edwards A., 52
Parke-Davis Company, 194
Parker, G. H., 32, 421
Parkinson's disease (paralysis agitans), 164, 225, 231, 272
Parmenter, D. C., 86
Pathology, In England, 103–104
Pavenstedt, Eleanor, 215, 233, 291–292, 295, 416
Pavlov, Ivan P., 153, 229
Peabody, Francis Weld, 91, 136, 137, 145, 148, 154, 395
Peary, Commodore, 34
Peck, Martin W., 202, 410, 411
Peirce, Charles S., 57
Peking Union Medical College, 90, 149, 179
Penfield, Wilder, 152, 169, 189, 221, 335, 418; Appreciation of Alan Gregg, 222; Attempts cervical sympathectomy in epilepsy, 187, 190–191; Publishes *The Cerebral Cortex in Man*, 279; Publishes *Cytology and Cellular Pathology of the Nervous*

Index

System, 172; Views on epilepsy, 191–192
Penwood, Dr., 65
Perkins Institute for the Blind, 307
Perry, Arthur, 14, 15
Perry, Bliss, 22
Peter Bent Brigham Hospital, 37, 38, 39, 43, 44, 67, 91, 95, 96, 136, 227, 301; Psychiatry at, 92, 144, 228; Stanley Cobb's internship at, 42, 48–49, 50
Peters, G. Quincy, 46
Pfaff, Franz, 38
Phenobarbital, 194
Phi Beta Kappa, 32, 43
Phi Rho Sigma, 48
Philadelphia State Hospital, 166
Phoenix Club, 20, 35
Pincoffs, Maurice C., 52
Play therapy, 291, 293, 296, 410
Pohl, Henrich, 102, 111, 113
Poiseville's Law, 188
Poliomyelitis, 53, 63–64
Ponkapoag, Massachusetts, 79–80
Pool, James Lawrence, 164, 404
Pope, Alfred, 256, 274, 418
Powers, Grover F., 52
Pratt, Joseph H., 39, 234
Prentice, Norman M., 286
Price, Charles P., 335
Prince, Gordon, 21, 31, 36, 45, 47
Prince, Morton, 31, 59, 118, 125, 200, 204, 206
Prudden, Dr., 100
Psychiatry, 170; Attitude of Fuller Albright toward, 272; At Boston City Hospital, 143–144, 145, 172–173, 178, 201, 220; Stanley Cobb's interest in, 69, 80, 83–84, 143–144, 145, 157, 161, 197; Education and training in, 251; Effect of psychoanalysis on, 216, 217; Effect of World War II on, 258, 259, 260; As liaison in a general hospital, 219–221, 240, 290, 413; At Massachusetts General Hospital, 82, 83, 144, 174, 177, 178, 201, 202, 203–204, 205, 220–229, 231–236, 269; New trends in, 219; Phases in therapeutic consultation, 223; Separation from neurology, 217–218, 260; Taught at Harvard Medical School, 222, 227–230, 249
Psychoanalysis, 41, 43, 49, 93, 125, 155, 161, 165, 170, 198, 199, 205, 275, 280; And academic affiliation, 202, 203, 218; Ambivalence of Eleanor Pavenstedt toward, 291, 292; As philosophy or science, 209, 210, 218; As a university discipline, 173, 202, 203, 204; In Boston after Putnam's death, 200, 207; Carl Binger's interest in, 174; Of Stanley Cobb, 155, 156, 173, 199, 200, 201, 202, 203; Stanley Cobb's interest in, 68, 121, 173, 174, 176, 200–204, 218, 258, 280, 288, 410–411, 414; And child psychiatry, 292–293; Mandel Cohen's opinion of, 216; Of Florence Clothier, 290; Felix Deutsch's opinion of, 215; Of Helene Deutsch, 213; Effect on the handling of psychiatric problems, 216, 217; Effect of World War II on, 216–217, 259, 260, 418; Growth of interest in, 216–217, 219; Jacob Finesinger's attitude toward, 169, 212; William Herman's interest in, 83, 142, 144, 172, 200, 202, 207; Integration with other neurosciences, 217; James Jackson Putnam's interest in, 49, 198, 409; Karl T. Lashley's opposition to, 206; At Massachusetts General Hospital, 206–207, 211, 269, 289; Adolf Meyer's views on, 54, 60; Opposition of Allan Butler to, 295; Qualifications for teaching of, 203; Harley Shand's skepticism of, 253; Standards for qualification as expert in, 199
Psychoneuroses, Pain sensitivity in, 246
Psychosomatic medicine, 38, 41, 150, 177, 201, 212, 214, 215, 225, 226, 244, 246, 247, 253, 274, 280, 283, 288, 304–305, 385; Course taught at Massachusetts General Hospital, 248; Liaison psychiatry as outgrowth of, 220; Role of "loss" in, 243
Psychosomatic Medicine, 275, 281
Pusey, Nathan M., 332
Putnam, Charles P., 50
Putnam, Irmarita, 116, 118, 121, 200, 201, 202, 203, 207, 236, 410, 411
Putnam, James Jackson, 39, 49, 69, 140, 198, 200, 207, 395, 408–409
Putnam, Lizzie, 198
Putnam, Marian, 198–199, 201, 208, 295, 303, 332, 408–409, 410; Establishes James Jackson Putnam Children's Center, 293–294
Putnam, Marion Cabot, 409
Putnam, Tracy J., 116, 121, 143, 145, 160, 161, 163, 164, 171, 234, 398,

Putnam, Tracy J. (continued)
405, 407; Director of New York Neurological Institute, 164, 194; Director of Neurological Unit at Boston City Hospital, 143, 177; And discovery of Dilantin as anticonvulsant in epilepsy, 193–194, 195, 196; Professor of Neurology at Harvard, 177, 193, 194
Putnam's Camp, 49–50, 198, 205, 408
Puys, France, 103, 107, 108

Quarton, Gardiner, 268, 269, 271, 281, 282, 283, 288, 311; Director of Stanley Cobb Laboratories at Massachusetts General Hospital, 269, 283, 288, 326, 421
Queen Square Hospital, see National Hospital, Queen Square
Quinby, Hosea N., 58, 61

Rackemann, Francis M., 38
Radcliffe College, 170
Rak, I. Paley, 164, 404
Ramon y Cajal, Santiago, 102
Randall, Guy C., 143
Rank, Beata, 293, 295, 296, 303, 420
Rank, Otto, 200, 293
Rasmussen, Andrew T., *The Cerebral Cortex in Man*, 279
Rawolfia, 321
Raynaud's Syndrome, 150, 177
Redfield, Alfred, 15, 16, 84–85, 151, 238, 311, 328
Reibnitz, Freifrau von, 114–115
Reid, John R., 285, 286
Reid, Mont R., 53
Rembrandt, 121
Renard Hospital, St. Louis, 323
Rexford, Eveoleen, 295
Rheims, France, 113
Rheumatology, 167, 271
Rhode Island Audubon Society, 328
Rhodes Cornelius P., 170
Ribble, Margaret A., 200, 410
Richardson, E. Peirson, 251, 260, 281, 283, 285, 310
Richardson, Henry B., 53, 64
Richardson, Maurice Howe, 39
Richter, Curt B., 53, 60
Rickards, Winston J., 286, 301
Riddoch, George, 106–107
Riggs, Austin Fox, 70, 330. *See also* Austin Riggs Foundation
Rivers, Thomas M., 53
Rizzo, Nicholas D., 286, 301, 420
Robbins, Eli, 252, 281

Robbins, Samuel D., 155, 161, 201
Robbins, William B., 39
Robey, William H., 39, 138
Rochlin, Gregory, 295, 298, 302
Rockefeller, John D., 36
Rockefeller Foundation, 37, 100, 135, 157, 176, 180, 183, 189–190, 205–206, 238; And development of hospital psychiatry, 220, 221–222, 413; Fellowships, 231, 232, 252; General Education Board, 123, 124, 126, 141, 142, 158, 402
Rockefeller Institute, 41, 100, 118, 201, 204, 205, 385
Rollins, Nancy (Mrs. McDonnell), 286, 301
Romano, John, 232
Romer, Alfred S., 311
Rose, Augustus S., 98–99
Roosevelt, Franklin D., 172, 175, 248
Roosevelt Hospital, 253
Rosenau, Milton J., 38
Rosenbaum, Milton, 216, 232, 281, 289
Rosenblueth, Arturo, 160
Rosenblum, Gershon, 286
Rosenow, E. C., 63, 64
Rosenwald Fund, 202
Ross, Joseph F., 245
Rossetti, Dante Gabriel, 107
Rotch, Thomas Morgan, 39
Rothschild, David, 410
Rouen, France, 108
Royal Post-Graduate Medical School at Hammersmith, 233
Royal Society, 120
Royal Victoria Hospital, Montreal, 189
Royden, Maude, 106
Rubens, P. P. 112
Rubin, Dr. (I. Paley Rak), 164, 404
Ruesch, Jurgen, 242, 252–253, 254, 286, 416
Ryks Museum, 121

Sachem (S.S.), 103
Sachs, Hanns, 169, 173, 202, 203, 204, 207, 212, 215, 410, 413
St. Botolph Club, 48
St. John's University, 42
St. Thomas's Hospital, London, 231
Salicylates, 145
Salmon Lectures, 275–276, 332
Salpêtrière, 109
Samuel W. Hamilton Award, 323, 331
Sanborn, Harvey, 410
Sanger, Margaret, 60

Index

Sargant, William W., 231, 232, 233, 241, 286, 414
Saslow, George, 251, 281, 415
Schaltenbrandt, George, 146, 147, 149, 176
Schwab, Dorothy Miller, 194
Schwab, Robert S., 164, 225, 231, 244, 404
Schwab, Sidney I., 390
Scoville, William Beecher, 286
Scripps Institute of Oceanography, 311
Seailles Family, 108, 110, 111, 113
Sears, David, 36
Sears, George, 39, 158
Seif, Leonhard, 155, 156, 161, 173, 200, 201, 202, 410
Shackleton, Sir Ernest, 35
Sham rage, 160
Shands, Harley C., 245, 252, 253–254, 272, 274, 286; *Thinking and Psychotherapy*, 254
Sharpe, William, 286, 301
Shattuck, Frederick Cheever, 38–39
Sherrington, Charles S., 68, 84, 101, 104, 107, 112, 120, 149, 153, 280
Shippen, Eugene R., 286
Sifneos, Peter, 281, 283; *Ascent from Chaos*, 282
Silbert, Louise, 233
Simpson, George G., 311
Skinner, B. F., 323
Skinner, James C., 281, 283, 284
Slater, Dr. 278
Slaughter, Frank, 164, 404
Sloane, Robert B., 285, 286, 287
Smell, Sense of, 276–277, 324–326, 328; In pigeons, 322–323
Smith, Archelaus Green, 2
Smith, Edith Cornell, 8, 9
Smith, Emma, 3
Smith, H. W., 246
Smith, Leonore, *see* Cobb, Leonore Smith
Smith, Lucy, 2
Smith, Philip Sidney, 8–9, 16
Smith, Richard M., 44, 45
Smith, Sidney, 8, 9, 65
Smith, William H. ("Big Bill"), 39
Sodium amytal, 210, 231, 411
"Soldier's heart," 65
Solomon, Earl G., 224, 281, 283, 286
Solomon, Harry C., 67, 96, 97, 135, 139, 160, 228–229, 249
Solomon, John Cobb, 335
Solomon, Philip, 405
Solomon, Stanley Cobb, 335

South Bay Wharf and Terminal Company, 3, 382
Southard, Elmer E., 38, 59, 87, 88, 92, 95, 139–140, 179, 181, 390
Spain, Emigrees from, 234
Spee Club, 20, 35, 41
Spielmeyer, Walther, 147, 156, 190, 401
Spiller, William G. 48
Stack, Dr., 111
Stafford-Clark, David, 286, 305–306, 371–376
Stammering, 200; *see also* Cobb, Stanley, Stammering problem
Steele, Mr. and Mrs., 119
Stevens, Janice R., 210, 411
Stevenson, George S., 65, 390
Stockholm, Harry, 275, 286
Stone, Simon, 164, 404
Stone and Webster Engineering Company, 21, 35
Storch, *see* Von Storch
Strauss, Maurice B., 171
String galvanometer, 38, 55, 56, 63, 65, 85, 89, 92; *see also* Electromyograph
Strong Memorial Hospital, 220
Stuttering, 225
Surgeon General's Office, 62, 64, 66, 67
Sutherland, George, 229, 286, 414
Suwa, Nozomi, 285, 286
Sweet, William, 270, 272, 320
Switzerland, Cobb's trip to, 117–119
Symonds, Sir Charles, 177–178, 219, 321, 405

Talbot, Fritz B., 45, 84, 181, 184, 185
Talbot, John H., 146, 147, 149, 151, 153, 188, 195, 225, 400
Talbot, Nathan, 298
Tate Gallery, 106
Taylor, Edward W., 39, 80, 82, 92, 139–141, 207, 396–397
Taylor, Eugene, 215
Taylor, John, 410
Taylor, Mariana, 226
Temperley, Charlotte, 154, 400
Tenner, Adolf, 184
Teuber, Hans Lucas, 312
Thayer, William S., 52
Thom Douglas A., 93, 155, 184, 406; Habit Clinic, 155, 290, 294, 295, 296, 416
Thomas, Henry, M., 52
Thomas, John Jenks, 125, 126, 136, 143
Thorpe, William H., 209
Tillman, William A., 286
Tillotson, Kenneth, 256, 290, 294

Tilney, Frederick, 66, 182
Timmins, Harvey, 47
Tisza, Veronica, 286, 301
Titchener, E. B., 204
Tobey, Mr., 155
Tokyo Medical College, 233
Tonsillectomy, 255–256
Tow, Peter M., 281, 284, 418
Towne, Alice, 154
Trethowan, William H., 271–272, 281, 282, 284, 417, 418
Troutwine, Charlotte, 176
Tuckernuck Island, 34
Tufts University, 125, 126, 136–137, 170
Tulane University, 220, 272
Turner, John M. W., 106
Typhus Research Commission, 41

Ulrich, A., 118
United States Public Health Service, 298
University of California at Los Angeles, 98, 233, 282, 285, 301; Brain Research Institute, 245
University of Chicago, 57, 220
University of Cincinnati, 165
University of Colorado, 220–221, 299
University of Georgia, 91
University of Iowa, 210
University of Maryland, 212, 268; Grants Cobb an honorary doctorate, 331
University of North Carolina, 232, 299
University of Pennsylvania, 163
University of Rochester, 220, 232, 284
University of Vienna, 213
U.S.A. General Hospital 11, 66, 67
U.S.A. General Hospital 14, 66
Utrecht, Cobb's visit to, 112, 121–122
Uyematzu, Schichi, 89, 93, 179, 182, 188
Uzman, Lahut, 417

Vacuum tube, 192
Valanne, Eero H., 286, 301
Van Amerongen, Suzanne, P., 286, 296, 301
Van der Hoop, J. H., 144, 200
Van Gogh, Vincent, 121
Van Riper, Walker, 325
Van Slyke, Donald D., 147
Vermeer, Jan, 121
Verzeano, Marcel, 285, 286
Veterans Administration Hospital, Boston, 214
Victoria and Albert Museum, 106

Vienna Psychoanalytic Institute, 208
Viets, Henry R., 160
Vitamin deficiency disease, 93–94, 96, 143, 153, 170, 171–172
Vogt, Cecile, 102, 113, 116
Vogt, Oskar, 68, 102, 113, 114, 115, 116, 146, 151, 153, 156, 166, 171, 184, 185, 398
Volkmann, D. L. V., 13, 14, 21
Volkmann School, 6, 13, 17, 21, 36, 384
Von Felzinger, John, 286
Von Storch, T. J. C., 163, 164, 173, 174, 404

Wadsworth, Harvey, 62, 65
Wahl, Charles W., 286, 301
Waldfogel, Samuel, 274, 286, 304
Walter, H. E., 31
Warren, John Collins, 36
Washburn, Frederick, 181
Washington University, 220
Watkins, Arthur, 245
Watson, Elizabeth Taylor, 6, 12
Watson, John B., 53, 56, 59
Weaver, Samuel, 173–174
Weber, Samuel G., 125
Wedrow, Earl M., 281, 284
Weed, Lewis H., 53
Weeks, A., 171
Weigert, Carl, 105, 115
Weil, Arthur, 115
Weinberger, Jerome, 287
Weisman, Avery, 223, 250, 251, 260, 281, 286
Weiss, Ruth S., 281, 284, 286, 301
Weiss, Soma, 216
Welch, William Henry, 43
Weld, Marion, 36
Well-baby clincs, 290
Wells, Frederick Lyman, 252, 254, 409, 416; *The Medical Examiner's Handbook*, 252
Wentworth, Mark, 143, 145, 172
Wermer, Harry, 286, 301
Whipple, Allen O., 189
Whiskin, Frederick E., 281, 284
White, Benjamin V., 225, 232, 286
White, Franklin, 39
White, Helen, *see* Cobb, Helen
White, James C., 270, 320, 321
White, LeMoyne, 252, 269, 281, 284, 411
White, Paul Dudley, 81, 244
White, William Alanson, 199
Whitehorn, John C., 215, 248

Whiting, Isabel, 225
Whitney, Byam, 34, 35, 46, 47
Whooping cough, 214
Wiertz Museum, 111–112
Wilbur, George, 410
Wilensky, Charles F., 234
Wilhelm II, Kaiser, 114, 200, 409
Williams, Carroll M., 311
Williams, Vernon, 254
Wilson, Karl M., 53
Wilson, S. A. Kinnier, 104, 105
Wilson's Disease, 104
Winkler, Cornelis, 102, 112, 121
Winters, Eunice S., 386, 387
Witmer, Helen, *Psychiatric Interview with Children*, 292–293
Wittels, Franz, 201, 385
Wolbach, S. Burt, 38, 170
Wolf, Irving, 286
Wolff, Harold G., 142, 144, 146, 148, 160, 168, 195, 399; European trip, 150; Relationship with Stanley Cobb, 147, 149–151, 153, 188, 331, 336
Wollan, Mr., 292
Woodall, Martin, 164, 404
Woods Hole, Massachusetts, 238, 282
Wool, Max L., 286
Worcester State Hospital, 57, 58, 59, 60, 61
Wordsworth, William, "The Rainbow," 336, 423
Works Progress Administration, 172, 175, 405
World War II, 239; And acceleration of medical education, 241; Stanley Cobb's anxiety over, 239; Cobb's work in war effort, 240, 248; Effect on study and teaching of psychiatry, 258, 259, 260; and growth of interest in psychoanalysis, 216–217, 260, 418; Psychiatric problems caused by, 258; And shortage of child psychiatrists, 295
Wrentham State School, 231
Wright, James Homer, 44
Wright, L. H., 183
Wundt, Wilhelm M., 204
Wyatt, Frederick, 254, 286
Wynne, Lyman G., 281, 284

Yakovlev, Paul I., 89–90, 94–95, 146, 148, 327, 391, 399
Yale University, 90, 120, 143, 153–154, 158, 164, 170, 201, 209, 401; Institute of Human Relations, 167, 219–220
Yankee from Olympus, 86
Yeshiva University, 331–332; Albert Einstein School of Medicine, 216, 232
Young, Brigham, 2
Young, David A., 232, 281
Young, Robert A., 233, 254, 286, 291, 294, 295, 416; Camp for psychoneurotic children, 291–292, 294

Zahle, Vagn, 286
Zeta Psi Club, 20
Zetzel, Elizabeth, 299
Zetzel, Louis, 299
Zucker, Joseph M., 286, 301